HANDBOOK OF CULTURAL AND CREATIVE INDUSTRIES IN CHINA

HANDBOOKS OF RESEARCH ON CONTEMPORARY CHINA

Series Editor: David S.G. Goodman, *Xi'an Jiaotong-Liverpool University, China*

China has undergone a period of intense and rapid social and economic change in its path to becoming a modern industrial superpower. This timely and exciting multidisciplinary series includes *Handbooks* that offer comprehensive overviews of the very latest research on contemporary China. Prestigious, high quality works of lasting significance, the *Handbooks* explore a range of issues affecting China in the 21st century. The emphasis of the series is on the most important concepts and research as well as expanding debate and indicating the likely research agenda for the future.

Titles in the series include:

Handbook on China and Developing Countries
Edited by Carla P. Freeman

Handbook of the Politics of China
Edited by David S.G. Goodman

Handbook of Chinese Migration
Identity and Wellbeing
Edited by Robyn R. Iredale and Fei Guo

Handbook on Class and Social Stratification in China
Edited by Yingjie Guo

Handbook of Cultural and Creative Industries in China
Edited by Michael Keane

Handbook of Cultural and Creative Industries in China

Edited by

Michael Keane

Curtin University, Australia

HANDBOOKS OF RESEARCH ON CONTEMPORARY CHINA

EE Edward **Elgar**
PUBLISHING

Cheltenham, UK • Northampton, MA, USA

Published by
Edward Elgar Publishing Limited
The Lypiatts
15 Lansdown Road
Cheltenham
Glos GL50 2JA
UK

Edward Elgar Publishing, Inc.
William Pratt House
9 Dewey Court
Northampton
Massachusetts 01060
USA

A catalogue record for this book
is available from the British Library

Library of Congress Control Number: 2016931734

This book is available electronically in the Elgaronline
Social and Political Science subject collection
DOI 10.4337/9781782549864

MIX
Paper from
responsible sources
FSC
www.fsc.org   FSC® C013604

ISBN 978 1 78254 985 7 (cased)
ISBN 978 1 78254 986 4 (eBook)

Typeset by Servis Filmsetting Ltd, Stockport, Cheshire
Printed and bound by CPI Group (UK) Ltd, Croydon, CR0 4YY

Contents

Figures

Tables

Contributors

Ruoyun Bai is Associate Professor of Media Studies at the University of Toronto. Her recent books include *Staging Corruption: Chinese Television and Politics* (University of British Columbia Press) and an edited volume, *Chinese Television in the Twenty-First Century: Entertaining the Nation* (Routledge, 2015).

Ming Cheung is Associate Professor in Media at the University of Adelaide, Australia. Her research centres on media design; she conducts research on visual communication, digital marketing and advertising, participatory social media, user experience design, design strategy and service innovation, design education and creativity, and intellectual property in design. She holds degrees in design, law, information technology, education, languages and music.

Yingchi Chu is a Fellow of the Asia Research Centre at Murdoch University, Perth, Western Australia, and teaches Media and Communication Studies. She is the author of *Hong Kong Cinema: Coloniser, Motherland and Self* (2003) and *Chinese Documentaries: From Dogma to Polyphony* (2007). Her recent publications include 'Self-hybridization: China as a Global Media Player' (2013); 'The Politics of Reception: Media in China and Western Critique'; and 'Dogmatic Documentary: The Missing Link' (2015). Her overall research focus is the emergence of critical discourse in China, with an emphasis on visual media.

Peichi Chung is an assistant professor in the Department of Cultural and Religious Studies, Chinese University of Hong Kong. Her research interests include new media industries studies, cultural policy, game studies and Asian popular culture studies. She has published works on media industry dynamics in various countries in the Asia Pacific.

Juncheng Dai is a lecturer in the National Centre of Cultural Innovation Research, Cultural Economics Research Institute, at the Central University of Finance and Economics, Beijing. He has been researching and publishing on economic and cultural geography and working on creative clusters, the creative class and cultural policies from geographical viewpoints.

Jeroen de Kloet is Professor of Globalisation Studies and Director of the Amsterdam Centre for Globalisation Studies (ACGS) at the University of Amsterdam. His work focuses on cultural globalisation, in particular in the context of East Asia. In 2010 he published *China with a Cut – Globalisation, Urban Youth and Popular Music* (Amsterdam UP). He wrote, together with Yiu Fai Chow, *Sonic Multiplicities: Hong Kong Pop and the Global Circulation of Sound and Image* (Intellect, 2013) and edited together with Lena Scheen *Spectacle and the City – Chinese Urbanities in Art and Popular Culture* (Amsterdam UP, 2013).

Anthony Y.-H. Fung is Director and Professor in the School of Journalism and Communication at the Chinese University of Hong Kong. He is also Pearl River Chair Professor at Jinan University at Guangzhou, China. His research interests and teaching focus on popular culture and cultural studies, popular music, gender and youth identity, cultural industries and policy, and new media studies. He has published widely in international journals, and authored and edited more than ten Chinese and English books.

Lauren Gorfinkel is a Lecturer in International Communication at Macquarie University. Her research is on Chinese media with a focus on television, music-entertainment and cultural programming, globalization, and the politics of national and ethnic identity. She is currently writing a monograph on *Chinese Television and National Identity Construction* (forthcoming, 2016).

Marina Guo is a cultural entrepreneur, academic and strategist. She is the Head of Arts Management at the School of Creative Studies, Shanghai Theatre Academy (STA), and Vice-Director of the John Howkins Research Centre on Creative Economy. She is currently CEO of STA InnoEdu and founder of Huashan Multiversity, which offers a capacity building talent development program and executive education for cultural creative sectors.

Eric C. Hendriks is a Dutch postdoctoral researcher in the Sociology Department of Peking University in Beijing. He investigates the globalization of self-help culture and has conducted fieldwork in the United States, Germany and China.

Christiane M. Herr is an architectural researcher and educator focusing on the areas of digitally supported design, conceptual design, structural design, design studio teaching and traditional Chinese approaches to creative thinking. Christiane is a German National and has worked and studied in Australia, Hong Kong, China and Taiwan for more than 13 years. In her PhD work at The University of Hong Kong, Christiane explored cellular automata as a means to establish architectural design support, which led to her strong interest in diagrams and designerly ways of seeing. In her recent research, Christiane has focused primarily on innovative approaches to structural design education in architecture. Her research focus in structural design emphasizes structural design pedagogy as well as research into qualitative aspects of structural design processes.

Vicky Ho is Assistant Professor in Creative Arts at The Open University of Hong Kong. She earned her PhD in Communication at the Chinese University of Hong Kong. She teaches communication, advertising and public relations, new media culture, and cultural industries. Her research interests include popular culture, media and religion, cultural industries, and cultural policy.

Ying Huang is an Associate Professor at Yunnan University of Traditional Chinese Medicine. Her research interests include Yunnan ethnic creative industries and ethnic traditional medicine culture. She has published two books and twenty papers in these areas.

Michael Keane is Professor of Chinese Media and Cultural Studies at Curtin University. He is Program Leader of the Digital China Lab. Michael's key research interests are digital transformation in China; East Asian cultural and media policy; and creative industries and cultural export strategies in China and East Asia.

Wei Lei has completed her PhD in the Faculty of Arts and Social Sciences, University of Technology Sydney. She submitted her doctoral thesis *Radio and Social Transformation in China* in December 2015.

Huailiang Li is Professor and Chair in the Faculty of Literature and Law at the Communication University of China. His work focuses on the trading of cultural products and services.

Wuwei Li (Professor) is a renowned economist, a national political leader and an independent thinker. Professor Li was formerly the Vice Chairman of the 11th China People's Political Consultative Council (CPPCC), the Deputy Chairman of The Revolutionary Committee of the Chinese Kuomingtang. He is Chairman of the Shanghai Creative Industries Association, the Director of Creative Industries Research Centre at Shanghai Academy of Social Sciences, and Director of the International Research Institute of Creative Economy at Donghua University. His best-seller, *How Creativity is Changing China*, has been translated into more than five languages and has been distributed nationally and internationally.

Yan Li is a doctoral researcher and professor at the Chinese National Cultural Industries Research Center (CNCIRC) in Yunnan University. He is also executive deputy director of the CNCIRC and dean of the

Cultural Industries Research Institute of Yunnan University. His research covers a wide range of cultural industries, ethnic art and cross-cultural comparisons. He has published five books concerning related areas and annual or biennial reports about China's regional cultural industries and Yunnan's cultural industries, as well as nearly 100 papers.

Bjarke Liboriussen is an Assistant Professor at the University of Nottingham Ningbo China's School of International Communications. His current research focuses on computer games and on the use of (digital) tools and technologies in China's creative industries.

Tim Lindgren is an Australian fashion designer who works in the global fashion industry where he has run his vertically integrated fashion label. Over the last ten years, Tim has also pursued his research interests in Shanghai, and most recently at the ARC Centre for Creative Innovation at the Queensland University of Technology where he gained his PhD. Tim is currently the Director of Fashion at the Queensland College of Art, Griffith University. His themes include creative entrepreneurship, aesthetics in design and brand building in China.

Ran Ma is currently teaching at the Global-30 'Japan-in-Asia' Cultural Studies Program, Graduate School of Letters, Nagoya University, Japan. Her research interests include Asian independent cinemas and film festivals, on which topics she has published several journal articles and book chapters.

Lucy Montgomery is Director of the Centre for Culture and Technology at Curtin University. She is also Deputy Director for Knowledge Unlatched, a not-for-profit organization working for open access to specialist scholarly books. Lucy trained as a China specialist at the University of Adelaide, before going on to complete a PhD in Media and Cultural Studies at Queensland University of Technology. Her work explores the role of digital technology and intellectual property in business model innovation in the creative industries. Her book, *China's Creative Industries: Copyright, Social Network Markets and the Business of Culture in a Digital Age* is published by Edward Elgar.

Eric Priest is an assistant professor at the University of Oregon School of Law, where he teaches and researches in the area of intellectual property law with a focus on copyright law in the information age and creative industry ecosystems in the US and China. Before joining the Oregon Law faculty in 2009, he earned a Master of Laws at Harvard Law School, where he also spent time as a fellow in residence at the Berkman Center for Internet & Society. He helped the Berkman Center develop the Noank

Digital Media Exchange project in China, a next-generation copyright licensing system for the legal distribution and transmission of digital works over the Internet. He also researched and analyzed Internet censorship and surveillance practices in several Asian countries for the OpenNet Initiative. Eric holds a Juris Doctor from Chicago-Kent College of Law and a BA, *summa cum laude*, from the University of Minnesota.

Zitong Qiu is an associate professor of the Media and Communication Research Centre at Ningbo Institute of Technology, Zhejiang University. Her research interests mainly cover youth and childhood studies and film studies. She recently published two articles in *China Media Report* and *Contemporary Cinema* about childhood in Indonesian independent cinema.

Xiang Ren is a Research Fellow in the Australian Digital Futures Institute at the University of Southern Queensland, where his research focuses on open access, digital publishing, and China's Internet media. He has published widely in these areas. He earned his PhD at the Queensland University of Technology with an outstanding doctoral thesis award. Prior to his academic career, he spent more than a decade working in the Chinese publishing industry as a Senior Editor and Sales Director. He is a well-known publishing commentator in China.

Florian Schneider PhD, Sheffield University, is Lecturer for the Politics of Modern China at the Leiden University Institute for Area Studies. His research interests include questions of political thought, governance, foreign policy, political communication, and digital media in the PRC, Taiwan, and Hong Kong.

Wanning Sun is Professor of Media at the University of Technology Sydney. She researches in Chinese media and communication, social change and inequality in contemporary China, and diasporic Chinese media. Her most recent monograph is *Subaltern China: Rural Migrants, Media and Cultural Practices* (2014).

Michael Alexander Ulfstjerne holds a PhD from the Department of Cross-Cultural and Regional Studies, Copenhagen University. Throughout 2008–9 Michael carried out fieldwork on Chinese creative industries, exploring local perceptions of originality and imitation, and more broadly the underlying dynamics within the scene of cultural production. Recent work builds on fieldwork in Ordos, Inner Mongolia, China and focuses on Chinese urbanism, debt, failed development projects and boom-bust cycles.

Jing Wang is Professor of Chinese Media and Cultural Studies and Director of New Media Action Lab at MIT. She is the Founder and Director of NGO2.0, which is now registered as a non-profit organization in Shenzhen. Her recent publications include 'TV, Digital, and Social: A Debate' (*Media Industries Journal* 1.3, 2015) and 'NGO2.0 and Social Media Praxis: Activist as Researcher' (*Chinese Journal of Communication*, 2015).

Qian Wang earned his PhD from the Institute of Popular Music, University of Liverpool. He is a lecturer at the School of Literature and Journalism, Yibin University. His research is mainly focused on Chinese popular music and related cultural scenes in PR China. He is the author of *The Crisis of Chinese Rock Music*.

Cindy Hing-Yuk Wong is Professor of Communications in the Department of Media Culture at the College of Staten Island, City University of New York. Her areas of research include global Chinatowns, diasporic Chinese media, film festivals, grassroots media and Hong Kong cinema culture. Her book *Film Festivals: People, Culture and Power in the Global Screen* (2011 Rutgers) offers the first comprehensive study of the global festival world. She is the co-author of *Global Hong Kong* (2005) and the co-editor of the *Encyclopedia of Contemporary American Culture* (2001); and has published in *Asian Cinema, American Anthropologist, Postscript, Velvet Light Trap*, and *Amerasia*.

Huan Wu works as an associate professor, School of Media and Design at Shanghai Jiaotong University. She obtained her doctoral degree from the School of Journalism and Communication, the Chinese University of Hong Kong. Her research interests are on ageing and communication, and creative industries. Her recent research concerns digital technology and its application among disadvantaged groups in mainland China.

Brian Yecies is a Senior Lecturer in Communication and Media Studies at the University of Wollongong. His research focuses on cultural policy, and the social, cultural, and industrial transformation of cinema in Korea, China and Australia. He is the author of *Korea's Occupied Cinemas, 1893–1948* (2011, Routledge) and *The Changing Face of Korean Cinema, 1960–2015* (Routledge, 2016) – both with Ae-Gyung Shim. He is also a chief investigator on the 2014–16 ARC Discovery Project 'Willing collaborators: Negotiating Change in East Asian Media Production'.

Lianyuan Yi is a PhD candidate in the Department of Cultural and Religious Studies at the Chinese University of Hong Kong. Her PhD dissertation is about the film censorship system of PRC since the reform of marketization.

Na Yi (Yeshi Lhamo), a Chinese Tibetan, is currently an associate professor in the Chinese Academy of Social Sciences, focusing on

Creative Industries Studies, Cultural Policy Studies and Tibetan Art History. Publications include five books of Tibetan art history, and the book *Exploration of Cultural Creative Industries Development in Ethnic Areas* (2014). She has also published more than 50 papers in these fields.

Xiaoming Zhang is a Professor at the Chinese Academy of Social Sciences. His research interests include cultural policy, cultural industries, and Economic Ethics. He has published books and papers on Economic Ethics, Chinese cultural industries, and the cultural market. He has been editor-in-chief of the *Blue Book of China's Cultural Industries* since 2001. He is currently doing research on the music industry and continues to study reform in China's cultural policy.

Elaine Jing Zhao is a Lecturer in Public Relations and Communications in the School of the Arts and Media, Faculty of Arts and Social Sciences at the University of New South Wales, Australia. Elaine has been researching and publishing on digital media, creative and cultural economy, user co-creation, informal media economies, and their social, cultural and economic implications.

Jane Zheng is an assistant professor at the BA Programme in Cultural Management at the Chinese University of Hong Kong. She obtained her PhD from the University of Hong Kong. Before joining CUHK, she was a postdoctoral fellow at the University of Technology, Sydney. She is one of the pioneering international scholars examining the phenomenon of creative industry clusters in China and her ongoing research interest rests on planning cultural resources in China's urban development.

Foreword
Stephanie Hemelryk Donald

Some things are best written in China. When the editor asked me to prepare a foreword to this book I was in Europe. From there, China has many faces but they are all slightly out of focus. Chinese creativity is shrouded by Chinese economic power, by a crashing market, or by disinterest. There, it's difficult to know what to say except the obvious. China's creative and cultural spheres of activity are essential topics for the contemporary media, culture and communications scholar and student. Read this book, please.

Here, six months later in Suzhou, everything is more distinct, and increasingly interesting. The Suzhou Industrial Park (SIP) houses Fortune 500 companies, Chinese and international universities, including the brand new but already international School of Music at Suzhou University, and is yet within a 30 minute drive of the old city of Suzhou, once one of the biggest and busiest capital cities in the world. Indeed it was only in 1860, during the Taiping Rebellion, that much of that historical fabric was destroyed. Now, SIP is the face of China's vision of accelerated modernization and leapfrog development in the region, but also another transformative version of the essence of Suzhou's entrepreneurial and cultural past. Down the road, Suzhou the old city has remaining charms, particularly architectural, of an earlier iteration of Chinese investment and trade. It is in the conjunction of these two Suzhous that one sees both the value of culture and the capacity of creativity in China now. Keane's introduction to this collection expertly presents the contradictions and crossover between culture and creativity in Chinese political and policy discourse. In this context, it all makes sense.

But also, as I write, news comes through that the Chinese Ministry of Trade (MOFCOM) has invested 200 million *yuan* in a rural e-commerce initiative. Peasants will be supported through new technology, better infrastructure and legal incentives to run e-platforms for trade that ousts the proverbial middleman. Although there are already skeptical commentaries about peasants' capacity to actually use the technology, I recall a grassroots initiative along similar lines in an Anhui bamboo-shoe factory way back in 2004. It didn't work because the infrastructure wasn't there, not for lack of entrepreneurial will or will to learn to use the equipment. The 2015 MOFCOM investment is an economic decision but it is one that will rely on the creative input of designers, gameification experts, and hardware producers if the peasant-farmers who need to make it work, are to have a real chance to do so effectively.

My point is that the discussions in this book from the perspective of Western and Chinese trained academics and commentators, are an invaluable source for thinking through how culture is translated through creativity and how creativity is bent to serve culture. The collaboration of the voices here demonstrates that perspectives and approaches do differ considerably across regimes of thought. The point is, to read both, and understand more.

Stephanie Hemelryk Donald
University of Liverpool
9 September 2015

Acknowledgements

This project had its gestation in mid-2013 as *The Handbook of China's Cultural Industries*. I took over as editor in 2014 with the new title. Stephanie Hemelryk Donald and Zitong Qiu started the roll call of contributors; I then brought others in. It has been a challenging journey and I would like to thank Stephanie in the first instance for asking me to come on to the project and Zitong for providing a perfect opening chapter. Alex O'Connell at Edward Elgar has been extremely supportive and patient.

Part of the challenge has been ensuring that all referencing is correct. My thanks go Yaoxia Zhu who provided me with great back up, checking the references and liaising with contributors, especially those in China. Having Chinese authors introduced a level of complexity, as requirements for referencing in the Chinese academy are not the same as those found in leading international presses. All chapters however were peer reviewed except those in Part II. We have used the Chinese pinyin Romanization system throughout.

1. Introduction
Michael Keane

A hundred years ago the New Culture Movement swept through China's coastal cities. The dynastical period presided over by emperors with their concubines and officials gave way to a heady period in which ideas such as democracy and science jostled with the legacy of Confucianism. Chinese culture was facing a crisis. Modernize or perish.

Chinese culture did modernize: it assimilated elements of Western Marxism, expurgated elements of Confucianism and under the stewardship of Chairman Mao set its course to liberating a nation. The idea that culture might be an industry was never countenanced: that was something bourgeois, evidence that the capitalists were evil. Cultural workers were the screw and cogs in a machine of progress measured initially by revolution and class struggle and later by economic reforms. When the economic reforms did come in the late 1970s, China emerged from its seclusion from the world. Culture, however, was still insulated from global market forces. This is no longer the case.

All societies need renewal; ways of thinking change, and governments inevitably look to the future. Ultimately renewal takes place when ideas gain purchase among communities, sometimes when governments are overthrown for a better development model, or sometimes they are incubated in creative or innovative milieus. But not all elements of society are willing to countenance destruction of traditions and old ways. In many instances ideas that regenerate societies come from outside national and cultural boundaries. As William Bernstein notes, over the course of history ideas from outside have contributed to economic growth; nations and societies have engaged in trade, exchanging skills and knowledge; at other times cultural values have been imposed though invasion and colonization (Bernstein 2008). The impact of some of these forces has been creative; at other times it has been destructive to cultural values. During the late 20th century, thanks to the rapid spread of information technologies, particularly the Internet, the international flow of ideas accelerated, challenging tradition, changing worldviews and confronting authoritarian regimes.

Much debate has ensued over the past three decades about the value of culture and the sustainability of cultural production in post-industrial societies. In the UK and parts of Europe the policy term 'cultural industries' was a timely response to these issues, an attempt to shore up the value of culture, whether by state subvention or commercial entrepreneurship. Other terms followed, namely the 'creative industries', the 'creative economy' and the 'creative class'. The travel of these policy terms internationally reveals much about national and regional development aspirations. In China these terms often manifest in ready-made solutions: policy is fast-tracked from afar and developments mimic international projects. Yet the gentrification of city districts, the commercialization of media, and the revitalization of tourist sites are in many respects a development façade; they have not yet led to Chinese culture achieving its international ambitions. Nonetheless, despite the lack of global recognition so far, momentum is gathering. The international profile achieved by a number of Chinese visual artists, and by some writers and performance artists in recent years, indicates that the nation is beginning to achieve results, albeit in a limited number of cultural fields. Moreover, the professionalization of China's cultural and creative industries owes much to the influx of foreign companies working in China.

In the early 2000s the introduction of 'creative' terminologies (industries, class, economy, cities) found fertile ground in the People's Republic of China. In Western developed economies the use of these terms precipitates debates about media ownership, entrepreneurship, industry sustainability, the casualization of cultural labour, outsourcing of production, and cultural diversity. In these debates, while the terms cultural and creative are often substitutable, there is room for conflicting points of view. For some the emphasis on 'industries' – and by extension commercialization – calls into question what counts as cultural, and for that matter, what can be measured as creative.

In China, however, the distinctions between culture, creativity and industry are more finely inscribed. Culture is directly associated with the hegemony of the state: it is place-specific, laden with historical significance, governed by conventions and micro-managed by censors. Creativity on the other hand is often associated with foreign content imported from Hollywood or from China's near neighbours South Korea and Japan. Creativity according to this account is liberating, offering a window of opportunity to break out of the constraints of state sanctioned culture. The need for indigenous creativity in China has become a mainstream topic in TV talk shows, on talk radio, in newspaper editorials and in numerous conference presentations.

The cultural and creative industries are accorded a prominent role in China's much-heralded shift to a consumption based economic model. Culture is set to become a 'pillar industry' by 2020, an industrial classification formerly reserved for construction, electrical and petrochemical industries, and auto manufacturing. At the time of writing in late 2015, culture's contribution was 3.4 per cent of GDP. The yardstick of a pillar industry is 5 per cent. Is this new leap forward possible?

To date the most widely cited literature on the cultural and creative industries is attributed to academics and policy consultants resident in the so-called Western 'free world.' Most applications of these 'industry terms' derive from early policy articulations of either the cultural industries (see Garnham 1990) or the New Labour government's creative industries task force in the UK (1990s–2000s); for this reason the terms largely reflect developments in Anglophone nations. The terms have far less traction in the US however, probably due to the dominance of the US entertainment industry complex.

The cultural and creative industries, while widely understood by governments, are sometimes devalued within the humanities; indeed, there is some suggestion that these are policy buzzwords of decades past. In China the terms are widely reported in national news and development reports, particularly as the nation scales up its international ambitions. It is therefore not surprising that Chinese scholars are attempting to present their side of the story to 'foreign' readerships (Li 2011; Xiang 2013; Xiang and Walker 2014). A number of accounts of cultural and creative industries in China, and Asia, have likewise added to the knowledge base (Keane 2007, 2011, 2013; Kong and O'Connor 2009).

International scholarship has advanced both critical and positive accounts of the cultural industries (Garnham 1990; Hesmondhalgh 2013; Hesmondhalgh and Pratt 2005; Oakley and O'Connor 2015); the creative industries (Hartley 2005; Hartley et al. 2013; Cunningham 2004; Flew 2012; Moeran and Alacovska 2012; O'Connor 2011; Pratt 2014; Caves 2000); the cultural economy (Scott 2000; du Gay and Pryke 2002); and the creative economy (Kong et al. 2006; Howkins 2002; UNCTAD 2010; Cunningham 2013). In some instances the terms are muddied; that is, there is no obvious difference. Elsewhere scholars have chosen to be specific, taking issue with definitions and industrial sectors.

Some critics of the creative industries point to their 'purely economic imperatives' and their association with neoliberalism (Oakley and O'Connor 2015). The term 'cultural industries' appears to offer a higher moral ground and be more enabling of critique. Yet it's hard to draw a clear line in practice because the terms are interchangeable. The conjunction of these terms in China as 'cultural and creative industries' (or cultural creative industries) is effectively a way to attenuate these ambiguities. Yet when used together the term 'cultural' always precedes 'creative'. Moreover, the official prescription from the Ministry of Culture in Beijing is 'cultural industries' (*wenhua chanye*). It is therefore worth considering why 'culture' (*wenhua*) carries so much weight in policy discourse. Why is culture, previously understood as 'ideology and related institutions and organizations', so important to economic transformation that it is accorded the status of a 'pillar industry'? And why have the cultural industries become a key component in the reform of education curricula as well as a driver of urban renewal over the past several years?

The answers to these questions have both domestic and international implications. In the first instance, the cultural industries (*wenhua chanye*) materialized as a national policy initiative as China's political leaders looked to shore up the nation's indigenous cultural resources in the lead up to World Trade Organization (WTO) accession in December 2001. Recognizing that China had grown strong in consumer manufacturing, the call went out in the late 1990s for cultural producers, workers, artists and designers to be more productive. The imposition of an industrial mentality had critics. Culture, some said, pointing to the vulgarity of Hollywood, was too important to be left to the market. Yet the problem was apparent: China needed to adopt a global market perspective if it was to hold back the forces of globalization. Several years later in 2007 as China's leaders endeavoured to promote a more attractive global image under the auspices of 'cultural soft power', a key challenge loomed: why was the nation's culture, which was symbolic of a great tradition and already building great industrial momentum, failing to attract global recognition?

One solution to making Chinese culture more attractive in the market-place has been to focus effort on ensuring that Chinese cultural producers absorb foreign ideas, best practice and know-how. The implications of cultural reform have extended across the whole nation, from the fast developing cities to the less developed western regions. The industrialization of culture has proceeded at breakneck speed together with massive government investment in public infrastructure. But will an industrial mentality improve the appeal of art, design and media products in an age when people are increasingly making and disseminating their own culture? Indeed, cultural officials, policy makers, participants, stakeholders and academics are at odds with how the cultural industries ought to function in China. Should cultural workers be free to imagine all possibilities as they do in liberal democracies? How should people's creativity be encouraged?

Calls for greater autonomy inevitably run up against the problem that these industries are by definition a product of government intervention. Indeed, the manner by which the cultural sector operates in China is sometimes difficult to equate with developments in liberal democracies. On the other hand we can speak of the cultural industries more politically as a development agenda, echoing the broad definition of culture in China: 'the sum total of all the material and spiritual wealth created by human beings in the course of the historical development of society' (Cihai 1989: 1731). Knowing what the 'cultural industries' represent on a national policy level in China is simple. They are underwritten by the view that Chinese civilization, and more specifically socialist civilization, supplies the appropriate norms and values for development. As one might expect in a nation that has long held artists to account and closed down opportunities for open expression of ideas, the guidelines for cultural industries remain prescriptive.

THE GENESIS OF THE CULTURAL INDUSTRIES

Before the cultural industries, and indeed the creative industries, scholars would refer to the 'culture industry.' Some still do in fact. In 1944, two left wing émigrés from Fascist Germany published *The Dialectic of Enlightenment*, describing how mass media, most typically Hollywood cinema, commercial radio, and advertising conspired to convince people that their wellbeing depends on owning the latest commodity (Horkheimer and Adorno 1972). Appearing in print prior to the global spread of broadcasting technologies, Max Horkheimer and Theodor Adorno's seminal work drew heavily on Marx's notion of commodity fetishism. Their critique of 'culture industry' remains influential to this day. Scholars often link the Frankfurt School's pessimism towards capitalism with contemporary developments. Without doubt the 'cultural industries', the 'creative industries', and the hybrid formulation 'cultural and creative industries' embrace capitalism and consumerism. Consultants, policy wonks and scholars rush to index development among nations, regions and locales, intent on showing how to increase the 'value-add' of culture in gross domestic product (GDP).

How then do we locate this critique of times past with the current economic and social transformations taking place in China? People in China are encouraged to spend more on cultural goods and services, to consume more in the name of national revival. The Frankfurt School position, on the surface at least, looks reasonable. But it's hard to draw comparisons across different time periods and political regimes. Much of the comparative difficulty is due to the nature of consumer demographics, the sheer scale of markets in China, and the fact that the state intervenes in almost all facets of commercial cultural production. This intervention is far removed from the brand of laissez-faire economics that led to the rise of the 'culture industry' in the US in the 1940s and critiques of neoliberalism today.

Momentum in China had been building during the late 1980s and early

1990s. Although cultural policy reforms in the mid-1980s managed to gradually instil the idea that the market was an effective arbiter of taste, little real autonomy was evident. During his 'southern tour' of the Special Economic Zones (SEZ) in February 1992, Deng Xiaoping announced that cultural and media units needed to be weaned off dependence on state subsidy. Signs of burgeoning commercial activity already had emerged in broadcasting and advertising along with consumption of overseas cultural products especially among younger Chinese. Publishing, independent film production and TV serial drama had witnessed moments of creative inspiration, typified by the Beijing hooligan writer Wang Shuo and a group of like-minded script writers and producers associated with him. At the time Deng made his southern tour all cultural production units (*danwei*) were state owned. The lack of commercial appeal of China's cultural sector was evident as audiences looked towards Hong Kong and Taiwanese (*gang-tai*) pop culture (see Gold 1993).

Deng's edict challenged public institutions to restructure and think about profit. Ideologically important institutions such as *The People's Daily* and China Central Television remained protected from market forces. In 1998, a time when China's broadcast media began to undergo further industrial consolidation (*jituanhua*), the Cultural Industries Division of the Ministry of Culture was established and charged with finding ways to turn culture into capital. In 2000, the cultural industries were inserted in the draft of the 10th Five-Year Plan for National Economic and Social Development (Xiang 2013). In 2001, the year the nation was admitted to the World Trade Organization (WTO), the State Council officially ratified the terminology 'cultural industries'. Joining the WTO was a great achievement for industrial and manufacturing sectors and in the following decade China's trade to the world expanded. In 1978, foreign trade had been worth US$ 20.6 billion. By 2010 the value was US$2.97 trillion (Yuan 2014). China had established itself as an industrial power, the world's largest exporter, on the back of an export orientation. 'Made in China' brands were proliferating internationally but at home Chinese culture was struggling to compete with the sophisticated media of East Asia and Hollywood. In 2005, the state media reported an alarming cultural trade deficit.

While the cultural industry had its underpinnings in China during the 1990s among critical intellectuals drawn to the anti-capitalist writings of the Frankfurt School scholars, by the time the term was ratified as national policy it had undergone a transformation. Scholars associated with the 'New Left' found global capitalism an easy target and in this endeavour they received support from international scholars on the left. This critique, however, did not extend to challenging state power in any overt or meaningful way. By the time the state moved in to legitimize the cultural industries many scholars were ready to follow the lead.

The genesis of the cultural industries coincided with 'national cultural security' (*guojia wenhua anquan*), an impassioned slogan aimed at resisting international pressures, mostly from the Motion Pictures Association of America (MPAA) to prise open cultural sectors. Because of the political origins of the cultural industries, projects that reflect government policy slogans have received, and continue to receive, substantial support in terms of tax benefits, publicity and low interest loans. When the cultural industries idea was incubated in Chinese Communist Party affiliated think tanks, regional governments were quick to realize that considerable economic advantage would accrue if artefacts and sites could be converted into tourism experiences. Regional governments were quick to appreciate how the policy blueprint of the central government could legitimize local real estate developments. Consequently many cities added cultural industry quarters and creative clusters to urban growth strategies (Keane 2011).

For the Chinese Communist Party, repackaging performing and visual arts, media, and tourism/handicraft sectors constituted a unified force against overseas culture, particularly pop culture. The term 'revitalization' (*zhenxing*) appeared frequently in cultural policy speeches during the mid-2000s. Despite extensive progress in many areas of media and cultural production post WTO accession, however, it was 2009 before the cultural industries were acknowledged as potential pillar industries (*zhizhu chanye*). The goal of 'actively developing cultural industries' appeared for the first time in the central government's work report that year. On July 22 the executive meeting of the State Council chaired by Premier Wen Jiabao discussed and approved the 'Cultural Industry Promotion Plan' as part of the drafting of the 12th Five Year Plan. The Cultural Industry Promotion Plan coincided with a renewed focus on the 'reform of the cultural system' (*wenhua tizhi gaige*), namely, how to reform public cultural institutions (*shiye*) to make them more enterprising and copyright compliant. In this 'revitalization' shiye should seek out ways to become commercial industries (*chanye*) wherever possible; the strongest chanye should be encouraged to list publicly.

The political responsibilities of the cultural industries are as evident now as they were a decade earlier. The Ministry of Culture's official publication outlining the 12th Five Year Plan opens with an interview with Minister Cai Wu. The Minister articulates a national strategy to double the annual revenue from cultural industries from 2010 to 2015. What is not detailed is the actual amount of state finance that goes into supporting these would-be pillar industries (Cai 2012). In a section of the document

entitled 'give impetus to cultural industries in order to become pillar industries of the national economy', we note the following wording:

> Cultural industries are an important channel for the satisfaction of people's
> diverse spiritual needs under the conditions of the socialist market economy;
> they constitute an important vehicle to bring about development and prosperity
> of socialist culture; they are the leaders among pillar industries and are strategic
> emerging industries in the national economy; they are a leading force in giving
> Chinese culture the impetus 'go out'; they are an important focal point to stra-
> tegically adjust the economy as well as a force to transform China's economic
> development model. (Cai 2012: 171)

In October 2011, during the 17th Meeting of the Sixth Plenary Session of
the Chinese Communist Party a new strategic plan for cultural reform and
development was devised. The so-called 'strong cultural power' (*wenhua
qiangguo*) strategy echoes national cultural security but emphasizes how
Chinese culture will go global (*zou chuqu*). This strategy endorses culture
that is in accord with the national identity of China.

What then does this entail? The 12th Five-Year Plan depicts culture as
the 'circulatory system of China's nationalities, the Chinese people's spiritual homeland' (Cai 2012: 6) The strong cultural power discourse builds
on this health and wellbeing metaphor, arguing that a 'healthy' circulatory
system will strengthen China's cultural sovereignty:

> China becoming a cultural power should not be the wishful thinking of an elite
> few but a common pursuit of all citizens. And just like the circulatory system
> national cultural strategy should circulate culture to every part of society from
> a national level down to a regional, business and local level. (Xiang 2013: 77)

The strong cultural nation strategy, like the 12th Five Year Plan, makes
frequent use of the term 'revitalization' (*zhenxing*). The emphasis on
Chinese civilization is evidence that this is an attempt to draw on the past;
for instance using Confucius Institutes abroad to disseminate appropriate Chinese cultural values (Xiang 2013: 80). In this model the massive
investment in establishing Chinese Central Television (CCTV) channels
overseas is predicated on the belief that they will disseminate approved
messages, even if they are drains on the Chinese public purse.

In looking for ways to grow China's cultural (and creative) industries
scholars in China accord a great deal of attention to international reports.
In particular, the demand for international textbooks on cultural management has precipitated a mini-translation boom. Much of the translated
literature is focused on the tangible elements of cultural production such
as value chains, marketing and cultivation of talent (*rencai*). Theories and
models of urban regeneration, as well as case studies of creative clusters

and creative cities find their way into Chinese university curricula and on to think tank reading lists. Delegations venture abroad to learn about the latest cluster developments while international scholar-consultants visit China, offering Western-style solutions that have limited chance of success due to the institutional complexity of Chinese governance and the effects of *guanxi* (personal networks).

ORGANIZATION OF PART I

The first part of the book is entitled 'the cultural and creative industries reconsidered.' The chapters address questions of how culture and creativity coexist as development discourses in China. In the first chapter Zitong Qiu draws on personal experience to explore how – and why – a distinctive 'Blue Book style' of presentation became the template for reporting on the cultural industries, displacing a theoretical approach evident among New Left scholars in the early 1990s, one that was overtly critical of globalization and the commercialization of culture. Prior to the late 1990s the term used for cultural industries was *wenhua gongye*, with the focus on labour (*gong*). In due course the default setting became *wenhua chanye*, emphasizing production (*chan*), hence the need to register productivity in data. Qiu's term 'remedy paradigm' aptly describes the propensity for academics to provide measured advice to government. The 'remedy paradigm' thus comprises development data, analysis of impediments, followed by recommendations, often extracted from international case studies. The key point here according to Qiu is that scholars are recruited to the cause of 'cultural development'; the 'remedy paradigm' style eschews the kinds of criticism of power one expects in international literature.

The tension between 'culture' and 'creativity' forms the subject of the chapter by Michael Keane. In China culture occupies the controlling position in the policy formulation 'cultural creative industries' (*wenhua chuangyi chanye*), implying that culture regulates creativity. In this chapter Keane draws on Chinese philosophy including *yin-yang* theory and the Confucian classic *The Great Learning* (*daxue*). Keane argues for a complementary conjoined term, creative-cultural industries, anticipating a dialectic in which nothing is ever complete; that is, creativity and culture co-evolve in a process of constant interplay: this interplay is now reflected in online networks and what is now known as the 'sharing economy', typified by crowdsourcing, collaborative production and network effects. Whereas the Chinese government's cultural industries model mandates order – and documents the ordering of successes, international models of innovation and creativity encourage disorder and disruption. More importantly in respect to China's ambitions to be a cultural power (*wenhua qiangguo*), Keane argues that both order and disorder are necessary to build competitive, robust sustainable industries. Creative-cultural industries are therefore the substance of 'digital China', a theme that recurs in several of the later chapters.

Jing Wang's chapter 'The makers are coming' situates this argument within debates around China's innovation system. Often associated with Web culture, the 'Maker Movement' is a global DIY phenomenon, encompassing online collaborating and sharing and the rapid prototyping of new products usually in informal networked communities. Wang's chapter investigates makers' projects that have emerged from below while critiquing the expedient association of the maker with the entrepreneur. Rather she argues that the concept of 'change-maker' is a more appropriate and important solution for China. Her chapter looks at three different models of 'makers as social innovators': innovation challenge contests for problem-solving projects shaped by NGOs and public interest organizations; the ThinkBig Initiative based on youth activism; and Enactus China, the national chapter of an international NGO promoting sustainable growth of communities through smart strategies designed collaboratively by college students, academic mentors, and business leaders.

China is a country where change has come at a rapid pace. Technology it seems is relatively cheap and younger Chinese are 'born digital'. Generational differences therefore are much debated within professions that are understood to rely on creativity. Liboriussen's chapter highlights why the concept of 'generation' is important in China. He argues that the concept is not only used by outside observers but by creatives themselves when they reflect on their practices. Examining the work practices of a number of successful artists and designers the chapter shows how the generational, the technological and the creative intertwine. Those born with computers, so-called 'digital natives', here categorized as 'post-1980s' (*balinghou*), illustrate a greater propensity to use digital tools in comparison to the '70s generation, who are more drawn to analogue tools. In his analysis Liboriussen reflects on the meaning of creativity as a 'travelling concept'.

The chapter by Michael Alexander Ulfstjerne extends this reflection, examining what happens when the discourse of creative and cultural industries arrives in remote destinations, not the larger Chinese coastal cities but the Chinese hinterlands. Using the travels of an iconic Danish sculpture, the 'little mermaid', and its appropriation as a symbol of modernity, Ulftsjerne argues that cultural and creative industries must be understood in the context of the place-specific modality of urban aspirations. Drawing on the case of the Inner Mongolian city of Erdos, sometimes referred to as a 'ghost city', the chapter shows the different ways that the discourse of cultural industries, municipal economies and private capital intersect in regional urban development. Drawing on several months of ethnography in Erdos, Ulftsjerne suggests that so-called 'prestige' or 'face-projects' (*mianzi gongcheng, zhengji gongcheng*) are not entirely bereaved of social creativity. Rather than simply lampooning Chinese local governments for their corrupted, superficial and deceptive appropriations of creative industries, Ulftsjerne says that we also need to encompass these urban facelifts in their capacity of managing social relations in a hierarchical system.

REFERENCES

Bernstein, William (2008), *A Splendid Exchange: How Trade Changed the World*. London: Atlantic Books.

Cai Wu (2012), *The Ministry of Culture's 12th Five Year Plan* (wenhua bu 'shier wu' shi qi). Beijing: Xinhua Publishing.

Caves, Richard (2000), *The Creative Industries: Contracts Between Art and Commerce*. Cambridge MA: Harvard University Press.

Cihai (1989), *Sea of Words*. Chinese Encyclopedia. Shanghai: Shanghai cihai chubanshe.

Cunningham, Stuart (2004), 'The creative industries after cultural policy', *International Journal of Cultural Studies* 7: 105–15.

Cunningham, Stuart (2013), *Hidden Innovation: Policy, Industry and the Creative Sector*. St Lucia: University of Queensland Press.

Du Gay, Paul and Michael Pryke (2002), *Cultural Economy: Economic Analysis and Commercial Life*. London: Sage.

Flew, Terry (2012), *The Creative Industries: Culture and Policy*. London: Sage.

Garnham, Nicholas (1990), *Capitalism and Communication: Global Culture and the Economics of Information*. London: Sage.

Gold, Thomas (1993), 'Go with your feelings: Hong Kong and Taiwan popular culture in China', *The China Quarterly* 136: 907–25.

Hartley, John (ed.) (2005), *Creative Industries*. Oxford: Blackwell.

Hartley, John, Justin Potts, Stuart Cunningham, Terry Flew, Michael Keane and John Banks (2013), *Key Concepts in Creative Industries*. London: Sage.

Hesmondhalgh, David (2013), *The Cultural Industries*, 3rd Edition. London: Sage.

Hesmondhalgh, David and Andy Pratt (2005), 'Cultural industries and cultural policy', *International Journal of Cultural Policy* 11 (1): 1–13.

Horkheimer, Max and Theodor, Adorno (1944/ 1972), *The Dialectic of Enlightenment*, translated by John Cumming. New York: Continuum.

Howkins, John (2002), *The Creative Economy: How People Make Money from Ideas*. London: Penguin.

Keane, Michael (2007), *Created in China: The Great New Leap Forward*. London: Routledge.

Keane, Michael (2011), *China's New Creative Clusters: Governance, Human Capital and Investment*. London: Routledge.

Keane, Michael (2013), *Creative Industries in China: Art, Design, Media*. London: Polity.

Kong, Lily, and Jason O'Connor (eds.) (2009), *Creative Economies, Creative Cities: Asian-European Perspectives*. Dordrecht: Springer.

Kong, Lily, Chris Gibson, L.-M. Khoo, and Anna-Louise Semple (2006), 'Knowledges of the creative economy: towards a relational geography of diffusion and adaptation in Asia', *Asia Pacific Viewpoint* 47 (2): 173–94.

Li, Wuwei (2011), *How Creativity is Changing China*, edited by Michael Keane, translated by Hui Li, Marina Guo and Michael Keane. London: Bloomsbury.

Moeran, Brian and Ana Alacovska (eds.) (2012), *Creative Industries: Critical Readings*. Oxford: Berg.

O'Connor, Justin (2011), *Arts and Creative Industries: A Historical Overview and an Australian Conversation*. Sydney: Australian Council for the Arts.

O' Connor, Justin, and Xin Gu (2006), 'A new modernity? The arrival of "creative industries" in China', *International Journal of Cultural Studies* **9** (3): 271–83.

Oakley, Kate, and Justin O'Connor (eds.) (2015), *The Routledge Companion to the Cultural Industries*. London: Routledge.

Pratt, Andy (2014), 'Creative industries and development: culture in development or the cultures of development', in C. Jones, M. Lorenzen and J. Sapsed (eds.), *Handbook of Creative Industries*. Oxford: Oxford University Press.

Scott, Allen J. (2000), *The Cultural Economy of Cities*. London: Sage.

UNCTAD (2010), *Creative Economy Report 2010*. Geneva: United Nations.

Xiang, Yong (2013), 'The 12th Five Year Plan and the transformation of economic development from the perspective of cultural industries', *International Journal of Cultural and Creative Industries* **1** (1): 74–80.

Xiang, Yong and Patricia Ann Walker (eds.) (2014), *China Cultural and Creative Industries Reports 2013*. Heidelberg: Springer.

Yuan Tao (2014), *On China's Trade Surplus*. Heidelberg: Springer.

PART I

THE CULTURAL AND CREATIVE INDUSTRIES RECONSIDERED

2. Doing Chinese cultural industries: a reflection on the Blue Book syndrome and remedy paradigm
Zitong Qiu

Few buzzwords in China today can compete with the cultural industries (*wenhua chanye*). The theme of many government-subsidized research projects, the cultural industries appear in the speeches of government officials and shape cultural policy and regulations at both central and local government levels. Often viewed as a 'sunrise industry' (*zhaoyang chanye*), the cultural industries have ignited public desire and passion for the revival of a 'strong cultural China' (*wenhua qiangguo*) riding on the back of national economic resurgence over the past three decades.

More significantly, the discourse of *wenhua chanye* has transformed the humanities in Chinese universities since 2000, the year that witnessed its official elevation to a national development slogan at the Fifth Plenum of the 15th Chinese Communist Party's Central Committee. Higher education institutions subsequently initiated 'cultural industries' majors at undergraduate level and research was conducted at postgraduate and doctoral levels. From 2001 onwards a steady stream of 'Blue Books' (*lanpi shu*) appeared – mostly development reports commissioned by editorial panels made up of industry practitioners and professionals, academics, and cultural industry-related officials.

This chapter takes the academic enthusiasm a step further in order to show the underlying socio-cultural transformations that condition shifting research orientations and intellectual positions. It asks: How should we understand the enthusiasm in academia for the cultural industries? What underpins knowledge production in the field in China? What concerns define the dominant paradigms and methodologies? Furthermore, what might the critical approach of cultural studies offer to this field of academic inquiry?

The chapter presents an insider account of the cultural industries in a university in Ningbo, a second-tier coastal city in Zhejiang Province. Between 2013 and 2015, I participated in two government funded research projects and was enlisted to write articles for two local Blue Books. I observed first hand the enthusiasm in academia for what I call the 'Blue Book syndrome'. I typify the mind-set that underpins Blue Book reports as a 'remedy-driven paradigm'. The chapter, however, is not an attempt to disparage the 'remedy paradigm' *per se*: it is widely used in development studies, policy studies and other social science disciplines. I want to draw attention to the overwhelming, if not monolithic use of the remedy paradigm in Chinese cultural industries research. In the mass production of Blue Books, there is a reliance on providing remedies; because this has become the norm it leads us to question the subjective positioning of intellectuals.

Before I delve into my experience as cultural industry researcher–Blue Book participant I want to explore tension between two approaches to the cultural industries. Until the late 1990s the word 'industry' was conventionally in Chinese translated as *gongye*, with an obvious emphasis on labour (*gong*) (see Keane 2013: 5–6). The role of labour was a central tenet of Marxism and Chinese socialism. The critique among humanities intellectuals at the time sided with the Frankfurt School's singular 'culture industry', an imported theoretical framework that captured the attention of a number of New Left scholars. With productivity superseding labour in both cultural policy and academic discourse by the turn of the century, the plural form of industries, expressed as *chanye*, displaced *gongye* (Liu and Huang 2013; Liu and Liu 2014).

The cultural industries (*wenhua chanye*) became the focus of political and cultural management under successive Five Year Economic Development Plans, the blueprints for national reform. As the cultural industries were elevated to national goals many intellectuals shifted camp from the critical school to align with government think tanks, taking advantage of the pecuniary benefits of such contract research. In line with the critical cultural studies approach I want to highlight problems associated with researching Chinese cultural industries. I argue that the research field of Chinese cultural industries requires multiple (and critical) disciplinary reflection and engagements. In doing this I will engage with the former usage, *wenhua gongye*.

BEYOND SEMANTIC CHANGE: FROM *WENHUA GONGYE* TO *WENHUA CHANYE*

Scholars of the cultural and creative industries have explored the relationship between 'culture industry' and the 'cultural industries' in liberal democracies, and the discursive transformation from the former to the latter. David Hesmondhalgh, in his book titled *The Cultural Industries* ([2002] 2013), emphasizes the highly complex, ambivalent and contested nature of 'cultural industries' that goes beyond the term's singular critical line fraught with Adorno and Horkheimer's cultural pessimism. Chinese critical scholarship has echoed this transformation, expanding it to examine significant changes that have occurred in China's cultural sphere. This transformation is clearly indicated in the semantic change from *gongye* to *chanye* in the academic field.

The discourse of *wenhua gongye* has clear references to Adorno and Horkheimer's Marxist critique of the industrialization and commercialization of the cultural realm in the US in the 1950s and 1960s. *Wenhua gongye* first gained momentum in academia in the 1990s, shortly after Horkheimer's *Critical Theory: Selected Essays* and Adorno and Horkheimer's *Dialectic of Enlightenment* were translated for Chinese audience readership (in 1989 and 1990 respectively). Largely thanks to New Left intellectuals who embraced the Frankfurt School's theoretical position, keywords such as 'mass production', 'profit-driven', 'false needs' and 'mass deception' were quickly picked up and used in the Chinese context. The intellectual response to the new formation of a profit-driven and industrial-thinking culture was most evident in a seminar convened in 1998 by *wenyi bao* (*Literature and Art*) entitled *The Problem of Chinese Cultural Industry* (*wenhua gongye wenti yantaohui*).

One of the dominant critical attitudes was articulated by Zhang Guofeng, a scholar based in the Chinese Academy of Social Science (CASS) (Zhang 1998). As the title of his article, later published in *wenyi bao* cogently suggests: 'The essence of cultural industry is a form of anti-culture'. Zhang's concern was two-fold. First, he considered that the flow of capital under the cover of culture only brought fundamental damage to Chinese culture, especially to popular cultural forms such as folk songs, literature and opera, forms largely played out in *minjian* society, a sociocultural space which roughly refers to a 'folk society' or 'people's society'. For Zhang, '*wenhua gongye* is a generic freak given birth by high-technology and capital' (in Zhou 1998). Zhang further claimed that the profit-driven nature of capital and commercialization would eventually culminate in an anti-culture (*fan wenhua*) process (Zhang 1998). Secondly, Zhang voiced ideological concerns over the capitalized culture formation, emphasizing that the insidious 'cultural violence' is more lethal than military force (in Zhou, 1998), anticipating the 'soft power debates' that would later gain credence.

Although other scholars at the seminar evinced slightly different attitudes towards China's cultural industry, there was strong acknowledgement of Adorno and Horkheimer's criticism. For example, in the words of literature studies scholar Cui Shaoyuan, we will 'fill . . . the bottle of "cultural industry" with our own [socialist] wine' (in Zhou 1998). Beijing Social Science Academy-based scholar Qian Guangpei argued that: '[If] capitalism can use "cultural industries", so could socialism' (in Zhou, 1998). This 'cultural industry with Chinese characteristics' thesis continues today. The core values are promoted by President Xi Jinping and are accentuated in a number of recent articles on China's cultural industries (for example, see Zhu and Liu 2012).

The strident theoretical critique of *wenhua gongye* was also a result of the 'high culture fever' (Wang 1996) and the broader 'theory fever' of the 1980s, the first decade after the nation's opening up. The need for new theories, often imported, was felt by both Chinese intellectuals and educated youth. At the same time new forms of popular culture were emerging in the 1990s. Prior to Zhang Guofeng's article, literary scholars including Jin Yuanpu (1994), Tao Dongfeng (1993), the Fudan University-based philosopher Zhang Rulun (1994) and other cultural critics drew heavily upon Adorno and Horkheimer's 'culture industry' to highlight problems in the commercialization of Chinese culture.

The scholarly vigilance directed towards *wenhua gongye* invariably shaped scholarly criticism of the highly commercialized and industrialized popular culture (*liuxing wenhua*) forms in the 1990s. For many the term *wenhua gongye* became synonymous with 'popular culture'. Chinese cultural critics' vigilance regarding *wenhua gongye* also resonates with the huge debate over the 'humanistic spirit' (*renwen jingshen da taolun*) that marked the 1990s, when television serials from Hong Kong and Singapore, and love stories and *wuxia* tales from Hong Kong and Taiwan rewrote the Chinese popular culture scene (Meng 2003).

The ideological concern about the industrialization of culture – and about the commercialization of Chinese socio-cultural lives in general – was particularly acute when youth and children were concerned. Youth studies scholars and educators constantly called for resistance to popular culture replete with Western ideologies (e.g., Gao (ed.) 2008; Liu 2003). In contrast with later popular cultural and fan studies in China, largely inspired by John Fiske's scholarship, this stream of youth studies, at the risk of reducing their research subjects, takes no consideration of young consumers' active yet very limited subjectivities and agencies. An example was youth educator Liu Jiliang, who argued that popular culture 'corrupts and degenerates values. Popular culture does not have any depth. It is a flattened, non-humanistic and anti-aesthetic culture' (Liu 2003: 141).

Over the past decade, the ideological concern that accompanied cultural industries has all but disappeared from scholarly discussion; on the other hand, when youth and children are concerned, the anti-culture nature of popular culture and 'cultural-contamination' theses have continued. A recent case occurred on January 29, 2015, when China's Minister of

Education Yuan Guiren told Chinese universities to shun textbooks that promote 'Western values' (BBC 2015).

The stridency of the Frankfurt School, explicit in *wenhua gongye*, lost its popularity and critical significance at the turn of the century. The waning of *wenhua gongye* was accompanied by the waxing of *wenhua chanye* in scholarly papers. Between 1990 and 1999, the annual numbers of articles on *wenhua gongye* and *wenhua chanye* were roughly equivalent. However, from 2000 to 2007, articles on *wenhua chanye* dramatically outnumbered those on *wenhua gongye*. Fewer academic papers discussing *wenhua gongye* appeared annually; albeit between 2007 and 2010 the annual figure increased to more than one hundred. In sharp contrast, thousands of academic papers addressing the topic of *wenhua chanye* were produced annually (see Liu and Huang 2013:112–113).

One of the reasons contributing to the radical change in numbers was the rise of competing approaches to cultural research. Some scholars contend that the rise of cultural studies scholarship in China led to the demise of Frankfurt School critique in academia (e.g. Zhao 2009; Liu and Huang 2013). For example, media and cultural studies scholar John Fiske's *Understanding Popular Culture* (1989) became a key theoretical tool: it was translated in 2001 and was well received by Chinese intellectuals. In comparison with the Frankfurt school's pessimism towards popular culture, Fiske offered an optimistic view of people's agency and how they created meanings and messages for the products they consume. For example, drawing on Fiske's optimistic view of popular culture, the now Saint Mary's College-based Chinese cultural critic Xu Ben (1996) published an array of Chinese articles in the mid and late-1990s constantly calling for a re-examination of the Frankfurt School's Marxist theory when consumers' active agency is considered. Tao Dongfeng, who largely drew upon Frankfurt School critique when criticizing Chinese popular culture in the early 1990s, turned to cultural studies scholarship as a theoretical resource. He actively introduced much cultural studies scholarship to the Chinese audience (Tao 2009).[1]

Cultural industry papers began to dominate and one could sense a change in scholarly positions. In an article on the rise and fall of cultural industry theory in China, the literary scholar Zhao Yong (2009) examined the change from *gongye* to *chanye* by exploring the repositioning among key cultural industries scholars. Jin Yuanpu, one of the early cultural critics to fiercely criticize China's *wenhua gongye* used to draw on the Frankfurt School's line of inquiry. Jin repositioned himself as an economist and as part of the government's think tank. In a later article advocating China's *wenhua chanye*, Jin (1998) bluntly foregrounds the thesis 'culture is economy, culture is market', using American cultural industries as a key point of reference throughout the article. Zhao stressed that the emerging discourse of *wenhua chanye* was incompatible with *wenhua gongye* theories. He lamented that what was criticized in the 1990s had become the object of applause.

The reasons behind the increasing numbers of academic papers on *wenhua chanye* and the change behind the scholarly position on producing academic articles favouring *wenhua chanye* over *wenhua gongye* are complex. The increasing political currency and legitimacy of the former term is obvious. It is a simple matter of compiling a historiography of the increasing importance of the term *wenhua chanye* in government proposals, reports and documents, and ultimately in official policies and statements appearing since the year 2000 (for example see Liu and Liu 2014). Since 2000, the government has prioritized the cultural industries in order to serve the national economy and bring about the 'realization of China's modernization' (*People's Daily* 2001). Thus, it is no coincidence that the soaring number of academic papers echoes the dominant political rhetoric.

Since the turn of the century, cultural industries research centres and the think tanks have attracted enthusiastic attention in Chinese universities and colleges. Government-sponsored research projects, many of which spring from think tanks, no longer criticize *wenhua chanye*, no doubt believing that such criticism would bring back the association with the out-dated Frankfurt School's criticism, i.e. the *wenhua gongye* theories. Most of the intellectuals' stance and their theoretical backups incessantly shy away from the *wenhua gongye* theories. This is observed and criticized by Zhao Yong:

> In a latent logic, nowadays, criticizing *wenhua gongye* is equivalent to criticizing *wenhua chanye*, hence it is equivalent to antagonizing [the political rhetoric of] 'vigorously develop cultural industries' and its related policy. [. . .] These criticisms [toward cultural industries] either have trouble and difficulty to get their critical voice heard, or lose their significance and [are] overwhelmed by articles extolling *wenhua chanye*. (Zhao 2009: 30, author's translation)

The fall of the Frankfurt School coexists with (neo)liberal intellectuals' theoretical critique of radicalism and 'grand narrative' sentiments at the time (for example, see Zhang 2008). Cultural industries' scholarship no longer referenced and acknowledged Adorno and Horkheimer's critique of culture industry. China's New Left intellectuals, who largely embraced and accommodated the Frankfurt School's criticism in China, have lost their power since the 1990s. This can be sensed from the leading Chinese New Left thinker and literary scholar Wang Hui's (2010:11–12) reluctance to use the title of New Left intellectual. He prefers to use 'critical intellectual' rather than New Left as the latter are seen as xenophobic and as encouraging a primitive and essentialist form of nationalism. Wang Hui's strategic positioning further reveals the ambiguous stance of the Chinese New Left. After Deng Xiaoping's inspection tour of southern China in early 1992, where he called for 'bolder and faster' strides toward developing the market economy, engendering a deeper and wider commercialization of Chinese industry, society and culture, neoliberal economics had become the official economics of the postsocialist state (Zhang, 2008), or what is elsewhere described as a '*national project*' (Rofel 2007: 20, original emphasis). For Zhang Xudong (2008), the emergence of liberalism marked intellectual life since the 1990s. New Left intellectuals who reject the 'national project' and free-market rationality were left high and dry as they could not emphatically criticize the dominant mode of postsocialist modernity promoted by the government.

THE BLUE BOOK SYNDROME: DOING CULTURAL INDUSTRIES IN NINGBO

The shift of scholarship from the critique of global capitalism towards its accommodation has impacted on the humanities. My insider story of 'doing Chinese cultural industries research' in a university in Ningbo shows how deep these changes are. Between 2013 and 2014, I participated in *The Blue Book of Broadcasting and TV Industry of Ningbo* (Ningbo Broadcasting, Film and TV Association (eds.) 2014) with a group of writers consisting of Ningbo media practitioners, academics and government officials. This local government funded research project laid claim to be the first Blue Book to examine the broadcasting industries (primarily radio, film and television) at the city level, in this way emphasizing the local specificity of the cultural industries.

Economic development constitutes a major focus of Blue Books. The Blue Book referred to above drew attention to broadcasting, film and TV industries – 'the core of Ningbo cultural industries', viewed through an economic prism. As the editors of the book state clearly: the driving force behind the development of these core industries is to 'facilitate . . . economic transformation and upgrade, and become the new engine to develop the economic society (*jingji shehui*)' (269). The mind-set of economic effectiveness (*xiaoyi*) is the primary approach. The Blue Book emphasizes how economic development will make Ningbo a culturally strong city (*wenhua qiangshi*), a message that is reminiscent of the national passion vis-à-vis the revival of a 'strong cultural power' (*wenhua qiangguo*) borne aloft by rapid economic growth over the past three decades. This economics-driven effectiveness mentality is not confined to this local book project. Numerous scholarly papers from various disciplines and Blue

Books about cultural industries strongly articulate the objective of serving national, provincial and local economies. It is not difficult to find journal articles, scholarly books, master and doctoral theses closely associated with keywords such as 'new economic growth point', 'economic transformation', 'economic development', and 'regional economy.'

In addition, Blue Books publicize 'new achievements and new developments' under the leadership of the Chinese Communist Party and local government. The primary materials including data are provided and carefully edited by party-supervised media practitioners at both county (*xiang*) and city (*shi*) levels. The editorial board provided explicit direction for the chapters I contributed. One high-profile editor asked me to change the subtitling into a standardized compositional formation so that the article would look neat and good. The book launch was held in the Bureau of Ningbo Brigade of Cultural Market Administrative Law Enforcement (*wenhua shichang xingzheng zhifa zongdui*), the government organ overseeing practices in the cultural sector, including media, sports and tourism. The importance of the Blue Book was highlighted by one of the government officials at the book launch who mentioned that 'foreign experts would like to read this book for its authoritative nature'.[2]

It was no coincidence that this double-focus – economic agenda and political guidance – underpinned the logic that ran through a similar Blue Book that appeared the same year: *The Blue Book of Ningbo Development: Report on the Development of Ningbo Cultural Industry* (Huang et al. 2014). The articulation of an economic-political agenda in these two Blue Books differed little from the Party-state's and the central government's steadfast commitment to economic development and continuing political management.

This double force that underpinned the logic of these local Blue Books reflects what Geremie Barmé (1999) has called 'corporate communism' – or how consumerism goes hand-in-hand with the ideological promotion of the Chinese Communist Party. *Wenhua chanye* delivers quantifiable economic benefits that are highly valued: moreover, local forces cooperate in producing such 'corporate communism', as they benefit financially from the growth of local cultural industries. Media studies scholar Wanning Sun (2012) reminds us that local, regional, and provincial level media require careful examination in order to understand the complex relations between media, culture and geography. I extend her approach to focus on different levels of cultural industries.

My experience of participating in the Ningbo Blue Book projects allowed me access to the motivations of individual intellectuals and editors; furthermore it allowed me to reflect upon the normative practice in Chinese academia when producing accountable knowledge of China's cultural industries, and more specifically the editorial practices that under-pin what is included in Blue Books, and what is excluded.

Such normative practice in Chinese academia is played out through a dominant research mind-set, what I call a 'remedy paradigm'. As well as extolling local and national successes, the contributors provide counter-measures, suggestions to 'remedy' existing problems. Such an approach is not unfamiliar to me. After two years of teaching both undergraduate and postgraduate level courses on 'Chinese Cultural Industries' in Ningbo, I learned that the most popular approach in student essays is in fact a 'remedy paradigm'. The approach is as follows: the current state of certain public cultural institutions and industries is provided; existing problems are pointed out; and finally advice is presented to remedy problems. Clearly, this remedy paradigm does not restrict itself to undergraduate or postgraduate students' course essays. Or to put it more precisely, students learn and acquire such approaches through the work of academics.

The remedy paradigm is more apparent in another type of article called *juece jianyi gao* (draft suggestions for policy making), often the key com-ponent of Blue Books and related research projects. My participation in the local government funded research project on Ningbo Internet compa-nies supervised by the Ningbo Cultural Industries Research Base, strongly favoured the *juece jianyi gao* model. These kinds of article provide 'rem-edies' for policy-making and may help in resolutions to existing problems, while maximizing the financial benefits to local cultural industries.

The remedy formula may differ across various articles. For example, comparative research (often between different regions, cities, nations or cases) in the academic field of cultural industries often ends with policy advice to government. Numerous scholarly articles offer the creative and cultural industries 'models' of Japan, UK, Europe and the US as a key point for referencing.

CONCLUSION: A CULTURAL STUDIES ENGAGEMENT

Over the past two decades the rapid growth of China's economy and the profit-seeking nature of marketization and commercialization has affected almost every sphere of society and culture. As one of the keywords in contemporary China, *wenhua chanye* conjures up the image of a prosper-ous China, one with modernization and commercialization as its guiding ethos. If, in the early stage of the post socialist era, the uptake of the Frankfurt School was a vestige of the extant high culture fever, the 'cul-tural industries' emerged as a reaction to China's joining the WTO in 2001 and the need to make Chinese culture stronger. The way to make China an economically and culturally 'strong nation' was rapid industrialization and marketization. Some scholars have argued that neoliberal economics became the prevailing mode in economic thinking and the official economic policies of the postsocialist state (Zhang 2008).[3]

In this sense, universities followed the cultural industries grant money that ensued from this national agenda. Many intellectuals developed a specific form of consultancy mostly for different levels of government based on data collection and mapping. This consultancy research was dressed up as cultural industries and presented in a series of Blue Books. The comparison with other countries and regions precipitated a remedial approach – providing suggestions to think-tanks. However, this approach is at odds with the theories inherited from Frankfurt School. In the same vein, this remedial approach generates discord among Chinese critical intellectuals who reject free-market rationality and the established social scientific approaches, and who experience discontent with social inequality and domestic social problems, and the disappointing consequences of China's economic reform.

In order to resurrect a critical agenda, questions of cultural and creative labour need to be reinserted and the negative consequences of China's economic reform need to be reconsidered. This chapter suggests that it is crucial to evoke the critical significance and the complex nature of the Frankfurt School and *wenhua gongye* discourse. Instead of viewing cultural industries as a 'modernization' process, it is important to question and problematize the over-determination of data-driven reports evidenced in Blue Books. As an academic inquiry the cultural industries requires a scholarly position that is not allied with government think tank or government-sponsored economists' perspectives.

NOTES

1. The rise of the audience and consumer as the dominant subject study echoes the shifting paradigm in communication studies in general: audience reception, intervention, and articulation are evaluated and studied. The rise of the audience and consumer agency was further stimulated by the Super Girl phenomenon. Super Girl (or Super Voice Girls, *chaoji nüsheng*) was an annual talent contest in Mainland China organized by Hunan Satellite Television between 2004 and 2006. With over 280 million viewers voting via their mobile phones at a given time, the show provoked research interest into fans as active cultural consumers and agencies, and largely triggered the transformation of the research paradigm from the production end to the consumption activities.
2. The author's own observations at the book launch.
3. The use of neoliberalism here is purely economic. Others have argued that it is difficult to envisage neoliberalism in China when institutions are so deeply managed by government (see Keane 2013; Nonini 2008).

REFERENCES

Barmé, Geremie R. (1999), *In the Red: On Contemporary Chinese Culture*. New York: Columbia University Press.

BBC (2015), 'China says no room for "Western Values" in University Education', accessed 30 January 2015 at http://www.theguardian.com/world/2015/jan/30/china-says-no-room-for-western-values-in-university-education.

Driscoll, Catherine (2010), *Modernist Cultural Studies*. Gainesville: University Press of Florida.

Fiske, John (1989), *Understanding Popular Culture*. London: Unwin Hyman.

Gao, Zhongjian (ed.) (2008), *dangdai qingshaonian wenti yu duice yanjiu* (*Research on Contemporary Youth Problems and Countermeasures*). Beijing: zhongyang bianyi chubanshe.

Hesmondhalgh, David (2013), *The Cultural Industries* (3rd edition). London: Sage.

Huang Zhiming et al. (eds.) (2014), *Ningbo fazhan lanpishu: Ningbo wenhua chanye fazhan baogao* (*Blue Book of Ningbo Development: Report on the Development of the Ningbo Cultural Industry*). Hangzhou: Zhejiang University Press.

Jin, Yuanpu (1994), *shilun dangdai de 'wenhua gongye'* ('Discussion of contemporary "cultural industry"'), *wenyi lilun yanjiu* **2**: 26–32.

Jin, Yuanpu (1998), *wenhua chanye: 21 shiji de xinxing gongye* ('Cultural industries: new industries of the 21st century'), *21 shiji* (*21st Century*) **6**: 37–8.

Keane, Michael (2013), *Creative Industries in China*. Malden: Polity.

Liu, Jiliang (2003), *qingshaonian jiazhiguan jiaoyu yanjiu* (*Research on Adolescents' Values Education*). Guangzhou: Guangdong jiaoyu chubanshe.

Liu, Hailong and Yalan Huang (2013), *shilun 'wenhua gongye' dao 'wenhua chanye' de yujing bianqian* ('On the discourse change from "cultural industry" to "cultural industries"'), *shanxi daxue xuebao (zhexue shehui kexue ban)* Shanxi University Academic Journal **36**, 2: 110–18.

Liu, Xinxin and Qingzhen Liu (2014), *cong wenhua gongye dao wenhua chanye* ('From cultural industry to cultural industries'), *dangdai chuanbo* (*Contemporary Communication*) **3**: 102–12.

Meng, Fanhua (2003), *zhongshen kuanghuan: shiji zhijiao de zhongguo wenhua xianxiang* (*Bacchanalia of Culture: The Clash of Cultures in Contemporary China*). Beijing: zhongyang bianyi chubanshe.

Ningbo Broadcasting, Film and TV Association, Ningbo Broadcasting, Film and TV Development Research Centre (eds.) (2014), *Ningbo Guangdian Lanpishu: Ningbo guangbo dianshi dianying fazhan baogao* (*Blue Book of Broadcasting and TV Industry of Ningbo: Report on Development of Broadcasting, Film and TV industry in Ningbo*). Beijing: Zhongguo guangbo yingshi chubanshe.

Nonini, Donald (2008), 'Is China becoming neo-liberal?' *Critique of Anthropology* **28** (2): 145–76.

People's Daily (2001), 'Cultural development concerns realization of China's modernization, rejuvenation of Chinese nation', accessed 3 January 2015 at http://english.cntv.cn/20111019/102118.shtml.

Rofel, Lisa (2007), *Desiring China: Experiments in Neoliberalism, Sexuality, and Public Culture*. Durham: Duke University Press.

Sun, Wanning (2012), 'Rescaling media in China: the formations of local, provincial, and regional media cultures', *Chinese Journal of Communication* **3**, 1: 10–15.

Tao Dongfeng (1993), *yuwang yu chenlun: dangdai dazhong wenhua pipan* ('Desire and decadence: criticism of contemporary mass culture'), *wenyi zhengming* **6**: 10–21.

Tao Dongfeng (ed.) (2009), *fensi wenhua duben* (*Fan Cultures: a Reader*). Beijing: Peking University Press.

Wang, Jing (1996), *High Culture Fever: Politics, Aesthetics, and Ideology in Deng's China*. Berkeley: University of California Press.

Wang, Hui ([2009] 2010), *bieqiu xinsheng: Wanghui fangtanlu* (*In search of Alternative Voices: Dialogues with Wang Hui*). Beijing: Peking University Press.

Xu, Ben (1996), *zouxiang houxiandai yu houzhimin* (*Towards Postmodern and Postcolonialism*). Beijing: Zhongguo shehui kexue chubanshe.

Zhang Rulun (1994), *lun dazhong wenhua* ('On popular culture'), *Fudan xuebao* **3**: 16–22.

Zhang Guofeng (1998), *wenhua gongye shizhi shi yizhong fanwenhua* ('The essence of cultural industry is a form of anti-culture'), *wenyi bao*, 28 July.

Zhang, Xudong (2008), *Postsocialism and Cultural Politics: China in the Last Decade of the Twentieth Century*. Durham: Duke University Press.

Zhang, Jie (2009), *dali fazhan 'wenhua chanye' jianjuedizhi 'wenhua gongye'* ('Vigorously develop "cultural industries" and resolutely resist "cultural industry"'), *Anhui wenxue* **7**: 378–80.

Zhao Yong (2009), *weijiechu shuoguo de sixiangzhihua: wenhua gongye lilun zai zhongguo de xingsheng yu shuailuo* ('The rise and fall of cultural industries theory in China'), *wenyi zhengming* **11**: 25–31.

Zhou Yuning (1998), *'wenhua gongye' wenti yantaohui jiyao* ('Summary of the seminar on the problem of the "Cultural Industry"'), *wenyi bao*, 14 April.

Zhu, Fuen and Na Liu (2012), *fazhan wenhua chanye shi jiakuai zhuanbian jingji fazhan de zhuolidian* ('Developing cultural industry is a key to accelerate economic transformation and development'), *lilun tansuo* **3**: 89–92.

3. The ten thousand things, the Chinese Dream and the creative←→cultural industries
Michael Keane

How should we assess the success of China's cultural and creative industries almost two decades after their inception?

Noting the evidence provided in government reports, many observers are impressed by the growth in the Chinese marketplace. Cinema box-office takings are rising, real estate values have climbed in cultural quarters and zones, the value of the visual art market has skyrocketed, artefacts and ethnic handicrafts are sold in increasing numbers on Taobao, and China's online media companies are scaling up their investment portfolios. Yet if we move beyond the data and talk to artists, media producers and investors there are indications of a larger story, one that is still unfolding. There is undoubtedly more growth to be had, particularly in international markets, but there is a great deal of disparity across sectors.

Along with the great expectations attached to domestic expansion, the import and export of cultural goods and services has come centre stage. In recent years there have been impassioned calls for China's 'cultural soft power' to be strengthened. The newest development slogan pressed into service is the 'strong cultural power' (*wenhua qiangguo*), in part reflecting a widely held belief that Chinese culture is the parent form in East Asian societies. In addition to hundreds of Confucius Institutes around the world, China exports performing arts, books, movies and documentaries about historical achievements and television programmes explaining Chinese ways of life.[1] One perspective is that international audiences will come to understand China in a new light when they see the 'real Chinese culture' (see chapter by Li Wuwei this volume). At the same time a view persists that China's outbound trade is too 'official' and too propagandist, resulting in negative consumer reaction rather than acclamation. The products that officially represent real Chinese culture in the export market align with the government's brand image, now celebrated in TV talent shows, talk shows and journalism as the 'Chinese Dream'. President Xi Jinping has declared: 'increasing national cultural soft power is related to the realization of the Chinese Dream.'[2]

As slogans go, the 'Chinese Dream' is a call-to-arms, urging Chinese nationals to collectively imagine a great future. Rather than a dream, however, it is an aspiration. While this aspiration is directed at what the media scholar Benedict Anderson (1983) referred to as an 'imagined community', the Chinese national community is now fragmented, both within the nation state itself and dispersed across many nations. The term 'Chinese characteristics', frequently used to show how China absorbs and adapts international ideas, loses its impact in the era of dispersed communities. In coining this term in 1992, Deng Xiaoping was describing a 'market economy with Chinese characteristics.' The changes Deng presided over affected the whole nation and led to increasing decentralization. In today's China numerous characteristics abound: distinctive development models, diverse market segments, and restless ethnic minorities.

The great expectation that China's culture will 'go out' confronts the reality that the world market is not responding with acclamation to the kinds of cultural goods that are being sent out. In the words of political scientist David Shambaugh: 'We witness a large and growing number of China's cultural activities abroad – but very little influence on global trends, minimal soft power, and a mixed-to-poor international image in public opinion polls' (Shambaugh 2013: 207). The official image offered to the world is invariably that of a well-ordered society, a nation with an ancient culture, beautiful landscapes and wonderful cuisine. The world has yet to see the evidence of 'creative China.'

In this chapter I explore challenges facing China as it attempts to propagate a new brand image, that of a great cultural power on the one hand, and an innovative creative nation on the other. Drawing on correspondences between nature and culture, between science and art, and technology and creativity, I propose an alternative way of understanding the role of the cultural and creative industries in China. Essentially, as we all know, from a policy perspective, the cultural and creative industries are grounded in the arts and humanities. Yet, with digital technology providing low cost tools and a never-ending variety of communicative affordances this foundation may not be so self-evident. In this context my intention is to reconsider the utility of the terms 'cultural' and 'creative', not only in China but elsewhere in the world. In the normal order of things in China 'cultural' precedes 'creative'; culture is civilizing and it orders the relations between people. With respect to industries, I believe it is now time to acknowledge a different ordering: I call this the creative←→cultural industries.

The synergy between creativity and culture is seldom canvassed in policy. The terms, together or separately, more often serve as normative indicators of development; hence a fascination with comparative indexes, the kinds popularized by Richard Florida (2002) for instance. Much focus, particularly in China, is directed to economic performance, reflecting a simple input-output model – cultural labour and investment, often from government as the input, and the commodity form as output. Bean counters couple the cultural and creative (industries) without any real consideration of how they actually function in the conjugal relationship. The data presented in Blue Book reports however is only a small part of the untapped 'people' resources. Delving deeper we find something more interesting about the relationship between creativity and culture.

In reversing the orthodox culture→creativity ordering I want to reconsider the role of grassroots collaboration. This leads to the question: is a harmonious creative society possible? Inevitably innovation comes from challenging the status quo. Is there a way therefore that the Internet – with its immense potential for generative innovation – can alter the 'China code'? Another way of saying this is: can Web 2.0, the sharing economy, crowdsourcing, collaborative production and network effects bring about a more creative←→cultural China?

Before considering the potentialities of platforms and the uses of collaborative media, I offer a traditional perspective on change. This leads to my key premise: that order and disorder are both necessary for creative expression, which is by definition unlimited. From a conceptual standpoint I argue that the relationship between creativity and culture is correlative and constantly changing; in understanding the nature of this relationship I will draw some observations about change, reform, novelty and continuity in China. The source of my enquiry is Chinese philosophy, or at least some elements of it. Understanding the application of traditional Chinese dialectics allows us to move from abstract metaphysical concepts to a deeper understanding of a 'world situation', namely the application of Chinese cultural policy. In using such a dialectical approach I believe it is possible to explain why the Chinese central government mandates the term 'cultural industries' and why it remains mistrustful of creativity.

THE PATTERNS OF THE PAST

While there is considerable literature on creativity – from creative people (types and personalities) to process, products, education and environments – very little work on process applies directly to the creative industries where the focus is on policy, products, environments and human capital. In investigating process I avoid the classic stage approach, namely problem solving, identification, definition etc. (Wallis 1926) and look at the role of scenarios, risk taking and recombination.

To give an example of the key idea I am exploring, consider the animated movie released by Disney/Pixar called *Inside Out* in 2015, a highly imaginative journey through the emotions of a child. The gestation of this challenging and 'risky' work took several years and was provisionally entitled *The Untitled Pixar Movie That Takes You Inside the Mind*. Making this animated movie presented a real challenge for the Pixar team: how to present a novel take on emotions and memory in a way that would attract both children and adults. During the period when the narrative was fermenting in the mind of screenwriter Pete Docter, he learned from a neuroscientist that 'only about 40 per cent of what we think we "see" comes in through our eyes' (Catmull 2014: 178). The remainder, some 60 per cent, is made up of patterns that we recognize from memory and past experience.

How does the past then impact on what we see and hear? Biologist E.O. Wilson says that the human sensory range is extremely limited compared to other animals; he says this limited sensory capacity provides great opportunities for the humanities because we rely on our memories (and imagination) to 'fill in'. There are so many ways for artists to spin stories. Yet Wilson believes that science and the arts are more similar than people generally believe: he says, 'what counts in science is the importance of the discovery. What matters in literature is the originality and power of the metaphor' (Wilson 2012: 276). He goes on: 'In the early stages of creation of both art and science, everything in the mind is a story' (Wilson 2012: 275); that is, the *written accounts* of scientific discovery and literature follow a similar process:

> In works of literature and art alike, any part can be changed, causing a ripple among the other parts, some of which are discarded and new ones added. The surviving fragments are variously joined and separated, and moved about as the story forms. One scenario emerges, then another.

CULTURE

So how do the scenarios emerge and converge? Let's look at culture first – after all, it is the dominant signifier. Echoing the statement by Wilson about the similarities of processes of discovery in science and the humanities, my point of departure is the relationship between nature and culture. Geoffrey Lloyd (2007: 131), a professor of ancient philosophy and science, observes that 'nature may be taken to correspond to what is universal, and culture with what varies from one group to another.' Lloyd also points out that the actual universality of this judgement was, and still is, open to dispute. In the Greek tradition nature became a normative term only as creation myths (e.g. Homer, Hesiod) gave way to a scientific approach to understanding the world. The separation of nature and culture in Western thought began from these pre-Hellenic origins, leading to the normative notion that what is natural or scientific is based on reason, and by extension culture is 'the realm of values, the relative, the subjective, the personal' (Lloyd: ibid).

For the ancient Chinese, nature and culture were represented by heaven and earth (*tiandi*) while the term 'ten thousand things' (or myriad things) (*wanwu*) captured the diversity of all beings and things. The emphasis was change, illustrated by variations in the patterns of things (*li*) and the idea of spontaneity or 'self-so' (*ziran*), a word also used for nature. The non-separation of nature and culture however was not confined to Chinese society: it is found in many non-Western contexts (Lloyd 2007; McLean 2009).[3]

Scholars are at loggerheads about how to define culture (see Williams 1988) but no such problems exist in China. Theories of culture (*wenhua*) in China have devolved from Marxist dialectics, Maoist revolutionary class struggle, and elements of Chinese tradition. In traditional China the Confucianists aspired to build and maintain a well-ordered society, which is not so different from modern times. Literature was a key element of governance, producing what Chad Hansen calls 'the *flow chart* of a civilization' (Hansen 1992: 75, italics in original). The Confucian rectification of names, roles and social responsibilities produced the *dao* (way): this manual for conduct was interpreted differently by the more irreverent Daoists (see below).

From this perspective culture is essentially a process of forming and reforming, patterning, and hence identifying or 'knowing the way' (*zhi-dao*). Enculturation occurs by a process of making distinctions (*shi-fei*) – 'this' not 'that' (Hansen 1992: 101). The Chinese philosopher Li Zehou uses the concept of 'sedimentation' to describe how material culture is distilled and condensed into aesthetic forms over time, embracing the 'social atmosphere' of various periods (Li 2010: xi). In the Chinese tradition he notes that the major themes are beauty and goodness, society and nature, feeling and form, art and politics.

In the modern age, the Chinese Communist Party (hereafter CCP) produced its version of the way (*dao*), called Marxist-Leninist Mao Zedong Thought. Of course, the CCP's cultural *dao* absorbed new variations over time. At the political level the standard definition is: 'Culture, in a broad sense, refers to the sum total of all the material and spiritual wealth created by human beings in the course of the historical development of society; in a narrow sense, culture refers to ideology and related institutions and organizations' (*Cihai*, Chinese Encyclopaedia 1989: 1731). This classic definition of culture presumes that there is a preordained purpose and people move from lower to higher understandings, guided by more enlightened 'model' individuals. But the above definition, while explaining the penchant for political terms like leader (*lingdao*) and people (*renmin*), doesn't tell us how people make actual cultural choices in China. We need a more evolutionary perspective.

Culture, or what we classify as such, is essentially made up of memories. Returning to the Pixar anecdote above, if we see about 40 per cent of the world through our eyes, how then do we make sense of the world? The answer is: we fill in from our cultural knowledge, much of which is memories of stuff we have learnt or been told, myths and legends, hearsay, etc., some of which is buried deep in our DNA and some of which comes to us through the media. Much of this cultural knowledge comes from social groups we belong to or affiliate with, and the languages we use to differentiate ourselves from other groups: this is what John Hartley and Jason Potts call 'demes' (Hartley and Potts 2014).

Individuals use communication to reduce complexity by creating a boundary between themselves and the outside world, and they are constituted through their act of communication with that environment. In so doing, they also construct the outside world through which they know themselves. Essentially this is how culture works: ideas are sorted into categories, some of which remain stable and some of which are transitory (Hartley and Potts 2014: 25).

According to Richerson and Boyd (2005: 49), people's decisions 'about which ideas to adopt or reject shape the content of culture'. Sometimes such decisions are unconscious. An evolutionary definition follows from this: 'Culture is information capable of affecting individuals' behaviour that they acquire from other members of their species through teaching, imitation, and other forms of social transmission' (ibid.).

In other words culture is knowledge. One's taste for creative goods and services is not given once for all time: it is dependent on repeated exposure, on repetition, reinforcement and experience. Reinforcement allows cultural tastes of one generation to be passed on to the next (Barbot et al. 2013). Moreover, if people are continually exposed to certain kinds of culture they might come to believe over time that there is no need for new and foreign forms. This was the rationale of cultural policy in China until recently. The strategy of the Chinese propaganda state under Chairman Mao was to repeatedly expose people to a narrative of progress, propagate cultural models, and deny access to foreign forms. In short, the Chinese Revolution proceeded by maintaining control of formats, genres and representations, and by punishing those who transgressed. After the 1980s when many people were exposed to new experiences through travel, study, and through watching Western movies, they began to question the guiding interpretations handed down by teachers and the media, the so-called 'engineers of the soul'. In the main, therefore, the emphasis in Chinese cultural policy, and the cultural industries, is to promote good and healthy representations of the well-ordered 'harmonious' society.

But as the philosopher and cognitive scientist Daniel Dennett (2013) notes, as well as seeing culture as the good things that are passed on it is also important to see the 'bad habits and ugly patterns'. The patterns of the past can restrict our ability to renew the way we think, make informed decisions and evaluate outsiders. Cultural evolution is part of a learning process: the production and consumption of movies, animation, comics, literature, music, painting, and art is to a significant extent socio-cultural. If our understanding of artistic endeavour is socio-cultural then it is understandable that some societies and communities are more embracing of creative experimentation, while others are more conservative.

CREATIVITY

Culture therefore is bound up with evolution: the 'socio-cultural' context is self-explanatory, groups come together and culture is made to 'fit.' Before proceeding to consider creativity within Chinese thinking I will identify three variants: 'combinational', 'exploratory', and 'transformational' (Boden 2013). According to Margaret Boden, a professor of cognitive science, combinational creativity is the 'generation of unfamiliar combinations of familiar ideas' (Boden 2013: 2); exploratory creativity involves 'new thinking styles' within a particular field of endeavour (for instance conceptual advances in poetry, painting or music); while transformational creativity evokes the quest for originality, the search for the new paradigm, even the new theoretical breakthrough in science. In actual fact most creativity is fundamentally combinational – and arguably much of this is uncreative. Applying these categories to China it is apparent that combinational creativity is widespread and is applicable to the breakout of *shanzhai* and maker cultures (see discussion below and in the chapter by Jing Wang). The reason that so much activity is combinational has something to do with the excessive fragmentation of markets in China: it is possible to take elements from one locale or region and localize. Recombination is a necessary first stage; the harder work is exploration and transformation.

Combination is ultimately about changing the order of things. Many combinations occur by chance; that is by experimentation, by playing with variations until they produce something new or culturally distinctive, a new melody for instance, a haiku. My first conjecture in this regard comes from *The Book of Changes* (*Yijing*),[4] a well-known Chinese divination practice that became a text of philosophical wisdom. During the Shang and Zhou dynasties in ancient China diviners dispensed advice to rulers.

Diviners evolved from shamans into Confucian officials, advisors and *junzi*, that is, men[5] of education and standing. Prior to the written records of governance in the classic books, the advisor would utilize a method of prediction by interpreting the cracks made on tortoise shells that had been exposed to heat. *The Book of Changes* evolved from these early divination practices, becoming a required study text for educated elites. In times of warfare elites with knowledge of ancient texts were in high demand.

The Book of Changes refers to changes (*yi*) in the world, not only natural changes but those introduced by humans. In this early manual for governance the meaning of dialectics (*bianzheng*) is represented in terms of several key Chinese concepts: *dao* (way), *yi* (change), *yin-yang*, and in particular, *biantong* (change with continuity) (Tian 2009: 514). The fundamental principle underpinning dialectical reasoning is that all activities are composed of *yin* and *yang* forces.[6] The complementarity (and opposition) of forces leads to all manner of 'world-situations' in which people find themselves: in other words, the *yin-yang* dynamic explains 'all things in their formation and transformation' (Cheng 2009: 72). The *yin-yang* concept also infuses the practice of Traditional Chinese Medicine (TCM). If *yin* and *yang* elements in the body are unbalanced for any period of time, for instance in the circulatory system, the resulting transformations will be detrimental to health.

While an in-depth discussion of *yin-yang* theory may lead into arcane abstractions, there is a fundamental principle at stake: that is, the relationship between *yin* and *yang* is 'mutually supporting, transforming, balancing, enhancing and furthering of the new' (Cheng 2009: 75). According to Chung-ying Cheng the *yin-yang* relationship is creative and productive: 'it is creative because it leads to new possibilities of realization and it is productive because it is generative of new things' (Cheng 2009: 75). In a highly imaginative collection of 64 short stories based on *The Book of Changes*, the novelist Will Buckingham (2015: 16) writes:

> To make use of the I Ching is to play at the boundaries of order between disorder. Nothing is both from order and disorder alone. For the arising of anything at all – solid bodies, stars, worlds, animals, human beings, poems, stories, in short that mass of phenomena that the Chinese designate as *wanwu*, or the ten thousand things – both order and disorder are necessary.

In the *Book of Changes* the first two hexagrams are *qian* (creative) and *kun* (receptive). In a commentary text called the *Xi-Ci*, it is said: 'The *qian* leads the great creation, the *kun* completes the creation of all things. *Qian* leads the simple quality of changing (*yi*), the *kun* is capable of completing by simply following' (Cheng 2009: 82). It is said that these fundamental hexagrams generate all of the ten thousand things through their interaction. The 'creative' and the 'receptive' therefore constitute two different aptitudes or dispositions: they are dynamically correlated – like day-night, expansion-contraction, impulse-response, change-nurture, and birth-completion. Importantly, Chinese philosophical thinking, unlike the Western tradition inherited from Descartes, did not separate the mind from the body: the *yin-yang* correlation connects 'heaven, earth and the myriad things' (Wang 2012: 12). Drawing from this I suggest that creativity and culture reflect these dialectical oppositions. In other words, culture is receptive of and completes creativity.

MAKE IT NEW

A second insight from classical Chinese texts comes from a Confucian text, *The Great Learning*. Dealing primarily with ethical behaviour, *The Great Learning* (sometimes called the *Ultimate Learning*) has enduring importance in Chinese social life. Along with the *Analects of Confucius*, *The Mencius*, and the *Doctrine of the Mean* (*zhongyong*), *The Great Learning* established prescriptive guidelines for people's behaviour as well as initiating the power-knowledge community of Confucian scholar-officials that would last until the end of the Qing Dynasty. In the commentary of the manuscript the following words can be found: 'The inscription engraved on Tang's bathing tub said, "Truly renew [yourself] each day. Day after day renew (yourself], and again, each day, renew [yourself]"' (*Daxue* 2012: 143).

King Tang was a legendary ruler in the Shang Dynasty in China. The anecdote about his bathing routines forms the subject of three different interpretations,[7] the most authoritative coming from Zhu Xi, the father of Neo-Confucianism, who noted,

> Tang took a man 'washing' his mind to get rid of evil to be like a man washing his body to get rid of dirt. Therefore he engraved his bathing tub with words saying that, for if one day you are truly able to wash away the dirt of old stains and renew yourself, then you ought to take what has already been renewed and every day renew it, and again, each day renew it. There cannot be the slightest interruption in this process.

The original intention of this commentary it seems is to constantly cleanse oneself by getting rid of the stains and habits of the past. In the second century BC, Qinshi Huangdi, the first emperor of China, made a conscious decision to cleanse the stains of the past by burning books and burying alive scholars who represented this past. The emperor was selective, burning books that he had no need for, while keeping those that were useful including the *Book of Changes*. In doing this, the emperor was able to reform and build an empire. The list of achievements include the standardization of a measurement system and written scripts, reinforcing 'legalism' within the administrative system and constructing the Great Wall and the Terracotta Warriors, now essential tourism resources counted as cultural industries.

In changing the China code the first emperor was well aware of *yin-yang* correlations. Returning to the metaphor of the 'ten thousand things', I believe we can draw a parallel with the modern technology of the World Wide Web where everything online seems instantly obsolete, where it is fashionable to constantly take on multiple identities and changing profiles, where nodes become networks, and where power laws overcome chance events.

While creativity is a buzzword of the ages, its relationship to reform, innovation systems, cultural branding and 'change-making' is relatively new. Rob Pope (2005) argues that the term 'creativity' surfaced as an object of public concern in the mid-twentieth century around about the time that the West saw its own cultural revolution along with the rise of the 'beat generation', and later the Beatles. Perhaps the origins of the creativity discourse as it applies to disruptive change can be located in modernism. The slogan 'make it new' underpinned the modernism movement in Western liberal democracies during the 1960s and 1970s.

'Make it new' is often attributed to the American-born poet Ezra Pound who was also a scholar of Chinese philosophy. In *Novelty, A History of the New*, Michael North recounts how Pound discovered it via translation in *The Great Learning*. According to a leading account of modernism (Gay 2008: 46), Pound's injunction to 'make it new' came to serve as a 'professional, almost sacred obligation' among practitioners (cited in North 2013: 162). In his 1936 translation *The Great Learning* Pound rendered the note on the bathing habits of the Shang dynasty ruler King Tang as 'to renovate', adding a footnote that this sagely advice was in fact to 'make it new'.[8]

'Make it new' is the *lingua franca* of China's 650 million 'netizens'.

ORDER AND DISORDER: INEXHAUSTIBLE CREATIVITY

In the opening section I observed that about 40 per cent of what we think we see comes through our eyes. I argued that we constantly make up our reality, drawing on the patterns of the past, including hard-wired fears and prejudices. We use our consolidated cultural memories, our group allegiances and linguistic systems, along with fragments of inherited and personal belief systems to make sense. In this way we order and archive our incoming thoughts as culture and separate ourselves from animals and other humans. The ordering of culture in epochs, categories, species, systems, periods, genres, fashions etc. is done by both scientists and artists, but more so by cultural elites.

While the cultural and creative industries in China are subject to a great deal of archiving, cataloguing and regulation, much informal activity is not registered. The former editor of the journal *Urban China*, Jiang Jun writes:

> To research China, we must look at its means of control . . . In an integrated archetype of traditional Chinese society, control is almost omnipresent. In this context, a discussion on 'informal China' cannot be limited only to the 'informal' aspect, but should look at the dialectical interaction between 'control' and 'out-of-control'. (Jiang 2006: 20)

In other words Chinese culture evolved from legacies of 'control' and 'out-of-control'.

The idea of order and disorder are intrinsic to Chinese culture and society. The precursor was the Warring States period in the Zhou Dynasty, a time when sages built careers dispensing advice to kings. Confucianism, despite suffering at the hands of the first Emperor, survived as a manual for social stability. Modern Chinese history is a record of disorder followed by order, from the White Lotus Rebellion, the Taiping Rebellion and Boxer Rebellion in the Qing Dynasty to the struggle against the Nationalists that eventually saw the formation of the People's Republic of China in 1949. Disorder is replayed constantly in popular culture, in Chinese TV serials and cinema, lest 'the common people' (*laobaixing*) forget. The foundation of Chinese cultural thinking is for this reason holistic, stressing the priority of the whole (the nation) over its parts.

Perhaps the most 'out-of-control' period, at least in modern Chinese history, was the so-called Cultural Revolution (1966–76). In many respects this was a time of unprecedented disruptive creativity, a time when many people took it on themselves to reinterpret policies (see Yu 2011), and for this reason the Cultural Revolution is very rarely the subject of TV dramas and movies. More often through history, control (censorship) was exerted over artists, writers and recently filmmakers. The governments of the dynastical period as well as modern day governments have attempted to define what constitutes Chinese culture, usually good and beautiful representations.

Earlier I spoke of Traditional Chinese Medicine (TCM) and the effects of an imbalance of *yin-yang* elements. While the complexities of TCM are not widely understood by all people in China, the fundamental principles are, particularly the idea that prescriptions for health should be holistic and inclusive rather than specific and exclusive, as in Western medicine (Ames 2011: 57). It is not surprising then that the metaphor of the healthy body permeates governmental discourse on the cultural industries. For instance, in the 12th Five Year Plan culture is depicted as the 'circulatory system of China's nationalities, the Chinese people's spiritual homeland' (Cai 2012: 6). The 'strong cultural nation' (*wenhua qiangguo*) discourse builds on this health and wellbeing (*yangsheng*) metaphor, arguing that a 'healthy' circulatory system will strengthen China's cultural sovereignty. This is not a discourse of radical change but more a reminder that everyone shares the same circulatory system and should self-regulate for the greater good of the nation.

China becoming a cultural power should not be the wishful thinking of an elite few but a common pursuit of all citizens. And just like the circulatory system national cultural strategy should circulate culture to every part of society from a national level down to a regional, business and local level (Xiang 2013: 77).

The dynamic correlation between order-disorder underpins the successful working of the creative industries in most countries. Moreover it creates economic value and soft power dividends. In other words creativity is valued in liberal democratic societies because it is inherently 'disorderly': the symbiotic relationship between disorder and order generates new and challenging cultural works. Looking back to China's past we can only imagine what might have been had Confucianism not triumphed over Daoism. The Daoists, while forming different schools, were largely sceptical of excessive order and the Confucian emphasis on ritual. The influences of Daoism on Chinese creative art (especially poetry and painting) are well known and have a close affinity with Chan (Zen) Buddhism. As the Daoist sage, Zhuangzi, noted: 'The existence of things is like a galloping horse. With every moment it changes. Every second it is transformed' (*Zhuangzi* Ch XVII, cited in Chang 2011: 73). The *Yijing* notes that the creative process is 'inexhaustible'. The last of the sixty-four hexagrams *wei chi*, meaning 'not completed', follows the sixty-third hexagram *chi chi*, 'already completed'.[9] A much-celebrated verse from *Laozi* tells us:

> The *dao* gave birth to the one, the one gave birth to the two, and the two gave birth to the three, and the three gave birth to the ten thousand things. Ten thousand things carry the *yin* and embrace the *yang*, and through the blending of *qi* (vital force), they achieve harmony. (translation by Shen 2003: 357)

While the meaning of this verse is sometimes disputed, Vincent Shen says that 'the one' is 'understood minimally as the beginning of being' whereas 'the two' represents the *yin* and *yang*, pairs of opposites such as being and non-being, or movement and rest. The three, and this is a key point in my argument, represents 'their interactive and dynamic interplay' (Shen 2003: 357).

CONCLUSION: RECODING THE CHINESE DREAM

So far I have endeavoured to show that creativity and culture exist in a correlative relationship. If this argument holds true it is probably futile quibbling about whether or not the terms 'cultural' or 'creative' industries are the better descriptor. Let's celebrate conjugality, preferably creative←→cultural industries. My argument is that the relationship is mutually dependent, correlative and unlimited in potentiality. One element (the creative) tends to be disruptive, and sometimes disorderly, the other (culture) tends to be orderly and ordering/harmonizing. The dynamic interplay comes into sharp focus as we move into an era of Web 2.0 platforms and collaborative culture, which offers increasing opportunities for recombination and sharing of 'talents, expertise, creativity and insights that were previously undervalued' (Chase 2015: 33). The key to this line of thinking is that a great deal of innovation comes from below, not from the big companies' research and development centres or government think tanks. People writing blogs, commenting on social media sites and uploading user-generated content contribute to the rapid increase in the combinational mode of creativity, or at least the volume of output: they may also bring about exploratory and transformational forms of creativity.

Interactive technologies have loosened the controls over official culture and made it more amenable to critique. Parodies (*egao*) flourish, generating myriad iterations (e.g. *Gangnam Style*). It is increasingly difficult to define a final form, if this ever were possible. Echoing Daoism and Zen Buddhism David Hall writes: 'Aesthetic events are momentary acts of creativity that come into being and at the point of full actualization cease to be in the fullest sense' (Hall 1982: 214). Of course, from a commercial and artistic sense, the final cut of the movie, the final overdub of the soundtrack, the final edit of the word on the page, these are the tangible IP that make the creative economy tick. Yet paradoxically originality relies on movement, continuous change. Liu (2003: 696) reminds us of how the *Yijing* deals with this: 'Changes mean creative creativity (*sheng sheng*)'. This is limitless, unbounded.

Never-ending acts of creativity are found in subconscious mental activity, in particular dreaming. The 'epistemological chaos' that pervades our lives in waking consciousness (see Buckingham 2014), finds fertile ground in which to play out in our dreaming hours. And vice-versa perhaps, our dreams pervade perceptions of reality. And while we can't control our dreams we are aware of conscious decisions. Without doubt our dreams are made up of memories, as are our cultural beliefs. Now the 'dream' metaphor has been given a new life in policy and a seemingly 'inexhaustible life' in online parody.

The Chinese Dream, like its counterpart the American Dream, with which it is often compared, is built on a solid material foundation – thousands of years of tradition, cultural memory and institutions: this is Li Zehou's sedimentation. It is a collective dream insofar as it is promulgated in the state media. Currently the collective dream is about national realization, China becoming a 'great cultural power' (*wenhua qiang guo*). The ethos of the American Dream is younger: its materialist foundation is a belief that everyone can obtain prosperity, and that opportunity awaits. In this dreamscape there is no requirement to become a singular cultural power. America has, and continues to absorb cultures from the world.

What these two dreams have in common, however, is stratification, consolidation and formation of empire: in the case of the US it is capitalism, in the case of China, socialism (albeit with capitalist underpinnings). The US model of capitalism was founded on industrialization, as now are China's cultural and creative industries.

Yet something quite significant is occurring that undermines these foundations: the crowdsourcing of creativity and innovation is occurring at pace, made possible by digital communication affordances, platforms, and the rapid transfer of ideas across national borders. The old model of top-down social structuring is changing and adjusting because of the grassroots forces of creative destruction – the new ten thousand things. While the system remains intact, largely thanks to cultural DNA and fears of social disorder, the inefficiencies, excesses, and rigidities of top-down models, both capitalist and socialist, are challenged by collaborative models of doing and making. These are the new 'ten thousand things', the present and future of creative←→cultural industries.

NOTES

1. Meanwhile, arguably the most successful Chinese television programme export is *If You are the One*, a reality style show about dating.
2. See Xi Jinping: 'Build a socialist strong cultural power, raise national cultural soft power' http://news.xinhuanet.com/politics/2013-12/31/c_118788013.htm.
3. In recent studies in the field of actor-network theory, scholars have problematized the divide between the natural and the social sciences, as well as rethinking the relations

between humans and non-humans (see Callon and Law 1995; Latour 2005). Other developments examining the integration of nature and culture from a 'Western' perspective include the field of research known as 'cultural science' (Hartley and Potts 2014).
4. Also known as the *I Ching and Zhouyi*.
5. *Junzi* were by definition male: in some respects *junzi* performed a creative function in Chinese political society by offering options to rulers. For a discussion see Tan (2015).
6. It is possible to construe that yin-yang theory positions the male above the female and that female (yin) aspects were bad or problematic; this perspective came into play under Confucianism but was not conventionally associated with the intention of the Daodejing where the yin elements of yielding, flexibility and submissiveness were equally powerful, in theory if not in practice.
7. Interpretations were by Zheng Xuan, Kong Yingda and Zhu Xi.
8. 'Renovate, dod gast you, renovate!', cited in North 2013. Other translations, including one by the Christian missionary James Legge, came closer to the original intention, which was to renovate oneself, from day to day, from moment to moment – although Legge's version positioned this renewal in relation to the Christian idea of being born again through Christ.
9. See Shu-hsien Liu (2003), entry for 'creativity' in *The Encyclopaedia of Chinese Philosophy*, p.696.

REFERENCES

Adorno, Theodor (1948), *Aesthetic Theory*, trans C. Lenhardt. New York: Routledge and Kegan Paul.
Ames, Roger T. (2011), *Confucian Role Ethics: A Vocabulary*. Hong Kong: The Chinese University Press.
Anderson, Benedict (1983), *Imagined Communities: Reflections on the Origin and Spread of Nationalism*. London: Verso.
Barbot, Baptiste, Mei Tan, and Elena Grigorenko (2013), 'The genetics of creativity: the generative and receptive sides of the creativity equation', in O. Vartanian, A.S. Bristol and J. Kaufman (eds.), *Neuroscience of Creativity*. Cambridge, MA: MIT Press, pp.72–93.
Boden, Margaret (2013), 'Creativity as a neuro-scientific mystery', in O. Vartanain, A.S. Bristol and J. Kaufman (eds.), *Neuroscience of Creativity*. Cambridge, MA: MIT Press, pp.1–18.
Buckingham, Will (2014), 'Communicating not-knowing: education, Daoism and epistemological chaos', *China Media Research* **10** (4) 10–19.
Buckingham, Will (2015), *64 Chance Pieces: A Book of Changes*. Hong Kong: Earnshaw Books.
Cai, Wu (2012), *wenhua bu 'shier wu' shi qi (The Ministry of Culture's 12th Five Year Plan)*, Beijing: Xinhua Publishing.
Callon, Michel, and John Law (1995), 'Agency and the hybrid *collectif*', *South Atlantic Quarterly* **94** (2): 481–507.
Catmull, Ed (2014), *Creativity Inc: Overcoming the Unseen Forces That Stand in the Way of True Inspiration*. New York: Random House.
Chang, Chung-yuan ([1963] 2011), *Creativity and Taoism: A Study of Chinese Philosophy, Art and Poetry*. London: Singing Dragon Books.
Chase, Robin (2015), *Peers Inc*. London: Headline.
Cheng, Chung-ying (2009), 'The Yi-Jing and yin-yang way of thinking', in Bou Mou (ed.), *History of Chinese Philosophy*. London: Routledge, pp.71–106.
Cihai Chinese Encyclopedia (*The Sea of Words*) (1989), Shanghai: Shanghai cihai chubanshe.
Daxue (2012), *Daxue and Zhongyong*, Bilingual edition, translated by Ian Johnston and Ping Wang. Hong Kong: Chinese University Press.

Dennett, Daniel (2013), 'The normal well-tempered mind', in John Brockman (ed.), *Thinking Big: The New Science of Decision-making, Problem-Solving and Prediction*. New York: Harper Perennial, pp. 1–17.

Florida, Richard (2002), *The Rise of the Creative Class*. New York: Basic Books.

Gay, Peter (2008), *Modernism: The Lure of Heresy*. New York: Norton.

Hall, David L. (1982), *The Uncertain Phoenix*. New York: Fordham University Press.

Hansen, Chad (1992), *A Daoist Theory of Chinese Thought: A Philosophical Interpretation*. New York: Oxford University Press.

Hartley, John and Jason Potts (2014), *Cultural Science: A Natural History of Stories, Demes, Knowledge and Innovation*. London: Bloomsbury Academic.

Horkheimer, Max and Theodor Adorno ([1944] 1972), *The Dialectic of Enlightenment*, translated by John Cumming. New York: Continuum.

Jiang, Jun (2006), 'Controlled by chaos: informal China', *Volume* (Archis) (2): 20–31.

Latour, Bruno (2005), *Reassembling the Social: An Introduction to Actor-Network Theory*. Oxford: Oxford University Press.

Li, Zehou (2010), *The Chinese Aesthetic Tradition*, translated by Maija Bell Samei. Honolulu: University of Hawai'i Press.

Liu, Shu-hsien (2003), 'Sheng: life or creativity', in Antonio C. Cua (ed.), *The Encyclopaedia of Chinese Philosophy*. New York and London: Routledge, pp. 695–96.

Lloyd, Geoffrey E.R. (2007), *Cognitive Variations: Reflections on the Unity and Diversity of the Human Mind*. Oxford: Clarendon Press.

McLean, Stuart (2009), 'Stories and cosmogonies: Imagining creativity beyond "nature" and "culture"', *Cultural Anthropology* **24** (2): 213–45.

North, Michael (2013), *Novelty: A History of the New*. Chicago: University of Chicago Press.

Pope, Rob (2005), *Creativity: Theory, History, Practice*. Abingdon: Routledge.

Richerson, Peter J. and Robert Boyd (2005), *Not By Genes Alone: How Culture Transformed Human Evolution*. Chicago: The University of Chicago Press.

Shambaugh, David (2013), *China Goes Global: The Partial Power*. Oxford: Oxford University Press.

Shen, Vincent (2003), 'Laozi' (Lao Tzu)', in Antonio C. Cua (ed.), *The Encyclopaedia of Chinese Philosophy*. New York and London: Routledge, pp. 355–60.

Tan, Charlene (2015), 'Understanding creativity in East Asia: insights from Confucius' concept of junzi', *International Journal of Creativity and Innovation*, DOI: 10.1080/21650349.2015.1026943

Tian, Chenshan (2009), 'Development of dialectical materialism in China', in Bou Mou (ed.), *History of Chinese Philosophy*. London: Routledge, pp. 512–38.

Wallis, Graham (1926), *The Art of Thought*. New York: Harcourt, Brace and Company.

Wang, Robin R. (2012), *Yinyang: The Way of Heaven and Earth in Chinese Thought and Culture*. New York: Cambridge University Press.

Williams, Raymond (1988), *Key Words: A Vocabulary of Culture and Society*. London: Fontana.

Wilson, Edmund O. (2012), *The Social Conquest of Earth*. New York: Liveright.

Xiang, Yong (2013), 'The 12th Five Year Plan and the transformation of economic development from the perspective of cultural industries', *International Journal of Cultural and Creative Industries* **1** (1): 74–80.

Yu, Hua (2011), *China in Ten Words*. New York: Pantheon Books.

4. The makers are coming! China's long tail revolution[1]
Jing Wang

INTRODUCTION

In February 2014, the US-based *Tea Leaf Nation*, a news site dedicated to Chinese citizens and social media, published an editorial 'It's official: China is becoming a new innovation powerhouse.' The title should surprise no one well informed of the scale and strategy of China's national innovation policies. Vacillating between an alarmist message that 'the world's factory is turning into an R&D machine' and a consolation sentiment that China will not out-innovate the US anytime soon, the article ponders statistics that seem to work in China's favour. Data reveal a spike in Chinese college graduates, from less than a million in 1999 to almost 7 million in 2013; more revealing, however, is the fact that 31 per cent of these graduates received engineering degrees, in stark contrast to the 5 per cent engineering degree recipients in the US In addition, other data show the US share of global R&D dropping from 37 per cent in 2001 to 30 per cent in 2011 while China's share jumped from a low 2.2 per cent in 2000 to 14.5 percent in 2011 (Wertime 2014). By way of downplaying these startling numbers, the editorial draws attention to the weakness inherent in Chinese-style education whereby rote learning is prioritized over creative thinking.

Not all is as it seems, however, and change is a constant in China. While contemplating these issues, I indulged myself in 'binge viewing' of a popular Chinese TV serial *Tiger Mom* (*huma maoba*) and stumbled upon the trend of 'creative education'. *Tiger Mom*, produced by Tianjin Satellite TV channel, is China's first serialized drama to pick up on the debates about schooling practices. In a country as heavily populated as China, passing the fiercely competitive college entrance exams has become the overriding goal, if not the only purpose, of education. Should China's generation of singleton children be put through the ordeal year after year, foregoing their happy childhoods? The episode ratings were surprisingly high and so it is worth asking: why was this kind of drama so popular? Why now?

The story revolves around a city couple – a disciplinarian mom and a low-key dad, their young daughter Qian Qian and her four grandparents. The family is torn apart on a daily basis by the warring education doctrines of Qian Qian's caretakers. The audience is led into a battlefield split between exam-score obsessed Confucianists and overseas-trained experts committed to a modern, creative pedagogy. While this was a well-crafted story, I couldn't wait for the full 46 episodes to unfold to find out the outcome of the competition. So I fast-forwarded to the finale where surprisingly, the militant mainstream ideologists were defeated by the new school of creative thinking; better still, it was an ending accompanied by the conversion of the diehard Confucian grandpa to the camp that trumpets the freedom of the mind and body and the new educational philosophy that emphasizes the necessity of giving children ample space to play and explore, getting their hands dirty and creating what their heart desires. The ratings success made me wonder if Chinese education is ready to undergo some subtle changes. Indeed, one of the climactic moments in the drama occurs in a conflict between the conservative and modern pedagogues: the daughter's hand-made, paper-cut bird mobile is smashed by her incensed grandfather who deems making things instead of studying a total waste of time. The reaction of the audience was revealing: their sympathy predominantly went to Qian Qian.[2]

To put this into context, it's worth examining the political winds blowing across Chinese national innovation culture. Since January 2015, news reporters have been propagating a new culture movement initiated by Premier Li Keqiang. In September 2014 and January 2015, in two consecutive meetings of the World Economic Forum in Davos, Li promulgated his now well-known slogan *dazhong chuangye wanzhong chuangxin* (mass entrepreneurship and mass innovation), seamlessly linking grassroots makers with national wealth. According to the premier, 'every cell in society' will be activated to innovate: moreover, the 'twin engine' of China's economic growth will rest on a scaled mobilization of individual makers and mass entrepreneurs (Li 2015).

Prior to his Davos speeches a well-planned domestic media blitz accompanied the premier on his visit to Chaihuo Makerspace in Shenzhen, China's high-tech manufacturing hub and a frontier of maker revolution. A subsequent series of statements and high-profile events propelled *chuangke*, 'makers,' onto the agenda of the Chinese national innovation system. In March, during the annual Two Sessions held by the PRC's top legislative and advisory bodies, the term 'maker' formally entered national policy discourse. Then on 'May Fourth', a historical milestone marking the anniversary of the 1919 student-led New Culture Movement, the premier delivered another poignant message, this time to the young makers studying at Tsinghua University, the Chinese MIT. Promising to clear up policy obstacles for SMEs, he said 'making and creating is no longer a privilege reserved for the elites but an opportunity afforded to the greater majority of people' (Li Keqiang zongli 2015). This measured statement implies nothing less than the shift of the government's pet policy project from creative industries – a top-down, closed, elitist line-up – to 'mass entrepreneurship' which is anchored on open innovation and made available to grassroots actors.

Makerspaces have 'popped up' – not only in first-tier cities but in Zhengzhou (Henan Province), Guiyang (Guizhou Province), and Ürümqi (Xinjiang Province). The term maker (*chuangke*) has entered the lexicon of new fashionable phrases. The fact that 'Tiger Mom' implicitly endorses the ethos of Maker Culture made me wonder whether the show would still be such a crowd pleaser if Premier Li had not championed the maker's cause. Regardless of the excellent timing of the broadcast though, winning the hearts of Chinese television audiences is no small victory. Children, the subject of this drama, watched the narrative unfold together with their parents and aging grandparents who are often the most stubborn gate-keepers of traditional pedagogy.

In this chapter I want to investigate the status of creativity in China by reflecting on 'maker culture'. I begin by first defining the concept and then situating Premier Li's Maker Initiative in the complex ecosystem of China's national innovation policy. I examine several makers' projects that have emerged from below. After scrutinizing the maker-driven startup culture, I argue that the official discourse of 'maker as entrepreneur' offers a limited value proposition. Only a small handful of young makers turn into entre-preneurs, and an even smaller number of entrepreneurs create businesses that actually hire paid staff.[3] The coupling of 'makers' and 'entrepreneurs' produces at best 'hope value'; it is a bubble that can burst any time.

The second half of this article thus realigns this policy discourse with an alternative term '*change*-maker', i.e. maker as social-change engineer. This does not have to be an either–or proposition. Makers can be both entre-preneurial and socially concerned and this hybrid is already in existence in China. I present examples that have successfully linked maker culture with social innovation programs driven by the utopian vision of young activists, many of whom are involved with nonprofit communities and public interest groups. Three different models of 'makers as social inno-vators' are analyzed: innovation challenge contests for problem-solving projects shaped by NGOs and public interest organizations; the ThinkBig Initiative that sits squarely on youth activism; and Enactus China, the national chapter of an international NGO promoting sustainable growth of communities through smart strategies designed collaboratively by college students, academic mentors and business leaders.

'MAKERS' AND 'MAKERSPACES'

At the outset it's important to establish a definition of 'makerspace' and the Maker Movement. Often associated with democratized innovation, the Maker Movement is inseparable from Web culture: think of garage culture moved to the Net. Chris Anderson identifies four major factors for this flourishing digital DIY movement: the new default of sharing and collaborating online; the appearance of digital desktop tools for hobbyists to design and prototype new products; the birth of a Web-based manufacturing model that functions like an on-demand cloud service enabling the emergence of a maker-driven market for one-off products; and the popularity of crowdfunding platforms that are creating a new class of mass investors willing to provide seed money for daring startups (Anderson 2012: 13, 21, 66, 77, 168).

This is not just amateur content creation, but the long tail of manufacturing, a twenty-first century mode of production anyone can access from Web browsers and scale up and down at will. The 'spaces' where these wide varieties of niche products are designed, prototyped and manufactured are called makerspaces – workstations usually stocked up with 3D printers, 3D scanners, laser cutters, and other metalworking and woodworking tools, and in the case of Shenzhen's Chaihuo Makerspace, open-source computer hardware like Arduino circuit boards. Central to the US concept of maker culture is the quadruple idea of make, create, hack and learn. The Maker Movement envisages a renewed interest in learning through tinkering and engineering.[4]

The Chinese definition of 'maker' is essentially functional. *The People's Daily* (*renmin ribao*) provides an official interpretation:

> Makers are devoted to innovation passionately. They control the production tools themselves. Taking 'user-innovation' as a core concept, they excel in discovering problems, unearthing (customer) needs, and providing solutions. Through creativity, design, and manufacturing, they offer a variety of products and services. (Yu and Deng 2015)

Conspicuously missing from the definition above is the spirit of collaborative engineering, and predictably, the pleasure principle of hobbyists and the educational perspectives of 'inventing to learn'. The emphasis is placed instead on a dry industrialist take on innovation. Significantly, three of the leading makerspaces in China – Chaihuo Makerspace (Shenzhen), Maxpace (Beijing), and XinCheJian (Shanghai, literally, the 'New Workshop') – define themselves as *dream factories*; they view makerspaces as venues for hackers to build dream machines,[5] places where 'makers from diverse backgrounds gather to brainstorm in teams and create visions,'[6] labs where they can 'experiment with new technology' and 'seek *pleasure* from making things collaboratively,'[7] and last but not least, open platforms for knowledge sharing and learning.

What then did Li Keqiang find in the makerspace that ignited his embrace of this movement? Whatever it was, it signals a watershed moment in state innovation policy that has embodied, over the past three decades, a well-focused national pursuit of rebranding China in the image of a creative nation. This triple shift – from 'made in China' to 'created in China' and now to 'making in China' – is perhaps a sign that innovation is now a societal concern: every maker should participate in this long tail revolution, not just state designated IT and creative industry clusters.

MILESTONES OF CHINESE INNOVATION POLICIES

In order to understand the context of Premier Li's Maker Talks, it's worth briefly noting China's catch-up game in innovation policy. Since 1988, a Chinese national innovation system has gradually taken shape. In that year the Ministry of Science and Technology (MOST) rolled out the Torch Program with the aim of establishing Science and Technology Industrial Parks, Software Parks, Science-Tech Business Incubators, and Productivity Promotion Centers.[8] A decade later in the wake of WTO accession, the 10th Five-Year Plan (2001–05) stipulated that R&D funding would be raised to more than 1.5 per cent of GDP (CPC Central Committee 2001). Then in 2006, innovation came centre-stage, the State Council unveiled a mid- to long-term plan (2006–20) to strengthen China's science and technology (S&T) development. Under this plan China would be an innovation-oriented nation (*chuangxing xing guojia*) by 2020 with the new leadership of Hu Jintao and Wen Jiabao endorsing the term *zizhu chuangxin* (independent or indigenous innovation) (State Council 2006).

Meanwhile in the cultural sphere the mood was buoyant and policy was being formulated at a rapid pace. Spurred on by a compromise term 'cultural and creative industries', Blue Books catalogued the excitement with cities racing against each other in reaching output targets; parks and creative clusters mushroomed all over the country. Then on the twentieth anniversary of the launch of the Torch Project in 2008, Minister of MOST Fang Gang announced that the Program would undergo major changes, one of which was a strategic shift from S&T centered initiatives to entrepreneurship-centric innovation projects (Fang 2008). Torch would continue to evolve in 2015 with 'makerspace' becoming a sub-category of 'S&T intermediary organizations'.

All those varying initiatives notwithstanding, China's national innovation system is not well integrated. Throughout the 2010s, policy makers
were to search for a formula of collaborative innovation that would eventually anoint the university as the primary engine for driving multi-sector
cooperative networks. In 2010, the Ministry of Education published a
new directive that allowed university science parks to take on the major
responsibility of setting up incubators and internship bases to house and
train students. Preferential policy treatments included seed funding, tax
reductions, and free office rentals for the first twelve months of the launch
of a new business (Ministry of Education 2010). To ensure outputs and
raise public consciousness about this new initiative, college student innovation contests were broadcast nation-wide by CCTV.[9] On 24 April 2011,
Hu Jintao attended the 100th anniversary of the founding of Tsinghua
University; his speech unveiled the concept of *xietong chuangxin* (cooperative collaboration). Less than a month later, the Ministry of Education
and the Ministry of Finance jointly launched 'Plan 2011',[10] which laid out
the infrastructure for strategic networked alliances, under which universities would cooperate with peer institutions, the corporate sector, local governments and international research organizations to engage in national
competitions revolving around four innovation categories: advanced
science and technology, preservation and reinvention of cultural heritage,
sector-specific innovations and creative design of regional development
plans (Ministry of Education 2011).[11]

The impact of the 2010 and 2011 policy decrees rapidly changed the
innovation landscape of universities and laid down a solid foundation for
maker policies, which similarly targeted college students by incentivizing
their entrepreneurial engagement. Since that time new academic programs
on innovation and entrepreneurship have sprung up in colleges all over
the country. Many new 'Schools of Innovation and Entrepreneurship'
(SIEs) were established in April and May of 2015, following the media
feeding frenzy about Li Keqiang's Shenzhen trip. Guangdong Province,
for example, released policies encouraging all provincially based colleges
to set up SIEs; and in an effort to double or triple the number of student-
entrepreneurs, it allowed youngsters interested in establishing startups to
take legitimate academic leave (Lei 2015). All this is crucial to hastening
the transformation of college students into makers.

Then came the policies well calculated to unleash the long tail effect of
China's grassroots creativity. In June 2015, in response to the Premier's
Maker Initiative, Shenzhen took the national lead in publishing a set of
experimental policies with the ambitious goal of creating 50 new maker-
spaces per year to reach a designated number of 200 by the end of 2017
(Shenzhen City Committee 2015). This was an unprecedented open call

for proposals targeting the entire city. Newly built or existing makerspaces with an expansion plan could receive up to $833,333 per recipient; an additional $500,000 is up for grabs for maker labs that wish to make hardware upgrades. Predictably, other cities are following Shenzhen's footsteps and preparing similar policy statements. The most eye-catching prize category is the $166,666 per recipient to qualified primary and middle schools, higher education institutions, and technical and apprentice schools that demonstrate a sound plan for integrating maker education into the curriculum and installing school-based maker labs (ibid.) Chinese authorities are apparently mindful of the role creative education plays in moving China up the ladder of innovation nations. Given time, tiger moms may lose their raison d'être as the whole society is mobilized to think and make things creatively.

COPYCAT OR BOTTOM-UP INNOVATION?

Meanwhile, complaints about the lack of creative impetus behind Chinese education, echoed in the TV serial *Tiger Mom*, are often accompanied by equally pungent criticisms of the *shanzhai* (copycat) phenomenon. The parallel, critics say, of a nation of rote learners to a nation of imitators producing counterfeit products is a blot on China's aspirations to be a creative nation.

Since the 2010s, however, the ideology of open innovation has paved the way for a revisionist interpretation of *shanzhai* to surface. A report in *Wired UK* describes *shanzhai* practitioners as 'guerrilla innovators' who apply 'as much innovation and ingenuity as their legitimate counterparts' (Johnson 2010). David Li, co-founder of the maker space XinCheJian, compares *shanzhai* with 'the Robin Hood spirit' that inspires 'legitimate and often quite innovative products' (*The Economist* 2013). Among the celebrity endorsers of *shanzhai* is Chris Anderson. Calling the bootleg business practice 'lightweight innovation', he echoes David Li's assessment and equates the phenomenon with the 'ultimate openness we in the open-source world are looking for' (Anderson 2012: 212). Proclaiming that 'a copy can be better than the original', Rainer Wessler, creative director of Frog Design, asked whether *shanzhai* has proved that the Western approach to innovation is outdated (Wessler, 2013).

Claiming that *shanzhai* and Open Source Hardware are 'twins separated at birth', David Li evokes a scenario in which the world of *shanzhai* converges with that of makers (Li 2014). Exactly how that happens however is left for speculation. Silvia Lindtner, co-founder of the Hacked Matter blog, argues that those two phenomena are complementary in essence. In her view, what we are witnessing is a natural partnership built between the founders of Chinese hardware startups (the makers' businesses) and the erstwhile *shanzhai* factories (Lindtner 2014). If we follow this logic, it appears Shenzhen's thriving maker culture owes a great deal to the bottom-up infrastructure and network ecosystem put in place by a myriad of *shanzhai* plants over the past decade.

Even if we cannot be conclusive about the tangible link between makers and *shanzhai* pirates, we can dig deeper into what distinguishes home-grown innovation from *shanzhai* by turning our attention to the changing profile of the new generation of innovators themselves. China's policy preferential treatments for indigenous innovation and university incuba-tors, as detailed in previous pages, have triggered a new round of startup fever embraced by the post-80s and post-90s generation, many of whom are college students or graduates, the 20- and 30-somethings. It is impor-tant to note however that not all makers are hardware tinkerers since software developers and digital platform builders are also included in the Chinese maker family.[12] The following section illustrates examples of young 'maker-entrepreneurs'.

YOUNG MAKERS AT A GLANCE AND HOMEGROWN STARTUPS

Long before Premier Li promoted makerspaces, embryonic communi-ties of makers had already sprung up here and there, joined by younger and younger participating members. One of the winning teams in a 2014 China-US maker contest that created 'Night Edge' – a laser and ultrasonic musical instrument – was spearheaded by a team of 15- and 16-year-old high school kids;[13] elsewhere a Wuxi based makerspace came up with a 'crazy crab' invented by a third grader who utilized what he learned from BIT@DIY to materialize the talking and crawling functions of the crab.[14] Under-age hobbyists aside, China is witnessing the rise of adult makers who are keen to turn themselves into full-fledged entrepreneurs. For example, Jason Wang made his name by raising funds on Kickstarter for Makeblock, an aluminum extrusion based construct platform that provides a set of flexible components – including slots, wheels, sensors, drivers and controllers, timing belts, and motors – for building robotics, machines, toys or even art-ware. When interviewed by *Wired*, Wang likens this combo kit to a 'Lego for adults' (Finley 2012).[15]

Not all 20-something makers are capable of following Jason Wang's example successfully. An increasing number of makers are creating robots; some are dull inventions like ticket-selling bots in movie theaters.

More newsworthy examples are actually platform and software creators. Sun Yan, the founder of SmellMe, is in his thirties, and like other young entrepreneurs he is a magnet attracting kindred spirits from the same age group. Sun rounded up an investment of US$ 7.8 million to roll out China's first pet social network *wenwen wo*,[16] a funny name that sounds like 'smell me' (Yan 2015). Pet owners can create profiles for their cute animals on the site, post fun snapshots and videos of their furry creatures, set up forum communities for pet-related topics, consult veterinarians on the site and brainstorm with specialists on pet food, pet nutrition, pet fashion and pet training. Most interestingly, users can initiate offline activities to plan pet walking in groups or orchestrate breeding schemes. The platform also incorporates features of e-commerce, rewarding dedicated users with in-site currency to purchase pet gifts on Taobao.com. SmellMe can be accessed via mobile apps. It boasts of having a user membership over 5 million.

SmellMe is but one of the hundreds, if not thousands of emerging startups in cities all over China. Where there is a gap in demand, there are competing startups. Venture capital investors are busy signing up carpooling apps, test-prep startups, various Internet-of-Things startups, efficiency apartment finders like Mofang and MogoRoom, services like Wifi Skeleton that unlock free connection to hotspots, on-demand valet parking services, beauticians to the doorstep app, fresh produce e-tailers, smart robot companions for homes, even a medical tourism app that connects Chinese tourists to overseas clinics for cosmetic surgery. With the boom of interest in online citizen entrepreneurship, new business categories like the training schools for startup zealots have also emerged. Chinaccelerator, a Shanghai based company founded in 2009 has already graduated seven batches of promising startup founders.[17]

Sun Yan and his teammates talked about their ambitions to grow SmellMe into an international brand. This brings to mind the meteoric rise of MyIdol, a Chinese startup whose overseas fame overtook its reputation in China. In the spring of 2015, the app broke into the German, US, Japanese, and Korean social media space and became the Internet's new obsession. MyIdol is a 3D avatar creator that helps a user to morph his or her face via selfies into computer generated cartoony bodies in self-select, dorky dancing and singing moves. Social feeds of hilarious and sometimes creepy snap shots and avatar pole-dancing videos have spread quickly over Twitter, Instagram, Tumblr, and Vine since April 2015. A favorite of mine is 'previously unreleased security footage of Bush gettin jiggy between meetings' on Vine (Lucythegoosey 2015). The fact that foreign users have no clues about what they pick on a menu written entirely in Chinese adds to the thrills of navigating in this 3D avatar milieu.

What is the startup behind MyIdol like? It's not easy to find them online because they seem to revel more in making things than promoting themselves. They are twenty-somethings, more idiosyncratic and creative than Sun Yan's team. When I finally found their site *AvatarWorks*, I was greeted by a unique self-introduction:

> Hi, you probably just found us, a charming company.
> She doesn't look like what you expected. She is neither a tech company nor an animation studio, and she's not a games company, either.
> She even waited for years before rolling out a single product.
> But she has a super cool lab and the best engineers to make high-quality animations and the most playful apps.
> She promises to be fun forever. (AvatarWorks 2015)

The startup's recent hiring announcement continues the playful speak. Claiming that they are a group of smart and goofy youths, they imagine themselves as an electric-saw wielding Don Quixote riding on a cross-country motorcycle, 'determined to cut off the gigantic windmill and make it our new toy' (AvatarWorks Hiring 2015).

CHANGE AGENTS AS MAKERS

The fun loving Avatar workers, exemplary makers in all respects, bring us back to the twin foci of this article – maker as entrepreneur and an alternative proposal of 'maker as change-maker'. If we find in SmellMe a team of entrepreneurs, then in the anonymous MyIdol crew we encounter Premier Li's ideal Maker – merry making original innovators who have left behind the shadow of the copycat ethos and brought change to a greed stricken startup culture in China.

However, AvatarWorks' playful employees are not strictly speaking 'change-makers'. On my cognitive map change-makers aren't merely engaged in changing corporate culture; they are above all, *civic-minded creative citizens* capable of building a genuinely creative society that presumably occurs at the third stage of China's 'creative century plan,' according to Liu Shifa's and Li Wuwei's futurist blueprints (Liu 2006; Li 2011). Where can we spot 'creative citizens'? And how do we characterize their activities? They are not quite the co-creative drivers of a 'user-led, demand-side' knowledge economy as John Hartley has speculated (Hartley 2010, xvii). Nor are they amateur content creators like Hu Ge (the maker of a sensational spoof) emerging from the sphere of 'grassroots recreation' in Michael Keane's terms (Keane 2011: 177–8). The problem is we don't know much about change-makers with a civic twist because they are completely left out of the vision of Chinese policy makers and mainstream Western media reports about social change in China.

A palpable generational shift is taking place in the nonprofit sector: the 40- and 50-somethings, middle-aged pioneers of Chinese philanthropy, have prized themselves in constructing a purist's vision of 'social innovation', one that is in essence anti-entrepreneurial and oblivious to new tech. The younger generation, especially those nurtured under the state innovation policies, takes a different approach to producing social good. Generally speaking, this new generation is social media savvy and entrepreneurial, and some of them are good at creating IT solutions to pressing social problems. It is a rare breed indeed because it's hard to be both a thinker and a doer successful in blending the visionary and the practical.

In fact, if I had not worked for six years in China's nonprofit sector and run a nonprofit organization there,[18] I would not have had access to the rich literature and sporadically emerging events involving social entrepreneurs of all ages, the most innovative of whom are 20-somethings. Although they are makers whose ingenuity rivals that of the founders of SmellMe and MyIdol, they have escaped mainstream media attention and received no endorsements from Premier Li.

There are currently three notable creative incubators of change-makers in urban China – Cinnovate, Enactus and ThinkBig. All three share the vision for cross-sector collaboration. Like other grassroots movements, they see the primary source of creativity originating in individuals. Therefore, for Cinnovate, ThinkBig, and Enactus, the starting point to identify talented citizen-individuals is making an open call for creative social strategies.

Cinnovate

In the summer of 2010 I met Joyce Zhou, a passionate, socially concerned manager at Intel Beijing, who subsequently spearheaded a series of social innovation challenges sponsored by her company and supported by foundations and the Ministry of Civil Affairs. Those were China's earliest social innovation tournaments and I was lucky to be involved as a judge for the initial two rounds of contests. The open competitions were part of an impressive corporate social responsibility (CSR) campaign that promoted an Intel style tech-fetishist view that 'Information Technology can advance and expedite social innovation'. The 2010 call for proposals reads, 'Do you know what ICT (Information Communication Technology) means to nonprofit organizations? Metaphorically, it gives wings to compassion and enables it to fly far' (Cinnovate 2010). Initially, contest prizes were given in three categories – Best Tech Development,

Best Tech Avant-Guard, and Best Tech Application. In 2011, other categories were added, including Best Collaborative Innovation. Intel China scored big in the public eye with those annual tournaments but they were discontinued in 2013 probably because of mixed results.

Many prizewinners failed to implement their proposed action, and some plans, although materialized, were not sustainable. Qifang Net, a 2010 contest winner, closed down without notice its P2P lending platform serving college students. In 2013, the founder was hunted down and forced to reckon with angry lenders. The scandal about his delinquency cast a shadow over newly established online philanthropy initiatives. Another 2010 winner, Rescue Minqin, an environmental NGO of which I was, and still am strongly supportive, failed to mobilize technology resources to deliver their proposed 'Plant Virtual Tree' platform. IT driven solutions are easier said than done. In the early 2010s, e-commerce was just taking off, techies and geeks had not yet formed communities, and cross-sector resources in technology were scarce to say the least. But a few successful pioneers also made their names, bringing public attention to the raw concept of social enterprise.

One of the most celebrated cases of 'technology as problem solver' was a 2010 Cinnovate winner, the Qiang Embroidery Help Center. The Qiang Center is an NGO specializing in minority cultural protection funded by Jet Li's One Foundation. Its earlier incarnation, an occupational service center for the Qiang women, was established in the immediate wake of the devastating Wenchuan Earthquake. Since 2008, the NGO has established embroidery stations one after another in small Sichuan villages with the goal of providing impoverished minority women with sustainable means of livelihood. The number of Qiang embroidery trainees went up to 168,000 in a few years.[19] Later, the founder of this organization opened up specialty embroidery retail shops from Chengdu to Suzhou, Beijing, Shanghai and Taipei, successfully turning the NGO into a social enterprise. They also built a B2C e-commerce store through Taobao.com and a B2B platform on Alibaba.com to reach multiple markets outside the remote county town. By modernizing a craft on the brink of extinction, ICT technology solved the problems of unemployment among rural Qiang women.[20]

More important, the Qiang Center overcame the difficulty of transporting embroidery instructors to mountainous areas by providing online video training.[21] Without leaving their home and quitting farm work, diligent Qiang women now have access to online instructions. This model of flexible employment was replicated by Qiang embroidery centers in other southwestern provinces – in Guizhou, Xinjiang and Sichuan where minority women are enlisted to reinvent the Miao, Kesai style, Shu and Tibetan embroidery traditions.[22] Digital communication not only popularized skill training at low cost, it also opened a window to the outside world and enriched the information flow in remote minority villages, benefiting not just the embroiderers themselves but other villagers as well.

Sporadic successes notwithstanding, founders of the Cinnovate tournaments soon found themselves caught in a dilemma. Initially set up as a mechanism encouraging grassroots NGOs to use IT means to solve social problems, the Cinnovate Award attracted a large number of government affiliated and well-endowed players in the following years. The integrity of the awards could not but be compromised by the entry of those rich and powerful official organizations that were picked and rewarded for half-baked ideas. Luckily, Cinnovate gained a second life in 2013 by bidding farewell to the contest formula. In its place, a new tradition of 'Innovation Week' was launched. Through an assemblage of fun inspiring workshops, speeches, activities, and offline interactive games, the new platform was designed to step up 'efforts to ignite public interest in emerging models of social innovation' (Cinnovate Center 2013).

'Be the change' is the new motto. Harnessing the creative power of individuals in transforming society was high on the agenda, and so is Cinnovate's desire to build 'a vibrant social innovation ecosystem' (ibid.). The 2013 Innovation Week was said to have drawn one thousand makers, philanthropists and members of nonprofit communities (Cinnovate Innovation Week 2013), not to mention talent-spotting venture investors that began to appear regularly in those events.

Although a praiseworthy pioneer of open innovation challenge contests and the originator of the Chinese term *chuang bian ke* (literally, maker-changer), Intel was not the only player in mid-2010s China that promoted the agenda of innovators as change-makers. To be frank, a CSR driven social innovation machine has its own vulnerabilities, among them the hubris of a multinational. A powerful company like Intel can be seen as guilty of paying lip service to 'cross-sector collaboration'. For when it comes to brainstorming at the table, its own voice dominates, leaving little room for other partners-in-name to play a significant role in shaping the agenda. In the end, building 'a vibrant ecosystem' for new philanthropy needs real and multiple collaborators and a networked vision not bound to a domineering mindset. That's perhaps the hardest lesson, and one that change-making incubators in China have yet to learn.

Enactus

Long before Intel Beijing promoted itself as a catalyst of Chinese social innovation, an international nonprofit organization, Students in Free

Enterprise (SIFE), has entered China and worked its way quietly through universities to help student-entrepreneurs create community empowerment projects. But it was not until 2012 when the CEO of SIFE changed its name to Enactus (Entrepreneurial: Action: Us) that a cross-sector alliance made up of college students, academic advisors and business leaders finally gained momentum. Working with a large number of leading corporate partners and more than 227 member universities in China, Enactus propagates the idea of leveraging entrepreneurial action to transform the lives of the disadvantaged as a way to enable sustainable social progress. Local Enactus chapters hold regular Business Competitions to identify talented students and train them as socially responsible, future business leaders. The goal is simple but powerful: Enactus student ambassadors make a pledge to leverage viable business concepts to help every person and community in need to 'live up to their fullest potential(s)' (Enactus 2015). Considering its enormous reach – 14,167 student participants by February 2014 – Enactus has made a bigger impact than Cinnovate (Enactus 2014, 15) in mobilizing Chinese youths to get socially engaged. Moreover, regional Enactus champions enter national competitions, and after rounds of tournaments, the winning teams advance to the prestigious Enactus World Cup and are given opportunities to be recruited by sponsoring companies. The three-stage value proposition of the platform – Community Programs, Leadership Connection, and Career Connection – forms a virtuous cycle. No wonder Enactus has grown at such lightning speed.

Lest you think short-term student outreach projects may be small in scale and their effectiveness not visible, Project Golden Pond will help make a different impression. The project, originated from Sun Yat-sen University, is the brainchild of an Enactus team that assisted tilapia fish farmers in a small Guangdong village to solve a pollution problem that plagued the village for years. Chemical overuse in ponds, isolated farming, and low winter harvests had taken their toll on the 750 families in the region who relied on this practice for their livelihood. After conducting rounds of research, the team discovered that planting ryegrass could bring villagers multiple benefits: it could improve the ecosystem of the ponds, enable the farmers not only to earn extra income by selling the grass but also create a new sideline business that supplies grass feed to local rabbit and cattle operations. Needless to say, since the implementation of Golden Pond Project, 'the average summer fish yield has risen from 18 tons to 23 tons' (Enactus 2015). Previously arid land is now utilized to plant ryegrass.

The Golden Pond project sounds almost like a fairytale. It is above all a case study that reminds us of a blind spot of techno-determinists: *not* all social problems call for technological solutions. The project also drives home the core value of Enactus's vision that entrepreneurial spirit and practice can transform people's lives. No less important, the success of Enactus foregrounds the importance of youth activism in China today.

Most of the time when we speak of urban youths, we think of them not as social change agents but consumers of cool fashion, hip hop, and animation. Marketers have churned out one study after another pondering how Chinese youths view luxury, drawing a very partial picture of China's millennials. The reality is more complex and less visible. Truly, if I had not created NGO2.0, a nonprofit organization that provides social media literacy training to grassroots NGOs (Wang, J. 2015), I would never have imagined the existence of the other China, where idealistic urban and rural youths are busy weaving their dreams as social engineers. Having trained and got to know hundreds of post-80s and post-90s NGO workers at our digital literacy camps (NGO2.0 2015), I now have a glowing faith in a kinder China to come. Just like NGO2.0's training camps that bring together like-minded youth activists, Cinnovate and Enactus provide a space for young activists to meet, collaborate, and form a community, which is where the real value of creative incubators lies. We all know that maker-entrepreneurs follow the law of the jungle, but change-makers thrive on collaboration.

ThinkBig

The Internet is filled with reports and academic papers on the connection between youth organizations, social action, and social movements in democratic societies. Chinese youth activists share the same utopian ideals as their Western counterparts and are deeply involved in a quest for equity and social justice, but they have to navigate carefully to steer clear of political landmines. Street demonstrations are certainly off-limits in China, but the state is tolerant of social service initiatives which are often equated with poverty alleviation and other state-endorsed social welfare categories. Mindful of the limits set for youth activism in China, Cinnovate and Enactus, both of which have international origins, put their programmatic emphasis on innovation and entrepreneurship, which is after all a state endorsed policy imperative over the past three decades, as I detailed in the first half of this chapter. Like all 'grassroots' activities in China, both platforms can function with relative political immunity probably because they have made partnerships with state organizations.[23]

I noted earlier that Enactus is perceivably a more influential platform than Cinnovate. Not only does it reach out to young people while they are still in their formative years, it doesn't target affluent regions exclusively.

A glance at the list of the 227 member universities reveals that Enactus cast its net far into western and central provinces, the less developed regions of China (Enactus 2014).

ThinkBig Initiative (*Zhongguo qingnian chuangxiang jihua*), the third model, is an indigenous Chinese incubator sponsored by a Hainan based corporate foundation committed to social innovation. It offers a slightly different model than Enactus and Cinnovate by prioritizing 'philanthropy' over 'entrepreneurship'. If we examine the origin of each of the three social innovation incubators, Cinnovate is the CSR arm of Intel, Enactus is backed by an international NGO, and ThinkBig is a young project supported by an indigenous Chinese company that bears no visible link to the government. It is operated by YouThink Center, a Chinese NGO, itself specializing in the sustainable development of youth activism. I take a special interest in ThinkBig because of its grassroots DNA. When I clicked open its website, I was greeted with this description: 'Based on our conviction that the individual is the primary target of our investment, we congregate and support young change-makers, and provide venture capital to youth philanthropy projects and youth driven social enterprises' (ThinkBig 2015).

I am delighted to find that the YouThink Center has taken over Cinnovate's slogan 'maker-changer' and fleshed it out with the ThinkBig project. Their main program is made up of five components – capacity training, international networking, project promotion and advocacy, youth community building, and incubating and investing. Founded in 2013, the Initiative is young. It has yielded 74 change-makers with a large percentage of talents concentrated in big cities. It's too early to tell if ThinkBig enjoys the kind of competitive advantage that can help them develop a sustainable community of young change-makers. The first two batches of funded projects span across multiple NGO issue areas such as welfare for people with disabilities, legal assistance, children's education, post-disaster psychiatric help, environmental protection, cultural preservation, AIDs and other health related issues, welfare for the elderly, urban and rural community development, animal protection, support for migrant workers and peasant employment, as well as a wide variety of youth activist categories. Not all projects fall into strictly defined maker categories. However, NGO2.0 and ThinkBig are planning a hackathon event whereby techies and interaction designers will be working side by side with ThinkBig youth activists to identify social problems that are susceptible to maker interventions.

CONCLUSION

The maker movement was a missing piece in the puzzle of Chinese innovation policy until spring 2015. Whether we are speaking of maker entrepreneurs or makers as change-making citizens, it is obvious that the government has now discovered the value of the individual, creative self-expression and grassroots energy in transforming Chinese economy and society. Creative industry clusters have come under the spotlight and it is now evident that they are not conducive to building a robust creative economy. Li Keqiang's maker slogan reminds policy pundits that a national innovation system is an ecosystem that needs to accommodate both the top-down superhighway approach and the messy centrifugal, bottom-up pathway that falls outside the purview of central planners. Where this new trend of democratized innovation will lead however is unclear. Whether the maker policy will succeed in reducing the high unemployment rate of college graduates is also unpredictable.

Meanwhile, the intrusion of an official discourse into an organic cultural phenomenon inevitably provokes anxieties, especially in the minds of purists. I have examined elsewhere the conceptual trap of dichotomous thinking in analyzing China. Binary pairs such as domination vs. resistance, state vs. society, communism vs. capitalism, power vs. subjugation, and the official vs. the grassroots, carry little analytical weight when they are applied to the Chinese case (Wang 2001: 98–99). We have already seen how Cinnovate and Enactus, both international entities, thrive in China in spite of, or perhaps because of, their formal partnership with governmental organizations.

One thing is certain: makerspaces will proliferate in China thanks to the government's blessing. Nobody can tell if a hundred potent ideas – and startups – will spring out of those state funded creative spaces. Will these suffer the same fate as the hundreds of lacklustre creative industry clusters? But that is beside the point. Perhaps we should all look elsewhere, to education, for clues about how to assess the productivity of a state-cosigned maker movement. There is ample evidence that something dynamic is happening in places out of media reach. Enthusiastic members of Chaohuo Makerspace are setting up colorful popup stations in shopping plazas, attracting kids and curious families. Universities are by no means the only privileged venues where makerspaces can systematically spread. Rudimentary makerspaces emerged long before 2015 in elementary schools and junior and middle highs, representing a less publicized grassroots effort made by tech enthusiast schoolteachers to introduce maker culture to the next generation: 'teaching children skills needed in a makerspace and let children build what they want' (Xie 2014; Wang,

Y. 2015: 81). Most surprisingly, the prototypes of 'maker education' are found not only in prestigious schools but also in schools of less developed regions (Wang ibid.). The onset of this phenomenon appears to be an attempt initiated by maker-teachers voluntarily.

Meanwhile creative education software is flooding into the market; among these are Yuantiku (a mobile Exam-coping software), Vipkid (an English learning app), Xueba (a homework answering tool), Mofangge (a crowdsourced learning app), and Geek Academy, a virtual IT university that exposes students in high schools and universities to playful learning routines. Chinese students are now given various creative means to improve their educational capital. Imagine a motion sensing software Hip-hop Tech that targets preschoolers! If Chinese makers continue the speed of producing innovative online education aids, and if primary and secondary school pupils are drawn to campus makerspaces, creative education will be a catching trend hard to stop even in the kingdom of rote learners. One has to wonder, if those erstwhile bookworms are transforming themselves into happy learners and creative thinkers, can a creative China be far from reach?

This chapter situates contemporary China's maker movement in the larger context of the Chinese national innovation system and unravels the double personae of maker – its entrepreneurial self and the activist self. In 2011, Michael Keane asked: 'How can we understand creativity in a way that accommodates policy and business while still engendering a sense of change, of variety, or value?' (Keane 2011: 169). The answer to Keane's prescient question lies in the steady rise of change-maker communities in urban China. Perhaps given time, Premier Li will be advocating a new maker culture that commends not only maker-entrepreneurs but the numerous change-makers and their happy emulators who are seizing opportunities to make the crown jewels of a creative society – social wealth and social good.

NOTES

1. I would like to thank Michael Keane for his excellent reading and editing of this piece.
2. See discussions about this TV serial on Chinese social media platforms. There are some lone defenders of the grandpa's action, but the majority of public opinion sides with Qian Qian.
3. The average number of employees per U.S. firm (with or without payroll) is just four! See Chris Rabb, *Invisible Capital: How Unseen Forces Shape Entrepreneurial Opportunity*, San Francisco: Berrett-Koehler Publishers, 2010, p. 1.
4. Sylvia Libow Martinez and Gary Stager (2013), *Invent to Learn: Making, Tinkering, and Engineering in the Classroom*. Torrance, CA: Constructing Modern Knowledge Press.

5. Beijing Maxpace on Douban, accessed June 2015 at http://site.douban.com/124037/.
6. Chaihuo Makerspace, accessed June 2015 at http://maker.eefocus.com/makerspace-orgnization/chaihuomakerspace.
7. Xin Che Jian, accessed June 2015 at http://xinchejian.com/about-2/?lang=zh.
8. This embryonic system developed as China acceded to the World Trade Organization and subsequently modernized its corporate governance structure, shifted investments from industrial to knowledge-based economy, and improved key framework conditions for innovation, including making a commitment to enforcing intellectual property rights protection.
9. http://v.youku.com/v_show/id_XNTM0MDA0OTIw.html?from=y1.2-1-105.3.4-2.1-1-1-3; http://v.youku.com/v_show/id_XMTEyMDM0ODYw.html; http://tv.sohu.com/20141105/n405785309.shtml; http://v.youku.com/v_show/id_XMTgwOTcwNTMy.html.
10. It is worth noting that Plan 2011 is an extension of Project 211 and Project 985, reform projects that focus on the development of talents and other innovation elements confined within the university.
11. One of the grant recipients is the Future Media Collaborative Innovation Center set up jointly by Shanghai Jiaotong University and Peking University in 2012, with partners spanning across the broadcasting, TV, information and communication, and Internet service sectors. It pulled in resources from a number of ministries – the Ministry of Education, MOST, SARFT, National Development and Reform Commission, and Standardization Administration of China. The resource sharing among ministries on such a grand scale speaks of its own symbolism – cross sector collaboration is no longer a theory and it also underscores the future direction of China's innovation plan. See Mai Qi (2014) Shanghai jiaoda weilai meiti wangluo xietong chuangxin zhongxin huo guojia rending ('Shanghai Jiaotong University's future media network cooperative innovation center received recognition from the state'), 22 October, http://bc.tech-ex.com/2014/exclusivenews/57780.html.
12. Chinese people are rather loose about the definition of makers, which include both hardware and software makers. Please see the definition of maker in http://baike.baidu.com/subview/371405/11140298.htm.
13. You can find the description of 'Night Edge' on the website for 'China-US Young Maker Competition', see http://www.chinaus-maker.org/en/staff/visible-interactive-electric-instrument/ 2014.
14. This crab was highlighted on the website for Shenzhen Maker Faire, http://www.shenzhenmakerfaire.com/szmf2014/post/category/workshop.
15. In April 2015 after receiving $6,000,000 from investors, his company grew from four founding members to a team of 80 employees.
16. See http://smellme.cn/index.html.
17. Not all China originated startups are founded and owned by indigenous Chinese inventors, for example, Origins, whose Mandarin speaking Swiss founder announced a cool, palm-sized solution to affordable air pollution monitoring. I did not include those foreign startups in the catalog listed above because my research focus is on homegrown innovation.
18. In 2009, I founded NGO2.0, a nonprofit organization that specializes in social media literacy training and nonprofit technology service. For details, see www.ngo20.org.
19. By April 2012, the Aba County held 141 training sessions and trained 16,800; among them 8,000 women mastered the skill. For details, see Wang Shuang, Zhenhou chongsheng qiangxiu, baqian xiuniang liaode ('The Rebirth of the Qiang Embroidery after the Earthquake: Eight Thousand Embroiderers One Thumbs Up'), 6 April 2012, accessed December 2013 at http://sichuan.scol.com.cn/dwzw/content/2012-04/06/content_3572849.htm?node=968.
20. Qiangxiu bangfu zhongxin: Zhuiqiu youxian lirun jiejue shehui wenti ('In pursuit of limited profits to solve social problems'), Huanqiu Net, 1 October 2013, http://hope.huanqiu.com/exclusivetopic/2013-10/4395825.html.

21. Abei zhou funu Qiang xiu jiuye bangfu zhongxin: Qiangxiu bangfu jihua ('Abei County's Qiang Embroidery Occupation Help Center: The Qiang Embroidery Project'), Sohu.com, 30 March 2010, accessed December 2013 at http://gongyi.sohu.com/20100330/n271211916.shtml.
22. See note 20.
23. Enactus has a partnership with Chinese People's Association for Friendship with Foreign Countries (CPAFFC), and Innovate's governmental partner is the Ministry of Civil Affairs. The depoliticized nature of CPAFFC made it much easier for Enactus to expand.

BIBLIOGRAPHY

Anderson, Chris (2012), *Makers: The New Industrial Revolution*. New York: Crown Business.
AvatarWorks (2015), 'About us', accessed June 2015 at http://www.avatarworks.com/.
AvatarWorks Hiring (2015), accessed June 2015 at http://special.zhaopin.com/pagepublish/48361852/index.html.
China–US Young Maker Competition (2015), 'Night Edge', accessed July 2015 at http://www.chinaus-maker.org/staff/visible-interactive-electric-instrument/.
Cinnovate (2010), Xin shijie' gongyi chuangxinjiang pingxuan huodong jieshao ('Introduction to Cinnovate's social innovation contest') Sohu.com 14 January, http://gongyi.sohu.com/20100114/n269582374.shtml.
Cinnovate Center (2013), promotion pamphlet.
Cinnovate Innovation Week (2013), http://www.huodongxing.com/go/siw.
CPC Central Committee of the Chinese Communist Party (2001), Zhonghua renmin gongheguo guomin jingji he shehui fazhan di shige wunian jihua gangyao ('The Essentials of the 10th Five-Year Plan of the National Economic and Social Development of the PRC')), http://www.china.com.cn/ch-15/15p8/2.htm.
The Economist (2013), 'Made in China', 30 November, http://www.economist.com/news/technology-quarterly/21590756-technology-and-society-china-has-its-own-distinctive-version-maker-movement.
Enactus (2014), 'Enactus China Program: 2013–2014', promotion pamphlet.
Enactus (2015), accessed June 2015 at http://enactus.org/project/project-2/.
Fang, G. (2008), Huoju jihua yao chengwei jianshe chuangxinxing guojia de yindao liliang ('Torch will become the guiding force for building an innovation nation'), 26 December, http://scitech.people.com.cn/GB/126054/141612/141614/8585872.html.
Finley, Klint (2012), 'Robotics hacker erects open source "Lego for Adults"', *Wired* 13 December, http://www.wired.com/2012/12/makeblock.
Hartley, John (2010), 'Foreword: Whose creative industries?', in Lucy Montgomery (ed.), *China's Creative Industries: Copyright, Social Network Markets and the Business of Culture in a Digital Age*. Cheltenham, UK and Northampton, MA, USA: Edward Elgar, pp. vi–xxvii.
Johnson, Bobbie (2010), 'Shanzai', *Wired UK* 7 December, http://www.wired.co.uk/magazine/archive/2011/01/features/shanzai.
Keane, Michael (2011), *China's New Creative Clusters: Governance, Human Capital and Investment*. London and New York: Routledge.
Lei, Yu (2015), Guangdong guli gaoxiao chengli chuangxin chuangye xueyuan ('Guangdong province encouraged colleges to establish innovation and entrepreneurship schools'), 1 April, http://tech.southcn.com/t/2015-04/01/content_121305369.htm.
Li, David (2014), 'The new shanzhai: democratizing innovation in China', *ParisTech Review* 24 December, http://www.paristechreview.com/2014/12/24/shanzhai-innovation-china/.
Li, Keqiang (2015), Chinese Premier Li Keqiang's Speech at 2015 Davos, 'Uphold Peace and Stability, Advance Structural Reform and Generate New Momentum for

Development', World Economic Forum, 21 January, https://agenda.weforum.org/2015/01/chinese-premier-li-keqiangs-speech-at-davos-2015/.

Li Keqiang zongli wusi qingnian jie gei Tsinghua daxue xuesheng chuangke huixin ('Premier Li Keqiang replies to the Makers of Tsinghua University on May Fourth'), (2015), accessed 25 September 2015 at http://news.tsinghua.edu.cn/publish/news/4204/2015/20150 504162305504431629/20150504162305504431629.html.

Li, Wuwei (2011), *How Creativity Is Changing China?* Michael Keane (ed.). New York: Bloomsbury Academic.

Lindtner, Silvia (2014), 'Hacking Shenzhen', *The Economist* 18 January, http://www.economist.com/news/special-report/21593590-why-southern-china-best-place-world-hardware-innovator-be-hacking.

Liu, Shifa (2006), Shishi chuangyi shiji jihua, kaizhan chuangyi Zhongguo xingdong ('Implementing the creative century plan, developing the creative China campaign'), http://blog.sina.com.cn/s/blog_506135de01008hgr.html.

Lucythegoosey (2015), 21 April, https://vine.co/v/ea1MbxW6q71.

Ministry of Education (2010), *Jiaoyu bu guanyu dali tuijin gaodeng xuexiao chuangxin chuangye jiaoyu he daxuesheng zizhu chuangye gongzuo de yijian* ('Opinions on the work by the Ministry of Education in advancing the education programs of innovation and entrepreneurship in universities and in facilitating self-employment of college students'), 4 May, http://www.moe.edu.cn/publicfiles/business/htmlfiles/moe/s4531/201105/120174.html.

Ministry of Education and Ministry of Finance (2011), 2011 xietong chuangxin zhongxin jianshe fazhan guihua ('The Development Guidelines for the Construction of the 2011 Cooperative Innovation Center Plan'), accessed June 2015 at http://www.moe.edu.cn/publicfiles/business/htmlfiles/moe/s7062/201404/167787.html.

NGO2.0 (2015), accessed June 2015 at http://www.ngo20.org/en/workshops.

Shenzhen City Committee of IT Innovation (2015), Shenzhen shi renmin zhengfu guanyu yinfa cujin chuangke fazhan ruogan cuoshi (shixing) de tongzhi ('Shenzhen city government's announcement of experimental policies regarding the acceleration of the development of makers'), 17 June, http://www.szsti.gov.cn/info/policy/sz/106.

The State Council of PRC (2006), Guojia zhong chang qi kexue he jishu fazhan guihua gangyao (2006–20) ('The essentials of China's fifteen-year plan for science and technology'), http://www.gov.cn/jrzg/2006-02/09/content_183787.htm.

ThinkBig (2015), accessed June 2015 at http://www.thinkbig.org.cn/website/aboutus.html.

Wang, Jing (2001), 'Culture as leisure, culture as capital', *Positions: east asia cultures critique* **9** (1): 69–104.

Wang, Jing (2015), 'NGO2.0 and social media praxis: activist as researcher', *Chinese Journal of Communication* **8** (1): 18–41.

Wang, Yu (2015), *Heike, Jike, Chuangke: Creativity in Chinese Technology Community.* Master of Science thesis, MIT, http://cmsw.mit.edu/heike-jike-chuangke-creativity-chinese-technology-community/.

Wertime, David (2014), 'It's official: China is becoming a new innovation powerhouse', *Tea Leaf Nation (Foreign Policy)* 7 February, http://foreignpolicy.com/2014/02/07/its-official-china-is-becoming-a-new-innovation-powerhouse/.

Wessler, Rainer (2013), 'Shanzhai's role in innovation strategy', *Insights China*, Collection No. 1, https://designmind.frogdesign.com/2013/04/shanzhais-role-innovation-strategy/.

Xie Z. (2014), Zhongxiaoxue chuangke kongjian liebiao ('List of elementary and middle school based makerspaces'), Sina microblog, 9 November, http://blog.sina.com.cn/s/blog_6611ddcf0102v7qt.html.

Yan X. (2015), Wenwen wo Sun Yan: yizhi gou yinfa de chuangye gushi ('SmileMe's Sun Yan: a story about entrepreneurship triggered by a dog'), 10 June, http://www.kusocial.com/22121.

Yu, J. and Deng W. (2015), 'Chuangke' yuanhe yin zongli dianzan ('Why did Makers receive endorsement from the Premier?'), 19 March, http://politics.people.com.cn/n/2015/0319/c1001-26715378.html.

5. Balinghou and qilinghou: generational difference and creativity in China
Bjarke Liboriussen

INTRODUCTION

Much discussion has ensued in recent times about creativity and innovation in Chinese society. Opinion is divided about people's propensity to express their creative aspirations in a society where the education system does not reward critical thinking. Government, policy advisors and educators often speak enthusiastically about nurturing China's 'creative talent' and courses have proliferated at institutions in the expectation that these will produce a new wave of creative talent. In the meantime, those who have established their own occupational status in the new 'creative economy' have taken different journeys. Based on focused interviews with Chinese animators, designers, artists and architects, this chapter traces nine such journeys. The interviews were conducted from April 2012 to January 2014 in Beijing and Ningbo as part of efforts towards understanding the role of tools and technologies in creative work, and how that role is changing with digitalization. Halfway through the series of interviews it struck me that much of the conversation with practitioners born before 1980 focused on the differences between growing up with and without computers. The 'older' interviewees would use their younger peer-competitor as a mirror image, regardless of what aspect of their work I expressed interest in. Thus generational difference became the main theme of the investigation. I chose two of the interviewees (VII and IX, see Table 5.1) because of their unique perspectives on generational differences, both having a parent who relied on creativity in their professional life.

'Generational difference' in China is a complex issue, even when confined to professions broadly understood to rely on creativity; for instance design, animation and sculpture. I do not make any claims about the representativeness of my limited sample, which cuts across a number of very different sectors tied together by 'creativity', a term that will be discussed shortly. The purposes of this chapter are more modest: to emphasise that the concept of 'generation' is important when considering creative work in China; to show that the concept is used not only by outside observers but by creatives themselves when they reflect on their practices; and

Table 5.1   List of interviewees

Number	Self-assigned title	Year of birth
I	Animator	1971
II	New media artist	1981 B
III	Graphic designer	1983 B
IV	Designer	1969
V	Animator	1971
VI	Designer	1967
VII	Architect	1982 B*
VIII	Creative director	1982 B
IX	Sculptor	1978*

Notes: B designates *balinghou*. An interviewee marked * is the child of a Chinese creative industries professional (VII: architect, IX: painter).

that the *generational*, the *technological* and the *creative* intertwine in such reflection.

My approach is informed by 'Grounded Theory' where the overall goal is to offer useful concepts inductively informed by – rather than veri-fied by – data (Glaser and Strauss, 1967), concepts that hopefully prove useful in further research but are not, in principle, representative beyond the collected data. My inclusion of two interviewees whose family back-ground made them interesting from the viewpoint of ongoing analysis is an example of 'theoretical sampling' (Corbin and Strauss, 2008, chapter 7) and, as perhaps the most important Grounded Theory characteristic of this inquiry, it has been important to find a fit between the concepts used by the researcher and practitioners, as is the case here with 'generation' and 'creativity'.

Although it actually goes against the chronology – the concepts were suggested by the data, not the other way around – the following section discusses 'generation' and provides more detail about the interview mate-rial. This is followed by a discussion of 'creativity', a concept which is underdefined in policy but which is a word used by the interviewees to make sense of their practices. With this background in place, I will then let the 'older' generation express their views on the use of tools in creative work and on the younger generation's perceived affinity with digital tools. The younger generation then responds, as it were, to the image that has been painted of them. The penultimate section sketches a comparison with the impact of digitalization on some creative industries in the UK, sug-gesting that the relatively more gradual introduction of computers allowed 'older' creatives more time to adapt their practices to digital tools, thereby softening some of the generational differences observable in China. The conclusion offers a brief summary highlighting how the interviewees are actually in broad agreement when it comes to the role of technology in creative work – analogue tools are seen to have significant advantages over digital tools – but they also employ technologies strategically as markers of creativity to attract new projects and to maintain leadership of ongoing projects.

GENERATIONS

For the sake of clarity, sociologists often use *birth cohort* or simply *cohort* instead of 'generation'. A cohort is a group of people born within a certain age range. In contemporary Mandarin, several cohorts are spoken of in terms of decade of birth. The best-known example is the *balinghou* – *ba* (eight) *ling* (zero) *hou* (after), meaning born 1980–89 – but use is also made of *jiulinghou* (1990–99) and *qilinghou* (1970–79) in that order of frequency. *Liulinghou* (1960–69) is as far back in time as the system seems to go, but usage is rare. *Linglinghou* (2000–09) is heard but is probably even rarer. In contrast to the members of a cohort, members of a *generation* are thought to share more than merely closely occurring birthdays. American examples include the generation of spoiled *Baby Boomers* growing up in an affluent, post World War II USA; comparisons are often made with the more disillusioned and ironic *Generation X* that followed.

When discussing the conditions under which a cohort becomes a generation in a significant sense, or 'generation as an actuality', Mannheim (2009: 182) focuses on the cohort 'being exposed to the social and intellectual symptoms of a process of dynamic destabilisation'. Mannheim gives the example of Germans growing up during the Napoleonic Wars. This cohort was 'sucked into the vortex of social change' (p. 183) since they, unlike those growing up before them, happened to live in interesting times. Although they do not make use of Mannheim, Cheng and Berman (2012) have described the *balinghou* by way of another 'dynamic destabilisation', namely globalisation. In other words, the 1980–89 *cohort* is the *balinghou generation* because it is the first to grow up in the new, globalised China, the China that began to emerge from the economic reforms of the late 1970s.

Balinghou can be seen as a supplement to two other generational labels, 'little prince' and 'little princess', which refer to another significant factor shaping China's urban generation:[1] China's one-child policy (Cheng and Berman, 2012: 104). Yet my interviewees never referred to the one-child policy. The decades-based designators of generation were used, but only occasionally. However, since the *balinghou* have become a focus for China's national reflection on the spiritual and moral effects of the country's rapid growth (see, for example, Liu, 2011), it is not unlikely that they inform the thoughts expressed in the interviews. In their review of the *balinghou* literature, Cheng and Berman (2012) rather dramatically state that 'underneath the single-hearted pursuit of pleasure and excitement among Chinese youth, there may very well have been an existential and moral crisis' (p. 105): this gives a broad sense of the tone of the discourse surrounding the *balinghou* (for a journalistic introduction to the *balinghou* in the media, see Palmer, 2013).

In the context of my interviews, the 'dynamic destabilisation' that produced a sense of generational grouping is nothing as broad as globalization, but rather the sudden introduction of computers. Although trained at the most prestigious Chinese art academies and design schools, some 'older' interviewees (I, IV, V) had never used a computer as part of their institutional training when graduating in the early 1990s. This straightforward distinction, before and after computers, informed answers not only to questions of training but also to broader questions of creativity and tool use. This was without exception done in contrast to the younger generation who grew up with computers.

I use *qilinghou* to describe interviewees born before 1980 (I, IV, V, VI and IX). Although interviewees IV and VI were born in 1969 and 1967 respectively and are thus not, strictly speaking, members of the 1970–79 generation, I include them in this cohort since they themselves used 'we' to signify groups consisting of themselves and persons born in the mid-1970s. The shared, generational experience is that of training without computers and now having to compete professionally with a younger generation who had the use of computers from the outset. I use *balinghou* to describe interviewees born after 1980 (II, III, VII and VIII). Since those four were born in 1981, 1982 or 1983, the designation can be used without caveats.

The interviewees are all successful in their various fields. Some of the older ones teach at the most prestigious art and design schools in China and have solved design problems of national importance, for example, the design of the medals awarded at the Beijing Olympics and the graphic identity of a national museum. Some of the younger ones run their own businesses and have significant online followings in Chinese social media. Access to the interviewees was gained in various ways. I have known a couple of them personally or professionally since the mid-noughties. Others were then contacted via snowballing. Most of them agreed to be interviewed thanks to a Chinese contact who is himself active as a professional artist.

Following Alvesson and Kärreman (2011), I refer to my interviews as 'empirical material' rather than 'data' to highlight how the interview material is constructed rather than found. There is much debate over the status of interview material (for an overview, see Silverman, 2011). In this particular case, a constructionist stance is a prerequisite for seeing any value in the interviews. I do not speak Mandarin, and only two of my interviewees were comfortable being interviewed in English. This added a professional interpreter to the interview. On top of this, my artist contact would often be present during the interviews and found it impossible, or at least very rude, not to make conversation with the interviewee; for example when I was preoccupied listening to the interpreter. This sometimes opened unexpected but highly illuminating lines of conversation.

The interviews loosely followed an interview guide centering on the opening themes of place, co-operation, sketching, training and tools (wherever possible I conducted interviews in work places). Analysis began as soon as each interview had been conducted. Coding took place as soon as the interview material had been transcribed and translated into English. Codes include handwork, the digital and 'flexibility vs. fixity'. Close attention to the use of 'I' and 'we' proved particularly productive for microanalysis of answers. Interviewees tended to generalize their own creative practices and modes of thought with a 'we', which I decided to label 'generation', defined through institutionalized training and whether digital technology had been absent or present through that training.

CREATIVITY

There is an overall sense amongst the interviewees that their success depends on 'open and bold thinking' (V) associated with phrases such as 'crazy', 'strange', 'discovery', 'inspiration' (IV), 'a fresh touch' (VIII) etc. I will refer to this mode of thought as 'creative'. It is a mode of thought that is at the centre of what David Hesmondhalgh refers to as the 'cult of creativity' in policy making aimed at national transformations from industrial and into 'knowledge' or 'information' societies (Hesmondhalgh, 2013, chapter 5). Such policy was pioneered by New Labour and subsequent UK governments' promotion of the 'creative industries' and was subsequently transferred to a number of countries including China. The concept of 'creativity' has thereby, as Keane (2013) puts it, taken a 'journey from the West' (p. 66). Or to use Bal's (2002) terminology: 'creativity' is a travelling concept, a concept that travels across both cultural and disciplinary borders and must be examined after each journey to be fully understood. It is also an example of what Bal would call a word-concept (2009: 21): a term sometimes used casually as an ordinary, everyday 'word', sometimes used as academic 'concept' – but most often used without specification of the exact meaning in both popular and academic discourse.

In this context, where the empirical material is interviews with practitioners and not policy documents or academic discourse, 'creativity' is a word-concept rather than a concept. It is used by the interviewees, sometimes explicitly, to capture something in between capacity and skill from which they draw their professional identity – and it bears repeating that it is described with words such as 'open and bold thinking' (V), 'crazy', 'strange', 'discovery', 'inspiration' (IV) and 'a fresh touch' (VIII). Another way the interviewees go about describing creativity is by contrasting it to un-creative work. Says interviewee I (animator, born 1971): 'I focus more on designing, creativity, simply the idea. The people who are good on computers will do the more detailed part'.

The obvious objection is that there is no reason why expert use of computers should stand in contrast to creativity, which raises a discussion that has recently found a popular, global audience. In the spring of 2014, actor Andy Serkis described the division of labour between himself and animators as follows: 'It's a given that [the animators] absolutely copy [the performance] to the letter, to the point in effect what they are doing is painting digital makeup onto actors' performances' (quoted in Woerner, 2014). Serkis made a name for himself playing roles such as Gollum in Peter Jackson's cinematic version of *The Lord of the Rings* (2001–03) and the title character in Jackson's remake of *King Kong* (2005), roles where his performances were recorded through a process known as performance capture (a term that has largely replaced 'motion capture') before animators created the non-human characters seen on screen. Read in context, Serkis's point about 'digital makeup' seems to be that motion capture technology has become much less intrusive since those early days, allowing him a greater degree of freedom as an actor, but some have read it as belittlement of the contributions of animators and other creatives who work with digital tools. This high-profile case illustrates how the discourse around 'creativity' can take on the character of a zero-sum game. If the actor, or as in some of my interviews, the animator or the designer, provides 'the creative element', workers who wield digital tools later on in the process might be denied their claim to 'being creative'. Across the interviews creative work is understood in contrast to the nuts and bolts, un-creative work of doing 'the more detailed part' (I); all of the interviewees speak very confidently of passing routine tasks on to others.

It is useful at this point to briefly refer to Csikszentmihalyi's (1996) five-phase model of creative work, which informed the original interview guide. Although Csikszentmihalyi stresses that actual creative work is more iterative than his model suggests, he nevertheless offers the following as a starting point for considering the various states of mind a person typically embodies at various points during creative work:

1. Preparation: 'becoming immersed' (p. 79) in the problem at hand.
2. Incubation: practitioners 'let problems simmer below the threshold of consciousness' (p. 79).
3. Insight: a solution enters consciousness.
4. Evaluation: practitioners 'decide whether the insight is valuable and worth pursuing' (p. 80).
5. Elaboration: 'This is what Edison was referring to when he said that creativity consists of 1 percent inspiration and 99 percent perspiration' (p. 80).

The five-phase model is useful for pinpointing the 'grunt' part of the process: the fifth, elaborative phase. The creatives themselves tend to focus on the early, idea-generating phases (1–3) when they describe their work, but also the fourth phase, evaluation: this is described by an interviewee in a 'creative' manner that allows him to maintain and justify a position of power. Interviewee V (animator, born 1971) describes how he 'was young in 2001 when my studio was newly established, so I was the core of our team while others were just helping me realize my ideas'. The distinction between 'ideas' and 'realization' fits the standard division of labour between 'creatives' and 'others'. But, says interviewee V, 'people grow old, so do I', and he now finds himself evaluating the ideas presented by younger employees rather than coming up with ideas himself. His work mostly consists of 'guidance' and 'aesthetic judgement' – or, to use Csikszentmihalyi's general term, evaluation. Following Rhodes (1983), this shift can be described as the result of an 'age effect', as opposed to 'cohort effect'. It is perceived to simply stem from interview V ageing, not from his belonging to any particularly cohort. The shift resonates to some extent with Mannheim's (2009) understanding of the younger generation's role in the cultural process: 'culture is developed by individuals who come into contact anew with the accumulated heritage. In the nature of our physical makeup, a fresh contact [always means] a novel approach in assimilating, using, and developing the proffered material' (p. 171).

  Both Mannheim and interviewee V find a universal mechanism at work: making 'fresh contact' with the material and finding novel uses for it (always) falls to the new generation. In 2001, interviewee V was that new generation; in 2012, it was his employees. But 'creativity', as a concept used by these particular practitioners, is a fluid term used to describe various elements of work in ways that tend to be associated with managerial power, or 'guidance', to use interviewee V's more polite word. This resonates, as illustrated with the Serkis example, with ongoing popular discourse where creativity is seen to be broadly associated with leadership, but stands in sharp contrast to scholarly use of the term 'creative worker'; for example when Hesmondhalgh and Baker (2011) note that in certain UK creative industries 'there is a strong tendency for creative workers to [be] experts and skilled workers with little or no supervisory or managerial powers' (p. 68). The difference stems from whether or not the fifth phase of elaboration is allowed to count as 'creative'. As this is the phase that has been most thoroughly digitalized this raises the question of how the creative and the digital connect.

QILINGHOU: HANDWORK AND SPIRITUALITY

When the *qilinghou* interviewees reflect on their training in the before-computers era, two intertwined aspects of creative work seem to reinforce each other: 'handwork' and 'spirituality'. The two terms are in-vivo codes chosen from interview VI (designer, born 1967).

For the *qilinghou* interviewees, handwork primarily means drawing with pens, pencils, brushes and airbrushes. Such handwork is under a certain amount of pressure from digitalisation. There is a note of defiance in inter-viewee I's (animator, born 1971) responses when she describes her way of working. She works in animation but her work routine does not involve digital animation directly. She insists on drawing with a pencil when she generates 'the idea' underlying the design solution, then scans her draw-ings and instructs employees in how to turn them into moving images, using software she cannot herself operate.

Across the *qilinghou* interviews, handwork is understood to be of great value to a creative person. Interviewee IV (designer, born 1969) holds that drawing is 'very essential' and 'very important' because it 'is an essential expression from your brain, through your eyes, from your brain to your hands, so this is a chain'. Drawing with a pen or brush – and by exten-sion, handwork in general – is seen to form immediate and fundamental connections between mind, senses and hands. The whole person becomes involved in the creative process in a fundamental way.

Interview IV's views are echoed by the other *qilinghou* interviewees but they centre their attention on the training necessary to obtain handwork skills, and the long-term effects of such training. Interviewee V (animator, born 1971) has to some extent embraced digital tools, boasting that he was the first in China to produce a short film shot entirely on a mobile phone (the film was later shown on national TV). Today, the digital (phone) camera has become one of his most important tools. But although the tools have changed, his training as a painter still informs his practice. It gives him an 'open view towards animation', allowing him the use of 'a wider range of methods', and '[provides] the foundation of my own general appreciation of beauty'.

This view is similar to that of interviewee VI (designer, born 1967) who talks of 'good foundation' and 'broad and deep [spiritual aspects]' in connection with the acquisition of handwork skills. The 'tough job' of acquiring the skills to, for example, 'draw a picture . . . with an airbrush and you can't even figure out whether it's a photo or a drawing' has a fundamental effect on the creative outlook of the person who requires such skills. Across the *qilinghou* interviews, this handwork-induced outlook is described as one of openness and flexibility. Handwork 'tools you use have more possibility to move and change' (IV), and those tool affordances are broadly understood to transfer into a creatively flexible outlook in the users who come to master such tools.

The *qilinghou* reflection on their own generation's tools and creative outlook is, without exception, performed with reference to the younger generation – the *balinghou* who grew up with computers. When interviewee I (animator, born 1971) talks of how a simple pen or brush allows for 'more possibility to move and change', this is done in explicit contrast to computers: 'we have good software, but still there are fixed tools and forms you have to choose'. The computer speeds the creative process up by offering a menu of choices but that choice is from a set of rigid, predefined options. The pen lets you 'create', the computer merely lets you choose, and the latter is only a shadow of true creation. (Some voices in Western architecture argue for the creative legitimacy of the act of choosing between options suggested by software. See Liboriussen, 2012.)

When interviewee V discusses the benefits of his training as a painter, he extends this to a preference for job candidates with a handwork background. He finds that animators working under him who have '[learned] computer animation directly from the beginning', without learning to draw and paint by hand 'are helping complete a project rather than creating something'. Again, the fundamental spark of true creation seems to be nurtured by handwork. There are, as interviewee I puts it, 'necessary [steps]' one must go through in order to get an 'idea', and the speed and ease of digital tools leads the creative worker to ignore those steps. What appears to be a digital shortcut turns out to be a cul-de-sac.

The *qilinghou* interviewees suggest that older handwork tools and training are more suited for creative work because they offer flexibility, whereas newer tools offer un-creative fixity: brush and sketchbook are pitched against computer and software. Flexibility and fixity are, however, relative terms, and this becomes clear in the case of photography. Interviewee I (animator, born 1971) is against the use of cameras in design work. He talks about 'the good habit of using sketch, writing notes' as opposed to 'taking pictures' with a smartphone or camera. The younger generation 'want things too fast and too efficient', he says. Photography is too fast compared to drawing, it does not allow the creative worker to take the 'necessary [steps]': following Csikszentmihaly (1996), these 'necessary [steps]' could be called phases of preparation and incubation, of 'becoming immersed' in the problem at hand and then '[letting] problems simmer below the threshold of consciousness' (p. 79). Interviewee V (also animator, born 1971) seems to agree with the basic sentiment that being 'too fast and too efficient' can be detrimental to creativity, but his old–new dichotomy of tools is animation–photography, not photography–drawing. In the eyes of this *qilinghou*, 'too fast and too efficient' would be to animate a sequence entirely 'on a computer', whereas the older, slower and better way of creating involves '[taking] a lot of pictures from real life' and then using these pieces of 'the real, material world' as 'creative elements' in animation. One *qilinghou's* too fast and efficient can be another's material and creative. Not only is the category of 'creative work' socially constructed, so is the category of tools that have affinity with creative work.

Underpinning the *qilinghou* descriptions of digital tools is an understanding of the perceived expert users of those tools, the *balinghou*. Here the most correct formulation would actually be '*balinghou* and *jiulinghou*'. The *qilinghou* interviewees are most definitely talking about people born in 1980–89 – the literal meaning of *balinghou* – but their understanding of 'the new generation' (VI) includes students they teach, and some of those students were born in the early 1990s. A finer distinction between those born in the 1980s and those in the 1990s does not, however, emerge from the empirical material. With this caveat I will stick to *balinghou*. What is important here is that unlike their predecessors, the *balinghou* grew up at a time when computers had become commonplace in urban China.

The *qilinghou* interviewees consider the *balinghou* 'lucky enough' (I) to grow up in a time not only of computers but of 'better living conditions' (VI) in general. The *balinghou* benefit from this in many ways. They have 'easy access to information' and this makes them 'more subtle and sensitive in thinking', 'smarter and more flexible in decision making' (VI). But whereas the *qilinghou* consider flexibility a core virtue of creative work, flexibility is not entirely positive as a personality trait. For a person, flexibility can easily become laziness, leading the creative worker to disregard the aforementioned 'necessary steps' (IV) of preparation and incubation. Although handwork mastery opens up the ability to be creatively flexible during the work process, interviewee VI maintains that one should exercise 'strong self-consciousness and motivation for improvement', be 'determined [and] persistent in doing one thing' to reach this level of mastery. First you work hard to achieve mastery of tools, then you exercise this mastery in a flexible way. It is not, the *qilinghou* interviewees seem to suggest, that the *balinghou* have *chosen* not to follow the tough path of handwork, spirituality, determination and improvement. That path is not open to them at all, since they have grown up under other conditions than the *qilinghou*. In short, the lazy *balinghou* taste for the fixed, fast and efficient is understood to be a cohort effect, not an age effect.

THE BALINGHOU FROM THE INSIDE

How does this criticism square then with the views and attitudes of the four *balinghou* interviewees? Interviewee VIII (who self-identifies as a 'creative director', born 1982) appears typically *balinghou* when she describes her work. She divides it into two categories: the work she does for money and the work she really cares about. As an example of work done for money, she produced a 'micro film' (contemporary Mandarin term for a short film distributed exclusively online) advertising robot vacuum cleaners for the appliance company Suning. The interviewee almost lost patience with me as I kept trying to understand the details of the work flow and communication involved in the Suning project: 'I want to earn my keep by doing what I really like to do instead of having to do things like the Suning commercial, which to me is just a tool for survival and a means to an end'. This is echoed by interviewees II (new media artist, born 1982) and III (graphic designer, born 1983) who talk at length about their very satisfying collaboration with a well-known folk/rock singer, an ongoing collaboration where they produce stage designs and album covers and the singer provides the musical content in something closer to a partnership than a traditional client-worker relationship. The notion that work can be fun or at least gratifying on a personal level never presented itself in the interviewees with members of the *qilinghou* generation.

At first glance the *balinghou* search for enjoyment and personal fulfilment in work might come off as self-centred or even hedonistic, with interviewee VIII making frequent use of 'passion' and 'passionate' when she describes what she is looking for in work. This view would be in accord with some of the general criticism of the *balinghou* generation. Interviewee VIII, however, connects her personal ambitions with an agenda of national improvement: 'We have many useful and practical things here [in China] but they are not made with aesthetic values'. She is not only working on expanding her already considerable online following to attract investors to her projects, but also to 'draw attention' to this lack of aesthetic sensibility in China. It is impossible to generalize from this single interview to an entire generation, but it can at least be observed that although it might be true that the *balinghou* are relatively more concerned with integrating self-actualization into their work, such ambition might connect with broader, societal concerns.

As for the *qilinghou* dichotomy of old-analogue-flexibility versus new-digital-fixity, the *balinghou* interviewees are in broad agreement; that is to say, they agree with the dichotomy as an evaluation of the usefulness of digital and non-digital tools in creative processes. Interviewee III 'prefers non-digital tools especially for doing graphic design with just a pen and paper', and interviewee II generally 'prefers to use a notebook rather than a computer' for keeping track of ideas. When I quietly observed interviewee II at work for about half an hour, the notebook did seem to be the locus of his work. He would, for example, write in the notebook, look something up on his smartphone, glue scraps of paper into the notebook, do a bit more hand writing, add a couple of sentences to a conversation taking place around him, look something up on the Internet (using the almost untouched cinema display-equipped Mac desktop computer in front of him), then return (always) to the notebook. When I asked him whether he had a favourite pen, he launched into enthusiastic endorsement of a very specific kind of Japanese pen with the capacity to write with six different colours. Interviewee III was also very attached to one particular pen: 'I only use this pen. This is the one I always use'. The importance of writing and sketching does not seem to have been forgotten by these particular *balinghou*.

The four *balinghou* would not agree that they get everything easy. There is, for example, disagreement between a *qilinghou* (VI) who holds that it is much easier to get accepted to an art academy today than in the 1980s, and *balinghous* who state that a high level of skill is required to get accepted (VIII) and that the academy training entails the challenge of '[facing] tremendous pressure and [growing] very fast' (II). A *qilinghou* (VI) speaks lyrically about '[inheriting] the [spirit], culture and humanity' of one of China's top schools for art and design, and the *balinghou* interviewees, who are graduates of these schools, do respect and appreciate their alma maters, but at the same time, the *balinghou* speak very highly of the importance of learning by doing and practice-led learning, for example by having accomplished practitioners come to the academy and do workshops. What some *qilinghou* see as disrespect for traditional training might be a *balinghou* interest in having training including more practice-oriented elements.

Although the *balinghou* interviewees would probably not recognize themselves from the *qilinghou* descriptions, they are aware of certain generational differences and are prepared to exploit them. Interviewee VII is a *balinghou* architect (born 1982) who occasionally works together with his mother who is also an architect. He does not consider his mother's traditional, handwork approach to sketching and drawing to be of any significance when it comes to the design process itself, but it becomes crucial when presenting projects to clients: 'Computer drawing is simple. Everyone can kind of make it but [hand drawn] sketches you have to like practice for years in order to make a very nice visualization'. The ability to make a 'very nice visualization' is 'not really necessary' but to a client, 'it means that you're a trained architect', and that might be what gets the contract. The young architects themselves might do all their work on computers and then have computer-generated sketches turned into hand drawn sketches for use in client meetings by skilled people working outside of the architecture firm. But 'if you really want to make the project convincing to them [the clients], you just make sketches in front of them when you talk to them', and that is where the skills of the interviewee's mother become very useful. Some *balinghou* appreciate the value of handwork but others, like interviewee VIII, take a very cynical stance towards it, exploiting its value as a marker of tradition and quality whilst discreetly dismissing its practical value.

'UK QILINGHOU'

Before concluding, I would like to briefly suggest parallels between the introduction of computers in China and in the West. Space does not allow a thorough comparison, but Dormer's (1997b) edited collection on the 'status and future [of craft]' in the United Kingdom provides an interesting starting point. Dormer's collection is based on material from the first half of the 1990s. By 1991, 'computing had become part of a technological "core" of course content' in UK design courses in higher education (Myerson, 1997: 178). Thus many of the contributors to this collection find themselves in roughly the same generational 'location' (as Mannheim [2009: 167] would have put it) as the *qilinghou*. Occupying roles as managers and teachers they argue for the value of handwork from a position of relative strength and observe the spread of digital technologies with a mixture of fascination and concern. Crampton Smith is quoted as saying that 'a pencil in the hand is like an extension of the brain' (Myerson, 1997: 180), anticipating interviewee IV's (designer, born 1969) comments about a '[chain] from your brain to your hands'. Crampton Smith also anticipates his criticism of the computer allowing for choice rather than creation: 'The computer always responds, offer options and alternatives . . . We're all lazy so we try different options instead of working it out' (quoted in Myerson, 1997: 179).

Also the point about creatives benefitting from traditional handwork training, even as they begin using digital tools, is anticipated in this edited collection:

> like many people who trained in a design profession during the 1950s or 1960s, [Ann Sutton] achieved a situation in which she . . . has the personal know-how of craft experience and she now [also] has the possibilities of computerised, distributed knowledge at her disposal.
>
> Many middle-aged designers in a similar position to hers (they may be weavers, engineers or architects) argue that they get the best out of the computer and its software if you are able to drive the tool rather being driven by it. (Dormer, 1997a: 145)

The 'personal know-how of craft experience', or what the *qilinghou* interviewees refer to as handwork, is seen as an enhancer of, and maybe even a prerequisite for, productive engagement with computers and software. There are, however, at least two big differences between the now middle-aged *qilinghou* and the middle-aged Britons of the early 1990s. The first is that computers entered the UK in a much more gradual way. In terms of technologies available during training, comparing a *qilinghou* born in 1970 and a *balinghou* born in 1980 is like comparing Britons born in 1950 and 1975. Following this, the middle-aged Britons might have had a better chance of adapting their own practices to new, digital tools, whereas there is a sense of strategic capitulation in the attitude of my *qilinghou* respondents. Knowing that they will never be able to keep up with them, they let the young have their computers and choose instead to focus on the values of handwork.

CONCLUSION

This has been a case study of 'creativity', as nine Chinese professionals who make their living 'being creative' understand the term, as opposed to how creativity is (under) defined during policy making and discussed as part of scholarly discourse. In the interviewees' understanding, creativity is tightly coupled with issues of generational difference (*qilinghou* and *balinghou*) and technology (analogue and digital). The exact way in which creativity, generations and technology intertwine will differ from case to case. The contribution of the case study is not to explain how such intertwining plays out in general but to highlight the three, connected concepts as useful analytical points of entry.

The *qilinghou* interviewed here see themselves as a group growing up under much tougher, pre-digital conditions than the *balinghou*, and they use these conditions to explain why they value hard work, handwork and 'spirituality' – as opposed to the *balinghou's* perceived laziness. The *qilinghou* explain their creative outlook and ways of working through a series of interrelated dichotomies: old-new, analogue-digital, flexibility-fixity, slow-fast, with the *balinghou* seen to be entangled with the new-digital-fixity-fast side of things. The *qilinghou* themselves see a connection between mastery of 'slow' analogue tools and a corresponding appreciation of the slowness of idea-generation: the *balinghou* are presumed to miss that connection because of their perceived affinity with the digital.

The *balinghou* interviewees are far less concerned with the *qilinghou* than vice versa. Although they are highly proficient with digital tools, the *balinghou* actually share the *qilinghou's* appreciation of analogue tools. Analogue tools allow for the flexibility of use, which is seen as crucial in the creative process. That being said, the *balinghou* are also capable of cynical use of traditional tools for merely strategic purposes, for example when presenting hand drawn sketches at client meetings in order to signal proper, traditional training.

The sense, shared by *qilinghou* and *balinghou* interviewees alike, is that analogue tools are superior for idea-generation, and this is carried over into a rejection of the idea that elaborative work can count as 'creative'; for example when the person who leads an animation project points to early, hand-made concept drawings as the only creative part of a project and everything that is subsequently done with digital tools as un-creative. Here the conceptual linking of analogue tools with creativity and flexibility – and in the mirror image: digital tools with un-creative fixity – is also part of the legitimisation of managerial power. Creative workers' thinking about their own creativity contains aesthetic reflections on beauty and newness but is also deeply embedded in much more mundane concerns over project and management hierarchies.

NOTE

1. The One Child Policy was strictly enforced in cities in the 1980s and 1990s; in the countryside people often had more than one child; special exceptions existed for national minorities.

REFERENCES

Alvesson, Mats, and Dan Kärreman (2011), *Qualitative Research and Theory Development: Mystery and Method*. London: Sage.
Bal, Mieke (2002), *Travelling Concepts in the Humanities: A Rough Guide*. Toronto: University of Toronto Press.

Bal, Mieke (2009), 'Working with concepts', *European Journal of English Studies* **13** (1): 13–23.

Cheng, Min and Steven L. Berman (2012), 'Globalization and identity development: A Chinese perspective', *New Directions for Child and Adolescent Development* 2012 (138).

Corbin, Juliet and Anselm Strauss (2008), *Basics of Qualitative Research: Techniques and Procedures for Developing Grounded Theory (3rd Edn)*. Los Angeles: Sage.

Csikszentmihalyi, Mihaly (1996), *Creativity: Flow and the Psychology of Discovery and Invention*. New York: Harper Perennial.

Department for Culture, Media and Sport (UK) (2014), Creative Industries Economic Estimates, accessed 23 July 2015 at https://www.gov.uk/government/uploads/system/uploads/attachment_data/file/271008/Creative_Industries_Economic_Estimates_-_January_2014.pdf.

Dormer, Peter (1997a), 'Craft and the Turing Test for practical thinking', in Peter Dormer (ed.), *The Culture of Craft: Status and Future*. Manchester: Manchester UP, pp. 137–57.

Dormer, Peter (ed.) (1997b), *The Culture of Craft: Status and Future*. Manchester: Manchester UP.

Glaser, Barney and Anselm Strauss (1967), *The Discovery of Grounded Theory: Strategies for Qualitative Research*. New Brunswick: AldineTransaction.

Hesmondhalgh, David (2013), *The Cultural Industries (3rd Edn.)*. London: Sage.

Hesmondhalgh, David and Sarah Baker (2011), *Creative Labour: Media Work in Three Cultural Industries*. Abingdon: Routledge.

Keane, Michael (2013), *Creative Industries in China: Art, Design and Media*. Cambridge: Polity Press.

Liboriussen, Bjarke (2012), 'On the origin myths of creativity, with special attention to the use of digital tools in architectural work', *Comunicação e Sociedade* 22: 16–32.

Liu, Fengshu (2011), *Urban Youth in China: Modernity, the Internet and the Self*. New York: Routledge.

Mannheim, Kurt (2009), 'The sociological problem of generations', in Lauren Cornell, Massimilliano Gioni, Laura Hoptman, and Brian Sholis (eds.), *Younger Than Jesus: The Generation Book*. Göttingen: Steidl, pp. 163–95.

Myerson, Jeremy (1997), 'Tornadoes, T-squares and technology: can computing be a craft?', in Peter Dormer (ed.), *The Culture of Craft: Status and Future*. Manchester: Manchester UP, pp. 176–85.

Palmer, James (2013), 'The balinghou', *Aeon Magazine*, n. pag, accessed 23 August 2015 at http://aeon.co/magazine/living-together/james-palmer-chinese-youth/.

Rhodes, Susan R. (1983), 'Age-related differences in work-attitudes and behaviour: a review and conceptual analysis', *Psychological Bulletin* **93** (2): 328–67.

Silverman, David (2011), *Interpreting Qualitative Data: A Guide to the Principles of Qualitative Research (4th Edn)*. London: Sage.

Woerner, Meredith (2014), 'Andy Serkis built a new world for "Dawn of the Planet of the Apes"', accessed 12 June 2015 at http://io9.com/andy-serkis-reveals-the-new-ape-world-in-dawn-of-the-pl-1553706020.

6. The artyficial paradise: municipal face-work in a Chinese boomtown
Michael Alexander Ulfstjerne

INTRODUCTION

In 2009, the Danish artist and professor Bjørn Nørgaard[1] received notice that Ordos, a resource-rich municipality in the Inner Mongolia Autonomous Region, was considering his work for a large art-theme park in a newly developed urban district. The communiqué asked Nørgaard to send photos of his earlier work to those responsible for selecting artists. After this review he was contracted to contribute an artwork to the 'International Friendship Park', located in the municipality's new flagship district, Kangbashi, although the curators required more detailed documentation of his work. Following this, Nørgaard and his colleague sent more pictures and awaited a follow-up. After a longer period with no response, they gathered that another artist might have been chosen for the task, or that the project had simply failed to materialize for some reason.

Then, towards the end of 2009 a notice arrived congratulating Professor Nørgaard, confirming that his artwork was nearly finished and, should he wish to make some smaller adjustments, he was indeed welcome. But in that case he should hurry. 'I thought we were supposed to go there to do some work. Then after a while of not hearing anything from them we reasoned that it didn't come through. Then we received the pictures!' In March 2011, Nørgaard explained to me how the artwork was manufactured in a sculpture production centre located in the outskirts of Beijing.[2] Those responsible for selecting artists had simply chosen an existing artwork and begun its reproduction from the photos they had received. Surprised to learn how his own creations had simply materialized without the slightest effort or knowledge thereof, he and his colleague asked to be included in the last process. Being well familiar with the scene of cultural production in China, Nørgaard explained:

> we stood there asking ourselves what the hell are they doing? Obviously they were happy with what they got [he received payment]. But if I hadn't been somehow familiar with China I would surely have gone ballistic. Yet I knew that it would be pointless to get wound up over that, a waste of time. So, we decided to go.

The artwork in question, 'The Genetically Modified Paradise', was initially created for Expo 2000 in Hanover, Germany. It was a collection of sculptures highlighted by a genetically modified edition of the iconic 'little mermaid', a tourist attraction in Copenhagen.[3] After the Expo, 'The Genetically Modified Paradise', including the mutated mermaid, was delivered back to Denmark and mounted in front of the National Agency for Enterprise and Construction, only a few hundred metres from her older sister, the unmodified Little Mermaid. It seemed that yet another family increase was well underway and that the mermaids now had a younger sister somewhere in in the periphery of Beijing, which would soon be on the way to Ordos municipality, alongside a large batch of other reproduced artworks.

Obviously, mermaids travel.[4] Or in this latter case the mermaid was unknowingly transmitted, transmuted from Copenhagen to the outskirts of Beijing, and on from Beijing to Ordos. Was she still the same mermaid? What did she bring with her and what was lost in transit? And finally, how did she cope with the new environment – one so distant from World Expositions as well as the familiar Copenhagen harbour – the sites her predecessors had explored?

The 'mermaid travelogue' was a legacy of the municipality's newfound interest in creative industries, and its aspirations to display and breed new cultural as well as international 'characteristics' (*tese*). By tracing the genetically modified mermaid's Chinese sibling into her new habitat, my aim in this chapter is to examine some of the repercussions that transpire when the discourse of creative and cultural industries arrives in new destinations. Not only insofar as the discourse of creative industries moves from a Western context to a Chinese one, as brilliantly portrayed by Jing Wang (2004), or the particular instruments and professional networks that enable policies to move and be implemented elsewhere (cf. Prince 2014), but particularly the move from the larger coastal cities in China to the hinterlands. Cultural and creative industries, I argue, must be understood in the context of the place-specific modality of urban aspirations in order to encompass the different ways that this development discourse intersects with municipal economies and private capital in Chinese urban regions.

Complementing research that deals with the 'cosmetic', 'inauthentic', or 'superficial' nature of upgrading (*shengji*) in contemporary Chinese urbanism (cf. Yu and Padua 2010; Bosker 2013:12) – including the local appropriations of cultural and creative discourse by government and speculators (Zheng 2010; Keane 2011, 2013) – I suggest that so-called 'prestige' or 'face-projects' (*mianzi gongcheng, zhengji gongcheng*) are not entirely bereft of social creativity. In doing so, I consider the gains of detaching oneself from normative assumptions about proper creativity or the notion that cosmetics or superficiality is necessarily bad. Instead of simply lampooning Chinese local governments for their corrupted, superficial and deceptive appropriations of cultural and creative industries we need to see these urban facelifts in their capacity for managing social relations. Municipal face-work, I will argue, needs to reference values attributed to Chinese faces and appearances (cf. Goffman 1967; Kipnis 1995; Yan 1996: 133; Wilson 2002; Hertz 2001).

This chapter draws specifically on seven months of ethnographic fieldwork I conducted between 2011 and 2014. Building on longer ethnographic sojourns in the Ordos municipality, my data includes interviews with various professionals connected to the planning, design and construction of urban projects in Ordos from 2008 to 2013. These included international architects, employees at the Ministry for Land and Resources, artists, financiers, urban planners and Chinese architects employed at the China Architecture and Design Research Group (Beijing). All of these informants contributed to my gaining a better understanding of the incentives that exist for appropriating cultural and creative industries by local developers and governments. To gain a better understanding of what paved the way for the mermaid's conspicuous arrival in Ordos the following provides some background of the city.

BECOMING A MUNICIPALITY

In 2001, the local administration changed its name from Yeke-juu league,[5] an ethnic administrative unit, to Ordos Municipality, a designation more in line with China's broader administrative system. Despite covering an immense territory (87,000 km^2) of mostly scarcely populated rural land, the nominal change to Ordos Municipality recalibrated the entire region as distinctly urban. Ordos' administrative upgrade served to incorporate the wider rural region into what Hsing calls an 'urban-dominant territorial governance system' (2010: 94). Following this change Ordos initiated an ambitious slate of urban transformations, ostensibly to divest itself of its poor and unsophisticated background. Abetted by a boom in local extractive industries, which had delivered windfall profits since the 1990s, local leaders sought to cement this transformation by expanding the city's narrow industrial base into new creative, cultural and scientific endeavours.

Attractive incentives prompt local governments and prefectures to apply for municipal status. These incentives mainly concern the expansion of local states' regulatory and fiscal ambit, including more autonomy to stipulate their own policies (Chien and Wu 2011: 133, 134; Chung and Lam 2009). In the quest for rapid development and higher revenue streams, local governments also seek to remove legal and administrative barriers that might obstruct growth, and in many cases instigate ambitious urbanization schemes. In Ordos municipal revenue generated from taxes and licences in the coal industry rose from 9.7 per cent of Municipal GDP in 2002 to 30.6 per cent by 2010 (OBS 2011; see also Zhang 2007: 30). By 2011, Ordos boasted the nation's highest per capita GPD. Local residents considered Ordos a Chinese Dubai – partly due to the city's resource-driven economy but also because of its ambitious schemes of modernist urbanization and prestigious landmark developments.

The inclination to modernize or expand urban territory is in no way unique to Ordos: it is common across China. This follows a change in the configuration of fiscal powers at local and regional level governments. One consequence of the fiscal decentralization policies issued by the central state since the 1980s is that sub-national level governments have gained more authority to devise economic policies, or what they believe are attractive economic policies.[6] Development crazes have followed in many of these regions, including Inner Mongolia (Bulag 2002: 212). Many of these crazes have bought into a widespread imaginary of the contemporary Chinese city. Anthropologist Uradyn E. Bulag writes: 'Cities have emerged as the centres where industrial miracles and "actions" occur, pointing towards a future utopia, departing from Mao's ideological ambivalence, and are represented in the media as an embodiment of modernity' (2002: 212). From the vantage point of regional governments, urbanization is therefore often seen as a pathway to economic success (Wu 2007: 9). Ordos Municipal Government's homepage illustrates this point well; it states:

> In recent years, Ordos carried forward the spirit 'transcending oneself, promoting civilization and achieving excellence' [. . .] so as to build a city with more vitality, strength, charm and harmony, and to enhance the development of politics, economy, culture and social welfare.[7]

Phrases like 'achieving excellence' or 'transcending oneself' were expressions that followed the municipality's attempts to leapfrog progressive states of urban development and catapult citizens into a more civilized, cultural and prosperous urban life. Rhetoric such as this has marked the ambition of Ordos as a frontier region to inscribe itself into the broader values of contemporary Chinese urbanism by bestowing large-scale urbanization schemes with contemporary values such as culture, social welfare and harmony.

Ordos' ambitious urban transformations were legitimized within a framework of rational planning – deeply rooted in the discourse of scientific development (*kexue fazhan*) and following the latest urban development trends. Yet beyond rhetoric that foregrounds the city's economic and cultural 'transcendence', the underlying incentives (to become a municipality and expand the urban territory) undoubtedly stem from the fiscal and economic benefits mentioned above. The rationale for invoking Danish mermaids into the Chinese periphery is therefore predicated on a broader restructuring of administrative and territorial powers. And, as I will argue next, the instigation of large-scale development projects at the urban fringe areas that would make up the future dwelling of the mermaid was both a product of latecomer imaginaries and conditioned by an opportunistic appropriation of the urban development policies of the times.

EXPANSIVE PLANS: THE NEW DISTRICT DEVELOPMENT

From the time Ordos changed its status to municipality the question of land took centre stage. Among the city's horizontal expansion plans, the most striking development was without doubt the Kangbashi New Area, one that was later held as emblematic of China's runaway real estate economy as it became infamous as one of China's modern 'ghost-cities'. Nevertheless, the city's leaders envisioned Kangbashi as the municipality's flagship project, a site to attract new industrial endeavours, one that would support the city in the long run. According to the local government, Kangbashi would serve as Ordos' new centre for 'politics, culture, finance, science and education, making Ordos one of the most charming cities in western China with her ideal, quiet and beautiful living and working environment'.[8] Moreover, Kangbashi was anointed to be a new administrative centre for the re-designated Ordos Municipality, with the preliminary capacity to house 300,000, the projected population for 2020.[9] Despite planners' and experts' warnings about the risk of constructing an entirely new urban area in a region that was foremost a net exporter of residents (Erdos Urban Development Strategy 2005: 28), it was nevertheless decided to follow through with the expansion of the city into the new area, located 27 kilometres southwest of Dongsheng District, the old administrative centre and main urban core of Ordos.

Initially, Kangbashi was the brainchild of the former highly revered mayor, and later Party Secretary of Ordos, Yun Feng.[10] In its early stages the area was intended as an Economic and Technological Development Zone called the Qing Chun Development Zone, following the pattern of numerous zoning developments around China. Later on this aim was modified, instead pursuing the rising trend of 'new town' (*xin cheng*) development projects (Woodworth 2012: 86), a trend that had become prevalent in the early 2000s. These 'new towns' were characterized by their mixed use including residential areas, commerce, industry, culture etc. bringing together a heterogeneous set of agents and interests (Hsing 2010: 114).

Upon entering the new area, expressways unfold into broad arteries of roads and avenues. In summertime roads leading in are clothed in flowers, decoratively planted to resemble ethnic ornaments and city slogans. Large sculptures are erected above these arteries. The planned area of 200 square kilometres includes an urban core of 31 square kilometres (Erdos Urban Development Strategy 2005). The urban core is conceived as a sun rising over a meadow and radiating outward. At the very heart, the massive 'Genghis Khan Square', 400 metres wide and 1.6 kilometres long (640,000 m²), connects the new municipal government's monumental new headquarters to a cultural area, including Ordos Performing Arts Centre, a library, the Ordos Museum and a cultural centre – all landmark projects that parade Ordos' new cultural ambitions, drawing clear lines to the region's cultural legacy[11] while also profiling itself through the use of renowned architects so as to index its international reach. At the bottom of the square a large man-made lake is located in a straight line directly beneath municipal headquarters, which, slightly elevated, oversees the district from its base on the massive square, surpassing Beijing's Tiananmen in size.

With its low density of construction Kangbashi expands outwards in ordered concentric circles opposed to the ad hoc chaotic sprawl of Dongsheng District, the earlier seat of the administration. Large green areas and parks stand in stark contrast to the general lack of leisure sites in Ordos' other urban districts. Everywhere police patrol and guide the scarce traffic; traffic signs are abundant. There is no litter to be seen and the large vacant spaces and spectacular designs stand out from the urban forms that were dominant earlier. Although the ample roads and overall design of the district appeal more to drivers and less to pedestrians, public buses serving commuters inside Kangbashi are free of charge. Compared with already existing urban districts in Ordos, Kangbashi is an almost perfect inversion.

One of the ways that Ordos has sought to rid itself of its mining boom legacy is to implement new policies to diversify its economy and expand its narrow industrial base. These include creative industries clusters, industrial parks, specialized industrial zones, zones for equipment manufacturing, car assembly and production areas, cloud computing and animation zones. New grand sports and cultural venues will host world-class events.

Altogether a total of more than 700 km² has been allocated as future zones for specialized production and industry.[12] All of these were planned and meticulously designed in collaboration with private and corporate stakeholders. To attract business, large plots in the newly converted urban land are allocated to influential enterprises. In some cases, as state functionaries working with land conversions explained to me, this even includes valuable stocks in the local resource industry. Beneficial conditions for taxation and rent have been offered to enterprises that venture into the new area.

The 2010–20 master plan[13] envisions a dual urban core made up of Dongsheng District to the northeast and Kang A (Kangbashi and its bordering region Azhen) to the southwest. As shown in the plan, the stretch between these two cores constitutes a central part of the area populated with the abovementioned industries, high-tech clusters, sports stadiums, and some residential areas.

In Ordos the authority obtained from the administrative upgrade is pertinent to the process whereby rural hinterland is converted to urban land, together with the new emphasis on urban planning and its plethora of buzzwords. Despite their claim to general applicability (cf. Prince 2014), 'mobile policies' that position culture and/or creativity as an economic driver are not implemented in a vacuum – even when, as in the case of Ordos, these policies are directed towards a brand new city in the making. Nevertheless, as I will argue next, there are other forces at play that help explain how plans, policies and cultural artefacts travel and are accommodated in new environments within a framework that considers a national hierarchy of cities.

MUNICIPAL FACE-WORK

Kangbashi was not merely a functional expansion in order to spur the industrial growth of the city. It was obviously also crafted as a showcase for urban planning, architecture, and the new municipality's economic development (cf. de Muynck 2009; Woodworth 2012; Bernstein 2008; Ulfstjerne and de Muynck 2012). A central way that local officials in Chinese municipal governments gain recognition in the context of intracity competition is through high-profile urban projects and the adjacent index of local real estate appraisal. You-tian Hsing describes how local leaders increasingly regard themselves as 'city promoters', in turn boosting the value of land:

> Mayors don suits and embark on road shows to promote real estate projects in
> their cities, and compete with one another to hire advertising gurus for help in

developing 'urban strategic development plans' aimed at improving the image of their cities and boosting their property values. (Hsing 2010: 9)

Beyond boosting tax and real estate-generated revenue, the symbolic display of these high profile projects is part of an emerging tendency whereby second and third tier cities in China attempt to leapfrog the progressive stages of urban development, pushing forward a wholesale transformation from an underdeveloped nowhere to becoming the place to live, consume, and invest (cf. Wu 2007: 1–19; Zhang 2006). Noting this trend, geographer David Harvey writes: 'Investment in consumption spectacles, the selling of images of places, competition over the definition of cultural and symbolic capital, the revival of vernacular tradition associated with places as a consumer attraction, all become conflated in inter-place competition' (1996: 298). As can be illustrated by Ordos' aim to launch itself as a 'model city' with its emphasis on being green, civilized, prosperous, creative, hygienic and liveable, creative industries are but one component in a wider set of more or less formally recognized upgrades.

How were these upgrades perceived on the ground? What were the most common ways to understand Ordos' government's urban aspirations?

From my interviews and observations among the new district's scarce pioneer inhabitants, it was obvious that few residents seemed to take much pride in these projects. Several of those I encountered expressed the view that such developments were fashioned to boost officials' chances of ascendance. Even the campaign to produce more civilized citizens to suit the new city was rationalized as something that was not intended for them – rather something that pertained to a political realm, often by reference to the term 'political prestige projects' (*zhengji gongcheng*) or 'face projects' (*mianzi gongcheng*), the latter term referring to the broader preoccupation with face which is incremental to a person's reputation and moral standing in China (Hsien-chin Hu in Kipnis 1995: 125; Yan 1996: 136–7).

Besides explanations that related these projects to the political realm, others pointed to the fact that both citizens and government in Ordos felt an urgent need to partake in the kind of rapid economic development that has characterized China's coastal regions – and when they finally did catch up, to show off their newly acquired wealth and status. The local government's investments in prestigious architecture, cultural and creative industries, and spectacular landmark developments were thus largely understood as a way the municipal government would mark Ordos' leap from a peripheral outpost to become known for its extravagance and excessive construction, the Chinese Dubai. One civil servant working in the National Ministry for Land and Resources' local department explained how, similarly to much of the general population who had acquired idle wealth through generous re-location compensation during Ordos' wholesale transformation,[14] the government was equally keen to show off: 'people who are relocated [in Ordos] often buy a nice car, an apartment, a fancy watch or take friends to nice restaurants. The local government can't do that. For them to show off they have to make new districts, crazy architecture. They are no different than the rest of us'. Another civil servant expressed the local authority's proclivity to flash their newly acquired wealth and fiscal power as a question of boosting their face, or as he phrased it, 'slap one's face until it's swollen in an effort to look imposing' (*da zhong lian chong pangzi*).

In the traditional Western use of the terms, concepts such as 'surface' and 'face' implicitly juxtapose surface with depth, or appearance vs. a hidden reality (for a critique see Miller 2005: 32). In his work on 'face-talk', Andrew Kipnis draws up a comparative genealogy of the meaning of faces and shows how the early translation from the Chinese words *lian* and *mianzi* into English 'face' came to designate the Chinese persona as false, indicating an 'absence of sincerity' (Smith in Kipnis 1995: 124). As Chinese people appear fond of 'face', they are assumed to value social appearance rather than that which lies underneath or inside. Kipnis' work moves beyond this impasse: he emphasizes how faces and face-work in China might be thought of more fittingly as 'constitutive visibilities': i.e. essentially relational, communicative and interactive. Kipnis observes how the size of one's *mianzi* (face), as implied in the metaphorical idea of a surface, is difficult to understand along a 'sincere-superficial' binary, but rather should be understood as the scope of one's communicative ambit. The larger the face, the greater communicative leeway is at hand. In this sense, concepts like *lian* and *mianzi* denote what Kipnis describes as 'the interactive surface from which human communication can begin' (Kipnis 1995: 131).[15]

In the light of increasing competitiveness among local governments across China, Kipnis' notion of 'constituent visibilities' spurs another reading of local governments' so-called 'face-projects': one less inclined to comprehend superficiality according to its otherwise derogative connotation. Existing hierarchies between local and regional governments dictate the appropriation of policy buzzwords and popular urban designs in a process that is equally communicative and strategic.

AN(OTHER) CREATIVITY – SHORTCUTS AND ARCHITECTURAL MIMICRY

Governments across the developed world, and increasingly in Asian countries (especially China), embrace creativity in city making. Creative industries are believed to be the new driving force for socio-economic development, the logic being that concentrations of a particular class of people engender innovative and creative practices that eventually will bring about a value generating process (Florida 2002). Historically, the clustering of creative individuals has taken more organic forms and entailed a degree of self-organization. Now, creative clusters are premeditated, 'artificially' produced in the process of strategic planning (Keane 2011).

Before cultural creative clusters had proved successful in attracting investment and raising the value of land, few municipalities looked upon the creative zeitgeist as anything but a waste of resources (Zheng 2010). Yet within a short period of time, creative clusters became a development model that could be implemented at the local level, with the key benefits being generation of tax revenues and real estate. This so-called 'creative estate' (see Keane 2011) brought local governments into a close relation with real estate developers who had bought into the most recent buzzwords in the rapidly changing landscape of urban policies and regulations, in turn, producing a local plethora of 'less warranted' creative sites; several of these never even materialized other than as online illusions crafted to raise the value of land, in turn, engendering an economy of 'unfinishing buildings' (Ulfstjerne 2016).

Yet in the heyday of Ordos' boom there was abundance of building. In order to accelerate the construction of the new urban areas, many designs and templates were simply copied and reproduced from other cities. This is not unique to Ordos. Replications of both national and international designs are seen widely across municipalities in China (cf. Yu and Padua 2007). In Ordos, one example of this trend was the 'International Friendship Sculpture Park' where Mr Bjørn Nørgaard together with several hundred other Western and Asian artists would be well compensated simply to have some of their earlier work displayed following its 'reproduction' in the Yidonghuan Sculpture Production Centre located in the outskirts of Beijing.

Contracted by artistic director, Miss He E, who was responsible for selecting artworks for the Ordos municipal government, most artists never oversaw or even encountered the works that were freighted on to Kangbashi from Beijing. Apart from the sculpture park, other examples included emulating the designs of bridges, squares, fun fairs and leisure parks, financial centres, cultural and creative industry zones etc. Yu Jie, one architect from the Chinese Architecture, Design & Research Group (CADREG)[16] who was contracted to create the master plan for a 200-hectare creative industry zone in Kangbashi New Area explained how their lack of experience and the contractor's demand for a quick process

Figure 6.1   Work team finishing Mr Bjørn Nørgaard's sculptures at the Yidongyuan Sculpture Production Centre

compelled them to 'borrow' from other designs. As the creative buzz had yet to gain potency at the time few had experience with creative industry zones. Nevertheless, within a month CADREG produced a 100-page booklet with the overall conceptual layout of the creative zone.

A common assumption that undergirds discussions about creative and cultural industries is that creativity and artistic production should be sincere, autonomous and uncensored. In China, as Jing Wang points out, none of the perceived preconditions for creative industries necessarily exist in the form initially conceptualized in the Western context: namely flat-hierarchy and bottom-up development, project-based work patterns, autonomous and avant-garde freelance producers etc. (Wang 2004: 12).

A related set of value orientations are evident among many planners and urban thinkers who insist that cities must grow naturally, rather than being transplanted from one place to another. Cultural elites and professionals (intelligentsia, architects, scholars, artists, journalists) often lament the loss of authenticity and proper identity in contemporary Chinese cities, at times measured by the widespread demolition of cultural sites and the proliferation of immense shopping malls and conference centres

(Zhang 2006: 469; Bosker 2013:3). As a logical consequence of this strand of thought the pace and scope of demolition-construction that character-izes contemporary Chinese urbanism is eroding the collective memory that adheres in particular historical spaces, an amnesia that is further deepened as urban identities are haphazardly transplanted from other cities. When urban designs are airlifted from one site to another they become detached from these cities' natural surroundings, with 'little, or any, sensitivity to their [new] physical or cultural context' (Yu and Padua 2010: 259). Seen through this optic the frenetic drive to capitalize on urbanization, in turn, makes the Chinese city superficial, its spaces uniform, commercialized, and unauthentic (Yu and Padua 2007). Although I am fairly sympathetic with this point of view, I wish to advance the idea of understanding this superficiality and copy-paste method of place making in a way that is less burdened by such value-laden connotations as imitation, superficiality, and inauthenticity.

Is there another way to understand these processes, one that pays closer attention to how urban designs, creative discourses, or even mermaids travel?

In a recent attempt to move beyond this impasse of interpretation Bianca Bosker (2013) turns to the Chinese tradition for appreciating copies 'as originals'. In light of a Chinese cultural and philosophical disposition to see reproduction as evidence of technology, skill and achievement, Bosker advances the idea that architectural mimicry can be understood as a sign of the transition from replication to innovation (Bosker 2013: 16). Bosker believes that such simulation is one way that China shows its technological and economic prowess – not only in regard to the capacity to duplicate, but also as an indication that China is on its way to catch up or even surpass the geographical origins of these simulac-rascapes (ibid: 17).

Bosker identifies pragmatic as well as symbolic reasons for why alien townscapes are simulated: first, developers and officials tap into the growing Chinese middle class newfound taste for what's exclusive and foreign (*yangqi*) (cf. Zhang 2010: 84; Wu 2007: 6). Second, accessible knowledge about construction, architecture, engineering, and planning related to Western urban forms is extensive, accessible and is now, after having been employed by the Chinese construction industry for some time, reproduced fast and with a lower cost (Bosker 2013: 70). Moreover, relating to the realm of political aspirations, the need for city mayors and local decision makers to produce as much as possible within a four-year frame provides some further explanation as to why entire townscapes and designs are imported wholesale. It saves time and effort: less basic design work is needed and architectural expenses are reduced. Beyond pragmatic reasons, the capability to almost instantly bring about forms that had taken years to develop in the West is perceived as a display of power.

Yet innovation, as I have suggested above, might happen at a completely different scale, one that is not just about whether a given design is original, borrowed, or a knock-off but is more understandable by reference to appearances and (sur)face work in the context of a city's aspirations. Imitation, in this light, is expressive and relates to tactics of recognition and the ceremonial order of an urban hierarchy.

Decisions about what can be built often revert to high standing officials. The taste for extravagance and gargantuan designs is common. Local governments spend excessively on duplicating the US Capitol Building, the Chrysler Building, the Eiffel Tower, or as in Tianjin, the Manhattan skyline. If architectural mimicry, as Bosker (2013: 87) argues, is a symbol of finally making it – a display of China's economic prowess and modernization – this then necessarily creates even larger incentives for producing similar cityscapes in the large parts of the country that feel less modern, outposts and so-called under-developed areas (*luohou*). It seems that the farther you get out into the provinces the less weight cultural connotations carry, i.e. the more freely designs float. Some might still invoke European antiquity and aristocracy while others – as Nørgaard's Artificial Paradise and his mermaid – are more up for grabs.

Figure 6.2   The mermaid's final destination: the International Friendship Park in Kangbashi, Ordos

MERMAID'S TRAVELOGUE

Reading the mermaid's travelogue as indicative of a broader appropriation, I have sought to shed light on pragmatic and symbolic reasons for why Western urban forms, including development policies, entire urban districts, and even Danish mermaids are replicated in the Chinese periphery. Rather than debate whether these forms are original or rip-offs, whether the mermaid is simply a third-tier mermaid or something in her own right, the chapter argues that we need to understand these travels beyond the binary of authentic vs. fake. With no regard to aesthetic inclinations, municipal face-work need not be opposed to sincerity and depth, but rather is adherence to a symbolic and communicative practice.

Against this background the emulation of the kind of urban designs and planners' buzzwords currently in vogue in first-tier or Western cities might be less about form, impact or even successful implementation, but pertain to the question of ascending in recognition and broadening one's communicative ambit. Although these designs may neither resonate as suitable to the local environment nor fit well with local populations' aesthetic dispositions, the new urban citizens of the Ordos municipality can nevertheless relate to the urgency of displaying the wealth and modernity that has finally arrived.

The radical modernization schemes that have changed a large part of Ordos' environment, the civilizing campaigns ubiquitous throughout the city, the new spectacular cultural venues, art centres and cultural clusters etc. are not only attempts to diversify the economy but are also attempts to distance the city from its background as a rough coalmining hub through municipal face-work. In Ordos, the pragmatic appropriation of form – from following suit on new district development to the fastidious re-production and installation of borrowed sculptures – in other words, everything that can imbue Ordos with an international flavour is also an attempt to boost the new districts' communicative ambit. Investment in 'appearances' is socially and politically constituted and constitutive.

Examining the industry of creative urban consultants, Russell Prince (2014) shows how abstract concepts such as creativity are rendered quantifiable, transformed into ready-mades that local governments can implement, rationalize, and measure (2014: 94). The face-work of municipalities, their superficial appropriation of development rhetoric and ad hoc acquisition of alien urban forms suggest a disregard for 'proper' creativity; in turn, this disregard potentially undermines hegemonic assumptions that exist among policy-makers; and it challenges the idea that these concepts can be applied anywhere with the intended effects. Prince does not see the trend of quantifying 'mobile policy' concepts as cultural and creativity as something static, but understands the field as one of fluidity, contention and emergence (2014: 99). Further, as knowledge necessarily is produced somewhere, its universality is compromised when translated, measured and transported elsewhere, a process that invites new conceptualizations.

The mermaid's travelogue is testimony to what happens when ideas about creativity travel, are copied, and implemented elsewhere. Ending up in so-called Chinese ghost towns amid hundreds of other sculptures one could speculate as to how they are perceived, or if they are recognized as something creative. When there are no conveyors of what 'proper' art is, what the right policy should look like, or authorities that judge the form or process of implementation, something entirely new might surface in this vacuum – or it might not rise to the occasion at all. What once bore traces of a Scandinavian mermaid might in the end amount to nothing other than relic-rubble in the peripheries of states, liberated from whatever cultural referent once framed it.

NOTES

1. Ethnographic data regarding the International Friendship Park and the mermaid's travels would not have been possible without the support, input, and assistance of Mr Bjørn Nørgaard and Mr Henrik Keil. Moreover, I also wish to extend my gratitude for the support of managers and employees at the Yidongyuan Sculpture Production Centre in Beijing, and the generous assistance and insights from civil servants in Ordos.
2. Interview conducted at Mr Nørgaard's residence and workspace, March 2, 2011.
3. The 'little mermaid' was a sculpture by the Danish artist Edvard Eriksen, based on the fairy tale by Hans Christian Andersen.
4. Danish mermaids are prone to visit China. The original 'Little Mermaid' spent six months in China as part of the Danish Pavilion at the Expo 2010 held in Shanghai.
5. Since the 1990s, several Inner Mongolian leagues have been transformed to prefecture-level cities, a process that is now taking place throughout most of the region and is referred to as 'league transformed to municipality' (*meng gai shi*).
6. For an in-depth analysis and overview of fiscal decentralization policies since reform, see Tsai 2004. Policies did not simply move toward an even greater level of local authority and decentralized system but have moved back and forth with shifting policies of taxation and systems of revenue collection and sharing.
7. OMG, accessed August 6, 2013 at http://www.ordos.gov.cn/english/eeds2/201207/t20120724_656109.html.
8. Accessed April 24, 2014 at http://www.ordos.gov.cn/english/ordos5/200908/t20090811_73261.html.
9. For more detailed information on Kangbashi's history, dates, development, and most central institutions see, accessed on April 24, 2014 at http://baike.baidu.com/view/1177473.htm. See also Woodworth 2012 for a more extensive analysis of design and development of Kangbashi.
10. Yun Feng was secretary of the Ordos Municipal Committee of the Communist Party of China and was the most central character behind Ordos's ambitious urban development through the years of rapid economic growth following the development of its natural resources.

11. The performing arts theatre was built in the shape of a traditional Mongolian headdress and the library was conceived as a collection of classic Mongolian texts.
12. Ordos Planning Bureau, accessed 20 August 2014 at http://www.ordosgh.gov.cn/ghzss/ztgh/201005/t20100525_186923.html.
13. The Master Plan was retrieved from Ordos Government homepage (Urban Planning Board). Several additional and accessible maps include more in-depth information about planning of new zones, industrial clusters, development of urban management systems, transportation planning, social services including the improvements of Ordos' educational, medical and cultural facilities. It also includes an overview of future engineering projects and natural disaster prevention, accessed 10 June 2014 at http://www.ordosgh.gov.cn/ghzss/ztgh/201005/t20100525_186923.html.
14. An unofficial policy, retrospectively called the 'Ordos model', granted relatively high relocation packages to those whose land was needed for modernization or expansion of the city. Compensation could include cash payments as well as modern apartments. Ordos' close association with idle wealth partly came from the way capital was redistributed.
15. In his work (1995) Kipnis distinguishes between *lian*, mainly related to a person's moral standing, and *mianzi*, which relates to prestige. While it is beyond the ambit of this chapter to engage in discussions about the rich connotations of these concepts, it mainly deals with the term *mianzi*, i.e. prestige.
16. CADREG is listed as a State-Owned Enterprise although smaller units seem to be more independent and project based. Local design institutes are responsible from changing sketch and conceptual design into construction design, complying with existing laws and building regulations. Before the '90s every design institute was state-owned and held a monopoly of construction – commissioned by central government's logistics and planning. In the last two decades these institutes underwent large changes: to cope with changing market demands, they deployed new strategies to become more flexible and catered to the private sphere. Some were fully privatized and others partly. One such strategy included making smaller project-based teams, working with a degree of independent units under the larger State-Owned LDI. For more information see Mapping China, accessed 6 June 2015 at http://www.culturalexchange-cn.nl/mapping-china/architecture/architecture-practice-china/state-owned-local-design-institutes-ldi.

REFERENCES

Bernstein, Fred A. (2008), 'In Inner Mongolia, pushing architecture's outer limits', *The New York Times*, 1 May, sec. Home & Garden, accessed 12 July 2015 at http://www.nytimes.com/2008/05/01/garden/01mongolia.html.

Bosker, Bianca (2013), *Spatial Habitus: Original Copies: Architectural Mimicry in Contemporary China*. Honolulu, HI, USA: University of Hawaii Press.

Bulag, Uradyn E. (2002), 'From Yeke-Juu League to Ordos municipality: settler colonialism and alter/native urbanization in Inner Mongolia', *Provincial China* 7 (2): 196–234.

Chien, Shiuh-Shen, and Fulong Wu (2011), 'The Transformation of China's urban entrepreneurialism: The case study of the City of Kunshan', *Cross Currents: East Asian History and Culture Review* 1: 95–116.

Chung, Jae Ho, and Tao-chiu Lam (2009), *China's Local Administration: Traditions and Changes in the Sub-National Hierarchy*. London: Routledge.

De Muynck, Bert (2009), 'Architecture on the move: urban and architectural design in Inner Mongolia', *Continuum: Journal of Media & Cultural Studies* 23 (2): 209–19.

Erdos Urban Development Strategy (2005), 'The Erdos Urban Region Development Strategy – a Report to the Municipal People's Government of Erdos'. Developed in collaboration with 'The World Bank (EASUR) and The Cities Alliance' and prepared by Chreod Ltd, March (www.chreod.com).

Florida, Richard (2002), *The Rise of the Creative Class. . . and How It's Transforming Work, Leisure, Community and Everyday Life*. New York: Basic Books.

Goffman, Erving (1967), *Interaction Ritual: Essays on Face-to-Face Behavior*. New York: Doubleday.

Harvey, David (1996), *Justice, Nature and the Geography of Difference*. Oxford: Blackwell.

Hertz, Ellen (2001), 'Face in the crowd: The cultural construction of anonymity in urban China', in Nancy Chen, Constance Clark, Susan Gottschang, and Elaine Jeffrey (eds.), *China Urban: Ethnographies of Contemporary Culture*. Durham, NC: Duke University Press, pp. 274–93.

Hsing, You-tien (2010), *The Great Urban Transformation: Politics of Land and Property in China*. New York: Oxford University Press.

Keane, Michael (2011), *China's New Creative Clusters: Governance, Human Capital and Investment*. London: Routledge.

Keane, Michael (2013), *Creative Industries in China: Art, Design and Media*. Cambridge: Polity.

Kipnis, Andrew (1995), '"Face": an adaptable discourse of social surfaces', *Positions: East Asia Cultures Critique* 3 (1): 119–48.

Miller, Daniel (2005), *Materiality*. Durham, NC: Duke University Press.

OMG (2011), *E'erduosi shi 2011 nian zhengfu gongzuo baogao* (*The City of Erdos Government Work Report 2011*), Ordos Municipality: Ordos Municipal Government.

OBS (2011), *E'erduosi tongji nianjian 2011* (*Ordos Statistical Yearbook 2011*). Ordos: Ordos Bureau of Statistics.

Prince, Russell (2014), 'Consultants and the global assemblage of culture and creativity', *Transactions of the Institute of British Geographers* 39 (1): 90–101.

Tsai, Kellee. S. (2004), 'Off balance: the unintended consequences of fiscal federalism in China', *Journal of Chinese Political Science* 9 (2): 1–26.

Ulfstjerne, Michael, and Bert de Muynck (2012), Ordos: A Chinese City Constructed in the Fast Lane, Solidere Multidisciplinary Design Department.

Ulfstjerne, Michael (2016), 'Unfinishing buildings', in M. Bille and T.F. Sørensen (eds.), *Elements of Architecture: Assembling Archeology, Atmosphere, and the Performance of Building Space*. Archeological Orientations, London: Routledge.

Wang, Jing (2004), 'The global reach of the new discourse: How far can "creative industries" travel?', *International Journal of Cultural Studies* 7 (9): 9–19.

Wilson, Scott (2002), 'Face, norms, and instrumentality', in Doug Guthrie and David Wank (eds.), *Social Connections in China*. Cambridge University Press: Cambridge, pp. 163–78.

Woodworth, Max D. (2012), 'Frontier boomtown urbanism in Ordos, Inner Mongolia Autonomous Region', *Cross-Currents: East Asian History and Culture Review* 1 (1): 74–101.

Wu, Fulong (2007), *China's Emerging Cities: The Making of New Urbanism*. Abingdon, Oxon; NY: Routledge.

Yan, Yunxiang (1996), *The Flow of Gifts: Reciprocity and Social Networks in a Chinese Village*. Stanford, CA: Stanford University Press.

Yang, Mayfair Mei-Hui (1994), *Gifts, Favors, and Banquets: The Art of Social Relationships in China*. Ithaca, NY: Cornell University Press.

Yu, Kongjian, and Mary G. Padua (2007), 'China's cosmetic cities: urban fever and superficiality', *Landscape Research* 32 (2): 255–72.

Zhang, Li (2006), 'Contesting spatial modernity in late-socialist China', *Current Anthropology* 47 (3): 461–84.

Zhang, Li (2010), *In Search of Paradise: Middle-Class Living in a Chinese Metropolis*. Ithaca: Cornell University Press.

Zhang, Zhanlin (2007), *shouru kuozhang zhong de difang caizheng Kunnan: shizheng lunyao* (*Expansionary fiscal policy and local government financial difficulties: case based discussion*). Beijing: minzhu yu jianshe chubanshe.

Zheng, Jane (2010), 'The "entrepreneurial state" in "creative industry cluster" development in Shanghai', *Journal of Urban Affairs* 32 (2): 143–70.

PART II

ADVICE TO GOVERNMENT, IDEOLOGY AND FUTURE CHALLENGES FACING THE CULTURAL INDUSTRIES IN CHINA

7. Editor's introduction
Michael Keane

The concerns of scholars in Mainland China differ in several important respects from their counterparts in liberal democracies, where the focus is often on issues of cultural and creative labour, media ownership, gentrification, intellectual property and gender. In many 'Western' accounts the spectre of neoliberalism is raised as a counterpoint to polemics of the benefits of the 'creative economy' that emanate from government think tanks and 'economic development' bureau. While neoliberalism certainly has traction in the developed 'liberal' economies particularly in respect to the 'creative industries', it makes little sense to speak of neoliberalism in the People's Republic of China, where the intervening 'visible hand' of the government in matters 'cultural' renders this imported term meaningless (Keane 2013; Nonini 2008). In addition, while issues of labour, gender and ownership are valid in China and likely to impact in the future, they hold less policy weight in China, where the government is tied to an explicit cultural development (*wenhua jianshe*) agenda.

Government closely monitors, regulates, subsidizes and promotes certain forms of culture in China; it categorizes sectors as cultural industries: these range from film making, print media, book and magazine publishing, television, tourism, advertising services, performing troupes, and Chinese opera, to ceramics. Each of these sectors has different characteristics, consumers, markets and regulatory systems. As the chapter by Qiu in this volume shows, Chinese universities and state-funded research centres publish annual reports known as Blue Books (*lanpi shu*) that purport to map, index and account for progress. Indeed, markets for cultural goods and services are expanding with urbanization and there is considerable good news to report.

For Part II we sought perspectives from scholars and policy advisors working in China. The intention is to recognize this work while acknowledging a different mode of analysis: those writing from within China adopt what one might refer to as 'administrative style.' These writers are seeking to identify areas of growth while calling attention to issues that require reform, usually in the form of policy recommendations. Many descriptive terms used in Chinese, when translated into English, imply a normative model of 'advice to government', which Qiu describes as the 'remedy paradigm'; for instance reports regularly include descriptions such as 'must' (*bixu*), 'upgrade' (*shengji*), 'construct' (*jianshe*), and 'rejuvenate' (*zhenxing*) as well as containing frequent usage of slogans informing China's domestic cultural ascendency and its globalizing agenda: 'going out' (*zou chuqu*), 'soft power' (*ruanshili*) and 'strong cultural power' (*wenhua qiangguo*). Another difference between this style of analysis and international scholarship is a high volume of data and a relative absence of scholarly references. For this reason these chapters were not peer reviewed. Most data presented in Blue Books comes from government sources and think tanks; in this way it feeds the scholarly system. Blue Book development reports therefore are mandatory reading in courses on cultural management in Chinese universities.

In reading these chapters readers should be aware of the conditions under which intellectual work is conducted in China, particularly in the field of culture. The inclusion of China-based scholars does not infer that they endorse the arguments presented by all scholars in this volume. Writers outside the mainland are inclined to adopt a critical approach. The contrast in approaches thus calls in question the different understandings of the cultural and creative industries and their role in society. To appreciate the way that the cultural and creative industries are framed in China, we need to consider the contrasting roles of 'scholar leaders' (*xueshuxing lingdao*) and 'leading scholars' (*xueshu lingxiu*). The former term refers to 'leaders with knowledge' while the latter cohort is made up of important scholars who have specialties in certain areas. Perhaps the roots of these distinctions can be traced to ancient times. In the Warring States period (500 BCE) in China, and certainly through the dynastical period (221 BCE to 1912), rulers sustained the employment of scholars, leading to extended systems of patronage, essentially building networks or 'lineages' of knowledge. Kings, dukes and emperors courted top scholar-leaders, usually persons with knowledge on a range of affairs of state who had read the requisite Confucian classics. As Lloyd and Siven point out in *The Way and Word*, 'patrons wanted neither basic research nor innovative perceptions, but advice and other services that would help their states survive if they were weak or grow if they were large' (Lloyd and Sivin 2002: 29). As to the burning question of innovation, Randall Collins writes, 'intellectual creativity is driven by opposition. . .when Chinese philosophy settles into a period of hegemonic consensus, that creativity freezes' (Collins 1998: 137). Of course the history of China over the past 2500 years is a case study in 'innovation by opposition' giving way to hegemonic consensus.

In modern times leading scholars may head up think tanks; or they may operate independent consultancies, especially if they are considered 'foreign experts'. Think tanks have become a common feature of the policy environment and they feature heavily in the cultural and creative industries in China. Think tanks, like the Chinese Academy of Social Sciences, are where we find scholar leaders. Zhu Xuefeng, a professor at the Zhou Enlai School of Government in Nankai University, maintains that think tanks are a window for the outside world to observe the Chinese political system and its processes (Zhu 2013). Think tanks influence policy-making and leading scholars working in these institutions rely on their patrons to survive. Policy makers also draw on multiple sources, thus providing a window of opportunity for the 'foreign expert.' Unquestionably, the closer one is to government, and the closer one's voice is to the prevailing orthodoxy, the more likely advice will be heard.

The nature of scholarship that informs the cultural industries (*wenhua chanye*) in China is both straightforward and complex. As Qiu has shown in Chapter 2, many scholars moved camps following the decision to adopt the description *chanye* over *gongye*. This semantic policy shift coincided with the initiation of cultural industry Blue Books. While it is easy for scholars outside China to downplay this administrative style as propaganda, within these 'industry reports' one does find criticism of the market and more measured critique of government strategy. Most accounts, however, are report-style, data-heavy and overly positive in respect to development, often disregarding issues that Western-based scholars would consider as important, even when they are translated for English readerships (see Xiang and Walker 2014). Readers outside China are often bemused by the lack of sharp critique. In recalling the role of scholars in Chinese academies however we also need to be cognizant of their positioning vis-à-vis funding bodies and their positions within their respective institutions.

In the first chapter Xiaoming Zhang (Zhang Xiaoming),[1] founding editor of the *Blue Book of China's Cultural Industries*, provides an overview of development since 2000, showing how China's cultural industry policy agenda developed from an increase in and diversification of urban consumption. A parallel development was China's response to cultural globalization, a fear that China would be infiltrated by Western culture following its accession to the WTO in 2001. The key value of the chapter is that the author carefully sets out the key stages of development and the relevant policies, while prudently pointing out areas that require attention by government, namely excessive intervention into the market.

In the following chapter, Wuwei Li (Li Wuwei), a leading spokesperson and policy advisor, argues that Chinese culture has the capability to reach world markets. Beginning with some of China's success stories, Li concurs with the importance of China's outward bound agenda in the cultural industries. Li provides comparative analysis of China's success and that of large Western media companies, showing that despite the euphoria about

China's large market, there is still a long way to go to become really competitive. Li advocates a number of measures to facilitate the internationalization of China's cultural 'enterprises' including enhancing originality, increasing technological and innovative capacity, adapting China's management system to international practices, transforming the government's role, adopting international marketing concepts, developing more cultural brands and getting overseas Chinese involved in the promotion of Chinese cultural products.

The third chapter in Part II also addresses the challenges facing China's culture 'going out'. Huailiang Li (Li Huailiang) from the National Research Centre for Chinese Cultural Trade at the Communication University of China looks at some of the successes of China's 'going out' policy while reiterating some of the concerns expressed by Prof Li Wuwei. The chapter sets out the policy frameworks underpinning China's going out strategy as well as calling attention to inherent weaknesses in the system. Of special interest is the analysis of policies that have attempted to allow China's cultural industries to develop collaborative partnerships. Li Huailiang points out some of the problems that China currently faces, among which are a lack of international market experience, a lack of high level managerial talent, and narrow markets, mostly located in East and South-east Asia.

The chapter by Na Yi (Yi Na) examines the recent strategy adopted on encouraging localized development, entitled 'characteristic cultural industries' (*tese wenhua chanye*), or more specifically 'one place, one product'. This policy is specifically aimed at the development of minority areas in western China that exhibit a weak economic base due to their dependence on a traditional mode of development. The government believes that the development of characteristic cultural industries will protect the legacy of traditional culture as well as being an important means of using culture as 'resource' to ensure that people are both wealthy and happy. One of the strategies is to encourage non-local enterprises to enter into local characteristic cultural industries, and encourage enterprises of other industries and private capital to engage in characteristic cultural industries by supporting small and micro businesses. Local people will also be encouraged to participate. The government has provided funds for the construction of the Silk Road Cultural Industry Belt and the Zang-Qiang-Yi Cultural Industry Corridor.

The following chapter by Yan Li (Li Yan) and Ying Huang (Huang Ying) examines Yunnan's ethnic cultural and creative industries. Located in the southern border region of southwest China, the province of Yunnan extends for more than 390,000 square kilometres and has a population of almost 46 million. Yunnan adjoins Vietnam, Burma and Laos.

The province is also geographically proximate to Thailand, Cambodia and India. Compared with the eastern coastal areas and middle regions of China, Yunnan is a late developer with less negative effects from industrial development and urbanization. Ethnic culture, infused into peoples' daily lives, includes oral transmission, ethnic songs and dances, traditional handicrafts, festival and events, and religious cultures, as well as villages and historical towns. Yet at the same time the development of Yunnan's ethnic grounded cultural creative industries relies too heavily on a market that is dominated by 'outside' cultural consumers. In other words, the local consumer market does not provide a solid foundation: there are insufficient products and creative services targeted at locals. The ethnic cultural creative industries are primarily centred around tourist areas, tourist cities and well-known sightseeing places.

The authors argue that globalization has been of great benefit. It has developed new spaces and has led to development of Yunnan ethnic-grounded creative industries. The foundations, opportunities, emerging spaces – as well as ideas, thoughts and development paths of these practical cases in this chapter provide a model for global cultural creative development.

As the process of urbanization increases in China there has been an unprecedented boom in the construction of cultural infrastructure. Galleries, museums, theatres and performing arts centres are appearing in China's cities, often as a result of urban regeneration strategies. In comparison with China, arts and cultural clusters in Europe took several decades to form an urban cultural ecology. In this chapter Marina Guo (Guo Meijun) outlines the nature of this rapid development and some of the impediments facing China's GLAM (galleries, libraries, arts and museums) sector. In particular she examines how China might use interactive media to encourage content innovation in the performing arts. Examples include digital museums, new media art museums, as well as digital theatres and concert halls. In addition to such innovation there is the potential of using big data to provide more customized services.

NOTE

1. The well-known scholars writing from within China are known by family name; here we have put both forms: family-given name and given name-family.

REFERENCES

Collins, Randall (1998), *The Sociology of Philosophies: A Global Theory of Intellectual Change*. Cambridge, MA: Harvard University Press.

Keane, Michael (2013), *Creative Industries in China: Art, Design, Media*. London: Polity.

Lloyd, Geoffrey, and Nathan Sivin (2002), *The Way and the Word: Science and Medicine in Early China and Greece*. New Haven and London: Yale University Press.

Nonini, Donald (2008), 'Is China becoming neo-liberal?', *Critique of Anthropology* **28** (2): 145–76.

Xiang, Yong and Patricia Ann Walker (eds.) (2014), *China Cultural and Creative Industries Reports 2013*. Heidelberg: Springer.

Zhu, Xufeng (2013), *The Rise of Think Tanks in China*, China Policy Series. London; New York: Routledge.

8. The cultural industries in China: a historical overview
Xiaoming Zhang

The development of China's cultural industries has proceeded together with reform and opening up, beginning in 1978. The concept of 'cultural industries' was introduced in the *Decision of the CCP Central Committee and the State Council on Accelerating the Development of the Tertiary Industry*[1] in 1992 during the 8th Five-Year Plan period; it was first used in the *Proposal of the CCP Central Committee on the 10th Five-Year Plan*[2] adopted in October 2000 by the 5th Plenary Session of the 15th CCP Central Committee. The term 'cultural industries' has been used in 'top-level policy documents' for more than fifteen years. This chapter traces the development of China's cultural industries since their inception and describes the current status quo and complexity of the cultural industries, as well as assessing development prospects over the next 5 to 10 years.

DEVELOPMENT: RISE OF CHINA'S CULTURAL INDUSTRIES

China's cultural industries emerged at the turn of the century, against the backdrop of modernization driven by reform and opening up. The cultural industries were an inevitable trend, as well as a proactive measure to cope with the forces of globalization with China joining the World Trade Organization (WTO).

Firstly, from a domestic perspective, the emergence of the cultural industries was a consequence of economic and social development, including increased incomes and changes in the structure of consumption. The income levels of urban and rural residents increased in the 20 years following reform and opening up (from 1978). By 1999, upon the completion of the 5th Five-Year Plan, per capita gross domestic product (GDP) had approached US$ 1,000: this led to a fundamental change in the structure of consumption. From 1978 to 1998, consumption levels increased from RMB 184 to RMB 2,972, an average annual increase of 7 per cent.[3] Moreover, the Engel coefficient fell below 50 per cent over the 1990s, marking China's transition to a 'well-off state'; it subsequently fell below 40 per cent among urban residents in the late 1990s, ushering in the era of affluence.[4]

A prominent feature of the structural change in consumption is a tendency to move away from expenditure on basic material goods, i.e. a fast-growing ratio of consumer spending is now directed to culture and education. From 1981 to 1997, the consumption patterns of urban residents underwent three stages: firstly, 'extensive consumption' was characterized by a considerable expansion of spending on subsistence items (mainly food and clothing); secondly, 'intensive consumption' saw a stabilization of such spending and an increase in household consumer durables; while 'extended consumption' led to people spending more freely on quality consumer products. In the third stage spending on necessities declined steadily while services consumption expenditure increased rapidly. For the first time, entertainment, culture and education overtook necessities in overall expenditure, changing the order of consumption practices to 'food, clothing, entertainment, culture and education'. Many people turned their attention to education, science and technology, tourism and cultural products.[5] As noted in the *2001 Blue Book of China's Society* (*2001 nian shehui lanpishu*) the fastest growing consumer sectors were education, entertainment, culture, transportation, communications, health care, housing, and tourism.[6] In effect, higher income levels and a changing structure of consumption, combined with strong demand for cultural goods, provided the decisive intrinsic motivation for the emergence of China's cultural industries.

Secondly, from an international perspective, new services were emerging with the knowledge-based economy: in the 1980s and 1990s globalization spread from the economic realm to the cultural sector. The cultural industries expanded worldwide, reshaping the overall pattern of globalization. In the mid-1990s, the Organisation for Economic Co-operation and Development (OECD) issued a number of documents addressing the knowledge-based economy and national innovation systems (NIS). In these documents, the OECD noted that member countries had entered the era of knowledge-based economy.

The knowledge-based economy is driven by digital information technology (DIT) and media industry convergence; the leading nation in this regard is the US. In 1995, the US Congress debated the *Telecommunications Competition and Deregulation Act* and adopted the new *Telecommunications Act* the following year: this legislation adopted competition as a fundamental basis for regulatory frameworks and opened the door to the world for US media giants. Ever since then the US media giants have had no shackles on their activities in the international market. In 1998, US exports of audio-visual technological and cultural products reached US$ 60 billion, assuming first position from aerospace-related exports. This indicated that the US had completed a new round of industrial restructuring, once again seizing the commanding heights, contributing to a new round of globalization (so-called McDonaldization)

Thirdly, as mentioned above, the development of the cultural industries was a policy initiative of the Chinese government, designed to cope with challenges accompanying accession to WTO in an environment of incomplete industrialization. The cultural industries have taken off in the 'post-industrial' era: they constitute a form of economic and cultural development in Europe and the US. In the context of global industrial development and restructuring, industrialization is a top priority for China. The accession to the WTO created opportunities for global industry relocation, but it also presented China with the challenge of opening its cultural services market. China's cultural institutions would be confronted with industrial competition, the effects of capital, as well as inevitable conflicts in cultural values. Nevertheless, it was a golden opportunity to effectively promote historical cultural reform and development, and bring about a transformation in the economic structure.

In balancing the advantages and disadvantages, the Chinese government made an important policy decision to develop the cultural industries. The *Proposal of the CCP Central Committee on the 10th Five-Year Plan,*[7] adopted in October 2000 by the 5th Plenary Session of the 15th CCP Central Committee, recommended to 'improve the policies for cultural industries, strengthen the construction and management of the cultural market, to boost cultural industries' and to 'push the convergence of the information industry and cultural industries'. This 'proposal' signified that 'sunrise' cultural industries of the kind that originated in the US and Europe would take off in China.

DEVELOPMENT STAGES

The stage development of China's cultural industries is dependent on the government's ongoing Five-Year Plans for Economic and Social Development as well as the tenure of political leaders. Taking into account major time cycles, we can observe three stages of development, fundamentally consistent with the 10th, 11th and 12th Five-Year Plans.

The first stage, from 2000 to 2005, witnessed the launch and piloting of reforms. As described above, the *Proposal* (*jianyi*) of October 11, 2000, called for efforts to 'push forward the convergence of the information and cultural industries'; in Section 4 of the document the *Proposal* called for efforts to 'speed up information integration into economic and social development' and to 'improve the policies for cultural industries, strengthen the construction and management of the cultural market, to boost cultural industries'; and in Section 15, the *Proposal* called for efforts to 'strengthen socialist spiritual civilization'.

In March 2001, in the *Report on the Outline of the Tenth Five-Year Plan for Economic and Social Development*[8] outlined by then-Premier Zhu Rongji in the 4th Session of the 9th National People's Congress (NPC), these recommendations were expressed as: 'deepen the cultural system reform and improve cultural and economic policies to promote the development of cultural industries'. The difference in expression between the *Proposal* and the *Report* is related to the strategy of information technology development and systemically connected to an emphasis on cultural work over the years, including cultural and economic policies, cultural market construction, and cultural system reform. The incorporation of cultural industries into top-level policy documents is of important strategic significance, marking the 'legalization' and the historic start of the cultural industries in China.

Cultural system reform was embodied in the requirement for 'earlier development of the overall planning for cultural system reform' in the Report to the 16th NPC on November 8, 2002. In accordance with this requirement, the pilot was initiated in 2003, involving 35 institutions and 9 provinces and cities and covering news media, publishers, libraries, museums, cultural centres, art troupes, film and television production companies, as well as printing, distribution and projection companies. The pilot program set out targets, methods and polices for both 'public welfare industries' (*gongyi shiye*) and 'business industries' (*jingyingxing chanye*). Upon completion of the pilot in 2005, the reform was extended nationwide.

Since 2000, China's cultural industries had been gathering momentum. The second stage, from 2005 to 2010, illustrated growth against prevailing trends and the recognition of culture as a pillar industry. Preferential policies initiated to support the reform of commercial enterprises introduced in the 2003 pilot cultural system reform accelerated development. With nationwide implementation in 2005, these policies further stimulated industrial expansion. According to statistics, from 2004 to 2010, the value of China's cultural industries grew from RMB 344 billion (approx. US$ 55 billion) to RMB 1105.2 billion (US$ 173 billion) and the absolute amount by RMB 761.2 billion (US$ 119 billion), an average annual increase rate of 23.6 per cent.

Of particular note is that the cultural industries exhibited growth against prevailing trends and a 'lipstick effect'[9] when economic growth fell below 9 per cent during the 2008 international financial crisis following a peak of 13 per cent the previous year due to WTO accession. Extraordinary growth was observed in film, television and new media, marking a rare bright spot in the national economy. This caught the attention of the economic authorities. In September 2009, the State Council Executive Meeting examined and adopted the *Plan on Reinvigoration of the Cultural Industries.*[10] In October 2010, the *Proposal on the 12th Five-Year Plan,*[11] passed in the 5th Plenary Session of the 17th CCP Central Committee, called for 'building cultural industries into a pillar of the national economy', officially highlighting the culture industries as a national strategic pillar.

The third stage from 2010 to 2015 witnessed a 'turning point' and 'gear change'. The target of building the cultural industries into an economic pillar is supported by market demand in China, particularly in light of the long-term short supply of cultural products. The critical issue is whether or not the development mode of cultural industries is appropriate and whether the policy stimulus applied to the cultural system leads to efficient production. It is in these two aspects that China's cultural industries are not yet ready. During the 12th Five-Year Plan period, substantive process has been made in the transformation of the development mode and adjustment of the economic structure. The shift in economic growth from 'high speed' to 'medium/high speed' is the 'new normal'. As this institutional policy reform, and its effects level off, the cultural industries encounter a 'substantial turning point' and the pace of development declines.

The idea of a 'turning point' in essence entails a 'gear change'. China completed the round of replacement of political leaders through the 6th Plenary Session of the 17th CCP Central Committee in October 2011, the 18th CCP National Congress in November 2012, and the 3rd Plenary Session of the 18th CCP Central Committee in September 2013. The *Decision of the CCP Central Committee on Major Issues Concerning the Deepening Reform,*[12] passed by the 3rd Plenary Session of the 18th CCP Central Committee, noted: 'let the market play a decisive role in the allocation of resources'. The primary keyword of the Cultural Policies section was changed from 'cultural industries' to 'cultural market', that is, to establish and improve the modern cultural market system. This shows that cultural industries in China are moving from government-led start-up stage to a market-oriented stage.

STATUS: COMPLEXITY OF CHINA'S CULTURAL INDUSTRIES

According to the data collected in the 2004, 2008, and 2013 economic censuses, in 2004 there were 318,000 legal cultural entities and 8.73 million employees, contributing RMB 344 billion (approx. US$ 54 billion) of added value and accounting for 2.15 per cent of GDP. In 2013, the figures read 918,500, 17.59 million, RMB 2.0081 trillion and 3.42 per cent respectively. Over the past 10 years, China has witnessed a nearly two-fold increase of legal cultural entities, a doubling of employees, and 4.8 increase of the added value of cultural industries. The status of cultural industries in China can be observed from the perspective of development, reform, and complexity.

DEVELOPMENT: 'COEXISTENCE OF LOW-LEVEL SHORTAGE AND EXCESS'

Due to low levels of economic development and the long-term planned economy, which suppressed the enthusiasm of cultural producers, there used to be a severe shortage of cultural services. About ten years ago the *Blue Book on Cultural Industries* (*wenhua chanye lanpishu*) noted the 'strategic shortage': actual cultural consumption in China was only one quarter of that of countries at the same level of development. Owning to sustained annual economic growth of 20 per cent or more over the ensuing three Five-Year Plans, the shortage of market supply eased significantly with some areas such as the animation industry even facing excessive investment and bubbles. The cultural market had entered a new era characterized by the coexistence of shortages and excess.

This coexistence can be further explained as shortage and surplus in a limited open market, one that is at a relatively low level of development. Here, the surplus is relative as the level of cultural consumption is significantly lower than that of countries at the same economic level. On the one hand, limited market openness leads to excessive investment and competition in the open market and inadequate investment in markets that are not open, resulting in insufficient supply. On the other hand, imperfect market mechanisms and heavy dependence on the government result in a large number of unsuccessful investments. The most discussed area is the lack of original content, which is attributed to limited market openness and unproductive government support in such fields as news and publishing. It can be seen that the peak of government-led investment has passed after 10 years of development. Large-scale reshuffles together with mergers and acquisitions will be inevitable with the change of impetus from government investment to social investment, the change of driver from investment to consumption, and a change of emphasis from quantity and scale to quality and efficiency.

REFORM: 'DUALITY OF REFORM AND DEVELOPMENT'

In effect, China's cultural industries have made considerable progress, which is mainly attributed to institutional relaxations (i.e. cultural system reform) and policy incentives (i.e. preferential policies). While the government's role has been significant, the contribution to cultural consumption from increased income level is much less. In other words, while development is in parallel with cultural system reform, the government intention to bring about 'development' lacks the support of market mechanism. The most observed phenomenon is motivation by 'performance': the 'visible hand' of administrative instruments intervenes in development and directly guides investment, inducing a man-made boom. This is an important reason to explain the rapid emergence of 'excessive shortages' in the cultural market. In the new situation, the cultural industries are also facing a 'transformation' of their development model, one that depends on the reform of the macro cultural management system – reconstructing relations between the government and the market.

From a logical point of view, cultural system reform is also aimed at development. The main trajectory of the post-2003 reforms has been to 'create market players' with the objective of 'separation of the management of public institutions and enterprises'. With initial results achieved, the next step is to build a 'modern cultural market system', to create a market environment in which restructured enterprises have fair, open and free competition. This forms the basis of the general task of 'establishing and improving a modern cultural market system' emphasized in the report to the 3rd Plenary Session of the 18th CPC Central Committee.

COMPLEXITY: ECONOMIC, POLITICAL AND CULTURAL CHALLENGES

The development and reform of China's cultural industries follow their own specific logic and trajectory: accordingly, complexity must be fully estimated.

Since their inception China's cultural industries have borne three historical missions: (1) as the main force of the modern tertiary industry, they participate in the strategic adjustment of the economic structure by promoting the new services; (2) as a central link of a new round of reform, they improve the socialist market economic system by pushing forward cultural reform; (3) as a component of political civilization construction, they deepen political reform through the implementation of people's cultural rights. Logically, the first mission rests on the second, while the second requires breakthroughs in the third.

In addressing this tripartite problem, many difficulties lie ahead. First, the development of cultural and creative industries in the 'post-industrial' era is 'incompatible' with economic environment as manifested in the difficulty for cultural enterprises in obtaining loans. Second, China's cultural management system has been seen as 'publicity-oriented cultural system'. It is an integral part of a political system that adheres to a 'stability-oriented principle', rather than a 'socialist market economy' that insists on 'development-oriented principle'. Should we emulate the former or the latter? Should we follow the logic of stability or the logic of development? A conflict often rises such that the publicity department demands a 'brake' while cultural and economic departments require an 'accelerator'.

China's cultural industries have grown out of the gaps between shifting institutional systems; they are engaged in multiple missions, entangled in multiple logics, hovering between the inexorable law of the market economy and the practical needs of the political system. The way out of this dilemma needs time and wisdom.

OUTLOOK: DEVELOPMENT OF CULTURAL INDUSTRIES IN THE 13TH FIVE-YEAR PLAN PERIOD

Looking to the future, the long-term prospect of China's cultural industries depends on the market while short-term prospects depend on policy.

Long-Term Prospect: Five Markets

First, as consumer services, the cultural industries have a huge space for development. In the 'new normal' of the 13th Five-Year Plan period, along with substantive progress in the transformation of macro-economic development patterns, the consumption environment will improve and cultural consumption will take off substantively, thereby creating a vast space for cultural development. According to the Ministry of Commerce, while China's actual cultural consumption exceeded RMB 1 trillion (US$ 0.16 trillion) in 2013, potential consumption was RMB 4.7 trillion (US$ 0.74 trillion), a gap of RMB 3.7 trillion (US$ 0.58 trillion). It is estimated that by 2020, the national demand for cultural consumption will total RMB 16.65 trillion (US$ 2.61 trillion), indicating the enormous potential.

Second, as producer services, the cultural industries will become a major fulcrum of development model transformation and economic restructuring. The transformation of development patterns through economic structuring and upgrading will drive the development of related industries. The demand for cultural industries as producer services is showing explosive growth amid the trend of integration of cultural industries with related industries. To address this demand, on March 14, 2014, the State Council issued the *Opinions on Promoting the Development of Cultural, Creative and Design Services and Integration with Related Industries*.[13]

Third, as new technology industries, the cultural industries will be driven by technological revolutions. The next 5 to 10 years will witness fundamental changes caused by technological progress. In 2014, Alibaba launched large-scale mergers and acquisitions of domestic cultural enterprises and was listed in the US; Tencent, Baidu and other Internet giants have also entered the core fields of the cultural industries. These moves have fully demonstrated the development opportunities pertaining to the integration of culture and technology.

Fourth, the modern cultural industries are urbanized industries: the new-type urbanization will bring enormous opportunities for cultural development. With a 50 per cent urbanization rate, up to 20 per cent of the population (260 million) will move from the countryside to urban areas. The demand for improving the built-up cities and building new cities opens up a huge space for cultural development.

Fifth, the overall enhancement of cultural trade will usher in global cultural development. In the next 5 to 10 years, China may witness a fundamental change in international cultural trade. According to the State Copyright Administration, in 2013, China imported 18,167 copyrights and exported 10,401 copyrights, so the ratio of imports and exports decreased from 1:10 at the turn of the century to 1:1.4. If the trend continues, China will become a net exporter of copyright in the next 5 to 10 years, characterized by 'copyright export and manufactured goods import'. It will make new contributions to the international cultural market by way of large-scale cultural consumption.

Short-Term Prospects: Three Policy Shifts

A fundamental judgment of the cultural policy environment during the 13th Five-Year Plan period is that the development of cultural industries will slow down with the arrival of the macroeconomic 'new normal', returning to a more normalized pace. 'Upgrading' will replace the practice of 'the more the better' in this new stage. In terms of policy orientation, the policies will become inclusive, stimulate producer demand, and focus on environmental construction.

The past 'preferential policies' aimed to facilitate reform; they utilized financial subsidies supplemented by tax incentives, while the 'inclusive policies' are focused on development and use tax incentives, supplemented by financial subsidies. Cultural policy will turn the focus from productive activities that meet consumer demand to productive activities that meet producer demand and give play to productive services, and further the policy will encourage cultural production and consumption activities in the whole society. Moreover, cultural policy will be oriented to environmental construction. Centering the construction of the modern cultural market system, the policy will involve opening the cultural market, promoting the rule of law, and fostering a cultural ecology, including supporting small and micro enterprises and encouraging cultural and financial cooperation.

DIFFICULTY: RELATIONSHIP BETWEEN INDUSTRIES AND THE MARKET

In the report to the 3rd Plenary Session of the 18th CCP Central Committee, the primary keyword of the Cultural Policies section was changed from 'cultural industries' to 'cultural market', implying that the basic policy orientation changes from 'development of cultural industries' to 'construction of [a] modern cultural market system'. The understanding of this change is fundamental to grasping the policy environment during the 13th Five-Year Plan period and critical to maximizing the policy dividend.

Under a sound market economy system, industrial policy can make up for shortcomings and foster strategic growth points, thereby boosting the national economy. However, where the market economy system is not perfect, industrial policy will be divorced from the market and distort market rules, resulting in resource configuration errors. China has an imperfect market economy and faces the dual task of reform and development. In this context, industrial development often interacts with the market mechanism. In a good scenario, industries help promote open markets and as a result industrial development can benefit from this impetus; in a bad scenario, industries deviate from the market law and the government will suffer the negative effects of such actions. Although cultural system reform was unveiled in 2003, the openness of the cultural market still lags behind policy intervention. As a result, the cultural industries have become more divorced from the market and have evolved into Government Performance Projects that depend on direct financial support. Therefore, the core task of reform during the 13th Five-Year Plan period is to re-build a reasonable relationship between the cultural industries and the cultural market and let the market play a positive role in resource allocation.

The key lies in the reform in production of cultural content and in the regulatory system. It is necessary to encourage public participation in cultural creation; to distinguish general cultural content from ideological content; and to develop classified and graded management measures to provide maximum protection of creativity. A large number of community agencies and industry associations that can perform (current) poorly managed government functions should be fostered in order to open up the liberal market space for creative behavior.

NOTES

1. *zhonggong zhongyang guowuyuan guanyu jiakuai fazhan disan chanye de jueding*
2. *zhonggong zhongyang guanyu 'shiwu' guihua de jianyi*
3. Liu Shijin et al. (2000), *General Idea about the 10th Five-Year Plan for the Development of Industries*. China Economic Press, p.112. In accordance with the mathematical knowledge of ordinary people, the level of consumption in 1998 was 16 times that of 1978, or in other words quadrupled, making an annual growth rate of above 14 per cent. However, this estimation obviously does not take into account inflation and other factors.
4. Ibid.
5. Ibid. pp.124–5, p.128.
6. *2001 Blue Book of China's Society*. Beijing: Social Sciences Publishing, 2002, p.18.
7. *zhonggong zhongyang guanyu 'shiwu' guihua de jianyi*
8. *guanyu guomin jingji he shehui fazhan dishi ge wunian jihua gangyao de baogao*
9. The term 'lipstick effect' here refers to a highlighting effect, a kind of superficial effect whereby one sector or industry stands out.
10. *wenhua chanye zhenxing guihua*
11. *shi'er wu guihua jianyi*
12. *zhonggong zhongyang guanyu quanmian shenhua gaige ruogan zhongda wenti de jueding*
13. *guanyu tuijin wenhua chuangyi he sheji fuwu xianguan chanye ronghe fazhan de ruogan yijian*

9. The challenges of China's culture 'going to the world'[1]

Wuwei Li

It's universally acknowledged that cultural prosperity constitutes a strategic development objective; today every country in the world is intent on developing and rejuvenating culture. China is implementing its own 'cultural empowerment' (*wenhua qiangguo*) policy. Against this backdrop Chinese cultural enterprises, as business entities in the cultural industry, are taking initiatives and finding ways to break through the confines of the domestic market in order to go global.

Cultural enterprises can establish an international presence either through culture-related trade or foreign direct investment: the former approach comprises trade in cultural products and services while the latter includes 'greenfield investments' and mergers and acquisitions. Foreign direct investment, moreover, entitles cultural enterprises to business entity status in the host country, guaranteeing a more effective way to spread Chinese culture.

THE BENEFITS OF GOING GLOBAL

Cultural products are characterized by an innate duality of economy and ideology. The presence of Chinese cultural enterprises globally can assist the world to gain a better understanding of Chinese values. Dalian Wanda's acquisition of the US-based cinema operator AMC Theatres' 5028 screens may help Chinese movies to access US theatre screens; in turn this may help US audiences to learn more about China through watching Chinese films. An American who has watched one hundred movies from China will understand that Chinese people are diligent and kind, and that the Chinese culture is tolerant and inclusive, and may dismiss the stereotype of China of being remote, bizarre and threatening. Movies, plays and novels that are engaging have proven to be more effective in disseminating Chinese culture than diplomatic delegations.

Further the Development of Cultural Industries and Accelerate Industrial Upgrading in China

Cultural industries gain a competitive advantage through low cost, low pollution and high added-value. Furthermore their industrial links and promotional capacity are enabling, and they are well positioned to merge with other industries so as to upgrade the industrial structure. Chinese cultural enterprises' global ambitions will bring not only economic benefits by selling cultural products and services but also opportunities to communicate and cooperate with their international counterparts to the advantage of both themselves and China's cultural industries as a whole.

Enhance China's Cultural Competitiveness and Raise the Level of Cultural Soft Power

Cultural soft power is a critical index of international competitiveness. China is the second largest economy in the world today and its culture should be attractive and influential, just as its economy is. To achieve this ambition an effective way is to allow more Chinese cultural enterprises to enter the international arena. There is no doubt the world will see the attractiveness and influence of Chinese culture when more people learn Mandarin in the Confucius Institutes that are now located all over the world, when more international viewers become fans of China's movies and plays, and when more Chinese cultural enterprises join Wanda to explore the market abroad.

Increase the Demand for Chinese Cultural Products and Services Abroad and Boost Domestic Employment

At present China is facing a tighter employment market against the backdrop of the global economic downturn. Effective avenues to providing more jobs include accelerating the globalization of cultural enterprises, expanding international markets and increasing demand for Chinese cultural products and services abroad. The development of cultural trade needs the involvement of more cultural enterprises and the participation of more talented people, especially graduates fresh out of universities who can find a space to exercise their imagination and creativity. At the same time the cultural industry won't sustain itself without the efforts of producers and merchants, which means more jobs in the employment market.

OPPORTUNITIES FOR CULTURAL ENTERPRISES TO GO GLOBAL

National Policy Support to the Cultural Industry in its Drive to Go Global

In recent years, China's government has attached unprecedented importance to the cultural industry, which in turn delivers unique opportunities for cultural enterprises. China's 'Cultural Industry Rejuvenation Plan' (*wenhua chanye zhenxing guihua*), issued on 22 July 2009, indicates that the government supports cultural enterprises to invest in, and run businesses abroad as well as participate in cultural activities that contribute to the development of cultural trade. Under this enabling policy, foreign investment in the areas of culture, sports and entertainment has increased ten times from RMB 19.76 million in 2009 to RMB 196.34 million in 2012.

On 18 November 2012 in a report to the 18th National Congress of the Chinese Communist Party, President Hu Jintao emphasized that cultural innovation (*wenhua chuangxin*) should be regarded as a crucial element of the self-improvement of the socialist system, thereby raising cultural innovation to the level of theoretical and policy innovation. On 28 February 2014, the *Implementation Plan for Deepening Reform of the Cultural System*[2] was approved with President Xi Jinping as the chair of the voting committee; the plan indicates that the government will increase investment in the cultural industries and strengthen support for cultural enterprises in their efforts to go global.

This has already been borne out by the Wanda Group's acquisition of AMC. The acquisition required a total fund of US$3.1 billion with US$2.6 billion used as an acquisition fund and US$0.5 billion as a complementary fluidity fund, which equates to RMB 19.6 billion in all, accounting for 9 per cent of the group's total assets of RMB 220 billion. This transaction would not have been possible without support from the banks in China. The banks helped Wanda obtain international loans by granting it a domestic merger and acquisition loan and by using domestic credit to guarantee the international financing.

THE ATTRACTIVENESS OF CHINA'S CULTURE TO THE WORLD

In recent years China has won the world's attention through its rapid economic growth and peaceful rejuvenation, dubbed 'the mystery of China' (*Zhongguo zhimi*). People from all corners of the world want to know more

Table 9.1   China's TV serials broadcast abroad (part)

TV serial	Time of broadcast	Countries broadcast
bailing gongyu (White Collar Apartment)	August 2002	South Korea
xin Shanghaitan (New Shanghai Bund)	July 2008	Japan
woju (Snail House)	2009	Southeast Asia
wode chouniang (My Ugly Mother)	February 2010	Mongolia
xin sanguo (The New Three Kingdoms)	May 2010	Japan
cang qiongzhi'ang (The Vault of Heaven)	June 2010	Japan
xifu de meihao shidai (The Prime Time of My Wife)	June 2010	Japan
Mufu fengyun (Turbulence of the Mu Clan)	December 2012	Philippines, Singapore, US, Canada
Jintailang de xingfu shenghuo (The Happy Life of Kintaro)	March 2013	Philippines, Japan, Singapore
xin shuihu zhuan (New Outlaws of the Marsh)	June 2013	Japan
wo shi tezhong bing 2 (I Am a Commando)	August 2013	US
Zhen Huan zhuan (The Legend of Zhen Huan)	July 2013	Japan, US
Lu Zhen chuanqi (Legend of Lu Zhen)	March 2014	South Korea
bubu jingxin (Scarlet Heart)	March 2014	South Korea, Japan, etc.
chunxia qiudong (Four Seasons)	April 2014	US

Source: Collected from relevant news reports.

about China and understand the reasons for its rapid development, as shown by popular reception of Chinese TV serials abroad.

Table 9.1 shows that since 2010, an increasing number of China's TV serials have been broadcast overseas, including in the US and Canada, in African countries, and in Asia. The *Prime Time of My Wife* won over African audiences with images of fashionable mothers-in-law in China; *I Am a Commando* has created a fresh impression on the American people about Chinese soldiers in the new age; *Four Seasons* even caused some enthusiasts to compare the Chinese uncle played by Yang Lixin in the serial with the role played by Kevin Spacey in *House of Cards*.

Table 9.2   Overview of the top five countries in terms of world cultural heritage sites

	Portugal	China	Italy	France	Germany
No. (items)	43	42	40	33	32
Percentage	4.9	4.56	4.33	3.76	3.64

Source: Wang Xiaodong *A Study on the Development Trajectory of China's International Cultural Trade (Zhongguo guoji wenhua maoyi fazhan lujin yanjiu) [J]* Price Monthly (Jiage Yuekan), 2012 (7).

Rich Cultural Resources

China, a multi-ethnic country of four ancient civilizations, boasts a time-honoured historical culture and kaleidoscopic ethnic customs and traditions, which in turn lay a solid foundation and provide valuable resources for its cultural enterprises' entry into the international market. Table 9.2 shows that China has 42 items on the world cultural and natural heritage list and was ranked second in 2011.

This means that China enjoys a great advantage in resources while pressing ahead with its aim to develop international cultural trade.

IMPROVING FINANCIAL SUPPORT SCHEME

China's incomparable foreign exchange reserves serve as a solid financial backing for the international ambitions of its cultural enterprises. The appreciation of the value of the RMB has helped lower the cost of foreign investment and the presence of more financial services agencies has not only provided cultural enterprises more opportunities to engage with their international counterparts but also accorded them more transaction insurance so as to decrease the transaction costs and risks. For example, it would be very hard for Wanda to find its overseas financing without support from the international branch of the Bank of China. Furthermore, the development of China's financial services agencies, represented by International Financing Limited Corporation of China (*Zhongjin Gongsi*) will bring China's cultural enterprises more professional and efficient services for overseas mergers and acquisition.

CHALLENGES FACED BY CULTURAL ENTERPRISES

Inadequate Overseas Investment Experience

According to statistics, 80 per cent of global capital flows are between developed countries or regions. Direct foreign investment wasn't a common practice for China's enterprises until a decade ago. For cultural enterprises the history is even shorter. Wanda's acquisition of AMC is the first large-scale foreign investment by a Chinese cultural enterprise, and it has attracted worldwide attention. Compared with it, Huayi Brothers' previous acquisition of a 9 per cent stake in GDC Technology (Hong Kong), which was listed in the US, was regarded as fiscal investment and failed to arouse much attention.

Direct overseas investments, particularly through mergers and acquisitions, face great legal and commercial risks. Legal risks refer to transaction risks incurred due to inadequate knowledge of international law, usually related to evaluation and approval, personnel placement, and transfer of property rights. The most risky area is evaluation and approval. Almost every country has set up procedures to evaluate and assess the legitimacy of acquisitions of cultural enterprises by foreign investors; those standards are quite indeterminate because of the ideological systems pertaining to different cultures. China's cultural enterprises face the prospect of considerable uncertainty before they can accumulate enough experience.

Investment risk is caused mainly by incorrect evaluation of the object of transaction. For instance, the value of intelligence-intensive enterprises relies on employees' creativity, whose unpredictability increases the risk associated with international-oriented mergers and acquisitions. One important reason for Wanda to target AMC in its first-time overseas acquisition is that the core value of AMC is dependent on tangible assets such as the theatres and cinema screens. It's easy for Wanda to form a comparatively accurate evaluation of those assets and manage them after acquisition. All this will be more difficult if the target is a film-production company whose value mainly consists in the creativity and innovation of employees including playwrights, directors, actors and producers.

INADEQUATE INNOVATION CAPACITY TO DEVELOP CULTURAL RESOURCES

China, which is still in the immature stage of the development of its cultural industry, needs to improve innovation capacity in order to produce high-quality cultural products that can secure a foothold in the world market. At present resource based traditional products take up a large share of cultural products exported abroad. However, the international ambitions of cultural enterprises won't come about without the convergence of high-tech and culture.

In 2012, the world-reputed West Lake attracted three million tourists to Hangzhou. Presenting China's culture successfully to tourists is a first step in winning worldwide attention. The scenic spot Songcheng, which is funded and developed by Songcheng Limited Corporation, is cited as a successful example in showing the charm of China's civilization through staging large-scale operas like the *Story of the Song Dynasty* and the *Warfare of the States of Wu and Yue*. In the performance of the *Story of the Song Dynasty*, the integration of music, dance and high-tech tells a story based on historical allusions and fairy legends, allowing audiences to travel through time and space to ancient times. The *Story of the Song Dynasty*, the most frequently performed work with the largest audience attendance up to now, is acclaimed as one of the world top three performances along with *Moulin Rouge* (Paris) and *O* (Las Vegas). Other successful examples include *Impression Liu Sanjie* in Guangxi, *Fox Fairy of Tianmen* in Zhangjiajie, and *Era – Intersection of Time* in Shanghai.

Nevertheless, China is still in the primary stages of cultural resources exploration. Some of China's cultural images and legends have become the inspiration of foreign cultural products such as the animation *Kung Fu Panda* and *Mulan* (US), and *The Three Kingdoms* and *Monkey King*, made by Japan and South Korea respectively. Now China has learnt her lesson and has been investing in the integration of culture and technology so as to maximize cultural resources. For example, Huaqiang Technology Corporation and OCT Group in Shenzhen have successfully developed popular theme parks such as Happy Valley and Fangte Happy World by incorporating technological elements within cultural products. Huaqiang's innovative capacity has helped it to attract business from Iran and countries in southern Africa.

Cultural Services Trade Deficit

China ranks first in terms of trade in cultural products, but it has a huge deficit in trade of cultural services. Table 9.3 shows the overview of trade volumes and balances from 1997 to 2006. As is shown, China maintained its position as the exporter with the largest trade volume in cultural products with a rapid growth rate during the period. Comparatively, the table registers a decreasing proportion of the trade volume in cultural services. While the total volume is now on the increase, cultural services trade is

Table 9.3 Overview of China's trade in cultural products and services (US$ million)

	1997	1998	1999	2000	2001	2002	2003	2004	2005	2006
Export trade volume of cultural products	22,861	23,425	24,261	28,474	28,845	35,022	41,919	50,143	61,360	69,983
Growth rate (%)	–	2.5	3.6	17.4	1.3	21.4	19.7	19.6	22.4	14.1
Import trade volume of cultural products	2,419	1,974	2,036	2,242	2,374	2,460	2,985	3,326	3,676	4,129
Total trade volume of cultural products	25,280	25,399	26,297	30,716	31,219	37,482	44,904	53,469	65,036	74,113
Growth rate (%)	–	0.5	3.5	16.8	1.6	20.1	19.8	19.1	21.6	14.0
Trade balance of cultural products	20,442	21,451	22,226	26,232	26,470	32,562	38,934	46,816	57,684	65,854
Export trade volume of cultural services	303	289	303	315	415	535	627	1,126	1,367	–
Import trade volume of cultural services	828	724	1,045	1,521	2,246	2,604	4,076	5,371	6,190	–
Total trade volume of cultural services	1,311	1,013	1,348	1,836	2,661	4,140	4,702	6,497	7,557	–
Trade balance of cultural services	–525	–435	–742	–1206	–1831	–3069	–3449	–4245	–4823	–
Proportion of cultural products trade	95.7	96.2	95.1	94.4	92.1	90.1	90.5	89.2	89.6	–

Notes: – means no data available.

Source: Fang Ying et al. (2012), 'Analysis of China's cultural trade structure and competitive capacity', Business Studies (shangye yanjiu), (1).

undergoing an expanding deficit margin, taking up a significant share in China's services trade deficit.

It's a big challenge for China's cultural enterprises to reverse the trend in their drive to go global.

Targeting Overseas Chinese as Main Consumers, Lacking an International Consumer Basis

China's cultural exports are largely confined to certain regions of Southeast Asia, the US, Canada, Australia and Europe where many overseas Chinese live. Thanks to cultural connections through language, diet and lifestyles, overseas Chinese have affinity for those products or services.

An example is the export of publication copyrights. In 2010, China exported 3600 categories of publication copyrights. The top five destinations were Southeast Asia, Taiwan, Hong Kong, the US and Canada, occupying around 67 per cent of the total. This shows that China has only secured rather restricted and concentrated destinations for its cultural exports.

On the other side, *The Legend of Zhen Huan* won a warm reception after being broadcast on Chinese TV stations in America. It will be reedited to screen on some English TV stations. This is a starting point for China's TV serials to attract international audiences but to make it happen there is still a long way to go. The language barrier necessitates the recourse to translation, which requires the engagement of various resources. The popularity of South Korean TV serials relies to some extent on support from the government and this in turn mobilizes various social sectors to help with translation and export.

Lack of International Influential Brands

The US has established and maintained its hegemonic cultural influence through the production of its regional brands such as Hollywood, business brands such as Disney and Fox; branded characters such as Snow White and Mickey Mouse; and movie stars like Tom Cruise and Brad Pitt. These are what China lacks at present. In all kinds of international cultural exchange activities, China still depends on its folk arts such as paper cuts, clay figurines, embroidery, lantern making or unearthed cultural relics to exhibit its culture. The lack of international influential brands makes it harder for China's cultural enterprises to gain a foothold in the international market. China needs more international stars like Jackie Chan and Jet Li to promote the influence of its films and facilitate their entrance to the international stage.

Lack of Scale Due to China's Short History of Industrialization and the Division of Production and Responsibility

China has long relegated culture to the category of public goods, to the neglect of its industrial attributes. As a result the cultural industry has been placed under the management of public institutions affiliated to central or local governments for the past decade instead of being managed as a business. The industrialization of culture is gradually coming into being through the entrepreneurial transformation of cultural public institutions and the authorization of private capital into the cultural industry. However, it is still in a primary stage characterized by small scale and limited effects. China's cultural industry used to be segmented into divisions and put under relevant administrative departments. As a result cultural enterprises were specialized in only one industrial segment for core business and lacked the capacity to produce a synergistic effect between industrial segmentations. For example, among companies listed in culture and media, there is rarely any connection between film and television, advertising, and publishing. Huayi Brothers Media Corp., a film production company, has nothing to do with publishing, while Guangdong Advertising Group Co., Ltd (Shengguanggufen) and BlueFocus Communication Group (Lanseguangbiao) specialize in advertising and do not engage in film and TV production.

The absence of economies of scale and synergistic effects makes it hard for China's cultural enterprises to compete with large media companies in America. Table 9.4 shows the great disparity between Chinese listed companies in film and TV production and their US counterparts in terms of annual revenue in 2012. The comparison between Huayi Brothers Media Corp. and Columbia Broadcasting System (CBS) is an example. The revenue earned by the latter is more than sixty times that earned by Huayi, although they are quite close in terms of the profit growth rate and net income from property. In addition to owning Columbia Film Production Company, CBS runs businesses like advertising, publishing, radio and television.

SUGGESTIONS TO CHINA'S CULTURAL ENTERPRISES

Enhance Innovative Capacity

The capacity for cultural innovation plays a pivotal role in enhancing companies' competitive strength and is also the lifeline to sustain them

*Table 9.4   Financial comparisons of Chinese and US film, TV and
entertainment production companies 2012*

Name of company	Main business	Net profit	Interest growth rate (%)	Net income from property (%)
Chinese (unit: RMB 100 billion)				
Huayi Brothers Media Corp.	13.86	2.44	20.46	11.53
Guangxian Media	10.34	3.10	76.46	16.59
Huace Media Group	7.21	2.15	39.64	14.15
US (unit: US$100 billion)				
Disney	422.78	61.73	17.40	15.53
Time Warner Inc.	279.5	30.19	4.61	10.10
CBS	140.89	15.74	20.61	15.41

Source: Listed companies' financial reports to the relevant stock exchange centres.

in the long run. A company will lose its soul if deprived of its reservoir of quality original works and pioneering staff who take the initiative to create. On the other hand, competitive companies can only exist in regions and countries which see the continuous birth of creative cultural products that are inspiring and have artistic glamour.

Strengthen Technology-Oriented Innovation

The approach of integrating technology into culture is the key to success for cultural enterprises. It's imperative for China's cultural enterprises to accelerate the integration between technology and culture so as to apply high-tech to the production and transmission of cultural products. In this aspect, the *Story of the Song Dynasty* and *Era – Intersection of Time* can be cited as successful examples, showing how to add technological elements to traditional performance for enhanced artistic flavour and better audience response. China's cultural enterprises must rely on 'knock-out products' in order to go global.

Reform the Management System and Transform the Governmental Function in Cultural Industry

Governmental guidance has played a critical role in the development of cultural enterprises in some advanced countries. It is not possible for any region or country to secure an advantageous place in international cultural trade without mobilizing a variety of social sectors including government, enterprises and non-governmental institutions from the fields of culture, technology research, foreign trade and law.

First, the government should shift its function from direct participation in the market to administrative management and place the running of the cultural industry into the hands of market agents; in this way cultural enterprises will have the opportunity to undergo the test of the market and become more competitive internationally. Second, China should change the industrial segmentation between different business divisions and support cultural enterprises to form synergistic effects across businesses. Last, China should stipulate and carry out proactive policies to facilitate the process of going global for cultural enterprises. Among these it should encourage the venture capital industry to increase its investment and improve governmental policy and financial support.

Develop an International Marketing Strategy and Produce More Internationally Recognized Brands

The maturity of the market economy mechanism has enabled advanced countries to produce and market cultural products in line with the law of the market. At present market operation mechanisms range from market research at the early stage to the exploration of marketing channels. The success of Hollywood worldwide boils down to its marketing strategies. While striving to realize their international ambition, China's cultural enterprises should take the initiative to learn from their international counterparts about their marketing concepts and techniques and strengthen the brand consciousness so as to enhance the added value and influence of their cultural products.

Get Overseas Chinese Involved to Promote Excellent Chinese Culture

Overseas Chinese play a significant role in promoting cultural trade owning to affinity for Chinese culture. According to the *Development Report of Overseas Chinese Entrepreneurs*, the population of overseas Chinese has grown from 4 million in 2000 to 44 million in 2009 and to some 48 million at present. Among them 6 million migrated abroad after China adopted the policy of reform and opening-up. These new migrants have changed the structure of overseas Chinese entrepreneurs and some have expanded their businesses to North America, Western Europe, Australia, and Japan. In addition, an increasing number of overseas Chinese entrepreneurs engage in production and commercial and trade activities, which helps to expand cultural trade and take it to a higher level. China should mobilize overseas Chinese to promote its culture if it wants to play a bigger role in the future in the area of international cultural trade.

Without the rejuvenation of culture, there will be no rejuvenation of the nation. China cannot become a powerful cultural nation until its cultural enterprises enter the international cultural market and gain a foothold through competition.

NOTES

1. The article is adapted from the author's theme speech at the sideline meeting of the third Conference. Editor: Cao Jinzhang. Translated by Zhu Yaoxia.
2. *shenhua wenhua tizhi gaige shishi fang'an*

10. Chinese culture 'going out': an overview of government policies and an analysis of challenges and opportunities for international collaboration
Huailiang Li

INTRODUCTION

Following China's formal entry into the WTO on December 24, 2001, the State Administration of Radio, Film and Publishing (hereafter SARFT or SAPPRFT) announced the first explicit articulation of the 'going out' (*zou chuqu*) strategy as it related to cultural industries. Further policies followed. These policies were meant to assist China's voice to spread globally, to ensure that China's radio, film and television programs would have a global presence, significantly changing the status quo, in which 'Western' film, radio and TV were strong while China's were weak.

The period from 2001 to 2012 saw the beginning and the evolution of China's cultural industry policy: in these ten years of rapid development and transformation the reform of the cultural system provided a powerful impetus. According to China's WTO commitments, China needed to increase the pace of opening its cultural markets. At the same time cultural enterprises were active in implementing the strategy of 'going out', enhancing China's capacity to participate in international cooperation and competition.

This chapter addresses the key policies and characteristics of China's cultural 'going out' program. It shows how the program has evolved and discusses the challenges and weakness of Chinese cultural products in the international market. The focus is on audio-visual media and performing arts. Data primarily come from national statistics and industry reports.[1]

KEY POLICIES

In July 2005, the central government issued *The Advice on Further Strengthening and Improving the Work of Exporting Cultural Products and Services*.[2] In 2006, the Office of the State Council followed up with another document, *Policies on Encouraging and Supporting the Production and Export of Cultural Products and Services;*[3] seven other institutions supported the release of this latter document.[4] These documents together outlined a number of support mechanisms for enterprises that sought to target international markets.

First, all enterprises engaging in the export of cultural products were accorded equal treatment, whether state-owned or private; in addition the government sought to harmonize statistics relating to the varieties of products exported. Second, the government would encourage enterprises to set up overseas offices that might facilitate exports of television programs and other cultural goods and services. Third, official organizations were established at the central and provincial level to assist; in this way cultural enterprises engaged in exports became eligible for preferential taxation policies. For instance, business taxes were waived or reduced in respect to overseas profits. Finally, organizations that demonstrated rapid progress in exporting were provided with awards.

In August 2009, the *Cultural Industry Revitalization Plan*[5] was implemented as part of the 11th National Five-Year Plan. It was significant because it marked the fact that the development of the cultural industry had risen to the national strategic level. The cultural industry was now the core of China's cultural soft power strategy. Then in April 2011, the Ministry of Culture issued *The 2011–2015 Comprehensive Plan to Promote the 'Going Out' of Cultural Products and Services.*[6] In the same month, the State Administration of Press and Publication (SAPP) issued the development plan for the news and publishing industry's 'going out' during this five-year period.

In October 2011, the Sixth Plenary of the 17th CCP Central Committee Congress examined and approved the Decision by the Central Committee of the CCP on *Deepening the Reform of the Cultural System, and Promoting the Development and Prosperity of Socialist Culture.*[7] This put forward the proposition that the cultural industry would become an important national 'pillar industry', and in this way would further the internationalization of China's culture.

The above documents constitute the main body of policies related to the 'going out' program. The current 'going out' related policy measures focus on export subsidies, tax incentives, and funding support, as well as utilizing national government to break through barriers to trade and create a relatively favorable international competition environment.

KEY CHARACTERISTICS AND ISSUES

In order to form an analysis of China's cultural trade structure, the following discussion differentiates between 'core cultural products and services' and 'related cultural products and services'. 'Core cultural products and services' have greater output, since they include trade in both tangible products and intangibles (copyrights). The core cultural products and services include film and television, music, media, publications, copyright, and cultural entertainment and leisure services. Related cultural products and services include arts and crafts, visual arts, new media, advertising services, architectural design, and research and development services.

Research on China's exports reveals that the category of 'design' accounts for more than 75 per cent of the total export of cultural products, followed by handicrafts, visual art and new media products; however, these are mainly low value-added, labour-intensive products. This highlights the advantage of low manufacturing costs. The proportion of the core cultural products, such as film and television, music, and publications, moreover, is very small; these three sectors together accounted for less than 2 per cent.

In the export structure of cultural services, advertising and market research accounted for more than 75 per cent; the proportion of core cultural services such as copyright and cultural entertainment services is very small, about 26 per cent and is continuing to remain in deficit. However, the export structure of China's cultural products is not rational. Knowledge-technology-intensive cultural products and services account for a very small proportion; cultural resources are not used efficiently; and there is serious waste and a lack of cultural branding.

UNIFORMITY IN CONTENT

An important problem is the relatively uniform characteristic of China's cultural trade exports. Kung Fu and action films, such as *Hero* (*yingxiong*), *The Promise* (*wuji*), *House of Flying Daggers* (*shimian maifu*) and *Ip Man* (*yewen*) have achieved good box office returns abroad. Chinese performing arts are accorded priority: in 2010 acrobatics accounted for almost half (47 per cent) of overseas performance programs. Over the past 20 years China has exported many ancient costume dramas, including martial arts dramas, history and adaptations of classics such as *The Romance of the Three Kingdoms* (*sanguo yanyi*), *The Dream of Red Mansions* (*honglou meng*), *The Smiling, Proud Wanderer* (*xiao'ao jianghu*), *The Demi-Gods and*

Semi-Devils (*tianlong babu*), *Yongzheng Dynasty* (*yongzheng wangchao*), and so on.

Book copyright output has been focused on traditional culture: the content mainly introduces Chinese traditional culture, including Chinese medicine, food and language. Other categories are less seen; for instance high-tech categories and those that reflect Chinese modernity are lacking. In the international market Chinese publications still occupy a marginal position, and only a few break into the international mainstream market; in addition, the domestic market and international market have different styles, which make it hard for the domestic press to integrate with international standards.

LOW EFFICIENCY

While the goal of trade is to seek profit, both social and economic outcomes are interlinked; paying attention to one kind of benefit inevitably weakens the other. There are several reasons for low economic returns on cultural products exported from China. Firstly, the government takes primary consideration of the social benefits at the sacrifice of the economic benefits when organizing its cross-cultural activities. Government-supported cultural exports are not market driven, and this can have the effect of creating a negative response internationally, which in some cases results in consumer resistance.

In addition, China's cultural industry illustrates a so-called 'buttons phenomenon', similar to that of the manufacturing industry. Because of the lack of independent brands, many enterprises can only engage in OEM processing, that is, exporting the 'parts' or 'components' rather than making new products; as a result many stay at the level of working for foreign companies. This inevitably leads to a business model of low value-added products and low yields, whereas the high added value is earned by foreign business. Cultural industries need to quickly transform from 'made in China' to 'created in China'.

Another factor is intense competition in the domestic market. This has a bad impact on the competitive environment. This kind of situation was prevalent in the manufacturing industry in the past: lacking competitive brands and products to compete for the limited international market share, domestic enterprises engage in heavy discounting, thereby killing each other's chances of success. Low price competition is also the result of inefficiency: a lack of adequate investment in product innovation and marketing has created a vicious cycle that is not conducive to Chinese soft power brands. This in turn impacts on the 'brand' association of Chinese culture.

Yet another problem is unfamiliarity with the pricing strategy of the international market. In 2011, the number of imported books, newspapers, periodicals, audio-visual products and electronic publications was 30.195 million and the revenue generated was US$425.08 million. In the same year exports of books, newspapers, periodicals and audio-visual products, and electronic publications totalled 15.575 million but the amount of revenue was only US$73.966 million. The exported volume was half the size of imports; yet the revenue from exports was less than one-fifth of imports.[8] In addition, the domestic publication industry used to focus on selling 'books'; only in recent years has there been awareness of copyrights. Through copyright trade the US earns more than $500 billion per year on average, accounting for 5 per cent of GDP; in contrast, China's copyright trade accounts for only around 1 per cent of GDP, less than RMB 100 billion.[9] The *Harry Potter* novels alone have earned tens of millions of RMB in royalties within China. Compared with China's novel *Red Poppies* (*chen'ai luoding*), one of the domestic market's leading best sellers, the foreign product earned more than one hundred times the royalties.

CONCENTRATION IN CERTAIN MARKETS

In Western developed countries there are many different kinds of cultural products and services; there are also many export regions throughout the world. Through cultural trade these countries are able to gain huge economic benefits while disseminating their 'cultural spirit'. In China the situation is not optimistic. Exports of cultural products are concentrated in certain countries and regions and this concentration is specific to the relevant cultural products. The geographic structure of China's overall trade in cultural products is mainly in the US, Japan, Europe and Hong Kong and other developed countries and regions. Core cultural products and services are exported to Hong Kong, the US, Britain, India, Japan, Germany, Australia, Taiwan, Malaysia, Singapore and Thailand.

Copyrighted materials are mainly exported to Hong Kong and Taiwan and several Asian countries: that is, the Chinese language limits market scope. Publications exports to Europe and the US have increased in recent years, but relative to imports from Europe and the US, the gap is very obvious. In regard to television, in 2010 the main export destinations were the US, Canada, Singapore, Hong Kong and Taiwan. The output to the above five countries and regions accounted for 79 per cent of the total. Performing arts services are exported to the US, Japan, Russia,

South Korea, Canada, Europe, southeast Asia, South America, as well as Hong Kong, Macao and Taiwan, but the main target markets are the US, Japan and Western Europe. In these countries the demand for culture is great and there are high returns: if trade is conducted well, this can lead to rapid expansion of markets.

Obviously, the current pattern of exports deviates from what is required for the designated international markets. Exports of China's cultural products and services are concentrated in a few developed countries as well as Hong Kong and Taiwan. The concentration of export market accounts for the narrow dissemination of Chinese culture. Cultural trade plays a very limited role in promoting China's culture and there is a need to establish more efficient cultural trade channels to realize the multiple diversified modes of development among markets in Asia, Europe, North America and other regions.

NARROW EXPORT CHANNELS

Because most of China's cultural enterprises are small scale, their financial strength is limited and they lack international market experience. Many lack the concept of a 'world market'; for this reason low investment and low risk trade has become their first choice approach for international business management. State-owned enterprises play a very important role in China's cultural exports. Yet China's large-scale cultural enterprises have not yet become competitive with their international counterparts. At present, domestic cultural products exports have three main channels: the first is domestic and well-known international cultural industry fairs, such as the Shenzhen ICCIE (International Cultural and Creative Industries Expo), the Frankfurt Book Fair, Tokyo Television Festival, the Korea Tomikawa International Cartoon Festival, the Tokyo International Anime Fair, and the Shanghai International Film Festival. Through these events it is possible to directly market excellent cultural products; for instance, in recent years, China has contracted more than 90 per cent of the copyright trade in the Beijing International Book Fair and the Frankfurt Book Fair.

The second channel is through using foreign agencies. These two channels have a certain effect but the limitations are obvious – they are just the primary stage. For cultural products and services to go out and for China to proactively seek overseas development and rapid growth in cultural product exports, it is necessary to focus on new technology and capital accumulation. This can occur in several ways, for instance, through joint creation, cooperation, publishing, franchising, joint ventures, electronic marketing and other market entry modes, as well as acquisition of overseas cultural assets.

In the performing arts industry, for example, many enterprises lack sufficient understanding of foreign markets: they lack segmentation and an overall grasp of the world market and the selection of target markets. Currently performances are sold to foreign performance companies, which organize and finance the operational planning: the Chinese enterprise only provides cultural labour, thereby earning a service fee.

In addition to government-backed projects, China's theatrical exports only invest in production; other aspects such as rent, travel, advertising and theatre props rely on investment from the foreign promoter. Due to this kind of 'non-investment' attitude among small and medium acrobatic troupes, foreign promoters have begun to undercut the price of some first-class performance groups and take about 70 per cent of the profit. Some of these have become successful performance brands with the help of the foreign party.

If performing arts groups want to enter overseas markets they should follow international commercial 'best practice' models. First, this entails cooperation, including joint ventures and acquisition of overseas assets. A second way is to register a performing arts company by foreign direct investment and in this way engage more directly in performance operations. Only a minority of China's performance enterprises are able to enter into overseas markets this way. A good example is the show called *Chun Yi: The Legend of Kung-fu* (*gongfu chuanqi*). In August 2009, the Tianchuang Company took out a loan from Beijing Bank of US$1 million and with an investment ratio of 67:33 with a Canadian promotion company it was able to break into one of the high end performance markets in the central London arts district. In 27 performances it achieved more than 60 per cent of ticket sales with average income of each performance recouping US$48,000.[10]

TALENT

In the 21st century, competition for talent is essential for competitiveness. Firms that effectively develop and utilize talent can assume the commanding heights of industrial development and remain dynamic. Because it pays attention to talent, the Apple Corporation has been able to achieve revolutionary innovations, lead industry trends and become number one in the world. The prominent characteristics of the cultural and creative industries are capital, human resources and intelligence. During the period of the 11th Five-Year Plan, China's cultural industries grew rapidly, output value doubled, increasing from **RMB** 100 billion (US$15.7 billion) in 2006 to **RMB** 200 billion (US$31.3 billion) in 2010.[11] However, during these five years cultural talent increased by only 10 per cent. Talent growth is therefore much lower than the growth of industries: the result is a widespread shortage of cultural industries talent.

The main problems are a lack of interdisciplinary talent and emerging industry professionals. Cultural management, particularly a lack of management talent, has a serious influence on the export of cultural products and services. Many cultural enterprises face financial difficulty and this is another factor that restricts development. Local governments and financial institutions do issue financial support policies and measures. However, financial institutions lack an understanding of culture while cultural enterprises don't understand financial aspects: this leads to the decoupling of these two fields and impacts on the financing of innovation.

In addition, because talent reserves are deficient, this restricts industry development. In Beijing, for example, the proportion of creative industry practitioners accounts for less than one thousandth of the total employment force. Not only are the reserves of talent lacking, the structural distribution is not balanced: there is a lack of top-notch talented leaders in the field of creative industries. By contrast, in New York cultural creative industries professionals account for 12 per cent of the total working population; in London the number is 14 per cent while in Tokyo the proportion is as high as 15 per cent.[12]

Many emerging sectors, such as the convention and exhibition industry, network game industry, copyright, digital media, animation, decorating and other industries, lack professional talent. As games, animation, film and television, copyright and other cultural industries develop towards the market the demand for creative talent will expand rapidly. In the endeavour to go global the creative industries need operational and management personnel with all-round capacities – with proficiency in foreign languages, expertise in film and television production and a knowledge of international cultural markets as well as international marketing strategies. This kind of specialized international cultural trade personnel in the domestic market is rare. It is a major issue when we consider that lack of cultural trade is one of the important bottlenecks restricting the export of Chinese cultural products. To speed up the pace of the export of Chinese culture, China needs to spend more time nurturing talent.

INDUSTRIES, POLICIES AND INTERNATIONAL COLLABORATIONS

Broadcasting

The 16th National Congress of the Communist Party of China established the direction of broadcasting and television industrialization. In 2004, SARFT issued an 'opinion' (*yijian*) to promote the development of radio, film and television industry, and further speed up the industrialization process. In accordance with China's WTO commitments, radio and television sectors were not directly opened but commitments were made in network, audio-visual services and advertising services; this in turn has affected broadcasting and television industries. Under the dual pressure of accelerated industrialization and accession to the WTO, the market has gradually opened in radio and TV. Non-public capital is allowed into some sectors under certain conditions. In media, Shanghai Oriental Pearl, Beijing Gehua Group, and Hunan Broadcasting System are engaged in international audio-visual cooperation.

The first area of reform is in regard to cooperation in TV shows and drama. In 1999, SARFT issued a document *Rules Regarding Foreign Participation in the Production of Radio and Television Program Activities*[13] in order to promote the healthy and orderly development of radio, film and television cooperation and to establish standards for foreigners to participate in radio, film and television program production. Then in 2004 SARFT issued a regulation on the administration of Chinese-foreign cooperative productions of TV series. In 2008 it subsequently published the *Regulations on Administration of Chinese-foreign Cooperative Production in TV Serial Drama*.[14]

Under these regulations radio and television stations, and units that hold television production licenses or permits for movie production, can hire foreigners to participate in the production of film and television programs, TV shows or movies, but may not hire foreigners to participate in production of news programs – this includes news, news commentary and news features. Subject to approval radio and television stations hire foreigners as experts to participate in foreign language teaching programs, and pay remuneration to, and hire foreign management experts in cultural and educational series. In 2004, the state promulgated the *Interim Provisions on the Administration of Chinese-foreign Joint Ventures and Cooperative Enterprises Producing and Distributing Radio and Television*:[15] the intention was to attract foreign investment into the audio-visual industries.

The second area of reform concerns the introduction of foreign media and programs. In 2004, SARFT promulgated new regulations and measures pertaining to foreign participation in China's audio-visual sectors. These included *Administrative Rules on the Operation of International Institutions Establishing Broadcasting and Television Stations in China*[16] and *Administrative Regulations on the Introduction and Broadcasting of International Satellite TV Programs*[17] and *Methods of Administration of the Landing Rights of International Satellite Channels*.[18] According to these documents radio and television agencies established by foreign institutions in China are required to apply for licensing permits. In addition, the regulations stipulate that foreign institutions are unable to establish radio and television agencies or editorial offices in China.

The new regulations allowed the introduction of foreign movies and TV series (including animation) and programs about education, science, and culture but not current affairs news programs. SAPPRFT (formerly SARFT) is responsible for the review and approval of foreign film and television dramas introduced into China as well as those TV programs transmitted by satellite. Programs are limited to international hotels rated as three-star and above, and apartments of foreign officials. Currently there are more than 30 such channels operating in China.

The third area concerns the 'going out' of radio, film and television. To expand China's radio and television coverage in foreign countries and to facilitate China's radio and TV culture abroad, in 2002 SARFT issued *Provisional Rules for the Administration of the Lease and Purchase of Channels and Establishment of Stations Abroad*.[19] China Central Television (CCTV) has received landing rights registration in 140 countries and regions and realized global satellite transmission coverage. China Radio International (CRI) transmits in 53 languages, has 22 whole frequency radio stations, 153 cooperation agreements with FM/AM radio, and 3158 overseas audience clubs: the coverage extends to more than 60 countries and regions.

Film

After WTO entry, China film entered into the important stage of deepening system reform and adjustment of industrial policy. In 2002, SARFT promulgated *Regulations on the Administration of Film*,[20] which served as the main document underpinning China's film industry policy. A licensing system was implemented to regulate film production, import, export, distribution, screening and public screening of movies. This system ensures that the management of the domestic movie market achieves maximum effectiveness, but to a certain extent this also hindered the development of Chinese film in line with international standards.

In regard to China-foreign co-productions, a project can be approved after the script is verified and a Chinese-foreign cooperative program permit issued. If the Chinese-foreign cooperative film project needs to import equipment, apparatus, film, or props, the Chinese parties are required to undergo import or temporary import procedures at customs while displaying the approval document issued by the State Council's Administrative Department for radio, film and television. The regulations stipulate that foreign filmmakers operating in China through forms of cooperation with Chinese partners need to abide by the laws and regulations of the People's Republic of China and respect the customs of the Chinese nation.

A second area is the importing and exporting of films. Film imports can be undertaken by those film import business institutions designated by SARFT. Films imported for theatrical release are required to be submitted for review. In addition, all films shown in domestic and foreign film exhibitions and international film festivals are required to be submitted to SARFT for examination and approval. At the same time, the government also has a policy to protect domestic films; the annual screen time of domestic film is set at no less than two-thirds of the total screen time. The government will strengthen the evaluation of domestic film screens each year and accordingly adjust the policy on foreign movie imports in order to encourage domestic film enterprises to produce and screen more films.

The third area is foreign investment. The film industry is constantly reducing the threshold on foreign capital in theatres: foreign enterprises are allowed to construct or renovate film theatres and engage in film screening in the form of Sino-foreign equity joint venture or a Sino-foreign cooperative but are not allowed to set up an exclusively foreign-owned film theatre or enterprise. Films screened in the foreign-invested theatres cannot be screened without a permit issued by SAPPRFT. Foreign invested enterprises are prohibited from screening counterfeit or pirated films and are prohibited from screening commercial videos, VCD, and DVD.

Performing Arts

After joining the WTO, significant adjustments were made in performing arts industry policies, the most significant being the removal of ownership restrictions. The institutional frameworks of the performing arts industry are contained in the *Regulations on the Administration of Commercial Performances*[21] and the *Implementation Rules for the Administration of Commercial Performance,*[22] and these have been continually revised to promote the reform of state-owned art troupes. Private performing art troupes have mushroomed and the dramatic rise of performance troupes has enhanced market competitiveness, further opening the market and facilitating international cultural exchange.

The first reform concerns performances organized, or performing arts institutions established by foreigners in China. In 2006, the Ministry of Culture announced the *Approval for Foreign Cultural and Artistic Performance Groups and Individuals in Song and Dance Activities*[23] in regard to undertaking commercial performances; this document specifies the application documentation and the time limit for approval when performance agencies, venue operations entities, and cultural and artistic performance groups invite foreign cultural and artistic performance groups or individuals to stage commercial performances.

In 2008, the State Council revised regulations concerning commercial performances. Investors from Taiwan region as well as other foreign investors can set up performance agencies and performance venue operations institutions with Chinese investors in the form of Sino-foreign joint ventures and Sino-foreign cooperative joint ventures. Chinese parties are required to maintain the principal role in the operation of such ventures. Artistic performance groups are not permitted to be established in the form of Sino-foreign joint ventures, Sino-foreign cooperative joint ventures or exclusively foreign-invested entities.

Foreign exhibition is another area that has seen changes. In 2004, the Ministry of Culture stipulated the *Notice Regarding Promotion of Commercial Cultural Product Exports in Performance and Exhibition.*[24] The policies entailed in this notice provide strong support for commercial performance and exhibition of cultural products and services as well as encouraging well-positioned entities to establish branch institutions abroad. It also encourages cultural institutions and enterprises to form a horizontal alliance with performance agencies abroad to establish international marketing networks. The government will provide financial support for those projects that are listed in the export catalogue of commercial performance and exhibition.

Animation

After China's WTO accession, foreign animation products began to quickly find ways into the domestic market. The Chinese market faced the risk of being eroded by the tide. The challenge for China in response to international competition in the animation market is to create animation products with Chinese characteristics. A number of measures and policies have been issued in the past decade in response to these challenges. The following is a summary of measures taken.

   The objective is to encourage the creation of high-quality domestic animation. In supporting the production of original animation, between 2002 to 2004, the state issued *The Tenth Five-Year Plan Period Development Plan for the Film, Television and Animation Industry*[25] and the *Notice on Strengthening the Administration of the Broadcasting of Imported Animation*[26] as well as other related documents. The intention was to support domestic cartoons as well as encourage cooperation between domestic and foreign companies in the making of animation. Foreign animation must not be broadcast before being submitted for approval by SAPPRFT. On channels screening animation, the ratio of domestic and imported animation is to be not lower than 6:4. Since September 1, 2006, all channels in China were restricted from broadcasting foreign animation or introducing foreign animated products between 17:00 and 20:00.
   A second area is related to the implementation of the 'going out' program for domestic animation products. An overseas service support system has been established to help animation products go abroad and attain a bigger market; the support includes subsidizing the costs of dubbing. Other avenues of support include funds for small and medium enterprises to take part in international exhibitions. The Import-Export Bank of China provides export credit support for promotion of Chinese animation seeking to enter the international market. In addition, there are tax subsidies that apply to animation that is successfully exported overseas and there is exemption for animation enterprises from revenue obtained from the export of their labour services.
   In addition, in 2009 the *Notice Regarding Tax Policies Supporting the Development of the Animation Industry*[27] exempted animation enterprises that independently developed and produced their own animation products and that need to import commercial products from paying customs duties and import value-added tax.

CONCLUSION

In the future China's cultural industry will make full use of the WTO membership platform to enter the global cultural market. China will adopt a more open attitude to participation in international cultural trade. Reducing the entry threshold for international counterparts will strengthen cultural exchange and cooperation and lead to complementary benefits and common development.

NOTES

1. Data compiled from the websites of State Statistics Bureau, the Ministry of Culture and the State Administration of Radio, Television, Film and Publishing.
2. *guanyu jingyibu jiaqiang he gaijin wenhua chanpin he fuwu chukou gongzuo de yijian*
3. *guanyu guli he zhichi wenhua chanpin he fuwu chukou ruogan zhengce*
4. The Ministry of Finance, the Ministry of Commerce, the Ministry of Culture (MoC), the People's Bank of China, the General Administration of Customs and Taxation, SARFT, and the General Administration of Press and Publications (GAPP).
5. *wenhua chanye zhenxing guihua*
6. *guanyu cujin wenhua chanpin he fuwu zouchuqu 2011–2015 nian zongti guihua*
7. *zhonggong zhongyang guanyu shenhua wenhua tizhi gaige, tuidong shehui zhuyi wenhua da fazhan da fanrong ruogan zhongda wenti de jueding*
8. 2012 *nian qiyue jiuri, xinwen chuban zongshu* (*Analysis Report of the Publishing Industry 2011*). Beijing: The General Administration of Press and Publishing, p. 9.
9. Cao Fenglan (2006), *Zhongguo tushu banquan shuchu qianlu manman*, ('A long way to go for China's publishing industry'), *Shenzhen shangbao*, 2016 nian shiyiyue shiwuri, *Shenzhen Business Press*, accessed 15 November 2006).
10. Han, Jie and Zhiwei Zhao (2010), *shuangxiang jiaoliu fazhan*, ('Mutual exchange and development'), *renmin ribao haiwaiban* (*People's Daily Overseas*), accessed 19 July 2010.
11. Zhu Jingruo, Zheng Shaozhong et al. (2011), *woguo shiyiwu qijian wenhua chanye kuaisu zengzhang* (*The rapid development of China's cultural industries during 11th five-year-plan*) *renmin ribao, renmin wang* (*People's Daily*, online edition), accessed 4 January 2011.
12. Fu Shaoqiang (2008), *lun woguo wenhua chuangyi chanye fazhan de xianzhuang yu wenti* ('On the situation and problems of the development of China's cultural creative industries') *xinwen zhanxian* (*Journalism Line*) **3**.
13. *guanyu waiguo ren canjia guangbo dianshi jiemu zhizuo huodong guanli guiding*
14. *zhongwai hezuo zhizuo dianshi ju guanli guiding*
15. *zhongwai hezi hezuo guangbo dianshi jiemu zhizuo jingying qiye guanli zanxing guiding*
16. *jingwai jigou sheli zhuhua guangbo dianshi banshi jigou guanli guiding*
17. *jingwai weixing dianshi jiemu yingjing, bochu guanli guiding*
18. *jingwai weixing dianshi pindao luodi guanli banfa*
19. *fu guowai zumai pindao he shetai guanli zanxing guiding*
20. *dianying guanli tiaoli*
21. *yingyexing yanchu guanli tiaoli*
22. *yingyexing yanchu guanli tiaoli shishi xize*
23. *waiguo wenyi biaoyan tuanti huo geren laihua zai feigewu yule changsuo jinxing yingyexing yanchu huodong de shenpi*
24. *wenhua bu guanyu cujin shangye yanchu zhanlan wenhua chanpin chukou de tongzhi*
25. *yingshi dongman ye "shiwu" qijian fazhan guihua*
26. *guanyu jiaqiang dongmanpian yinjin he bofang guanli de tongzhi*
27. *guanyu fuchi dongman chanye fazhan youguan shuishou zhengce wenti de tongzhi*

11. Ethnic cultural industries and the 'one place, one product' strategy
Na Yi

INTRODUCTION

In January 2008, the author attended a Creative Industries High-Level Panel Meeting held by United Nations Conference on Trade and Development (UNCTAD) in Geneva and delivered a presentation entitled 'Chinese Cultural and Creative Industry: Development and Policies'. The presentation for UNCTAD discussed the uneven development of Chinese cultural and creative industries noting similarities and differences in the developed eastern, the developing central and the underdeveloped western regions. In addition, the presentation suggested that developing central regions and underdeveloped western regions can develop their own cultural and creative industries based on local conditions. This chapter, which draws on the presentation at UNCTAD, provides more detail about this topic and discusses how the Chinese government is providing industry assistance for ethnic cultural industries while ensuring the protection of intangible cultural resources.[1]

Two Dimensions of the Term 'Ethnic' in China

When people mention ethnic cultural industries in China, they may be referring to two different understandings: a political context and/or a globalization perspective. China's 56 ethnic nationalities are dominated by the Han majority: the other 55 'ethnic minorities' (*shaoshu minzu*) comprise just 8.49 per cent of the population (NBSC 2011). Normally when the term 'ethnic affairs' (*minzu shiwu*) is used in China, it refers to minority affairs. This is a political usage.

China is one of the earliest states to sign the UNESCO *Convention on the Protection and Promotion of the Diversity of Cultural Expressions*. In contrast to France and Canada, China not only fights against globalization by the US, but also 'Western' cultural influence more broadly. In this context China used to refer to all local industries as 'ethnic', not just the 55 ethnic minority groups.[2] This is the globalization perspective.

TO ENCOURAGE LOCALIZED DEVELOPMENT IN DIFFERENT REGIONS

Similar industrial structures, simplistic development patterns, as well as over-exploitation and ineffective use of cultural resources: these are all factors hindering the development of cultural industries in local regions, especially in small and medium cities and counties. Seeking to solve these problems in 2015, the central government launched an ambitious plan to develop what is now called 'characteristic cultural industries' (*tese wenhua chanye*). The key strategies are localization and branding.

Localization is fundamentally concerned with the identification of resources, the selection of lead industries and positioning of products in consumer markets. Distinctive cultural resources, regional 'characteristics' and the potential brand positioning of the respective localities will determine strategies and function as resources for future development. Under this plan China will develop regional cultural industry belts; in turn the regions will promote the trade of cultural products both domestically and into overseas markets. Branding, in terms of policy strategy, is best explained by the 'one place, one product' strategy (i.e. one place = county, township, village). This is aimed at fostering influential and competitive local brands. The 'characteristics' (*tese*) fall into three categories: local cultural resources, distinctive regional characteristics and national characteristics. Such a plan is a roadmap for creative transformation of the countryside.

This policy is specifically aimed at the development of minority areas in western China that exhibit a weak economic base due to their dependence on a traditional mode of development.

CHARACTERISTIC CULTURAL INDUSTRIES – CHARTING A LOCAL PATH

The thinking behind this policy dates several years. In 2014, the Ministry of Culture and the Ministry of Finance of China jointly issued a document called the *Guiding Opinions on the Promotion of Development of Characteristic Cultural Industries*,[3] defining principles, objectives, tasks and policy security measures for the development of 'characteristic cultural industries'. In the policy the term 'characteristic cultural industries' refers to an industrial development mode that provides cultural products and services with distinctly regional characteristics (and national features) by virtue of unique local cultural resources. In the past decade China has issued many policies to encourage and accelerate the development of cultural industries with regional and national characteristics. This new strategy is a culmination of previous policies and secures their implementation through allocation of project funds.

The policy is directed to the fact that China abounds in rich indigenous cultural resources. By 2014, China had listed 4295 state-level key cultural relics protection units, 45 world heritage areas, 113 state-level historic and cultural cities, 181 state-level historic and cultural towns, 169 state-level historic and cultural villages as well as 1219 state-level intangible cultural heritages; all of these are regarded as sources of innovation for the development of characteristic cultural industries. Another important factor is that the development of these industries will lead to job creation. The cultural resources are found in a vast number of villages and towns. The low entry threshold can drive employment in rural areas, in this way playing an important role in the provision of jobs and contributing to the transformation of the economic development mode of both urban and rural regions in the mid-west of China.

An example is the fine arts and craft production sector. Statistics indicate that during the 12th Five-Year Plan, the number of enterprises above 'designated size'[4] in handicraft production will reach 8,000, while the total industrial output value of enterprises (both above and below 'designated size') will amount to 1,500 billion RMB (US$ 236 billion). The number of rural processing workers will number 20 million with annual growth estimated to be 22 per cent. The most important factor is that industries such as the ceramics of Jingdezhen, the New Year paintings on kites of Weifang, the wood carvings of Dongyang and the silver and bronze ware of Heqing, have already served as significant economic resources in the development of many Chinese regions.

Furthermore, the government believes that the development of characteristic cultural industries will protect the legacy of traditional culture as well as being an important means of using culture as a 'resource' to ensure that people are both wealthy and happy. The development of traditional and characteristic cultural resources is therefore closely related to the lives of local people. As society changes, many traditional production practices, lifestyles and culturally rich environments are starting to fade away. To protect the cultural legacy of regions more effectively, the goal is to develop such 'characteristic' cultural products and services. Moreover, by incorporating the ethos of protection and inheritance of these resources, cultural value can be transformed into economic and social value.

Currently emphasis is on the development of six cultural industrial systems, including artworks, entertainment, cultural tourism, festivals, cultural clusters and towns, and exhibitions, all of which reflect regional characteristics and national features in their products and services. In respect to the concept of development, the proposal is for 'originality-oriented, trans-industry integration' (*chuangyi yinling kuajie ronghe*). Particular focus will be given to the importance of creative design in the improvement of the quality of products and services in order to upgrade the structure of characteristic cultural industries and extend industrial chains. In addition, emphasis is given to the integrative development of characteristic cultural industries with industries such as architecture, gardening, agriculture, sports, catering and garments, the cultivation of new types of products and the creation of a completely new industrial form.

In relation to regional development, the focus of the policy is both rural and urban areas, leading to the formation of regional belts of 'characteristic cultural industries'. It is clear that the priority of development is given to certain regions including the route along the Silk Road, the Zang-Qiang-Yi Cultural Industry Corridor,[5] and the South-to-North Water Diversion Landscape Belt.[6] The purpose is clearly to promote the integration of cultural industries and the tourist industry.

In terms of policy, the plan requires breaking down the separation of regions and industries. This can be effectively done by encouraging non-local enterprises to enter into local characteristic cultural industries, and by encouraging enterprises of other industries and private capital to engage in characteristic cultural industries by supporting small and micro businesses. Local people will also be encouraged to participate. Funds have been provided for the construction of the Silk Road Cultural Industry Belt and the Zang-Qiang-Yi Cultural Industry Corridor. Funds will be leveraged to promote the upgrading and transformation of characteristic cultural industries and products. Public service platforms will facilitate investment and financing for such projects.

PRODUCTIVE PROTECTION: A GAME BETWEEN HERITAGE PROTECTION AND INDUSTRIAL DEVELOPMENT

A general survey on intangible cultural heritage was carried out in China from 2005 to 2010, producing the following benchmark data:

- The number of intangible heritage resources in China is nearly 870,000;
- 1219 of these are included in the 'Directory of State-level Intangible Cultural Heritage';
- 36 are included in the 'Directory of Masterpieces of Intangible

Cultural Heritage of Humanity' and the 'Directory of Intangible Cultural Heritage that Need Urgent Protection';

- China has the largest number of intangible cultural heritages included in the UN directories;
- 1488 people are included in the Directory of Representative Inheritors of State-level Intangible Cultural Heritage;
- 11 experimental areas of state-level cultural ecology protection are established;
- 41 'Demonstration Bases for Productive Protection of State-level Intangible Cultural Heritage' are established;
- 1499 million RMB central finance had been invested specific to the protection of intangible cultural heritage accumulatively by 2011;
- *Intangible Cultural Heritage Law of the People's Republic of China*, the first law of China that protects intangible cultural heritage, was put into force on June 1, 2011.

The concept of 'productive protection' (*shengchanxing fangshi baohu*) is aimed mainly at the protection of traditional skills, the processing of traditional Chinese medicine and intangible cultural heritage of traditional art. It has attracted great attention. Officially, it means active and effective protection of production, and the processes by which traditional Chinese medicine is prepared, as well as the protection of intangible cultural heritage under the condition that traditional manual production laws and modes of operation are obeyed and authenticity and integrity, core manual skills and traditional processes are secured. 'Productive' refers to the property, cultural connotations and skill values embodied in intangible cultural heritage items that are brought into existence through manual creation. The processes and core skills associated with these cases of intangible cultural heritage need to be protected, inherited and carried forward.

Though both are under the administration of the Ministry of Culture, 'productive protection' (of intangible cultural heritage) differs from characteristic cultural industries. They are therefore given different names and administered by different means, even though they are directed at similar cultural resources and developed with similar methods.

The administrators that put forward the concept of 'productive protection' have emphasized the difference from 'characteristic cultural industries'. In their opinion the focus on cultural originality in the latter is generally put on production and the management concepts of the products. Originality and creativity drive the economic value of such cultural products through the market system. However, the emphasis of intangible cultural heritage protection is on the 'type of protection', especially the 'process of production'. Attention is given to practical craft production – a link that implies and expresses core skills and the cultural connotations of intangible cultural heritage. This is an important difference between the two.

In fact, 'productive protection' stresses manual production and creative design – core factors in the development of cultural resources. It is in opposition to the relentless force of business development that exploits cultural resources. For instance, the unchecked spread of printed Tibetan Thang-ga has impacted severely on the market for Thang-ga made by the traditional handicraft method using precious natural minerals.

An illustrative example of productive protection is the 'Integrated Project for Inheritance and Development of Traditional Handicraft Culture in Linzhi, Tibet'. Linzhi is a little lower in altitude than other regions of Tibet and is inhabited by a dozen ethnic groups including Zang, Han, Hui, Manba, Lhoba, Nahsi, Lisu and Tulung. It is home to nine types of intangible cultural heritage and sixty-three intangible cultural heritage protection projects.[7] An academic team comprised of experts and designers from the Department of Intangible Cultural Heritage in the Ministry of Culture have provided support in regard to design, operation and management and have helped realize the overall inheritance and development of handicraft culture and associated life values.

Hardly viable villages, nearly lost skills, arcane formulas, environmental damage by chemical dyes, and local culture-irrelevant artwork manufacture – all these are problems encountered by the academic team when they started the survey in Linzhi in 2012.

Linzhi is inhabited by over 2000 Lhoba people who have various languages but traditionally no form of writing. With a particularly sparse population, Lhoba is faced with the possibility of losing its traditional culture, which has been inherited orally over generations. Lhoba costume and Linzhi Tibetan clothes and ornaments are typical items of state-level intangible cultural heritage of Linzhi Prefecture. According to the consensus of the academic team, textiles and costumes are highlights of the intangible cultural heritage of Linzhi. But their inheritance is challenged by many problems: quality of materials is not guaranteed; inheritors have less knowledge on the skills and are unable to judge the market; and most importantly, production sites are short of raw materials.

It is almost impossible and unsustainable to get all raw materials handmade by inheritors. Hence, the academic team turned to the woolen mill of Linzhi. The first modern enterprise of Tibet and a Tibet support project of Chinatex Corporation, it was shut down in the late 1990s. During its construction in 1965, over 600 employees and their families moved together with the mill to Tibet. The government of Linzhi Prefecture has offered help to recover the productivity of the mill, by purchasing relevant equipment and providing new jobs in raw material processing, such as dyeing, spinning and fabric production.

The academic team also established the 'Linzhi Demonstration Base of Tibetan Costume Textile Technology Inheritance' in Zhenba village, where the tradition of people making their own Kongpo Tibetan costumes survives. Forty-seven women villagers received training in more than 30 kinds of manual sewing skills, and became adept in processing and making creative designs. Additionally, over 50 villagers of Kasimu village and Zengba are now able to prepare Tibetan wool to supply materials for the production processes of Zhenba. Moreover, the academic team improved the Tibetan wood loom to make the wool tighter, which avoids the deformation of materials in later processing.

In the meantime, Lhoba Costumes and Manufacture Skills Inheritance Institute, the Pengren Qude Temple Tibetan Incense Workshop, the Langxian Jindong Tibet Paper Workshop, and the Motuo Manba Traditional Bamboo Ware Inheritance Institute and other similar programs were carried forward gradually. The six project sites along the sides of Yaruzampbo River together constitute a modern platform that promotes the inheritance and development of traditional skills. The entire project is based on the principle of respecting the lifestyles of local people and organizing production nearby; evaluating fully the capacity of production and the environment; promoting skill inheritance; improving product quality; and restricting the scale of production.

After two years of effort, local people have raised their incomes and embraced a new life in harmony with the environment, working nearby and seeing no change in basic lifestyle. Particularly, Lhoba women have enjoyed the progress brought by modern social development, thanks to the inheritance and development of traditional skills. This is of significant importance for Lhoba, with so sparse a population.

But blind pursuit of tradition is also a problem. It is difficult to improve product quality while protecting the environment in production. During the spinning process, the best vegetable dyes were selected from foreign countries to avoid environmental contamination. Therein lies a problem. As Linzhi is located in the plateau, where boiled water cannot reach 100°C, every kind of dye must be retested to create the ideal plateau colors. Without modern equipment, Lin Jihua, director of Linzhi textile mill, solved the problem of using vegetable dyes by virtue of his experience and indigenous methods, and under the guidance of experts from Beijing Institute of Clothing Technology, succeeded in the core technical processing of staple yarn textiles. He was surprised to find plants growing in the places where vegetable dye wastewater was discharged, which was definitely impossible before. He was excited about this and proud of the efforts over two years.

The Jindong Tibet paper project is in the most urgent need of rescue and conservation. Emerging in the seventh century, Tibet paper is among the first group included in the *Directory of State-level Intangible Cultural Heritage* in 2006. The outstanding Tibet paper was used exclusively to make official documents, and to preserve Confucian classics and paper currencies in ancient times. Shrub silk daphne, the raw material for the project, grows in a fragile environment, has a long growth cycle and has been scarce due to papermaking since ancient times. As the most exquisite kind of paper in Tibet, Jindong Tibet paper is endangered because of high cost, low output and the passing of inheritors. Arriving in Linzhi, the academic team interviewed elderly inheritors, orally recorded the production process, conducted experiments over and over again, and improved the quality up to that of the original Tibet paper. Due to the slow growth of raw materials, the academic team did not develop Jindong Tibet paper on a large scale. Instead, they made reasonable designs, such as making high-grade chrome paper and ownership stamps, and connected these plans with other parts of the project to constitute a solid, integrated and high-quality cultural ecology system.

LADDER-TYPE DEVELOPMENT MODEL

Like China's economic and social development, China's cultural industry development exhibits a strong local innovative color. From an institutional point of view, China's reform and development is conducted mainly in the 'central' and 'local' levels. As for major industrial development strategies, it is usually the case that the central government determines the major policies, and then the locale determines the specific implementation measures based on their financial capacity. In the development process, there is also a strong learning and competition mechanism between local governments. This modernization development of China can be seen as a 'double competition' model of market players and local administrative bodies, almost unprecedented in human history. This pattern of development is the major factor driving the rapid development of China since its reform and opening up; it also provides a diversified strategic development path for post-industrial China.

As the success stories on China's urban development cited in the report testify, China's cities are becoming the 'creative field' and 'testing ground', thereby attracting the world's attention. It can be imagined how diversified China's development will be when the industrialization target has been achieved, the 'GDP' straitjacket on local governments has been lifted, and regional cultural resources and community cultural tradition (the so-called 'intangible cultural heritages') become a new source of development. The booming Western 'cultural industry' in recent years has already made the development prospects clear to us.

China's governments at all levels will set about developing the '13th Five-Year Plan for Cultural Industries'.[8] In the face of a new stage of development, those in power in each region and each city should conduct more research into local characteristic resources, development stages, development environments, strengths and weaknesses, and then set their own development goals and development strategies accordingly. What the development of cultural and creative industries at home and abroad provides us is just ideas and methods rather than ready-made samples to be copied, and each region has to plan, to innovate, to manage and to practice in accordance with its own actual situation before finding the most suitable 'one'. In the new stage of development, China must reflect on and abandon the previous GDP competition, homogeneous competition and repetitive construction in the development of cultural industries.

'Local development path' is the theme of the United Nations' *Creative Economy Report 2013 (Special Edition)* and indeed the ultimate choice of Chinese cultural industries over the past 15 years of development. The Chinese government introduced a series of new cultural industries policies in 2015 and took it as one of the major reform objectives to 'promote cultural industry to be a pillar industry of the national economy'. This indicates that the development trend of Chinese culture and creative industries in the future will break from the single development mode in order to encourage different regions to choose cultural and creative industry development patterns consistent with local cultural traditions and economic development. In addition it will break trade barriers to encourage innovation and creativity with independent intellectual property rights in different sectors.

NOTES

1. All data in this chapter comes from the NBS (National Bureau of Statistics of China), 'The Sixth National Population Census Data Released', available at www.stats.gov.com, Retrieved April 28, 2011.
2. These so-called 'local industries', are those enterprises established in China, managed by Chinese (including overseas Chinese), and owning the whole brand, as well as having headquarters in China and maintaining control of finance.
3. *tuidong tese wenhua chanye fazhan de zhidao yijian*
4. Before 2011, 'enterprises above designated size' referred to the main business income of RMB 5 million and above; since 2011 it refers to the main business income of RMB 20 million and above.
5. Including seven provincial regions: Sichuan province, Guizhou province, Yunnan

province, Xizang (Tibet) Autonomous Region, Shaanxi province, Gansu province and Qinghai province.

6. The South-to-North Water Diversion Project is a multi-decade infrastructure mega-project in China. Ultimately it aims to channel 44.8 billion cubic meters of water annually from the Yangtze River in southern China to the more arid and industrialized north through three canal systems. The 'belt' above means the central route. The main canal is 1, 246 km, and it is built on the North China Plain so that gravity will allow the water to flow all the way without the need for pumping stations. This route runs from Danjiangkou Reservoir on the Han River, a tributary of the Yangtze River, to Beijing. There are 12 sites on this route planned to be cultural industries projects.

7. Three are national-level intangible cultural heritage projects, 38 are provincial-level, 22 are country-level.

8. The 'five-year plan', as a part of China's national economic plan, is mainly to plan major construction projects nationwide, productivity distributions and proportions of national economic components, thereby providing the direction and objective for national economic development. Since the first five-year plan in 1953, China has compiled a total of twelve 'Five-Year Plans', and currently the '12th Five-Year Plan' is under implementation.

12. Globalization and ethnic grounded cultural creativity in Yunnan
Yan Li and Ying Huang

Located in the southern border region of southwest China, the province of Yunnan extends for more than 390,000 square kilometres and has a population of almost 46 million. Yunnan adjoins Vietnam, Burma and Laos. The province is also geographically proximate to Thailand, Cambodia and India. Geographically southeast below the Tibetan Plateau, Yunnan neighbours Sichuan, Tibet, Guizhou and Guanxi. Its physical topography includes high mountain ranges, sunken basins and deep-cut valleys. Longitudinally from south to north, the high mountains pass into long impressive river systems; the vast drop in altitude from the mountain ridges to valleys results in considerable geological and ecological diversity.

As well as being synonymous with biodiversity, Yunnan has been a focal point of regional human migration throughout history. In addition to the Han, it is home to 25 ethnic minority groups: these belong to four major ethnic families: Diqiang, Baiyue, Baipu and Miao Yao. Among these ethnic minorities 15 are unique to Yunnan: Bai, Hani, Dai, Jingpo, Lisu, Naxi, Achang, Jinuo, Wa, Deang, Bulang, Pumi, Dulong and Nu. Different development levels of these ethnic groups have led to a variety of living styles; the distinctive geographic environment allows ethnic minorities to mingle but still maintain their lives and customs in small settlements. The varied climates of Yunnan, as well as distinctive living spaces, modes of production and lifestyles have produced a rich ethnic culture in Yunnan. Compared with the eastern coastal areas and middle regions of China, Yunnan is a late developer with less negative effects from industrial development and urbanization. In the process of modernization it is therefore imperative that ethnic cultures, along with their legacies and ways of life, should be preserved and inherited.

UNESCO's *Convention for the Safeguarding of Intangible Cultural Heritage* defines 'intangible cultural heritage' as 'the practices, representations, expressions, knowledge, skills – as well as the instruments, objects, artefacts and cultural spaces' (OECD: Paris, 17 October 2003, 32nd session). In Yunnan these include oral traditions and forms of expression including language, performing arts, social practices, rituals and festive events, knowledge and practices concerning nature and the universe, and traditional craftsmanship. Among ethnic minorities in Yunnan, many myths and epic legends are handed down; for example, the Dai people cite more than 500 narrative epics; other ethnic minorities also claim distinctive myths, epics and stories.

More than 180 ethnic musical instruments are used in Yunnan including windpipes and beaten, plucked and string instruments; in addition to nearly 100 ethnic and folk songs in totally different styles, there are more than 300 dances. The variety in geographical environment, climate, different modes of production and living has led to extremely colourful ethnic costumes. Colours, styles, decorative patterns and embroidery vary among four major ethnic families: Diqiang, Baiyue, Baipu and Miaoyao. Within each ethnic family, the apparel of different groups is distinctive. Traditional craftsmanship is an important part of ethnic culture, and includes artefacts made from metal, wood and grass, mud, stone, cloth and paper. These handicrafts, which are still manufactured in large quantities, are used in various forms of production, in people's daily lives as well as in religious rituals. Rituals and festive events play an important role in ethnic group identity, congregation and entertainment. Every minority group in Yunnan has different rituals and festive events and these serve as vehicles for communication with other ethnic groups.

Ethnic culture, infused into people's daily lives, includes oral transmission, ethnic songs and dances, traditional handicrafts, festival and events, and religious cultures, in villages and historical towns. This diversity constitutes a complex cultural ecosystem. Ethnic minorities' culture can be viewed as the totality of their lives: all kinds of culture permeate through products without obvious economic property. In the late 20th and early 21st century, China has achieved rapid economic growth. Yunnan has also integrated into the global economy, which has in turn provided new opportunities for these comparatively closed ethnic areas. Its geographical environment, together with the diversity of ethnic cultures, and eco-surroundings relatively undamaged by progress, has enabled Yunnan to develop into a very important tourist destination in China. The influx of tourism has led to rapid development of tourist industries and ethnic culture is the primary object for tourists' experience. Creativity has in turn transformed ethnic culture: products formerly for the 'self' have transformed into products and services for the 'other'. Integration of global cultural consumerism with Yunnan ethnic cultures therefore not only brings about a new kind of modernity in the province, but also becomes a way of grounding the province's creative industries. It is possible to identify three forms of ethnic creative industries in Yunnan: grounded ethnic performance creativity, ethnic tourist arts and crafts creativity, and traditional rituals and festive events creativity. These three original forms engender creative forms of expression as well as providing material economic benefits.

ETHNIC SONGS AND DANCE

With their plentiful variations, the songs and dance performances of the 25 ethnic minorities served mainly as self-entertainment for people – as well as for their 'gods' until the 1980s. For this reason traditional songs and dance played a very significant role in people's productivity, in their lives and in folk religion. They represent a complete cultural transmission system: for each ethnic group these songs and dances were common in their daily lives, imperceptibly influencing the cultural legacy; men and women, old and young were able to sing and dance, and the inheritors of the traditions, as well as prominent singers and dancers, were highly respected. Since such songs and dances are important cultural activities, their distinctive legacy has manifested in major festivals, in religious rituals and in daily recreation.

In the 1990s, the Chinese government effected its opening up policy, accelerating the pace of economic development in ethnic areas as well as providing construction and improving infrastructure and modern transportation. In the subsequent expansion of tourist industries in Yunnan, ethnic songs and dance found new ways of expression: the principle of entertaining 'self and gods', transferred to entertaining the 'other'. Yunnan's ethnic songs and dances now adopt stagecraft, commercial performance elements and modern set designing; combining with technology and popular aesthetics, the art forms have utilized innovation and creativity. Since 2003, large-scale song/dance performances have emerged and become popular. At present, there are about 100 performances of different varieties and types, found primarily in tourist cities and towns such as Kunming, Lijiang, Dali, Xishuangbanna and Tenchong (Table 12.1). In Xishuangbanna alone, the estimated number of performing shows is about ten.

In catering to tourism, most performance productions absorb local ethnic cultures, including elements found in traditional and classical dances, myths, legends, love stories, religious cults, natural cults and tributes to labour; with the help of modern stage aesthetics, lighting, and other stage technologies they produce a striking visual impact, an aesthetic totally different from what one finds in metropolitan life. Locality, diversification and distinctiveness have merged as ethnic traditions encounter mass tourism consumption; the conversion from products for entertaining 'self and gods' to products of 'grounded' performance

Table 12.1   Yunnan's major ethnic performances and distribution

City or Town	Repertory
Kunming	Dynamic Yunnan (Yang Liping), Peacock (Yang Liping), Sounds of Yunnan (Yang Liping), Jixin Banquet, Fubao Paradise
Dali	Dali-A Fantasy (Chen Kaige), Butterfly Dream
Lijiang	Mountain River Show, Impression Lijiang (Zhang Yimou), Flying Colourful Clouds, Forever Love in Lijiang, Love Song from Flower Chamber, Naxi Ancient Music
Shang-ri-la	Tibetan Myth (Yang Liping)
Tengchong	Mysterious Tengchong
Xishuangbanna	Lancang-Mekong River Bonfire Show, Xishuangbanna Super Song-Dance Show, Duogeshui Song-Dance Party, Unforgettable Night with Dai Pretty Girls, Affinity with Water

has been accomplished; the result is seen in economic benefits and job opportunities. In this way ethnic performance has become a new cultural economy form.

Lijiang currently lays claim to six in-residence performances: *Mountain River Show, Impressions of Lijiang (Zhang Yimou), Flying Colourful Clouds, Forever Love in Lijiang, Love Song from Flower Chamber* and *Naxi Ancient Music Performance*. From early 2000 to September 2014, the investment cost of these shows amounted to RMB 328 million (US$52 million): together they employed 1,221 people, producing a total of 20,221 performances with audience numbers totalling 17,120,000. The overall income received was RMB 1,933,580,000 (US$307,405,400) and the tax returned was RMB 197,530,000 (US$30,740,540). From 2000 to 2010, the Naxi Ancient Music Performance retained a 75 per cent yearly average attendance with 9,000 shows and audiences of 1,500,000 in total: this brought in more than RMB 5,000,000 (US$794,000) in yearly profit and tax.

Without doubt Yang Liping is the most representative figure in Chinese ethnic dance. For a long time Yang was concerned with innovation and creativity in ethnic dance. She identified and nurtured ethnic minority inheritors of traditional song and dance from different groups and areas and sought to combine these legacies with the cultural elements of her artistic brand to innovate the 'primitive (aboriginality)' concept of ethnic song-dance art. In this way the first large-scale ethnic performance, *Dynamic Yunnan*, was conceived. Since its inception in August 2003, Dynamic Yunnan has been performed nearly 4,000 times to over 4 million people: it is now a symbolic project of Yunnan creative industries and is listed as a 'China national performance masterpiece'. From 2012

Table 12.2   Statistics of Impressions of Lijiang *over five years*

Year	Show total	Audience numbers	Income (million RMB)
2010	768	1,500,000	180
2011	905	2,010,000	230
2012	929	2,084,400	233
2013	899	2,081,100	240
2014	987	2,350,000	250

Source: Jiang Chengxian (2015) 'Impression Lijiang hit a record high audience, Lijiang Hotline', available at http://www.lijiangtv.com/article/52079-p-1.html, February 3.

Source: Photographer Liu Jianhua.

Figure 12.1   Impressions of Lijiang *by Zhang Yimou, 1*

to 2013 new works of the *Peacock* and *Dynamic Yunnan* (an upgraded version) were launched with higher added value from creativity, art and ethnic culture. On October 23, 2014, the Yunnan Yang Liping Culture Communication Corporation went public and was listed in NEW OTCBB of China stock market: it became the first dance performing company on NEW OTCBB.

In 2014, the Hangzhou Songcheng Tourism Development Co. Ltd

Source: Photographer Liu Jianhua.

Figure 12.2   Impressions of Lijiang *by Zhang Yimou, 2*

originated another performance called *Forever Love in Lijiang* using the 'cultural theme park + large-scale performance' model. Since it opened to the public from 21 March 2014 to 31 December of the same year, 504 shows were shown, bringing in a total audience of 1,850,000, as well as more than RMB 100,000,000 (US$15,898,251) to the Songcheng tourist area of Lijiang.

At present, almost 20 large-scaled ethnic grounded song-dance performances can be seen in the major tourist cities and scenic spots of Yunnan. However, in the wake of intense competition, problems have arisen such as shortage of investment into content creativity and a lack of inspiration: this has led to a decline in ticket sales, lower seat occupancy, lower performance rates and ultimately declining profits. Some shows have been rendered obsolete by market forces. Meanwhile new shows keep appearing with better combinations of songs and dance, enhanced with new technology and stage aesthetics, in this way generating more added value.

Source: Photographer Liu Jianhua.

Figure 12.3 Yang Liping performing the Peacock Dance

THE TRANSFORMING OF UTENSILS FOR PRODUCTION

Traditional handicrafts assume an important role in people's lives – as utensils and tools for production, in people's daily living and in religious practice. The comparatively closed geographic environment of Yunnan, combined with different means of production and various minority religions has led to a diversity of handicrafts, albeit not on a large scale. In the past, organization of production was done by individuals, among families, and within the villages; while these products bore features of ethnic culture they were primarily practical. In the 1980s industrially manufactured utensils and tools flooded into the market and ethnic handicrafts were squeezed out or disappeared. On signing up to UNESCO's *Convention for the Safeguarding of the Intangible Cultural Heritage*, central and local governments of China listed traditional handicrafts as an important form of intangible heritage. Since the end of the last century, when the Chinese government started to promote tourism, traditional handicrafts began to transform; the production has changed from practical utensils and tools used in local lives to tourist art crafts catering to popular tastes. In converting from practical uses for the 'self' into cultural consumption for the 'other', the symbolic meaning is magnified and strengthened; ethnicity, modernity, fashion elements and traditional skills open up vast space for the development of traditional ethnic handicrafts, and many traditional crafts have been protected or even creatively modified. Traditional ethnic handicrafts are therefore an important form of Yunnan ethnic creative industries.

According to government statistics, in 2013, the added value of Yunnan traditional handicrafts accounted for 13.7 per cent of the total added value in creative industries, proving to be the sector with the most potential among the ten major categories of creative industries. At the end of 2013, among 319 provincial key cultural enterprises, there were 29 handicraft companies associated with manufacturing and sales of ethnic art crafts; seven of these had primary business income exceeding RMB 100 million (US$15,898,251) and 11 were listed among the 103 large or medium-sized enterprises. Statistics from Yunnan Provincial Handicrafts Trade Association shows that in 2012, handicrafts production output reached RMB 10 trillion (US$1,589,825,100) (jewellery and jade excluded) with a 12–15 per cent yearly sales increase. In all there were 2,200 manufacturing companies, and 7,000 sales enterprises with 400,000 employees, more than 300 of which held handicrafts certificates.

There has been a five-in-one system of 'Gold-Wood-Earth-Stone-Cloth' in Yunnan handicrafts creativity industries which includes folk inheritors, families, traditional villages, medium and small-sized enterprises as well as a whole system of prominent distribution markets and production, creativity, collection and distribution. With an increase in ethnic features, added value from creativity, production scales are expanding continuously.

Among the many traditional handicrafts in Yunnan, metal crafts have achieved noticeable progress in recent years; higher added value comes mainly from industries like speckle copper, speckle tin, black copper with silver ornaments and traditional knife tools. Historically Xinhua Village in Dali's Heqing County was a typical Bai local village manufacturing stirrups, farming tools and daily wares. In the past craftsmen from Xinhua went to other ethnic areas of Yunnan to explore new sales markets, in this way providing metal wares to other ethnic groups for living, clothing, decoration and religious purposes. Those craftsmen in turn learned skills from these ethnic minorities during their travels and this laid the foundation for later market expansion. Since the 1980s, Xinhua has developed from a local production-oriented handicrafts village into a market-oriented centre for tourist creations, their production and distribution. Initially, 60 households participated in handicrafts manufacturing; today 987 households among the total of 2,879 villagers are involved in the creation, production and sale of silver products. Xinhua has become well known in China and internationally as an ethnic silverware brand name. Xinhua silver creation and production can be seen in most scenic sites in China.

Yunnan is the most important wood producing and processing area in China. Wood and bamboo handicrafts are important ethnic handicraft types. A complete traditional handicrafts creation system, including furniture design, production, tea tables, tea set design, wood-cutting, root carving, decorations and traditional architecture design has come into existence. Jianchuan County of Dali is the most prominent traditional wood cutting production district. Almost 10 per cent of Jianchuan's total population, employing 12,000 persons, is in the wood cutting business. With 1,500 self-employed householders and 15 professional processing factories, Jianchuan County's wood-cutting and related businesses bring an annual output of more than RMB 200 million (US$31,796,502).

Earthenware is another very important form of Yunnan ethnic handicraft. Jianshui purple pottery, Huanning black ceramics, and Xishuangbanna's slow-wheel ceramics have transformed from being daily use commodities to craft and artistic pottery. Jianshui purple pottery is representative of a coalition of artists, calligraphers and painters with pottery crafts. In 2014, there were 329 registered pottery manufacturing and marketing enterprises and individual operators with a total of 8,000 employees; the pottery sector's annual output in Jianshui County was RMB 800,000,000 (US$12,718,600). Jewellery, jade and accessories assume an important role among Yunnan traditional ethnic handicrafts. At the end of 2012, 3,400 registered jewellery companies were operating in Yunnan with more than 15,000 merchants, employing nearly 1 million practitioners; in 2012, gross sales of jewellery and jade (raw jade and metal excluded) was RMB 31,700,000,000 (US$5,039,745,600).

Tie-dyed fabric and embroidery represent a significant concentration of traditional handicrafts and productivity. As sectors benefiting the people, they support farmers in remote areas to improve their condition, for instance by helping village women with extra money. Local governments are guiding the development of tie-dyed fabric and embroidery to cater to the tourism market and are promoting creativity and commercialization of these crafts. Among the various ethnic districts in Yunnan, nearly 1 million women are engaged in embroidery. At the end of 2013, there were 56 Yi ethnic people's embroidery associations in Chuxiong Yi Autonomous Prefecture; among a total of 330 households, 34 had annual incomes of more than RMB 300,000 (US$47,694). Mouding County, within Chuxiong Yi Autonomous Prefecture, had a sales volume of 45,400 pieces, realizing RMB 13,620,000 (US$ 2,165,341) output in 2013.

ETHNIC RITUALS AND FESTIVE EVENTS

Ethnic rituals and festive events are collective carnivals of China's minority cultures; as well as group identification they play important roles in trade, cultural exchange and religious activities. The 25 ethnic minorities in Yunnan each have unique and influential festivals and events. With more and more tourists coming into Yunnan, creative elements have been injected into festivals and events: these events have changed from being local celebrations to 'cultural experience' festivals.

Yunnan traditional ethnic festivals have evolved considerably. Besides demonstrating ethnic culture, building a platform for cultural trade

Table 12.3   Major festivals and exhibitions in Yunnan

	Major representative festivals and exhibitions
Cultural creativity exhibitions	Kunming China Expo, China International Tourism Trade Fair, Kunming China Pan-Asia International Food Expo, China-South Asia Expo, Kunming China Pan-Asia Stone Expo, Kunming China International Flower Expo, Southeast Asia Commodity Expo; Yunnan Cultural Industry Expo, Yunnan Pu'er Tea International Trade Fai, Yunnan International Education Expo, Jinsha River Strange Stone Art Expo, Yunnan Kunming International Jewellery Festival, Yingjiang China International Jewellery & Jade Raw Material Expo, Kunming Real Estate Trade Fair, Yunnan Tea Trade Fair
Traditional ethnic festivals and events	Dehong Jingpo Munao Folk Song Festival, Stone Forest International Torch Festival, Miao People's Flower-hill Climbing Festival, Dali Bai Ethnic Festival (Lunar March Bazaar), Xishuangbanna Dai People's Water-splashing Day, Chuxiong Yi People's Torch Day; Asia Micro-Film Festival, Dali China Orchid Expo, China-Burma Baobo Carnival, Yi People's Makeup Competition Day, Jianchuan Shibaoshan Mountain Bai Folk Song Festival
Modern creativity festivals	Lijiang Snow Mountain Music Concert Festival, Dali Erhai Lake Strawberry Music Concert Festival, Dali International Photography Exhibition, Luoping Rape Flower Cultural Tourism Festival, Yunnan Cangyuan Va People's Carnival, Mojiang – China Tropic of Cancer Twins and Hani Sun Festival, Nie'er China International Music Festival, Kunming Seagull Cultural Festival, Kunming China International Cultural Tourism Festival and Kunming Carnival, etc.

and promoting local economy, they are also an important part of Yunnan's cultural creativity. Traditional festivals like Xishuangbanna Dai People's Water-splashing Day, Chuxiong Yi People's Torch Day, Yunnan Cangyuan Va People's Carnival, Dali Bai Ethnic Festival (Lunar March Bazaar), and the Dehong Jingpo Munao Folk Song Festival are achieving wider influence, bring development in accommodation, dining, shopping, travel, recreation and entertainment. During Chuxiong Yi People's Torch Day in 2015, Chuxiong, the capital of Yi Autonomous Prefecture, received 402,140 visitors with a value of RMB 101,424,700 (US$16,124,753). Modern creative festivals like Lijiang Snow Mountain Music Concert Festival, the Dali International Photography Exhibition, the Luoping Rape Flower Cultural Tourism Festival, the Asia Micro-Film Festival, and the Mojiang – China Tropic of Cancer Twin and Hani Sun Festival combine local knowledge, traditional ethnic song and dance, ethnic handicrafts, recreation and traditional catering culture with modern music, dance and bar culture. The reputations of these festivals have spread, creating a cultural branding effect.

The Lijiang Snow Mountain Music Concert Festival, combining modern rock music with ethnic music, kicks off each year during the October golden week holiday period. Many back-packers come to Lijiang and the festival takes place at the foot of Jade Dragon Snow Mountain. Rock bands and artists from all over the world share a carnival atmosphere with back-packers under the snow mountain around the Naxi ancient town. The festival provides a good opportunity to experience Lijiang culture; Lijiang and Dali have now become destinations for Chinese folk music creators. Thanks to Internet and mobile technology their interaction fosters local cultural and creative activities in the ethnic areas. Local customs play a role; for instance, there are reportedly many twins born in Mojiang, a small town traversed by the Tropic of Cancer. Near the town is the 'twin well'. The Mojiang – China Tropic of Cancer Twins and Hani Sun Festival is based on legend and the human biological phenomenon of twins. It combines Hani minority culture with the local knowledge of Mojiang and takes place during Labour Day holidays in May every year. It attracts millions of tourists and draws considerable revenue; in 2013, over three days of celebration, 1,784,000 tourists from within China and international destinations came to Mojiang, bringing in RMB 278,290,000 (US$44,243,243).

CONCLUSION

In the interaction between politics, economy and culture in China a new spatial configuration can be observed: the east coastal areas, the middle areas and now the western areas. Most minorities are concentrated in the western areas, which lag behind in economic development and urbanization but enjoy a better ecological system and are home to a density of ethnic cultures. Yunnan, possibly the best-known western region of China, has developed a range of cultural products and services embodying locality, ethnicity and modern creativity, a reference and example for China's other western ethnic areas. In conclusion, three aspects illustrate the value of creativity for ethnic minorities:

First, thanks to the existence of abundant cultural resources, the development paths mentioned in this chapter are opening up new spaces for economic development for ethnic groups, which are latecomers to the creative economy. Due to comparatively weak industrial foundations in some ethnic areas, these pathways and approaches are providing employment opportunities, allowing the region to leapfrog industrialization and move into modern service industries.

Second, cultural creativity produces products and services with local characteristics and flavor; ethnicity differentiates culture and plays an important role in this era of global mass production of culture and cultural services, offering new opportunities that are not available in metropolitan centres.

Third and finally, the practice of ethnic cultural creativity aligns with UNESCO's call for protecting intangible cultural heritage and diversity through cultural creativity. The development of grounded ethnic cultural creative industries in Yunnan has definitely promoted the cultural legacy, developed the dissemination of ethnic cultures, advanced their international influence, and enhanced ethnic peoples' self-confidence and affection toward their own culture.

Globalization has occurred at a rapid pace and brought with it development of ethnic cultural creative industries. The successful cases mentioned from Yunnan in this chapter are illustrative and are worthy of further research to probe their multi-layer meanings and values. Even so, while we are at the initial stage of researching Yunnan's ethnic grounded creative industries, it is necessary to draw attention to problems that need further attention in order to bring about sustainable development. We conclude with three areas of concern.

First, the development of Yunnan's ethnic grounded cultural creative industries relies too heavily on a market that is dominated by 'outside' cultural consumers. In other words, the local consumer market does not provide a solid foundation: there are insufficient products and creative services targeted at locals. The ethnic cultural creative industries are primarily centred around tourist areas, tourist cities and well-known sightseeing places. For example, ethnic performances, handicrafts and rituals and festive events are concentrated in Lijiang and Xishuangbanna. Current trends of demassification and diversification in tourist consumption will inevitably lead to changes in the types of ethnic cultural creative activities and services provided. Whether or not Yunnan's creative industries can adjust, innovate and develop remains to be seen.

Second, similarities in products and services represent a serious problem. A reliance on a tourist consumption-oriented market brings with it risks. While some creative products and services have modern, fashionable and scientific designs, most are based on local elements. The weakness is a lack of artistic and cultural-added value. As a consequence the competitive power of products is comparatively weak. Most ethnic song-and-dance programs are performed in certain clubs or bars; these troupes and bands are not able to expand their market influence by touring. Many ethnic creative handicrafts originate in daily lives: they are uncomplicated and are deficient in art, design and handicraft skills, as well as artistry and creativity. Meanwhile, another constraint is the weakness of branding and market presence. Ethnic rituals and festive events also illustrate problems such as a lack of planning and control during the creative process: the essential meaning of the ritual can dissipate due to the pursuit of economic benefits; this in turn can lead to a shortfall in the tourist experience.

Third, in promoting cultural creative industries, the local government aims at achieving economic efficiency in order to promote commercial development in ethnic regions without paying enough attention to the protection and inheritance of ethnic cultural resources. Commercial development not only causes damage to fragile cultural resources but can have negative effects on sustainability. Lijiang Ancient Town, the core of the World Heritage of Naxi Dongba culture, is now a tourist, recreational and commercial centre. It has seen dramatic changes in its traditional way of living. Many of its aboriginal residents have moved from their old town, where they lived for generations. The ancient town's unique cultural value disappears with the loss of its traditional lifestyle. In ethnic regions and historical towns like Dali, Lijiang, Xishuangbanna and Tengchong, tourist real estate projects are emerging; these have led to more congestion, forcing people out of traditional cultural living spaces. The destruction of ethnic traditional historical and cultural spaces results in a disappearance of cultural diversity as well as weakening the developmental roots of ethnic grounded cultural creative industries.

Globalization has been of great benefit. It has developed new spaces and has led to development of Yunnan ethnic grounded creative industries. The foundations, opportunities, and emerging spaces, as well as ideas, thoughts and development paths of the practical cases in this chapter, provide a model for global cultural creative development. In Yunnan the relationships between the 'self' and the 'other', between locality and globalization, between ethnicity and nation, between tradition and modernity, capital and culture, space and ethnic rights, government power and citizens' rights illustrate the vitality of cultural creative industries and their influence on China's ethnic regions.

13. Cultural organizations in China: creating digital platforms for success
Marina Guo

The construction of cultural facilities in China is taking place on an unprecedented scale. As a result of urban planning and urban regeneration strategies, clusters of galleries, museums, theatres and performing arts centres have mushroomed in a short frame of time. In comparison, arts and cultural clusters of the same scale in Europe, such as London's West End, took centuries to form.

The sheer scale and speed of theatre, museum and cultural tourism has surprised the world. Every year approximately 100 museums are built in China. In 2011, the number of newly constructed museums was 386, or approximately one every day. By way of contrast, the peak of the museum construction in the US occurred in the mid-1990s. However, even in the heyday, the US only added between 20 to 40 museums each year. Guo Xiaoling, the curator of the Capital Museum in Beijing believes there is a long way to go if China is to be regarded as a 'strong cultural power' (*wenhua qiangguo*). He says that China needs at least 43,000 more museums before it catches up with the world standard, that is, 21 times the current number.

According to Jeffrey Johnson, director of the China Megacities Lab at Columbia University's School of Architecture:

> China is undoubtedly experiencing both a boom in new museums and popularity. This is a critical moment to assess the museum and its potential role in contemporary China. Is it defined as part of a historical continuum of past museum culture in China or is it a radical break? Are museums in contemporary China more products of a globalized (i.e. Western) consumer culture or are they inventions reflecting local conditions, traditions and desires? (Johnson 2012)

Johnson believes that construction is too fast; at the same time as curators are struggling to collect exhibits, audiences are slow in responding. Johnson believes that many new art museums will go out of business, or open intermittently. Unfortunately, these predictions have been verified by cultural projects in some cities.

Certainly, the feverish cultural construction is a reflection of the phased development of China's cultural and creative industries. Moreover, it is an embodiment of the local implementation of national strategy. Cultural facilities often become iconic landmarks that represent a city's image; of course, they also perform public cultural service functions.

The success of a cultural cluster or art complex lies not in the completion of one or a group of high standard facilities but in how to effectively activate such space, endow it with cultural resonance and vitality, enable its role in economic, social and cultural life, and bring cultural value to the community, even to the city. A potential negative consequence of the large-scale construction of cultural facilities is the imbalance of hard and soft infrastructure: this imbalance can be attributed to three deficiencies: cultural content, art management competency and local cultural consumption. A lack of cultural content leads to operating difficulties of cultural organizations (including venue operation): this deficiency is a stark contrast to the hard infrastructure. Putting more cultural facilities on the plan or into operation means that there is more demand for content; however, China's current 'soft power' in terms of cultural content, art management professionals, and management level lags behind the rapid growth of cultural infrastructure. In time these short-term problems may be resolved along with long-term investment.

The slowness of delivering cultural content constitutes an opportunity for mature foreign cultural organizations. Many are exploring business opportunities in China, hopeful of applying their experience and new technology in design, arts management and creativity. British governmental institutes and industry associations in particular have urged enterprises to participate in China's 'cultural development'. Organizations like UK Trade & Investment (UKTI) and the British Council have contributed to improving international cooperation between China and Britain in the cultural and creative industries. A typical case comes from the northeastern city of Tianjin where a world-class artistic centre in the Binhai New District opened to the public in 2015. The local government commissioned the Lincoln Center (US) to provide consultancy in design, construction, program planning, operation and training. Elsewhere the new West Bund cultural corridor in Shanghai's Xuhui district has drawn attention from design agents, consultancies and media enterprises in China as well as from the US, Britain, Japan and Denmark. Cultural organizations that proactively seek internationalization are more likely to develop and overcome the label 'first-class venue but third-class management'.

Indeed, planning and construction of cultural facilities needs to abandon the orthodox idea of 'hardware first and software second'. The West Kowloon Cultural Zone in Hong Kong provides a case worth studying: M+ is a museum situated in this project, emblematic of Hong Kong's modern visual culture. M+ museum is expected to open in

2017. The government has invested HK$21.6 billion: 15 exhibiting pavilions are planned or under construction. The managing concept of M+ museum is content first and venue second. The M+ cultural organization was established in 2012; it started participating in the design and planning of the museum; in 2013, M+ established an online virtual museum, fostering its audience by 'non-venue operation'; it explored different modes of public engagement and exhibition planning under the absence of a concrete museum. For domestic arts and cultural organizations, this development concept is worth learning.

HIGH-END ART MANAGEMENT TALENT SHORTAGE BECOMES THE BOTTLENECK FOR DEVELOPMENT

The development boom in grand theatres, performing arts centres, museums and art galleries has spread from first- to second- and third-tier cities, following a cluster development model. In Beijing, the Temple of Heaven (Tiantan) and the Bridge of Heaven (Tianqiao) performing arts clusters are currently under construction. Wuhan, Hangzhou, and Zhongshan are establishing museum clusters. Cultural organizations need to recruit many arts managers to operate such venues and facilities. Currently, management talent is not lacking; sometimes supply surpasses demand. However, what is really in short supply are arts management professionals with understanding and competence in both arts and business, as well as international experience. As mentioned above, internationalization in China has become a kind of irreversible momentum. You need to 'go global' and proactively seek international collaborations, not to mention the fact that a lot of foreign institutes and artists are making overtures to China. In fact, economic benefits, social effectiveness and elevation in management brought by international cooperation in all forms are reasons why domestic cultural and arts institutes are reluctant to decline international cooperation. For emerging art forms, such as contemporary art, musicals, modern dance and art works that originate from the West, international standard professionals and management talent are in short supply in China.

Contemporary art museums have a recent history in China and are mainly located in first-tier Chinese cities: overall they account for only 2 per cent of total museums. Despite their small numbers they are seen as indicators of the future of China's museums and galleries. My own research has shown that contemporary art museums and galleries are rapidly becoming display and exchange platforms of contemporary culture by presenting new art forms and new media forms. For this reason curatorship has become one of the most popular majors in recent years. Since it is closely related with art history and aesthetics only a few art universities or art schools can offer such programs. It appears that the occupation of 'curator' will be a rare resource for some time yet: there is evidently a market shortage in professional curators, in terms of both quality and quantity.

A lack of operational experience in international projects is an important factor leading to problems in the performing arts. In January 2014, the musical *Chicago* cancelled its schedules in seven cities in China due to a failure to achieve agreement on technical requirements for performance between the local presenters and rights-owner. Disgruntled audiences sought refunds and the *Chicago China Tour* fizzled out. As a result the Chinese presenters incurred great losses; the US$2 million they paid to the American party for the project order and the upfront fees of RMB 30 million (approximately US$5 million) was lost.[1] The lesson learned is that experienced and internationally informed arts managers are indispensable. Their aesthetic judgment, market evaluation, business negotiation ability, as well as cost control and planning execution all play a vital role in contemporary art management practices.

Developing comprehensive art management talent has always been a concern in academia and the industry. On 22 January 2014, Premier Li Keqiang presided over the standing meeting of the State Council, which confirmed policies and measures to hasten the convergence of cultural creativity, design services and related industries. Among policies and measures, the second one specified:

> . . . implement supporting plan for cultural creative and design service talents. Support new approach of talent development in combining degree-granting education parallels with occupational training, and to integrate creative design with business management, so as to foster more talent. (China State Council Report 2014)

Government, education circles and cultural organizations are attaching growing importance to capability building in arts management. A growing number of universities have offered programs in cultural and art management. Leading industry players such as the National Center for the Performing Arts and the Capital Museum have initiated practice-based arts management training programs.

FUND PREDICAMENT FOR MANAGING CULTURAL FACILITIES

The architectural design and equipment configuration of cultural facilities require certain 'foresight' in order to adapt to the increase in demand over the next decade or even longer. Investment in large cultural projects is normally divided into construction (or restoration) cost and operational cost. The construction cost of a grand theatre or a performing arts centre may be several hundred million RMB, even as much as several billion RMB in some elite projects. Likewise, the construction cost of a gallery or museum is at least tens of millions and sometimes several billion RMB. For instance, the investment in Beichuan National Earthquake Ruins Museum is estimated to be RMB 2.3 billion (approximately US$400 million). As a kind of urban public cultural construction, the investment into such facilities mainly comes from fiscal appropriation. As the cultural development and financial reform deepens, more private funds are being injected into the cultural and creative industries, and thus investment in private museums/galleries and small commercial theatres is increasing substantially these days.

Chinese arts and cultural organizations are mainly state-owned; only a few adopt a mixed system of public-private partnership. Private museums and commercial theatres, however, are purely commercial concerns. When cultural organizations take over the operating and management of a cultural facility, the operational budget becomes a problem urgently in need of a solution. Should a public cultural institution continue to ask for financial support from the government? Or should it seek profit in the market? This is a dilemma because the cultural and arts market is endowed with 'market failure'. Pure commercial pursuit moreover may result in various malpractices leading to a net loss in social welfare. Believers in market failure argue that culture needs intervention.

There is no unified answer to the question of whether or not a cultural institution should be 'close to culture' or 'close to business'. Due to market failure, cultural and arts markets need the 'visible hand' of government to correct an imbalance in the investment structure. Subsidies by government or dedicated financing are a sort of effective remedy for market failure and can ensure the orderly operation of cultural organizations. In early 2008, the National Museum started comprehensive free access. The central government provided RMB 2 billion (approximately US$350 million) annually for this free access; this fiscal investment significantly promoted arts development and urban public culture service.

Developing private museums is an effective supplement to public museums and art galleries. From 1996, when Ma Weidu was granted approval to establish the first private museum in China, the Guanfu Classic Art Museum, to 2009 the number of private museums registered with the cultural heritage sector across the nation has totalled 386.[2] Museums constructed by private investment can be mainly divided into three categories: firstly, those established by cultural relic collectors who invest in venue construction jointly with local government: the collector himself/herself can be therefore 'upgraded' from a collector to the owner of a private museum; secondly, by entrepreneurs whose museum and exhibits can be themed by their own industry; thirdly, by culture lovers who consider operating a private museum as a kind of realization of personal value. However, maintaining a museum is much more difficult than establishing one. After operating for a period of time, private museums often encounter funding shortages; some have had no choice but to close. 'Keeping the museum open by business' is a strategy of many private museums. In other words, some owners support the museum by their real estate businesses and some others by business profits, which are not stable and can be cut off at any time.

CULTURAL ORGANIZATIONS MARCH TOWARD DIGITAL TRANSFORMATION

Nowadays, it is an indisputable fact that 'science and technology are changing our life'. Communication, work and lifestyle are all altered due to scientific and technological innovations. Arts are also changed by science and technology. Digital media technologies have transformed creative industries such as music, publishing, films and TV, as well as design, in a radical way. When interviewed by the Global New Prominent Award of CCTV Finance Channel, Prof. Huang Changyong, the vice-president of Shanghai Theatre Academy and Director of the Metropolitan Culture Audit Center (MCAC), stated,

> In the contemporary information era, science and arts are the two sides of one coin. Be it scientific innovation or art creation, it is inseparable from the creativity of humankind. Apart from this, neither side is rootless. Science and technology are really a huge boost for art creation.

Scientific innovation provides new solutions for creating and transmitting creative content and cultural products. Firstly, artistic creation has a wide variety of possibilities thanks to its facilitation by digital media technology. Digital content from cross-disciplinary cooperation provides diversified options for cultural organizations in developing more innovative cultural products. The digitalization and interactive trends of digital museums, new media art museums, immersive science and technology museums, 3D virtual museums, digital theatres, digital concert halls and other cultural facilities cater for the ever-changing demands of the audience. For any cultural venue, content is ultimately the core equation.

At the end of each year, the Global New Prominent Award of the CCTV finance channel develops an inventory of global scientific and technological achievements of the year. In 2013, besides scientific and technological innovation and design innovation, the Award added a cultural innovation section. *The Sound of the Universe*, jointly presented by the British Royal Philharmonic Orchestra and 59 Production received the CCTV's Cultural Innovation Award. The *Sound of the Universe* is an interactive music installation artwork located in the British Natural History Museum. In addition to the high end theatre sound system and 360° large screen display, the interactive technology enables visitors to participate in 'conducting' and 'instrument playing', by which they gain an immersive music experience, or download apps to learn orchestral music, or learn popular scientific knowledge through interactive images. The cooperation between orchestras, media companies and museums realizes digitalization and collaborative innovation and achieves realistic, immersive and interactive effects.

AUDIENCE INVOLVEMENT WITH NEW MEDIA AND SOCIAL MEDIA

By utilizing new media, interactive design, and other digital media technologies, cultural organizations are able to provide different new experiences in audience engagement and in addition absorb and explore audience involvement by means of non-traditional media platforms. The Pew Research Center in the US issued a report on *New Media and Museum Audience Participation* in 2013 by conducting an online survey of the 1224 arts organizations receiving support from the US National Endowment for the Arts. The survey showed that

> network and social media has already permeated in every aspect (exhibition planning, exhibition, education, charity and activities) of the operation of cultural organizations such as museums, becoming integral constituents to the American art field. A majority of organizations utilize social media for online activities, exhibition promotion, ticketing, fund raising, audience comments and interaction, and it is evident that new media has greatly improved audience involvement and the depth of understanding of museums and their exhibits.

In the US 78 per cent of arts organizations surveyed believed that digital technology is essential to improve audience engagement; 92 per cent of the respondents agreed that 'science and social media allows better participation of audience when visiting the museum and makes the audience structure more diversified' (83 per cent).[3] In fact, opening up new access for participation does not 'dilute' the value of the exhibits. In China, arts and cultural organizations' engagement in the digital technical field is just beginning. However, the growing momentum cannot be taken lightly. Increasingly traditional museums, art galleries, and libraries are actively digitalizing their collections, exhibits and archives. The popularity of new media accelerates exhibition and activity improvement through the Internet and mobile technologies and enables customization in experiences, ticketing and merchandising. Some pioneer cultural institutions provide online education, guide services or convening of online seminars through new media, stimulating audience participation so as to elevate the popularity and service efficiency of the organization. In this way they are better able to cater to the public requirements and better fulfill the mission of cultural organizations.

Social media provide new approaches for audience engagement in the arts. The transformation of the cultural organizations is realized by taking advantage of social media to facilitate an emotional relationship with audience; for instance, to attract audience through social media before, during and after the events. However, as well as positive benefits, there are also negatives in terms of the influence of social media on cultural and arts organizations. The positive functions of social media are mainly evident in drawing more participants to events, thus improving box office and the popularity of the organization; moreover, social media can enable an organization to exchange information with its industry counterparts, patrons and audience, and expand publicity. However, social media increases platform operational costs; this leads to new challenges from public opinion. Members of the public may post negative opinions or complain about the services of an exhibition or performance event. Nevertheless, on the positive side, such opinions may be the force to drive improvement of the services provided. In a wider cultural field, digital heritage, digital culture and digital tourism all need to explore new platforms to facilitate audience participation. In fact, there is still great potential in the media communication sector of the value chain for Chinese culture.

BUSINESS MODEL INNOVATION

Business model innovation in cultural organizations requires new breakthroughs in strategic positioning, core values, and resource management. It is important to cater to unsatisfied demand and realize the 'Blue Ocean' that exceeds existing benefits. This chapter suggests that it is necessary to incorporate cultural facilities into the preliminary stage of urban planning, or to reach an understanding between decision makers (e.g. government cultural departments), investors (e.g. state-owned enterprises) and managers (e.g. cultural organizations) before proceeding with venue restoration. Other opportunities in business model innovation for cultural organizations include reconnecting digital content and audience participation, forming new business arrangements with stakeholders, bringing new value to the audience and generating new sources of revenue.

An example worth considering is the National Theatre in London. Its 50-year celebration in 2013 marked a comprehensive digital transformation due to successful business model innovation. The *NT Live* (National Theatre live) project and *War Horse* toured performances and the copyright revenue accounted for nearly one-third of its total annual income. The live broadcast of the theatre integrated traditional art forms as well as new entertainment forms. The National Theatre paved the way for digital performing arts in the UK with its *NT Live* HD (high definition) screening running in 60 British cinemas and more than 170 foreign cinemas. This case illustrates that seizing the business opportunities brought by digital technologies will not only generate social economic benefits but will also support the transformation of traditional cultural organizations. Live broadcasting is further discussed below.

TRENDS IN INNOVATION-DRIVEN CULTURAL DEVELOPMENT

Cultural organizations need to pay attention to three trends in utilizing scientific and technological innovation to advance cultural development: first, the application of big data in cultural resource management; second, performing arts can be extended from theatre live shows to cinematic broadcasting; and third, mass collaboration can be triggered by the Internet-of-Everything and cloud culture.

Big Data Application

2013 was coined the first year of big data; since then big data analysis has accelerated in the cultural and creative industries. One of the major functions of big data lies in assisting cultural enterprises and arts organizations to 'activate cultural resources', converting assets and artifacts into digital forms. Artworks, exhibits, collections, performance programs, intangible heritage and other historical and cultural resources are digitalized and incorporated into information management systems. Big data technology utilizes data collection, data integration, data mining, smart application and other functions to provide customized services in managing cultural resources.

The big data revolution also helps cultural enterprises to develop their transformation strategies. The Artron Group, headquartered in Shenzhen, used to be a printing company. In the past decade it seized an opportunity in digital media and cultural development, proactively seeking industrial restructuring to shape a unique business model of 'traditional printing + modern IT technology + culture and arts'. In 2013, Artron took a stride to incorporate big data technology in its core strategy by building the 'China Artwork Database' in collaboration with HP. By data collection, mining and application management, it successively launched products including e-publications, online previews of auction and digital antique catalogues. Artron's big data application was extended to artistic creation and research, artwork trading and collection as well as the whole process of the industrial chain. Big data not only helps organizations to better predict the market but spill-over effects of big data analysis benefit arts education and academic research, presenting significant positive externalities.

From Stage to Screens

Following the digitalized transformation in film and TV, radio, publishing and animation, this chapter argues that performing arts will be the next sector experiencing significant digitalization. Specifically, the live performance of music, theatre, dance and other performing arts is becoming live broadcasting in cinemas or on the Internet. In the United States, watching HD opera in the cinema has been popular for some time now. The lifestyle changes in cultural consumption of the global younger generation will rapidly spread to China in the next few years.

Met HD Live is a 21st century pioneering undertaking in the classical arts. It changes the communication form of performing arts, creating a brand new entertainment genre. The Metropolitan Opera House ('the Met') in New York launched its 'HD opera' project in 2006, applying cutting-edge visual and sound technologies in opera performance. Every performance season, the Met provides around 10 operas to millions around the world, who watch the HD operas in cinemas and local theatres, enjoying the aesthetics of this art form at the same time as those sitting in the Metropolitan Opera House. Aside from cinema broadcasting, the Metropolitan Opera House also promotes radio broadcasts, iPod downloads, and Met online video promotions, and organizes free live broadcasting in Times Square and the Lincoln Center. The HD Opera

Table 13.1   Comparison of the digital transformation of well-known performing arts organizations in China and internationally

Content provider	Partner in technical production & distribution	Digital broadcasting platform	Sharing method	Programs introduced by Shanghai Grand Theatre
Metropolitan Opera House	NCM Fathom	Theatre, cinema and Internet	Live broadcasting, prerecording, HD broadcasting	*The Magic Flute* *Turandot* *La Boheme* *The First Emperor* *Madame Butterfly* *AIDA* *Ring of the Nibelungen*
National Theatre London	BY Experience	Theatre, cinema and Internet	Live broadcasting, prerecording, HD broadcasting	*Frankenstein*
Shakespeare's Globe Theatre	Arts Alliance Media	Theatre, cinema and Internet	Live broadcasting, HD broadcasting	None

project of the Metropolitan Opera House has expanded to five continents and has been screened in 1900 cinemas in 60 countries, with audiences up to 10 million as of April 2012. From 2010 to 2012, the income of annual cinema box office was US$60 million, contributing 27 per cent of the total annual income for the Metropolitan Opera House.

Shanghai Grand Theatre was the first domestic arts organization in China to introduce digital performing copyright HD broadcasting. Since August 2011, Shanghai Grand Theatre has introduced seven operas of Met HD Live and one drama, *Frankenstein* from the National Theatre London, attracting large young audiences. This marked the beginning of live screening of internationally produced performing arts into China's domestic theatres.

The digital transformation of the last fortress of the cultural industry, the performing arts, is the next important trend for the convergence of culture and technology. This chapter suggests that the future trend in performing arts will manifest as follows: firstly, value-added digital content will become an important source of revenue with big data analysis playing an important role in audience development; secondly, transmedia digital storytelling will incorporate high technology and new media into every link of the value chain of the performing arts; thirdly, smart trends will occur in cultural venues: digital theatres and digital concert halls will be the future spaces for performing arts, blending real space and virtual space.

MASS COLLABORATION TREND TRIGGERED BY INTERNET OF EVERYTHING AND CLOUD CULTURE

The Internet of Everything (hereafter IoE) will connect everything which has yet to be connected, including humans, data, and processes. IoE is a new representative of next generation scientific development following from Mobile Internet (see chapter 26 by Ren, this volume) and the Internet of Things. Cisco maintains that the next stage of Internet development is the network formed by the integration of human, processes, data and material objects. What the IoE is capable of realizing is not only represented by an increase in the sheer number of connected objects, but also a sharp increase of influential network effects and the ability of each node in the networks to connect 'with everything'. Compared with the traditional Internet or the Internet of Things, IoE enables enterprises, organizations and society to acquire more complete, accurate, timely and valuable information, to downsize operational costs, to increase decision making ability and efficiency, and to improve consumption and life experiences.[4]

To introduce the IoE concept to cultural organizations, it is therefore necessary to establish a 'mass collaboration' model within the framework of cloud culture as the management mechanism; that is, cultural organizations are no longer isolated culture providers or venue suppliers, but a hub connecting cultural production, cultural communication and cultural consumption in the value chain. The cultural resource network will be the 'Internet of everything', connected everywhere, not a simple link on a linear industrial chain. No matter whether this is scientific and technological innovation or cultural innovation, the subjects and objects (users) of the service are human or the society made up of humans. Mass collaboration therefore requires managers of cultural organizations to change their conventional linear thinking. They should establish people-centred behaviour and a society-centred cultural ecology so as to construct a smart network where people-to-people, people and objects, real space and virtual experience, and material and data can coexist, in doing so realize timely, interactive and mobile connectivity between people (audience, consumers etc.), objects (exhibits, artworks, creative products etc.) and spaces (museum, theatre, cultural relics etc.). It is suggested that the competences of a cultural organization will grow according to whether they can connect, integrate and collaborate with various external resources and nodes, thereby creating maximum overall benefits.

CONCLUSION

The French literature master of the 19th century, Flaubert, once said: 'science and arts break up at the foot of the hill but meet again at the peak.' In the course of human progress and history, science and technology have always accompanied the arts. The mission for cultural and arts organization is to provide creation, display and exchange platform for new thinkers, new works and new forms; these are the essence of human wisdom and scientific achievements; they stimulate us to ceaselessly create and innovate; they facilitate the convergence of scientific and technological innovation; and they raise cultural creation to new heights.

NOTES

1. Hu Fang, 'Who can manage the grand theatres?', *China Culture Daily* 7 September 2013.
2. Fang Jiaxi, 'Private museums expect policy breakthrough', *Economic Information Daily* 24 December 2010.
3. Li Huijun, 'US released survey report on new media and audience engagement in museums', *China Culture Daily* 4 February 2013.
4. http://www.ceconline.com/it/ma/8800069526/02/

REFERENCE

Johnson, Jeffrey (2012), 'The museumification of China', *Leap*, 18, available at http://leapleapleap.com/2013/05/the-museumification-of-china/

PART III

TRADITIONAL CULTURAL AND CREATIVE INDUSTRY SECTORS IN FLUX

14. Editor's introduction
Michael Keane

Significant changes have occurred in the past decade in the management of China's media and cultural sectors. Some sectors have resisted structural change but the trend towards commercialization and digitalization is irreversible. The adjective 'traditional' preceding the term cultural and creative industries sectors therefore requires some clarification in an era of convergent media. In the context of the ensuing discussion the term describes well-established cultural pursuits that have been central to social life for decades but which have recently come into the spotlight and are expected to deliver economic dividends; often these are government-funded institutions (*shiye*) as much as enterprise or industry formations (*qiye*).

The 'traditional sectors' addressed in this section are broadcasting (television and radio), film, animation, music and publishing. The most significant change is the marketization and commercialization of cultural production. For instance, the commercial imperative in media production has changed how people work, how funds are allocated to production, and the way that content is regulated; moreover, it has allowed content to reach hitherto unacknowledged audiences. Unquestionably, the rapid ascent of online platforms is challenging the role that these media play in people's daily lives, in particular changing the way that content is distributed and accessed, a theme that is dealt with in considerable depth in the following section. The rise of the market and its complexities offers new opportunities to engage in research into Chinese production culture.

Another important factor that is producing flux, and with it disruption, is the fact that Chinese companies are seeking to export cultural products and services to many parts of the world; tension is understandable because the success of these ventures abroad is constrained by domestic regulatory forces and framed by official perceptions of what is 'good content'. Nevertheless, the requirement that China become a cultural exporter is having noticeable impacts on market activity, stimulating the development of private and semi-private companies and associated content and distribution entities.

In liberal media systems journalists, producers and businesses are accorded considerable autonomy; that is, market activities are not unduly constrained by politics. However, under the cultural system that evolved in the planned economy, media practice was perceived as an injection of propaganda from the Party to the masses. As media channels expanded during the mid-1980s, Mao's famous image of the masses as 'blank sheets of paper' began to change to accept the inevitability of market forces. By the 1990s the speed of reform had increased and as overseas nations looked to penetrate the market, the Chinese government went ahead with a series of reforms in the media and cultural industries, which by 2003 had come under the rubric of the 'reform of the cultural system' (Lee 2000; Zhao 2008; Keane and Sun 2013; Zhang 2011).

The top down model of media regulation through institutions including the Central Propaganda Department (CPD), the State Administration of Radio, Film and TV (SARFT, now SAPPRFT), the Ministry of Culture (MoC) and the State Administration of Industry and Commerce (SAIT) has been the default setting. The Chinese government's attempts to regulate expression make it an easy target for critics.

The first chapter in this section, by Florian Schneider, examines the complexity of cultural regulation as it applies to China's media industries. Schneider makes two observations about the nature of cultural governance: the first is that the role of state and Party has changed, from institutions that govern cultural content in a straight-forward fashion to agencies that now use market mechanisms and soft controls to influence the wider framework in which cultural production takes place. Schneider's second observation is that cultural production involves a wide range of actors in collaborative efforts to produce and disseminate culture. The chapter shows why mass-delivery systems, such as TV broadcasting, play such an important role in the CCP's political communication strategy. The focus of the discussion is how authorities regulate broadcasting and the mechanisms deployed to ensure that audiences are informed while at the same time protected from harmful 'ideologies.' Following this discussion the chapter turns to the collaborative aspect of cultural production in China and the challenge that digital media pose for the Chinese leadership.

The second chapter, by Peichi Chung and Lianyuan Yi, examines the relationship between the Hong Kong film industry and the Mainland in the context of the CEPA (Closer Economic Partner Agreement). In recent years co-produced Hong Kong films have attained commercial success in the Chinese market. The trend points to a new regional influence of Hong Kong cinema, comparable to the success within Asia during the 1970s and 1980s. This chapter focuses on the subversive impact that co-production brings to the history of Hong Kong cinema. It also serves to redefine Hong Kong's status as a cultural production centre that leads the development of film production in Asian popular culture. While much discussion has concentrated on the disappearance of Hong Kong's identity because of the industry's emphasis on reaching into the Chinese market, Chung and Yi review the possibility of Hong Kong's transformation into becoming a global centre of co-production. The chapter analyses political and economic factors that contribute to the particular style of filmmaking in co-produced films. It outlines the regulatory system that creates the particular censorship industry environment for Hong Kong-China co-produced films.

With the general decline of the working environment in the US film industry since the 1990s, and the global industry's transition to digital production, distribution, and exhibition in the early-to-mid-2000s, there has been a sharp diverting of production away from Hollywood toward new centres of transnational cultural production, also known as global media capitals. China (Beijing, Shanghai and many other first and second tier Chinese cities) and indeed South Korea (Seoul and Busan) are now among the growing list of global media capitals into which transnational cultural production is flowing. In particular, China has become the new and largest wild frontier, a stimulating environment where film companies and practitioners are now heading in droves.

With these developments in mind, Yecies' chapter introduces some recent examples of collaboration and technological transfer between the Chinese and Korean film industries; because much of this joint activity has occurred behind the scenes, the sheer volume of these efforts has frequently gone unrecognized. More and more Chinese firms and filmmakers are opening new doors by looking beyond the limitations of the local market to the wider Asian region, especially to Korea, and are thus aspiring to internationalize Chinese cinema. To shed more light on this important and growing trend in international filmmaking, the chapter investigates the increasing levels of co-operation in co-productions and post-production work between China and Korea since the mid-2000s, following a surge in personnel exchange and technological transfer. It explains how a range of international relationships and industry connections is contributing to the consumption strength and expansion of China's domestic market and synergistically transforming the shape and style of Chinese cinema.

One of least performing sectors of Chinese media in terms of international sales is documentary. Yingchi Chu's chapter places the recent commercial documentary *A Bite of China* (*shejian shang de Zhongguo*) within the historical and generic trajectory of the evolution of Chinese documentary filmmaking. Chu discusses the notion of self-hybridization and argues that successful self-hybridization is possible only where a powerful cultural tradition is threatened by the kind of cultural imperialism that is exerted by European and especially US cultural production. In this respect

China is well placed to defend its culture globally by adopting a strategy of self-hybridization. What this means for the new commercial exports, such as *A Bite of China*, is above all two things. One is the use of foreign languages, for instance, imitations of BBC documentary style, aiming to secure the success of Chinese documentaries as export commodities. At the same time, Chinese producers are opting for a deliberate reduction of the intricacies of traditional Chinese culture for ease of cross-cultural consumption. As a result, Chinese cultural products are now increasingly evident in the commercial production of documentaries showcasing China's country, people and culture.

The chapter by Lei, Gorfinkel and Sun examines a largely understudied sector of China's cultural industry – radio broadcasting. The authors show how the radio industry has adapted to shifting social, cultural, political and market demands in Mainland China with a focus on urban- and rural-oriented radio programs. To date limited attention has focused on how media products have constituted and contributed to ongoing urban-rural divides. This chapter makes a contribution to the understanding of China's cultural and creative industries in relation to state policies and commercialization in urban and rural China with a focus on traffic radio, a particular urban-oriented radio genre, and rural radio, illustrated with examples from Beijing Traffic Radio and the Beijing-based national rural channel, The Voice of the Countryside (*xiangcun zhi sheng*) during 2013. The authors argue that while the urban-oriented radio channels focus on establishing radio as a commercial cultural enterprise (*wenhua chanye*), rural-oriented broadcasting has emerged as a result of a push towards creating a non-commercial cultural public service for the masses (*wenhua shiye*). While urban-oriented programs have run as profitable enterprises aiming to capture middle class audiences, for instance aiming to meet the desires of the new population of private car owners, the relative neglect of radio services for rural audiences has led to the state stepping in to create an entirely new nationally run rural channel.

Vicki Ho and Anthony Fung look at the Chinese animation industry as it struggles to compete with restrictions on content and the inroads of foreign animation. Over the last decade, in the wake of the influx and popularity of overseas animation, particularly content accessed through the Internet, Chinese authorities have jumpstarted the domestic animation industry by implementing various support policies in relation mostly to production. Despite some short-term success, these local productions soon fell out of favour with audiences. The fundamental reasons according to Fung and Ho are censorship, unrealistic market goals, and more practically the close connection of animation production with the state which ultimately manages the content and ensures these works constitute propaganda. As local audiences lose interest, they turn to other local or global content online.

Qian Wang and Jeroen de Kloet look at the market for commercial pop music. They identify three interconnected developments that have transformed China's music industry since 2001. First, the purported 'rise of China' that has come with increased self-confidence and different modes of soft power; second, the global crisis, or more specifically shifts within the music industry, partly related to the emergence of digital technologies, which are gradually rendering the CD obsolete and instigating processes of media convergence; and third, processes of intensified globalization and regionalization of the media industries, forging transnational and regional modes of cooperation and feeding into celebrity culture. Wang and de Kloet show how the Chinese music industry has transformed from being a secondary market in East Asia towards becoming the main consumer market. They look at the role of television programmes like *Voice of China*, *I am a Singer* and *Idol*, and their related celebrity culture. These formatted shows have not only changed the business model of the music industry, they also profit from strategic alliances with national media and Internet platforms.

The final chapter in this section, by Eric Hendriks, looks at a traditional industry sector that is finding new ways to diversify. The topic is the burgeoning self-help industry. Although the self-help industry has a centuries-long tradition in the Anglo-American realm, this particular, commercial type of life advice is relatively new in Mainland China, first emerging in the wake of Deng Xiaoping's reforms. Hendriks' chapter outlines the young history of US-style self-help in Mainland China and discusses the glocalized character of Chinese self-help culture. Hendriks examines the structural transformation of the Chinese book market and mass-mediated public sphere that enables and continues to facilitate the prominence of the self-help industry on the Chinese Mainland. Finally, Hendriks sketches self-help's role in public life, which involves touching upon its limited autonomy and weak delineation as a cultural field, its relatively privileged position vis-à-vis institutionalized religion, and its significance as a source of guidance to uprooted individuals chasing after the 'Chinese Dream' in the rat race of China's new market economy.

REFERENCES

Keane, Michael and Wanning Sun (2013), *Chinese Media: Critical Concepts in Media and Cultural Studies*. London: Routledge.

Lee, Chin-Chuan (ed.) (2000), *Money, Power, and Media: Communication Patterns and Bureaucratic Control in Cultural China*. Evanston, IL: Northwestern University Press.
Zhang, Xiaoling (2011), *The Transformation of Political Communication in China: from Propaganda to Hegemony*. Hackensack, NJ: World Scientific.
Zhao, Yuezhi (2008), *Communication in China: Political Economy, Power, and Conflict*. Lanham, MD: Rowman and Littlefield.

15. The cultural governance of mass media in contemporary China
Florian Schneider

INTRODUCTION

The People's Republic of China (PRC) has one of the most carefully regulated media environments in the world. The Chinese state and the ruling Chinese Communist Party (CCP) take an unapologetically authoritarian stance when it comes to controlling the production and flow of culture: for China's political leadership, it is of crucial importance to 'correctly guide public opinion'. This is true for political issues, such as news reporting on sensitive current affairs or international relations, but also for cultural expressions that might constitute 'ideological challenges' to Chinese sovereignty or cultural identity, which the leadership views as matters of 'national security' (Ng 2014).

Foreign media tend to interpret media controls in the PRC as the workings of a monolithic authoritarian apparatus that is trying to win a 'cat and mouse' game (Economist 2013) with the 'forces of freedom of expression' (Sudworth 2013). Such assessments can also be found in academic accounts, where Chinese media workers and government officials are at times seen as 'unapologetic spouters of lies' (He 2008: 38). There is of course much to criticize about censorship and propaganda in the PRC today. However it would be misleading to view such information control solely as top-down acts by the state. The reality of cultural regulations is far more complex, and it is the purpose of this chapter to capture some of this complexity.

In the following I will argue that attempts to regulate culture in China have continuously evolved over the past decades. More specifically, the leadership has adapted its strategy for managing cultural expression to China's changing social, economic, and political environment, and this has had two major effects: the first is that the role of state and Party has changed from institutions that govern cultural content in a straightforward fashion to agencies that now mainly use soft controls and market mechanisms to influence the wider framework in which cultural production takes place; the second is that cultural production involves a wide range of actors in collaborative efforts to produce and disseminate culture.

I will refer to this strategy as 'cultural governance', a term I am borrowing from Michael Shapiro (2004), and which here describes collaborative attempts to regulate society by regulating its cultural parameters.

To illustrate this approach towards mass communication, I take my examples from TV broadcasting, mass-media events and digital media. After a short introduction to the logic behind Chinese cultural controls, I review why mass-delivery systems such as TV broadcasting have played such an important role in the CCP's political communication strategy, and I take a look inside the Party's vast propaganda system. The subsequent section looks at the Chinese state: how exactly do the authorities regulate broadcasting, and what mechanisms do they deploy in their endeavours? The chapter then turns to the collaborative aspect of cultural production in China. In the final part I discuss the challenge that digital media pose for the Chinese leadership. I conclude by arguing that China's media management is likely going to deal with this challenge the same way it has dealt with previous ones: by remaining highly adaptive and creative.

THE LOGIC BEHIND THE PRC'S EVOLVING CULTURAL CONTROLS

To understand what shapes Chinese cultural governance today, we need to view cultural controls in a historical perspective. Censorship and propaganda in the PRC are by no means contemporary phenomena, so we should first travel back into China's past to examine how the leadership's current strategy has evolved from earlier perspectives.

For political leaders in China, it has long been imperative to take charge of political communication and exert interpretive sovereignty over systems of meaning. While this is arguably also true of political communication elsewhere (cf. Callahan 2006), Chinese political thought has placed a particularly high premium on 'cultivating' morally correct conduct. Traditional Chinese thought of the Confucian persuasion, for instance, posits that individuals generally emulate the actions of others, and that the sage ruler consequently needs to set a positive example through superior moral conduct (Munro 1969: 190). Such pre-modern logic later found fruitful ground in the 20th century, when consecutive Chinese leaders fused 'this Confucian belief with the Leninist concept of a vanguard whose task is to enlighten the people and help them to see their own interests' (Zhao 1998: 26). During the Republican era, when the CCP and the rival Nationalist Party (KMT) were vying for power in a China torn by civil war, each side used political rhetoric 'to provide guidance to followers' and create their respective 'ideological regime' (Zarrow 2005: 211).

A particularly ardent supporter of Leninist 'thought reform' (*sixiang gaizao*) was Mao Zedong, who outlined a programme to control cultural representations in his famous speech at Yan'an (Mao 1942). After the CCP had defeated the nationalists and Mao had established the New China in 1949, his programmatic view of culture became a major influence on early PRC politics. Iconic propaganda and appeals to revolutionary role models would later find their most radical interpretations during the early years of the Cultural Revolution, when leaders assigned 'violent meanings to words as part of a political project with devastating psychological and physical consequences' (Mitter 2004: 210).

Despite these consequences, the legacy of Maoist cultural politics remained alive throughout the subsequent decades (Brady 2008: 35–39). The leader generations after Mao held fast to the idea that the Party needed to reform China through 'ideological work': Deng Xiaoping famously argued that propaganda was 'imperative for all revolutionary work'; his successor Jiang Zemin stressed that the media should function as 'the mouthpiece of the Party'; and Hu Jintao was unambiguous about the idea that 'correct guidance of public opinion' was 'beneficial to the Party, the country, and the people' (Zhang 2011: 31). Xi Jinping has recently followed in these footsteps with his campaign to promote the 'Chinese Dream' and through sanctions against media workers and citizen journalists who report too critically about contemporary affairs. The Leninist view of media and culture thus still informs Chinese politics to this day and this is evident from recurring mass campaigns, the continuing use of role models like revolutionary martyr Lei Feng, or the strong belief that the 'quality' (*suzhi*) of citizens should be raised through cultural means (cf. Jacka 2009).

In the post-Mao era, this continuing moralist view of culture has become aligned with increasing awareness among CCP cadres that the Party needs to justify its rule over China to its citizens. For China's leaders, this arguably perennial need came violently to the fore with the collapse of the former Soviet Union and the traumatic events around Tiananmen Square in 1989. The Party has since attempted to improve its political legitimacy by taking a multi-tier approach, which includes political reform and economic development, but also maintaining a strong emphasis on ideology (Shue 2004). As Brady (2008: 1) has pointed out, 'in the post-1989 period, propaganda and thought work have become the very life blood (..) of the Party-State'.

In post-socialist China, the CCP leadership has realized two things: that propaganda is most effective when it is attractive, and that over a billion pairs of eyes possess huge commercial potential. Much like in any other sector of reform-era China, the leadership has consequently been following a dual-track approach. On the one hand, it has updated its management strategy: in this case refining censorship mechanisms and creating increasingly sophisticated propaganda that often resembles advertising or PR. On the other hand, it has opened up the state-dominated media sector to the market, turning China's cultural and creative industries into a pillar of economic success. In 2010 alone, the sector reportedly produced the equivalent of US$172 billion (Chen 2012), which is more than the annual GDP of a small national economy like New Zealand. A defining element in China's media management today is thus the ongoing challenge to balance the bottom line with the Party-line (cf. Zhao 1998, 2008), in other words to guarantee that China's cultural and creative industries succeed commercially whilst producing didactically healthy and politically correct content.

MASS MEDIA AND THEIR ROLE IN CCP PROPAGANDA

Mass communication technologies such as broadcasting have played an important role in this regard. Television in particular appealed to the CCP. As a delivery technology TV broadcasting promised to relay centrally produced messages instantaneously and simultaneously to a vast mass-audience, regardless of people's level of literacy. It was this promise that informed the so-called 'Great Leap of Broadcasting Work' under Mao in the late 1950s, and that led to the establishment of the PRC's first television station in 1958. In those early years, television nevertheless had a hard time competing with cinema or radio, and only privileged cadres owned a TV set. Also, at the time the PRC neither possessed production facilities to create TV content nor the necessary technical expertise to make its Great Leap of Broadcasting a reality (Lull 1991: 20).

It was not until the reform era that the CCP under Deng rediscovered television as a delivery system of information and set in motion a development strategy that would turn television into the most important propaganda method for reaching Chinese households: the authorities made television sets available to the public at subsidized prices, and they encouraged every province and major city, along with many county-level governments, to found their own television stations. By the turn of the millennium, China possessed roughly 2000 such stations (Redl and Simons 2002: 19) and reportedly had a TV penetration rate of about 94 per cent (SARFT 2002).

The state-funded expansion of TV broadcasting has been accompanied by market reforms, and by attempts to carefully adjust the broadcasting and content production sectors (Zhao 1999). Two seemingly contradictory trends in this regard have been the liberalization and simultaneous re-centralization of the burgeoning broadcasting industry. The authorities have on the one hand cut subsidies to TV stations, prompting these state-owned enterprises to adopt professional business models, make their own programming choices, and recoup expenses through advertising sales. On the other hand, the state has dismantled many of the smaller stations and merged others to create a more manageable number of conglomerates (Zhao 2000). Examples include the Shanghai Media Group (SMG), Hunan Broadcasting System (HBS), and the official national broadcaster China Central Television (CCTV). This move to create conglomerates has partially been motivated by commercial concerns, since these large enterprises often incorporate both production and distribution facilities and can therefore profit from economies of scale. At the same time, such institutions are easier to manage, due to the wider reach of their hierarchical structures and the fact that the top officials in charge are also Party officials.

THE CCP PROPAGANDA SYSTEM

This brings me to the complex system of controls that the CCP uses to manage China's mass media. It is important to remember that the Party and the state are separate institutional systems, even if they are often conflated into one 'party-state'. The two systems indeed work in unison, but each has different functions. At the risk of oversimplifying processes that are in reality highly complex, Party institutions are generally responsible for making programmatic and personnel decisions while state institutions are responsible for fleshing out and implementing these decisions. In line with Marxism-Leninism, the CCP sees state institutions as tools that it deploys to manage China's progress along the road to socialism. The state, and consequently its system of state-owned enterprises, is thus subordinate to the Party.

I will return to the state, its administrative organs and its policies in a moment. First, allow me to take a look at the CCP's propaganda system. Contrary to the state and its institutions, which are organized in a fairly transparent fashion and make their decrees publicly available, the intricate workings of the Party's various issue-related political 'systems' (*xitong*) are far murkier. This is also true for the propaganda system. Each of these systems consists of a secretive leadership small group (*lingdao xiaozu*) and sprawling personal networks that crisscross the PRC's state and societal institutions at all levels of administration, making them 'virtually invisible on China's organization charts' (Lieberthal 2004: 233). What happens inside such a xitong is considered internal communication, and what little we know of the propaganda system, we know from personal interviews, leaked memos, leaders' memoires, or from attempts to reverse-engineer the decision-making processes that led to certain regulations or propaganda content. Shambaugh (2007) and Brady (2008) have each provided insightful studies of how the propaganda system is structured, so I will only highlight some of its most important features and explain how the Party system links up with state organizations (see Figure 15.1).

At the top of the propaganda system stands the opaque Central Leadership Small Group on Propaganda and Ideological Work, which is run by one of China's most powerful men: a member of the CCP's Politbureau Standing Committee. During the Hu Jintao administration, the head of this small group was Li Changchun. Since the transition of power to Xi Jinping in 2013, the group has been headed by Liu Yunshan. While the small group decides about major policy directions, the actual administrative centre of the propaganda system is the CCP Propaganda Department (*zhong-gong zhongyang xuanchuanbu*), which is now officially called the 'Publicity Department' to avoid any negative connotations that the word 'propaganda' (*xuanchuan*) might have in foreign languages. This central propaganda department is de facto responsible for the content management of all media outlets, education institutions and cultural organizations in China. Under Hu Jintao it was run by Liu Yunshan, and, after Liu's promotion to head of the small group, the department has come under the purview of his former deputy Liu Qibao.

As is generally the case for the CCP's structure, the relation between Party committee and administrative department is reproduced at lower levels of China's bureaucracy. This means that each province, municipality or autonomous region possesses a propaganda department under its own respective local CCP committee. While these lower-level institutions are beholden to directives from higher levels, they possess considerable autonomy and are responsible for media management in their own geographical locale. In this sense the CCP's cultural governance should not be interpreted as a 'grand strategy' that uniformly affects all parts of Chinese society, but as a loose framework of parameters that local agents implement in ways that suit their respective situations.

This creates highly diverse outcomes, including infamous propaganda blusters of crudely made images or videos that become the laughing-stock on Chinese social media. Examples from 2011 are a CCTV news broadcast that visualized Chinese air force drills by using footage from the Hollywood movie Top Gun, or a poorly edited image that allegedly showed local officials in Sichuan Province inspecting a road – only that the propaganda workers had failed to add the cadres' shadows. However, the CCP's diffuse approach to propaganda also leads to highly sophisticated PR, and events like the Beijing Olympics Opening Ceremony or the Shanghai Expo are testament to this.

How then do Party propaganda departments influence China's cultural spheres? Three mechanisms are noteworthy here (cf. Lieberthal 2004: ch. 7). Firstly, the Party is linked to the state through a system of overlapping responsibilities, which in practice means that many officials on the state side also hold positions on the CCP side of the bureaucracy. This practice of 'interlocking directorates' assures that the top levels of all state organizations (including government agencies, TV stations, and state-run production companies) are staffed by Party cadres. Aside from retaining administrative control of these organs, it allows the Party to streamline communication with the state institutions. Secondly, the Party maintains so-called Party core groups in every major organization in Chinese society, including any private enterprises that are run by Party members. These groups function as personnel departments and also allow leading cadres within an institution to coordinate their work. Finally, through its personnel politics across the state sector, the CCP creates pressure for media workers to conform to the Party-line. As Brady (2006: 63) points out, 'the Central Propaganda Department and its provincial branches have the power to authorise the hiring and firing of senior managers in the media and other propaganda related sectors', regardless of their function, rank or affiliation with the Party. For media workers in China this means that offending Party officials can hamper career advancement, lead to a cut in one's performance-based salary bonuses or can even get the respective employee fired.

STATE REGULATIONS AND CHINA'S MASS MEDIA

As discussed so far, the CCP maintains a range of controls over China's cultural sector, particularly where that sector is state-owned, but it also stays in control of the cultural sphere through the various government agencies that regulate media content (Figure 15.1). For broadcasting, two types of government institutions are important. The first are agencies that govern radio and television directly. Within the central government this task falls mainly to two ministry-level agencies under the PRC's State Council: the Ministry of Information Industries (MII) and the State Administration of Press, Publication, Radio, Film and Television (SAPPRFT), which was created out of the former State Administration of Radio, Film, and Television (SARFT) and the Government Agency of Print and Publication

PARTY-STATE CONTROL

- Interlocking Directorates
- Patronage and Guanxi
- Nomenklatura and Bianzhi
- Party Core Groups
- Direct Information Links

Central CCP Structure

National Party Congress
全国代表大会
(over 2000 representatives)

CCP Central Committee
中央委员会

CCP Politbureau
中央政治局

Politbureau Standing Committee
政治局常务委员会

General Secretary
中书记

CCP Secretariat
中央委员
会书记处

CCP Central Propaganda Department
中共中央宣传部

Central Leadership Small Group on Propaganda & Ideological Work
中央宣传思想工作领导小组

Central State Structure

Premier
国务总理

The State Council
国务院

Other Ministries

MII
工业和信息化部

SAPPRFT
国家新闻出版广电总局
&
SIIO
国家互联网信息办公室

Xinhua News Agency
新华通讯社

CCTV
中央电视台

Broadcasting Sector

State Production Company

Provincial TV Station

Conglomerate

Firm

Firm

Provincial TV Station

State Production Company

Local TV Station

Conglomerate

Firm

Firm

Local TV Station

Production Sector

State Production Company A

State Production Company B

Private Production Company A

Private Production Company B

Guerilla Production Company A

Guerilla Production Company B

PRODUCTION CONTROLS

HARD MECHANISMS
- Company permits
- Production permits
- Distribution permits
- Prime-time regulations

SOFT MECHANISMS
- Market bureaucratism
- Financial interests
- Regime of uncertainty
- Ideology

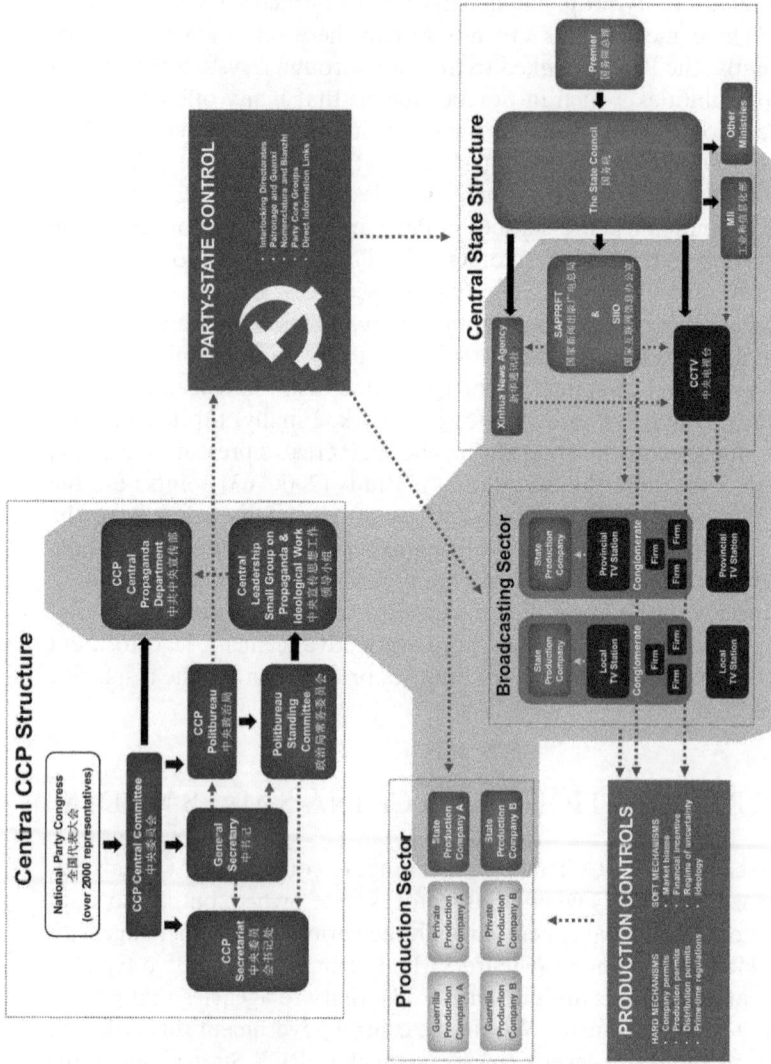

Source: Adapted from Schneider 2012: 170.

Figure 15.1 Government and Party control over China's mass media: the case of television

(GAPP) in 2013. Officially, the MII is in charge of 'planning, administration and technical standards of broadcasting and telecommunication', and the SAPPRFT, like its predecessor the SARFT, 'regulates content, CCTV and the development of the cable system' (Harrison 2002: 170). While the two institutions have a history of overlapping responsibilities that can at times lead to jurisdictional conflicts (Redl and Simons 2002), at the level of content it is the SAPPRFT and its equivalent provincial Bureaus of Radio and Television that govern production and broadcasting. It is also these SAPPRFT institutions that are responsible for censoring TV and print content (for online information, this task falls to the State Internet Information Office, or SIIO). In other words, censorship in China is conducted by ministry-level agencies under the State Council.

The second group of government agencies that shape mass media and broadcasting are those organizations that are indirectly linked either to cultural production or to specific policy issues. These organizations need to provide their consent when content touches on their area of expertise. Most prominently, this includes China's Ministry of Culture, which is responsible for art and literature, cultural events, and national history. However, depending on the topic at hand, it can also include other agencies. For instance, TV programming that deals with China's ethnic minorities would have to be approved by the State Ethnic Affairs Commission, and educational programming for minors would need the approval of the Ministry of Education.

To illustrate how the tools of cultural governance are evolving in China, it helps to take a closer look at the SAPPRFT and how it manages TV broadcasting content. This agency is responsible for regulating the industry by approving which production companies should be established or closed, and it influences TV content through a system of production permits, distribution permits, import controls, broadcasting regulations and censorship committees. Take, for example, the government's system of permits (cf. Schneider 2012: 164–7). Producing TV content in China first requires a production permit (*zhizuo xukezheng*). Large state-owned production companies, which are tied to the Party and have their own censorship mechanisms built into the company structure, receive a general permit for their 'work unit' (*danwei*), which entitles the unit to produce any content it sees fit. Approximately 100 central state agencies possess such a general permit, including state-owned enterprises like the China Teleplay Production Centre, CCTV and the China Film Group Corporation, but also various academic institutions, a number of ministries and the armed forces. The permit allows these agencies to take a leading role in producing content; it is these institutions that are largely responsible for producing official 'main melody' (*zhuxuanlü*) propaganda content. Propaganda programmes that promote the PRC's police, for example, are often directly designed and created by China's Ministry of Public Security whereas content that presents the armed forces in the right light is at times produced by production units within the People's Liberation Army (PLA).

In contrast to these large, state-approved production units, smaller private companies that make up a large part of TV production need to apply for individual permits for each of their projects. This private industry has diversified immensely since the early 2000s, and the SAPPRFT keeps track of the many cultural projects through its system of temporary production permits. Officially, these permits are meant to assure that the market does not become oversaturated with short-term fads that might create investment bubbles (for example when a particularly popular format engenders a large number of copy-cats). They are also meant to make the private companies legally accountable to their investors – an issue that has received increased government attention following a number of industry scandals. Production permits are therefore also an attempt by the authorities to create contractual obligations within the industry. Nevertheless, the implicit threat of denying or revoking production permits creates pressure to conform to official expectations and many private producers keep a careful eye on what the authorities approve of to maximize their sales to the state-owned TV stations.

This sales process is governed through a second kind of permit, the distribution permit (*faxing xukezheng*). To obtain a distribution permit the content producers send their finished product to a local Bureau of Radio and Television where the respective censorship committee checks the content for excessive violence, explicit sexual conduct, references to drugs or gambling and politically sensitive themes like ethnic tensions, CCP legitimacy or China's territorial integrity. If any part of the programme causes offense, the censorship committee will inform the production company of its concerns and provide time for revising and resubmitting the product. In practice, producers often coordinate their work with the censors from the very start of the production process to avoid costly delays at the distribution stage.

Overall, Chinese distribution controls are highly 'localized'. Take, for example, the case of popular TV dramas (Schneider 2012): due to the volume of content that is today produced in China (tens of thousands of hours), the pragmatic approach has been to allow distribution if any one of the local Bureaus of Radio and Television have approved a programme. This means that production companies submit potentially controversial programmes repeatedly to different local bureaus until one of them approves their series. What ends up being broadcast is thus often a matter of negotiation rather than of top-down directives.

In addition to its system of permits, the SAPPRFT counts on market dynamics to create incentives for wholesome and inoffensive content, and it manipulates these market dynamics to achieve the desired result. Since China possesses a large number of private producers who need to sell to a relatively small number of state-run TV stations, the market is highly competitive on the supply-side. This market bias works in favour of the SAPPRFT and its preferred indirect approach to governing. For instance, the agency issues general guidelines for what can and cannot be aired between seven and ten p.m., which in Chinese is known as the 'Golden Time' (*huangjin shijian*). With TV stations depending on prime-time programming for their advertising profits, the agency is able to influence the demand for certain genres and formats. The SAPPRFT has thus at times forbidden crime dramas or imperial-era court dramas during prime time and then relied on the TV stations to relay this decision to producers through the market.

This system of market incentives and government checks works very effectively: the SAPPRFT and its subordinate agencies approve most of the TV content that passes through the system and it is very rare that a programme or show starts airing on Chinese television only to be banned later. Such cases exist, but they are detrimental to the authorities, since they draw unwanted attention to the issues the CCP considers 'sensitive'. Rather than letting the situation escalate, the system therefore prompts those who wish to be part of China's lucrative mass-media industry to cooperate with the authorities and self-censor their content before it ever reaches the screen (cf. Hassid 2008).

CULTURAL GOVERNANCE AND SOFT POWER: COLLABORATIVE EFFORTS TO MANAGE PUBLIC OPINION

China's authorities rely heavily on private actors in a liberalized market to create cultural content. This is true not only for the SAPPRFT, but for the PRC's cultural governance approach as a whole. The Party and the state try to solicit the support of media professionals rather than coercing them, and in many cases cultural production is either created collaboratively between public and private actors or is 'outsourced' by the state to private specialists. For the Party, such collaborations are beneficial in several ways. They bring together expertise that CCP propaganda workers do not necessarily possess, they legitimate cultural production by involving a wide range of actors, and they promise to turn a profit. Most importantly: they create content that appeals to audiences in ways that traditional propaganda may not.

It would therefore be misleading to refer to the kind of cultural production that involves public and private interests as 'propaganda', even though such productions often reproduce what we might call dominant discourses. These discourses are not necessarily the outcome of explicit CCP intervention. Good examples are popular TV productions, for example historical epics or teen dramas, which tend to create visions of history and contemporary society that are compatible with (though not necessarily identical to) the CCP's interpretations. The CCP is exceedingly successful at aligning the interests of screen writers, directors, producers, marketing experts, programming directors, and other cultural producers with its own: creating fun yet 'healthy' content that sells.

This logic also extends to foreign audiences, for which the CCP propaganda system reserves a separate branch, replete with its own administrative institutions (cf. Brady 2008: 156). China's foreign public relations have the goal to improve China's image abroad, and as such generally avoid content that might offend audiences by being too obviously 'propagandistic'. Take the example of the Beijing Olympics Opening Ceremony, which was arguably a milestone in Chinese PR. To appeal to both domestic and foreign audiences, the Party outsourced the ceremony to a committee under the auspice of the Ministry of Culture that included non-Party members from the PR and advertising industries. The committee members were given the general goal to brand the Chinese nation as a harmonious and civilized power. They then embarked on a four-year endeavour that involved commissioning thirteen proposals on how to implement the project, transferring the practical decisions to a director's team under the leadership of renowned film-maker Zhang Yimou, and coordinating the rehearsal with numerous state agencies, Party officials, and entrepreneurs. Before the actual performance, the ceremony was further revised, following test-screenings before officials, artists, critics, intellectuals, groups of 'common people' (*laobaixing*) and foreign cultural advisors. When the world tuned in for the spectacular show on 8 August 2008, no aspect of the mega-event had been left to chance, and yet no state or Party institution was singularly responsible for the content.

Other good examples include the foreign channels of CCTV or China Radio International as well as the English-language version of China's official news agency Xinhua. These state-run media outlets attempt to provide the kind of open discussion that they believe appeals to audiences socialized through foreign media systems, while still framing the issues to tell the official Chinese side of the respective story. In fact, these channels often allow critical discussion of topics that would be strictly regulated within the PRC, such as the situation in Tibet or Xinjiang. China's Ministry of Culture tends to take a similar stance towards academic collaboration and cultural exchange, and its Confucius Institutes often invite foreign scholars critical of the CCP to give lectures to foreign audiences. All of these practices suggest that China's leadership has come to a similar conclusion as Joseph Nye, who has famously argued that states need to pay attention to their 'soft power'. As Nye has pointed out, such attempts are unlikely to succeed if they are engineered explicitly by the state – in Nye's words (2011: 83): 'the best propaganda is not propaganda'. As far as its foreign PR is concerned, the CCP seems to try and take this advice to heart.

MASS MEDIA AND THE DIGITAL CHALLENGE

The CCP has been very successful in establishing its cultural hegemony across China's media system, often through negotiation with and tacit consent from Chinese media workers (Zhang 2011). However, the CCP's cultural governance approach is very much tailored to a world of mass media, where a small number of professional media outlets broadcast their authoritative messages to a vast audience through delivery technologies that can be monitored by the state. The authorities have adapted to changes in this media environment, for instance by making use of soft controls, but these adaptations are informed by an understanding of media and culture that reflects the realities of 20th century mass communication. China's cultural governance is built around a paradigm of one-to-many communication, and this paradigm is currently confronted with a series of challenges from the many-to-many communication patterns that digital media increasingly afford their users.

These challenges affect both the production and the dissemination of culture. On the dissemination side, digital media make it possible to quickly copy content and spread it almost instantaneously through non-hierarchical, diffuse communication networks. On the production side, Chinese Internet users are highly adept at manipulating cultural templates and creating user-generated content, and they consequently pose a real competition to professional media workers. Since Internet users are neither tied into the CCP's propaganda system nor motivated by the kind of commercial incentives that govern China's professional cultural industries, their activities do not necessarily lend themselves to the kind of cultural governance mechanisms that have proven effective in the past.

How then has the leadership been dealing with these challenges? Overall, the authorities have translated their strategy for mass-media management to China's digital networks and this is visible in the State Council's programmatic 2010 White Paper on the role that the Internet should play in China. According to the document (Information Office

2010), the purpose of the Internet is to spread 'China's splendid national culture', 'publicize government information', and help 'the government get to know the people's wishes'. In other words, the 2010 roadmap for China's Internet management is an extension of the CCP's existing Leninist ideology of how to think about information. The paper's emphasis is consequently on national development, cultural security, and social stability.

The resulting authoritarian model of information management includes a range of coercive mechanisms, such as blocking access to webpages, removing online posts or arresting contentious bloggers (cf. Deibert et al. 2010: 449–87), but these hard controls are deployed inconsistently by local authorities (Wright 2014) and are again augmented by a range of soft measures. For instance, the authorities attempt to reproduce the kind of commercial conglomeration that has served them so well in the mass-media sector. On China's web, the major sources of information are websites either by established news organizations like the People's Daily Group, Xinhua.net, and the Nanfang Group, or large accredited enterprises like Tianya, Sohu, Sina or Caixin. While these latter organizations are private businesses, they are nevertheless legally liable for the content on their websites and are consequently under pressure to self-censor and to manage user content. A particularly interesting case is the popular independent news service Caixin, which is known for its investigative journalism. In late 2013, state-backed China Media Capital bought a major stake in the company, bringing it officially under the leadership of the same manager who also heads the Shanghai Media Group (Frater 2013). Whether this move will affect Caixin's independence was not clear at the time of writing, but such financial manoeuvres at the very least suggest that the authorities continue to experiment with ownership structures to manage China's media.

The authorities seem to follow a similar centralization strategy when it comes to social media. The state blocks foreign social networking and media sharing services such as Facebook, YouTube and Twitter, and instead nurtures private Chinese enterprises that develop local alternatives. Examples include the social media platform Renren, the video hosting service Youku Tudou, the microblogging service Sina Weibo, and Tencent's mobile messaging service WeChat. These various services provide spaces for diverse cultural exchange and political dissent (cf. Herold and Marolt 2011; Yang 2009; Zheng 2008), but they nevertheless depend on the state for their licencing and are consequently subject to PRC media controls.

For the Chinese state this arrangement is again doubly advantageous since it creates strong, internationally competitive champions of industry while allowing domestic discussions to take place in walled gardens that can be monitored and censored for unwanted content. That the authorities remain innovative and adaptable when it comes to managing digital culture is apparent from the campaigns against 'online rumours' that have characterized cultural governance under Xi Jinping's leadership (cf. Kaiman 2013): the authorities have been experimenting with various mechanisms to curb the spread of content through China's digital networks, and this has included mandatory real name registrations and sanctions for inappropriate tweets.

The degree to which the CCP and the Chinese state have been able to rein in discussions in digital China demonstrates that views of the Internet as a motor of political change may be overly optimistic. The Chinese authorities are constantly refining their technical, economic, and legal toolset to reshape digital China in the image of the PRC's mass-media system. Contrary to John Gilmore's argument that 'the Net interprets censorship as damage and routes around it', China's censorship regime has been fairly effective at managing Chinese digital spheres.

CONCLUSION

In this chapter I have argued that managing cultural expressions across different media in China is a collaborative effort. This effort leads to highly diverse cultural content, but it also provides the authorities with the means to set certain parameters within which other actors then manage their own conduct. The combination of these measures makes for a relatively effective system, which only rarely has to actively deploy 'hard' measures to censor content, and which can largely rely on its 'soft' mechanisms to assure compliance. The CCP today tries to avoid coercive top-down interventions and crude propaganda. Instead, it takes on a leadership role in China's cultural and creative industries and 'educates, informs, persuades, and discourages' China's pluralist and media-savvy citizens (Zhang 2011). This is what allows the CCP to retain control over an increasingly complex system of cultural production and 'guide public opinion'.

The issue with this model is not whether or not it works, but what it costs. I am not referring simply to the large sum of money that the Chinese government spends annually on domestic security measures, which include censorship efforts (Reuters 2012). More importantly, by applying a mass-media rationale to digital communication, the Chinese authorities are trying to buy social stability at the price of potential innovation and creativity. We should of course be wary of overemphasizing the novelty of digital media, but information and communication technologies such as mobile phones, cheap computers and the infrastructure of the net afford users with ways to engage culturally that are arguably different from established mass media and their broadcasting logic. As Benkler (2006: 272) has shown, the major economic benefit of digital connectivity is that individuals are no longer 'consumers and passive spectators', but can become 'creators and primary subjects' who exchange their innovative user-generated content freely.

This potentially beneficial effect, however, is reduced when users only access digital networks to retrieve vetted information without sharing controversial ideas because they fear repercussions. In other words, by restricting the 'noise' that accompanies networked communication, the authorities are also restricting the emergent properties of networks, which are precisely the properties that produce serendipitous innovations. This should be a major concern to the PRC's State Council, which co-produced a 2013 report with the World Bank on China's economic future. The report lists innovation and creativity as crucial ingredients for turning the PRC into a high-income country (World Bank 2013).

The PRC's cultural policies thus remain torn between the conflicting goals of social control and open knowledge exchange. As long as the priority remains with the former, the Party will continue to pay a high price for its cultural governance model. However, it should also be pointed out that the Chinese leadership recognizes the need to create a 'knowledge economy', and that many of the private enterprises it collaborates with keep re-negotiating the boundaries of media controls in China. To give an example, in early 2014 the company behind the popular app WeChat publicly criticized China's domestic censorship practices for injuring its user-base abroad. Such conflicts of interest between public and private actors are characteristic of collaborative governance approaches, but judging by the adaptability of the CCP and the Chinese state, it seems reasonable to assume that the authorities will continue to refine their cultural governance approach to bring digital communication into the fold of CCP management without alienating business elites. After all, the Party considers it its historical obligation to both 'correctly guide public opinion' and strengthen China's economy. Its leadership is painfully aware that squaring this circle of political and economic interests is very much a matter of political survival.

REFERENCES

Benkler, Yochai (2006), *The Wealth of Networks – How Social Production Transforms Markets and Freedom*. New Haven and London: Yale University Press.

Brady, Anne-Marie (2006), 'Guiding hand: the role of the CCP Central Propaganda Department in the current era', *Westminster Papers in Communication and Culture* **3** (1): 58–77.

Brady, Anne-Marie (2008), *Marketing Dictatorship – Propaganda and Thought Work in Contemporary China*. Plymouth: Rowman & Littlefield.

Callahan, William A. (2006), *Cultural Governance and Resistance in Pacific Asia*. Abingdon and New York: Routledge.

Chen, Keyu (2012), 'Culture is new growth source', *China Daily* 10 January, retrieved 19 March 2014 from http://www.chinadaily.com.cn/business/2012-01/10/content_14412469. htm.

Deibert, Ronald, John Palfrey, Rafal Rohozinski, and Jonathan Zittrain (eds.) (2010), *Access Controlled – The Shaping of Power, Rights, and Rule in Cyberspace*. Cambridge MA and London: MIT Press.

Economist (2013), 'The machinery of control: cat and mouse', *Economist Special Report: China and the Internet* 6 April, retrieved 19 March 2014 from http://www.economist.com/news/ special-report/21574629-how-china-makes-sure-its-internet-abides-rules-cat-and-mouse.

Frater, Patrick (2013), 'Li Ruigang's CMC buys stake in Caixin Media', *Variety* 19 December, retrieved 19 March 2014 from http://variety.com/2013/biz/news/li-ruigangs-cmc-buys-stake-in-caixin-media-1200978643/.

Harrison, Mark (2002), 'Satellite and cable platforms: development and content', in Stephanie Hemelryk Donald, Michael Keane, and Hong Yin (eds.), *Media in China – Consumption, Content and Crisis*. London and New York: RoutledgeCurzon, pp. 167–78.

Hassid, Jonathan (2008), 'Controlling the Chinese media – an uncertain business', *Asian Survey* **48** (3): 414–30.

He, Qinglian (2008), *The Fog of Censorship: Media Control in China*. New York: Human Rights in China.

Herold, David K., and Peter Marolt (eds.) (2011), *Online Society in China: Creating, Celebrating and Instrumentalising the Online Carnival*. Abingdon: Routledge.

Information Office of the State Council of the People's Republic of China (2010), 'The Internet in China', 8 June, retrieved 19 March 2014 from http://www.china.org.cn/government/whitepaper/node_7093508.htm.

Jacka, Tamara (2009), 'Cultivating citizens: suzhi (quality) discourse in the PRC', *Positions* **17** (3): 523–35.

Kaiman, Jonathan (2013), 'China cracks down on social media with threat of jail for "online rumours"', *The Guardian* 10 September, retrieved 19 March 2014 from http://www.theguardian.com/world/2013/sep/10/china-social-media-jail-rumours.

Lieberthal, Kenneth (2004), *Governing China – From Revolution through Reform (2nd edn)*. New York and London: W.W. Norton.

Lull, James (1991), *China Turned On: Television, Reform and Resistance*. London and New York: Routledge.

Mao, Zedong (1942), zai Yan'an wenyi zuotanhuishang de jianghua ('Talks at the Yan'an Forum on Literature and Art'). Speech held in Yan'an on 23 May 1942, retrieved 19 March 2014 from http://news.xinhuanet.com/ziliao/2004-06/24/content_1545090.htm.

Mitter, Rana (2004), *A Bitter Revolution: China's Struggle with the Modern World*. Oxford: Oxford University Press.

Munro, Donald J. (1969), *The Concept of Man in Early China*. Stanford: Stanford University Press.

Ng, Teddy (2014), '"Cultural threats" among five focuses of new national security panel, Colonel says', *South China Morning Post* 14 January, retrieved 19 March 2014 from: http://www.scmp.com/news/china/article/1404926/cultural-threats-among-five-focuses-new-national-security-panel-colonel.

Nye, Joseph S. (2011), *The Future of Power*. New York and Philadelphia: Public Affairs.

Redl, Anke, and Rowan Simons, (2002), 'Chinese media – one channel, two systems', in Stephanie Hemelryk Donald, Michael Keane, and Hong Yin (eds.), *Media in China – Consumption, Content and Crisis*. London & New York: RoutledgeCurzon, pp. 18–27.

Reuters (2012), 'China domestic security spending rises to $111 billion'. Retrieved 19 March 2014 from http://www.reuters.com/article/2012/03/05/us-china-parliament-security-idUSTRE82403J20120305.

SARFT (2002), *shiye fazhan, 2002 nian tongji* (*Enterprise Development, 2002 Statistics*), Beijing: SARFT. Retrieved 15 May 2006 from http://www.sarft.gov.cn/manage/publish-file/51/1095.html.

Schneider, Florian (2012), *Visual Political Communication in Popular Chinese Television Series*. Leiden and Boston: Brill.

Shambaugh, David (2007), 'China's propaganda system: institutions, process, and efficacy', *China Journal* **57** (January): 25–60.

Shapiro, Michael J. (2004), *Methods and Nations – Cultural Governance and the Indigenous Subject*. New York and London: Routledge.

Shue, Vivienne (2004), 'Legitimacy crisis in China?', in Peter Hays Gries and Stanley Rosen (eds.), *State and Society in 21st-Century China: Crisis, Contention, and Legitimation*. New York and London: RoutledgeCurzon, pp. 24–49.

Sudworth, John (2013), 'Chinese web activists see new pressure from censors', BBC Online 17 May, retrieved 19 March 2014 from http://www.bbc.com/news/world-asia-china-22566821.

World Bank (2013), *China 2030 – Building a Modern, Harmonious, and Creative Society*. Retrieved 19 March 2014 from: http://www.worldbank.org/content/dam/Worldbank/document/China-2030-complete.pdf.

Wright, Joss (2014), 'Regional variation in Chinese internet filtering', *Information, Communication & Society* **17** (1): 121–141.

Yang, Guobin (2009), *The Power of the Internet in China – Citizen Activism Online*. New York: Columbia University Press.

Zarrow, Peter (2005), *China in War and Revolution 1895–1949*. London and New York: Routledge.

Zhang, Xiaoling (2011), *The Transformation of Political Communication in China – From Propaganda to Hegemony*. Singapore: World Scientific Publishing.

Zhao, Yuezhi (1998), *Media, Market, and Democracy in China: Between the Party Line and the Bottom Line*. Urbana and Chicago, IL: University of Illinois Press.

Zhao, Bin (1999), 'Mouthpiece or money-spinner? The double life of Chinese television in the late 1990s', *International Journal of Cultural Studies* **2** (3): 291–305.

Zhao, Yuezhi (2000), 'From commercialization to conglomeration: the transformation of the Chinese press within the orbit of the Party State', *Journal of Communication* **50** (2): 3–26.

Zhao, Yuezhi (2008), *Communication in China – Political Economy, Power, and Conflict*. Lanham, MD: Rowman & Littlefield.

Zheng, Yongnian (2008), *Technological Empowerment – The Internet, State, and Society in China*. Stanford: Stanford University Press.

16. The regionalization of co-production in the film industries of Hong Kong SAR and Mainland China

Peichi Chung and Lianyuan Yi

INTRODUCTION

Since 1997, the Hong Kong film industry has shifted emphasis from local production to offshore co-production in Mainland China. The number of films produced in Hong Kong decreased – from 94 films in 1997 to only 42 in 2013 (Poon 2014). The catalyst was the enactment of the Mainland and Hong Kong Closer Economic Partnership Agreement (hereafter the CEPA) signed in 2003. The CEPA is essentially a treaty that allows Hong Kong products, companies and residents preferential access to the Mainland market.[1] Since that time the Hong Kong film industry has undergone a process of Sinicization (Lie 2014; Chung 2012b), which is evident in the growing cross-border trade relations between the two sides. In 2015, five co-produced movies, *zhuo yao ji* (*Monster Hunt*, 2015), *xiyou: xiangmo pian* (*Journey to the West: Conquering the Demons*, 2013), *xiyouji zhi danao tiangong* (*The Monkey King*, 2014), *Aomen fengyun 2* (*The Man from Macau II*, 2015), *zhiqu weihushan* (*The Taking of Tiger Mountain*, 2014), *shier shengxiao* (*CZ12*, 2012) topped the list of the top ten most profitable 'Chinese movies' of all time in the Mainland market. The theatrical success of these films on the Mainland, however, has not translated into the same level of box office performance in Hong Kong.

The trend toward co-production reflects uncertainty about the current status of the Hong Kong film industry. From the Mainland perspective, Hong Kong's co-production ambitions have a positive influence on the structure of the Chinese film industry (Zhan 2013). Echoing this point, Davis (2010) points out that China's film industry has enjoyed a boom in production, investment and international participation, particularly as many Hong Kong enterprises are in hot pursuit of joint ventures in order to enter the Chinese market.

Meanwhile co-production has sparked intense debate in Hong Kong about the marginalization of the Hong Kong film industry's achievements. Up until the mid-1990s Hong Kong was regarded as the 'Hollywood of the East' because of its central position in Asian filmmaking. Many filmmakers, academics and observers argue that since 1997, Sinicization (that is, the increasing dominance of Chinese-style stories among Hong Kong co-produced films) is contributing to the disappearance of 'Hong Kong elements'. A pragmatic response therefore is to release two copies of films, creating an alternative version when films do not pass the censorship gauntlet in the Mainland. According to He (2010) filmmakers can maintain aesthetic autonomy. With HK filmmakers becoming more familiar with China's film review process this strategy has increased. In the case of *qieting fengyun* (*Overheard*, 2009), a film about internal politics of police corruption, two copies were distributed; one of these included a final anti-corruption scene to appease Mainland officials. In 2011, a sequel, *qieting fengyun 2* (*Overheard 2*, 2011) managed to circumvent cuts during the censorship review: but only one copy was distributed. While it might be suggested that the filmmaker achieved creative freedom, more likely this was a case of understanding the limits.

In this chapter we examine the predicament that the Hong Kong film industry encounters because of its unavoidable integration with the Mainland. We look at how Hong Kong subjectivity is impacted through co-production, drawing on the framework of Asian film regionalization. The argument is that Hong Kong-PRC film co-production is characteristic of an emerging China-centric regionalism in the Asian filmmaking business. In some respects this regionalism resembles the runaway productions that transpired when Hollywood internationalized much of its global production to the world market in the 1980s (Christopherson 2005), sometimes referred to as the 'new international division of cultural labour' (Miller et al. 2005). The difference between Hong Kong and Hollywood, however, lies in the way in which the new 'runaways' treat political and cultural issues. The Sinicization of Hong Kong films signifies that Hong Kong sees its market as the sub-region of China, in turn demonstrating the intra-Asian character of Asian regionalism.

In this chapter we explain how the CEPA has impacted on the two industries (Mainland and Hong Kong) and more specifically, its impact on creative freedom since 2003. We conclude by discussing some alternative filmmaking strategies that could potentially resituate Hong Kong as a hub within an extended Asian market while maintaining the CEPA framework of cooperation between Hong Kong and China's film industry.

HONG KONG FILM AND ASIAN FILM REGIONALIZATION

A number of authors have analysed co-production as a filmmaking strategy adopted by Hong Kong filmmakers in pursuit of pan-Asian production projects (Chan 2011; Leung 2013; Teo 2008). Due to political, geographical and cultural realities, Hong Kong film has always been seen as crossover cinema. Pugsley (2013) argues that Hong Kong cinema draws from an extended intergenerational interaction with Japanese, European and Hollywood cinematic styles. This 'de-localization' makes it difficult to definitively categorize Hong Kong cinema within the conceptual framework of 'national cinema' (Chan 2011). For instance, Hong Kong filmmakers engage in various forms of regional co-production. Filmmaker Stephen Chow worked with Thailand GTH director Banjong Pisanthanakun on a Thai-China thriller movie. *Xianggang zai* (*Aberdeen*, 2014) is a Hong Kong film co-produced with five other countries (including the PRC); it centres on local storytelling. Hong Kong's history as a British colony and its current status as a Special Administration Region (SAR) of the People's Republic of China situates its cinema as a historically boundary-crossing industry (ibid.).

The chapter focuses on co-productions, specifically looking at how Hong Kong filmmakers are making films for a Chinese market and the learning processes that are involved in this transition. Leung (2013) believes that Hong Kong filmmakers encounter a 'China complex' whenever they address capitalist Hong Kong and socialist China in their storytelling. Adjusting to a Chinese environment, some filmmakers will self-censor in order to pass the film board review required by the State Administration of Press, Publication, Radio, Film, and Television (SAPPRFT). Some choose to adopt multi-layered tactics, such as circulating pirated DVDs in order to evade 'ideological purification'. Other filmmakers contract with Hong Kong producers; in disengaging with the Sinicization movement, they produce low-budget films for the local Hong Kong market (Leung 2013).

In *East Asian Screen Industries*, Davis and Yeh (2008) categorize Hong Kong co-production into five clusters: Euro-Asian alliances, intra-Asian co-producers, pan-Chinese co-producers, pan-Asian program packagers and Hollywood-Asia ventures. These five clusters represent a form of localism that East Asian film industries practice in order to nurture production and connect specific filmmaking resources to given markets. According to Davis and Yeh, each co-production cluster reflects a different type of organizational activity. Among these organizational groups, pan-Chinese co-producers most actively support the funding and production of Chinese-language films. The companies that engage in Hong Kong-China co-production include Media Asia, Empire Motion Pictures, Sil-Metropole Organization, Universe Entertainment, MVP Company Ltd, Pegasus Motion Pictures and Film Workshop Company. These companies initially developed their businesses in Hong Kong, extending gradually into co-production and now excel on the Chinese market. Filmmakers who 'go north' to make co-produced movies look to achieve market success in China by producing mega-budget movies that fit the popular tastes of the film-going public in the genres of action, romance, drama and comedy (Leung, 2013). The Emperor Entertainment Group, in particular, has formed an alliance with the second largest film group in China, Shanghai Film Group, to set up SFG Emperor Culture Development, in this way expanding local business.

Theoretically, the analysis of Sinicization in Hong Kong film production refines Asian regionalization in two ways. First, it updates existing concepts of film regionalization in Chinese-language communities. Since the 1970s, Hong Kong's film industry has maintained a global identity as a transnational Chinese cinema serving overseas Chinese communities (Hau and Shiraishi 2013). From the perspective of pan-Asian regional geopolitics, Cantonese popular culture served as an early form of regional productivity emerging from 'East Asia'. Hong Kong also became a hub in a multi-sited network of Mandarin-language films (ibid.). Within these milieus Hong Kong filmmakers tended to deploy a cosmopolitan representation of Hong Kong to establish 'location identification' with the predominantly urban, transnational Chinese audiences that make up the world of Sinophone cinema (Donald 2005).

In addition, the transnational connections that unite cultural industries in the geographic regions of Taiwan, PR China, Hong Kong and the Chinese communities of Southeast Asia collectively form what Chua (2001) calls 'Pop Culture China', extending into other parts of Southeast Asia. To be specific, the Pang Brothers' collaboration with Thailand's film industry and the Shaw Brothers' joint venture with a Malaysian film distribution company, Astro, reveals Hong Kong's central place in the regional geography of filmmaking since the 1970s. However, this form of Asian regionalism is a result of the reworking of pre-existing, complex transregional production and consumption relationships within Hong Kong's early pan-Asian network (see Curtin 2007). Thanks to the recent spate of co-productions with Mainland China, Hong Kong's film industry has undergone a transition that shows its ability to reinvent itself; it is making films that successfully circulate beyond its original sphere of influence; it is entering into new niche markets in China, despite some losses of overseas markets in Taiwan and Southeast Asia (Hau and Shiraishi 2013).

The second theoretical consideration points to how Sinicization is functioning as a new model of hybridization in inter-Asian cultural flows. In addition to Hong Kong popular culture, other forms of East Asian film regionalization, including Japanese and Korean, have reached across borders to achieve cosmopolitan success (Chua 2008). Asian filmmakers sometimes borrow ideas, themes and nuances that are regionally popular when they produce their own versions of popular films. It is believed that such elements in stories are more likely to bring domestic box office success; for instance, the remake of the Hong Kong movie *genzong* (*Eye in the Sky*, 2007), into the Korean action movie, *Cold Eyes* (2013), shows the influence of Hong Kong cinema in the popular filmmaking of South Korean cinema.

This extended level of hybridization diversifies inter-Asian regional flows. Formerly these flows emphasized popular culture originating from the production centres of Hong Kong, Japan and Korea. Michael Curtin (2011) uses the idea of 'socio-cultural variation' to explain the local capability of media capitals such as Hong Kong. Essentially this means that Hong Kong has been able to diversify its film-making. In establishing itself as a 'media capital', Hong Kong became a sender of diverse content that absorbed Asian elements (ibid., p. 551). Previously, Asian popular cultures grew within a national context before extending to regionalization. In addition to this, and 'creative migration', agglomeration of media production capacity enables a location to export media content outside its national market. Japanese content producers have established a pan-Asian cross-cultural reach; this is enabled by the 'cute' culture of much Japanese anime and manga. Regionally circulated animation, comic books and live-action films collectively register a particular cultural signal that Iwabuchi (2002) considers 'odourless' but uniquely Japanese. In addition, the Japanese government now adopts a 'cool' Japan strategy to promote its content industry (Choo 2012). Similarly, the Korean wave extends pan-Asian regionalization as part of a national soft power strategy. The Korean government's film import quota system provided industrial support, allowing Korean film to establish a domestic market presence. The protectionist film policy allowed Korean film (and other pop culture) to compete with US-led global culture in both local and regional theatres (Shim 2008). Korean regionalization raises an important question about the ever-changing experience of 'Asianness' among pan-Asian audiences. The popularity of Korean television dramas in China, Japan, Taiwan and Southeast Asia reveals the contested field of hybrid Asian regionalization and the inculcation of representative modern sensibilities and Asian virtues in Asian popular culture (Lee and Ju 2011). The question becomes: what effect will the China market have on these sensibilities?

The rapid growth of the Chinese market is reshaping film regionalization in Asia. Asian filmmakers are testing the co-production formula, looking to bring China's 1.3 billion consumers into their filmmaking territory. Hong Kong's venture into China-centred film co-production complicates the diversity of pan-Asian film regionalization. The recent success of Hong Kong-China film co-productions appears to be bringing a more Chinese dimension to Asia's multi-centred popular cultural flows within East Asia.

GOVERNMENT-CORPORATION DILEMMA WITHIN THE FRAMEWORK OF CEPA

The Mainland Hong Kong Closer Economic Partnership Agreement (CEPA) underpins the cultural policy framework that governs Hong Kong's cultural collaborations, including film co-production, with Mainland China. CEPA is an economic agreement between the government of the Hong Kong Special Administration Region (HKSAR) and the Central People's Government of the Republic of China (PRC). The agreement was signed in September 2003 and took effect in January 2004. The main purpose was to eliminate tariffs and non-tariff barriers between Hong Kong and Mainland China by following economic principles under the political framework of 'One Country, Two Systems'.[2] Specific regulation related to Chinese-language film co-production in the CEPA regulation covers the areas of distribution, employment, language and content. Table 16.1 lists details of the regulation.[3]

According to CEPA regulations listed on the website of the Hong Kong Trade and Development Council (2014), the Hong Kong government utilizes CEPA to achieve its main goal of boosting the local economy. This rationale also pertains to the development of Hong Kong's cultural and creative industries. The category of film, video and music is one of eleven sectors that Hong Kong government classifies as part of its knowledge-based economy. These eleven sectors include: (1) art, antiques and crafts; (2) education and library, archive and museum services; (3) performing arts; (4) film, video and music; (5) television and radio; (6) publishing; (7) software, computer games and interactive media; (8) design; (9) architecture; (10) advertising; and (11) amusement services. As audio-visual content has long been a vibrant creative sector, the government of Hong Kong utilizes the CEPA to allow Hong Kong service suppliers to enjoy privileged access to the Mainland's motion-picture market. In production, CEPA stipulates that HK-China co-produced film cannot be restricted by the film quota system. In achieving recognition as local film,

Table 16.1   CEPA regulation of Hong Kong-China film co-production

Regulation category	Regulation content
Distribution	Hong Kong Chinese-language film co-productions receive exemption from the quota system governing imported foreign films if the film passes a review of the film review board. Cantonese versions of Hong Kong-Mainland co-productions may be distributed and screened in Guangdong Province.
Employment	The definition of 'Hong Kong co-produced film' refers to a Chinese-language film made by companies registered in the Hong Kong Special Administration Region. More than 50% of a film's production employees should include Hong Kong residents.
Language	Mandarin is the official language in a co-produced movie. Since January 2014, Hong Kong-mainland co-productions of dialect-version movies may be distributed and screened on the Mainland after obtaining the approval of relevant Mainland authorities, on the condition that filmmakers also provide standard Chinese subtitles.
Content	At least one-third of the main cast must be Mainlanders. There is no requirement for the proportion of principal creative personnel from Hong Kong. The movie's story should take place in specific mainland locations stipulated in the co-production agreement.

Source: Hong Kong TDC Research web site.

Hong Kong co-produced film companies benefit from the distribution advantage.

In practice, however, HK co-produced films need to receive approval from China Film Group (CFG) and the China Film Co-Production Corporation (CFCC); both of these are government entities. Yet the CEPA regulation allows Hong Kong service suppliers to freely circulate Hong Kong-produced movies in the Guangdong area. In regards to management, Hong Kong service suppliers may set up wholly owned or joint-venture enterprises on the mainland to produce video and sound recording products. These companies have free access to capital resources and can obtain funds to make co-produced film from any country of origin. In distribution, Hong Kong's joint venture enterprises can vertically integrate their audio-visual production with film distribution; these companies have obtained the approval of relevant mainland authorities. For instance, Dadi Digital Cinema Corporation is a Hong Kong film distribution company, ranked as the fourth largest theatre chain in China. The company is also one of the second largest film distributors following the Dalian Wanda

Group and two other government owned companies, Shanghai United Circuit and China Film Stellar Theatre Chain. In addition, the well-known Hong Kong celebrity Jackie Chan owns eleven theatres under the name 'Jackie Chan International Movie Theatre' in cities including Beijing, Guangzhou, Changzhou, Tianjin, Luoyang and Shenyang.

The CEPA's main goal is to maintain closer economic ties between Hong Kong and Mainland China. Yet two factors are contributing to the attenuation of Hong Kong's film industry under the regulatory framework of CEPA. The first, censorship, establishes organizational borders for Hong Kong film companies (Leung 2013). Censorship seeks to institutionalize China's popular culture to ensure that the public follows the moral imperatives of the Communist party-state. The relevant authorities from the Propaganda Department of the CCP Central Committee and the SAPPRFT act as gatekeepers of Chinese standards, monitoring approved viewing content for the public, and scrutinizing politically sensitive themes in films made by co-production ventures (ibid.). The government's draconian censorship system causes Hong Kong filmmakers to struggle to maintain artistic integrity in the films they produce, while its top-down form of state control sets up barriers for Hong Kong filmmakers who insist on freedom of expression. Popular genres such as ghost, cop and triad movies have been absent in Hong Kong co-produced films because of the restrictions on violence and superstition (Sala 2003; Szeto and Chen 2013). However, since the 2010s Hong Kong filmmakers have started to master their screenwriting to bring Hong Kong film genres into the Chinese market. The box-office success of police genre films in China such as *han zhan* (*Cold War*, 2012) and *du zhan* (*Drug War*, 2013) indicates a creative breakthrough for Hong Kong filmmakers after a decade of localizing their co-production to the Chinese market.

Hong Kong-China co-produced films undergo the censorship review process in two stages. In the first stage Hong Kong co-produced movies need to navigate a script review before production. The script needs to receive approval from both the China Film Group and the SAPPRFT. The second stage occurs in the final cut after the film completes shooting (Cain 2011). During the first stage the Film Censorship Board has about fifteen days to respond to the film's content; the SAPPRFT then follows with review comments and requests for modifications. Sil-Metropole Organization Ltd. is the only Hong Kong-based film company that receives an exemption from the Chinese government. The exemption is because of the close funding connection that Sil-Metropole Organization Ltd. has with the Chinese government. Hong Kong productions produced by Sil-Metropole are considered as made-in-China films. Its film script does not need to be submitted for censor review. The notable case is the

Hong Kong police action film, *han zhan* (*Cold War*, 2012), as the script was not reviewed before its release.

Another important consequence of the CEPA is labour migration from Hong Kong to China. In the 1980s, Hong Kong had the third largest film industry in the world, next in scale to Hollywood and India; by 1993 it was producing 200 movies. Soon after, however, the industry declined thanks to the Asian financial crisis and a later deliberate attempt to yield to the Chinese market under CEPA (Curtin 2007; Fung 2013). Although Hong Kong filmmakers tend to choose to follow filmmaking within the Chinese political system, the Hong Kong-China co-production model draws attention to the structural dangers facing the Hong Kong film industry (Szeto 2014). Hong Kong's film industry under CEPA suffers from a loss of junior talent at the entrance level; many migrate to China for jobs. From the late 1990s to 2008, the city's industry faced disintegration, given its severe shortage of young talent needed to continue local production in Hong Kong.

INDUSTRY PERFORMANCE UNDER CEPA

A review of the structural change from 2003 to the present leads to further understanding of the impact of CEPA – in particular Hong Kong's contribution to the growth of the film industry in China. According to interviews with industry insiders, the 1997 Asian financial crisis and the decreasing size of the domestic film market under the threat of Hollywood impacted the Hong Kong film industry during the 1990s. A review of the ten-year box office record of Hong Kong-China film co-production since 2003 reveals the influence of the CEPA on the film industry's structure.

Table 16.2 reports the box office revenue of the top ten most profitable co-produced movies in China from 2003 to 2014. The market scale of these films presents a sharp contrast in box office performance between Hong Kong and the Mainland. Organizational collaboration shows Hong Kong's reliance on local companies to complete production in China. *xiyou xiang mo* (*Journey to the West*, 2013), for instance, is the most profitable Hong Kong-China co-produced movie, collecting RMB 1.246.26 billion (US$ 195.41 million) market revenue in China. The film's box office take in Hong Kong, however, was only 1 per cent of the box office in the Mainland. This difference surely explains why many Hong Kong filmmakers are fully integrating with the industry in China.

The influence exerted from closer integration with the Mainland is evident in Table 16.3 (below), which compares the numbers of films

Table 16.2   Top ten co-produced films and their box office performances in China and Hong Kong, 2003–14

Rank	Title/Year	Box Office in China (million **RMB**/US$)	Box Office in HK (million HKD/US$)	Production company
1	*zhuo yao ji* / Monster Hunt (2015)	2387.54/374.37	9.67/1.25	EDKO Film (HK) Tencent Video Dream Sky Entertainment Co. Ltd
2	*xiyou xiangmo pian* / Journey to the West: Conquering the Demons (2013)	1246.26/195.41	28.12/3.63	BinGo Group (HK) Village Roadshow Asia (CN) ChinaVision Media Group (CN) EDKO Film (HK)
3	*xiyouji zhi danao tiangong* / The Monkey King (2014)	1044.63/163.8	25.28/3.26	Beijing Variety Star Media (CN) Mandarin Films (HK)
4	*Aomen fengyun 2* / The Man from Macau II (2015)	974.33/152.77	28.41/3.66	Mega-Vision Project Workshop Limited Bona Film Group Sun Entertainment Culture Limited
5	*shier shengxiao* / Chinese Zodiac (2012)	878.98/137.82	11.52/1.49	Huayi Brothers Media Group (CN) JCE Entertainment (HK)
6	*zhiqu weihushan* / The Taking of Tiger Mountain (2014)	822/128.89	/	Bona Film Group Huaxia Film Distribution Bayi Film Studio
7	*huapi: II* / Painted Skin: II (2012)	726.5/113.92	8.97/1.16	Ningxia Film Group (CN) Huayi Brothers International (HK)
8	*siren dingzhi* / Personal Tailor (2013)	712.1/111.66	0.36/0.05	Huayi Brothers Film Group (CN) Huayi Brothers International (HK)
9	*rang zidan fei* / Let the Bullets Fly (2010)	674.3/105.73	11.34/1.46	China Film Group (CN) Emperor Motion Pictures (HK)
10	*tangshan da dizhen* / Aftershock (2010)	665.05/104.28	14.87/1.92	Shanghai Film Group Emperor Motion Pictures (HK)

Source: www.entgroup.cn.

Table 16.3 Comparison between the number of Hong Kong co-produced films and the total films produced in China, 2003–14

Year	No. of HK-China co-production films	No. of non co-produced HK films	No. of total films produced in China	Total box office in China (million RMB/US$)	Box office of top ten HK-China co-produced film (million RMB/US$)	Ratio of top ten HK-China co-produced films to total annual film production in China
2003	28	54	140	1,010/158.37	–	6/–
2004	41	47	212	1,514/237.39	324/50.8	8/21.4%
2005	30	27	208	2,046/320.81	527.9/82.77	10/25.8%
2006	29	35	208	2,620/410.82	726.5/113.92	8/27.7%
2007	31	35	320	3,327/521.67	725.3/113.73	9/21.8
2008	25	37	406	4,341/680.67	1,539.1/241.33	10/35.5
2009	20	37	456	6,206/973.1	1,480/232.06	7/23.8
2010	33	33	526	10,172/1,594.97	2,320.7/363.89	7/22.8
2011	28	32	558	13,115/2,056.43	2,354.9/369.25	7/17.9
2012	33	15	745	17,073/2,677.05	2,807.9/440.28	7/16.4
2013	28	15	640	21,769/3,413.38	4,193.22/657.5	7/19.3
2014	27	23	618	29,639/4,647.4	2,446.57/383.62	3/8.25

Source: *China Film Yearbook*; EntGroup (www.entgroup.cn)

produced in both Hong Kong and China between 2003 and 2014. CEPA's film policy benefits large-scale Hong Kong film companies that co-produce Chinese language films. From 2003 to 2014 China's film industry grew fourfold. In contrast Hong Kong production declined, particularly in regard to local production (i.e. not co-produced film). Although the number of Hong Kong-China co-productions has remained stable in growth, the number of non co-produced Hong Kong films decreased drastically from 54 films in 2003 to just 15 in 2013.

Among the twenty or so major companies that now engage in co-productions in Hong Kong and China, more than 90 per cent of their films have earned higher revenue in the Mainland than in Hong Kong. Major Hong Kong film companies like Emperor Entertainment Group and Media Asia have excelled in the Mainland market; they are now the top producers of blockbusters. Small and mid-size movie companies continue to produce low budget films primarily for the Hong Kong market. These filmmakers face challenges as consumers turn away from local movies. Local film distribution also faces competition from Hollywood. Only a small number of Hong Kong movies like *laogang zhengzhuan* (*Mr. Cinema*, 2007), *guima kuangxiang qu* (*Fantasia*, 2004) and *tong meng qiyuan* (*Wait Till You're Older*, 2005) have gained higher revenues in Hong Kong than in China. Exceptions include history and action films like *Ye Wen* (*Ip Man*, 2008) series and Kung Fu action genre films of *jizhan* (*Unbeatable*, 2013), *aomeng fengyun* (*The Man from Macau*, 2014) and *han zhan* (*Cold War*, 2012). These films are popular genres in the current film market of Hong Kong.

Hong Kong and Mainland film industries show another level of deviation during the aforementioned co-production period. This difference is evident in a comparison of Tables 16.4 and 16.5. As Table 16.4 shows, Hong Kong's distribution market has made minimal progress in the numbers of box office revenue and multiplexes. Because of the rising cost of theatre rental, multiplex numbers have decreased in the past decade. Movie theatres are able to maintain stable revenue return by raising ticket prices and increasing the showing of 3D movies in local theatres. There is no doubt that Hollywood movies collect the major share of the movie market. *Iron Man 3* (2013), *Avengers* (2012), *Transformers 3* (2011), *Toy Story 3* (2010) and *Avatar* (2009) have been the highest grossing films in Hong Kong.

Comparatively, Table 16.5 suggests a rapid transformation of the filmmaking environment in respect to consumption, distribution and exhibition. Within ten years of the CEPA implementation, China's film market expanded from RMB 1,010 million (US$1,58.37 million) to RMB 2,9639 million (US$4,647.4 million) worth of market revenue. The number

Table 16.4   Box office, number of screens and multiplex theatres in Hong Kong, 2003–11

Year	Box office revenue (million HKD / US$)	No of multiplex theatres	No of screens
2003	896/115.58	57	188
2004	954/123.07	57	197
2005	941/121.39	48	207
2006	944/121.78	47	181
2007	950/122.55	47	182
2008	1,096/141.38	49	190
2009	1,170/150.93	49	201
2010	1,337/172.47	47	208
2011	1,395/179.96	46	204

Source: Hong Kong Theatres Association Ltd (www.hktaorg.com).

Table 16.5   Box office, number of screens and multiplex cinemas in China, 2003–14

Year	Box office revenue (in million RMB / US$)	No of multiplex nationwide	No of screens nationwide
2003	1,010/158.37	1,140	2,285
2004	1,514/237.39	1,188	2,396
2005	2,046/320.81	1,243	2,668
2006	2,620/410.82	1,325	3,034
2007	3,327/521.67	1,427	3,527
2008	4,341/680.67	1,545	4,097
2009	6,206/973.1	1,687	4,723
2010	10,172/1,594.97	2,000	6,256
2011	13,115/2,056.43	2,800	9,200
2012	17,073/2,677.05	3,680	13,118
2013	21,769/3,413.38	4,583	18,195
2014	29,639/4,647.4	5,598	23,670

Source: China Film Yearbook and EntGroup (www.entgroup.cn).

of multiplex cinemas has grown from 1,140 to 5,785, and the number of screens has increased from 2,285 in 2003 to 23,670 (as of end of 2014).

In regard to the above data there are significant changes in both industries in box office revenue and the number of screens and theatres since 2003. It is too early to conclude that Hong Kong's integration with the Mainland will make the latter's film industry more successful.[4] Meanwhile, co-production is the main path of development and will continue to be the most important filmmaking strategy in Hong Kong. With China predicted to become the world's biggest film market in 2020 (Child 2012), Mainland films have become more transnational. Such transformations bring sophisticated cultural reflection on the potential of local filmmaking to detach place-bound identities in their internationalization process for the global market.

ALTERNATIVE FILMMAKING FOR A HONG KONG-CENTRED INDUSTRY TRANSFORMATION

As mentioned above, other kinds of filmmaking have filled the vacuum created by the Hong Kong-China co-production relationship. The market environment created under the CEPA maps out the boundaries of alternative filmmaking in three ways. The first is at the level of government. Those responsible for film policy in Hong Kong face the challenge of facilitating an environment that promotes both filmmaking and film going. The government provides assistance to areas that are less explored in commercial filmmaking.

According to our fieldwork interviews with Hong Kong film industry professionals the Hong Kong government focuses on planning activities in order to brand the industry. Film policy aims at increasing filmmaking productivity; it provides funds to small and medium budget filmmakers as well as training new talent in producing, directing, scripting, lighting and choreographing.

The major government film related office, the Film Development Council (FDC), offers services such as funding support, facilitation guarantees and post-production licensing to the film community of Hong Kong. The FDC has provided partial financing to fund 47 film projects with a total investment of 133 million Hong Kong dollars since the launch of the Film Development Fund in 2007. The office also collaborates with the telecommunication sector to experiment in the 3D exhibition of virtual concerts and international sport events. Hong Kong's theatres are gradually disappearing in many local administrative areas. Old theatre buildings are replaced by shopping complexes as the city goes through the regeneration process of urban renewal.

Many FDC administrators we spoke with recognize that the Hong Kong film industry has historically explored offshore markets. The industry is currently overcoming stagnation but the FDC office considers such low moments natural as an industry grows through its lifecycle. The FDC applies a market-led approach, trying to maintain minimum government intervention to implement policies aimed at maintaining satisfactory outcomes in co-production between Hong Kong and China, while at the same time promoting funds for niche-filmmaking. The latter approach allows young filmmakers to explore secondary markets under the overall co-production structure of CEPA.

The second way of maintaining filmmaking outside Hong Kong-China co-production is at the level of the film company. Particularly in film distribution, Hong Kong's alternative strategy works around the centralized control of China's state-entrusted film companies. Similar to its film censorship process, the Chinese government monitors foreign content with officers reviewing at various levels of the Ministry of Culture, SAPPRFT and the Film Censorship Board. Likewise in film distribution, Hong Kong companies face unpredictable review results when they apply for license approval.

As mentioned above, the CEPA offers Hong Kong film companies better access to the Chinese market compared to other 'foreign' companies. The agreement has lifted the restriction on the number of Hong Kong films that can be imported into China. However, in practice, Hong Kong film companies still face the same degree of restriction as before when applying for film license approval. There is a lack of transparency in the current structure as most foreign films released in theatres are distributed by the two state-owned companies, China Film Group and Huaxia Film Group. The China Film Group, in particular, is the major company entrusted to release Hollywood films in China. The two companies often release Hollywood films with Chinese titles taking up the majority of theatre screens during popular hours; while Hong Kong co-produced movies are left to compete with Hollywood for the rest of the screens. This dominance of both state-owned companies discounts the benefit that Hong Kong companies enjoy in film distribution under the CEPA.

Consequently, alternative strategies for film distribution can only work in a larger political context, one in which Hong Kong is exempted from the quota restriction in the foreign film category in China. As Hong Kong theatres are diminishing in number, local film companies need to explore the potential of digital film distribution to enlarge the market of Hong Kong films. Now as Hong Kong companies begin to build theatres in China, the distribution of Cantonese language films is increasing. The achieved outcome in film distribution shows in Hong Kong's film circulation of non co-produced films. These films also receive higher distribution in the Southern part of China under the new revision of the CEPA regulation in 2013.

Thirdly, in respect to labour issues, labour migration from the

Hong Kong film industry to Mainland China is critical. Similar to labour issues in California when Hollywood moved offshore to other locations, Hong Kong's film industry faces the problem of industrial disintegration due to labour migration. In addition, the industry illustrates the problem of wage gap, as it grows tougher for new talent to enter. According to CEPA regulations, Hong Kong-China co-production needs to include a Chinese actor or actress to be the main lead in the film. In Hong Kong, because A-list actors and actresses such as Andy Lau, Stephen Chow and Jackie Chan still enjoy a high reputation in Chinese and overseas Asian markets, the diminishing size of the Hong Kong film industry constitutes a new barrier of entry for local talent; put simply there is a lack of jobs for the small scale market for non co-produced Hong Kong films. Alternative strategies therefore require a closer inter-sectorial integration between film and other industries in Hong Kong.

CONCLUSION

The chapter has drawn attention to concerns about the current development of non co-produced films in Hong Kong. It calls for a new perspective to examine the impact of CEPA on Hong Kong's film industry. The chapter contends that evaluation of the Hong Kong film industry should include the extended impact of the Hong Kong film industry on other film industries in Asia. Effective policy needs to consider the implementation of supporting policies to maintain Hong Kong's industry value chain outside CEPA's regulation framework. Alternative filmmaking should maintain the possibility of integration among sectors with other support so that more talents can participate to produce local films with a larger scale of value chain in film production and distribution.

Theoretically, Hong Kong's Sinicization in regional filmmaking under the CEPA re-conceptualizes the hybridity of Asian film regionalization. Sinicization allows Hong Kong films to become crossover cinema in Asia again. It reconnects Hong Kong film and pan-Asian audiences together through blockbuster Hong Kong-China co-productions. We argue that the level of pan-Asian regionalization in Hong Kong-China co-production movies is illustrative of a reintegrated film culture that is culturally Hong Kong-based but yet also politically Chinese. The chapter uses the CEPA to make a case for regional cultural policy in Asia. It concludes with an emphasis on alternative filmmaking where social voices in independent cinema can represent the local in the multi-dimensional filmmaking environment that CEPA creates for the Hong Kong film industry.

NOTES

1. CEPA is a government document that was signed by the Chinese authority and the government of the Hong Kong SAR to reduce tariffs in trade.
2. The exclusions of the World Trade Organization (WTO) framework are stated in the CEPA document under Article Four. The information is available, accessed 4 May 2014 at http://tga.mofcom.gov.cn/article/zt_cepanew/subjectaa/200612/20061204078587. shtml.
3. The URL for the CEPA web site is available, accessed 4 May 2014 at http:// hong-kong-economy-research.hktdc.com/business-news/article/Research-Articles/ CEPA-Supplement-X-and-Hong-Kong-s-Cultural-and-Creative-Industries/rp/ en/1/1X486E8M/1X09W3ZS.htm.
4. Filmmaker Zhang Yimou made a comment that film talent from Hong Kong has contributed to China's film industry development in the past decade.

REFERENCES

Cain, Robert (2011), 'How to be censored in China: a brief filmmaking guide', accessed 28 April 2014 at www.indiewire.com/article/how-to-be-censored-in-china-a-brief-filmmaking-guide.

Chan, Ka Ming (2011), 'Crossing the transnational Hong Kong cinema co-production: production culture, policy, business, and individual practitioners', Ph.D. Thesis, The Chinese University of Hong Kong.

Child, Ben (2012), 'China will be the world's biggest market by 2020', *The Guardian*, accessed 5 May 2014 at www.theguardian.com/film/2012/nov/29/china-biggest-film-market-2020.

Choo, Kukhee (2012), 'Nationalizing "cool": Japan's global promotion of the content industry', in Nissim Otmazgin and Eyal Ben-Ari (eds.), *Popular Culture and the State in East and Southeast Asia*. London: Routledge, pp. 85–105.

Chow, Vivienne (2013), 'See the bigger picture on the film industry', *South China Morning Post*, accessed 5 May 2014 at www.scmp.com/news/hong-kong/article/1262366/see-bigger-picture-film-industry.

Christopherson, Susan (2005), 'Divide and conquer: regional competition in a concentrated media market', in Greg Elmer and Mike Gasher (eds.), *Contracting Out Hollywood: Runaway Productions and Foreign Location Shooting*. Lanham: Rowman & Littlefield Publishers, pp. 21–40.

Chua, Beng-Huat (2001), 'Pop culture China', *Singapore Journal of Tropical Geography* **22** (2): 113–21.

Chua, Beng-Huat (2008), 'Introduction East Asian TV dramas: identifications, sentiments and effects', in Beng-Huat Chua and Koichi Iwabuchi (eds.), *East Asian Pop Culture: Analysing the Korean Wave*. Hong Kong: Hong Kong University Press, pp. 1–12.

Chung, Stephanie Po-yin (2012a), taojin shinian zoujin kaoyan shike – tan xianggang yingren de beipiao xianxiang ('Trials after ten years golden rush: on the phenomenon of Hong Kong filmmakers "Going to the North"'), *jintian* (*Today*) 99: 1–15.

Chung, Stephanie Po-yin (2012b), guangying liushi: xianggang dianying zoujin dazhongguo shidai ('Hong Kong movies and the Chinese market') *dangdai dianying* (*Contemporary Cinema*) 4: 127–30.

Curtin, Michael (2007), *Playing to the World's Biggest Audience: The Globalization of Chinese Film and Television*. Berkeley: California University Press.

Curtin, Michael (2011), 'Chan is missing: Hong Kong creatives in China's orbit', *Media Fields Journal* 5, available at <http://www.mediafieldsjournal.org/chan-is-missing/>.

Davis, Darrell William (2010), 'Market and marketization in the China film business', *Cinema Journal* **49** (3): 121–5.

Davis, Darrel William and Yueh-Yu Yeh (2008), *East Asian Screen Industries*. London: British Film Institute.

Donald, Stephanie Hemelryk (2005), 'The *Ice Storm*: Ang Lee, cosmopolitanism, and the global audience', in Greg Elmer and Mike Gasher (eds.), *Contracting Out Hollywood: Runaway Productions and Foreign Location Shooting*. Oxford: Rowman & Littlefield, pp. 140–56.

Fung, Anthony (2013), 'Introduction', in Anthony Fung (eds.), *Asian Popular Cultures: The Global (Dis)continuity*. New York: Routledge, pp. 1–18.

Hammond, Stephan (2000), *Hollywood East: Hong Kong Movies and the People Who Made Them*. Lincolnwood: Contemporary Books.

Hau, Caroline S. and Takashi Shiraishi (2013), 'Regional contexts of cooperation and collaboration in Hong Kong Cinema', in Nissim Otmazgin and Eyal Ben-Ari (eds.), *Popular Culture Co-Production in East and Southeast Asia*, Singapore: NUS Press, pp. 68–98.

He, Hilary Hongjin (2010), 'One movie, two versions: post-1997 Hong Kong cinema in Mainland China', *Global Media Journal* **4** (2): 1–16.

Hong Kong Trade and Development Council (2014), 'Film entertainment industry in Hong Kong', accessed 5 May 2014 at www.hong-kong-economy-research.hktdc.com/business-news/article/Hong-Kong-Industry-Profiles/Film-Entertainment-Industry-in-Hong-Kong/hkip/en/1/1X000000/1X0018PN.htm.

Iwabuchi, Koichi (2002), *Recentering Globalization: Popular Culture and Japanese Transnationalism*. Durham and London: Duke University Press.

Jin, Dal Yong and Dong-Hoo Lee (2012), 'The birth of East Asia: cultural regionalization through co-production strategies', *Spectator* **32** (2): 26–40.

Klein, Christina (2007), 'Kung Fu Hustle: transnational production and the global Chinese language film', *Journal of Chinese Cinema* **1** (3): 189–208.

Lee, Soobum and Hyejung Ju (2011), 'The meaning of Korean dramas in Japanese fandom: re-emerging sentiment of "Asianness"', in Do Kyun Kim and Min-sun Kim (eds.), *Hallyu: Influence of Korean Popular Culture in Asia and Beyond*. Seoul: Seoul National University Press.

Leung, Yuk Ming Lisa (2013), 'Re-nationalizing the transnational? The cases of exiled and warlords in Hong Kong-China film co-production', in Nissim Otmazgin and Eyal Ben-Ari (eds.), *Popular Culture Co-productions and Collaborations in East and Southeast Asia*. Kyoto: Kyoto University Press, pp. 115–35.

Liang, Shao, Chuck Kwok and Omrane Guehami (2010), 'National culture and dividend policy', *Journal of International Business Studies* 41: 1391–414.

Lie, Fu (2014), 2007: xianggang dianying jiqi yu zhongguo dianying wenhua xingeju zhong de yinsu, ('HK film and the facts in new pattern of Chinese film culture in 2007'), *dangdai dianying (Contemporary Cinema)* 3: 54–7.

Miller, Toby, Nitin Govil, John McMurria, Ting Wang and Richard Maxwell (2005), *Global Hollywood 2*. London: British Film Institute.

Pond, Steve (2013), 'Will Oscar voters see the wrong version of "The Grandmaster"?' *The Wrap Covering Hollywood*, accessed 2 May 2014 at www.thewrap.com/will-oscar-voters-see-wrong-version-grandmaster.

Poon, Daniel (2014), 'Film entertainment industry in Hong Kong', accessed 29 April 2014 at http://hong-kong-economy-research.hktdc.com/business-news/article/Hong-Kong-Industry-Profiles/Film-Entertainment-Industry-in-Hong-Kong/hkip/en/1/1X000000/1X0018PN.htm.

Pugsley, Peter (2013), 'Hong Kong film as crossover cinema: maintaining the HK aesthetic', in Sukhmani Khorana (ed.), *Crossover Cinema: Cross-Cultural Film from Production to Reception*. New York: Routledge, pp. 3–13.

Sala, Ilaria (2003), 'CEPA and Hong Kong film: The mixed blessing of market access', *China Rights Forum* 4: 75–77. Available at http://www.ln.edu.hk/mkt/staff/gcui/Hong%20Kong%20Film%203.pdf.

Shim, Doobo (2008), 'The growth of Korean cultural industries and the Korean Wave', in Beng-Huat Chua and Koichi Iwabuchi (eds.), *East Asian Pop Culture: Analyzing the Korean Wave*. Hong Kong: Hong Kong University Press, pp. 15–32.

Szeto, Mirana M. (2014), 'Sinophone libidinal economy in the age of neoliberalisation and mainlandisation: masculinities in Hong Kong SAR New Wave cinema', in Audrey Yue and Olivia Khoo (eds.), *Sinophone Cinema*. London: Palgrave Macmillan, pp. 120–46.

Szeto, Mirana M. and Yun-Chung Chen (2013), 'To work or not to work: the dilemma of Hong Kong film labor in the age of mainlandization', *Jump Cut: A Review of Contemporary Media* 55, accessed 4 May 2014 at www.ejumpcut.org/currentissue/SzetoChenHongKong/ text.html.

Teo, Stephen (2008), 'Promise and perhaps love: pan-Asian production and the Hong Kong-China interrelationship', *Journal of Inter-Asia Cultural Studies* **9** (3): 341–58.

Throsby, David (2009), 'Explicit and implicit cultural policy: some economic aspects', *International Journal of Cultural Policy* **15** (2): 179–85.

Zhan Qingsheng (2013), chanyehua gaige shinian zhongguo dianying hepaipian fazhan beiwang (2002–2012) ('The memorandum of China co-production film from 2002 to 2012'), *dangdai dianying (Contemporary Cinema)* 2: 39–47.

17. Chinese transnational cinema and the collaborative tilt toward South Korea*[1]

Brian Yecies

Transnational exchange has long characterized the 'internationalization' of the global film industry. Collaboration takes place among production companies, practitioners and co-investors. Stories and locations are subject to change; they can be traded off in contractual negotiations. In the past most projects occurred in the US for the simple reason that 'Hollywood' spelled the dream destination for industry workers and aspiring actors alike. However, with the general decline of the working environment in the US film industry since the 1990s, and the global industry's increasing adoption of digital production and post-production methods since the early-to-mid-2000s, there has been a sharp shift of production away from Hollywood toward new centres of transnational cultural production, such as Beijing, Shanghai, Mumbai and Seoul.

The focus on cultural and creative industries and the excitement about China's media 'going out' (*zou chuqu*) is impacting not just on flows of content but on flows of expertise. China has become the new and largest media frontier where in spite of (or perhaps because of) the Communist Party's control, one senses a dynamic 'global experiment of modernity' resulting from the 'displacement and reappropriation of expertise' (Giddens 1994: 59) from elsewhere. International film companies and practitioners are now heading to China in droves; together with the expansion of multiplex cinemas, the increase in local audience numbers, and investment in joint projects, this has enabled the Chinese film market to become the second largest in the world (in terms of box office revenues) after the US (Pulver 2013; Qin 2015). In turn, this transnational migration of human capital and know-how across all corners of the Chinese film industry is contributing to a new 'ecology of expertise' (Ong 2005), which operates according to a simple but 'fluid logic of assemblage' (Berry 2013); in other words, films are now made in multiple locations. The end result is a contribution to the professionalization of Chinese media and media produced in China.

With these developments in mind, this chapter introduces some recent examples of collaboration and technological transfer between the Chinese and Korean film industries; because much of this joint activity has occurred behind the scenes, the sheer volume of these efforts has frequently gone unrecognized. More and more Chinese firms and filmmakers are opening new doors by looking beyond the limitations of the local market to the wider Asian region, especially to Korea, and are thus aspiring to internationalize Chinese cinema. The internationalization of the Chinese film industry – and the evolution of a 'Chinese transnational cinema' – is leading to new kinds of assemblage involving Korean colleagues and firms on an increasing scale, although not without teething problems.

To shed more light on this important and growing trend in international filmmaking, this chapter investigates the increasing levels of co-operation in co-productions and post-production work between China and Korea since the mid-2000s, following a surge in personnel exchange and technological transfer. It explains how a range of international relationships and industry connections is contributing to a new ecology of expertise, which in turn is boosting the expansion of China's domestic market and synergistically transforming the shape and style of Chinese cinema.

SEEDING GUANXI AND BLAZING NEW TRAILS

Over the last five years a small number of Korean film companies have contributed to the making of nearly one-third of the top-performing films at the Chinese box office. At the centre of this development – at least initially – have been a handful of Korean nationals who studied directing, producing, editing, and theory at the Beijing Film Academy (hereafter BFA), beginning in the early 1990s. These students were part of the first wave of Koreans allowed by their government to study in China after bilateral relations began to thaw in the post-Cold War era. Among the earliest cohort of BFA graduates, who learned valuable language and cultural skills in China, are Yi Chi-yun (aka Edward Chi-yun Yi), director Kim Jeong-jung, Chloe Park (producer, CJ E&M China), Kim Pil-jeong (manager, Korean Film Council, China), film critic Do Seong-hi, and Peter Ahn (VFX producer, Dexter Digital), to name only a few.

In their own ways all these figures have been central to the creation of new personal and industry 'networks' (*guanxi* in Chinese) between the two countries. Throughout the 1990s, these Korean students studied alongside and developed close relationships with critically acclaimed Sixth Generation 'enfants terrible' of Chinese cinema filmmakers such as Jia Zhangke, Wang Xiaoshuai, and Zhang Yuan. These Chinese and Korean classmates, who are now at the helm of their respective industries, were taught by some of the most distinguished Fourth and Fifth

Generation Chinese filmmakers, including Xie Fie, Tian Zhuangzhuang, Chen Kaige and Zhang Yimou.

These aspiring Korean filmmakers and BFA students grew up on a steady diet of landmark Fifth Generation Chinese films such as Chen Kaige's *Yellow Earth* (*huang tudi*, 1984), *King of the Children* (*haizi wang*, 1987), *Life on a String* (1991), and *Farewell My Concubine* (*ba wang bieji*, 1993), and Zhang Yimou's *Red Sorghum* (*hong gaoliang*, 1987), *Ju Dou* (1990), *Raise the Red Lantern* (*dahong denglong gaogao gua*, 1991), and *The Story of Qiu Ju* (*Qiu Ju da guansi*, 1992), which were shown on television and in cinemas, and also distributed more widely on videotape. (Xie Jin's *Hibiscus Town* (*furong zhen*, 1986) and *Red Sorghum* were among the first Mainland Chinese films officially released in Korea in 1989, introducing this new wave of Chinese cinema to eager filmmakers and audiences alike.) Considering these films' popularity in Korea and the universal acknowledgement of their artistic merit, it is little wonder that aspiring Korean filmmakers were drawn to Beijing to study at the BFA, Asia's most prestigious film institute. After completing their studies, these Korean graduates returned home and applied their training to improve the quality and diversity of the local Korean industry, as well as the sheer quantity of domestic films produced. After proving themselves at home and becoming recognized for their craft, they began filtering back to China to assist the rise of the new wave of Chinese cinema through their established networks there.

Ultimately the depth of *guanxi* that Korean filmmakers had nurtured in China in the early-to-mid-1990s led to the flowering of relationships with both the state-controlled and budding commercial sectors of the Chinese film industry. As a result, when the Pusan International Film Festival (hereafter PIFF, but known today as BIFF) – the largest festival and market in the world for Asian cinema, and a key networking location for promoting Asian films to the global film industry – was launched in 1996, established linkages with the Chinese film industry proved invaluable. Festival programmers tapped into established personal networks, and also began building new networks of their own for the benefit of the industry as a whole.

During the 1990s, members of the inner circle of the Mainland Chinese film industry added new layers to the networks developing between Chinese and Korean filmmakers. Major directors including Xie Jin, Zhang Ming, Zhang Yimou, Jia Zhangke, Zhang Yuan, Wang Xiaoshuai and their entourages visited Korea under the auspices of PIFF, networking with Korean industry figures attending the festival. In 1996, Chinese film and television director and producer Zhang Yuan (a BFA graduate) was invited to be a jury member for the New Currents Award at the inaugural PIFF. And in 1997, Shan Dongbing of China Film Export & Import Corporation – the single largest (state-run) company of its kind – sat on the jury for PIFF's NETPAC (Network for the Promotion of Asian Cinema) Award, while Sixth Generation director Zhang Ming was a jury member for the New Currents Award, an award he had himself won the previous year for his contemporary social drama *In Expectation* (1995, aka *Rainclouds Over Wushan*). In addition to these three directors, the festival was attended by numerous guests from all sectors of Greater China's film and entertainment industries during the 1990s.

In the East Asian context, the development of these *guanxi* networks has provided the seedbed for the rapid growth of collaboration between Chinese and Korean filmmakers after 2001, and for the Chinese film industry's tilt toward Korea more generally.

Today, the world's major film industry players, whether from Hollywood, Korea, East Asia or China itself, are jockeying for a share in the rapidly unfolding economic and cultural dream that is the Chinese market: a privileged position that up until a few years ago was open only to filmmakers and firms from within Mainland China. Unquestionably, the 'opening up' of the burgeoning Chinese film market has played a significant part in writing the latest chapter of the Chinese film industry's own expansion into international markets. Since China joined the WTO in 2001, cooperation between the Chinese and Korean film industries has gradually generated a momentum that has drawn them increasingly closer together, enabling Korean filmmakers to become 'wider, deeper, more tightly [enmeshed] with China' (*Korean Cinema Today* 2012: 30). In recent years this relationship has blossomed in a number of areas, including a handful of formal co-productions overseen by Korean Film Council (hereafter KOFIC, a quasi-government organization charged with promoting and supporting Korean Films at home and abroad), and a much larger number of informal collaborations, including the use by Chinese companies of Korean post-production and visual effects firms, co-financing, the sharing of cast and crews, and the shooting of particular scenes or even entire films on location in one or both countries.

It is especially notable that the number and kinds of bilateral collaborations have multiplied steeply since 2009, following the establishment of a KOFIC branch office in Beijing. In 2011, KOFIC chairman, Kim Ui-seok, publicly underscored the necessity of pursuing globalization activities of this kind (Kim 2011). Although the bulk of Chinese–Korean collaborations were occurring outside of this official channel, nevertheless, under Kim's leadership, in 2011 KOFIC and KAFA (Korean Film Academy) launched a small and exclusive (but nevertheless high-profile) industry networking event known as KAFA China Pre-biz. This event brought a select group of Chinese and Korean film people together in Beijing to forge new relationships, primarily with an eye to their own future projects, and to learn more about each other's markets. Partly as a result of the significant networks established at this event, as well as the continued hosting of Chinese industry delegates at BIFF, the value of China's official film imports from Korea has taken off: US$731,000 in 2012; US$1,757,000 in 2013; and a massive US$8,206,000 in 2014.[2]

A sharp upturn for the Korean film industry, and film industries around the globe, occurred in early 2012 when the Chinese government increased the number of foreign feature films permitted to share in domestic box office profits from 20 to 34; as a result the market for Korean films in China expanded even further.[3] At the same time the numbers of multiplex screens have continued to rise in China, reaching around 23,600 at the end of 2014: in 2014 alone 1,015 new cinemas and 5,397 new screens were added, revealing a truly remarkable acceleration in growth, up from an estimated 1,500 modern multiplex screens in 2008.[4] According to *The Hollywood Reporter*, Mainland China's cinemas showed a 'tenfold increase' between 2002 and 2012: from 1,300 to 13,000 (Tsui 2012). This trend is bound to continue considering the size of China's population, which now is reaching 1.4 billion. The number of films exhibited in 3D has risen sharply too and new box office revenue-sharing records have been set in this area. Most importantly, the 2014 signing of the China–Korea co-production treaty has classified co-produced films as local films, thus further expanding Chinese–Korean international film encounters – and Korea's share of the massive Chinese box office. Bilateral collaborations can only increase following the signing of this landmark treaty. In short, a large slice of the contemporary Korean film industry has become part of the 'Chinese dream'. China has become a unique stepping stone for the further globalization – and perhaps continued survival – of major sectors of the Korean film industry.

The Chinese film industry's recent 'tilt' toward Korea is the product of a long sequence of developments. With the growing popularity of Korean cultural contents in Asia – the so-called Korean Wave – one of the most notable areas of film collaboration in the 2000s was the export of acting talent. Since 2003, an increasing number of Korean actors, including Kwon Sang-woo, Kim Hee-sun, Song Hye-gyo, Jung Woo-sung and So Ji-seup, have accepted invitations to appear in Chinese productions, eager to expand their profiles among new pan-Asian audiences.[5] In turn, directors such as Jackie Chan have increased the potential commercial value of their films by casting these popular stars. *Seven Swords* (*qi jian*, 2003) and *The Myth* (*shenhua*, 2005) starred leading ladies Kim So-yeon and Kim Hee-sun respectively, while popular singer and television actress Jang Na-ra appeared in *Girls' Revolution* (*maque yao geming*, 2007), directed by San Dao and co-staring Jaycee Chan (Jackie Chan's son). More recently, Choo Ja-hyun starred in the crime thriller film *The Boundary* (*quancheng tongji*, 2014), directed by Wang Tao.

A number of established Korean directors have also been able to re-boot their careers in China. Director Hur Jin-ho (aka Heo Jin-ho), well known for *Christmas in August* (1998) and *One Fine Spring Day* (2001), has directed two Chinese films, *A Good Rain Knows* (*haoyu shijie, 2009*, aka *Season of Good Rain*) and *Dangerous Liaisons* (*weixian guanxi*, 2012). Both films were produced by Beijing-based Zonbo Media, blending the commercial acumen of Zonbo's president Chen Weiming with the artistic vision of director Hur. Around the same time, Ahn Byung-ki, Korea's leading horror film director, best known for *A Nightmare* (2000), *Phone* (2002) and *Bunshinsaba* (2004), and also the producer of *Speed Scandal* (2008) and *Sunny* (2011), which were both box office hits in China, entered the Chinese market. He has directed a Chinese trilogy based on his 2004 hit film, *Bunshinsaba* (2012), *Bunshinsaba 2* (2013), and *Bunshinsaba 3* (2014) – one of the earliest domestic horror series released in China. Finally, in 2015, Korean director Chang Yoon-hyun, known for the thriller *Tell Me Something* (1998), is directing the transnational thriller *The Peaceful Island*, a co-production produced by CJ E&M, China's C2M and Huace Media and Hong Kong's Media Asia Group. Although these are all seasoned directors with strong track records, their reputations had faded in Korea after a cohort of younger, ambitious directors pushed them out of the spotlight. As a result, they struggled to find new projects at home and turned their attention to China where more than 600 films were produced in 2014, signalling a need for experienced directors to capitalize on the opportunities presented by the burgeoning Chinese film industry.

Over time and as Chinese cinema's local and global profile continued to expand, the nature and scope of joint Chinese–Korean projects became increasingly sophisticated. Productions featuring Chinese locations include: the historical action-swordplay epic *Musa* (*wushi* aka *The Warrior* 2001, aka *Musa, the Warrior*), written and directed by Kim Sung-soo and co-produced by Cha Sung-jae (Sidus) and Zhang Xia (deputy managing director of the Beijing Film Studio), with major support from CJ Entertainment and state-run China Film Group, and shot on location in the desert lake area of Zhongwei, the Liaoning highlands, and the ancient city of Xingcheng; CJ Entertainment's fantasy–action drama *The Legend of Evil Lake* (2003); the historical action-swordplay movie *Shadowless Sword* (2005), directed by Kim Young-jun and co-financed by Taewon Entertainment and US-based New Line Cinema (shot at Hengdian

World Studio); and the historical action-adventure drama *Demon Empire* (aka *The Restless*, 2006), produced by Nabi Pictures and directed by Kim Sung-soo, with visual effects by Seoul-based Macrograph. (*Demon Empire* was also shot at Hengdian World Studio.)

In short, the abovementioned films stand as watershed productions, films that have inspired further collaborative ventures between the Chinese and Korean film industries that have continued to grow in both strength and scope. Further collaboration between Chinese and Korean film-makers followed these projects, including a growing number of Korean firms that have provided production and digital post-production services in China, at a fraction of the cost of similar work undertaken for most Hollywood blockbusters.

In 2007, a new watershed in international film collaboration was celebrated when BIFF (then known as PIFF) screened Feng Xiaogang's *Assembly* (*jijie hao*, 2007) as the festival's opening offering. The prominent position given to this action-war drama, a co-production between China, Hong Kong and Korea, at BIFF represented a new level of recognition for the collaborative efforts of the Greater Chinese and Korean film industries. Not only were Huayi Brothers and Media Asia Films, *Assembly*'s producers, the largest and most progressive film companies in China, but the festival screening showcased the close involvement of Korean action and post-production digital effects specialists in the film (coordinated by MK Pictures); such features would soon come to typify Korea's deepening contribution to Chinese cinema.

From this moment on the large scale sharing of technical staff and technological transfer between China and Korea signalled the birth of an advanced form of film collaboration. Replacing the patterns of the recent past, where one partner commonly maintained leadership of a co-production project, China and Korea were showing how it was possible for groups of international crew members to be brought together through personal and industry networks to complete creative projects as a team. This is not to claim that colleagues from both countries shared intimate details of every aspect of the film during the pre-production, production, and post-production stages of *Assembly*, rather that levels of collaboration, mutual respect and *guanxi* had reached unprecedented heights since members of both film industries had worked alongside each other on *Musa* in 2001.

In early 2006, when Feng Xiaogang was conceiving the *Assembly*, he and his core production and planning team looked to Kang Je-gyu's Korean War blockbuster hit *Taegukgi* (2004, aka *The Brotherhood of War*) as a model to emulate. Not only did *Taegukgi* look, sound, and feel like the Hollywood blockbuster *Saving Private Ryan* (1998), which was made on a budget of around US$70 million, but it was produced for around 18 per cent of that figure. To help bring *Taegukgi* to China, Feng and his team collaborated with Korea's MK Pictures, which was exploring ways of capitalizing on the momentum generated by the production of *Musa* in China five years earlier.

MK Pictures assisted the project by offering Feng producer Edward Chi-yun Yi, a BFA graduate who coordinated the work of specialized teams from Korea. Yi had extensive networks in both the Korean and Chinese film industries and had developed an intimate knowledge of their inner workings. In addition to speaking Chinese and understanding Chinese culture, he knew the right people for this project – namely, the key executives and crewmembers who had worked on *Taegukgi*. In 1996, on returning to Korea after completing his studies at BFA, Yi was appointed production manager on director Kang Je-gyu's *The Ginko Bed*. Then in 1999, he was involved in the pre-production of *The Anarchists*, scouting locations in Shanghai. He was also a line producer during its production at Shanghai Film Studio's newly built 62-acre film production and theme park complex, with heavy assistance from local art director Zheng Changfu and producers Zhong Zheng (of *Purple Butterfly*, *zi hudie*, 2003) fame) and Fu Wenxia. As one of the active producers on *Assembly*, Yi was responsible for bringing together a Korean team of action and stunt coordinators, as well as technical experts in special effects, make-up, sound effects and sound editing – teams which had worked together previously on *Taegukgi*. Given that this was the first time such a large number of Korean technicians and other specialists had worked on a Chinese blockbuster, there was much for both sides to learn from each other. As a result the Korean film industry was made aware of the burgeoning need in the Chinese industry for the type of expertise and advanced technical skills and training that Korean practitioners had amassed since *Shiri* had splashed across the big screen in 1999.

Listing the numerous films made in China with input from Korean practitioners following the release of *Assembly* is a near-impossible task. Although, what the list does show is that Koreans have left their mark on a plethora of genres including *wuxia* (martial arts), comedies and fantasies, contemporary and period dramas, romantic and black comedies, thrillers and horror films and war films. In reality the number of Chinese–Korean film encounters of all varieties far exceeds the list of co-productions offered by KOFIC and other studies of Chinese and Korean cinema in international markets.[6]

Having said this, since *Assembly*, Yi has continued to work as a producer with some of China's leading commercial directors and has introduced an increasing number of fellow Korean film practitioners to Chinese film projects. In 2008 and 2009, Korean special effects and make-up company MAGE, in concert with special effects company Demolition and the Seoul-based Dolby film sound-mixing studio Bluecap Soundworks, worked extensively on John Woo's *Red Cliff I* (*chibi*, 2008) and *Red Cliff II* (2009), helping to realize the director's full creative vision for the series. In 2010, these same three firms, along with other Korean action consultants and stunt coordinators, helped to re-create the striking disaster sequences and soundscapes in Feng Xiaogang's *Aftershock* (*Tangshan da dizhen*, 2010), a film about the 1976 Tangshan earthquake and its devastating aftermath. In addition, Busan-based AZ Works, headed by Lee Yong-gi, 'grandfather of colour grading' in Korea, received the visual effects award at the Hong Kong Film Awards for its contribution to Tsui Hark's *Detective Dee and the Mystery of the Phantom Flame* (*Di Renjie zhi tongtian diguo*, 2010). While working on these and additional projects, Yi (and others following in his footsteps) came to appreciate that Korea was far ahead of China in terms of advanced digital production and post-production technology and techniques. As a result, Korean companies and practitioners began concentrating their activities in this lucrative frontier territory.

Between 2009 and 2015, Korean practitioners working in China continued to consolidate their skills while gaining valuable experience in the rapidly expanding Chinese film industry. During this period, Seoul-based Digital Idea and Beijing-based Lollol Media worked on the visual effects and digital intermediary (aka DI or colour grading) work for Tsui Hark's top-performing 3D film *Flying Swords of Dragon Gate* (*gui lunmei*, 2011) as well as *CZ12* (aka *Chinese Zodiac*, *shi'er sheng xiao*, directed by Jackie Chan, 2012) and *The Chef, The Actor, The Scoundrel, chuzi xizi pizi*.[7] In addition, Korea's CJ Powercast, Next Visual Studio, and Lollol Media (along with Chinese firm Phenom Film) played major roles in the VFX and 2D/3D digital intermediary work on director Wuershan's supernatural fantasy–action romance *Painted Skin 2: The Resurrection* (*huapi er*, 2012), inspired by the classic Liao Zhai Zhi Yi collection of supernatural tales.[8]

Thus far, the biggest box office sensation resulting from Chinese–Korean collaboration is Stephen Chow's *Journey to the West: Conquering the Demons* (*xiyou xiangmo pian*, 2013), an action-comedy directed by Stephen Chow and Derek Kwok Chi-Kin, which returned a gross profit of US$192 million. For this action-packed 3D production, Korean companies Macrograph and Moneff, in concert with the Korean VFX farm run by Los Angeles-based Venture 3D, completed the spectacular visual effects; Seoul-based Locus Corp. was responsible for key CGI scenes as well as the film's ancillary character-licensing products. The next big collaborative hit was *The Monkey King* (*da nao tian gong*, 2014), which conquered the box office with US$168 million. A total of 11 Korean companies worked on this film, including CG firms Dexter Digital, Digital Studio 2L, Digital Idea and Macrograph, helping *The Monkey King* to become the second runner-up at the box office in 2014, behind *Transformers: Age of Extinction* and the Chinese romantic comedy/road movie *Breakup Buddies* (*xinhua nufang*) directed by Ning Hao.[9] In their respective credits, *Journey to the West* and *The Monkey King* boast the longest list of Korean companies and practitioners of any films produced in China, demonstrating the increasing scope of the ongoing internationalization of Chinese cinema.

Clearly the list of Korean companies and individuals contributing to Asian blockbusters that exemplify Chinese cinema's upward technological trajectory is burgeoning. In particular, Yi and other producers, who have stayed and worked in China as long-termers, are now setting their sails to catch the winds of change blowing across China – gradual changes that have come about as a result of government regulations that have opened up the film industry and that may or may not continue in the same direction in the future. I call these post-production pioneers 'effects inbetweeners' – a play on the name of the visual effects clean-up artists in the animation industry's pre-digital (traditional) era.

EFFECTS INBETWEENERS

Since 2002, China's annual film production figures have soared, with an average annual growth rate of 20 per cent; in 2010, with 526 productions to its credit, China became the third largest producer of films in the world (Entgroup 2012). In 2014 this figure had reached 618. The rapidly expanding number of films being produced on an annual basis in China (Frater 2015) is ensuring that there is no shortage of DI and visual effects work for both domestic and international practitioners and firms.

Between 2013 and 2014, Forestt Studios, a full-service post-production company based in the Qikeshu Innovation Park area of Chaoyang District in Beijing, and run by experienced Korean DI expert Ethan Park, completed a series of films of its own. Forestt specializes in colour grading for feature films (to which it has recently added full-scale sound post-production), and is one of the few Chinese companies that can meet the highest international standards for 2D and 3D high-resolution (4K real-time) digital intermediate service. The firm's lengthy filmography includes the romance *My Lucky Star* (2013), a prequel to the 2009 official Chinese–Korean co-production *Sophie's Revenge, feichang wanmei* (produced by Beijing Perfect World Co. and CJ Entertainment), directed by

US-born Dennie Gordon and starring Zhang Ziyi and Leehom Wang; and the Chinese–Hong Kong action crime thriller *A Chilling Cosplay* (2013, aka *−197°C Murder*), by director Wang Guangli and producer Wong Jing. With Park at the controls, Forestt also made major contributions to Wang Xiaoshuai's *Red Amnesia* (*chuangru zhe*, 2014). In all, Forestt Studios completed around 20 films in 2014 and another 15 in the first quarter of 2015, and there are another 10 films in the pipeline for completion before the end of 2015.[10]

As one might expect, Chinese directors and producers inspire Korean DI and visual effects technicians in different ways from their Korean counterparts, pushing them to satisfy a different set of aesthetic values and production needs. Simply put, China's landscape colour palette is unlike that found in Korea; in particular, the colours of land and sky, the shapes of mountains and rivers, as well as people's reaction to the natural world all differ in significant respects from their Korean equivalents, further challenging Korean professionals to explore alternative artistic and creative terrain.

This trend has been strengthened by the relaxation of official censorship regulations. In July 2013, China's State Administration of Press, Publication, Radio, Film, and Television (aka SAPPRFT, formerly known as the State Administration of Radio, Film, and Television or SARFT) announced that it would confine its scrutiny to inspecting a story summary prior to granting a filming permit, thereby eliminating 20 distinct components requiring government approval, including the thorough assessment of film scripts (Xinhua 2013).[11] With this changing policy landscape in mind, the somewhat surprising censorship approval granted to the psychological mystery thriller-drama *Double Xposure* (*erci baoguang*, 2012) offers a timely opportunity to assess the potential for technical and artistic creativity in the Chinese film industry under a relaxed censorship regime. A case study of its post-production context offers insights into how and where Korean practitioners are making a mark on Chinese cinema in a potentially volatile policy environment.

Double Xposure (2012), director Li Yu's fifth and most aesthetically ambitious feature film to date, is a quintessential example of an evolving transnational cinema – one that is being created through an assemblage of international collaborators drawn from across China's new ecology of expertise. Her exploration of thriller and road movie conventions, which marks a departure from her earlier documentary and realist style, makes the film a significant new addition to 'China's genre revolution' (Elley 2015). In this visually stunning film, Li uses the flashbacks, illusions and hallucinations involving sex, adultery, violence and murder experienced by the protagonist Song Qi (played by Fan Bingbing) to disorientate the audience. Song Qi, an ambitious cosmetic surgeon, experiences emotional turmoil after learning that her closest friend is having an affair with her boyfriend. Her life becomes more disjointed when she discovers that she has a psychological disorder. Song embarks on a road trip in search of her past and as a means of uncovering her deeply repressed thoughts. The second half of the film in particular is marked by a sense of ambiguity, detracting from the overall cohesion of the story. Despite its provocative content, or perhaps *because* the film's controversial scenes are presented as the protagonist's paranoid delusions, *Double Xposure* managed to satisfy government censorship (after several rounds of negotiations).[12]

Double Xposure is an excellent example of the ways in which, in contemporary Chinese cinema, film genres are being expanded with the aid of the sophisticated technical support and creative input offered by Korean practitioners. The film was shot on five different formats (which were tested in advance along with an iPhone 4 camera): primarily with the Alexa digital film camera, but with flashback, helicopter, and underwater sequences shot on a combination of 35mm (for aerial photography) and Super 16mm analogue, and Canon 5D, GoPro (for CCTV footage), and RED MX (for high-speed shots) digital film cameras. The crisp, clean, cold look that these filming techniques created for the scenes set in the present day reflected the sterile atmosphere of the cosmetic surgeons' operating theatre, to give one example. This aesthetic forms an effective contrast to the aged, analogue-style appearance of the flashbacks and historical sequences, initially replicated through digital film noise, but eventually given a more authentic 'grainy' look through the use of Super 16mm film stock. Specifically, the DI was used to enhance the 'cold' feeling of the appropriate sequences by increasing the blue and green tints, and then to create a desaturated and low-contrast colour effect near the end of the film when Song Qi emerges from her delusions and into a more natural but still ethereal setting on a beach. Even for a veteran colourist like Park, with seven years' experience in the industry – which he has shared with me in multiple interviews, the DI process involved made *Double Xposure* the most challenging and interesting film he had worked on to date.

Once the footage had been digitized using state-of-the-art equipment, DI specialist Park, working on the project exclusively in Beijing, created artificial scratches and dust spots on the film, removed grain from other shots, and applied motion and edge blur for the dream sequences as well to simulate camera shake and add 'highlight glow' to close ups of Song Qi. Park's attempts to differentiate sequential shots, while also using particular colours to signal emotions displayed by the characters, provided additional challenges. The shared vision that marked the pair's relationship, along with Li Yu's confidence in Park's talent and ability, as seen in his work on her previous film *Buddha Mountain* (*guanyin shan*, 2010), enabled Park to experiment freely with colour grading and correction techniques, processes that were new not only to him as one of Korea's most experienced DI experts, but also to Chinese cinema. Park dedicated 20 days to completing the DI for *Double Xposure* over a three-month period, taking breaks between processing each quarter of the film in order to maintain a fresh perspective on the work and to push his, and cinematographer Florian Zinke's ideas even further, achieving just the kind of creative response to the material that producer Li Fang had hoped for.[13]

For *Double Xposure*, Park – who had also worked closely with Li Fang on *Buddha Mountain*, which required three months' worth of DI, resulting in a wholly unconventional visual style, and German-born cinematographer Florian Zinke, a graduate of the Beijing Film Academy – pushed their joint creative endeavours in a new direction. Building on their combined track record, the team developed a unique visual style that veered away from the direction taken by recent unconventional Korean thrillers such as the horror-thriller *H* (2002, about an urban serial killer), Kim Jee-woon's *A Tale of Two Sisters* (2003), and Park Chan-wook's *Thirst* (2009).

More recently, Forestt Studios under Park's creative direction completed the post-production and digital effects for Sixth Generation nonconforming *enfant terrible* Chinese arthouse auteur director Lou Ye's Chinese–French co-production *Blind Massage* (*tui na*, 2014), a drama told from the perspective of blind masseurs and masseuses. *Blind Massage*, which received script approval from SAPPRFT before production began, is director (and BFA graduate) Lou Ye's eighth feature film but only the third that censors have approved for release in China.[14] It won Asia Pacific Screen Awards' Jury Grand Prize and the Taipei Golden Horse Film Festival Award for best feature film, best adapted screenplay, new performer (Zhang Lei), cinematography, film editing, and sound effects, as well as the Silver Berlin Bear for Jian Zeng's outstanding artistic contribution to cinematography at the 2014 Berlin International Film Festival. Truth be told, and without providing a disservice to the ways that Jian Zeng shot the film, whilst the Silver Bear explicitly celebrates individual achievement, the film and its filmmakers owe a debt of gratitude to Park, who is uncredited on *Blind Massage* in IMDB, for his skillful and ingenious treatment of the film during post-production. Hence, it is no wonder there is a small picture of Park holding the Silver Bear hanging on the wall in Forestt Studios.

In order to create an innovative look for the film, and also to manage the multiple grading applied to nearly every single shot, Park and his team of junior assistants required 60 days, about six times as long as a film with more conventional DI, to colour it, guided in each scene by the tempo of the background music and the natural sound layer. This was a novel approach for Park and for DI more generally (certainly in China and Korea, but also internationally), given that conventional DI involves a single consistent grading for each shot. Furthermore, many colourists turn off the audio while working to avoid the soundtrack influencing their colouring style. As a result, in *Blind Massage* the soundtrack and the colour palette flow in unison as if they were two halves of a single breathing rhythm, raising provocative questions about what blind people 'see' in their imaginative world. To gain further understanding of this synesthetic rhythm in a real-life setting, Park visited numerous 'blind massage' parlors in an attempt to experience this world for himself. Limited space here prevents further analysis of how Park fully implemented his own visions into the DI and how it impacted the cinematography, however, suffice it to say that with or without Jian Zeng and Lou Ye's tacit knowledge, Park propelled the film's visual aesthetics (and cinematography) way beyond the conspicuous frame.

CONCLUDING THOUGHTS

This chapter has attempted to show how a new ecology of expertise involving Korean firms and practitioners working with Chinese colleagues is enabling China to 'catch up' to Hollywood by drawing technological expertise and knowledge through selective collaborative ventures. In many ways this fluid assemblage of human capital, which typifies the global playing field, is presently enabling the Chinese and Korean film industries gradually to challenge global markets that were once dominated by US firms and practitioners.

The opportunity for Korean film practitioners to work on the abbreviated list of Chinese films discussed here has grown from tiny seedlings – the contacts and friendships (aka *guanxi*) that a handful of aspiring Korean filmmakers made while studying at the Beijing Film Academy during the early-to-mid-1990s. The professional inroads made by these now major Korean industry players have enabled themselves and others throughout the Korean film industry to become some of the most active practitioners and companies in China today. In this way Korean cinema is continuing to expand its boundaries, leveraging off talent and expertise deployed outside of Korea's national borders.

Working behind the scenes, Ethan Park (aka Park Sang-soo, not to be confused with the colourist Ethan Park working in the US industry) is one of the key figures in understanding the nature of the collaborative relationship between the Chinese and Korean film industries, and the ways in which the institution of Korean cinema is being absorbed by the Chinese film industry, at least in part, and often without acknowledgement. Park studied film editing at Dongguk University (Seoul) and in 2006 joined post-production company HFR where he specialized in colour grading and DI, skills that were in high demand as a result of the ongoing transition to digital workflow practices. Park's English-language skills landed him a key role as a DI producer on CJ E&M's first China–Korea co-production, *Sophie's Revenge* (2009). In the same year he urged HFR to open a Beijing branch, and Park moved to China to apply the skills that he had mastered while working on several dozen top-grossing Korean films.[15] After leaving HFR, he teamed up with Yi Chi-yun at rival post-production firm Lollol Media in Beijing, thus gaining further experience in the local market and expanding his industry and personal networks. Park is currently CEO of Forestt Studios, known for both its commercial work and highly creative arthouse genre-bending films.

Post-production practitioners like Park are pioneer digital colourists: that is, they manipulate the colours of a film during the post-production and final printing processes, which are now completely digitized (and known as digital intermediary or DI). DI, which has become an essential medium for filmmaking across the globe, enables filmmakers to manipulate a film and prepare it for digital projection before it is distributed to cinemas or processed for other screen formats. Park is one of the select few practitioners who has 'coloured' and, following the industry's transition from analog to digital equipment, digitized the bulk of Korean feature films, both commercial and independent, made by the leading producers, including such leading directors as Bong Joon-ho, Park Chan-wook, Kim Jee-woon and Lee Myung-se. This remarkable achievement has come hard on the heels of his role in pioneering Korean cinema's transition to digital equipment and workflow processes between 2002 and 2005.

While working in China, Park has explored numerous opportunities offered by new types of film projects that have enabled him to enhance his skills. The pathway that he has taken and the timing of his entry into the Chinese market has coincided with the large-scale expansion and transformation of the Korean film industry. At the same time a wave of change is sweeping through the Chinese film industry, although some practitioners are yet to appreciate the rapidly changing policy environment in which they are now operating. Be that as it may, there is no doubt that this transformation of the Chinese film scene is being driven by commercial imperatives and achieved in large part by the leveraging of creativity from outside China, notably from Korea, one of the country's most significant trading partners. In this way new avenues are being created for alternative production and distribution ventures within China's independent cinema as well as the mainstream commercial environment.

Against this background of large-scale collaboration, and bearing in mind that international film co-productions have become commonplace around the globe (and that visual effects experts rarely receive full credit for their post-production artistry), fine-tuning the working relationships between international partners still presents a challenge for Chinese cinema. In the cases of *Double Xposure* and *Blind Massage* a pinch of Korean technical skill and ingenuity has proven to be a key ingredient in producing a successful dish, especially where the creation of original and dynamic colourscapes and intriguing accents to cinematography has been a critical factor. Just as a new breed of Korean films produced after the success of *Shiri* achieved a high level of production values and narrative diversity, contemporary Chinese films are becoming known for their innovative visual styles and growing diversity of genres and stories. The increasing collaboration between the two countries, especially cooperation in post-production work, is raising the bar in terms of technical quality, leading to increased value in the marketplace.

Whilst industrial and technological change is always the product of multiple factors and variables, as well as teams of creative practitioners, it is undeniable that a handful of Korean technicians have created new pathways that have smoothed the Chinese film industry's transition to digital workflow practices to advanced international standards. In the recent past, DI was a cost-prohibitive luxury offered by a small number of US, Canadian and Australian firms working with a select group of leading Chinese directors and their big-budget films. However, the arrival of Park and other Korean practitioners (working for Korea-based companies such as CJ Powercast, Dexter Digital, Digital Idea, Digital Studio 2L, Macrograph, Moneff, and SK Independence, etc.), coupled with lower costs and a high level of technical capability, has enabled both established and emerging Chinese filmmakers to utilize this key process. These technical specialists have provided a set of readily transferable and economical resources in the form of core skills, knowledge, and technological expertise that are a match for the high-end infrastructure and capabilities generally associated with Hollywood productions while complementing and strengthening the existing capabilities of Chinese filmmakers and technicians.

In sum, the collaborative ventures that Korean producers and directors pursued in tandem with their Chinese colleagues throughout the 2000s have entered a new stage with the advent of a host of new opportunities in the post-production arena. In 2015 China is still the new wild frontier, a stimulating environment that nevertheless presents Korean practitioners with many challenges, including opportunity costs – the sharing of trade secrets and intellectual property, among other things. If industry headlines are anything to go by, however, this is a small price to pay given that there seems to be 'No End in Sight for China Film Sector's Rapid Expansion' (Coonan 2013). In these ways, both Chinese and Korean national cinemas are undergoing a major makeover as Chinese filmmakers and firms leverage the fresh aesthetic qualities and export-oriented expertise for which Korean cinema has become celebrated around the globe since the censorship of domestic films was ended by the Korean government in 1996 (Yecies 2008; Yecies and Shim 2011). In this new cultural and commercial arena, Korea's global experience and success with its own brand of soft power has been instrumental in developing its collaborative relationship with China.

NOTES

* An earlier version of this work appears in: Yecies, B. and Shim, A. (2016), 'Korean transnational cinema and the renewed tilt Toward China', in B. Yecies and A. Shim (eds.), *The Changing Face of Korean Cinema, 1960–2015*. New York: Routledge, pp. 227–50.

1. This chapter draws on research currently being conducted in an Australian Research Council Discovery project *Willing Collaborators: Negotiating Change in East Asian Media Production* DP 140101643. The author thanks producer Yi Chi Yun, and post-production practitioners Ethan Park, Lee Yong-gi, Kim Hyeong-seok, Peter Ahn, and Choi Young, as well as Chinese industry representatives Shan Dongbing (former International General Manager, Le Vision Pictures), Michelle Yeh (Producer, East Light Film), Mia Zhang (Creative Producer, Walt Disney China and formerly with Yunnan Film Group), and April Fang (April Harvest Productions) for sharing their insights on this topic.

2. According to a major KOFIC report, film exports to Hong Kong are listed separately from those to the PRC; the value of exports to Hong Kong also increased from US$832,700 in 2012 to US$2,755,624 in 2014. Taken together, these figures show an unprecedented increase in total exports to Greater China. See KOFIC 2015, 48.

3. The government also allows a small number of flat-fee foreign films on China's big screens. Between 2012 and 2014, over 100 additional films were approved for import – each recouping a one-off payment without taking a cut of the box office revenue. One advantage of the flat-fee system is that the film's original foreign producer/distributor receives the fees up-front and is not dependent on a local partner to report box office income accurately – a besetting problem for parts of the global film industry today.

4. Jibu, Bian (2015), 'China Passes US at Movie Box Office', *China Daily* 3 March, accessed 3 March 2015. at http://m.chinadaily.com.cn/en/2015-03/03/content_19709880.htm.

5. Other recent cases of Korean actors working in China include Jung Woo-sung starring alongside Michelle Yeoh in *Reign of Assassins* (2010), Kim Hee-sun in *The Warring States* (2011), Kwon Sang-woo in *Chinese Zodiac* (2012), Song Hye-kyo in *The Grandmaster* (2013), *The Crossing* (2014), and *The Crossing 2* (2015), as well as K-pop boy band Super Junior singer and actor Choi Si Won, in *Dragon Blade* (2015).

6. On the Kobiz (Korean Film Business Zone) website run by KOFIC, a total of 28 films are listed in the Korea–China co-production category, beginning with *Seven Swords* in 2005. The co-production area listed include co-producing, co-financing, location,

production services and talent exchanges: accessed 20 September 2015 at www.kobiz. or.kr/jsp/production/productionCaseList.jsp.

7. The total gross profit earned by *The Flying Swords of Dragon Gate* was US$100 million. See Marsh, James (2012), 'China Beat: Tsui Hark & Bona Exploring 3D Together', *Twitchfilm* 12 May, accessed 31 March 2015 at http://twitchfilm.com/2012/05/china-beat-tsui-hark-bona-3d-projects.html.

8. *Painted Skin 2*'s box office takings exceeded US$108 million, overtaking Jiang Wen's *Let the Bullets Fly* (US$106 million) and Feng Xiaogang's *Aftershock* (US$106 million) and becoming the highest-grossing Chinese film of 2012. See Anonymous, 'Painted Skin 2 Becomes Highest-Grossing Chinese Film Ever' *Screendaily* (28 July 2012), accessed 31 March 2015 at http://www.screendaily.com/territories/asia-pacific/painted-skin-2-becomes-highest-grossing-chinese-film-ever/5044809.article.

9. See www.boxofficemojo.com/intl/china/yearly/.

10. Prior to establishing Forestt, Park also worked on Wang's *Chongqing Blues* (2010), as well as Zhang Yuan's celebrated *Beijing Flickers* (2012).

11. The easing of restrictions only applies to films dealing with 'ordinary' subjects – those avoiding matters connected with 'diplomacy, ethnic topics, religion, military, judiciary, historical figures, and cultural celebrities'.

12. Earlier, the cuts to Li's *Lost in Beijing* demanded by the censors had fundamentally altered the story written by Li and her co-writer and producer Li Fang. (The film was later banned outright.)

13. In the digital environment, the DI process normally takes around seven days to complete, or five days for a rush job. Not only did Park's work on *Double Xposure* amount to more than double the number of working days usually spent on the DI for a film (which usually involves around 80% grading and 20% adjusting the work according to feedback received from the director and/or producer), but it also marked an innovative approach to the workflow process.

14. Lou Ye's notable filmography includes *Suzhou River* (2000, initially banned by SARFT), *Purple Butterfly* (2003, approved), *Summer Palace* (2006, banned), *Spring Fever* (2009, banned), and *Mystery* (2012, approved).

15. For HFR's China branch, Ethan Park and Lee Yong-gi purchased and installed state-of-the-art digital post-production equipment, costing upwards of US$500,000 (depending on the film scanner, recorder and digital projector chosen, as well as upgrades and options, but not including the cost of building a suitable studio space – a project which they also oversaw). The pair have transferred state-of-the-art technology in China, thus contributing more than creative ideas to the local ecology of expertise. Park and Lee relocated to Beijing in 2009 and 2011 respectively, and in 2015 they and a growing number of Korean colleagues are among the most sought-after DI and visual effects experts in China.

REFERENCES

Berry, Chris (2013), 'Transnational culture in East Asia and the logic of assemblage', *Asian Journal of Social Science* **41** (5): 453–70.

Coonan, Clifford (2013), 'No end in sight for China film sector's rapid expansion', *The Hollywood Reporter: Busan Daily Edition #3* (6 October): 2.

Elley, Derek (2015), 'China's genre revolution', *Film Business Asia* 23 July, accessed 6 January 2015 at www.filmbiz.asia/news/chinas-genre-revolution.

Entgroup (2012), *China Film Industry Report 2010–2011*, Entgroup, accessed 20 September 2015 at www.entgroup.cn/uploads/reports/2011123123.pdf.

Frater, Patrick (2015), 'China surges 36% in total box office revenue', *Variety* 4 January, accessed 26 Feb 2015 at http://variety.com/2015/film/news/china-confirmed-as-global-number-two-after-36-box-office-surge-in-2014-1201392453/.

Giddens, Anthony (1994), 'Living in a post-traditional society', in Ulrich Beck, Anthony Giddens, and Scott Lash (eds.), *Reflexive Modernization: Politics, Tradition and Aesthetics in the Modern Social Order*. Cambridge, UK: Polity Press in association with Blackwell, pp. 56–109.

Kim, Hyeol-lok (2011), 'Kofic Chairman Kim Ui-Seok, "Globalisation is not a choice, but a necessity"' ('Kim Ui-Seok Yeongjin Wiwonjang "Geullobeoreun Seontaek Anira Pilsu"'), *Star News* 14 April, accessed 1 March 2015 at http://star.mt.co.kr/view/stview.php?no=20 11041408173701359&type=1&outlink=1.

KOFIC (2015), *2014 Film Industry Overview* (*2014 Yeonghwa Saneop Gyeolsan*). Seoul: KOFIC.

Korean Cinema Today, Busan Special Edition (2012), 'Wider, deeper, more tightly with China', Vol. 14 (October), Seoul: Korean film Council (KOFIC): 30.

Ong, Aiwa (2005), 'Ecologies of expertise: assembling flows, managing citizenship', in A. Ong and S.J. Collier (eds.), *Global Assemblages: Technology, Politics and Ethics as Anthropological Problems*. Malden, MA: Blackwell, pp. 337–53.

Pulver, Andrew (2013), 'China confirmed as world's largest film market outside US', *The Guardian* 22 March, accessed 20 February 2015 at www.theguardian.com/film/2013/mar/22/china-largest-film-market-outside-us.

Qin, Amy (2015), 'China overtakes U.S. at the box office', *New York Times* 2 March, accessed 20 September 2015 at http://sinosphere.blogs.nytimes.com/2015/03/02/china-overtakes-the-u-s-at-the-box-office/?_r=0.

Tsui, Clarence (2012), 'Why more movie theaters in China could be bad news for Hollywood', *The Hollywood Reporter* 7 December, accessed 2 March 2015 at http://www.hollywoodreporter.com/news/chinese-movie-theaters-why-more-399173.

Xinhua News Agency (2013), 'China cuts 20 approval items for film, TV sectors', *China Daily US Edition* (ChinaDaily.com.cn) 17 July, accessed 20 September 2015 at http://usa.chinadaily.com.cn/china/2013-07/17/content_16789815.htm.

Yecies, Brian (2008), 'Planet Hallyuwood's political vulnerabilities: censuring the expression of satire in *The President's Last Bang* (2005)', *International Review of Korean Studies* **5** (1): 37–64.

Yecies, Brian and Aegyung Shim (2011), 'Contemporary Korean cinema: challenges and the transformation of Planet Hallyuwood', *Acta Koreana* **14** (1/June): 1–15.

18. Chinese documentary: towards commercialization

Yingchi Chu

INTRODUCTION

Documentary has played an important role in nation building in China. Nowadays, however, the role of documentary is changing, as are its practitioners and investors. While retaining its role as a vehicle of state propaganda, documentary makers are embracing new formats and seeking out audiences in keeping with the challenges of 'cultural system reform' (*wenhua tizhi gaige*) on the one hand, and 'going out' (*zou chuqu*) on the other. As a cultural industry sector that has largely underachieved in comparison with international counterparts, the challenge now is for documentary makers to seize the moment.

If we accept John Grierson's definition of documentary as 'creative treatment of actuality' (Izod and Kilborn 1998: 427), China is one of the biggest documentary producers worldwide, generating between 7,000 and 10,000 hours annually for television alone (He et al. 2014: 6). These figures include traditional documentary formats as well as reality shows and travel documentaries. Television remains the most prolific producer of documentary. At the same time there is a noticeable decrease in film formats and an increase across digital media platforms. The majority of Chinese documentaries are screened via three nation-wide, dedicated television channels, in addition to provincial and city channels. Since the 1990s, so-called 'New Documentary' and independent documentaries have captured the attention of a small but influential circle of fans in China at festivals, as well as critics and scholars abroad (see Ma and Wong's chapter in this volume; Berry et al. 2010). More recently, a number of Chinese mainstream documentaries have entered the international market. In 2013, China Central Television (CCTV) distributed a selection of 84 documentaries to 51 countries and 14 airlines (CDRC, 2015, 127). Amongst these, *A Bite of China* (*shejian shang de Zhongguo*, 2012) and *China's Mega Projects* (*chaoji gongcheng*, 2012) have been screened in South Korea, Belgium, Poland, Australia, the United States and Germany (CDRC 2015: 127; Cheng Chunli 2014: 92–3).

This chapter presents an overview of Chinese documentary, arguing that while it remains under the control of the Chinese government, it is moving inexorably towards embracing the principles of commercialization.

HISTORICAL OVERVIEW: FROM DOGMA TO POLYPHONY

Since the period of Mao Zedong, documentary film has played a decisive political role in the education of the Chinese population by adopting Lenin's motto of documentary as 'the visualization of political theories' (Gao 2003:131; Fang 2003: 205; Shan 2005: 142–5). Since then the documentary industry has been controlled throughout the production process from scripting, filming, and editing to distribution and exhibition (Fang 2003; Shan 2005). Documentary topics were routine responses to government edicts, while filmmakers had to adopt a monolithic pattern for documentaries, identifiable by a shared 'dogmatic formula' (Chu 2007: 53ff.; 2015). Only when Deng Xiaoping's agenda of the Four Modernizations took hold in the 1980s did the documentary scene change from its dogmatic style towards the presentation of a cinematic 'polyphony of voices'; this style became popular in the early 1990s (Chu 2007).

This stylistic transformation led to the evolution of three strands of documentary film. First and foremost, there is 'mainstream government-sanctioned documentary' with its official system of production, distribution, and exhibition, as well as concomitant commentary, festivals and awards. The second strand comprises 'semi-independent documentary', operating partly within and partly outside the system. Documentaries of this second strand are identified by their focus on marginal and ordinary people, and the representation of minorities under social change with a presentational process favouring observational documentation. This strand is exemplified by the New Documentary Movement of the 1990s (Lü 2003; Berry et al. 2010), and by the Yunnan based ethnographic and community oriented film production. Some of these filmmakers collaborate with state-owned TV stations, government institutions, and overseas funding bodies, such as in joint ventures between the Yunnan Social Science Academy and the US Ford Foundation, and neighbouring countries like Vietnam (Bao 2014).

As a reaction to an aesthetics of grand national themes with monolingual narration, non-diegetic music and montage illustrating political ideology, the New Documentary Movement developed a cinematic style identified by Luke Robinson as '*xianchang*', an emphasis on contingency in location shooting, the here and now of filmed subjects, and what is accidental and ultimately uncontrollable. For Robinson, the cinema of *xianchang* announces a 'clear post-socialist sensibility' (Robinson 2013: 72), exemplified by Wu Wenguang's *Bumming in Beijing* (*liulang Beijing*, 1990), and Duan Jinchuan's *No 16 Barkhor South Street* (*Bakuo nanjie shiliu hao*, 1996) straddling both inside and outside the system, as do some films from the Shanghai and Beijing television documentary programs *Documentary Editing Room* and *Oriental Horizon* of the 1990s (see Berry 2009). While the New Documentary Movement ended in the late 1990s (Lü 2003, 23), semi-independent documentary making has continued to the present as outsourced or commissioned work, and is flourishing today.

The third strand, 'independent documentary', operates outside the official film culture (Qian 2012; Robinson 2013; Viviani 2014). Its filmmakers define themselves as strictly autonomous, their documentaries being sustained by small circles of artists, film buffs and self-funded exhibitions. Internationally, independent documentaries have appealed to audiences at film festivals in Australia, North America, Europe and the rest of Asia. Independent documentary was a more radical response to the domination by mainstream ideology and presentational modes, financing, production and screening. The result was the prolific production of documentary critique of social woes, environmental degradation and alternative versions of history (Meng 2015; Viviani 2014; Voci 2010). A few striking examples of this kind are the powerful *West of the Tracks* (*tiexi qu*, 2003), directed by Wang Bing, Hu Jie's *Looking for Lin Zhao's Soul* (*xunzhao Lin Zhao de hun*, 2004), Ai Xiaoming's *Our Children* (*women de haizhi*, 2009), and more recently Chai Jing's *Under the Dome* (*qiongding zhi xia*, 2015). However, the New Documentaries, ethnographic films, and independent documentaries have not captured the imagination of mass audiences in China and so have remained marginal phenomena. This is so partly because the former are primarily concerned with documenting social change and cultural specificity, while the latter is disinclined to sacrifice its main objective of critique to commercialization, quite apart from the fact that the government has prevented independent documentaries from entering the market.

Viewing the development trajectory of Chinese documentary since its dogmatic phase, it is evident that an orientation towards the market is emerging in tune with broader trends of commercialization in the cultural industry. This is partly a consequence of government policies since the economic reforms of the 1980s, the separation of production and screening in the 1990s, the transformation of media and cultural institutions into industries in 2003 and 2004, and furthermore, an effect of China's 'soft power' policies of 'going abroad' since the early 2000s (Keane 2013, 2015; Chu 2014; Nye 2005; Sun 2015). However, this shift should not blind us to the fact that Chinese documentaries retain their roots in two broadly shared convictions: that traditional aesthetics in the arts should continue its responsibility to produce good citizens and that the doctrine of documentary as 'visualization of politics' is still valuable. This commitment is reflected in the continuing dominance of subject matter and narratorial guidance, as well as didactic editing. In four decades of evolution since the establishment of the People's Republic, Chinese documentary has had no real competitors, enjoying undivided government support. Yet over the last three decades, a growing tension has emerged between its ideological stance and its failure to satisfy market expectations. With the spectacular exceptions of some documentaries, such as *A Bite of China* or *China's Mega Projects*, the box-office revenue and ratings of documentaries still lag well behind those of the fiction film.

POLICY: PROMOTION AND RETARDATION

Today, the Chinese government remains firmly in charge of the documentary industry and cultural industries more broadly. The Central Publicity Department (CPD), the Ministry of Culture (MoC) and the State Administration of Publication Press Radio Film Television (SAPPRFT) issue policies relating to subject matter, production, exhibition, trading, awards, training and consumption, with the objective of 'strengthening the soft power' of Chinese culture (Gao 2014: 49). SAPPRFT invests in the documentary infrastructure, secures screen space and ensures that overseas competitors do not swamp the domestic market. In 2010, the government announced its policy of 'Speeding up the development of the documentary industry' (*guanyu jiakuai jilupian chanye fazhan de ruogan yijian*), followed in 2013 by 'Improving 2014 satellite TV programming' (*guanyu zhuohao 2014 nian dianshi shangxin zhonghe pindao jiemu bianpai he beian gongzuo de tongzhi*), reserving a minimum of 30 per cent screen time for non-fiction programs, and more importantly, no less than 30 minutes for domestic documentaries in each of the 34 satellite channels. At the same time, the Beijing and Shanghai documentary channels were permitted to join in, making three documentary channels available nation-wide. This leaves an annual gap of some 6,000 additional hours of film to be filled (Gao 2014: 47).

To meet demand SAPPRFT has promised to stimulate documentary production on its China Documentary website, inviting the public to submit proposals for production and marketing. SAPPRFT also aims to strengthen copyright protection, safeguard screening for the new media, and secure the domestic market for Chinese products. A screening ratio of 7:3 has been set in favour of Chinese over imported documentaries and training programs have been introduced for young people to get involved in the industry. To gear up production, interest free loans and low tax concessions, especially for documentaries targeting overseas markets, are now available. In line with 'going abroad' (*zou chuqu*) policies, SAPPRFT is encouraging exchanges with non-Chinese industries, boosting mainstream production on Chinese topics by forging links between governments, documentary associations, marketing agencies, and research institutions abroad (Gao 2014: 46–50). SAPPRFT also promises to continue its policy of separating production from screening to allow private companies to work with the official system. However, such support is granted on condition that the documentaries so produced comply with official guidelines of 'promoting patriotism, history and culture, and ocean consciousness', the latter referring to the spread of Chinese culture abroad (Gao 2014: 49). The 2015 budget of RMB 11.5 million (approx. US$2 million), for example, was earmarked for the selection of projects such as *Hundred Years: The China Dream, China: Our Story* and *Seeking Dreams: the Chinese*. There is also a modest budget for short documentaries dedicated to topics like *The China Dream*, publicizing China's reforms and progress (Gao 2014: 49). For this purpose, a special archive for short documentaries has been established by SAPPRFT for downloading and screening.

Unfortunately, increased production by itself does not guarantee high approval ratings. In the wake of the policy of the 30 minutes compulsory screening on satellite TV, a survey conducted by the Chinese Documentary Research Centre (CDRC) found that while the 18:00 to 1:00 ratings in three out of nine channels had slightly improved, those in six other channels had dropped (CDRC 2015: 124). This kind of audience reaction should not be surprising. Globally, documentaries are in fierce competition with fiction genres and other forms of entertainment, such as singing competitions, dating programs and game shows, especially during prime time. In spite of policies promoting a documentary screen culture and increased production, the Chinese documentary market so far remains small, although optimism is in the air. The potential vitality of documentary creativity cannot be tapped as long as the government continues to insist on the genre's didactic ideological function. Likewise, because of the government's continued blocking of documentaries produced outside the system, especially those raising social concerns, as did *Under the Dome*, China's full creative potential cannot be unleashed. This situation has produced an unhealthy tension between the official directives endorsing cultural industries and their marketization, on the one hand, and the reality of a stagnating documentary production, on the other.

INDUSTRY: RATTLING THE CHAINS

Albeit still ideologically oriented, the 2010 and 2013 policies mark the beginning of Chinese documentary on the way to commercialization. The challenge for the documentary industry now is to comply with government guidelines and yet to produce documentaries that attract high ratings in competition with fiction genres, dating programs and singing competitions. Popularity is now the name of the game. But the competition for audiences is no longer the prerogative for TV stations alone. Owing to the availability of new forms of entertainment, TV audiences have been in decline. This has put pressure on TV stations to experiment with overseas formats to boost domestic ratings (Keane 2015). At the same time, the documentary industry has benefitted from the accessibility and interactive nature of the new media. For instance, Chinese YouTube-like sites such as Youku Tudou, QQ, Sohu, and iQiyi are providing a novel platform for independent documentaries and a forum for consumer feedback.

The message then is loud and clear: documentary production must now prioritize the market. But so far the Chinese producers have not yet quite learnt the golden rule of 'no genres, no market'. Cheng Chunli, a marketing expert, reminds the industry that 'successful overseas documentary channels have illustrated the importance of regularity and marketization. Individual style is not sufficient. Individual style must be able to transform into a genre' (Cheng Chunli 2014: 96). Unfortunately, the bulk of Chinese documentaries are still designed to fit into specialized, predetermined subject categories for TV programs, such as *renwen lishi* (biography, culture and history), *shehui jishi* (society), *ziran dili kexue tansuo* (nature, geography, science, exploration), *wenxian jilu* (compilation), and *zhenlun* (political theory). A CDRC survey of provincial TV stations between 2012 and 2013 shows that biography, culture, and history account for about half of all documentaries. About 20 per cent are about contemporary society and everyday living; compilations and political theory documentaries make up a further 20 per cent, with nature and geography topics adding 10 per cent and science providing less than 5 per cent (He et al. 2014: 15). While genre diversity by itself does not guarantee a greater variety of topics, markets tend to identify with genres rather than subject matter. More importantly, genre is now accepted as a pathway to success. For documentary makers this means exploiting sub-genres such as music/concert recordings and reality show formats (Liu and Han 2014: 305), a judgment confirmed by Chinese documentary researchers who are calling for a broader definition of documentary and its division into sub-genres (Liu 2014: 228–38; Li and Zheng 2014: 239–46; He 2014: 247–57).

Although the government has expressly welcomed investment from the commercial industry and private productions to help filling the available screen time slots, currently commercial productions find it difficult to gain access to the domestic market, let alone government regulated exports. Fewer than 20 TV stations out of 300 have the budget to purchase documentaries from commercial producers, while the private commercial industry is too small to compete (Cheng Chunli 2014: 95). A survey conducted by CDRC in 2012 and 2013 shows that only 11 per cent of the screened documentaries on TV are commissioned, around 20 per cent are purchased, and the rest are made by TV stations themselves (He et al. 2014: 13–14). Nonetheless, the CDRC is confident that the commissioned documentaries are on the rise as a result of government provision of additional TV screen time (He et al. 2014: 14). Commercial companies like *Sanduotang* signed a number of contracts with CCTV and Hubei TV in 2013 to 2014. In 2013, *Daluqiao* produced 2,700 hours of documentaries and, impressively, signed contracts with the BBC, the United States, Germany, and Spain for documentaries showcasing China (He et al. 2014: 26).

Predictably, once private companies have full access to the documentary market, the acceleration of commercialization is irreversible. Learning from the West is likewise strengthening the trend towards marketization. In developing its soft-power strategies, China has acknowledged the need to understand the kind of Western industrial processes employed by the BBC and the Discovery channel. Chinese documentary filmmakers are being encouraged to study trends in the global cultural market. The results so far have been positive. In 2012, CCTV documentaries earned US$2.2 million in overseas revenue, a 140 per cent increase over the previous year (Cheng Chunli 2014: 92). In 2013, CCTV documentaries were screened in mainstream channels in Germany, France, Italy, Belgium, Poland, the US, Australia, and in Asian and African countries. In the process of aligning itself with international standards, China is well on the way towards regularization and marketization.

Another significant boost for the documentary industry has come from digital convergence in the new media. Since it is impossible to ignore online feedback and the quantity of clicks, the industry now has a 'reliable' measuring device for gauging the degree of popularity of its documentaries. Today, iQiyi, QQ, Youku Tudou, and Sohu all offer online documentary channels, as well as participating in documentary production, hosting documentary festivals, and assisting with judging and awards (Li and Xu 2014: 192). Documentaries such as *Travelling* (*lüxin* 2013) and *Entering Tibet* (*jinzhang* 2014) are not only popular online, but are also screened on CCTV. Slick online documentaries tend to be depoliticized and entertaining, participatory and interactive, appealing to a large audience. Since the early 2010s, documentary Internet sites have been utilized for 'crowd-funding' or 'crowd-sourcing'. In 2014, Hangzhou TV and its Huashu Digital Television Media Group launched a 'user pays' digital documentary channel with the declared aim to 'educate by entertainment' and satisfy peoples' curiosity about history, nature, health, exploration, and science. The Group envisages the editing of overseas documentaries to suit domestic tastes and invite Discovery specialists (Chen Yonghua 2014: 299). Thus, digital media convergence has radically foregrounded the consumer, with significant consequences for the changing face of the Chinese documentary industry.

MODE OF PRESENTATION: CRITIQUE AND COMMERCIALIZATION

As indicated, independent documentary has been eking out a marginal existence outside the documentary mainstream. One can hardly call it an industry; its production is largely self-funded and its products are rarely seen in the commercial and public space. Some of these works are circulated underground, and occasionally they are viewed at unofficial festivals. On 23 August 2014, the government abruptly terminated the famous Beijing Independent Film Exhibition, which had been operated by artists and fans for a decade. The event, however, had always been under police surveillance. The reason for the termination goes to the heart of the issue. True independent documentary film making in China sees its *raison d'être* as social and political critique, in opposition to government guidelines. Independent documentary as critique is consistent with the topics and evolution of modes of presentation, focusing on the injustices of industrialization, urbanization and modernization, and the theme of disharmony in opposition to the propagandist utopia of a harmonious China. The emergence of a distinct mode of presentation is well suited to this agenda, from observation to participation, from copying reality to intervention, from critical commentary to social activism.

However, while rapprochement with the documentary mainstream looks unlikely, some independent documentary filmmaking has been able to find financial support abroad; for example, Wu Wenguang gained funds from the German Goethe Institute, Swiss Film, and Holland's Borneoco for the organization of 'Village Documentary' and the 'Folk Memory Project', teaching DV skills to peasants from nine provinces and creating a 'folk archive' recording rural history and village elections. Encouraged by exhibitions of his films in Italy in 2015, Wu Wenguang continues to plead for an 'independent road' for Chinese documentary, complementing the official 'highway construction'. Given the commitment to critique, commercialization looks undesirable for Chinese independent documentary film.

In contrast, a largely monological Chinese government perspective dominates mainstream documentaries, even if since the 1980s their mode of presentation has undergone some significant transformations. Increasingly, the incorporation of interviews has livened up the scripted and montage style of political lecturing, without however being able to break the ideological mould of those films. So not surprisingly, the lack of competing views and critical perspectives has drawn some cynical feedback. Some documentaries produced by the Ministry of Propaganda and CCTV as recently as 2011, such as *Flag* (*qizhi*, 2011) depicting 90 years of history of the Chinese Communist Party, and the 2012 screening of *The Road of China* (*Zhongguo zhi lu*, 2012) have been greeted by a low number of clicks on Youku Tudou, and drawn such comments as 'Am I watching science fiction?' Celebrating patriotism, documentaries like *I Love You, China* (*wo ai ni, Zhongguo*, 2009) and *It's All About the Nation* (*Zhuguo zhi shang* 2001), where footage is mixed with interviews recalling the personal sacrifices of Chinese citizens made in the service of dignity, security, and national prosperity have not fared much better in terms of audience response.

A significant portion of mainstream documentary has toned down political lecturing, favouring the dissemination of knowledge. This is well illustrated by the TV documentary series *Money* (*huobi*, 2012), consisting of ten 45-minute episodes dedicated to the history of money. In a similar vein, *The Golden Times* (*huangjin shidai*, 2012) is an eight-episode series exploring the relationship between humans and gold, made for the CCTV economics channel. It discusses the effects of money on humans, including the global money order, inflation and economic crises. The presentational process is characterized by some 200 interviews with scholars and a Nobel Prize winner. *The Gold Brick Countries* (*jinzhuang zhi guo*, 2012), also made by the CCTV, is about developments in China, Brazil, Russia and India, showing how the changes in these countries affect the world economically and politically. A recent and highly topical documentary is *China, Dashi* (*da shi Zhongguo*, 2011) in which CCTV records the last 20 years of China's stock market and how it has affected society. Surprisingly, science only makes up 3 per cent of mainstream production. When science does become a topic, it is typically presented in relation with social and ethical concerns, for instance, *Warm and Cold We Share Together* (*huanqiu tongci liang ren*, 2012) a science ethics film addressing the relation of humans and their environmental history. Another example of this presentational mode is the 15-episode series *Seeking Water for China* (*wei Zhongguo zhao shui*, 2010), completed by Chinese National Geographic after three years of field work by Chinese non-government scientist Yang Yong, who had spent 20 years studying China's rivers and lakes.

A further step in the freeing up of mainstream documentaries is the cinematic promotion of tourism. Here it is often local governments that take on the role of main producer. For example, *Longxing River* (*Longxing Jiang* 2010) produced by the Heilongjiang Provincial government, in cooperation with China News and Documentary Film Studio, CCTV, and Heilongjiang TV, entertains the viewer with Manchu scenery, ski resorts and an attractive dose of local culture with a view also to attracting investment domestically and from abroad. The five episodes of *Kangba is Blessed* (*tianci kangba* 2013) made by the Sichuan Provincial government, the Propaganda Ministry, Sichuan TV, and Tibetan Satellite TV, celebrates Kangba national minority culture across Qinghai, Tibet, Sichuan, Yunnan and Gansu. Once more promoting local tourism, *Watching Hainan* (*wang Hainan*, 2012) also commissioned by CCTV, was produced by the largest non-government documentary company in China, *Sanduotang*. With an eye on its commercial potential and high ratings, Sanduotang employed BBC cinematographer Irmin Kerck for filming the underwater attractions around tropical Hainan Island, a ploy that guaranteed its commercial success.

A highly successful lure for attracting Chinese audiences to these mainstream documentary films is to play to shared and deeply felt cultural memories, rather than political nationalism. This device has made several recent Chinese documentaries attractive to a large section of the population, as for instance in *The Forbidden City 100* (*gugong 100*, 2012), a series of 100 six-minute vignettes telling the story of the Chinese royal families. Another large and commercially oriented production is *Porcelain/China* (*chi*, 2012), a series of two fifty-minute documentaries, co-produced between CCTV, the British Museum and the Victoria and Albert Museum, documenting the history of China's export trade. Likewise, *The Power of Sport* (*tiyu de liliang* 2012), a record of how much the Olympics have changed Chinese attitudes towards sport, has had considerable public appeal. Also tapping into national emotions is the Hanban-produced *5000 Years of Chinese Characters* (*woqian nian hanzi* 2013), a part of China's soft power campaign promoting Chinese language and the work of Confucius Institutes around the world.

The path towards documentary commercialization, then, is reflected in the gradual transformation of the earlier lecturing style (see Berry 2009) into a very different mode of presentation, including dramatization, a broadening of topics, advances in visual presentation, and most recently, the use of digital convergence in multimedia technology (*jiaohushi*), promoted by such online companies as CNTV, Sohu, LeTV, Youku, Tudou, PPTV or PPS (Keane 2015: 142). This shift is what makes a playful documentary like *Hitch-hiking to Berlin* (*dache qu Berlin* 2010) particularly attractive among the young audience. In its twenty episodes of 26 minutes each the film records the adventures of an American youth, Kyle Johnson, who gives up his job in a finance company in 2009 to hitchhike from Beijing to Berlin to see his girlfriend.

A documentary popular both in China, and in some overseas markets, is *China's Mega Projects* (2012), which records the construction of the Shanghai Centre Building, the Beijing underground, and the Hong Kong-Zhuhai-Macao Bridge. The political message of China as a super power is made palatable by major concessions to filmic commercialization (Müller 2013). But by far the most successful documentaries in the new commercial format are a succession of 'taste and bite' films, such as *A Taste of Jiangnan* (*Jiangnan weidao*, 2013) focusing on the cooking culture of the region south of the Yangzi River, and the equally popular *A Bite of Chongqing* (2012), both in the wake of the commercial triumph of *A Bite of China* (*shejian shang de Zhongguo* 2012; cf. Inglis and Gimlin 2009).

A brief summary of this program will suffice to conclude this overview of Chinese documentary on the way to commercialization. *A Bite of China* is arguably the most successful documentary food program of global television. The reasons for its domestic and international triumph, including its screening at the Cannes film festival, cannot just be traced to its culinary displays. Rather, its main attraction is precisely that it transcends the very genre it seems to belong to, using the cooking template merely as a viewer's guide through the diverse regions of China, their contrasting geography, history and culture and the rich variety of human relationships. It is its combination of Chinese pedagogic documentary made easy on the eye by a seductively commercial mode of presentation that has had the ratings racing to the top in China and guaranteed the program's global appeal. Screened first on CCTV in May 2012, this seven-episode documentary is well suited to reviving the flagging interest of Chinese audiences in documentary film (Liu 2014, 233) while at the same time fulfilling its task as persuasive conveyor of China's 'soft power' message by demonstrating its 'global communicability' (Yang 2015: 409–411). Perhaps most importantly for the Chinese cultural industry, *A Bite of China* confirms that there need be no contradiction between quality documentaries and commercialization.

CONCLUSION

The conclusion, then, seems inevitable. If Chinese mainstream documentary wants to capture the imagination of its mass audiences, it must embrace the idea that documentary genres are part of popular culture. This demands a choice of subjects that satisfies the needs of education via entertainment by novel modes of presentation on TV and the Internet. Documentaries can be made attractive by multiple perspectives, dramatization, increased audience participation, feedback via ratings, and by including animation, gaming, staging and CGIs. The production process must adopt advanced forms of industrialization, with production and screening kept separate. Attractive branding is essential for channelling audience expectations, while growing regional demand can be met by local TV productions. Such measures are necessary if documentary film channels are to recoup costs.

In addition to reforms in domestic production, internationalization cannot be avoided. While China's 'soft power' campaign has had some success, the globalization of documentary production has lagged behind. There is a vast international market ready for the consumption of Chinese-made documentary shows and films. In this respect the concept of 'self-hybridization' deserves attention (Chu 2013). By toning down the intricacies of traditional Chinese culture, which so far have been the limited province of an elite trained in Sinology, the commercialization of matters Chinese can be made internationally attractive to mass audiences without necessarily violating cultural essentials. Such self-hybridized documentaries can assist China in penetrating a lucrative global market. Chinese documentary production, then, can very much benefit from the objective identified by documentary producer Liu Wen as the mission of CCTV to provide a 'global perspective, universal value and international expression'.

To be sure, China is entitled to commercially successful self-documentation of the kind represented by *A Bite of China*. And there is no reason to think that this commercializing trend is going to change in the foreseeable future. However, from a broader perspective of socially and politically advanced societies, the evolution of Chinese documentary will not be able to benefit from its full potential as long as independent documentary remains relegated to its present shadow existence. Given the technological advances in lightweight, portable equipment, documentary by its very nature is conducive to fostering a polyphony of democratic voices. It would be undesirable if a combination of official control and the wholesale commercialization of documentary in the name of 'cultural industry' were to drown out the voices of *critique*. Only when independent *critique* becomes a legitimate player in China's emerging public media sphere, will society at large be able to appreciate the valuable contribution made by a diversification of Chinese documentary modes of presentation. And only in this way can we see the true 'creative treatment of actuality' in China.

REFERENCES

Bao, Jiang (2014), *Xianxiang xue yinxiang minzhu zhi de tupo* ('Breakthrough of the phenomenology audio-visual ethnography'), in Suliu He, Ke Liu, Ning Li and Hunwa Wang (eds.), *Zhongguo jilu pian fazhan baogao 2014 (Annual Report on the Development of Chinese Documentary 2014)*. Beijing: Social Sciences Academic Press (China), pp. 258–75.

Berry, Chris (2009), 'Shanghai Television's documentary channel: Chinese television as public space', in Ying Zhu and Chris Berry (eds.), *TV China*. Bloomington: Indiana University Press, pp. 71–89.

Berry, Chris, Xinyu Lu and Lisa Rofel (2010), *The New Chinese Documentary Film Movement: For the Public Record*. Hong Kong University Press.

CDRC (Chinese Documentary Research Centre) (2015), *jilupian canye de shuju toushi* ('The data insight of documentary industry'), in Suliu He, Ke Liu, Ning Li and Hinwa Wang (eds.), *Zhongguo jilu pian fazhan baogao 2014 (Annual Report on the Development of Chinese Documentary 2014)*. Beijing: Social Sciences Academic Press (China), pp. 119–29.

Cheng, Chunli (2014), *Zhongguo jilupian 'zouchuqu' tanshu yu duice yanjiu* ('"Go to the world" of the Chinese documentary'), in Suliu He, Ke Liu, Ning Li and Hinwa Wang (eds.), *Zhongguo jilu pian fazhan baogao 2014 (Annual Report on the Development of Chinese Documentary 2014)*. Beijing: Social Sciences Academic Press (China), pp. 91–103.

Chen, Yonghua (2014), '*Qiusuo jilu' shuzi gaoqing pindao: Zhongguo jilupian fazhang xin moshi* ('"Qiusuo Channel": new development model of Chinese documentary'), in Suliu He, Ke Liu, Ning Li and Hinwa Wang (eds.), *Zhongguo jilu pian fazhan baogao 2014 (Annual Report on the Development of Chinese Documentary 2014)*. Beijing: Social Sciences Academic Press (China), pp. 296–304.

Chu, Yingchi (2007), *Chinese Documentaries: From Dogma to Polyphony*. London and New York: Routledge.

Chu, Y. (2013), 'Self-hybridisation: China as a global media player', *Media Asia* **40** (4): 344–53.

Chu, Yingchi (2014), 'The politics of reception: "Made in China" and Western critique', *International Journal of Cultural Studies* **17** (2): 159–73.

Chu, Yingchi (2015), 'The dogmatic documentary: the missing link', *The New Review of Film and Television Studies* **13** (4): 403–21.

Fang, F. (2003), *Zhongguo jilu pian fazhan shi (A History of Documentary in China)*. Shanghai: China Drama Publisher.

Gao, Weijin (2003), *Zhongguo xinwen jilu dianying shi (History of Chinese Newsreel and Documentary Film)*. Beijing: The Central Communist Party Historical Materials Publisher.

Gao, Changli (2014), *yi Zhongguomeng zhuti daoyin Zhongguo jilupian fanrong fazhan* ('Guiding the development and prosperity of Chinese documentary by the themes of Chinese Dream'), in Suliu He, Ke Liu, Ning Li and Hinwa Wang (eds.), *Zhongguo jilu pian fazhan baogao 2014 (Annual Report on the Development of Chinese Documentary 2014)*. Beijing: Social Sciences Academic Press (China), pp. 46–51.

He, Mingming (2014), *woguo jilupian de neixing guannian sibian* ('Speculation of documentary types in China'), in Shuliu He, Ke Liu, Ning Li and Hinwa Wang (eds.), *Zhongguo jilu pian fazhan baogao (2014) (Annual Report on the Development of Chinese Documentary 2014)*. Beijing: Social Sciences Academic Press (China), pp. 247–57.

He, Suliu, Ke Liu, Ning Li and Hinwa Wang (2014), *2013 nian Zhongguo jilupian chanye fazhan yanjiu baogao* ('Research report on industrial development of Chinese documentary 2013'), in Shuliu He, Ke Liu, Ning Li and Hinwa Wang (eds.), *Zhongguo jilu pian fazhan baogao (2014)* (*Annual Report on the Development of Chinese Documentary 2014*). Beijing: Social Sciences Academic Press (China), pp. 1–38.

Inglis, David and Debra Gimlin (eds.) (2009), *The Globalization of Food*. New York: Bloomsbury.

Izod, John and Kilborn, Richard (1998), 'The documentary', in John Hill and Pamela Gibson (eds.), *The Oxford Guide to Film Studies*. Oxford: Oxford University Press, pp. 426–33.

Keane, Michael (2013), *Creative Industries in China: Art, Design and Media*. London: Polity.

Keane, Michael (2015), *The Chinese Television Industry*. London: British Film Institute & Palgrave.

Li, Ning and Jin Xu (2014), *2013 nian xin meiti jilupian zongshu* ('Review of new media documentary 2013'), in Shuliu He, Ke Liu, Ning Li and Hinwa Wang (eds.), *Zhongguo jilu pian fazhan baogao (2014)* (*Annual Report on the Development of Chinese Documentary 2014*). Beijing: Social Sciences Academic Press (China), pp. 189–99.

Li, Zhi, and Youxian Zheng (2014), *jiaohushi jilupian de xushi yanjiu* ('Research on the narration of interactive documentary'), in Suliu He, Ke Liu, Ning Li and Hinwa Wang (eds.), *Zhongguo jilu pian fazhan baogao (2014)* (*Annual Report on the Development of Chinese Documentary 2014*). Beijing: Social Sciences Academic Press (China), pp. 239–246.

Liu, Hongmei (2014), *chumeng zhi shang de shijie* ('The world beyond Truman'), in Suliu He, Ke Liu, Ning Li and Hinwa Wang (eds.), *Zhongguo jilu pian fazhan baogao (2014)* (*Annual Report on the Development of Chinese Documentary 2014*). Beijing: Social Sciences Academic Press (China), pp. 228–38.

Liu, Ke and Fei Han (2014), *jilu fan wai pian: yinshi shengtai lian zhong de gao guangdian* ('Side story of documentary: highlights in the entertainment value chain'), in Suliu He, Ke Liu, Ning Li and Hinwa Wang (eds.), *Zhongguo jilu pian fazhan baogao (2014)* (*Annual Report on the Development of Chinese Documentary 2014*). Beijing: Social Sciences Academic Press (China), pp. 305–12.

Lü, Xinyu (2003), *jilu Zhongguo: dangdai Zhongguo xin jilu yundong* (*Documenting China: The New Documentary Movement in China*). Beijing: Sanlian Shudian.

Meng, Jing (2015), 'Personal camera as public intervention: remembering the Cultural Revolution in Chinese independent documentary films', *Studies in Documentary Film* 9 (2): 143–60.

Müller, Gotelind (2013), *Documentary, World History, and National Power in the PRC: Global Rise in Chinese Eyes*. London and New York: Routledge.

Nye, Joseph (2005), *Soft Power: The Means to Success in World Politics*. New York: Public Affairs.

Qian, Ying (2011), 'Just images: ethnic and documentary film in China', *China Heritage Quarterly* 29, accessed 20 July 2015 at http://www.chinaheritagequarterly.org/scholarship.php?searchterm=029_qian.inc&issue=029.

Qian, Ying (2012), 'Power in the frame: China's independent documentary movement', *New Left Review* 74: 105 23.

Robinson, Luke (2013), *Independent Chinese Documentary: From the Studio to the Street*. London: Palgrave Macmillan.

Shan, Wanli (2005), *Zhongguo jilu dianying shi* (*The History of Documentary Film in China*). Beijing: Film Press.

Sun, Wanning (2015), 'Slow boat from China: public discourses behind the "going global" policy', *International Journal of Cultural Policy* 21 (4): 400–418.

Viviani, Margherita (2014), 'Chinese independent documentary films: alternative media, public spheres and the emergence of the citizen activist', *Asian Studies Review* 38 (1): 107–23.

Voci, P. (2010), *China on Video: Smaller-screen Realities*. Abingdon, UK: Routledge.

Wang, Xiaolu (2011), *Zhongguo duli jilupian de qiyue jingshen* ('The contractual spirit of Chinese independent documentary'), *Film Art* 5: 93–98.

Yang, Fan (2015), '*A Bite of China*: food, media, and the televisual negotiation of national difference', *Quarterly Review of Film and Video* 32: 409–25.

19. The urban-rural divide in China's cultural industries: the case of Chinese radio

Wei Lei, Lauren Gorfinkel and Wanning Sun

INTRODUCTION

During most of Mao-era China (1949–76), newspaper readership was limited to political and educated elites. Television was still in its developmental stage. The dominant mass medium, radio broadcasting, was firmly under the control of the Chinese Communist Party and part of the hierarchically and bureaucratically organized national propaganda system (Liu 1975). During this time radio played a key role in the mission of building a socialist society, a society that aimed to eliminate inequalities between rich and poor, and between urban and rural Chinese. After the implementation of economic reforms from the late 1970s, the state gradually began applying a system of marketization to the broadcasting sector. Among the first Mainland Chinese radio stations to change their approach was Guangdong People's Radio, which had to compete with the more entertaining and less preachy style of the Hong Kong-based channels that local audiences could receive from just across the border. The launch of Pearl River Economic Radio in 1986, which mirrored the style of its Hong Kong counterparts, including well-known personalities, talk back, economic news and pop music, was a great success and led to many other local radio channels across China following suit (Chan 1994). Due to massively reduced funding from the state, broadcasters at all levels were reshaped to operate as part of a state-owned but market-funded system. Whilst still having to negotiate with social and cultural requirements requested by the state, radio broadcasting nationwide concentrated most of its energy on becoming financially self-sufficient and, where possible, on generating further revenue in order to establish a profitable enterprise.

Radio programmes are produced with economic as well as political, ideological and cultural considerations. Broadcasters have shifted their attention to their audiences, classifying them by economic status rather than as political subjects. Different types of radio programming are now created for affluent urban consumers and less affluent and rural audiences. Guided by a profit incentive, producers and financers of cultural products

259

and services put greater effort into programming that targets China's newly affluent urban population. The commercialization of the media sector has meant that the Chinese state's political commitment to 'satisfy the masses' spiritual and cultural needs' (Zhao 2008: 109) – meaning the provision of cultural products to people across various boundaries such as gender, class, race, educational level and location, has been largely under-delivered. One crucial demographic which is both politically significant and enormous in size but neglected by the commercialized media is the rural population.

Since 2002, in an attempt to deal with this disparity, policies targeting the cultural sector began to place greater emphasis on national cultural development (*Zhongguo Gongchandang* 2011). A state-led 'cultural public service' (*wenhua shiye*) drive focused on providing non-commercial cultural products and services for 'the masses' to appreciate and participate in (Zhao 2008). At the same time the state has continued to promote the development of a market-oriented cultural economy in the form of the 'cultural industries' (*wenhua chanye*), of which media broadcasters represent a significant component (Zhao 2008). In this chapter, we ask how specific radio outlets respond to the state-made distinction between cultural public services (*shiye*) and cultural enterprises (*chanye/qiye*) in the process of addressing rural and urban audiences.

During the early 1990s a wave of radio reforms led to the establishment of numerous radio channels at national, provincial and municipal levels (Xu 1993; Liu 1994; Wang 1996; Zhou 1993). These channels were established around generic themes thought to be most attractive to advertisers, including news, business and finance, music, arts and entertainment and traffic. They targeted audiences with disposable incomes who were able to purchase the products and services that were promoted during the shows. Rural China, however, which was politically and economically marginalized during the economic reforms, was far less affected by such developments. It was not until the early 2000s that provincial radio stations (e.g. Shandong radio station, Shanxi radio station, Hubei radio station) launched separate rural-oriented radio channels. This initiative came after the State Administration of Radio, Film and TV (SARFT),[1] the national media regulator, began to emphasize the need to enhance rural media production and consumption as a core part of its agenda. While many local rural-oriented channels ended up as commercial entities, SARFT pushed for the development of a non-commercial cultural public service. The result was the establishment of the centrally administered national rural radio channel, The Voice of the Countryside (*xiangcun zhi sheng*) (Zhao 2008). This Beijing-based channel runs alongside the existing China National Radio suite of channels, which feature the popular national channels, The Voice of China (*Zhongguo zhi sheng*) and The Voice of the Economy (*jingji zhi sheng*); both these channels have become commercialized and favour an urban audience. Other national channels include one aimed at minority ethnic groups and another targeting the population of Taiwan.

In examining how the rural-urban disparity is embodied in the restructuring of the radio domain in an era of rampant commercialization, we pose a number of questions: How have economic imperatives transformed urban-oriented radio? How have urban-oriented radio stations become enterprises? What has been the effect on content production? Why was The Voice of the Countryside launched as a commercial-free cultural public service and how does its role as a cultural public service provider shape its content? Moreover what differences exist between cultural public service and cultural industry-oriented programming?

For this chapter, we have selected one urban-oriented channel – Beijing Traffic Radio (*Beijing jiaotong guangbo*) – and one rural-oriented channel – The Voice of the Countryside – to scrutinize these questions. Beijing Traffic Radio is one of the most successful examples of the traffic radio genre, a radio format that targets urban audiences and which has proved profitable across many major Chinese cities. A product of the shift towards a commercialized society, which has led to urban affluence and a dramatic increase in vehicle ownership, it clearly fits the cultural enterprise model. We compare it with The Voice of the Countryside, which claims to be the first national channel to provide a commercial-free cultural public service ('zhongyang renmin guangbo xiangcun zhisheng jianjie' 2013) and which also targets the previously neglected rural audience. Considering the lack of channels specifically catering to rural audiences, we suggest that 'rural radio' can be seen as a genre in its own right.

TRAFFIC RADIO AS A CULTURAL ENTERPRISE: A PRIMARY PROFIT MAKER IN A MUNICIPAL RADIO NETWORK

As a cultural enterprise the traffic radio genre is simultaneously shaped by state-led urbanization, regulatory policy and commercially oriented media reforms. The escalation of commercial urban-oriented traffic radio channels across China directly correlates with the dramatic increase in private car ownership, especially in the major cities. Mirroring rising incomes, the number of private household cars has grown rapidly since the 1990s. In 2007, private vehicles nationwide numbered over 15 million ('Zhongguo siren jiaoche' 2009); by the end of 2012, the numbers had soared to over

53 million with a growth rate of 22.8 per cent on 2011 figures (Qian and Liu 2013). In 2012, Beijing registered over 4 million privately owned vehicles ('erlingyi'er nianmo' 2013). Along with the promotion of the car industry by the state (Committee on the Future of Personal Transport Vehicles in China 2002), car ownership is a symbol of social status, wealth and a modern lifestyle among the newly affluent urbanites (Zhang 2008). As seen previously in the American radio industry, the growing number of people with access to automobiles was recognized as a key opportunity to revitalize radio listenership at a time when television had taken over radio as the prime broadcast medium in the family home.

Traffic radio emerged in China in the early 1990s to facilitate the very practical need of traffic management in Shanghai. At the time large-scale urban construction projects designed to transform Shanghai into an international city were disrupting normal traffic conditions (Huang 1992). Regulations restricting the launch and operation of new radio channels resulted in co-operation between radio stations and the local bureau of traffic management, which supplied traffic updates. Over time, traffic radio not only offered regular traffic updates, but also included weather reports, talk shows, and a variety of news, current affairs and music pro-grammes to keep listeners interested, with advertising underpinning the core of its operations. The launch of traffic radio in significant cities like Shanghai, and later Beijing, provided a new format for other city-level radio stations, which were desperately searching for new innovative radio approaches to attract both listeners and advertisers. Rather than operating as a form of public service, traffic radio became a commercial enterprise – even in areas that do not suffer from traffic congestion. Provincial sta-tions also created their own traffic radio channels, even though the traffic problem only usually pertains to the capital city of provinces, as Beijing Traffic Radio director Wang Liang (2002: 22) explained:

> Basically traffic radio in our country is urban-oriented. However, as its main aim is to make money, provincial- and city- [level radio channels] in some regional areas have also launched it. In theory, it is a waste of radio resources. . .At present, provincial traffic radio mainly covers the traffic in the provincial capitals. Functionally, radio stations at the provincial capital city level only would be enough to fulfill the need.[2]

At the time of writing, there was a traffic radio channel for most major cities, and for each provincial and autonomous region except for the Xizang Tibetan Autonomous Region. Provincial examples include Shandong Traffic Radio, the Inner Mongolia Voice of Traffic, and the Qinghai Traffic and Music channel.

As mentioned above advertising is the dominant model for generating revenue in the traffic radio business. For instance, in its early days, Beijing Traffic Radio, the focus of the discussion below, adopted a series of business strategies, such as performance-based rewards, to encourage staff to make more advertising deals (Wang 2002). In order to encourage advertising agencies to place more advertising, they made a deal that 70 per cent of any extra advertising revenue earned above the original target would go to the advertising agencies (Wang 2002). Market researchers have shown how traffic radio has grown into a primary profit-making channel for provincial and municipal radio networks, especially those located in the eastern coastal regions (Ma 2009; Huang 2007). In 2010, advertising revenue generated by traffic radio accounted for over 34 per cent of the total advertising revenue of the radio industry (Huang 2012). Beijing Traffic Radio, the nation's most lucrative traffic radio channel, and the station that serves China's most congested city, generated over RMB 60 million (US$10 million) in 2000 (Huang 2007). With rapid growth in subsequent years, revenue reached RMB 280 million (US$46.7 million) in 2006 (Huang 2007), nearly RMB 400 million (US$66.7 million) in 2009 (Luo 2010), and RMB 710 million (US$118.3 million) in 2010 ('erlingyiling niandu' 2011).

Beijing Traffic Radio's publicity claims that its core listenership is between 30 and 50 years old, with males outnumbering females, and primarily focused on drivers and passengers. It says that the largest group of listeners has an income bracket of over 5000 RMB per month (US$825), with the second largest group having between 3000 RMB (US$495) and 5000 RMB (relatively high salaries compared to the average monthly income in China). Its promo also claims that these listeners have a strong consumption power and aim to pursue a quality of life (*Beijing jiaotongtai guangbo zixun* 2009). In other words, the urban poor, who are unable to afford cars for private and leisure purposes and who include many rural-to-urban migrant workers, are not the target audiences of this channel.

Complementing the efforts of radio stations to gain the interest of urban consumers who are increasingly accessing radio in their private cars is the car industry's growing interest in the medium of radio. Alliances between traffic radio and the car industry have given rise to programmes concerning the purchase and use of private cars. The programme Car World (*qiche tianxia*) on Beijing Traffic Radio, which has grown into a trademark programme of Beijing Traffic Radio since it was first broadcast in 2002 (Liang 2013), is a typical case that demonstrates this mutual influence. Car World is a daily programme. Advertising slots occupy no less than half of the airtime during its broadcast from 10 to 11am. There are usually three or four advertising sections during the programme: at the beginning, the middle, and the end. In one episode in 2013, the first section had 21 advertisements interspersed with a brief news and information segment (*xinwen zixun*), traffic updates and a weather and air quality report. The second section had 27 advertisements following news and traffic update, and the third section, 33 advertisements after another traffic update. The products and services advertised included domestic furniture, house painting, food and clothes as well as cars and car-related components and services. The non-advertising segments focused on a car club in which car industry professionals and car owners discussed car-related issues. Table 19.1 provides a weekly breakdown of sections from Car World.

Table 19.1   Weekly programme schedules on Car World (qiche tianxia)

	Title of Section	Details
Monday	New Car 3+2 (*xin che 3+2*)[a]	Introduces a recent new product in the car industry.
Tuesday	You Can Buy a Car! (*hui mai che*)	Listeners are invited to communicate and bargain with a car salesperson to arrive at a deal. Following the deal all listeners can join the club and purchase the car for the same price as agreed to on-air.
Wednesday	Wednesday Drawing Room (*zhousan huikeshi*)	Discussion of car-related issues such as new regulations and policies with invited guests and media practitioners with an expertise in the car industry.
Thursday	Car Arena (*qiche jianghu*)	Discussion of listeners' complaints and how they are dealt with by car sales companies.
Friday	Car Life (*che shenghuo*)	Introduces and promotes upcoming car group tours and activities.
Saturday	Car Jack (*cheshi qianjinding*)	Discussion of car-related experiences and stories with invited guests in the form of a chatty and light-hearted group talk. For instance, in one episode, an in-studio hostess and three guests talk about the last person they would want to sit with in the passenger seat while they are driving. Another episode features a discussion on the 'gender' of private cars.
Sunday	Car Fashion (*che ying feng shang*)	Invites professional staff from the car industry to talk about cars and car-related trends.

Note: 3+2 is likely to be an adaptation from the Chinese term *sanyan liangyu* (lit: in two or three words, meaning 'in brief'). The short description of the Monday section is *sanyan liangyu dui hua Liang Hong*, meaning a brief dialogue with Liang Hong. Liang Hong is the female host of Car World, http://www.fm1039.com/2013/04/20130408143415.htm.

Traffic radio energetically promotes the culture of the car, sometimes as a kind of parody of public service. Despite the overwhelming tone of the programme being driven by advertising and encouraging consumption through the naturalization of the car as a basic and essential everyday commodity, it is nonetheless significant to note subtle and occasional attempts by the host of Car World to re-frame the focus away from mere commercialization towards other more public-service oriented aims relating to unity, nationalism and support for government policies. The host, for instance, explained that the aim of a car fair co-sponsored by Beijing Traffic Radio was 'not to make a profit, but to make you happy, and establish our brands' (15 October 2013). The slogan 'unity is power', a term widely used during the Mao era to mobilize national unity and encourage agricultural and industrial productivity, and which continues to be used in official discourse to promote national unity, is appropriated throughout the programme as it calls on listeners to bargain with car dealers. Advertisements also call on audiences to 'group-purchase' cars, stressing a 'collectivist' message in what is otherwise a promotion of an individualistic and private-ownership oriented culture.

With the economic capacity of on-air advertising reaching its limit because of the restricted airtime that can be allocated to advertising, the culture of car consumption has led Beijing Traffic Radio to engage in off-air commercial business activities to maximize its profits. Since the 2000s, Beijing Traffic Radio has established a number of sub-limited companies ('Beijing jiaotong guangbo' n.d.). These multiple sources of revenue range from promotions for the consumption of car-related products and services as well as other everyday commodities. For instance, Beijing Traffic Radio is actively engaged in cultivating and developing a self-drive tourism market. One of the most financially successful cases is the Beijing Traffic Radio 1039 Car Club. '1039' which is used in its programmes and mentioned widely on Beijing traffic radio refers to its frequency number 103.9. 1039 Car Club is a sub-section of the program Car World. This program has helped build a company, which provides car-related services including car workshops, advertisements for second-hand cars and promotions for the self-drive tourism market. Self-drive tourism covers domestic and international travel. For example, in 2007, borrowing the title of a classic Chinese novel 'Journey to the West' (*xi you ji*), in which a monk and his three disciples travel to India to seek a Buddhist text, the club launched the 'Journey to the West' event in which participants travel to the Western Chinese province of Xinjiang. It also launched an overseas tour entitled 'Self-drive on the east coast of America' (*Meiguo xihai an zijia*) (Development Centre 1039 car club 2008).

The promotion of self-drive tourism has already extended to other traffic radio channels, including but not limited to those on Shenzhen Traffic Radio and Dalian Traffic Radio (Chen 2008; Jie 2008; Pan 2008; Pan and Zhang 2008; Pei and Liu 2008; Qin and Xie 2007). In addition, in connection with its self-drive tourism initiatives, Beijing Traffic Radio has also established co-operation with around 900 commercial businesses. For instance, it issued a 1039 prepaid shopping card, which offers consumers discounts on purchases in shopping malls, restaurants, supermarkets, movie theatres, fitness centres, hotels, petrol stations and on car services. The commercial value of traffic radio far outweighs its value as a civil service designed to facilitate traffic order. Beijing Traffic Radio has spent significant energy conceiving its advertising business and entrepreneurial activities – arguably much more than the energy spent on creating radio content.

Echoing the extent of radio commercialization, other provincial and municipal radio stations throughout China have launched 'private car radio' (*sijia che guangbo*) channels (e.g. Henan provincial FM 99.9 private car radio; Zhengzhou municipal private car radio; Sichuan sijiache guangbo; Chengdu kuaile sijiache guangbo; Fujian 987 sijiache guangbo) as part of their business activities, which individualize programming for specific groups or families of private car owners. Jiangsu Traffic Radio (in east China) envisages a future of traffic radio in which 'profit generating from extended services will exceed profit from radio advertising' (Ma 2009). In a nutshell, traffic radio has taken advantage of the growth of private car-related consumption by the growing number of affluent urban car owners.

THE VOICE OF THE COUNTRYSIDE IN THE NAME OF A CULTURAL PUBLIC SERVICE (*GONGGONG WENHUA FUWU*)

While traffic radio proliferated across China's urban areas and became a forerunner in income generating radio services, rural-oriented programming was increasingly neglected. This created a void that the state has attempted to fill; significantly it has attempted to do so with a fundamentally commercial-free model. The Voice of the Countryside is probably the channel with the least economic interest of all radio channels in China. Its emergence and presentation in the context of an overwhelmingly commercialized radio domain is explored below.

In general, rural audiences have faced a relative lack of access to diverse media services. A renewed attempt to provide programming specifically directed at rural audiences came in 2003 when SARFT called for the media to provide services to rural areas. New initiatives in rural-oriented broadcasting were connected with the government's announcement of 2005 as 'The year of serving the countryside' (Zhang 2005). The initiative was also a response to a notice calling for the continuation of the *cun cun tong* project, which explained the need to consolidate and promote access to television and radio in every village (SARFT, the Committee of Development and Reform and the Ministry of Finance 2004). This notice was proposed by multiple top institutions including SARFT, the Committee of Development and Reform and the Ministry of Finance and was approved by the State Council in 2004. In addition, a series of announcements since 2004 has ensured that the 'three rural issues' (*san nong*), referring to issues surrounding agriculture, rural areas and farmers, were a top priority of the central government.[3] Establishing a rural public service system, which includes radio and television, has been a focus of the central government's cultural services agenda (Zhongguo Gongchandang 2011).

Rural radio channels have been launched at different levels, beginning with provincial and local rural radio channels in the early 2000s. These channels (e.g. Shandong countryside channel, Shanxi rural radio, Hubei rural radio) were not immune to commercialization; they too were required to make money to fund station operations. As a result, sub-national rural radio channels also produced programmes mixed with advertising. Particularly widespread was the advertising of medical and agricultural products. The launch of the national-level channel, The Voice of the Countryside, in 2012 followed the release of an official statement calling for the construction of a commercial-free, rural-oriented cultural public service channel as part of a broader focus on developing China's cultural industries. As Wang Qiu (cited in Xiao 2012), the then director of China National Radio, expressed in an interview at the launch of The Voice of the Countryside,

> The Sixth Session of the Seventeenth Central Committee restressed constructing a rural-oriented public service system, providing various public services (*gongyi fuwu*) that include radio and TV broadcasting to peasants. This is a direct requirement addressed to us. Secondly, our country is an agricultural country with a population of 1.3 billion. As a national radio station, we have the responsibility and obligation to do this job well.
>
> The Voice of the Countryside is a centrally administered channel. Its aim is to meet the 'public interest' (*gongyi*) as part of the project of 'radio broadcasting benefiting the rural' (*guangbo huinong*). While consumer-oriented advertising in post-Mao era China has been dominant, all media across China have simultaneously been required to run government initiated 'public service advertising campaigns' (*gongyi guanggao*) (public service announcements), which aim to promote good virtues, manners and behaviour, and remind the public to fulfill

their public responsibilities. While less space is given to such campaigns in the commercialized media, The Voice of the Countryside has been instructed by the central government to play an instrumental role in promoting 'socialist cultural development and cultural prosperity' (*tuidong shehui zhuyi wenhua da fazhan da fanrong*) ('Zhongyang renmin guangbo diantai' 2012).

The notion of cultural service is manifest in programming on the national rural broadcaster. Although it is difficult to get a sense of the listenership of The Voice of the Countryside due to the lack of official data and the fragmented locations of listeners, the devices used to access The Voice of the Countryside shed some light on the profile of its listeners. In addition to listening via affordable analogue technologies (via AM720) and loudspeakers in public places in rural areas, The Voice of the Countryside has also been made available via digital and online technologies. In 2014, The Voice of the Countryside cooperated with China Telecom (*Zhongguo dianxin*), one of the largest state-owned telecommunication operators, to launch a radio reception service called Tianyi – The Voice of the Countryside China (*Tianyi-Zhongguo xiangcun zhisheng*). The service, launched initially in China's southeastern Jiangxi province, enables customers to access The Voice of the Countryside via their China Telecom landline and mobile phones, particularly the Tianyi (literally: Sky Wing) brand mobile phones, which China Telecom also owns (Liu Xianzhong 2014). A report issued by The Voice of the Countryside extolled the advantages of mobile phone-based reception in overcoming the problems of limited transmission and interference often encountered in traditional radio transmissions, which enabled rural dwellers to more easily access policy information from the top as well as relevant scientific knowledge. The manager of China Telecom in Jiangxi, Zhao Hongyou, cited in the report, relayed plans to further cooperate with The Voice of the Countryside in order to promote its reception in rural areas in other provinces. A local, Wu Xiaoyu, from Zhufang village, Qiaoshe town, Xinjian county also expressed appreciation of the smooth reception from the mobile-phone service as well as the useful content in the programmes that gave peasants an understanding of important policies concerning their interests and needs. The implied message was that given their lack of access to information on policy previously, rural citizens were often left vulnerable and under-protected, and important policies were often not fully implemented (Liu Lu 2014).

The types of listeners who contribute to on-air programmes include plant growers and poultry farmers, as well as rural students; they also include people who live in urban areas but maintain connections with rural areas. Those who have migrated to urban areas for study, work or marriage engage with the channel. Listeners include children and elders.

Listeners who participate in on-air and online initiatives tend to comprise a relatively affluent, educated sector of the rural population who have access to the telecommunication tools required to receive and engage with the channel, who already have a basic understanding of science, technology, and the law, and who appreciate contemporary entertainment. Listeners who participate also have enough social capital to take the initiative to seek help from the media, with one listener, for instance, posting a request online for The Voice of Countryside to help deal with a local issue related to limited access to basic infrastructure in his or her hometown.

The Voice of the Countryside has seventeen programmes, which are divided into four categories – news and information, feature, talk, and arts and entertainment. As a national broadcaster, news programmes on The Voice of the Countryside are closer to the ideology of central authorities and wider in scope than those on sub-national rural radio channels. Rural news coverage, for instance, emphasizes rural China as a place where living conditions and social welfare are constantly improving. Broadly speaking, programmes on The Voice of the Countryside are sympathetic to the plight of rural Chinese and speak about rural China with affection and as a place of hope. This sense of optimism is embodied explicitly in one of its slogans 'seek golden hope!' (*zhuixun jinse de xiwang!*). The 'golden hope' of rural China is exemplified through emphasis on the economic, social and cultural progress made in rural areas.

News reports acknowledge and confirm the legitimacy and credibility of the national policies issued by the central authorities. Positive developments are framed as the direct result of direct government efforts to correct the massive disparity and tensions produced by capitalist exploitation and structural inequality between rural and urban China. Reports on social and economic achievements in rural China are routine news items in programmes such as 'The Three Rural Issues Morning Paper' (*san nong zao bao*) and 'The Three Rural Issues of China' (*san nong Zhongguo*). For instance, reports cover reforms in a number of provinces and cities promoting increased educational fairness through dropping the household registration system that previously limited individuals from participating in university entrance exams outside of their designated hometowns, which especially affected offspring of rural-to-urban migrant workers. Reports also cover broader health care and pension issues relevant to the rural population and associated with the government's medical and social welfare reforms.

News programmes also discuss agriculture-related polices issued by the central authorities. Agricultural policies on land reform (*tudi gaige*), urbanization (*chengzhenhua*) and family-based farmland (*jiating nongchang*) are discussed as playing a vital role in the progress and development of rural

China (Xia and Chen 2014). Following the third plenary session of the 18th Central Committee of Chinese Communist Party, held in Beijing from 9 to 12 November 2013, an online campaign co-sponsored by The Voice of the Countryside and the China Agricultural Bank, entitled 'The spirit of the third plenary session of the 18th Central Committee enters towns and villages' (*shi ba jie san zhong quan huijing shenru xiangcun*), introduced and explained these newly issued polices to local rural residents. In a letter celebrating the launch of The Voice of the Countryside, former Premier Wen Jiabao explicitly expressed the view that the channel was playing a key role in propagandizing the three agrarian policies of the central party and government ('Zhongguo xiangcun zhisheng' n.d.).

The function Wen Jiabao attached to this channel is 'propaganda' (*xuanchuan*), that is, in the Chinese sense of providing clear information. New policies, which may be intellectual or abstract, are translated by experts into language easily understood by rural residents. This is often done through explanation with reference to concrete cases brought up by rural participants. For example, the land reform policy was explained via a series of questions such as 'can a household apply for a contract for more farmland when they have a baby?' Interpretation of these policies on The Voice of the Countryside generally comes in the form of news featuring opinions and comments from intellectuals and officials who belong to party or governmental institutions or universities. For instance, one discussion in 2013 concerned how the framework of reform from the third plenary session of the 18th Central Committee would benefit peasants and asked what else needed to be done. It involved the expert opinions of the Chief Economist of the National Information Centre, a professor of the Central Party School, the Dean of the China Rural Research School of Central China Normal University, and the Vice Dean of the School of Agriculture and Rural Development at Renmin University of China/Head of the Department of Industry Policy and Regulation in the Ministry of Agriculture (He 2013). Despite the rhetoric of rural participation, the model is still clearly top-down. Peasants are told what is happening and have little real say in the policy making process. The greater involvement of the state and institutionalized knowledge workers on The Voice of the Countryside frames 'ordinary' participants as absorbing the knowledge of urban-based experts relatively passively compared to the market-led public participation on Beijing Traffic Radio, which invites listeners to participate more as savvy and active consumers.

Dr. Agriculture Online (*nong boshi zai xian*) is an exemplary case in The Voice of the Countryside's promotion of science and technology to rural audiences. The programme's title and the slogan 'Experts in agricultural technology by your side [lit: next to your ear]' (*nongji zhuanjia zai erbian*) reveals the interaction between agricultural specialists as a source of authoritative knowledge and peasants as recipients of this knowledge. This programme encourages listeners to participate by calling and leaving their questions off-air or sending text messages or microblog posts (*weibo*) via the Internet. A typical example comes via a mobile phone text message from a listener in Langfang, Hebei (a province neighbouring Beijing), who requests the host to 'Please ask Dr. Agriculture' to explain the types of companion plants that could be planted beside his pear trees ('Dr. Agriculture Online' 2013). While Q&A segments with experts are common on radio stations throughout the world, and experts provide a valuable source of information and education for listeners, the limited chance to hear the actual voice of 'ordinary' rural people in this show contributes to its top-down nature. The host usually reads out the questions and comments on behalf of participants and an expert (mostly from urban institutes) provides answers and suggestions. Occasionally a pre-recorded off-air question is broadcast on the programme.

The cultural public service model of The Voice of the Countryside makes possible the commitment of the state to rural China by ensuring a close focus on agricultural and rural issues in a way that benefits rural Chinese people without commercial distraction. At the same time, this cultural public service model defines the kind of knowledge and tools rural China needs in order to fit into the expanding market economy and be part of a state-defined modernization. The Voice of the Countryside supplements the other (commercialized) channels on the national radio network by offering a space specifically geared towards tackling the problem of rural-urban cultural inequality. For instance, although The Voice of China, the flagship channel of the national radio network and the primary national news channel, reaches the whole population and carries significant public responsibilities, the fact that it carries advertisements means that more attention is inevitably given to urban issues and angles where politically, economically and culturally influential groups are concentrated. In comparison, The Voice of the Countryside is where news on rural issues finds its place.

CONCLUSION

More than three decades since China's economic reforms began, economic interest has in many ways overtaken former social and cultural priorities, and urban-rural disparity has become a feature of Chinese society. This chapter has shown how in the radio sector an uneven cultural economy has likewise been established along urban-rural lines.

Since the early 1990s, radio broadcasting has embraced the state-approved and market-oriented expansion in its move towards a cultural economy, with traffic radio being the exemplary case. However, this market-oriented sensitivity and adaptability has been selective and calculative, favouring the social trends of affluent urban residents. Media policy makers in contemporary China have become gradually aware that such a cultural economy has resulted in the marginalization of rural China. A failure to cater to the rural majority could challenge the political legitimacy of the Chinese Communist Party and social stability at large. The launch of The Voice of the Countryside represents one state-approved attempt to address this issue. In this case, a cultural public service model has been re-introduced to supplement the dominant commercial model in an effort to achieve ideological, political, social, and cultural equilibrium.

Both traffic radio and rural radio are the outcome of the development of China's cultural economy and its cultural industries. Traffic radio emerged at a time when the top-down market-oriented media reforms swept the media landscape. In the years that followed, it has made progressive efforts to establish cultural enterprises. Its alliance with the car industry has extended from on-air programmes to off-air businesses. The logic it produces is a culture of consumption favouring spending power. The rise of traffic radio as a cultural industry has resulted in the marginalization of news and current affairs, which nonetheless continue to be offered in a minimal way to legitimate the media's expected public service role. Advertisements, music, traffic and weather updates, and chatty talk shows dominate the programmes. The commercial-free Voice of the Countryside has emerged as a solution to deal with the marginalized status of rural China in the media, as well as the failure of the commercial media to address issues of concern to rural publics.

NOTES

1. In 2013, SARFT was amalgamated with the National Administration of Press and Publication to form a new national institution called the State Administration of Press, Publication, Radio, Film and Television of the People's Republic of China (SAPPRFT) as a result of an institutional restructure.
2. All translations in this article are the authors' own unless otherwise indicated.
3. The notion of the 'three agrarian issues' was first discussed in 1996 by the economist Wen Tiejun who examined two fundamental contradictions constraining the development of rural areas in China (Wen 1996). In 2000, Li Changping, then chairman of a township-level Chinese Communist Party committee in central China's Hubei province, submitted a letter to the then Premier Zhu Rongji to state the seriousness of the three agrarian issues, in which he argued that 'peasants are really suffering, the countryside is really poor, and agriculture is really in danger' (Li 2002). The 'three agrarian

issues' has since been prioritized as part of the national agenda by the top authorities, and has been formally used in both official and academic discourse.

REFERENCES

Beijing jiaotong guangbo (n.d.) *jiaoguang chuanmei jianjie* ('A brief introduction to the Beijing Traffic Radio company'), accessed 30 November 2014 at http://www.fm1039.com/gywm/index.htm.

Beijing jiaotong tai guanggao zixun (2009), *Beijing renmin guangbo diantai jianyao jieshao* ('A brief introduction to Beijing radio station'), accessed 30 November 2014 at http://blog.sina.com.cn/s/blog_5ed987040100dh15.html.

Chan, Joseph Man (1994), 'Media internationalization in China: processes and tension', *Journal of Communication* **44** (3): 70–80.

Chen, Zhiping (2008), *shendu ronghe zhong zhuiqiu guangyi duoying: Dalian jiaotong guangbo zijia you huodong qianxi* ('Purchase multiple meanings and successes in deep integration: a brief analysis on self-driving activities organized by Dalian traffic radio'), *Zhongguo guangbo* (*China Broadcasting*) 6: 23–5.

Committee on the Future of Personal Transport Vehicles in China, National Research Council National Academy of Engineering – Chinese Academy of Engineering (2002), *Personal Cars and China*. Washington, DC, USA: National Academies Press.

Development Centre of 1039 Car Club of Beijing Traffic Radio (2008), *yi mei jie you shi, cu chanye fazhan: tan Beijing diantai jiaotong guangbo 1039 qiche julebu de zijia you yunying* ('Rely on advantages of media, promote industry development: the operation of self-driving tour by development centre1039 car club of Beijing Traffic Radio'), *Zhongguo Guangbo* (*China Broadcasting*) 6: 17–19.

Dr. Agriculture Online (*nong boshi zaixian*) (2013), *nong boshi bangbang tuan: lishu jian zhong shenme zuowu hao* ('Dr. Agriculture assistance group: what is the appropriate companion plant beside pear trees'), accessed 30 November 2014 at http://zgxczs.cnr.cn/nbszx/201310/t20131028_513955760.shtml.

erlingyi'er nianmo Beijing shi siren qiche bao you liang 407.5 wan liang ('The number of privately-owned cars reaches 4.075 million by the end of 2012') (2013), accessed 30 November 2014 at http://www.askci.com/news/201302/10/101535460121.shtml.

erlingyiling niandu quanguo guangbo guanggao shouru 10 qiang ('The top 10 radio stations with the most advertising revenue in China in 2010') (2011), accessed 30 November 2014 at http://www.crftv.com/showNewsInfo.asp?NewsID=6249&borderid=16.

He, Peng (2013), *Zhongguo zai qihang: gaige, shixian gengduo quanli de fenxiang* ('China sets a second sail: reform, achieving the sharing of more rights'), accessed 30 November 2014 at http://zgxczs.cnr.cn/xcjd/201311/t20131114_514136358.shtml.

Huang, Mingxing (1992), *kongzhong 'honglü deng': ji Shanghai renmin guangbo diantai jiaotong xinxi tai* ('On-air red and green light: traffic information radio on Shanghai radio station'), *xinwen jizhe* (*Journalism Review*) 1: 14–17.

Huang, Xueping (2012), *Zhongguo guangbo meiti de guanggao chuanbo jiazhi* ('The advertising value of radio broadcasting in China'), *Sound and Screen World: Advertising Man* 6: 53–5.

Huang, Yiqiu (2007), *FM 103.9 de 1/8 he 7/8: fang Beijing jiaotong guangbo diantai taizhang Qin Xiaotian* ('1/8 and 7/8 of FM 103.9: interview with Qin Xiaotian the director of Beijing Traffic Radio'), *chuanmei* (*Media*) 3: 25–7.

Jie, Ting (2008), *wanshan jizhi baozhang cujin zijia you jiankang fazhan* ('Complete security mechanism promotes health development of self-driving tour'), *Zhongguo guangbo* (*China Broadcasting*) 6: 22–3.

Keane, Michael (2004), 'Brave new world, understanding China's creative vision', *International Journal of Cultural Policy* **10** (3): 265–79.

Li, Changping (2002), *yige xiang dangwei shuji de xinlihua: gei Zhu zongli de xin*

('A township-level party chairman's heartfelt words: a letter to Premier Zhu'), accessed 30 November 2014 at http://news.sohu.com/45/42/news204704245.shtml.

Liang, Hong (2013), *zhuanye xing guangbo jiemu ruhe qieru shehui redian huati: yi Beijing jiaotong guangbo 'qiche tianxia' jiemu wei li* (How radio programmes specializing in one subject engage in high-profile social issues: take "qiche tianxia" on Beijing traffic radio for example), *qingnian jizhe* (*Young Journalists*) 18: 75–7.

Liu, Alan (1975), *Communications and National Integration in Communist China*. Berkeley, Los Angeles, London: University of California Press.

Liu, Lu (2014), *tianyi Zhongguo zhi sheng shangxian, rang guangbo huinong shengji* (The launch of mobile phone-based application called "Sky Wing" The Voice of The Countryside, upgrading [the project] of radio benefiting rural China), radio broadcasting transcript, The Voice of The Countryside, China National Radio, accessed 30 June 2015 at http://country.cnr.cn/cover/201401/t20140130_514775252.shtml.

Liu, Suqin (1994), *rexian dianhua zai guangbo xuanchuan gaige zhong de diwei he zuoyong jiqi fazhan qushi* (The place and function of telephone hotline in radio propaganda reform and its development trend), *Zhongguo guangbo dianshi xuekan* (*China Radio & TV Academic Journal*) 5: 30–32.

Liu, Xianzhong (2014), *jiangxi dianxin chuangxin nongcun guangbo chuanbo fugai moshi* ('Jiangxi provincial company of China Telecom innovates the transmission and reception mode of rural-oriented radio broadcasting'), accessed 2 July 2015 at http://jx.people.com.cn/n/2014/0129/c186330-20498324.html.

Luo, Xiaobing (2010), *bu zhi shi 'jiaotong' guangbo: Beijing jiaotong guangbo jingying fenxi* ('More than traffic radio: analysis of the business of Beijing Traffic Radio'), accessed 30 November 2014 at http://www.meijiezazhi.com/zt/yw/2012-04-04/2863.html.

Ma, Caihong (2009), *Zhongguo jiaotong guangbo fazhan licheng* ('The history of the development of traffic radio in China'), *xinwen zhishi* (*Journalistic Knowledge*) 4: 21–4.

Pan, Li and Yanling Zhang (2008), *dui zijia you jingying moshi yu tuiguang de zai sikao* ('Rethinking on modes of self-driving tour management and promotion'), *Zhongguo guangbo* (*China Broadcasting*) 6: 25–6.

Pan, Yonghan (2008), *Shenzhen jiaotong guangbo zijia you qishi* ('Inspiration from self-driving activities organized by Shenzhen traffic radio'), *Zhongguo guangbo* (*China Broadcasting*) 6: 19–20.

Pei, Jianping and Yifan Liu (2008), *yanshen de guangbo jingying: bufen shengshi diantai jiaotong guangbo zijia you moshi dajia tan* ('Extended radio broadcasting business: a collection of papers on modes of self-driving business in some of provincial and municipal traffic radio'), *Zhongguo guangbo* (*China Broadcasting*) 6: 14–15.

Qian, Cheng and Zheng Liu, (2013), *Zhongguo siren jiaoche baoyouliang da 5308 wan liang* ('The number of privately-owned cars in China in 2012 reached 53.08 million'), accessed 30 November 2014 at http://news.xinhuanet.com/2013-02/22/c_114771978.htm.

Qin, Xiaotian and Xianjin Xie (2007), *jiaotong guangbo fazhan licheng yu sikao* ('Thoughts on and track of the development of traffic radio'), *xiandai shiting* (*Contemporary Audio-Visual Arts*) 1: 39–42.

SARFT (The State Administration of Radio, Film and TV), The Committee of Development and Reform and the Ministry of Finance (2004), *guanyu gonggu he tuijin cuncuntong guangbo dianshi gongzuo de yijian* ('Opinions regarding reinforcing and promoting radio and television service available in each village'), accessed 30 November 2014 at http://www.gov.cn/gongbao/content/2004/content_62906.htm.

Wang, Liang (2002), *jingying jiaotong guangbo de jige guannian wenti* ('A number of view issues about the management of traffic radio'), *Zhongguo guangbo dianshi xuekan* (*China Radio & TV Academic Journal*) 8: 22–24.

Wang, Pei (1996), *jiushi niandai guangbo jiemu gaige, fazhan tezheng ji zouxiang* ('Reform, development features and the direction of radio programs in the 1990s'), *Zhongguo guangbo dianshi xuekan* (*China Radio & TV Academic Journal*) S1: 89–91.

Wen, Tiejun (1996), *zhiyue 'sannong wenti'de liangge jiben maodun* ('Two fundamental contradictions that constrain the development of the "three agrarian issues'"), *jingji yanjiu cankao* (*Review of Economic Research*) D5: 17–23.

Xia, Enbo and Chen, Jiangnan (2014), *Li Guoxiang: ba zhengce jiedu gei nongmin gei tamen yijian weiquan wuqi* ('Li Guoqiang: interpret policy for peasants, give them a weapon to protect rights and interests'), accessed 30 November 2014 at http://country.cnr.cn/cover/201401/t20140108_514602198.shtml.

Xiao, Z.T. (2012), *woguo diyi tao quanguo xing duinong guangbo pinlv Zhongguo xiangcui zhi sheng zhengshi kaibo* ('The official launch of the first national rural-oriented radio channel The Voice of the Countryside'), radio broadcast transcript, China National Radio, accessed 30 November 2014 at http://china.cnr.cn/xwwgf/201209/t20120926_511004370.shtml.

Xu, Guoping (1993), *guangbo xinfeng: rexian dianhua* ('Radio broadcasting's new wave: telephone hotline'), *Zhongguo jizhe* (*Chinese Journalist*) 6: 20–22.

Zhang, Haitao (2005), *anzhao kexue fazhan guan de yaoqiu, quanmian jiaqiang nongcun guangbo dianshi gongzuo: zai guangbo dianshi dui nong fuwu gaoceng luntan shang de jianghua* ('In accordance with the requirement of scientific development, fully reinforce the rural-oriented radio and television service: a speech at the high-level forum concerning rural-oriented radio and television'), speech transcript, accessed 30 November 2014 at http://www.sarft.gov.cn/articles/2005/06/17/20070910174338600455.html.Zhang, Li (2008), 'Private homes, distinct lifestyles: performing a new middle class', in in Li Zhang and Aihwa Ong (eds.), *Privatizing China: Powers of the Self, Socialism from Afar*. Ithaca, New York, USA: Cornell University Press, pp. 23–40.

Zhao, Yuezhi (1998), *Media, Market, and Democracy in China: Between the Party Line and the Bottom Line*. Urbana: University of Illinois press.

Zhao, Yuezhi (2008), *Communication in China: Political Economy, Power and Conflict*. Lanham: Rowman & Littlefield.

Zhongguo gongchandang di shiqi jie zhongyang weiyuanhui diliuci quanti huiyi (The Sixth Plenary Session of the 17th Central Committee of the Chinese Communist Party) (2011), *zhonggong zhongyang guanyu shenhua wenhua tizhi gaige tuidong shehui zhuyi wenhua dafazhan dafangrong ruogan zhongda wenti de jueding* ('The Chinese Communist Party Central Committee's resolution on several significant issues of deepening cultural system reform, promoting great socialist cultural development and prosperity'), *Xinhua News Agency*, accessed 30 November 2014 at http://news.xinhuanet.com/politics/2011-10/25/c_122197737_5.htm.

zhongyang renmin guangbo diantai wenhua fazhan gongcheng zai jing qidong ('The launch of cultural development project of China National Radio in Beijing') (2012), radio broadcast transcript, China National Radio, accessed 30 November 2014 at http://www.cnr.cn/zgzb/wh/zy/201208/t20120823_510667854.shtml.

zhongyang renmin guangbo diantai Zhongguo xiangcun zhi sheng jianjie ('A brief introduction to The Voice of the Countryside on China National Radio') (2013), accessed 30 November 2014 at http://zgxczs.cnr.cn/xczt/gbhn/point/201310/t20131025_513939379.shtml.

Zhongguo siren jiaoche bao you liang chaoguo 1, 500 wan ('The number of privately-owned cars in China exceeds 15 million') (2009), *Xinhua News Agency*, accessed 30 November 2014 at http://auto.163.com/08/0229/15/45SNDQQN000816HJ.html.

Zhongguo xiangcun zhi sheng kaibo yishi ('The opening ceremony of China's The Voice of the Countryside') (n.d.), accessed 30 November 2014 at http://www.cnr.cn/zgzb/xczskb/.

Zhou, Hongjun (1993), *diantai xuanfeng* ('The whirlwind of radio stations'), *xinwen aihaozhe* (*Journalism Lover*) 6: 4–6.

20. Animation industry in China: managed creativity or state discourse?*
Anthony Y.-H. Fung and Vicky Ho

INTRODUCTION

Globally speaking, animation is one of the fastest growing media content sectors. According to Research and Markets (2015b), the output of the global animation industry reached US$ 222 billion in 2013. Countries with a strong animation production tradition such as the US and Japan have maintained a strong position globally. Major animation markets include the US, Canada, Japan, China, Britain, France, South Korea and Germany. In 2010, Pixar's *Toy Story 3* established a record for the top-grossing animated film, reaping US$ 1.06 billion from its box office worldwide. In 2014, Disney's *Frozen* surpassed the record with an international gross of US$ 1.27 billion, becoming not only the highest grossing animated film but also the fifth highest grossing film of all time.

Apart from its economic significance, animation is a sophisticated form of creative work. Oscar (Academy Award) recognition dates from 1932 for animated shorts while animated features have been awarded since 2001. The animated films *Beauty and the Beast* (1993), *Up* (2009) and *Toy Story 3* (2010) were nominees for Oscar Best Picture. Animation as a form of entertainment content has increasingly appealed to various audience segments beyond children, including teenagers, adults, and the whole family. Adult animated series like *The Simpsons*, *King of the Hill* and *South Park*, for instance, have become prime time successes.

International competition in animation has been intense. Today we are looking at not just leading studios like Pixar, Disney and DreamWorks but also other influential content brands, such as Blue Sky, Sony and Illumination. In the European market, France, Spain, Germany and Britain are leaders. European studios have produced animated content for television and animated shorts while striving for breakthroughs in animated features. Outsourcing and co-production are the key trends of the global industry. Nowadays, about 90 per cent of all US television animation is made in Asia (Research and Markets, 2015a). Studios in China and India are popular co-production partners of Western and Japanese studios. But while Japan maintains its position as animation leader, many other Asian countries are striving to develop their local animation industries. The South Korean government has announced investment of US$ 345 million in its animation industry by 2019 to break into the international market (*The Korea Times*, 2015).

China is keen on growing an internationally respected animation industry, one that can match up with global players. In this chapter we trace China's efforts and outcomes so far. We examine the development of the Chinese animation industry under government support on the one hand and ideological control on the other. We also discuss the implications that state policy has on creative expression in animation and how a lack of creativity in turn impacts on the global competitiveness of China's animation industry.

CHINA'S ANIMATED AMBITIONS

Thanks largely to considerable government support over the last decade, China's animation industry has recorded remarkable growth. In 2013, the total output value (television, film, derivatives included) exceeded RMB 90 billion (approximately US$ 14.5 billion) with a year-on-year increase of around 21 per cent (Research and Markets, 2014). Domestic animation is promoted by broadcasting channels at various levels. China Central Television (CCTV) has diligently promoted animation through its Kids Channel and online platforms such as the *Animation Chart* (*donghua rebobang*). *Booney Bears* (*xiong chumo*), *Pig Man* (*zhu zhu xia*) (a piglet-turned-superhero), and *Pleasant Goat and Grey Wolf* (*xiyangyang yu huitailang*) are some of the most popular domestic animation series both on TV screens and the big screen.

Since 2012 China has been the home of Oriental Dreamworks, a joint venture between DreamWorks Animation (DWA) and China Media Capital, Shanghai Media Group and Shanghai Alliance Investment. As one of the most highly capitalized Sino-US joint ventures in the content industry, the Shanghai-based Oriental Dreamworks aspires to 'produce entertainment in China for China, and for export to the rest of the world' (Oriental Dreamworks 2015). There are high hopes that the partnership will create an impetus that will take Chinese animation to the next level. The much-anticipated *Kung Fu Panda 3*, co-produced by Oriental Dreamworks and DWA, is scheduled for a global release in 2016. The creative mastermind of the project is still DWA, whereas Oriental Dreamworks contributes feedback for cultural relevance as well as contributing production capacity. In any case China is obviously gearing up its animation industry and eyeing the global animation market. The question is, does the Chinese animation industry have what it takes to impress the global audience?

China's animation industry manifests several marked differences from its foreign counterparts. In China the animation industry is combined with comics and is conventionally referred to as the *dongman* industry (*dong* stands for *donghua* which means animation, and *man* stands for *manhua* which means comic). When China adopted the cultural and creative industries rhetoric in the early 2000s, the government recognized that the *dongman* industry was under-developed and moved quickly to implement policies to facilitate growth. The *dongman* industry is subsequently known as 'a creativity-focused industry with a wide range of forms, from animation to comic and movie' (Ministry of Finance et al. 2006): these include publication, film, TV, theatre production, costumes, as well as toys and games related to cartoon images. Yet, under the *dongman* umbrella, development in animation is much more rapid than in comics.

In China, animation has long been stigmatized as childish, immature and as a kind of subculture or entertainment that distracts children from their studies. Parents and teachers are particularly concerned that some animation may spread undesirable attitudes and behaviour such as violence and improper attitudes to romance. Such ingrained ideas of the effects of animation have constrained the development of homegrown animation despite its over 80 years of existence in China. Moreover, even though the government has stepped up its support for the industry, policies have continued to regard animation as a child-oriented medium. Unlike many Western countries, there is no animation classification system in China and thus all animation content is evaluated with the default criteria as children's media. This one-size-fits-all approach to regulation has resulted in limitations on genres and themes available in the market. Moreover, the government has used various measures in its attempt to control animation content, measures which despite the rhetoric are not conducive to the cultivation of creativity in the industry.

FROM GOLDEN ERAS TO CULTURAL MIMICKING

The origins of Chinese animation date to the Wan brothers' short black and white work *Uproar in the Studio* (*danao huashi*), which was made in 1928. The four Wan brothers (Wan Laiming, Wan Guchan, Wan Chaochen, Wan Dihuan) are widely recognized as the founders of Chinese animation. They virtually monopolized Chinese animation until 1941 with a range of animated works including advertising, entertainment and propaganda films. The first feature-length animated film in

China, and the world's fourth, *Princess Iron Fan* (*tieshan gongzhu*), was made by the Wan brothers, based on a chapter from the Chinese novel *Journey to the West* (*xiyouji*). Chinese animation experienced two 'golden eras', 1950–64 and 1976–80s including experimentations with Chinese fairy tales and Chinese art techniques. Works in the first golden era include *Pigsy Eats Watermelon* (*zhubajie chi xigua*) (1958), *Little Tadpole Looks for Mamma* (*xiao kedou zhao mama*) (1960), *A Clever Duckling* (*chongming de xiaoya*) (1960), and *Havoc in Heaven* (*danao tiangong*) (1961) among others. Various traditional art and craft techniques such as ink painting, paper cutting, and paper folding are incorporated in these works.

The production of Chinese animation stalled during the Cultural Revolution, only resuming post-1976. During the so-called second golden era, artists who had been oppressed during the Cultural Revolution were eager to show their talent and thus exerted an extraordinary level of energy in producing their best works (Lent and Xu, 2010), including *Story of Effendi* (*A fan ti de gushi*), *Three Monks* (*san ge heshang*), *Ne Zha Conquers the Dragon King* (*Ne Zha nao hai*), and other works. Chinese animation works of these golden eras are said to exhibit 'very high levels of aesthetics and experimentation' (Lent and Xu 2010: 116).

Along with the implementation of the reform and open policy of China, CCTV introduced the Japanese animation *Astro Boy* in 1980. Overseas animation entered from various countries. *Doraemon* and *Ikkyu-san* came from Japan; *The Smurfs*,[1] *Mickey Mouse* and *Transformers* entered the Chinese market from the US. During the early 1990s animation production in China was mainly shared among Beijing Television, China Central Television (CCTV) and Shanghai Animation Film Studio. However an obvious gap existed between Chinese animation and its foreign counterparts; for example, only four domestic animation works totalling 195 minutes were produced in 1993. Local production was limited in terms of length and themes. *40 Kids Songs in Cartoon* (*katong tongyao sishi shou*) was the longest running cartoon at the time with 40 episodes but each episode was under two minutes and its content was mainly educational. In the 1990s, imported animations such as *Sailormoon* from Japan were far more popular than Chinese animation products. As well as appearing on official television channels, foreign animation penetrated the Chinese market illegally through pirated forms. This import of foreign content occurred because of weak intellectual property protection. Although domestic studios tried to increase production, the most popular pre-release pirated VCD in the early 2000s was Pixar's *Toy Story 2* (Donald 2002). The attractive characters and stories of foreign animation captured the hearts of the children born after the '80s. In face of the invasion of foreign animation culture, China strove to boost its domestic animation production as a counter force.

However, when the Chinese animation industry tried to catch up with its foreign counterparts, the attempt was characterized by intense cultural mimicking. The 1990s saw the initial commercial developments of China's cultural sectors and most cultural workers had limited ideas or experience in how to turn culture into business. At the same time, because of lower labour costs, many Japanese animation companies were outsourcing their work in Asian countries, including China. Many Chinese artists worked on tasks such as drawing the backgrounds and colouring the animations. These uncreative and time-consuming jobs were not helping Chinese artists to gain genuine insights into the creative process. The result, more-over, was a lingering Japanese influence. Many Chinese animation works produced thereafter were copycats, especially of Japanese animation. For example, the Chinese animation *Music Up* (*wo wei ge kuang*) (2001) was said by its producer to be a 'Chinese edition of *Slam Dunk*' (Ng 2002). Taking into account the success of the US, other Chinese animations imitated American animation. The animated film *Lotus Lantern* (2000) resembled Disney's *Pocahontas* for its indigenous characters (Donald 2005) while China's first 3D digital animated film *Little Tiger Banban* (2001) was modelled after *Toy Story* (N/A, 2009). In more recent times a Chinese animated film *The Autobots* (*qicheren zhongdongyuan*) (2015) was widely criticized because it was adjudged to be a copycat of *Cars*.

GOVERNMENT SUPPORT FOR THE ANIMATION INDUSTRY

The development of the Chinese animation industry after 2000 has been largely driven by government policy. Since 'The Notice of Strengthening the Import and Management of Animated Films'[2] was issued in March 2000, the government's attention to the animation industry has been evident. In 2002, the State Administration of Radio, Film and Television (SARFT)[3] issued the first animation related document, entitled 'Development Plan on the Animation Industry During "The 10th Five"'.[4] It outlined the major challenges faced by China's animation industry between 1996 and 2000, including: (1) insufficient domestic animation production; (2) poor quality of domestic animation production; (3) frag-mented institutions and immature systems; (4) immature industry struc-ture. This document showed that the government recognized the need to strengthen the local industry. Important policies followed and were out-lined in the 'Suggestions on the Development of the Animation Industry'[5] in 2004, which marked the year as a key moment for the development of the animation industry in China.

One important aspect of government support is to increase domestic animation production and distribution by developing an 'animation broadcast system'. Between 2004 and 2009, the state established four satellite channels dedicated to animation. To increase the airtime for domestic animation, the regulation limited the ratio between domestic animation and imported animation on TV channels at no less than 6:4. TV stations were allowed to extend advertising time as an incentive to broadcast locally produced animation. These policies have maintained a steady internal demand for local animation. With the expansion of broadcasting hours, television became the major outlet for local animation content. The government has also provided domestic animation studios with subsidies for original animations that are broadcast on television. The amount of subsidy varies by location and is dependent on the level of the TV stations that broadcast the animation. For instance, studios with animation content broadcast on CCTV receive higher subsidies. For enterprises in Hangzhou and Shanghai, subsidies are allocated by the local government and by 'national bases' (see below) in which many of the enterprises are located. Because of the high production cost of animation and the low returns from selling to TV stations (TV stations pay far less to buy local animation content when compared to foreign ones), these subsidies are important to the survival of local animation businesses.

In addition, various license and identification systems have been established to boost the status of local animation businesses. SARFT has issued the license of 'National Animation Industry Base' to animation production centres since 2004. The identified industry bases are expected to operate as industry clusters to develop talent and encourage business activities. As the major production force in local animation, they can enjoy financial and taxation privileges from the government. The Ministry of Culture also began the accreditation of animation enterprise in 2009 and started to identify 'key animation businesses' and 'key animation products' in 2010. Animation companies have to achieve certain targets of sales revenue, export revenue, awards, and overall animation product quality in order to qualify as key animation businesses. For example, key animation businesses must record an annual sales revenue of RMB 10 million or above from animation products. In 2010, eighteen companies from seven provinces and municipalities were listed as key animation businesses. Hunan province in south China came top in the provinces as it housed six of the key animation businesses, while Beijing came in second with three key animation businesses. As for the key animation products, 35 animation products from 10 provinces and municipalities were awarded in 2010. Hunan again topped the list with 13 awarded products from seven companies (MOC 2010). In terms of performance by business, both Zoland Cartoons from Zhejiang and GreatDreams Cartoons from Hunan were prominent with four key animation products.

Government support has yielded notable numerical growth in the industry. The output volume of the local animation industry recorded a 47 per cent year-on-year increase since 2005 after the implementation of the 'Suggestions' in 2004. From 2005 to 2009, the number of provinces producing animation doubled while the total number of animation output increased fourfold. In 2010, although the number of provinces producing animation slightly reduced from 22 in the previous year to 19, the output volume continued to grow by almost 30 per cent. There were 23 National Animation Industry Bases in 2010. The performances of the animation bases varied: some animation bases recorded remarkable output growth, some grew steadily, but there were also some animation bases with zero output. This raises the question: Do more production entities mean China's animation industry is thriving?

As we can see government policies to boost local animation rely heavily on regulating imported products, creating internal demand and subsidizing local businesses rather than introducing a sustainable environment to stimulate creative local works. As a result animation businesses have little motivation to become truly creative. The government will pay them as long as they produce something, no matter good or bad, or if they manage to make a deal with television channels. Settling for mediocre products is detrimental to the Chinese animation industry: instead of investing in producing quality animation, some animation businesses simply feed on government subsidies to survive. Some even offer their animation to television channels for free in order to receive government subsidies. An incident was reported in 2010 in the media concerning an animation segment broadcast in the late hours (11pm–1am) on CCTV Kids' channel, which was subsequently criticized as a platform launched only for the subsidy but with no real audience (Liu 2010). Some animation businesses operate in a 'migratory bird' *(houniao)* mode, meaning they would seek out locations with better subsidy policies to register, not for business expansion but simply to benefit from better subsidies.

DIRECT AND INDIRECT MECHANISMS OF CONTENT CONTROL

While government support has failed to stimulate a creative environment, a further hindrance to creativity in the Chinese animation industry is content control. As mentioned, animation in China has always been targeted at children. Children are regarded as vulnerable and easily susceptible to 'spiritual pollution' *(jingshen wuran)* and corrupting forces. Therefore, in the eyes of the Chinese government, animation content has to be carefully guarded to avoid such polluting influences and to serve as a tool of morality building in children. The Chinese government has set up several censorship and recommendation systems as mechanisms to manage animation content.

In 2004, an approval system was established in order to censor the subject matter of domestic animation. Animation businesses must first propose the content of the animation and receive government approvals before going to production. Another censorship mechanism is the distribution permit. SARFT issued the 'Notice relating to the implementation of the domestic TV animation distribution permit system'[6] in October 2005. Local animation businesses must obtain the distribution permit in order for their animation to be shown on television; the above notice specifies the conditions under which a distribution permit will not be issued to domestic animation. In general, content deemed to be jeopardizing national sovereignty and national interest or promoting pornography, gambling, violence or criminal behaviors is prohibited.

Apart from censorship, SARFT started implementing the 'Methods to recommend excellent domestic animation' in 2005.[7] Animation enterprises are encouraged to submit their works and SARFT would make the final judgment of recommendations. These recommended animations are prioritized for screening on television channels at all levels. As we shall discuss in the following section, the recommendation list indicates that the recommended works are often based on their relevance and alignment to the state's ideology. Two other award projects were launched after 2008, namely 'The children products and national animation development funding scheme (on trial)'[8] and 'The national original television animation and animation talent development scheme (on trial)'.[9] The judging criteria for the two schemes are similar: out of the domestic television animations that are recommended by SARFT, the selection will be based on ideology, artistic quality, public interest and the brand popularity of the animated image. The criteria also state that 'serving the people and serving socialism' *(wei renmin fuwu, wei shehui zhuyi fuwu)* is the direction of judging and that 'social welfare is to be prioritized, in order to achieve the convergence of social welfare and economic viability' (SARFT, 2008). This illustrates that these award and incentive schemes, while encouraging a certain level of creativity in the animation products, are still largely ideological in nature.

The recommendation and awards systems are important mechanisms to control animation content. While censorship only stipulates what to avoid in the content, the award systems exemplify the government's preferred line, which may serve to guide the creation of animation content. Indeed, since the implementation of the regulations, there has only been one reported incident in which a domestic animation on air was banned. In 2007, the domestic animation *Rainbow Cat and Blue Rabbit (hongmao lantu)* was banned by CCTV rather than by direct order of the government authority SARFT because of parental concern about violent scenes in the animation. In fact this action is a kind of self-censorship by the broadcast channel rather than direct intervention from the government. Yet the animation later received the First Class award in excellent domestic animation, and screening subsequently resumed afterwards. Of course, foreign animation still faces relatively strict censorship. But in the local industry, incentives are more effective than sanctions in regulating animation content. By referencing the reward criteria and exemplary works, animation companies can identify a formula for animation content that can earn the favour of authorities. It is not mandatory to embed ideological themes in animation, but many companies self-initiate to follow suit. In the following, we discuss two of the most popular and most awarded domestic animations, the *Rainbow Cat and Blue Rabbit* series and the *Pleasant Goat and Grey Wolf* series, to illustrate how the mechanism serves to promote the dominant ideological discourse.

EXEMPLARY ANIMATION AND IDEOLOGICAL CONTROL

Rainbow Cat and Blue Rabbit, made by GreatDreams Cartoon Media Company, was named Excellent Domestic Animation nine times between 2005 and 2011. The series started off with episodes depicting individual short stories with the two major characters, the rainbow cat and the blue rabbit; it later developed the characters' adventures in more sophisticated contexts such as the *wuxia* world, outer space and the underwater world. The rainbow cat and the blue rabbit are role models for children as they each embody various virtues. The rainbow cat was brave, persevering and wise while the blue rabbit was friendly, kind and loving. The rationale for the recommendation of this animation included creative, aesthetic and ideological elements. The animation was complimented for its captivating narratives and humorous presentations that drew the attention of children. Technically, the animation also received recognition for its graphics, color and animation style. A few of its sub-series, such as *The Legend of the Seven Warriors (hongmao lantu qixia chuan)*, *To the Ends of the World (hongmao zhang jian zou tianya)*, *The Sword of Brightness (hongmao la tu guangming jian)*, utilize *wuxia* themes and incorporate traditional Chinese cultural elements.

However, a crucial rationale for the government's endorsement of *Rainbow Cat and Blue Rabbit* was pedagogical value. As mentioned in the recommendation, the executional merits were commended because they were conducive to inspiring its child audience and helping them to develop a positive character in a relaxing and entertaining atmosphere. The underlying messages of the series often emphasizes the triumph of justice over evil and the personal growth of the major characters, but the more defining factor for its success would be its alignment to the 'harmonious society' (*hexie shehui*) discourse in China. The notion of the harmonious society, which means 'to maintain social stability through proactively leveraging positive influences, strengthening the creativity of society, mediating the interest of multiple parties and facilitating collaboration among people', has become an important element of the state discourse since 2004. In the face of various social problems in China, the harmonious society discourse serves to control social unrest and maintain the ruling capacities of the Party state.

Several of the recommended sub-series of *Rainbow Cat and Blue Rabbit* carried the message of the harmonious society through the storyline. For example, in *The Legend of the Seven Warriors*, the seven warriors headed by the rainbow cat and the blue rabbit cooperate to get rid of the villain, the evil tiger, in order to maintain harmony in the forest. Another sub-series *Adventure Under the Sea* portrays how the characters survive various difficult situations in the sea and illustrates how terrestrial animals and aquatic animals can eventually gain mutual trust and get along with each other in harmony. While the settings of the stories may vary, they have a common thread in emphasizing the importance of building a harmonious society, which is in line with the state discourse.

The second example, *Pleasant Goat and Grey Wolf*, made by Creative Power Entertainment Corporation, depicts the story of how the goat community deals with the neighbouring wolves in order to protect their homeland. It was named Excellent Domestic Animation twice between 2005 and 2011, but also received other national animation awards. Again, the series was awarded not only because of its interesting plot and characters, the witty and humorous presentations, which could be considered the creative elements, but also because the storyline matches with the notion of harmonious society. The message of harmonious society is embedded in *Pleasant Goat and Grey Wolf* in three aspects. First, the story highlights the bonding within the goat community and the non-violent and creative method as an ideal way for resolving conflict. Second, it emphasizes harmony between humans and the environment. Third, the grassland, which is the context of the story, is symbolic of contemporary China in which various social problems and tensions do exist, but with wisdom and collective efforts problems can be overcome (Fung 2013). Pleasant Goat in the story combines positive traits including kindness, bravery, intelligence, and modesty, to name just a few. The likeability of Pleasant Goat makes it an undeniable role model for kids; the desired behaviour of harmonious resolution of conflicts is therefore more easily ingrained in children's minds.

The brand image of the Pleasant Goat has also translated into success on the big screen. The first feature film of the series, *Pleasant Goat and Grey Wolf: The Super Snail Adventure*, released during the Chinese New Year in 2009, grossed over RMB 8 million in the box office. Its sequel in 2010 achieved over RMB 1 billion in the box office, setting the record for local animated film in China, although later surpassed by the 3D animated film *Boonie Bears* in 2011. Since then sequels of the Pleasant Goat have been released during the Chinese New Year. In fact, this animation has become so successful in China that it attracts kids, teens, college students and adults alike. Some of the plots and jokes actually reference the reality of the social conditions in China today, and thus arouse a different level of pleasure in the adult audience. Some also find the villain Grey Wolf admirable in certain aspects since Grey Wolf is not constructed as an utterly wicked character in the story. There is even a popular saying that one should 'learn from Pleasant Goat in the being and from Grey Wolf in the doing' (Cao and Wang 2010). This illustrates that the built-in ambivalence of the animation, while not subverting the cultural order, may aid the popularization of animation into different audience segments.

According to Gorfinkel (2012) the idea of harmony can be adapted to different kinds of 'indoctrintainment' depending on the perceived audience. The above examples show how the discourse of peace and harmony can be easily embedded in animation. By endorsing animations that promote politically correct messages in modern and engaging ways, the government is able to guide an animated culture to circulate state discourse to the audience of children. Of course, when the state renews its official line of dominant discourse, the preference for the embedded message in animations will also change. Under the leadership of Xi Jinping since 2013, China's new guiding principle of state governance nowadays is the 'Chinese dream' – 'the great revival of the Chinese people'. This was quickly incorporated in the directions for producing animation content. Government officials were reported to highly encourage animation businesses to focus on the theme of the 'Chinese dream' in upcoming animation series (State Administration of Press, Publication, Radio, Film and

Television – SAPPRFT 2013). Various competitions to recruit ideas for 'Chinese dream' themed animations flourish these days. Without doubt, this kind of ideological advice offered to producers greatly limits originality and inspiration in animation content.

CHINESE ANIMATION AND GLOBAL COMPETITION

Under government support the output of the Chinese animation industry has unquestionably increased significantly. In 2010, China topped the world in animation output, surpassing the US and Japan. According to the *Report of the Development of the Chinese Animation Industry 2013*, the total length of Chinese animation output in 2011 reached a historical high of 260,000 minutes (Xinhuanet 2014). Although the number retracted to 220,000 minutes and 204,000 minutes respectively in 2012 and 2013, China's animation output in terms of minutes is still impressive. However, the export performance of Chinese animation is far from triumphant. The strongest export record of Chinese animation was achieved in 2010 with US$ 18.1 million. In the subsequent two years, the number quickly shrank to only around US$ 5 million to 6 million (Keane 2015). In short, pedagogical content simply does not sell well to the international audience.

The enterprises that created *Rainbow Cat and Blue Rabbit* and *Pleasant Goat and Grey Wolf* are among the successful examples in the Chinese animation industry, but the so-called breakthroughs of these companies are still largely confined to the local Chinese context. In 2008, the Hunan-based GreatDreams Cartoon Media Company, which produces *Rainbow Cat and Blue Rabbit*, merged with Sunchime,[10] once the most successful animation company in China, which created the locally well-known *Blue Cat* series (Keane 2009). The Guangdong-based Creative Power Entertainment Corporation, which produces *Pleasant Goat and Grey Wolf* is now owned by Guangdong Alpha Animation and Culture, one of the leading Chinese animation enterprises today. This enterprise, formerly an animation derivative business, transformed its operations successfully. Alpha Animation achieved sales revenue of RMB 17 billion (US$ 2.7 billion) and a net profit of RMB 2.89 billion (US$ 455 million) in the first three quarters of 2014. While these mega animation groups are forming, it is too soon to claim that they are catching up in the international scene. Although the *Pleasant Goat* series was aired overseas in 52 countries, including Singapore, India and Australia, it can hardly fulfil the aspiration of making the Pleasant Goat icon a Hello Kitty or even a Mickey Mouse equivalent.

Even in the local market Chinese animation lacks competitiveness in face of international rivalry, especially when it comes to teenage audience segments. Teenagers in China have continued to seek out foreign animation content because of better quality and wider genre diversity. In 2006 and 2008, SARFT further tightened its policy in restricting the airtime of imported animations. According to this edict television channels are not able to screen any foreign animation films during prime time; nor can they show segments introducing or displaying foreign animation works during prime time. The restricted hours were extended from 5–8pm in 2006 to 5–9pm in 2008. Despite this quota, teenagers can easily access foreign animation content thanks to the rapid development of online video sites. These videos are usually made available through downloading or purchasing from overseas sources, as well as through sub-titling by 'fansub' groups and sharing on the net. Popular online video sites such as Youku and Tudou are able to obtain exclusive rights from Japanese media to broadcast popular Japanese animation in China. These sites allow netizens to view popular Japanese animation such as *Naruto*, *Bleach*, *Gin Tama* and *Gundam* legally in real time on online video sites. The Internet is an alternative channel for teenagers to access foreign animation; at the time of writing there were no government restrictions on the amount of foreign animation on the Internet.

CONCLUSION: MANAGED CREATIVITY IN THE ANIMATION INDUSTRY

China began to ramp up development of its cultural and creative industries in the early 2000s; however, the adoption of the term 'creative industries' in the policy discourse in China is not without some degree of tension. While the Chinese government appreciates the promises of wealth creation, talent renewal and industrial progress promised by the creative industries discourse, the concept of creativity is essentially problematic for China (see Chapter 3 by Keane in this volume). In the Western context, the term creativity entails a kind of

> 'artistic' sensibility and practice – breaking the rules, 'thinking outside the box', 'coming from left field', etc. – which links to the aesthetic of the 'revaluation of all values', 'the shock of the new' and the agonistic struggle with the existing order which characterizes the modernist and avant-garde traditions (O'Connor and Gu 2006: 273)

This kind of creativity is mostly nurtured in a stimulating environment with favorable social conditions for free expression and a general openness to novel ideas. Yet these conditions are frail in China with an authoritarian, risk averse political regime. Scholars such as Jing Wang (2004) are not optimistic about the transplant of the Western concept of creative freedom in China and see it as a compromise: 'where creative imagination and content are subjugated to active state surveillance' (p. 13).

From our review of the animation industry and its rapid development in China, we conclude with the idea of managed creativity. Drawing from the discipline of business management, Bilton (2010) has discussed the concept of 'manageable creativity' borne out of the historically opposed categories of 'management' and 'creativity.' He examines how both business and cultural policy rhetoric has rendered a notion of manageable creativity through redefining creativity 'in managerial terms, as a business commodity and as a management competence' (p. 257). But beyond the economic model, it may be worthwhile to look at how the attempts 'to tame or domesticate unpredictable. . .processes of creativity within a framework of predictable policy outcomes' (p. 266) play out. In the context of China, creativity is managed to serve the political end. In other words, the government has tried to tame the creative process for creating predictable political outcomes.

Behind the various measures to manage animation content we have discussed in this chapter, the ultimate boundary for the animation industry is the government's instruction that animation is fundamentally ideological content targeting China's young population. According to our interview with the organizer of China's International Animation Festival in Hangzhou,[11] the industry closely follows the prescribed approach; the ideological boundaries ensure they do not deviate. Content that may be considered ideologically sensitive is removed. A common strategy to avoid sensitive topics is to cast the plotline in a world of fantasy, and this is why many Chinese animations have their stories designed around communities of animals rather than human beings, as seen in the various examples that appeared in this chapter, from *Rainbow Cat and Blue Rabbit*, *Pleasant Goat and Grey Wolf* to *Boonie Bears*, *Pig Man* and numerous others. These imagined settings with animals as the central characters provide a relatively 'safe zone' because the content is not directly linked up with real life situations. In this sense creativity for the Chinese animation industry is about how to tell new stories within an ideological boundary. Some opt to recycle ancient Chinese legends such as the stories of *Sun Wukong* (the Monkey King) from *The Journey to the West* as these stories provide imagined settings that do not touch on social reality. The blockbuster *Monkey King Hero is Back (xiyou ji da sheng gui lai)* (2015) which topped the animation box office record in China (breaking the record set by *Kung Fu Panda 2* in 2011) again proves that the formula of the Monkey King is almost never going to miss. However, this common practice of serial adaptation evidently does not help in any real way in developing innovative content creation.

In this chapter we have examined the development of the Chinese animation industry and its implications for success in the international arena. To date government support for the industry has only fuelled quantitative growth. The reality however is that many policies stifle the kind of creative culture necessary for successful animation businesses. Although many enterprises have rushed into the industry, it seems that few are motivated by the creative vision to produce high quality work. What's worse, the managed creativity exhibited in the Chinese animation industry means that creativity is encouraged insofar as it is consistent with the government agenda. It ought not to be shocking or disruptive. Whenever possible, it is deployed to circulate the state discourse. These hindrances to creativity must be tackled for the Chinese animation industry to develop in a sustainable way and further to thrive globally. While animation audiences nowadays are becoming more diverse and more sophisticated, constantly seeking something edgier and more groundbreaking, the Chinese animation industry is still pulled back by the concept and policy that view animation as a children-oriented medium and a propaganda tool. Unless this can be changed, there is little real hope for Chinese animation studios to create animation content that will appeal to an international audience.

NOTES

*   This chapter is fully supported by a grant from the Research Grant Council of HKSAR (CUHK14402914).
1.   *The Smurfs* originated as a comic series in Belgium and was later produced as a popular television series by an American animation studio in the 1980s.
2.   *guanyu jiaqiang donghuapian yinjin he buofang guanli de tongzhi*
3.   The authority was known as the State Administration of Press, Publication, Radio, Film and Television (SAPPRFT) after 2013.
4.   *yingshi donghuaye shiwu qijian fazhan guihua*
5.   ('Suggestions') *guanyu fazhan woguo yingshi donghua chanye de ruogan yijian*
6.   *guanyu shixing guochan dianshi donghuapian faxing xuke zhidu de tongzhi*
7.   *youxiu guochan donghuapian tuijian buochu banfa*
8.   *shaoer jingpin fazhan zhuanxiang zijin ji guochan donghua fazhan zhuanxiang zijin pingshen banfa (shixing)*
9.   *guochan yuanchuang dianshi donghuapian ji guochan donghua chuangzuo rencai fuchi zhuanxiang pingshen banfa (shixing)*
10. The Hunan Sunchime Cartoon Archive Development Limited Company, known as Sanchen in Chinese.
11. Personal interview, 29 April 2015.

REFERENCES

Bilton, Chris (2010), 'Manageable creativity', *International Journal of Cultural Policy* **16** (3): 255–69.

Cao, Rong and Na Wang (2010), *zuoren yao xue xiyangyang, zuoshi yao xue huitailang* (*Learn from Pleasant Goat in the being and from Grey Wolf in the doing*). Beijing: kexue chubanshe.

Donald, Stephanie Hemelryk (2002), 'Crazy rabbits! Children's media culture', in Stephanie Hemelryk-Donald, Michael Keane and Hong Yin (eds.), *Media in China: Consumption, Content and Crisis*. London: RoutledgeCurzon, pp. 128–39.

Donald, Stephanie Hemelryk (2005), *Little Friends: Children's Film and Media Culture in China*. Lanham, MD: Rowman and Littlefield Publishers.

Fung, Anthony (2013), '*Pleasant Goat and Grey Wolf*: Creative industry, market and the state-animated modernity in China', *International Journal of Cultural and Creative Industries* **1** (1): 54–65.

Gorfinkel, Lauren (2012), 'Promoting a harmonious society through CCTV's music entertainment television programming' in J. Lee, L. Nedilsky and S. Cheung (eds.), *China's Rise to Power: Conceptions of State Governance*. New York: Palgrave Macmillan, pp. 71–90.

Keane, Michael (2009), 'Between the tangible and the intangible: China's new development dilemma', *Chinese Journal of Communication* **2** (1): 77–91.

Keane, Michael (2015), *The Chinese Television Industry*. London: British Film Institute, Palgrave.

Lent, John A. and Ying Xu (2010), 'Chinese animation film: from experimentation to digitalization', in Ying Zhu and Stan Rosen (eds.), *Art, Politics, and Commerce in Chinese Cinema*. Hong Kong: Hong Kong University Press, pp. 111–25.

Liu, Qiong (2010), *yangshi shaoer wuye bo donghua re zhengyi meiti zhiyi gei shui kan* ('Controversies on animation broadcast at midnight on CCTV Kids Channel: who's the audience?'), accessed 30 November 2014 at http://ent.sina.com.cn/v/m/2010-07-21/12 423024276.shtml.

Ministry of Culture (MOC) (2010), *wenhuabu guanyu gongbu 2010 nian di yi pi tongguo rending de zhongdian dongman chanpin mingdan de tongzhi* ('Notice about the first batch of key animation products 2010 from the Ministry of Culture'), accessed 30 November 2014 at http://www.gov.cn/zwgk/2010-09/02/content_1694450.htm.

Ministry of Finance et al. (2006), *guanyu tuidong woguo dongman chanye fazhan de ruogan yijian* ('Several opinions of the State Council on promoting development of animation industry in China'), Beijing: State Council of the PRC, accessed 9 May 2014 at http://www/cpll.cn/law7113.html.

N/A (2009), *2001 nian zhongguo di yi bu sanwei shuzi dianying* ('2001: China's first 3-dimensional digital film'), accessed 11 December 2014 at http://www.comicyu.com/html/DMZT/GCDH60ZN/JDSJ/2009/09/30484.shtml.

Ng, Wai-ming (2002), 'The impact of Japanese comics and animation in Asia', *Journal of Japanese Trade and Society* July/August: 1–4.

O'Connor, Justin and Xin Gu (2006), 'A new modernity? The arrival of "creative industries" in China', *International Journal of Cultural Studies* **9** (3): 271–83.

Oriental Dreamworks (2015), 'About Us', accessed 6 July 2015 at http://www.oriental-dreamworks.com/odw-about-our-film-studio.

Research and Markets (2014), *Global Animation Industry 2014: Strategies, Trends and Opportunities*, accessed 2 February 2016 at http://www.researchandmarkets.com/reports/2880694/global-and-chinese-animation-industry-report#pos-5.

Research and Markets (2015a), *Asian Animation Industry 2015: Strategies, Trends and Opportunities*.

Research and Markets (2015b), *Global and Chinese Animation Industry Report 2015: Strategies, Trends and Opportunities*.

State Administration of Press, Publication, Radio, Film and Television (SAPPRFT) (2013), *Nie Chenxi kaocha guangzhou dongman qiye yaoqiu tuidong zhongguomeng zhuti donghuapian chuangzuo* ('Nie Chenxi visited animation enterprises in Guangzhou and requested the promotion of "Chinese Dream" themed animation creation'), accessed 22 May 2015 at http://www.sarft.gov.cn/articles/2013/12/23/20131223162533150493.html.

State Administration of Radio, Film and Television (SARFT) (2008), *guanyu woguo dongman chanye de ruogan yijian* ('Suggestions on the development of the animation industry'), accessed 30 November 2014 at http://www.sarft.gov.cn/articles/2007/02/27/20070914165147430508.html.

The Korea Times (2015), 'South Korean government to invest $345.8 million in animation industries by 2019', accessed 22 May 2014 at http://www.koreatimesus.com/s-korean-govt-to-invest-345-8-million-in-animation-industries-by-2019/.

Wang, Jing (2004), 'The global reach of a new discourse: how far can "creative industries" travel?' *International Journal of Cultural Studies* **7** (1): 9–19.

Xinhuanet (2014), *guocan donghua dianshi nianchanliang lianjiang jinru you liang zhuan zhi 'huandangqi'* ('Consecutive drop in yearly domestic animation output, "change of gear" from quantity to quality'), accessed 30 November 2014 at http://news.xinhuanet.com/newmedia/2014-05/04/c_126457708.htm.

21. From 'Nothing to My Name' to 'I Am a Singer': market, capital, and politics in the Chinese music industry
Qian Wang and Jeroen de Kloet

Mainland China is becoming more important as a source of artists and repertoire for us. I think that in coming years the popularity of artists from mainland
China could be the same as those performers from Taiwan who currently dominate the Mandarin music scene.
Sunny Chang, chairman and CEO Greater China, Universal Music (IFPI
2014a: 11)

INTRODUCTION

I am a singer (*wo shi geshou*) is a Chinese talent show broadcast by Hunan
Satellite TV, based on a Korean format. In the third season broadcast
in 2015 the winner of the show, Han Hong, a well-known singer from a
Tibetan background, won by performing a duet with Hong Kong pop idol
Eason Chan. Renowned for the wide range of her voice, Han previously
performed in the closing ceremony of the Beijing Olympics. Among other
contestants she also ended up in front of Sitar Tan (or Tan Weiwei), who
performed together with the godfather of Chinese rock, Cui Jian – singer
of the by now legendary song from the 1980s titled 'Nothing to My Name.'
This song is generally considered to mark the start of China's rock culture.

Whereas in the past talent shows like *The Voice* functioned as a possible
stepping stone towards a music career, *I am a singer* operates on a different
logic: the audience adjudicates if the singer is worthy of stardom. The show
attests to the importance of the media – in this case a combination of television and the Internet – in the making or breaking of a pop star. The show
also alludes to the regional entanglement: that is, it takes a Hong Kong
pop star, a Tibetan singer, a Korean format and a provincial satellite TV
channel to produce a national winner. Finally, the show underlines that
it is not so much CD sales that matter, but rather the manufacturing of
a pop stardom that smoothly traverses different media platforms, ideally
including cinema, television, Internet and live performance.

Three interconnected developments have transformed China's music
industry quite radically since 2001, the year the nation entered the World

293

Trade Organization. First, the purported 'rise of China' has presented increased self-confidence and different modes of soft power in which culture and creativity play a constitutive role; second, the global economic crisis, or more specifically shifts within the music industry, partly related to the emergence of digital technologies, are gradually rendering the CD obsolete and instigating processes of media convergence; and third, processes of intensified globalization and regionalization of the media industries, are forging transnational and regional modes of cooperation and feeding into celebrity culture.

In this chapter we analyse these three developments, taking the music industry in Mainland China as our focus. We show how this industry has moved from being a secondary market in East Asia towards becoming the main consumer market. This has regional implications: the music industry is increasingly entangled with Hong Kong and Taiwan. Moreover, the regional neighbours cannot ignore the Mainland market. Television programmes like *Voice of China*, *I am a Singer* and *Idol*, and their related celebrity culture have played an important role in growing the power of the Mainland music industry. These formatted shows have not only changed the business model of the music industry, they also profit from strategic alliances with national media and Internet platforms.

Talent is slowly moving to the Mainland. While this may hold potential for creative change in the Mainland, much of this talent now – and even more so in the future – is being appropriated by what Fung terms a 'state-global media complex' (Fung 2008: 84). Considering the importance of regional partners from Korea, Taiwan and Hong Kong, a more precise term might be a state-global-*regional* media complex.[1] As we will show in our analysis, regionalization comes with frictions, disjunctures and cultural anxieties; at the moment this makes it impossible to speak of the rise of a Greater China music industry. We also show how convergence with other media is more profitable for television and new media companies than it is for the music industry itself.

We begin with a brief introduction on changes taking place in the music industry, introducing the concept of convergence. Then we move on to discuss the role of the state in the Chinese music industry. We illustrate with two cases that explore the complex relationship that oscillates between support and censorship: music talent shows on TV and music festivals. In the following section we delve deeper into the workings of the Chinese music industry; here we draw on interviews with industry professionals in China to analyse their views on the increased involvement of Hong Kong and Taiwan as well as the convergence with other media platforms. In the final section we analyse the unexpected rise of folk singer Song Dongye and the stardom of Hong Kong pop singer G.E.M. Deng Ziqi.

Both careers are related to music TV shows and new media technologies, but the stars differ in how they navigate between the Mainland, Taiwan and Hong Kong, as well as within the music industry itself.

AN INDUSTRY IN FLUX

According to Wikström (2009: 4), 'the music industry during less than a decade has completely shifted its centre of gravity from the physical to the virtual – from the Disk to the Cloud.'[2] Over the past decade we have witnessed the invention of new business models, first primarily for downloading (e.g. the iTunes store), after that increasingly for live streaming (e.g. Spotify). In China, likeminded services such as *Youku* and *Xiami* have enabled a move away from music carriers to digital platforms. Wikström (2009: 5–8) identifies three important shifts in the music industry: first, the move from control towards connectivity; second, a move from product to service; and third, a shifting balance between professional and amateur, with the latter gaining power. As we will show in this chapter, we witness similar changes in the case of China – but with some specific modifications, highlighting two processes: the continuing controlling role of the nation-state, and the regional entanglement that comes with intensified levels of cooperation, and simultaneously produces tensions and disjunctures.[3]

In effect, the music market is shifting dramatically, making it increasingly difficult to analyse total revenues. Music now is more often the product through which one brands the star. One good example is Korean pop star Psy, whose global hit *Gangnam Style* was downloadable for free, resulting in mass circulation (Mahdawi 2012). *Gangnam Style* was made to be copied, 'by doing so, he allowed the song to be co-opted by any group who wanted to use it for their own cause. Thousands took up the challenge and made the song their own' (Globalization 2012: online). This example is relevant for China, a country often perceived as a place of copyright infringement. Since China entered the World Trade Organization in 2001 the issue of piracy has been a concern for artists. It goes beyond the scope of this chapter to critique the discourse of copyright infringement – a discourse that generally serves the industry more than artists (see Pang 2012). The image of China as a pirating country has inspired continuous attempts by the state and the industry to 'improve' the situation and secure copyrights.

Data from *2014 Chinese Music Industry Report*, conducted by Zhao Zhian at the Communication University of China, show that total market revenue reached RMB 271 billion in 2013, including RMB 44 billion from the digital music market, RMB 14 billion from live shows, but only RMB 650 million from physical products, which clearly displays the complete transformation of the Chinese music industry under the pressure of market and industry convergence.[4] Although 650 million online users contributed 5.6 per cent increase in China's digital music market in 2014,[5] the ease and convenience of getting music for free through new media pushed digital piracy levels up as high as 99 per cent.[6] In turn such infringement had the effect of inspiring the search for new and different business models; one of these is to aim for increased convergence between different media platforms, including CD, DVD, television and Internet.

Convergence has changed the music industry worldwide. The rapid development of technology has forced the creative industries, especially media industries, to change their business models in order to deal with the challenge from new technologies and the demand of consumers' participation. As Jenkins notes, 'digitalisation set the conditions for convergence; corporate conglomerates created its imperative' (2006: 11). Jenkins rightly points out that 'convergence refers to a process, not an endpoint' (ibid. 16), which includes 'a top-down corporate-driven process and a bottom-up consumer-driven process' (ibid. 18). Whereas the first alludes to the integration of different media platforms, the second dimension refers to the appropriation of media content by audiences, especially fan communities. In his words:

> media companies are learning how to accelerate the flow of media content across delivery channels to expand revenue opportunities, broaden markets, and reinforce viewer commitments. Consumers are learning how to use these different media technologies to bring the flow of media more fully under their control and to interact with other consumers. (Jenkins 2006: 18)

Jenkins writes of viewer commitments, but we can by the same token speak of listener commitments. In his view 'convergence culture' opens up the possibility for politics as new forms of participation while collaboration generates social power. Consequently, participatory power inserts itself into the entertainment system – and by extension into the political process. Couldry, however, points out the weakness of Jenkins' theory, arguing that 'the term "convergence *culture*" blurs important processes of differentiation and stratification and so blocks a better understanding of the politics of convergence' (Couldry 2011: 487). Like Couldry we are hesitant in celebrating an emergent participatory culture. This is particularly so in the case of China, where the nation-state continues to hold a strong control over the production of culture, while simultaneously stimulating its intense commercialization. Before we move to the particularities of the music industry in China it is important to reflect upon the role of the nation-state. We will do so through exploring two different cases: reality music shows and music festivals.

MUSIC AND THE STATE

Between November 7 and 10, 2013, the Beijing municipal bureau of copyright and the national music industry park co-organized the first China music industry conference in Beijing. The theme of the conference was 'Innovation, Openness, and Win-win', and a wide range of issues, including policy, capital, media, market, digitalization, creativity and education were discussed. In recent years twelve so-called 'music industry parks', five in Beijing, one in Shanghai, two in Guangzhou, two in Shenzhen, and two in Chengdu, have been developed to construct a stable infrastructure for what is hailed as the wonderful future of the Chinese music industry. This policy of clustering follows a general trend of the creative industries policies in China. In the desire to move from 'made in China' to 'created in China' (cf. Keane 2009), both the national government as well as municipalities have over the past decade developed a strong creative industries policies – as this book analyses. Since 2005, the number of official 'creative industry clusters' in Shanghai has grown to around 90 in number (O'Connor and Gu 2014: 1; see chapter by Zheng in this volume). The music industry parks that have been developed nationwide thus fit into a general policy in support of the creative industries (Keane 2009, 2012, 2013). As Keane (2013: 93) writes, 'despite the prominence given to such clusters, the evidence suggests that most are underperforming and are in effect real estate developments'.

Music parks – like the East Chengdu Creative Music City, Shenzhen Dameisha Music Industry Park, Guangzhou Risheng Music Industry Park, Shanghai Music Valley and Beijing China Music Valley demonstrate China's strong desire to become a new powerhouse of popular music for the sake of economy, culture and soft power. Yet while China is often perceived to be lagging behind particularly in terms of pop music,[7] it is currently making quite a leap forward. First, China has become an important consumption market for popular music and audiences are willing to pay a lot for live performances. Second, the Mainland is becoming increasingly important in the production of music, not least because of the success of reality music shows on TV. This trend started in 2005 when *Super Girl* (*chaoji nüsheng*), produced by Hunan Satellite TV became a nationwide hit.

Such reality shows build on foreign formats (see Keane 2015); moreover, they are an example of convergence culture because they make use of different media platforms; they engage, but also capitalize on the audience through mobile voting; and they help produce new music stars like Li Yuchun, winner of the first series in 2005. The production of music and stars is no longer under the control of the music industry: it involves jury members and audiences. Indeed the Li Yuchun phenomenon in 2005 demonstrated the power of convergence in reshaping the Chinese music industry and capitalizing on participatory culture. This presents a way to mitigate piracy, as the revenues come not only from the sale of CDs and downloads of music, but also from advertising revenues and profits made through SMS voting. Yet the show operated on a tight rope; not only did its tremendous popularity raise the concern of the central government, its use of a 'national' voting system together with the androgynous image of Li Yuchun, which turned her into a gay icon, were further reasons for concern.

Internationally the show was indeed hailed as a playground for democracy, but as Meng argues convincingly (2009: 269): '[A]s long as institutionalized channels for civic engagement and political participation remain tightly controlled in China, the rather misplaced enthusiasm on the democratic implications of *Super Girl* is an indication of how far China is from democracy rather than of how close it has come. . .' The show received a lot of critique, from media professionals as well as government officials, for being too vulgar and low. Consequently, as de Kloet and Landsberger (2012: 144) show, the state intervened in the show:

> for the 2009 show, scandals about the judging panel members and the girls were to be avoided, the behaviour of the girls needed to be monitored, crying-together scenes were not allowed, the show could not be broadcast in prime time, it had to be finished before the end of the summer holidays, and voting through the Internet or text messaging was no longer allowed.

Yet a complete ban would be tricky, causing unrest and running against the state's own policies towards media commercialization.

Subsequent talent shows like *I Am a Singer* are continuing the success of *Super Girl*. As mentioned before, the most significant difference is that *I Am a Singer* features professional singers, with support from colleagues, who join the contest. The show is profoundly regionalized with supporters and contestants coming from other places and countries as well. This attests to the increased regionalization of the music industry in China, a development we will analyse below.

A second development that has changed the face of the music industry in China, and that involves a curious involvement from the nation-state, is the increase in big music festivals. Shen Lihui is a typical Beijing entrepreneur in that he combines different roles: he was the lead vocalist of the band Sober, owner of a bar, founder and director of indie record label Modern Sky and organizer of the Strawberry Music festival. Like many of his generation, he knows how to navigate between the permissible and the impermissible, being confronted at times with bans, censorship and last minute cancellations of festival permits, but always managing to continue playing the game. This makes him a prolific figure in the local music industry. While the idea of large scale outdoor music festivals was something almost unthinkable until the end of the 1990s – after all, the Party wants to avoid large gatherings of people no matter whether they are music fans or *Falungong* members – they have mushroomed all over China since the 2000s with the backing of creative industries' policy.

During the May holiday many youth will go to Tongzhou Park, located far from the centre of Beijing, to join the Strawberry Music festival. The festival hosts rock bands like The New Pants and Zuoxiao Zuzhou. They attract thousands of visitors, and at times magical moments happen, for example during Zuoxiao Zuzhou's closing concert in 2010. While police kept the audiences under control, on screen they were offered fragments from the Ai Weiwei documentary *Let Feng Jenghu Go Home* (2009) about the Chinese economist and human rights writer and blogger. The audience instantly recognized these fragments and started to applaud and cheer loudly. This combination of a clearly articulated political critique among a crowd that was so visibly under control by the police attests to the complexities and contradictions of the possibility for doing politics in China.

But as Jeroen Groenewegen-Lau (2014) shows in his analysis of music festivals, such a political reading of these festivals fails to acknowledge the complex entanglement between the state and the cultural industries in China. Groenewegen-Lau shows how in the first decade of the 2000s, bands started to earn big money for their performances; a performance by Miserable Faith in 2011 earned the band a fee between RMB 50,000 and RMB 100,000. Groenewegen-Lau quotes organizer Shen Lihui (p. 5):

> The last couple of years a lot of bands earned over a million a year. Accounts are easy to settle. For instance if thirty of the fifty music festivals book you and you earn thirty to fifty thousand a show, you'll make more than a million. Only now they've become rock stars. In the past they were rock aspirants. Stars are wealthy because of the market. Only then they can perform for years without disbanding.

Groenewegen shows how city governments started to support festivals financially as part of city branding tactics. Such support remains fragile; for example, the 2015 Strawberry festival was cancelled. But in general the festivals are now state supported events (like many similar festivals elsewhere in the world); they are the result of creative policies that help produce a 'middle ground where the state, the market, and the people negotiate conflicts' (Groenewegen 2014: 25).

The state, the media and the music industry are thus deeply implicated with one another. Apart from simply banning festivals, there are many other ways in which censorship is taking place. Elsewhere, de Kloet (2010) has elaborated on how bands manage to circumvent the censors, for example by linguistic tricks (printing different lyrics than those that are sung), or by the release of illegal or pirated versions, resulting in what can best be described as a cat and mouse game between musicians, music industry and censors. This game has become probably even more complicated with the increased entanglement with Hong Kong and Taiwan.

REGIONALIZATION OF CHINA'S MUSIC INDUSTRY

In the early 1990s, both global and regional companies entered the Mainland music market. While unsuccessful in their ambitions at the time, they did create a space for local companies like Modern Sky (see de Kloet 2010 for an analysis of this local turn). With China's accelerated opening up since the late 1990s, 'foreign' companies have once more moved into the market.[8]

Sony music was the first of the Big Five; it entered China in 1997, and immediately flexed its capital muscle to sign prominent Mainland stars such as Liu Huan, Han Lei, Chen Ming and Mao Ning. Warner, EMI, BMG and Universal made their move a little later, likewise targeting big names for immediate rewards with no interest in new faces. The Big Five believed that their advantage in capital operation and marketing expertise would help them to conquer the Chinese market, but they failed to understand the workings of the market, including piracy issues. This paved the way for a stronger involvement from regional partners, especially from Hong Kong and Taiwan. Producers, lyric writers as well as musicians increasingly work across these three localities. As the IFPI writes (2014b: 37), 'in the absence of a developed market for sales of recordings or performance rights, labels working in China rely heavily on management and live performance income. Most big-selling artists are developed out of Taiwan, dubbed the "Hollywood" of the region.'

According to Sunny Chang of Universal Music Greater China, 'the vast majority of the deals his company signs include management rights. He says an artist in Greater China typically generates 40 per cent of their income from digital revenues, 30 per cent from physical sales and 30 per cent from non-recording income, such as live performance or sponsorship' (IFPI

2014a: 21). We earlier quoted his prediction that the Mainland will play an increasingly important role as producer of talent. When Mainland pop diva Na Ying performed at the Hong Kong Coliseum in 2001, it was regarded by some as a turning point: finally Mainland pop stars had penetrated the Hong Kong and Taiwan market; the business flow was now multi-directional. One important reason why Na successfully transformed from a stereotyped Mainland singer on CCTV into a pop diva is her collaboration with musicians and record companies from Hong Kong and Taiwan dating back to 1993. However, to mark Na's performance as the beginning of an equal relationship is perhaps an overstatement; while China is becoming more important as a consumption market, Hong Kong and, especially, Taiwan remain the key players in the music industry.

Based on interviews with four professionals in the music industry of Mainland China, our analysis shows that this increased cooperation with Hong Kong and Taiwan is accompanied with frictions and disjunctures.[9] The former manager of Warner and Universal Music Xiang Zheng believes that increased regional cooperation as well as convergence with media industries brings more damage than benefit to the Chinese music industry. After participating in many *gangtai*[10] pop star tours around China, such as Soda Green (*Suda Lü*), Xiang feels that the cash mainly flows from China to Hong Kong and Taiwan. Wang Feng – the number one Chinese pop/rock star, is the highest paid musician in China. He received RMB 14 million for a concert at the Shanghai Stadium in 2013. Yet the Taiwan pop/rock band Mayday (*wuyuetian*) earned RMB 20 million for their concert at the National Stadium in Beijing in the same year.[11] In Xiang's view the increased entanglement between China, Hong Kong and Taiwan is a 'gold rush' for *gangtai* pop stars and record companies; the mainland offers them a lucrative market, far greater than Hong Kong or Taiwan. For instance, when Faye Wong (Wang Fei) had her comeback tour in 2010, ticket prices ranged from RMB 300 to RMB 2500 in Beijing, compared to HK$280 (RMB 220) to 980 (RMB 770) in Hong Kong. The profit margin differential makes the Mainland the new central stage of Chinese popular music. Wong took full advantage of this; she performed thirty-eight concerts in the Mainland and only three in Taiwan and five in Hong Kong.

The words of former manager of Jingwen Records Li Zhuohui resonate with a similar mistrust in regional cooperation; he thinks that the current situation might destroy the future development of Chinese popular music and cites three reasons. First, he claims that record companies from Hong Kong and Taiwan only care about financial rewards from China's market and are not interested in supporting local music cultures. Second, industrial experience and expertise will influence the musical taste of

Mainland audiences and inspire the majority of Mainland musicians to imitate a *gangtai* style and lose their assumed 'own artistic taste and value.' Third, in a similar vein, Chinese musicians will consciously decolour their Mainland Chinese identities in terms of aesthetics, ideologies and politics.

What interests us in his words is not so much whether this is indeed happening, but more so the articulation of a *perceived essential cultural difference* between the Mainland and Hong Kong and Taiwan, a difference that is ridden with power. The cooperation is viewed more in terms of cultural imperialism, rather than cooperation. What these words thus tell us is how *perceived* cultural differences produce a culture of mistrust and hinder cooperation. In other words, the increased cultural entanglement is ridden with conflicts, ambiguities and contradictions, rather than gesturing towards a shared Sinophone future. Li Zhuohui and Xiang Zheng are both convinced that this entanglement will level music cultures, but it is unlikely to lead to a shared social culture.

But these cultural anxieties do not only play out on the Mainland. Musicians and music professionals in Hong Kong and Taiwan articulate cultural differences, coupled with a fear that the Mainland will completely overwhelm them in the near future.[12] For example, when Taiwan students protested against a trade deal with China in March 2014, and formed the Sunflower Movement, Taiwanese musicians and singers such as Zhang Xuan made a public appeal in support of the students and rejected cooperation with the Mainland. Although they claimed that the uploading of a song called 'Stand Up' (*qilai*) on their website was caused by hackers, Taiwan pop/rock band Mayday (*wuyuetian*) was still criticized in the Mainland media for being hypocritical as they need the Mainland market while they simultaneously express hostility to the Mainland.[13] In the fall of 2014, pop stars Anthony Wong and Denise Ho played a crucial role during the Umbrella Protest in Hong Kong, a role that has since seriously impacted their careers as they cannot perform in the Mainland anymore. These cases show that it is far too sweeping to speak of an emergent shared creative industry between Hong Kong, Taiwan and Mainland China. While their music industries increasingly overlap and work together, this cooperation is fraught with cultural conflicts and anxieties.

In our interviews the trend of media convergence was met with critique and some scepticism. On a positive note, the former marketing director of Modern Sky, Ding Taisheng, thinks that while convergence between the media industry and the IT industry has caused a serious decline of sales of music products in conventional forms, such as CD and DVD, it has also created new forms of music products and consumption, which offer more opportunities to indie musicians to break into the mainstream market. Guo Bo, project manager of Modern Sky, agrees with Ding and claims that convergence diversifies the contents, styles, forms and business models of China's music industry and helps generate better financial rewards.

On a more pessimistic note, Xiang Zheng and Li Zhuohui argue that convergence will cause a further decline of the Chinese music industry. Xiang says that in 2012 music related revenues were RMB 39 billion for China Mobile and RMB 8 billion for China Unicom in comparison to RMB 500 million for all record companies. The Chinese music industry did not benefit from convergence. In 2013, only six Mainland record companies could make a profit.

According to Xiang and Li, while the concert-tour market has developed rapidly in recent years, this has been captured by the television industry. Wang Qian's (2013) research shows that CCTV's *The Same Song* (*tong yi shou ge*) show bypassed the music industry, and instead generated its own financial and ideological benefits.[14] Winners of talent shows like *Sing My Song* (*Zhongguo hao gequ*), and the *Voice of China* (*Zhongguo hao shengyin*) are all obliged by contract to release their music as part of a company affiliated to the television company, and not part of China's music industry. When some popular contestants including Zhou Bichang, Chen Chusheng, Shang Wenjie, Zhang Jie, He Jie, and Wang Xiaokun want to quit their TV entertainer identity and become musicians, lawsuits are often the only solution. In 2013, according to Xiang Zheng, the concert tour market was worth more than RMB 5 billion. However, the television industry occupied the biggest part of the market, the *gangtai* music industry was second, then came Modern Sky and the Midi Music School; only a very small part of the market was left to other Chinese record companies.

The Internet also is said to undermine the music industry. The music division of China Mobile, for example, is located in Chengdu, and has been transformed into Migu Music label, which has more than 1400 music business partners with 3 million copyrighted repertoires, 700 million users and 120 million members. Migu Music had occupied 75 per cent of the digital music market in China in 2012.[15] New technologies and devices make fair competition impossible between the Chinese telecom industry and the Chinese music industry, and allow organizations and people in power to profit and benefit from the Chinese music industry illegally.[16] The twelve music industry parks around China, in Li Zhuohui's opinion, mainly serve the government and state-owned units. They possess resources which ordinary music business organizations do not have, but contribute little to the Chinese music industry and fail to compete with the *gangtai* music industry. Under these circumstances, it is claimed to be difficult for 'ordinary' Chinese music business organizations to survive and produce good music.

FROM BRANDS TO RESISTANCE TO BRANDING

Two final cases further illustrate the music industry in China: the sudden and unexpected rise of folk singer Song Dongye, and the stardom of Hong Kong pop singer G.E.M. Deng Ziqi. Both are connected to the increased importance of music TV shows and both showcase the importance of new media for producing a solid fan base, but whereas the first gestures towards an intensified integration between the Mainland, Taiwan and Hong Kong, the second confronts us with its political tensions and frictions.

June 29, 2013, was the birthday of Song Dongye's grandmother who had passed away shortly before; in order to escape from the silence of sadness at home Song went to a gig that night. When he came out of the club he noticed that the number of his *weibo* followers had increased to over one thousand. At that moment he could not imagine how a talent show, which he did not attend, would completely change his life from a mere nobody to a new idol revered by urban youth. A few hours previously, Zuo Li had performed his song 'Miss Dong' on Hunan satellite TV's *Super Boy*. Programme producers had noticed a number of contestants performing this song at the audition and they realised its potential popularity; they selected Zuo whose cuteness and rumours over his love life made him the ideal performer for the song. It opened the door to the mainstream market for Song Dongye and his fellow urban folk musicians. Industrial veteran Lu Zhongqiang believes,

> Song Dongye's success is mainly due to the space unconsciously pushed by the TV platform. Judging from the present condition, the best approach for indie music to reach the mainstream market is still TV, regardless of talent show or variety show, TV can completely change the fate of indie music. (Li 2014)

Modern Sky released Song's first official album *The North of Anhe Bridge* in 2013. A number of songs from this album subsequently became the theme songs of films, TV series, and computer games. Song and Modern Sky director Shen Lihui even appeared together in a Dell advertisement. But instead of fully cooperating with the media industry, Song publicly avers to resisting it. For example, when Hunan Satellite TV repeatedly demanded to acquire the copyright of 'Miss Dong' because they felt that they made this song and Song successful in 2013, Song rejected the proposal and refused to participate in shows produced by Hunan Satellite TV.

Song refuses to be assimilated into the mainstream pop sphere. In fact, he signed the contract with Modern Sky under the condition that he will also remain a member of Mayouye – a loose organization and a label for urban folk music. Song would attend cultural awards ceremonies, such as Lu Xun Culture Awards, which he won in 2013, but he declines invitations to attend commercial pop music ceremonies. Song claims publicly and repeatedly that he is still a *chou diaosi* (stinky loser), a gesture stressing his alleged grass roots background, thereby authenticating his expression, and differentiating him from pop stars, and thus securing his own market.

Websites and apps, such as *douban* and *xiami*, have become the vital communicative devices for today's youth culture. By June 2015, Song's music had been listened to more than 73 million times, remarkably high when compared to Wang Feng (87 million) and A Mei (83 million) on *xiami*.[17] Acknowledging this potential source of income, three IT giants in China, Baidu, Alibaba, and Tencent have restructured their music business divisions in recent years, aiming at intensified convergence between music, media and IT.

Song's fame reached Hong Kong and Taiwan and a number of famous Taiwan musicians and stars attended his two sold-out concerts in Taipei in 2014. Liu Ruoying, a veteran actress and singer in Taiwan, performed with him on stage. Writing in the Taiwanese newspaper *Want Daily* (*wang bao*), Shen (2014) believes that in comparison with political heroes like Cui Jian, Song represents a different image of China, as a member of a generation who chase their dreams and struggle in China's cities. Shen writes quite hyperbolically,

> Song's music is like a gentle call of the time. Song writes about the trivial feelings in order to warm and melt the ice in our hearts. Luckily, Song passes this warmth to the heart of young people in Taiwan. . . The stories in his music have nothing to do with politics and the country's future, but can make the Taiwan audiences gradually feel the profound cultural identity of Chineseness shared by both sides of the Taiwan Straits.

A Taiwan audience member watched Song's concert and wrote, 'I have never been to Beijing till today. I cannot understand the story of that city, and do not know how that demolished Anhe Bridge looks like, but I know there is my own private Anhe Bridge in my heart' (quoted in Henhenhong, 2014).

The case of Song shows how media convergence and regional integration can work together; his resistance to commercialization authenticates his music, which helps explain his appeal beyond the Mainland. If the success of Song was unexpected and exceptional in that it overcame regional tensions and disjunctures, at least on the level of reception, the case of G.E.M. Deng Ziqi demonstrates how regional integration and media convergence can both benefit and restrict a musician's career.

Deng has been well known in Hong Kong since 2008, but *I Am a Singer* season two in January 2014 turned her into a superstar. Deng subsequently released a mainland version of *The Best of G.E.M. 2008–2012* in February 2014, which sold over one hundred thousand copies on the first day, demonstrating the market power of China.[18] In May 2014, Deng entered into the 2014 Forbes list of Chinese celebrities for the first time at the position of 91.[19] Among 27 cities Deng toured in 2014, 22 were in the Mainland where she had 28 concerts, in comparison with seven concerts outside of China.[20] Her music videos were watched more than 100 million times on Youtube in August 2014, which made her the first Chinese pop star to reach this milestone.[21]

In April 2014, Deng received the *Kids' Choice Awards – Favorite Asian Act*, voted by her 9.4 million Mainland *weibo* followers. In accepting the award, she said: 'being the first nominated Hong Kong singer and represent China, it is my honour to receive this award'. Some Hong Kong media and netizens were quick to criticize Deng for her choice of expression; they insisted that she should only represent Hong Kong, and labelled her as 'giving in' to the power of the Mainland. Others argued that because Deng was born in Shanghai and moved to Hong Kong at the age of four, she might not qualify as a Hong Kong singer.[22] The political tensions between the Chinese government and Hong Kong are here mapped onto one singer, revealing the anxieties that accompany regional integration of the music cultures.

This is further exemplified during the Umbrella Protests in the fall of 2014. On September 27, 2014, the first weekend since the start of the protest, Deng posted a message with a smiley picture on Twitter: 'It is Saturday now. Tomorrow will be a new start, what will you do during the weekend?' This message, devoid of any reference to the protests, met with strong critique. A Hong Kong netizen replied, 'I will fuck your mom. Can you have a little bit of common sense and conscience?' A Taiwanese netizen wrote, 'You do not care about your hometown people after getting rich yourself!' Only very few Hong Kong fans defended her, 'She only talks about music, not politics here. She is just a singer.' Deng posted the same message and picture on *weibo*, and a typical reply from her Mainland fans reads, 'I am of course missing you. I will listen to your beautiful music, spread it to the entire world, and make everybody know that you are the best.'[23] Under pressure, Deng later posted another message to wish everyone at the protest to remain safe, which quickly inspired rumours that Deng was a supporter of the protest. This consequently angered many Mainland fans. Netizens appealed to ban her and boycott her Mainland tours. It wasn't until Deng performed on CCTV's Chinese New Year Gala in February 2015, watched by audiences totalling 690 million,[24] that the storm around her finally calmed down.

After her first performance on *I Am a Singer* in January 2014, Deng asked her manager Tan whether it would be possible to have 5 million fans in China. By June 2015, the number of her Sina *weibo* followers was 17 million, as well as 6.5 million on Tencent *weibo*, and one million on Baidu *tieba*. Each of her *weibo* messages will be roughly reposted 8,000 times, commented on 10,000 times, and liked 100,000 times in the Mainland. These numbers are quite staggering – as numbers often are when they concern the PRC. They help explain why the Mainland is such an attractive market for pop singers.

CONCLUSION

We opened this chapter with a quote from Sunny Chang, manager of the Greater China branch of Universal, predicting the rise of China as a producer of music. What our analysis shows, however, is that such a picture tends to present Greater China as a harmonious unity, whereas there are in fact important cultural differences, if not conflicts and disjunctures. We have drawn attention to the increased importance of the Mainland, both in terms of consumption as well as production. This market surge is connected to the popularity of music talent shows on TV as well as the prominent role new media plays in the everyday lives of Chinese youth. Hong Kong and Taiwan remain crucial, and are more and more inspired, or forced, to cooperate with the Mainland. These processes of media convergence, digitization and regional integration create moments of shared cultural understanding, but also ideological fault lines, tensions and cultural anxieties.

In addition, the Chinese nation-state continues to control the production of culture tightly, but also in contradictory ways. For example, Cui Jian rejected an invitation by CCTV to perform during their 2014 Chinese New Year Gala because he was not allowed to sing his politically charged 'Nothing to My Name.' Yet, it was exactly this song that Deng selected at the final show of *I Am a Singer* in April 2014. If it takes a Hong Kong star to perform a politically sensitive song from a Beijing singer in the Mainland, what does this say about politics? Meanwhile, the local music industry in China is struggling to cope with the increased power of television and new media companies, as well as with the consolidation of power from Taiwan and Hong Kong. For the music industry, this will continue to be a hard and difficult battle and we expect that intensified cooperation, across media and across political boundaries, will prove key to their survival. But while the stakes are high, not all actors are equally powerful.

NOTES

1. We use the term 'regional' to refer to the entanglement with especially Hong Kong and Taiwan. This runs the danger not only of ignoring other localities (such as Singapore, South Korea and the Chinese diaspora), it may also run the danger of glossing over the regionalization *within* China. More study is required to delve deeper into the differences between music industries within China.
2. Some care is needed here, as the IFPI reports that in Germany, CD sales still make up over 50% of the revenues of the music industry (www.ifpi.org).
3. Contrary to expectations, it is important to observe that, when compared to the music markets of the US, Japan and even The Netherlands, the combined music market of Mainland China, Hong Kong and Taiwan turns out to be a marginal one in terms of revenue (de Kloet 2010: 190). In 2013, China only ranked 21st in terms of music sales (IFPI 2014b).
4. Data is from news report on *Economic Daily*'s website, accessed June 5, 2015 at http://www.ce.cn/culture/gd/201411/14/t20141114_3905292.shtml. We do not include all figures here, such as RMB 28 billion for musical instruments, RMB 37 billion for live show equipment, and RMB 46 billion for musical training, education etc.
5. Data is from <IFPI Digital Music Report 2015>, page 29.
6. Data is from news report on Sohu, accessed on Jun 5, 2015 at http://it.sohu.com/20150104/n407506487.shtml.
7. China has since the 1980s been perceived as the place for Chinese rock music, more so than for example Hong Kong, but the market for rock music is comparatively small (de Kloet 2010).
8. Interestingly, China uses different terms than either Hong Kong or Taiwan. From the perspective of China, Chinese language popular music is referred to as *Zhongguo liuxing yinyue* (Chinese popular music) as the Chinese government wants to consolidate the authority over issues related to China and Chinese culture. Yet, from the perspective of other countries and regions, Chinese language popular music is referred to as *huayu liuxing yinyue* (Sinophone popular music), which acknowledges the cultural and linguistic connection with China and simultaneously clarifies the political and ideological independence from China. In practice, *Zhongguo* and *huayu* are often interchangeable, and this intertextuality creates the vital flexibility and ambiguity of terminology, enabling intensified business collaboration.
9. They are Li Zhuohui (former general manager of Jingwen Record / founder and general manager of 1919 theatre which is a national music theatre and a part of the 1919 national music industry park, interviewed on May 7, 2014), Xiang Zheng (former marketing director of Warner Music and Universal Music / Vice president of Musikid, interviewed on March 12, 2014 and May 6, 2014), Guo Bo (Project manager of Modern Sky, interviewed on March 12, 2014), and Ding Taisheng (former marketing director of Modern Sky / independent director, founder of the Weirdo Image, interviewed on March 10, 2014).
10. *Gangtai* is a term referring to pop stars from Hong Kong and Taiwan.
11. Regarding the reliability and accuracy of those data, Xiang Zheng explains that the data cannot be 100 per cent correct, but in comparison with well adjusted official reports, Xiang believes that his data are more reliable because he gets them through his daily and personal communication with industry professionals. Xiang has developed a very good personal network within the Chinese music industry and the Chinese creative industries. In order to evade taxes, Chinese business organizations often adjust figures in financial reports when possible, for example, the audience number of the 2013 Strawberry Music Festival was estimated around 300,000 by the media, but in Modern Sky's official report, the number was less than 90,000.
12. It is interesting that a 2015 survey conducted by the University of Hong Kong revealed that 67 per cent of Hong Kong's 7 million people do not consider themselves Chinese. Accessed June 5, 2015 at http://www.dw.de/hong-kong-distances-itself-from-tiananmen-square-memorial/a-18494300.

13. From news report on Netease, accessed June 5, 2015 at http://ent.163. com/14/0326/11/9O8S3HP100031H2L.html.
14. The problem, however, of notions like 'music industry' and 'media industry' is that they tend to generalize too much, something that can also be said of the idea of convergence. For example, when Hunan TV starts a unit to promote and develop music, why would this not be counted as part of the music industry (just as music companies like Sony also have different divisions)? More detailed analysis is required to unpack the workings of the industry, in particular the role of gatekeepers and mediators that operate on the boundaries of different media (e.g. TV and music), and on the boundaries of different places (e.g. Taipei and Beijing).
15. From Migu Music website, accessed July 11 5, 2014 at http://www.migu.cn/ help/184_1024.html, accessed July 11, 2014.
16. For instance, several officials of Migu Music were arrested for bribery and corruption in 2010. Chairman Li Hua was given a suspended death sentence for over RMB 16 million ill-gotten gains, Ma Li's takings were over US$17 million, Ye Bing's were over US$50 million, and general manager Li Xiangdong's were reported as several hundred million RMB, but believed to be over one billion RMB which was double the revenue of all Chinese record companies in 2012. Information and data are from news reports, accessed June 10, 2014 at http://www.c114.net/news/118/a830146.html; http://news.21cn.com/zhuanti/domestic/zydfb/2012/03/03/11021252.shtml.
17. All data is from Xiami official website, accessed on June 5, 2015 at www.xiami.com
18. Data is from news report on Sina, accessed June 6, 2015 at http://ent.sina.com. cn/y/2014-02-25/15054102238.shtml.
19. Data is from news report on Sina, accessed June 6, 2015 at http://ent.sina.com. cn/s/2014-05-04/16564136222.shtml.
20. Data is from Deng Ziqi's Baidu Baike encyclopedia (accessed June 6, 2015): http://baike. baidu.com/link?url=VkwX6v2ts5YlHmLsNRAwm09miJw0nnrGcxaIsolt1JSDMIBB EGSVGknt1V9Tp9-CnhKsTGHbN0pVn5kC7xwaia4_5.
21. Data is from news report on Tencent, accessed June 6, 2015 at http://ent. qq.com/a/20140829/060351.htm.
22. Information and data are from news report on Chinanews and Sina, accessed June 6, 2015 at http://www.chinanews.com/yl/2014/04-02/6020786.shtml, http://ent.sina.com. cn/y/2014-04-10/22064125042.shtml.
23. Information is from news report on Malay Eunited, accessed June 6, 2015 at http:// www.uniteddaily.com.my/?q=node/86475.
24. Data is from news report on Phoenix new media, accessed June 6, 2015 at http://sports. ifeng.com/a/20150220/43204325_0.shtml_zbs_baidu_bk.

BIBLIOGRAPHY

Couldry, Nick (2011), 'More sociology, more culture, more politics; or, a modest proposal for "convergence" studies', *Cultural Studies* **25** (4–5): 487–501.
Fung, Anthony (2008), *Global Capital, Local Culture – Transnational Media Corporations in China*. New York: Peter Lang.
Globalization (2012), *Gangnam Style Takes the World By Storm*, accessed 20 May 2015 at http://www.globalization101.org/gangnam-style-takes-the-world-by-storm.
Groenewegen-Lau, Jeroen (2014), 'Steel and strawberries: how Chinese rock became state-sponsored', *Asian Music* **45** (1): 3–33.
Henhenhong (2014), *Song Dongye: Taibei dui Beijing xin de xiongxing huanxiang* ('Song Dongye: the new masculine imagination of Taipei about Beijing'), accessed 15 December 2014 at http://ent.qq.com/original/views/v603.html.
IFPI (2014a) *Investing in Music – How Music Companies Discover, Nurture and Promote Talent*, accessed 5 June 2015 at www.ifpi.org.

IFPI (2014b) *IFPI Digital Music Report 2014 – Lighting Up New Markets*, accessed 5 June 2015 at www.ifpi.org.

Jenkins, Henry (2006), *Convergence Culture: Where Old and New Media Collide*. New York and London: New York University Press.

Keane, Michael (2009), 'Great adaptations: China's creative clusters and the new social contract', *Continuum*, **23** (2): 221–30.

Keane, Michael (2012), *China's New Creative Clusters. Governance, Human Capital and Regional Investment*. London: Routledge.

Keane, Michael (2013), *Creative Industries in China*. Cambridge: Polity.

Keane, Michael (2015), *The Chinese Television Industry*. London: BFI Palgrave.

de Kloet, Jeroen (2010), *China with a Cut – Globalisation, Urban Youth and Popular Music*. Amsterdam: Amsterdam University Press.

de Kloet, Jeroen and Stefan Landsberger (2012), 'Fandom, politics and the Super Girl contest in a globalized China', in Koos Zwaan and Joost de Bruin (eds.), *Adapting Idols: Authenticity, Identity and Performance in a Global Television Format*. Farnham: Ashgate, pp.135–50.

Li, Chun (2014), *Song Dongye: ai ku de nanhai weishenme neng hong* ('Song Dongye: why is a cry-baby so popular?'), *Nan Du Zhoukan* (*Southern Weekly*) Vol. 37.

Mahdawi, A. (2012, September 24). 'What's so funny about Gangnam Style?', *The Guardian*, accessed 5 June 2015 at http://www.guardian.co.uk/commentisfree/2012/sep/24/gangnam-style-south-korean-pop.

Meng, Bingchun (2009), 'Who needs democracy if we can pick our favourite girl? Super Girls as media spectacle', *Journal of Chinese Communication* **2** (3): 257–72.

O'Connor, Justin and Xin Gu (2014), 'Creative industry clusters in Shanghai: a success story?', *International Journal of Cultural Policy* **20** (10): 1–20.

Pang, Laikwan (2012), *Creativity and its Discontents: China's Creative Industries and Intellectual Property Rights Offenses*. Durham, NC: Duke University Press.

Qiu, Liben (2014), *yinfu, zhengzhi, ruanshili* ('Musical notes, politics, and soft power'), *Yazhou Zhoukan* (*Asia Newsweek*), accessed 5 June 2015 at http://blog.ifeng.com/article/30412075.html.

Shen, Xuechen (2014), *Song Dongye chuanda lingyizhong Zhongguo xiangxiang* ('Song Dongye represents another image of China'), *Wang Bao* (*Want Daily*) 7 April.

Wang, Qian (2013), 'Double hegemony: market and ideology control of "the Same Song"', *Journal of Creative Communication* **8** (1): 15–28.

Wikström, Patrik (2009), *The Music Industry*. Cambridge: Polity.

22. China's self-help industry: American(ized) life advice in China
Eric C. Hendriks

INTRODUCTION: THE SELF-HELP INDUSTRY REACHES CHINA

During the Cultural Revolution (1966–76), the Chinese Communist Party (CCP) sought to monopolize the field of life advice in order to ensure that people's imagination, values and aspirations would be wholly socialist. The Party disseminated an official literature on how a good socialist was supposed to live. Socialist life advice was meant to replace the life advice of China's religious and philosophical traditions. Meanwhile, capitalist ideology was to be blocked out completely. To the Maoists, American self-help books – from Dale Carnegie's *How to Win Friends and Influence People* (1936) to Norman Vincent Peale's *The Power of Positive Thinking* (1952) – were squarely in the capitalist category. Hence they were banned.

When Deng's reformist faction gradually opened China's economy and society, the Party's attempt to monopolize life advice quickly faded. The destruction of the Cultural Revolution, followed by the implosion of Maoist socialism, left an ideological and spiritual hole in the heart of Chinese culture (Bell 2008; Gittings 2005). The public sphere, though still strictly monitored by the Party-state, opened up to alternative, non-socialist sources of life advice once again. Confucianism resurfaced in the 1990s and early 2000s (Bell 2008; Billioud and Thoraval 2008, 2009; Yang 2007). Further diversifying the field of life advice were the new international competitors carried in by the global popular culture that began flooding China.

Most prominent among these new competitors are the teachers, products and life teachings of the US-oriented, global self-help industry. The global self-help industry is a new player within the millennia-old, but now fully commercialized and mediacentric Chinese field of life advice. In only two decades US-style self-help culture, and with this the figure of the self-help author-speaker or 'self-help guru,' has skyrocketed to prominence in the book market, mass media and public life in general (Hendriks in press). Yu Dan's advice title *Confucius from the Heart* (*Yu Dan lunyu xinde*) sold over eleven million legal copies in Mainland China before being exported all around the world. Though the exact size of the Chinese market for self-help books is unknown, 'supplementary educational books,' of which self-help is the dominant component, counts for 34 per cent of the Chinese market for printed books. This equates to an annual revenue of RMB 18.2 billion (US\$ 3 billion) (Open Books 2011). By contrast, in Germany (the country where the most reliable and precise statistics are available[1]), self-help accounts for only 5.7 per cent of the total book market, or € 544 million Euros (US\$ 600 million). Some commentators suggest that the Chinese love for American and 'American'-style self-help titles reflects people's attempts to cope with the brutal social and economic turbulence of contemporary China (Barry 2010; Campanella 2008: 293).

The rapid rise of the self-help industry in Mainland China is particularly spectacular – and ironic. China after all continues to be socialist in name and is also commonly imagined as the paradigmatic 'Eastern Other,' while the self-help tradition could be seen as the very archetype of Western capitalism and liberal/libertarian individualism. This chapter will first try to define 'self-help' as a cultural industry. Second, it will outline the history and composition of China's 'glocal' self-help industry. Third, it will touch on the complex relationship between the structural transformation of the Chinese book market and media, on the one hand, and the glocalization of self-help into China, on the other. Last, it will sketch out self-help's presence in Chinese public life.

DEFINING SELF-HELP

It is difficult to get at a precise definition of 'self-help.' This is because the international self-help industry is marked by a heterogeneity of authors/teachers, schools/companies and life teachings, as well as a broad range of advice topics – which cover everything from careers, dating and parenting to health and spirituality. Yet, a number of broadly shared tropes, discourses, and legitimization strategies loosely bind all these together. First, there is the stress on nourishing a positive attitude. A positive attitude is commonly recommended as pragmatic and sensible – but it can inflate into a metaphysical principle, as in the prominent New Thought school, which has a century-old tradition running from Emma Curtis Hopkins (1849–1925) to Rhonda Byrne's *The Secret* franchise (2006 onward). The New Thought school centres on the metaphysical notion that positive thinking is a spiritual force capable of literally producing miracles. Second, self-help foregrounds challenges and opportunities as these relate to the individualized human being, thereby de-emphasizing social problems and providing possibilities for collective action (McGee 2005;

Ehrenreich 2009). The message is that you can – and should – change your own life; worrying or complaining about society is just a waste of time, even counterproductive. Third, modern self-help follows the format of the therapeutic discourse which first brands the reader/client as unhealthy or dysfunctional and then proposes solutions and cures (Illouz 2008). Fourth, self-help preaches that, by means of disciplined self-improvement, one can and should undergo a personal transformation. In one's disciplined quest for self-improvement, one is typically supposed to be guided by the example set by the self-made 'self-help guru' (Hendriks 2012).

Historically, this now globalizing self-help culture, though heterogeneous and diverse, has its primary roots in the eighteenth and nineteenth century Anglo-American world. Identifying the first major self-help bestseller is an arbitrary endeavour. Candidates are Benjamin Franklin's *The Way to Wealth* (1758) and Samuel Smiles' *Self-Help* (1859). The latter resembles a manifesto and is the book that provided the tradition with its name. Firmly grounded in the liberal-bourgeois tradition, the early self-help literature instructed men on how to attain wealth and success, celebrating the legendary figure of the 'self-made man' who moved from rags to riches through discipline, creativity and perseverance. The same basic ethos of liberal-bourgeois individualism has remained dominant in self-help's long history. Nowadays commentators tend to label this ethos 'neo-liberal,' but given the historical continuity on this point, the 'neo'-prefix seems unnecessary.

That said, the self-help cultural industry did transform in three ways. First, the range of themes and audiences broadened. Self-help began to cater to female readers and clients too, as well as to an expanding number of niche markets. Second, psychological and therapeutic discourse – which had been absent from early self-help, with its straightforward rags-to-riches narratives – engulfed modern self-help in the twentieth century (Illouz 2008: 155). Last, the self-help industry conquered the globe, spreading far outside of the English-speaking world, the West, and the realm of liberal democratic regimes (Hendriks in press).

Research covering self-help outside of the English-speaking world remains scarce, however. Almost all research focuses on the US (McGee 2012: 686–7). Key studies of the American self-help industry include Starker's *Oracle at the Supermarket: The American Preoccupation with Self-Help* (1989), Sandra Dolby's *Self-Help Books: Why Americans Keep Reading Them* (2005), and Micki McGee's *Self-Help Inc.: Makeover Culture in American Life* (2005). Journalists report that US-style self-help culture has reached places as unlikely as Saudi Arabia (Billing 2008) and the Islamic Republic of Iran (Fassihi 2008). Meanwhile, a number of pioneering social-scientific studies touch upon self-help culture in

Australia (Wright 2010), Israel (Illouz 2008), Britain, Mexico, Argentina and Trinidad (Nehring 2009a, 2009b; Nehring et al. 2015), Russia (Salmenniemi and Vorona 2014), and Germany and Mainland China (Hendriks in press). Still, self-help's globalization remains a largely unexplored and generally underestimated socio-cultural phenomenon, perhaps in particular in relation to its rise in Mainland China.

THE RISE OF CHINA'S GLOCAL SELF-HELP INDUSTRY

The field of Chinese self-help is 'glocal' in character, consisting of a heterogeneous mixture of self-help author-speakers, teachings, products and discourses from a variety of countries, mainly Mainland China, Taiwan and the US. Of the top-hundred bestselling books in the 'psychological self-help' (*xinli zizhu*) category, around 30 per cent derive from China, the rest from Western countries and predominantly the US (Open Books 2011). Translated American titles covered 37 per cent of the top-ten slots between January 2010 and December 2011 (Open Books 2011). Only a few bestselling titles derived from countries other than China, Taiwan and the US (Open Books 2011; see Figure 22.1). The two most prominent foreign authors in this 'other' category (Figure 22.1) were the Israeli Tal Ben-Shahar and the Australian Rhonda Byrne.

In the early and mid-nineties, when the self-help field first emerged on the Chinese Mainland, Taiwanese authors were predominant. These early

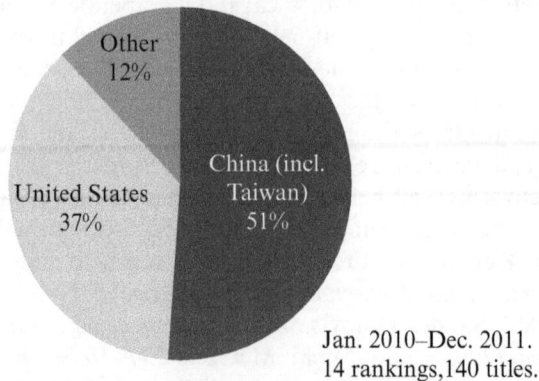

Other 12%

United States 37%

China (incl. Taiwan) 51%

Jan. 2010–Dec. 2011.
14 rankings,140 titles.

Source: Open Books (2011).

Figure 22.1 Origin of top ten self-help bestsellers in China

days were 'the era of Liu Yong' (Open Books 2008: 111). Between 1998 and 2001, Liu's book titles on self-actualization, communication skills and parenting covered on average three of the top-ten slots in monthly self-help bestseller rankings (ibid.). Why were Taiwanese authors and their book titles so predominant on the Mainland directly after the Mainland opened up its market for life advice in the wake of Deng Xiaoping's reform policies? Taiwan, being much more capitalist and Americanized than its mainland brother, already housed its own glocal, US-oriented self-help industry, while belonging to the Chinese Mandarin linguistic-cultural region. These two factors combined appear to have enabled Taiwanese self-help author-speakers such as Liu Yong, Li Kaifu and Zeng Shiqiang to be among the first to move in when new commercial and educational opportunities emerged on the Mainland. Affiliated with the culture and fluent in Mandarin, they quickly entered the PRC's mass media, while publishers eagerly transliterated their writings into simplified Mandarin characters.

Taiwanese self-help author-speakers serve as a bridge between the West and Chinese culture. An example is self-help author-speaker and management professor Zeng Shiqiang. Zeng has been teaching on the Mainland from 1990 onwards. He has a strong personal connection to the Anglosphere; he was educated in Britain and the United States. Simultaneously, however, Zeng claims to teach the 'authentically Chinese way,' offering a Confucian and harmony-oriented approach to management, causing some mainlanders to celebrate him as 'the father of Chinese management.' In connection to this, he also presented a lecture series on CCTV-10 explaining *The Book of Changes* (*yijing*). He argues that this classical religious text from the fourth/third century BCE offers insights that are relevant to modern management (Zeng 2007). On such occasions, Zeng dons the traditional style mandarin jacket of pre-socialist China – instead of a Western business suit, symbolizing his allegiance to 'traditional China.' The result is a curiously hybrid discourse, one that has American self-help written all over it yet is symbolically connected to Chinese tradition.

The Taiwanese author-speaker Li Kaifu sides more fully, or more openly, with Western modernity. Li, who holds dual Taiwanese and American citizenship, has worked in the management of Apple, Microsoft and Google, but more recently started up his own venture capital fund on the Chinese Mainland. During the nineties, he began providing career advice to Chinese youngsters on the Mainland, authoring books such as *A Walk Into the Future* and *Be Your Personal Best*. More broadly, he campaigns on education reform. Li believes that the Chinese education system produces quantity but not quality. Therefore he argues for a focus on creativity and individualism in Chinese education (Li 2006, 2008, 2009). In a sense, Li is encouraging mainland students to become more 'Western', or at least more like the idealized picture of Western students.

In the early 2000s, translated English-original self-help titles, most of which derived from the US, engulfed the Chinese field. Spencer Johnson's *Who Moved My Cheese?* topped the Chinese bestseller rankings in 2001. Later Anglo-American bestsellers on the Chinese book market include Will Bowen's *A Complaint Free World* and Rhonda Byrne's *The Secret* (Open Books 2011). Each of these stirred up media hype upon its Mandarin release and, subsequently, an army of native, glocal emulators. These glocal emulators are mainland self-help authors who reiterate the key ideas, concepts and slogans of their respective Anglo-American examples. Chinese bookstores overflow with Mandarin-original books on topics such as 'emotional intelligence,' a concept popularized by American psychologist Daniel Goleman; coping with change, discussed in reference to Johnson's 'moved-cheese' allegory; and the art of controlling one's destiny through the power of 'positive thinking,' as propagated by Will Bowen and Rhonda Byrne (Hendriks in press). In such instances it is possible to directly trace lines of discursive influence running from American to Chinese self-help.

For all its Americanized overtones, it is significant that native Chinese self-help has gained in prominence and creative assertiveness vis-à-vis international self-help. Whereas in 2004 translated foreign titles accounted for 45 per cent of the top hundred self-help bestsellers in China, the numbers dropped to between 20 to 30 per cent in the period from 2006 to 2011 (Open Books 2011). The glocal Chinese field was picking up steam. Bestselling self-help authors from the mainland include Bi Shumin, Wu Ganlin, Wu Weiku, Ma Yun, Li Yanhong, Wang Fang and Bai Yansong.

Illustrative of the glocalization of self-help in China is the development of China's *Psychologies* magazine. The Chinese edition of the international magazine *Psychologies*, which offers self-help advice and pop-psychology infotainment, increasingly ran locally produced items rather than translated items imported from the other national editions. After its founding in 2006, the Chinese edition initially mainly contained Mandarin translations of imported foreign items. By 2012, however, the proportion of translated foreign items had sunk to about 10 per cent and locally produced content had correspondingly risen to 90 per cent. Wang Yuling, the features editor of the magazine's Chinese edition notes: 'As our Chinese team matured and attained a deeper understanding of the value of our work, we began to run more localized topics that truly reflect urban Chinese people's life conditions' (Wang 2013).

STRUCTURAL TRANSFORMATION AND CULTURAL FLOWS

The rise of a glocal self-help industry in Mainland China has been enabled by the structural transformation of Chinese society. In the new China, despite the continued rule of a political Party that calls itself 'communist,' global commerce comes pouring in, and the influence of civil society and business elites has grown rapidly. As Kin Chilau notes: 'If, before market reforms, individuals were regarded as existing only for the collective under the leadership of the Communist Party, now, with market reforms, individuals are encouraged to pursue their self-interests as entrepreneurs under the shadow of the Communist Party' (Kin 2004: 214). Correspondingly, Chinese public life has manifested a commercial and thoroughly un-socialistic character (Gittings 2005), one that is subsumed with a new individualism (Yan 2009). These are preconditions for the self-help industry gaining in prominence.

Of specific importance to the rise and staggering prominence of the self-help industry in China is the commercialization of the Chinese book market (Rohn 2010) and media system (Sparks 2010). After consecutive rounds of free-market reforms, profit-seeking and partly privately owned book and television markets have emerged (Fung 2008; Hao et al. 2004; Zhu 2012). Since the 1990s commercially oriented television broadcasters, especially satellite channels, have proliferated in Mainland China (Keane 2015). In a parallel fashion, the national broadcaster CCTV began to cater to the market in the early 1990s, exchanging its traditional propaganda content for content containing more subtle traces of propaganda and hidden censorship (Fung 2008, 162; Sun 2002; Zhao 2011: 143–74, 159–60).

A similar story can be told about the book market and other media markets. Privately owned publishing houses have spread all over China since their legalization in 1995, while the state bookseller, Xinhua, now fully caters to the market (Häntzschel 2007: 51; Rohn 2010: 183). Though direct foreign investment in publishing houses is still illegal, foreign investors can invest in every part of the retail and distribution network, such as bookstores. Also they can sell product licensing to certified Chinese publishers. Most typically, a Chinese publisher buys the right to sell a Mandarin translation of an English-language book title from a large, international media cooperation, the biggest of which are News Corporation, Disney, and Bertelsmann (Rohn 2010: 183, 187). Piracy, however, remains rampant (ibid. 182).

The structural transformation of Chinese society and its media system have created the necessary conditions for the emergence of a US-style self-help industry. Yet the relationship between the two developments is more complex. Because of the pervasive socio-cultural impact of the structural transformation, the following ambivalence emerges: it is difficult, if not impossible, to clearly differentiate the direct influences of American and international self-help discourses, trends, products and styles upon Chinese self-help culture, on the one hand, from the adaption of Chinese publishers and authors-speakers to the new structural conditions, on the other. Of course, there are indeed many traces of direct cultural influence, as when Chinese authors explicitly cite the power-of-positive-thinking philosophy of *The Secret*, humanistic psychology, the commercial wing of the Emotional Intelligence school, or point to Johnson's 'cheese' metaphor for missing new opportunities due to obsessing over lost entitlements. Yet, in cases where such explicit discursive links are absent, it is possible for a Chinese self-help teaching or product to obtain a deceptively 'Americanized' appearance due solely to the fact that it is well-adjusted to the new structural conditions of China's commercialized media and book markets. Raw commercialism is then easily mistaken for direct American cultural influence. Consider that many of the typical traits of books in the US-oriented self-help tradition – namely accessible language, catchy slogans, a personalized focus on the author's own life, and upbeat life lessons – may also simply be reflections of a heightened sensitivity to market demand.

Illustrating this ambivalence, it is difficult to know where to place Yu Dan's 'self-help' take on Confucianism. Yu Dan starred in blockbuster episodes of the television series *Lecture Room* on CCTV, in which she presented the Confucius classic the *Analects* to a general audience (2006a; also see Zhu 2012: 163–6). As mentioned in the introduction to this chapter, her book *Confucius from the Heart*, which was based on the television presentations, became a major bestseller and was exported all over the world. Yet the Confucius she presents to the public is not the classical ethicist and political philosopher. Rather her Confucius resembles a motivation coach in the American self-help tradition, catering to the everyday needs of the modern individual. Tellingly, the Mandarin book cover states: 'The true meaning of the *Analects* of Confucius is to tell us how we can live as happily as our hearts and souls desire' (2006b, my trans.).

Reviewing Yu Dan's book, Confucian philosopher Daniel A. Bell, based at Tsinghua University, writes, 'Her account is complacent, conservative, and supportive of the status quo. Confucius must be turning in his grave' (Bell 2008: 174). Dissident intellectual and Nobel laureate Liu Xiaobo brands Yu Dan, 'a pseudo-scholar . . . with a sales pitch that combines tall tales about the ancients with insights that are about as sophisticated as the lyrics of pop songs' (2013: 189). Many criticisms by Chinese intellectuals, including Zhao Yong's in the *Southern Metropolitan Daily*, dismiss Yu Dan's Confucianism in a similar vein (Zhu 2012: 164).

Yet is the direct influence of American self-help partly to blame for Yu's complacent, individual-centred Confucianism? Her book does seem to 'model itself on some of those "American" self-help books' (Bell, email correspondence 19 September 2009); yet it does not explicitly cite the American self-help tradition. Hence, similarities may simply reflect the fact that, due to China's commercialization and individualization, the structural conditions under which players operate in the Chinese book market have grown more similar to those of the US.

Hence, the rise of self-help culture on the Chinese Mainland is an over-determined phenomenon. China's commercialization and individualization has opened the door for the import and glocal appropriation of American self-help culture; yet, simultaneously, that same structural transformation already has a socio-cultural impact on its own that mimics the effects of the former. Since these two developments – that is, China's structural transformation and engulfment by cultural flows from the Anglo-American realm – would plausibly have similar effects on the field of life advice, the two become indistinguishable in practice. One result is that US-style self-help culture has both an *extensive* and an *elusive* presence within the Chinese field of life advice and within Chinese society and public life more generally.

SELF-HELP IN CHINESE SOCIETY AND PUBLIC LIFE

Embedded in larger processes of commercialization and individualization, self-help's tentacles reach from the book market and numerous mass media platforms into the business world, journalism, formal education, Chinese medicine and popular philosophy. This extensive outreach is enabled by implicit Party approval and apparent consumer demand which in turn seems to be in some respects a response to challenges confronting individuals in China's competitive and non-egalitarian economy. Under these conditions, self-help author-speakers sell the Chinese public politically conformist and marketable advice on how to live the Good Life in the new China.

In the media Chinese self-help author-speakers appear on a wide variety of platforms, the most important of which is the edu-tainment television program *Lecture Room* which hosted lectures by self-help author-speakers such as Zeng Shiqiang, Bi Shumin and Yu Dan, and, occasionally, foreign, 'inspirational' speakers such as Bill Gates (Hendriks in press). Celebrity journalists such as Wang Fang and Bai Yansong have also authored self-help books (Wang 2010, Bai 2010), while prominent self-help author-speaker Bi Shumin frequently provides 'journalistic' commentary on broader public issues such as land ownership reform or China's relationship to the West (2009a, 2009b). All this blurs the distinction between journalism, including relatively critical journalism, and self-help. My comparative study of self-help culture in China and Germany reveals that the social roles of journalist, public intellectual and self-help author-speakers are significantly less distinct from each other in China, perhaps because of the relatively weakly developed state of its public sphere (Hendriks in press).

Equally porous are the borders between self-help and the 'official knowledge' of academia, formal education, medical institutions, and state-accredited psychotherapy. In these porous border areas you find media philosophers such as the above-mentioned Yu Dan, as well as Chinese medicine teachers such as Ma Yueling who use self-legitimization strategies that are (semi-)charismatic rather than rational-bureaucratic or traditional (in the Weberian sense). Such players tend to be particularly controversial among academic philosophers and medical authorities, respectively. Likewise, scholars of emotional intelligence such as Zeng Guoping, a professor in Chongqing's business school, draw on academic prestige while strongly catering to the market, thereby provoking the ire of academic psychologists. All these kinds of players stand in between commercial popular culture, on the one hand, and formal education and established knowledge traditions, on the other.

An even broader trend intersecting with the rise of self-help is the surging of commercial psychotherapy. Long suppressed under Mao, the surge of psychotherapy in the twenty-first century has engendered a staggering 'psychoboom' in the private market (Huang 2014, 2015). From 2005 onward, hundreds of thousands of new therapists entered the Chinese market with basic certificates supplied by commercial agencies (but accredited by the state). Meanwhile, the more established psychotherapists began giving nationwide lecture tours and offering psychological services to corporations such as employee training programs (Huang 2015: 14–17), while some even starred as counselors in 'psychotherapeutic' talk shows on television (Huang 2014: 195). Given the commercial and media-oriented habitus of many or even most of these therapists, and the discursive overlap provided by humanistic psychology and NLP, the new field of commercial psychotherapy should be seen as partly overlapping with China's self-help field.

All of the above indicates that the Chinese self-help industry is a 'heteronomous cultural field,' to apply Bourdieu's field theory. Alternatively, if one instead conceptualizes the whole of life advice as a cultural field, then self-help is a particularly heteronomous *sub-field* within that larger field of life advice. In the Bourdieusian conception, a cultural field is a 'microcosm' in which players compete for status according to a unique set of rules (Bourdieu 2005 [1996]: 31). Cultural fields are not, however, impenetrable systems isolated from the rest of society. Rather each field is only partly autonomous. The status game of each field is to a certain extent guided by the field's own distinct rules or principles (*nomoi*) (Bourdieu 2005 [1996]: 32–33; Bourdieu 1993: 181). Conversely, a field is heteronomous to the extent that its inner status game is skewed by principles from its socio-cultural surroundings; that is, by outside forces. Fields can be more autonomous or more heteronomous depending on the social circumstances (Bourdieu 1993: 40; Hallin 2005). Self-help is a strongly heteronomous field or, conversely, a heteronomous segment of the field of life advice (depending on your conceptualization), particularly in China (Hendriks in press), because it extensively overlaps with, and shades into the economic, academic and journalistic fields while also depending on political approval to enter the mass media.

What should not be overlooked here is that heteronomous fields – though by definition weakly delineated – are not necessarily without influence. To think in terms of strong-autonomous versus weak-heteronomous is erroneous. Highly autonomous fields can be 'isolationist': able to ward off the heteronomizing influence of external status games but simultaneously relatively non-influential. Similarly, highly heteronomous fields can, precisely because of their weak delineation from their societal surroundings, strongly impact adjacent socio-cultural fields. An example of the latter kind of field is journalism. In many national contexts, journalism – though itself heteronomized by politics and the market – heavily heteronomizes the status dynamics of other socio-cultural fields (Benson 1999: 466). Likewise, self-help in China is also highly heteronomous in nature *and* prominent, if not also influential.

Benefitting the public prominence of self-help in China is that it receives tacit Party approval whereas institutionalized religion, perhaps the main competitor of the secular self-help industry, suffers under severe (though selective) political suppression. Specifically targeted are fifteen religious movements and organizations deemed 'evil cults' by the Party-state. These include the home-grown Falun Gong, which, under the charismatic leadership of Li Hongzhi, clashed with the Party in 1999, as well as various Christian and Muslim organizations (Zhu 2010: 477). Particularly suspect are Catholics with extra-national loyalties to the Pope, and Uyghur Muslims, associated with separatism and anti-Han revolt in China's northwestern region.

In comparison, self-help is a 'safe option.' In fact, according to one account the Party elite may be hoping that by 'continuing to ply rebellious youngsters with idolatry and apolitical popular culture,' the latter could be kept from turning to political activism (Fung 2008: 160). For that purpose, nothing could be more useful than the depoliticizing narratives of self-help author-speakers who reframe every social issue as an individual challenge to be overcome through individual self-improvement rather than collective action or policy reform. In any case, the fact that the Party-state continues to keep a range of religious competitors out of the media and public life indirectly benefits the self-help industry.

In addition, people's insecurities under China's competitive economy arguably further demand for individual life guidance of the type offered by US-style self-help author-speakers. Urban China is 'a brutally competitive, almost Darwinistic place; the weak, feeble, unintelligent, or unskilled are quickly crushed and cast aside' (Campanella 2008: 294). Social welfare is limited, while income inequality in China, with a Gini index of 47, now even surpasses that of the US (*CIA World Factbook* 2014). It appears that one of the symptoms of the new Chinese socio-economic regime, which confronts Chinese urbanites with opportunities as well as increased economic risks and insecurities, is that people are en masse turning to self-help advice: 'The significant market in self-help and management titles is a clear reflection of the new insecurities of life in China, caused by the increasingly competitive pressures of a rampant market economy' (Barry 2010).

In this light it is unsurprising that business self-help – including the themes of entrepreneurship, management and career advancement – is so prominent within the Chinese self-help industry. Providing exact percentages is difficult, because all depends on how one defines 'business self-help.' Yet even the most conservative possible estimate of the share of business self-help bestsellers – which disregards bestseller rankings of economic and financial advice titles (parts of which could legitimately be included) and instead only includes titles labelled as 'psychological self-help' – still puts the share of business self-help at 28 per cent of bestselling self-help titles (Open Books 2011, monthly top-50 rankings). The equivalent German number is a mere 8.2 per cent (*Branchen Monitor* 2014). In describing public life in China's metropolises, Campanella reflects on the striking presence of business and career self-help: 'Today the tycoon has replaced the worker or soldier – or Chairman Mao – as the new cult hero in China. Chinese bookstores overflow with 'How I Earned My Fortune' titles by self-made millionaires. . .' (2008: 293).

Many of China's most prominent 'business gurus' derive from China's booming IT branch. Examples are Li Kaifu, Ma Yun and Li Yanhong.

Li Kaifu, as mentioned above, served as a top-level manager for Apple, Microsoft and Google before he started his own venture capital firm. Ma Yun started the online retail company Alibaba (an eBay clone) and oversaw its growth into an Internet company worth hundreds of billions of dollars and employing tens of thousands of people worldwide. Among his many media activities, he starred as 'judge' and counsellor in a reality show on television in which young entrepreneurs contested for venture capital. The accompanying self-help book, based on the transcript of the television show, wore the title *Ma Yun's Comments on Starting a Business* (*Ma Yun dianping chuangye*). Finally, the media-savvy Li Yanhong – who co-founded Baidu, the Google clone that has become China's most widely used search engine – authored a book purporting to teach 29 principles for success in business and life.

Chinese author-speakers and books in the business self-help category are similar to their Anglo-American counterparts in combining autobiographical (or better: auto-*hagio*graphical) narratives with practical advice and illustrations. Moreover, they equally tend to celebrate the virtues of the self-made man, the classical, liberal-bourgeois exemplar of ethical perfection. In fact, the Chinese businessmen celebrated by Chinese self-help are reminiscent of the rags-to-riches industrialists and inventors celebrated by early self-help authors such as Timothy Shay Arthur (1809–85) and Samuel Smiles (1812–1904). These similarities point toward deeper structural parallels. The cradle of the self-help industry – the United States and the British Empire of the late eighteenth and nineteenth centuries – was a world marked by rapid industrialization, urbanization, economic dynamism and the socio-economic rise of the bourgeoisie, and hence presented people with radically new socio-economic opportunities, risks and insecurities. It was a world of winners and losers – not unlike China today.

CONCLUSION

In the wake of the pro-market reforms of the 1980s and 1990s, contemporary China witnessed the rise of a media-saturated, commercialized and increasingly individualized society. With global commercial popular culture, the discourses, teachings, teachers and products of the international, US-oriented self-help industry came flowing in. After an initial phase in which the mainland mainly imported Taiwanese self-help content and translated American books, the mainland gave birth to its own, glocal self-help industry. As the glocalization of self-help discourses, traditions and styles complexly interacts with the growing commercialization, mediatization, psychologization, and individualization of Chinese society at large, it is difficult to keep these processes apart. This is just one of the reasons why Chinese self-help is heteronomous in the Bourdieusian sense, with its outer borders weakly delineated, and its societal outreach extensive as well as largely elusive and unidentifiable.

The following four factors appear to further self-help's prominence, influence and societal outreach in Mainland China. First, the commercialization of the book and media markets prepared the ground for the self-help industry. Second, self-help is sucked into the spiritual vacuum in Chinese culture that was left by the Cultural Revolution and the subsequent implosion of Maoist communism. Third, political suppression keeps some of self-help's would-be religious competition from entering the mass media.

Finally, self-help sells answers to people's individual challenges under the 'Darwinian' competition of twenty-first century China. In response to the new socio-economic regime, Chinese urbanites have, in a cultural sense, become the 'New Americans' – to borrow a phrase from Campanella (2008: 293) – in that they live in fear of losing out while also nourishing an obsession with 'winners,' specifically with the classical liberal-bourgeois icon of the self-made man. Self-help culture feeds into people's strenuous quest for the 'Chinese Dream,' to draw on President Xi Jinping's trademark slogan. Though the official CCP doctrine behind this voguish slogan is surprisingly convoluted and conventional, recycling the Party's perpetual ideology of collective modernization, the phrase 'Chinese Dream' already tells its own story: it plays on the imagery of the good-old 'American Dream.'

NOTE

1. Most of the available statistics about the size of self-help book markets are unreliable, because the criteria for including a certain book title as 'self-help' are either unspecified or fully dependent on the strategic, often even opportunistic, self-labeling of authors and publishers. The latter method entails defining 'self-help' as whatever calls itself 'self-help,' which leads to a drastic underestimation of the actual size of the self-help book market. After all, many self-help titles are marketed as 'academic psychology,' 'spirituality' or 'philosophy,' and thus fall outside of the data set. Germany is currently the only major country for which I managed to collect reliable and precise statistics. The German statistics do not draw on the narrow, strategic self-labeling by publishers and authors, while also differentiating between advice categories (which the Open Books statistics about China lack). If one defines the advice categories of 'health,' 'spirituality,' 'life help, everyday' and 'law, career, finance' as forming the core of the self-help genre, then self-help covers 42.9 per cent of the total German advice (*Ratgeber*) market and 5.7 per cent of the total German book market, electronic and print (*Branchen Monitor* 2014).

REFERENCES

Bai, Yansong (2010), *xingfu le ma?* ('*Are You Happy?*'). Yangtze River Literature and Art Publishing House.

Barry, Virginia (2010), *Red, the New Black: China-UK Publishing*, Report to the Arts Council England, accessed 28 February 2014 at http://www.artscouncil.org.uk/publication_archive.

Bell, Daniel A. (2008), *China's New Confucianism: Politics and Everyday Life in a Changing Society*. Princeton: Princeton University Press.

Benson, Rodney (1999), 'Field theory in comparative context: a new paradigm for media studies', *Theory and Society* **28** (3): 463–98.

Bi, Shumin (2009a), *wo ba guotu jiao yu shui?* ('Who did I protect the land for?'), op-ed. in *Beijing Evening News* 24 Augustus 2009, accessed 1 November 2010 at http://www.bjd.com.cn.

Bi, Shumin (2009b), *Zhongxi wenhua wei sha goutong bu chang* ('Why it is so hard for China and the West's culture to communicate with each other'), newspaper interview, *Beijing Evening News* 11 December 2009, accessed 1 November 2010 at http://www.iguoxue.cn.

Billing, Soren (2008), 'Relationship self-help book is Saudi best-seller', accessed 3 January 2015 at http://www.arabianbusiness.com/relationship-self-help-book-is-saudi-best-seller-81889.html.

Billioud, Sébastien and Joël Thoraval (2008), 'The contemporary revival of Confucianism', *China Perspectives*, accessed 17 December 2014 at http://chinaperspectives.revues.org/4123.

Billioud, Sébastien and Joël Thoraval (2009), '*Lijiao*: The return of ceremonies honouring Confucius in Mainland China', *China Perspectives*, accessed 17 December 2014 at http://chinaperspectives.revues.org/4927.

Bourdieu, Pierre (1993), *The Field of Cultural Production: Essays on Art and Literature*. Randal Johnson (ed.), Cambridge: Polity.

Bourdieu, Pierre (2005 [1996]), 'The political field, the social science field, and the journalistic field', in Rodney Benson and Erik Neveu (eds.), *Bourdieu and the Journalistic Field*. Cambridge, UK: Polity.

Branchen Monitor Buch (2014), 'The German Publishers and Booksellers Association', statistics for first quarter of 2014, accessed 19 April 2015 at http://www.boersenverein.de/792842/.

Campanella, John (2008), *The Concrete Dragon: China's Urban Revolution and What It Means for the World*. Hong Kong: Princeton Architectural Press.

CIA World Factbook (2014), 'Distribution of family income', accessed 28 April 2014 at https://www.cia.gov/library/publications/the-world-factbook/rankorder/2172rank.html.

Dolby, Sandra (2005), *Self-Help Books: Why Americans Keep Reading Them*. Urbana: Illinois University Press.

Ehrenreich, Barbara (2009), *Smile or Die: How Positive Thinking Fooled America and The World*. London: Granta Books.

Fassihi, Farnaz (2008), 'Positive thinking in Tehran: youth embrace self-help movement', *The Wall Street Journal* 30 June 2008, accessed 18 March 2013 at http://online.wsj.com/article/SB121479169997914947.html.

Fung, Anthony (2008), *Global Capital, Local Culture: Transnational Media Corporations in China*. New York: Peter Lang.

Gittings, John (2005), *The Changing Face of China: From Mao to Market*. Oxford: Oxford University Press.

Hallin, Daniel (2005), 'Field theory, differentiation theory, and comparative media research', in Rodney Benson and Erik Neveu (eds.), *Bourdieu and the Journalistic Field*. Cambridge, UK: Polity, p. 224–44.

Häntzschel, Alexander (2007), 'Markt mit Potenzial und Hindernissen' [A market with potential and challenges], *Horizont* 35, 30 Aug. 2007.

Hao, Gui, Gert Kopper, and Kristin Kupfer (2004), *Massenmedien in der Volksrepublik China (The Mass Media in the People's Republic of China)*. Dortmund: Project.

Hendriks, Eric C. (2012), 'Ascetic hedonism: self and sexual conquest in the seduction community', *Cultural Analysis* 11, accessed 20 September 2015 at http://socrates.berkeley.edu/~caforum/volume11/pdf/Hendriks.pdf.
Hendriks, Eric C. (in press), *Knowledge Wars: The Global Competition between Self-Help Gurus and Institutional Authorities*. Leiden: Brill.
Huang, Hsuan-Ying (2014), 'The emergence of the psychoboom in China', in Howard Ching (ed.), *Psychiatry and Chinese History*. London: Pickering and Chatto, pp. 183-204.
Huang, Hsuan-Ying (2015), 'From psychotherapy to psychoboom: a historical overview of psychotherapy in China', *Psychoanalysis and Psychotherapy in China* 1: 1-30.
Illouz, Eva (2008), *Saving the Modern Soul: Therapy, Emotions, and the Culture of Self-Help*. Berkeley: University of California.
Keane, Michael (2015), *The Chinese Television Industry*. London: BFI Palgrave.
Kin, Chilau (2004), 'What kind of knowledge do we need?' Interview with Kin Chilau by Tani E. Barlow, *positions: East Asia cultures critique* Spring, 12: 1.
Li, Kaifu (2006), *Zhongguo yanjiusheng duo 21 shiji xuyao de rencai shao* ('There are too many graduates, but too few real talents to fulfill the needs of 21st century China'), *Xinmin Evening News*, print publication, online 15 November 2006, accessed 12 November 2010 at http://cul.sohu.com/20061115/n246409199.shtml.
Li, Kaifu (2008), *Zhongguo xuesheng mei gexing, quefa chuangxin* ('Chinese students lack personality and creativity'), *Yangzi Evening News*, print publication, online 2 March 2008, accessed 12 November 2010 at http://tech.163.com/08/0302/10/4618UOF8000915BF.html.
Li, Kaifu (2009), *Li Kaifu tan Zhongguo fazhan 'zui xuyao': chuangxin shi buke huo que yi huan* ('Li Kaifu discusses the "most urgent" prerequisite for China's development: innovation'), interview, *People's Daily* overseas edition, print publication, online 14 October 2009, accessed 12 November 2010 at http://www.ce.cn/macro/more/200910/14/t20091014_20193190.shtml.
Link, Perry, Richard Madsen and Paul Pickowicz (2002), editorial introduction to *Popular China: Unofficial Culture in a Globalizing Society*. Lanham, MD: Rowman and Littlefield.
Liu, Xiaobo (2013), *No Enemies, No Hatred: Selected Essays and Poems*, Perry Link (ed.). Harvard: Harvard University Press.
McGee, Micki (2005), *Self-help, Inc.: Makeover Culture in American Life*. New York: Oxford University Press.
McGee, Micki (2012), 'From makeover media to remaking culture: four directions for the critical study of self-help culture', *Sociology Compass* 6 (9): 685–93.
Nehring, Daniel (2009a), 'Cultural models of intimate life in contemporary urban Mexico: a reading of self-help texts', *Delaware Review of Latin American Studies* 10 (2), accessed 26 February 2014 at http://www.udel.edu/LAS/Vol10-2Nehring.html.
Nehring, Daniel (2009b), 'Modernity with limits: the narrative construction of intimate relationships, sex and social change in Carlos Cuauhtémoc Sánchez's *Juventud En Éxtasis*', *Sexualities* 12 (1): 33–59.
Nehring, Daniel, Emmanuel Alvarado, Eric C. Hendriks and Dylan Kerrigan (2015), *Transnational Self-Help: Self-Help Books and the Politics of Contemporary Social Change*. Basingstoke: Palgrave.
Open Books (2008), *kaijuan shi zhounian* (*The Tenth Anniversary Digest*). Beijing: Open Books.
Open Books (2011), Chinese National Research Institute. Beijing: Open Books.
Rohn, Ulrike (2010), *Cultural Barriers to the Success of Foreign Media Content: Western Media in China, India, and Japan*. Frankfurt am Main: Peter Lang.
Salmenniemi, Suvi and Mariya Vorona (2014), 'Reading self-help literature in Russia: governmentality, psychology and subjectivity', *The British Journal of Sociology* 65 (1): 43–62.
Sparks, Colin (2010), 'China's media in comparative perspective', *International Journal of Communication* 4: 552–66.
Starker, Steven (1989), *Oracle at the Supermarket: The American Preoccupation with Self-Help Books*. Transaction: New Brunswick NJ.
Sun, Wanning (2002), 'Semiotic over-determination or "indoctritainment": television,

citizenship, and the Olympic Games', in Stephanie Hemelryk Donald, Michael Keane and Hong Yin (eds.), *Media in China: Consumption, Content and Crisis*. New York: Routledge-Curzon, pp. 116–27.

Wang, Fang (2010), *wo shi aiqing ke daibiao* (*I'm Love's Advocate*). Nanjing: Jiangsu Phoenix Literature and Art Publishing.

Wang, Yuling (2013), interviewed by Eric C. Hendriks at Hearst China, 18 June 2013, Beijing.

Wright, Katie (2010), *The Rise of Therapeutic Society: Psychological Knowledge and the Contradictions of Cultural Change*. Washington: New Academia.

Yan, Yunxiang (2009), *The Individualization of Chinese Society*. London: Berg.

Yang, Fenggang (2007), 'Cultural dynamics in China: today and in 2020', *Asia Policy* (4): 41–52.

Yu, Dan (2006a), *Yu Dan lunyu xinde* (*Confucius From the Heart*), seven television episodes on seven consecutive days, CCTV-10 *Lecture Room*, February.

Yu, Dan (2006b), *Yu Dan lunyu xinde* (*Confucius From the Heart*). Beijing: Zhonghua shuju.

Zeng, Shiqiang (2007), *Zeng Shiqiang du jingdian xilie: yinjing yu rensheng* ('Zeng Shiqiang on *The Book of Changes and Life*'), June, television program, CCTV-10 *Lecture Room*.

Zhao, Yuezhi (2011), 'Understanding China's media system in a world historical context', in Daniel Hallin and Paolo Mancini (eds.), *Comparing Media Systems Beyond the Western World*. Cambridge: Cambridge University Press, pp. 143–74, 159–60.

Zhu, Guobin (2010), 'Prosecuting "evil cults": a critical examination of law regarding freedom of religious belief in Mainland China', *Human Rights Quarterly* **32** (2): 471–501.

Zhu, Ying (2012), *Two Billion Eyes: The Story of China Central Television*. New York: The New Press.

PART IV

ASSESSING DIGITAL LIVES, CONSTRUCTING CREATIVE FUTURES

23. Editor's introduction
Michael Keane

From the time of their inception in 2001 China's cultural industries were unwaveringly material, following the blueprint of industrialization (*chanyehua*) laid out in the national Five-Year Economic Development Plans. The objectives were pragmatic: construct physical environments, build more theme parks, produce more artefacts to sell to tourists, turn over buildings to artists and label them creative clusters, and hopefully in the process stumble across some innovation.

Then came the injunction: China needed to 'upgrade' (*shengji*) rather than just build. But something occurred in the interim that was a game changer. The Internet had become an unstoppable force: its users were young, most born in single child families and disinclined to be altruistic. In the past most of the energy of the government was focused on regulating the Internet, making sure that it was amenable to control, employing thousands of people to take down posts that were deemed offensive and to report miscreants whose conduct was not 'harmonious'.

Ideas such as the 'convergence of technological innovation and cultural creativity' (*keji chuangxin yu wenhua chuangyi ronghe*) suddenly came to the forefront in think tanks. The state reacted, commissioning a wave of incubators and experimental bases. Designated 'creative technology' projects included the Tsinghua Science and Technology Park in Zhongguancun, Beijing, sometimes referred to as China's Silicon Valley, as well as parts of the Zhangjiang Science and Technology Park in Shanghai. The broader landscape soon was rapidly populated by wannabe digital parks and clusters, some focused on digital outsourcing such as Ningbo Digital Technology Park, Chengdu Tianfu Software Park and the Wuxi National Digital Film Industry Park and some on 'big data' such as Xi'an Fengxi Xincheng.

In China GDP dominates everything. While economic data may often be suspect there is no doubt that the government aspires to keep GDP indicators stable. In the past this has been achieved largely by the strength of 'made in China' exports. But like many tales of progress, there is more than one side. Despite the suggestion that technology is now changing China and that China is moving closer towards developing a service-led consumer economy, it is clear that the economy still relies heavily on physical infrastructure and physical labour. Hundreds of millions of people want work: without the guarantee of labour China would have social disruption on a large scale.

THE DIGITAL TURN: A TECHNOLOGICAL 'NEW LEAP FORWARD'

Much discussion now focuses on how the whole of Chinese society can 'upgrade', particularly in regard to the millions of people with low levels of education living outside the large urban centres. Human capital is a significant challenge. The aging of China's population, a consequence of the One Child Policy established in 1978 by Deng Xiaoping, is having a direct impact on the numbers of people registered in work. Such a decline is to be expected over time but combined with increasing minimum wages and growing average incomes, the nation is moving inexorably closer to what economists call the 'Lewis Turning Point.' This occurs when the economy can no longer create wealth by adding cheap labour. As a report from Access Economics points out, the challenge now is to generate added-value through increased efficiency, innovation and high-value production (Crabbe 2014).

China is a more technologically connected society than ever before; it has leapfrogged stages of development by adopting and adapting technologies. In 2015 China had more than 700 million Internet users. By 2012, according to Access Economics, 242 million people had purchased goods and services online (Crabbe 2014); 55.4 million of these purchases were transacted on mobile phones. Indeed the rapid growth of mobile purchases, from 'negligible' in 2009, is evidence of a connected society.

Can new technologies solve the problem or will they add to the challenges facing China as more of its low cost production moves to cheaper locations? For many people concerned about how Chinese culture can be bootstrapped to technological progress and exert greater influence globally, this idea about the convergence of technology and culture appeared to offer great hope, representing the coming together (or convergence) of two quite different approaches to development.

As the chapters in this volume show, new kinds of connections are now being thought through and applied, at least in policy, business and skills training. China is borrowing ideas – and technology – from the rest of the world, and innovation is occurring in unlikely places. Apps are the new currency, from those that enable people to find taxis to apps to allow people to purchase online, to those that allow people to watch content and engage with traditional Chinese culture. This is only the tip of the iceberg.

China is setting its course for a digital revolution and it is spilling into the cultural and creative industries.

The digital turn in the cultural and creative industries is an important moment. The reasons behind this can be traced directly to central government policy documents, the most relevant being *The Outline of the Program for Innovation in National Culture and Technology*, which emerged from state think tanks during the drafting of the 12th Five-Year Plan for Economic and Social Development. In May 2012, the Central Propaganda Department head Liu Yunshan, then newly elected to the Political Bureau of the Chinese Communist Party's Central Committee, spoke about the importance of shifting the mode of cultural development and promoting the competitiveness of Chinese national culture on the global stage.

The most significant application of convergence culture has come with the state's Internet+ agenda, formally announced by Premier Li Keqiang in March 2015. The goal is to 're-boot' China's economy, a goal endorsed by the leaders of China's online companies, particularly Alibaba (Jack Ma/Ma Yun), Baidu (Robin Li/Li Yanhong) and Tencent (Pony Ma/Ma Huateng). The plan is even touted as the 'uberisation of the Chinese economy.'[1] The technological frontier includes next generation information networks, core electronics, high-end software and new information services. Particularly in coastal cities such as Beijing and Shanghai the emerging technologies of mobile Internet, cloud computing and big data are driving the 'upgrade' of cultural and creative industries.

THE CONNECTED SOCIETY IN CHINA

While technological convergence is undoubtedly changing China, policy makers are yet to really grasp its significance. Furthermore, businesses are struggling with change and the task of managing intellectual property in rapidly moving digital sectors; labour markets are changing as consumer spending increases with millions buying commodities online rather than from bricks and mortar shopping arcades; meanwhile TV programs, films and games are more accessible online than through state-owned media outlets and many of these media sectors are cashing in despite high rates of piracy.

On the physical front the factories have not gone away; of course some manufacturing has moved to Vietnam and parts of Africa; elsewhere in China many factories are directly 'connected' to the outside world. They produce goods that are distributed to consumers online through Taobao, China's equivalent of eBay. The factories symbolize China's industrious revolution (see Keane 2013). As people move online to purchase goods, retailers become 'e-tailers'. People from countries around the world source cheaply-made products from factories in China, even while the 'end of cheap China' (Rein 2012) is imminent.

This leads to the question: Is the convergence of technological innovation and cultural creativity just a slogan or does it have the capacity to produce meaningful change? Are we seeing a transformation or just a restructuring of the economy? Evidently, there is cause for optimism. According to a 2014 report by McKinsey & Company there are six million e-merchants listing products on Taobao.[2] This is having a strong impact on private consumption while at the same time accelerating innovation in services, in advertising and marketing, payment systems, warehousing and IT systems. This surely is a manifestation of the creative economy however defined – and it is driven by technological innovation.

Digital technologies are transforming the relationship between culture, creativity and innovation, exemplified by the BAT grouping of companies (Baidu, Alibaba and Tencent). Thanks to the entry of these cash-rich IT-based companies into the market, new forms of production, distribution and consumption have evolved for screen-based content. Alibaba for instance have established Taobao Movies (an online app for ticketing and social networking) and Yulebao (a film crowdfunding model), along with its online retail site, TMall. In doing this Alibaba intends to consolidate its move into content. It has established Alibaba Pictures Group and has made its first Hollywood movie investment, partnering with Paramount Pictures to make and promote the studio's next instalment of the *Mission Impossible* franchise in China. The title of Alibaba's own book, now adopted as a university media text, tells it all – *Internet Plus: from Information Technology to Digital Technology* (Gao 2015).[3]

Convergence, and the greater latitude provided to new media than to traditional media by China's regulators, have allowed incumbents to experiment with form, content and business models. The developments in television related content that are now happening in China reflect global changes. BesTV, Youku Tudou, iQiyi, PPTV, Netease, and LeTV are China's answer to Netflix, Hulu, Amazon and Google TV. They are commissioning and buying original content on an unprecedented scale.

These technologies are transforming Chinese culture and society and people's ways of interacting with information. While dramatic changes have taken place in the way that people in China live, work, play and interact with government, employers, peers and family members, the fact remains that the development master plan is underpinned by a deep seated acceptance of the need for social order; for instance new regulations issued by the media regulator State Administration of Press, Publication, Radio and Television (SAPPRFT) in 2014 require all content streamed on video sites to undergo scrutiny.

CHAPTERS

The chapters in Part IV address the issues of 'digital lives and creative futures' in different ways. A particular problematic area across China for China's digital society is intellectual property. As a signatory of the WTO, China is obliged to manage violation of intellectual property. Commercial digital service providers such as Youku Tudou, Netease, Sina and Tencent are taking down pirated content from their sites, realizing that international collaboration and investment depends on observing the rules of the game. China's smaller-scale enterprises also realize that they have to break away from the model of simply replicating by learning to monetize the IP generated from the content or technology they create.

The first chapter, by Lucy Montgomery and Eric Priest, provides some historical background to the drafting of China's copyright law, initially adopted in 1990 and further revised in 2001. Following this overview, the authors examine the impact of uneven media sector reform on China's 'born-digital' copyright industries, characterized in this chapter by the film, television, music and publishing sectors. Montgomery and Priest argue that the new distribution possibilities enabled by the Internet and mobile technologies have changed the game, such that many illegal operators have come to see the benefits of copyright compliance. In other cases established played have banded together to promote the benefits of compliance and challenge infringers. The end result has seen a radical shakeup of the media environment (see Zhao and Keane 2013). The rapid development of online portals such as Youku Tudou, Sina.com and 51.com was made possible by their ability to provide unlimited free content, much of which was pirated. However, their continued popularity depends on their ability to attract viewers and thus generate advertising revenues. By 2009, the 'free ride' was over. Like their counterparts internationally, the major sites began to expurgate content that was not copyright compliant. In order to maintain their presences they then began to outlay large sums purchasing attractive licensed content. A consequence of the crackdown on piracy has been the production of shorter films, now financed by companies like Youke and Tencent, once again following the international trend set by YouTube, Google, Netflix and Amazon (see Cunningham and Silver 2013). At the end of the day businesses, policy makers and users in China are facing the same kinds of challenges as their counterparts in more mature open markets.

Ruoyun Bai's chapter then looks at changes in broadcasting. Bai argues that the Chinese television industry is currently characterized by three distinct yet overlapping developments – commercialization, concentration and digital transformation. This chapter discusses the structural changes of Chinese television by focusing on these three developments over the past decade. Bai argues that these changes are turning Chinese television into a capital-intensive, profit-oriented entertainment industry that simultaneously absorbs and is absorbed by a new platform of capital accumulation, the digital media.

The commercialization of Chinese television, which was set in motion by Deng Xiaoping's market reform in 1978, forged ahead as the Chinese state allowed market forces to play an increasingly larger role in the broadcast sector in the wake of China's entry into WTO in 2001 and the launching of the so-called 'cultural system reform' in 2003. Concentration refers to the rapid and still ongoing formation of several large media groups. These conglomerates, formed around the most influential television networks such as CCTV, Hunan Satellite TV, Jiangsu Satellite TV, and Zhejiang Satellite TV, dwarf the other television networks by a large margin and are flexing muscles to dominate the national television market. Aside from commercialization and concentration, digital transformation is rapidly changing the face of Chinese television. Faced with the aggressive entry of new media businesses into the audio-visual sector, Chinese television networks are struggling to remould themselves by exploring synergistic opportunities with digital media and communication technologies, and/or entering into strategic alliances with digital media giants.

Xiang Ren's chapter concerns one of the real growth areas – publishing. Over the past decade the emergence of the mobile Internet and mobile publishing have enabled people to read anytime, anywhere, and with multiple devices. Ren shows how freedom has generated a huge emerging new readership for the digital publishing industry in China. Combined with social media and user co-creation, mobile reading is a catalyst for innovations in the publishing business and culture more broadly. Ren's chapter reviews developments and future prospects for China's digital publishing industry in the age of the mobile. The chapter starts with an overview of the development of the technologies of the mobile Internet. It examines the status quo of digital publishing in China, arguing that mobile reading is becoming a fast-growing revenue-earning business for the Chinese digital publishers in China, who have been struggling to achieve commercial sustainability. The chapter maps the structure of the Chinese mobile reading industry by identifying major forces ranging from traditional publishers, telecommunication companies, online literature giants, to various digital start-ups. The chapter conceptualizes mobile reading in the context of an evolving reading public in the digital age, drawing insights from cultural studies and evolutionary economics. It further discusses the significant role of mobile publishing and reading in widening the reading public and enabling population-wide creativity, which are essential for building a creative economy in China.

Elaine Zhao moves the discussion of convergence to mobile devices such as smartphones and tablets, as well as more ubiquitous broadband and wi-fi networks that afford new viewing experiences in different scenarios, across various platforms, providing viewers with 'networked engagement' with the content they choose. These emerging affordances offer an opportunity to theorize convergence and connected viewing experience. Zhao's chapter examines various attempts to integrate the mobile into the viewing experience and extend it beyond the living room. She looks at several initiatives in the industry, including text messaging for interactive experiences, the development of innovative mobile apps, the marriage of soft- and hardware, and the integration of social apps in content distribution. The chapter provides an analysis of the impact of socially networked viewing on content production strategies as well as changes in distribution and promotion strategies.

The chapter by Ming Cheung addresses the disparity between the growing e-commerce culture in China and the lack of consumer trust in online purchases. It considers whether China's regulatory measures are sufficient to protect the rights of online consumers. If the answer is negative, then what does the gap between expectations and reality imply? The chapter examines how Alibaba's Taobao, one of the leading e-marketplaces in China, has attempted to narrow this gap by designing and implementing a self-regulated consumer rights protection system in its website. The chapter concludes with a discussion of the significance of consumer rights protection and its possible future impact on China's sustainable development in e-commerce and integration into the global online economy.

When the business leaders of China's Internet companies talk about the synergies between the Internet and cultural industries, very few references are made to older adults. Most attention is focused on youth demographics, the heaviest consumers of online sites and social media. As other chapters in this volume have shown, the fast adoption of digital technologies by China's one child generation (those born after 1980) provides a partial picture of China's digital cultural industries. However, if we are to gain a comprehensive understanding of the cultural and creative industries in China it is important to represent all citizens of China. Wu illustrates how older adults in China participate in digital cultural industries. Elderly people are avid consumers of TV drama; they participate enthusiastically in cultural activities such as communal dancing in parks; and many uphold traditional cultural values. But when it comes to digital culture, the question remains: how do they participate? Moreover, what is the potential of this growing demographic? How is their social capital maintained through digital culture? These are missing parts of the puzzle.

NOTES

1. 'Internet Plus, China's official strategy for the uberisation of the economy', Innovation is Everywhere, accessed 22 September 2015 at http://www.innovationiseverywhere.com/internet-plus-chinas-official-strategy-for-the-uberisation-of-the-economy/.
2. 'China's e-tail revolution', McKinsey, accessed 22 September2015 at http://www.mckinsey.com/insights/asia-pacific/china_e-tailing.
3. This phrase from 'information technology to digital technology comes from Alibaba founder Jack Ma.

REFERENCES

Crabbe, Matthew (2014), *Myth-busting China's Numbers: Understanding and Using Chinese Statistics*. London: Palgrave MacMillan.
Cunningham, Stuart and Jon Silver (2013), *Screen Distribution and the New King Kongs of the Online World*. London: Palgrave Macmillan.
Gao, Hongshui (ed.) (2015), *hulianwang + cong IT dao DT* (*Internet Plus: from Information Technology to Digital Technology*). Beijing: China Machine Press.
Keane, Michael (2013), *Creative Industries in China: Art, Design, Media*. Cambridge: Polity.
Rein, Shuan (2012), *The End of Cheap China: Economic and Cultural Trends that Will Disrupt the World*. New Jersey: John Wiley and Sons.
Zhao, Elaine J. and Michael Keane (2013), 'Between formal and informal: the shakeout in China's online video industry', *Media Culture and Society* 35 (6): 724–41.

24. Copyright in China's digital cultural industries
Lucy Montgomery[1] and Eric Priest

INTRODUCTION

Economic and cultural sector reforms and engagement with international markets initiated by Deng Xiaoping since 1990 led to the rapid development of the PRC's copyright law. Since China joined the World Trade Organization in December 2001, affluent Chinese consumers have become an important target market for both Chinese and international firms trading in creative and cultural products. While enforcement remains problematic, Chinese creators and businesses are adept at navigating the intellectual property system – developing business strategies that engage with the possibilities of digital technologies and copyright licensing; using copyright to support expansion into new markets; and adapting distribution approaches to reflect lessons provided by first-movers in digital spaces.

This chapter explores how and why copyright's role is expanding and changing in China, focusing on recent developments in digital content markets. It considers the impact of uneven media sector reform processes on the emergence of 'born digital' copyright industries in China. There are signs that the commercial benefits of copyright compliance are beginning to outweigh the advantages of operating outside the intellectual property system for many Chinese stakeholders. We argue that these developments – in particular the emergence of widespread exclusive licensing practices – signal a watershed moment for China's cultural and creative industries, highlighting the potential for digital technology to create new markets for legitimate content and services, as well as the importance of global dynamics in the development of digital era copyright industries. We also caution, however, that despite the adaptability and innovation shown by many players in China's digital culture ecosystem – which includes professional creators, publishers, and key distributors and intermediaries, the sustainability of that ecosystem remains uncertain. Low revenues and the continued prevalence of free, unlicensed content pressure the business models of entities throughout the ecosystem.

Producing economic growth in a market-capitalist system demands much higher levels of individual freedom in relation to production and consumption than existed under a planned economy. However, cultural sector reform in China has not led to a system that is wholly based on either the freedom of the market or rule of law. In reality, copyright enforcement remains weak, government-protected monopolies persist, and pervasive state intervention and censorship constrain producers and frustrate consumers. China's cultural economy remains transitional and important differences exist between the ways in which businesses operate in this market and the strategies of their counterparts in mature markets. State protected monopolies, in particular, are limiting the extent to which copyright is able to operate as a mechanism for rewarding investments in creativity, and large portions of what are often regarded as 'core copyright industries' remain centrally controlled.

MEDIA REFORM AND THE EMERGENCE OF CHINESE COPYRIGHT INDUSTRIES

Internal pressures to decentralize production, combined with exogenous pressure by foreign governments – especially the United States – to protect their authors' works, led to the drafting and adoption of the 1990 Copyright Law. The drafting process took more than a decade and was among the most contentious in PRC history (Alford 1995), in part because of conservative officials' concerns over the wisdom of granting private rights in information goods and incentivizing private sector production (Song 2014: 270). The Copyright Law amendments were part of a broader intellectual property reform overseen by Deng Xiaoping's government, and were closely linked to wider efforts to strengthen China's trading relationships and pave the way for eventual entry into the WTO in 2001. In 2001, the Copyright Law underwent a comprehensive revision to conform to international standards and ensure compliance with various copyright treaties, foremost being the WTO's Agreement on Trade-Related Aspects of Intellectual Property Rights (TRIPs). The Copyright Law was revised again in 2010 as a result of the findings of the WTO Dispute Settlement Body in a case initiated by the United States.[2]

An important element of China's economic reform process has been the marketization, privatization, and deregulation of large parts of the cultural system (Keane 2013). As government subsidies for state-run publishing houses, cultural troupes, film studios, and media companies were withdrawn, advertising, subscription, and box office revenues became vital to the survival of many cultural sector firms. A growing number of both private and international stakeholders have also been granted space to operate, particularly in the co-production of content. Although the Chinese government continues to maintain tight control over media censorship and ownership, entrepreneurial collaboration between the state and private and foreign investors is now an important element of China's cultural production system (Akhavan-Majid 2004; Keane 2013).

The film industry has been engaged in a process of commercialization and reform since the early 1990s. The policy changes facilitating more private investment in film production have more than compensated for the withdrawal of funding from state-owned studios (Hui 2006: 63; Montgomery 2010; Frater 2015). Similarly, China's music industry has made a remarkable transformation from a system dominated by state-funded cultural troupes dedicated to writing and performing a limited repertoire of propaganda songs during the 1980s (Kraus 2004: 9) to the vibrant, digitally driven, contemporary domestic music scene that exists today (Montgomery 2010; Peto 2014). Reform of the publishing industry has been slower. Official approval for many of the practices widely adopted by publishers over the last thirty years remains a legal grey area. Television has experienced two fundamental reforms: the separation of broadcasting and production in 1999, which allowed private companies to produce more entertaining programmes for sale to state-run TV stations; and the establishment of competition within a national market between central and local TV stations through cable and satellite TV networks.

Firms operating in all of these areas face the challenge of developing business models capable of monetizing content. In this context, copyright assumes an important role as a device capable of turning creative works into products that can be traded in a commercial market. In a post-reform era, copyright attaches property rights to creative works, allowing them to be acted on in an entrepreneurial fashion: to be bought and sold, to generate income, and to form part of a wider creative economy. As Chinese entrepreneurs and creative professionals become more conscious of the value of their creative assets and the intellectual property rights that help to define them, their willingness to act proactively to protect these assets is increasing.[3]

Although impressive progress in relation to the growth of a copyright culture has been made, unauthorized use of creative content is common, among both media firms and the public. A clear example of this can be found in the publishing industry. The Nobel Prize winning novel *One Hundred Years of Solitude* has been in print in China since 1985, selling millions of copies and assuming a place as a literary classic for both Chinese readers and writers. This is remarkable, given that a Chinese publisher first acquired translation rights for the book in 2011.[4] Chinese textbook publishers, who preside over an enormous market, regularly fail to pass on royalties to authors, both Chinese and foreign.[5] In the music industry, hit pop songs from Hong Kong and the United States as well as classical songs are regularly translated and performed by Chinese artists without the authorization of copyright owners,[6] and television broadcasters air foreign films and other content without permission.[7]

This culture of unauthorized reuse has spilled over into the habits of media firms with access to the wealth of user-generated content now available online. Blogs, amateur video content, music, and photos are all regularly re-published and broadcast through traditional media channels without authorization from, attribution, or payment to authors. Difficulties with copyright impact on even the largest media organizations: according to Huayong Zhao, CEO of China Central Television (CCTV), CCTV '. . .is one of China's biggest victims of copyright infringement, as well as one of the biggest infringers of others' intellectual property' (Liu and Bates 2008: 5).

A key challenge for the growth of a culture of respecting copyright in China relates to the power of copyright owners in a system where content production has largely democratized but distribution channels remain tightly controlled. Content distributors such as bookshops, cinemas, digital portals, and television stations are often government owned, either wholly or in part, and enjoy powerful state protected monopolies. For example, distribution of foreign films in China is limited to a state-owned duopoly, and distribution of the most lucrative digital music product – mobile 'ringback tones' – is limited to state-owned mobile service providers. Such entities are difficult to hold to account and are able to dictate their own terms to smaller players in the value chain, extracting large profits while taking few risks. In the case of the digital music industry, copyright owners receive less than 3 per cent of digital music revenues.[8] Even the largest Chinese film studios receive only about 40 per cent of the box office return their films generate.[9] Chinese copyright industries also lack the infrastructure for reliable royalty distribution and sales auditing, making it difficult for copyright owners to ensure payment of negotiated shares of revenue. In this context, individual creators have very little hope of securing favourable terms of use or obtaining meaningful copyright enforcement.

THE CHALLENGES OF UNAUTHORIZED DISTRIBUTION

Strict restrictions on content importation and distribution, consumer appetite for new and higher quality content, and the low cost of pirated media has long fuelled demand for pirated content. The high rates of piracy in China deeply trouble businesses and policy makers in nations that rely on copyright as the basis upon which content can be exported, such as the United States. Grey distribution channels have also provided Chinese consumers, artists, and the next generation of media professionals with access to uncensored international films, music, and literature at affordable prices much earlier than official reform processes might have allowed. The rich availability of content has helped to speed the development of the nation's hardware industries, creating domestic demand for DVD players, e-book readers, computers, smartphones, and tablets. It has also helped to provide Chinese creative professionals and audiences with semiotic tools to build upon as they make the shift from propaganda machine to market-driven entertainment industries with aspirations to reverse cultural import deficits and begin exporting Chinese creative and cultural products. Nevertheless, widespread piracy poses significant impediments to the growth, stability, and independence of China's domestic creative industries (Priest 2014).

The challenge of reining in unauthorized distribution and encouraging consumers (and businesses) to make a shift to legal channels is being made greater by the Internet and developments in digital technologies for making, copying, and sharing. China is now home to the world's largest population of Internet users: more than 640 million.[10] There are also more than one billion mobile users, nearly 20 per cent of whom have 3G services.[11] Open and networked digital technologies are making it difficult to control the distribution of content in all markets. In China, the International Intellectual Property Alliance estimates that 99 per cent of music accessed online is 'pirated',[12] while local commentators estimate that the illegal online literature industry is ten times larger than its legally regulated counterpart (Ren and Montgomery 2012). Internet search engines like Baidu and large e-commerce portals like Taobao play an essential role in the grey value chain of digital piracy in China, improving the discoverability of unauthorized content and providing digital platforms for the unauthorized sale of pirated DVDs and books.

China's copyright protection challenges are not lacking enforcement activity; rather, China suffers from poor enforcement. China in fact has the greatest volume of intellectual property enforcement in the world (Dimitrov 2009). The Chinese government's preferred method of tackling unauthorized distribution over the past two decades has been highly publicized enforcement campaigns involving seizure of unauthorized content and the arrest and prosecution of pirates. While such campaigns are intended to reassure foreign governments and copyright owners with images of seized goods being destroyed by conscientious authorities, the efficacy of such campaigns is doubtful. They tend to be poorly coordinated, and they aim to produce short-term, readily quantifiable victories rather than address the root causes of endemic infringement. They are also part of a complex landscape of state control over content and its distribution. Anti-piracy campaigns have been connected to campaigns targeting 'pornography, illegal publications and piracy' (*saohuang dafei*), intended not just to address concerns over intellectual property rights, but also to strengthen the government's control over cultural production and the media. Furthermore, in the absence of serious penalties and consistent enforcement, these campaigns have little impact on highly profitable, often highly organized illegal distribution activities.[13]

Copyright owners may sue infringers in court in addition to seeking remedies through administrative copyright enforcement. However, judicial enforcement, although improving, still fails to provide meaningful deterrence in many copyright cases. Even when plaintiffs succeed in demonstrating copyright infringement, the damages awarded are too low to deter ongoing infringement. Between 2006 and 2009, for example, the average copyright damages awarded were just RMB 31,000 (US$5,000), and are often less than 10 per cent of damages claimed by plaintiffs (Priest 2014; Sepetys and Cox 2009).

Unauthorized distribution is a threat not just to the profitability of international copyright owners but also to Chinese content industries. In addition to direct economic losses associated with lost sales (which can be difficult to calculate), widespread unauthorized distribution can reduce monetization options for smaller and independent domestic producers, distort market signals sent to producers, and disproportionately expose producers to exploitation by intermediaries (Priest 2014). Further, the scale of unauthorized distribution in China means that those operating within the bounds of the legitimate system are forced to compete for audience time, attention, and spending power with free or very cheap, uncensored material. Access to affordable copies of the latest audiovisual productions from all over the world has greatly increased the media literacy of Chinese audiences, raising standards for local producers who often have less experience than their foreign competitors (although that is rapidly changing) and who are hamstrung by China's censorship system. Chinese content producers thus have a very real interest in better copyright enforcement, at least in part because piracy is such a powerful source of competition.

CHINESE COPYRIGHT INDUSTRY BUSINESS MODEL INNOVATION

The challenges of enforcing copyright in analogue contexts are rapidly being overtaken by the need to find business models capable of functioning profitably in networked digital landscapes. China's publishing industry provides a salient example of the impact of digital technologies and business model innovations that arise in response.

E-Book Publishing

Mobile distribution, creative users, crowd-sourced content, and micropayment models are transforming the publishing industry. In 2013, China's total volume of book retail sales was RMB 50 billion (US$8.2 billion), an increase of 10 per cent compared to sales in 2012. Most of the growth was driven by online bookstores, which grew 20–30 per cent over 2013. E-books are available at much lower prices than in other markets: around RMB 8 (US$1.30) for the average retail book (Publishing Technology 2015). The volume of titles purchased by Chinese readers is vast and growing. According to Patrick Dodd, Managing Director of Nielsen China, China has an annual e-commerce growth rate of 120 per cent – making it the fastest growing, and soon to be the largest, e-commerce market in the world. The intention of these consumers to purchase an e-book doubled between 2011 and 2014, from 26 to 51 per cent (China Internet Watch 2014).

Continued state censorship in China's print publishing market is also helping to drive authors and readers towards innovative digital models of both production and consumption. Books published in traditional print formats must comply with censorship processes before an International Standard Book Number (ISBN) can be issued. As a result, many readers are turning to serialized fiction made available via online literature portals or microblogging sites, which provide greater freedom for experimentation by both authors and readers. Serialized fiction is ideally suited to mobile reading – providing content in small chunks that can be enjoyed while waiting for a bus or standing in line at a coffee shop.

Freemium fiction sites like Qidian.com allow authors to register for free and to create stories in installments of up to six thousand characters. Readers are able to download these stories without charge – at least at first. If a work becomes popular, authors can choose to become VIP members of a site, which enables them to charge readers for accessing content. Readers are generally given free access to the first installments of a VIP story. If they choose to keep reading, they then pay between

.02 and .07 Yuan to read each new installment, with revenue split between authors and websites.

Authors are obligated to sign a formal contract with sites when they join as VIP members. These contracts generally assign exclusive digital distribution rights to the online literature site, in return for the site's commitment to promote and make the work of the author available to readers via their platform. VIP authors are also able to earn additional revenue through VIP bonus programs, which award a cash bonus to authors voted most popular by readers each month, as well as through reader tipping.[14] Licensed adaptation and distribution of popular works across multiple platforms and in different formats is a growing source of income for both online literature portals and some authors (Zhang 2010). However, while sites may invite popular authors to enter into an individually negotiated contract assigning rights to adaptation for print, screen, and games in advance, standard VIP contracts allow authors to retain these rights.

The vast majority of authors that publish works via online literature websites make very little, if any money. But these sites have also created a new generation of literary superstars with a loyal online following that has translated into lucrative fan-bases for print editions, computer games, and film adaptations. In December 2014, the ninth edition of the China Writers Rich List (similar to the annual Forbes Rich List) named 34-year-old Zhang Jiajia as China's highest earning author. Zhang rose to prominence with a collection of bedtime stories for adults posted on the microblogging site Weibo. Having secured an online following, the stories were published as a single volume: *I Belonged to You* (*cong nide quan shije luguo*) earning Zhang RMB 19.5 million (US$3.1 million) in 2014. The author subsequently secured a deal to turn five of the stories in the collection into films, including one which he will direct under guidance from Hong Kong director Wong Kar-Wai (Publishing Technology 2015).

Online Video Portals

Seismic shifts in the business models of Chinese Internet video portals in recent years are evidence of copyright's important role in the development of that market. These shifts, which emerged in 2009, are serving as a watershed for online copyright enforcement, as well as for the wider commercial development of China's digital creative industries, particularly film and music.

From their inception in the mid-2000s China's major online video streaming portals, including Youku.com, Tudou.com, Sina, Sohu and 56.com have emerged as powerful competitors to traditional television platforms (see Keane 2015; Zhao and Keane 2013). Their success has been built on their ability to provide consumers with access to unlimited free popular content (Priest 2015: 186). Because the websites generate revenue through advertising, their profitability depends on their ability to attract viewers. Professionally produced content plays a key role in attracting viewers to these sites because it is more popular among Chinese audiences than user-generated content (Priest 2015: 186).

Until 2009, domestic and international copyright owners had little success in tackling the unauthorized distribution of their content. As noted above, even if copyright owners prevail in court, the damages awarded in Chinese copyright litigation are typically too low to deter infringement. Chinese online video portals are also notorious for gaming the 'notice and takedown' processes provided for by Chinese copyright regulations, using these provisions to complicate and delay takedown of popular content while infringement persists (Priest 2014: 474–5). Before 2009, the result was a seemingly endless stream of 'pirated' video content available to users through mainstream video streaming sites, and little if any market for the licensed distribution of popular works. In 2009, the free ride for the major Chinese video streaming sites screeched to a halt. They began purging their services of unlicensed content, and spending unprecedented sums acquiring distribution licenses from copyright owners. The sudden change in habits was not precipitated primarily by fear of legal liability or a desire to evolve into pay-per-view businesses. Rather, copyright owners succeeded in shifting the behaviour of these sites by threatening their ability to attract the advertising revenue that is their economic lifeline.

In autumn 2009, frustrated by the ineffectiveness of copyright infringement litigation against video streaming websites, a consortium of domestic and foreign copyright owners launched a sustained offensive against the advertisers that used these sites. The copyright owners targeted major transnational consumer brands in particular. The offensive involved both extralegal and legal pressure tactics, including suing major transnational brand owners such as The Coca-Cola Company and Pepsico for contributory copyright infringement after their ads appeared with unlicensed content (Priest 2015). While the lawsuits were hastily dismissed, they grabbed the attention of international brand owners, who are themselves owners of valuable intellectual property and frequently battle infringement in China. The tactic worked. Major brands openly pledged not to advertise on known 'pirate' sites, pressuring video websites into compliance.

The overnight shift in the demands of major advertising clients for copyright compliance left websites scrambling to fill their services with attractive licensed content. Having resolved to pay for licenses, the sites sought to outmaneuver competitors by hosting the most desired blockbuster content on an exclusive basis. The result was a bidding war among major online video sites for exclusive licenses to prized content,[15] and a corresponding 'bubble' in video content licensing fees. In 2009, when the major Chinese video portals were still rife with piracy, the licensing fee for online distribution of the most popular show in China – a dramatic serial called *Latent* – reportedly cost US$1,500 per episode. Subsequent competition for exclusive licenses drove up prices so much that by 2011 the cost of the then-most-popular television drama *Palace* was US$290,000 per episode (Wang 2012). Websites alternately sued one another to protect their sizable investments in content and formed alliances to pool licenses and stabilize licensing costs. The two largest online video websites, bitter rivals Youku.com and Tudou, even merged in 2012 to pool resources and stave off ruination in the face of soaring content fees.

Video websites' post-2009 shift to licensed content, and the corresponding licensing bubble, has had three significant effects on audiovisual content producers in China. First, the meteoric rise in content fees resulted in a revenue windfall for copyright owners, including domestic and international film studios and television companies, to the tune of hundreds of millions of dollars from Chinese Internet streaming services that prior to 2009 paid virtually nothing to content owners (Priest 2014: 486–7). This has facilitated investment in newer, higher quality domestic works, and increased competition among domestic producers.

Second, streaming websites' shift to licensed content has provided a new monetized distribution channel for films and television programs in China. Just a few hundred domestic films are approved for theatrical release each year in China. Anyone whose film is not among those had little hope of recouping their investment,[16] since endemic piracy has all but destroyed legitimate DVD sales and other secondary markets for video content. Likewise, obtaining distribution on traditional TV in China is difficult due to strict censorship regulations governing TV production. Further, even shows that are distributed on television do not necessarily stand to make significant revenue from broadcast royalties. Instead, producers of popular shows often rely on ancillary revenue streams such as trademark licensing.[17] As discussed below, censorship rules have generally been far less strictly enforced with regard to content distributed online, as compared with theatrical releases and television broadcasts. Now that the major online streaming platforms pay licensing fees, filmmakers are developing 'web-native' films, particularly with mobile distribution in mind (Wan 2014). Currently, advertising revenue still comprises the bulk of filmmakers' online streaming royalties,[18] but web streaming companies have been eager to transition to a predominantly pay-per-view or subscription model and Chinese viewers are increasingly willing to pay for access.

Third, the high licensing costs and the need for better market differentiation have driven Chinese video sites to develop original content in-house. Chinese websites seek to emulate major video streaming services in the West such as Netflix and Amazon, which develop cutting-edge original, exclusive content including *House of Cards*, *Orange Is the New Black*, and *Transparent* to drive up subscriptions. Chinese video websites develop original content by culling the best talent from among their millions of content contributors. Companies such as Youku Tudou Inc. and Tencent support promising filmmakers with capital, professional services, marketing, and access to powerful social media platforms and hundreds of millions of viewers. Scouting and investing in talent for online productions has led companies like Youku to create content for release on its own platform. Moreover, the lines between Internet and 'traditional' film production are rapidly blurring: Youku, for example, has begun producing films for theatrical release with its 2014 hit, 'Old Boys: Way of the Dragon,' based on the smash hit web movie 'Old Boys.' Other Internet media companies such as Alibaba (itself a recent investor in Youku Tudou Inc.) and Tencent are aggressively investing in domestic film studios and feature films projects for theatrical release. In August 2015, Youku announced that it planned to invest US$1.6 billion in original content production through 2018 (Horwitz 2015a).

The key driver of this surge in energy and investment surrounding video production in China is the shift of video streaming sites from a free-for-all of unlicensed content to a copyright compliant model based on exclusive licensing (see Zhao and Keane 2013). This change is being made possible because video streaming sites that now pay for exclusive licenses have become stakeholders in a copyright compliant ecosystem. For each video website to recoup its substantial investment in content, it needs its competitors to respect its exclusive rights. While lawsuits between the major players over infringement of rights remains part of the landscape in China's video streaming industry, it is not the primary reason why, as Sohu CEO Charles Zhang recently proclaimed, '[Online video in China] is an industry with law and order' (Coonan 2014). For the exclusive licensing model to work, more than legal enforcement is needed. As social psychologist Tom Tyler and numerous legal scholars including Cass Sunstein argue, laws function best when they effectively promote and shape behavioural norms (Tyler 1990: 23; Sunstein 1997: 61). The major video sites are by and large complying with copyright law out of self-interest, producing a widespread change in behavioural norms in the online video streaming industry (Priest 2015). As we discuss below in relation to China's music industry, many of the same major players in online video are also operating in the online music space. There is evidence that the copyright compliance norms now emerging in relation to video have begun to take hold in the online music industry as well.

Online Video: A Haven from Censorship?

China's online streaming sites have enabled a mass, monetizable market for independently produced films and videos that are not subject to a formal censorship review process and are not strictly monitored. All content developed for television broadcast and theatrical release is required to undergo strict scrutiny by the State Administration of Press, Publication, Radio, Film and Television (SAPPRFT), which regulates audiovisual production, distribution, and broadcast. SAPPRFT is notorious for its opaque film and television content regulations, sweeping discretionary power over audiovisual content, and micromanagement over the creative process. However, SAPPRFT has taken a more hands-off approach to controlling web-native video content. SAPPRFT does not review scripts or even the videos themselves before they are posted online, hence creators feel far more creative freedom when producing for the web. SAPPRFT's comparatively lax approach to online video has even extended to foreign films and television programmes. In recent years, such hit Hollywood television series as *The Walking Dead* and *House of Cards* have been among the most popular shows in China, available uncensored through online streaming websites Youku and Sohu, respectively, despite transgressing SAPPRFT dictates against violence, horror, and overtly political themes.[19]

Nevertheless, SAPPRFT's lack of proactive control over web-native video content does not indicate that the space is censorship free. In fact, SAPPRFT keeps both the video producers and the websites in line by imposing on them legal liability for a video's content, ensuring at least two levels of self-censorship to discourage pornography, nudity, and seditious content. A danger inherent in self-censorship is that SAPPRFT's cryptic rules and erratic enforcement might encourage producers to err on the side of caution, resulting in over-censorship. In practice, however, the market has provided some counterbalance, since in the highly competitive online video environment, innocuous, insipid fare will attract few viewers. Producers of web videos appear willing to push the envelope – to a point – in order to stand out. There are lines that few producers dare to cross, however. In the words of web film director Jin He, 'Don't shoot pornography or nudity and don't talk about the Party or politics. Other than that, anything goes' (Lei 2012).

The Uncertain Future of Online Video Portals in China

The trend toward copyright compliance and exclusive licensing in the online video space has been a boon for copyright owners and even independent content creators, but its effect on the long-term viability of the video websites themselves is unclear. Online video in China is now a US$4 billion a year industry, but content licensing fees are onerous, and the major video streaming sites remain unprofitable. Youku Tudou Inc., for example, which runs the popular sites Youku.com and Tudou.com, spends nearly 50 per cent of its budget on content, the vast majority of which goes to licenses. While advertising revenue in China's online video industry is rising rapidly – a 50 per cent year-on-year increase between 2014 and 2015 – it still falls far short, as Youku's net losses over the same period have doubled. Other online video companies enjoy more financial stability, but only because they have deep-pocketed parents, such as the video offerings from Internet giants Tencent and Baidu.

Thus, the trend toward greater investment in user-generated content is more than a differentiation strategy: it is a survival strategy. Investment in original content produces permanent assets (unlike the licensing deals that typically expire within one to three years) and, most importantly, is less expensive than purchasing licenses from other companies. In Youku's case, original productions already reportedly account for 50 per cent of its offerings. Web video companies are betting their future that they will become the primary producers of popular content and that licensing will become a niche aspect of their business models. Even so, it will be some years before video advertising revenue will be sufficient to sustain these sites.

That means hope for business model success lies, at least for the near-to-mid term, in the video sites' ability to convince users to pay for content. There is some evidence to warrant optimism in this regard. iQiyi, Baidu's online video service, launched an original series in 2015 titled *The Lost Tomb* (*daomu biji*) by making the first episode available for free and releasing a new free episode each week. However, viewers that signed up for iQiyi's premium subscription service had immediate access to all twelve episodes from the first season. The show was a hit and helped iQiyi increase subscriptions by more than 700 per cent in 2015. Subscription options have been available on such services for years getting little traction with consumers and generating negligible revenue, but some observers believe *The Lost Tomb* marks a turning point (*Global Times* 2015).

Despite tremendous gains in the major streaming sites' battle against unauthorized content online, the greatest obstacle to the development of successful subscription models continues to be the ready availability of unlicensed content. While the major video streaming services in China are largely piracy free, as discussed above, unlicensed content remains abundant on smaller websites, and consumers are increasingly using cloud storage services to share content privately. As long as free, unlicensed content remains accessible with relative ease, pay models for video websites will have difficulty gaining traction. In a recent survey of Chinese netizens, 40 per cent reportedly said they would not pay to watch a movie online, and another 26 per cent would consider paying only RMB 3 (US 50 cents) or less (*Global Times* 2015).

The lesson learned from China's online streaming sites' emphasis on copyright compliance and exclusive licensing appears to be that while this strategy benefitted sites in the short-to-medium term, it is not sustainable as long as China's online video industry remains primarily advertising-supported. Copyright compliance and exclusive licensing helped Chinese streaming sites benefit by facilitating closer relationships with advertisers. However, the effects of exclusive licensing in this context might well be counterproductive long-term. Exclusive licensing in a highly competitive environment begets price inflation, and online video advertising revenues have failed to keep pace. Moreover, hosting exclusive content has done little to truly differentiate the services in consumers' minds or build brand loyalty for the websites. Many Chinese consumers are apt to hop from one site to another in pursuit of their preferred content. Online video services are not abandoning their exclusivity strategy, however. They are merely adjusting it to be more cost-effective and sustainable.

Digital Music

Compared with the film and television industries, China's music industry has had far more difficulty locating an effective monetization model. Digital music is exceedingly popular in China: according to government estimates, more than three-quarters of China's 600 million Internet users listen to music online. The challenge for music copyright owners is motivating this enormous fan base to pay for recorded music. Ubiquitous free recorded music online – most of it unlicensed until recently – has conditioned consumers to expect unlimited free access to music downloads and streams. Pay access music services have therefore enjoyed little traction in China. Even the free, fully advertising-supported, licensed music download service that Google launched in China in 2009 foundered because users already had ample sources of free music downloads, most of which were unlicensed (Priest 2014: 525).

Nevertheless, Chinese consumers have proved willing to pay substantial sums for music in one peculiar context: mobile phone 'ringback tones'.[20]

Ringback tones are monetizable because they are integrally tied to mobile phone services. They are not susceptible to piracy because they are centrally controlled and broadcast by mobile service providers. Mobile phone subscribers can add a ringback tone service to their account for an additional fee. Chinese mobile providers gross over US$4 billion annually in ringback tone fees. That amount is comparable to what the recording industry grosses annually in the US market, which ranks first in the world in recorded music sales. If Chinese mobile providers were to split the ringback tone revenue equally with music copyright owners, China would instantly rank third in the world in recorded music revenue behind the United States and Japan, and ahead of Germany and the United Kingdom. But Chinese mobile providers keep 98 per cent of ringback tone revenue, passing along a mere 2 per cent to copyright owners. Since the service is controlled by a duopoly (China Mobile and China Unicom), the copyright owners have little leverage. This is especially true since ringback tone revenue, as meager as it is, accounts for a substantial percentage of record labels' income. As a result, copyright owners are able to wring less than US$100 million annually from China's vast music market (Priest 2014: 496).

Widespread infringement of music online, long a major obstacle to monetization for record labels, has been slowly improving. For years the largest alleged infringer of music copyrights was Baidu, the Chinese Internet search giant, which provided free downloads to vast amounts of music through its MP3 search feature. In 2011, the international major labels – Universal Music, Sony, and Warner – settled with Baidu, ending years of contentious litigation. In return for payment and Baidu's commitment to develop a premium paid-access tier, the labels granted Baidu blanket licenses to lawfully distribute their content. Ultimately, the Baidu deal, in the words of Universal Music's international business head Max Hole, was not 'fantastically successful' but it was 'a start' (Cookson 2014).

The Baidu deal, and the trend toward licensing and copyright compliance among the major Internet video sites, set the stage for a spate of more recent music-oriented deals with major Chinese Internet portals. Music copyright holders watched with great interest the rise in video licensing fees spurred by exclusive licensing and fierce competition between video streaming sites. In hopes of driving up the value of their content and enlisting powerful Internet companies as stakeholders and copyright enforcers, record labels are granting exclusive rights to major Chinese web companies. In 2014, Warner Music and Sony both granted Internet giant Tencent the exclusive right to distribute their recordings online in China. Other web portals that reportedly have acquired exclusive licenses from domestic and South Korean pop labels include Alibaba, NetEase, and Kugou. In a trend reminiscent of the early days of exclusive licensing by Chinese video websites, music streaming providers such as Tencent, NetEase, Kugou, and Alibaba have actively sued one another to enforce their exclusive licenses (Horwitz 2015b).

The websites acquiring exclusive digital music licenses plan to be more than just online streaming services – they plan to be music rights management companies. Major Internet players such as Tencent envision eliminating smaller, unlicensed competitors by coercing them to pay licensing fees or suing them out of existence. As Chinese music industry expert Ed Peto (2014) observes, '[W]e will see these few major players – with the support of the government – being able to shut down or license any rogue sites or apps, leaving a handful of services who will in turn most likely have been consolidated into one of the fiefdoms.'

Whether the exclusive licensing strategy will ultimately be a net positive for music copyright owners or the websites, however, is unclear. By all indications, exclusive licensing practices have yet to fuel a bubble in music copyright valuations. The long-term benefit of exclusive licensing for websites is also questionable: it is not clear that hosting exclusive music content drives brand loyalty among consumers, particularly as long as exclusive licenses are spread among numerous providers. There are strong incentives for one major Internet company, such as Tencent, to monopolize the online music market by acquiring exclusive licenses to the bulk of popular music content in China. There is a very real danger, however, that consolidation of market power in one or two monopsony intermediaries will drive licensing fees downward, as is evident from the mobile ringback tone example.

CONCLUSION

Digital technologies and the open and networked architecture of the Internet are creating new challenges for copyright in all markets. In a brave new digital world in which the role of copyright in processes of value creation, innovation, and trade in creative works is not yet fully understood, businesses, policy makers, and users in China face many of the same challenges as their counterparts in more mature markets. Rather than simply managing a shift from analogue to digital technologies, China's cultural and creative industries must come to terms with the role of copyright in the context of other complex changes in media regulation and markets, as well as rapidly changing access to technology and evolving patterns of user engagement with content. All of this makes China one of the most exciting places in the world for those interested in understanding the conditions necessary for the growth of vibrant creative industries and relationships between legal frameworks, like copyright, and creative and cultural economies of a digital age. It also makes it one of the most challenging markets in the world for businesses that depend on copyright to define their products and to enable their trade.

As China's cultural and creative industries become more commercially focused, the role of copyright and exclusive rights in every aspect of China's creative economy is becoming more pronounced. On paper, China's copyright law now has much in common with copyright laws that exist elsewhere in the world and China's policy makers, creative professionals, and businesses are becoming conscious of the value of recognizing and protecting intellectual property rights. China remains the subject of robust criticism from trading partners for its failure to effectively enforce copyright. However, while trade relations remain an important factor, international pressure is no longer the main driver of copyright's development in China. As local creative industries become more deeply invested in protecting and monetizing creative works, the ecosystem is shifting.

Most players in China's digital creative ecosystem – from individual creators to publishers to online intermediaries – still seek sustainable monetization models in this environment. Somewhat counter intuitively, however, their business model innovations all betray a familiar and decidedly 'twentieth-century' device: rights of exclusion. Publishers of online e-books might not charge for access to their serials, but they monetize them by selling exclusive film rights, which are in turn monetized via the most venerable exclusive right of all: the right to permit or exclude one (a paying customer) from entering a controlled space (the movie theatre). Internet video portals appear to have tied their future to exclusive rights, acquired either through the creation of original content or through licensing from other content owners. Music portals are adopting a similar approach. To date, the rise of exclusive licensing has been a boon for many creators and content owners, but it remains unclear whether exclusive licensing models will enhance or destabilize China's digital creative ecosystems in the long term. Exclusive licensing can engender bidding wars that drive up content licensing fees unsustainably. Exclusive licensing can also concentrate too much power in one or a handful of intermediaries, leading to downward pressure on content licensing fees and exploitation of creators.

Ultimately, however, the biggest obstacle to sustainably monetizing China's digital creative industries may not be the proliferation of exclusive rights, but rather the ongoing challenges with enforcement of those rights. So long as paying for content is effectively 'optional' for consumers, most will choose not to pay. Many digital services offering original or licensed content must then rely on online advertising revenue, which is presently insufficient to cover costs. In short, the future viability of the online creative ecosystem is unclear if consumers remain unwilling to pay for content and can readily acquire access to unlicensed copies online.

NOTES

1. The author would like to acknowledge the advice and support of Dr. Xiang Ren, Research Fellow at the Australian Digital Futures Institute at the University of Southern Queensland, particularly in relation to the sections on Chinese digital publishing.
2. The WTO Dispute Settlement Body found that China's failure to accord copyright protection to works that had not been submitted for censorship approval constituted a breach of the nation's obligations under several international conventions, which China accepted (Mara 2009; World Trade Organization 2010).
3. This is evident in the rise in formal copyright registration that has taken place since 1995. Although copyright registration is optional in China, it can make seeking enforcement easier. In 2010, the NCAC held records for 359,871 formally registered creative works, accessed 20 August 2015 at http://data.chinaxwcb.com/epaper/2011/2011-09-07/14116. html, as compared with just 2,915 registrations in 1995 when the service was first launched, accessed 20 August 2015 at http://file.lw23.com/f/f7/f70/f703b86a-b95c-45ea-b572-14824d4047a9.pdf.
4. Accessed on 25 September 2015 at http://www.sipo.gov.cn/mtjj/2011/201107/t2011 0715_611351.html; http://book.sina.com.cn/news/a/2010-09-15/1045273290.shtml.
5. Accessed on 25 September 2015 at http://www.chinanews.com/cul/2012/05-23/3909660. shtml.
6. Accessed on 25 September 2015 at http://www.zhiyiwang.com/news/show_8506.html.
7. See some examples, accessed on 25 September 2015 at http://www.chinanews.com/ yl/dyzx/news/2008/12-10/1481860.shtml; http://news.xinhuanet.com/zgjx/2008-12/05/ content_10460006.htm; http://ent.sina.com.cn/m/c/2005-12-23/0250938212.html.
8. Accessed on 25 September 2015 at http://www.techweb.com.cn/internet/2012-11-16/1255656.shtml; also see Yang 2012.
9. Accessed on 25 September 2015 at http://ent.sina.com.cn/m/c/2012-11-16/02393789083. shtml.
10. Accessed on 25 September 2015 at http://www.cac.gov.cn/2015-02/03/c_1114237273. htm.
11. 'According to the Ministry of Industry and Information Technology, mobile phone users in China reached 1.06 billion by the end of July 2012, of which 183.8 million subscribed to 3G network services' (Shen 2012).
12. International Intellectual Property Alliance (IIPA) (2012), '2012 Special 301 Report on Copyright Protection and Enforcement,' http://www.iipa.com/ rbc/2012/2012SPEC301CHINA.PDF, accessed 28 September 2015.
13. According to Jason Berman (2005), Chairman of the International Federation of the Phonographic Industry (IFPI), see http://www.ifpi.org/content/section_news/20050209. html.
14. Abrams (2013).
15. The video streaming sites with the greatest market share at the end of 2009 were Youku, Tudou, Ku6, PPStream, PPLive, UUSee, and 56.com (Ding 2010).
16. An exception came in the form of foreign distribution. Chinese films that secured a coveted spot in a foreign film festival, or that appealed to the Chinese diaspora, had a chance of earning revenue in foreign markets. This, however, had the effect of incentivizing Chinese filmmakers to produce content not for domestic audiences but to appeal to foreign critics and consumers (Barmé 2000: 190–92; Pickowicz 2012: 316).
17. In this regard, one of us recalls a conversation in 2007 with the producer of an extremely

popular Chinese animated television series. According to the producer, he lost money every time China Central Television (CCTV) aired an episode of his show. CCTV paid him no royalties, but it cost him about US$15 to deliver the master to the broadcaster. Nevertheless, the national broadcast was important because it promoted the show and its characters, catalyzing a lucrative business licensing the characters for use on myriad consumer products.

18. This advertising revenue may come in the form of payments by the websites to copyright owners, but often comes in the form of product placement advertising, for which the video producer strikes a deal directly with the advertiser to feature its products or services in the video.

19. In 2015, SAPPRFT imposed tighter restrictions on the distribution of foreign content, including that foreign works (including Hong Kong productions) must be submitted to SAPPRFT for approval and that foreign content can comprise no more than 30 per cent of a video streaming site's total content. The requirement that domestic videos must comprise at least 70 per cent of a site's content is likely animated as much by economic protectionism as by concern over information control (Priest 2014: 482–3).

20. Ringback tones are songs or other recordings that a caller hears while waiting for the call recipient to answer her mobile phone. Ringback tones are essentially 'hold music' that the mobile phone company plays for the caller while he waits for the recipient to answer.

REFERENCES

Abrams, Dennis (2013), 'Scandal rocks China's largest online literature site', *Publishing Perspectives*, Growth Markets blog, 5 June, accessed 20 August 2015 at http://publishing-perspectives.com/2013/06/scandal-rocks-chinas-largest-online-literature-site/.
Akhavan-Majid, Roya (2004), 'Mass media reform in China', *Gazette* **66** (6): 553–65.
Alford, William (1995), *To Steal a Book is an Elegant Offense.* Stanford: Stanford University Press.
Barmé, Geremie (2000), *In the Red: On Contemporary Chinese Culture.* New York, NY: Columbia University Press.
China Internet Watch (2014), 'Chinese consumers strong intention for online purchase with higher buying rates than browsing', accessed 28 August 2015 at http://www.chinainternet-watch.com/8763/online-purchase-intentions.
Cookson, Robert (2014), 'Streaming is the answer for Chinese music industry', *Financial Times*, Digital Media blog, 28 May, accessed 19 September 2015 at http://www.ft.com/intl/cms/s/0/60255bc6-e4c0-11e3-894f-00144feabdc0.html#axzz3mAEF04xG.
Coonan, Clifford (2014), '"Saturday Night Live" Launches on Chinese Video Site Sohu', *Hollywood Reporter*, 2 January, accessed 19 September 2015 at http://www.holly-woodreporter.com/news/sat urday-night-live-launches-chinese-668177.
Copyright Law of the People's Republic of China 1990, promulgated on 7 September by the 7th National People's Congress, amended at the 24th Session of the Standing Committee of the 9th National People's Congress on 27 October 2001.
Dimitrov, Martin (2009), *Piracy and the State: The Politics of Intellectual Property Rights in China.* Cambridge: Cambridge University Press.
Ding, Yining (2010), 'Websites vie for profit from free online video streaming', *Shanghai Daily*, China blog, 10 March, accessed 15 August 2015 at http://beta.adchina.com/Newsletter.aspx?dl=20100402145833166.pdf.
Fitzgerald, Anne and Brian Fitzgerald (2004), *Intellectual Property in Principle.* Sydney: Lawbook Company.
Frater, Patrick (2015), 'China rising: how four giants are revolutionizing the film industry', *Variety*, Film blog, 3 February, accessed 28 August 2015 at http://variety.com/

2015/film/news/china-rising-quartet-of-middle-kingdom-conglomerates-revolutionizing-chinese-film-industry-1201421685.

Global Times (2015), 'Online video sites bet Chinese viewers ready to pay for content', 16 August, accessed 20 September 2015 at http://www.globaltimes.cn/content/937332.shtml.

Hong, Junhao (1994), 'Mao Zedong's cultural theory and China's three mass-culture debates: a tentative study of culture, society, and politics', *Intercultural Communication Studies* 4: 87–104.

Horwitz, Josh (2015a), 'The "YouTube of China" is acting more and more like YouTube', *Quartz* 7 August, accessed 20 September 2015 at http://qz.com/474656/the-youtube-of-china-is-acting-more-and-more-like-youtube/.

Horwitz, Josh (2015b), 'China's major music streamers are suing the hell out of each other – and that's a good thing', *Quartz*, 22 July, accessed 21 September 2015 at http://qz.com/459551/a-whirlwind-of-lawsuits-among-chinas-internet-giants-might-tear-through-the-nations-piracy-habit-too/.

Hui, Desmond (2006), *Study on the Relationship between Hong Kong's Cultural and Creative Industries and the Pearl River Delta*. Hong Kong: Centre for Cultural Policy Research, University of Hong Kong.

Keane, Michael (2013), *Creative Industries in China: Art, Design and Media*. Cambridge: Polity Press.

Keane, Michael (2015), *The Chinese Television Industry*. London: British Film Institute and Palgrave Macmillan.

Kraus, Richard (2004), *The Party and the Arty in China: The New Politics of Culture*. Lanham, Boulder: Rowman and Littlefield.

Lei, Tang (2012), 'Micro-movies move toward mainstream', *News China*, Cultural Listings blogs, November, accessed 15 July 2015 at http://www.newschinamag.com/magazine/move-toward-mainstream.

Li, Yufeng and Catherine W. Ng (2008–09), 'Understanding the Great Qing Copyright Law of 1910', *Journal of the Copyright Society of the USA* 56: 767–88.

Liu, T. and B. Bates (2008), 'Copyright in China: implementation issues in electronic media', paper presented at the 2008 IAMCR conference *Media and Global Divides*, Stockholm, Sweden, 20–25 July.

Mara, Kaitlin (2009), 'Parties accept WTO Dispute Settlement Report on China IP Protection', accessed 20 August 2015 at http://www.ip-watch.org/2009/03/24/parties-accept-wto-dispute-settlement-report-on-china-ip-protection/.

Montgomery, Lucy (2010), *China's Creative Industries: Copyright, Social Network Markets and the Business of Culture in a Digital Age*. Cheltenham, UK and Northampton, MA, USA: Edward Elgar.

Mun, S.-H. (2008), 'Culture-related aspects of intellectual property rights: a cross-cultural analysis of copyright', Doctoral thesis, Austin: The University of Texas.

Peto, Ed (2014), 'Glaciers aligning: progress in the Chinese digital music industry', *China Music Business*, 13 March, accessed 20 September 2015 at http://www.chinamusicbusiness.com/article/china-great-digital-music-leap-forward/.

Pickowicz, Paul (2012), *China on Film: A Century of Exploration, Confrontation, and Controversy*. Lanham, MD: Rowman and Littlefield.

Priest, Eric (2014), 'Copyright extremophiles: do creative industries thrive or just survive in China's high piracy environment?', *Harvard Journal of Law and Technology* 27: 467–541.

Priest, Eric (2015), 'Acupressure: the emerging role of market ordering in global copyright enforcement', *SMU Law Review* 68: 169–242.

Publishing Technology (2015), 'Five trends in Chinese publishing that will change your view of China', accessed 28 August 2015 at http://www.publishingtechnology.com/2015/03/five-trends-in-chinese-publishing-that-will-change-your-view-of-china/.

Ren, Xiang and Lucy Montgomery (2012), 'Chinese online literature: creative consumers and evolving business models', *Arts Marketing: An International Journal* 2 (2): 13.

Sepetys, Kristina and Alan Cox (2009), *Intellectual Property Rights Protection in China: Trends in Litigation and Economic Damages*, accessed 10 July 2014 at http://www.nera.

com/content/dam/nera/publications/archive1/PUB_IPR_Protection_China_0109_final.pdf.

Shen, Jingting (2012), 'China had 1.06b mobile phone accounts', *China Daily*, Business/Industries blog, 28 August, accessed 28 September 2015 at http://www.chinadaily.com.cn/business/2012-08/28/content_15713316.htm.

Song, Hongsong (2014), 'The development of copyright law and the transition of press control in China', *Oregon Review of International Law* 16: 249–305.

Sunstein, Cass (1997), *Free Markets and Social Justice*. New York, NY: Oxford University Press.

Tyler, Tom (1990), *Why People Obey the Law*. New Haven, CT: Yale University Press.

Wan, Adrian (2014), 'Chinese directors find greater freedom online making micro movies', *South China Morning Post*, Arts & Entertainment blog, 9 January, accessed 23 August 2015 at http://www.scmp.com/lifestyle/arts-culture/article/1401565/chinese-directors-find-greater-freedom-online-making-micro.

Wang, Fei'er (2012), 'The copyright clash', *Global Times*, Business blog, 12 January, accessed 21 September 2015 at http://www.globaltimes.cn/content/691864.shtml.

World Trade Organization (2010), 'China – Measures Affecting the Protection and Enforcement of Intellectual Property Rights', accessed 20 August 2015 at http://www.wto.org/english/tratop_e/dispu_e/cases_e/ds362_e.htm.

Yang, Yang (2012), 'A record tailspin in music industry', *China Daily*, Business/Industries blog, 30 June, http://www.chinadaily.com.cn/cndy/2012-06/30/content_15538349.htm.

Zhang, Anna (2010), 'Shanda literature: making money from copyright', accessed 28 August 2015 at http://www.chinaipmagazine.com/en/journal-show.asp?id=574.

Zhang, Yingjin (2004), *Chinese National Cinema*. New York, NY: Routledge.

Zhao, Elaine Jing and Michael Keane (2013), 'Between formal and informal: the shakeout in China's online video industry', *Media, Culture and Society* 35 (6): 724–41.

25. Commercial and digital transformation of Chinese television
Ruoyun Bai

INTRODUCTION

Commercial television in China has evolved out of a geographically and administratively fragmented broadcasting system owned by various levels of government. At each stage of development the state has played a crucial role creating conditions for, and modulating the speed and boundaries of commercialization. In this way the television system commercialized in the 1980s and 1990s without letting go its core mandate, i.e. serving as the Chinese Communist Party's (hereafter CCP) mouthpiece. The coexistence of two core directives – politics and profit – led to a dual identity. Television was meant to be a public institution (*shiye*) run as a business enterprise (*qiye*). This dual identity provided ideological legitimacy for commercial television while allowing stations to profit handsomely from a rapidly expanding national economy and consumer society. Meanwhile it also imposed a limit to how far commercialization could proceed.

In the wake of China's accession to the World Trade Organization (WTO), the dual identity began to dissolve as a result of political, economic and technological forces. Chinese television has remained state-owned-and-regulated but it is no longer 'a public institution run as a business.' Then what does the new identity look like and how is it achieved? In this chapter I review the commercialization of Chinese television from the analytical standpoint of 'dual identity.' Two key cultural policies deserve special attention: (1) the 'cultural system reform' and (2) the 'media convergence' reforms within the ambitious state initiative called 'Internet+.' In a sense, commercialization in the new century has been about reducing the ambiguity and uncertainty regarding the commercial nature of Chinese television. Leaving the 'public' baggage behind, a small number of broadcasters are rapidly remolding themselves to integrate with the frontiers of the privately dominated Internet economy (see Keane 2015).

SETTLING THE IDENTITY ISSUE THROUGH BIFURCATION

Within the vaguely defined *shiye*-qua-*qiye* model that prevailed in the 1980s and 1990s, Chinese television stations were required to be financially self-sufficient while submitting to the CCP's propaganda needs and government control. Yet divergent political and economic interests made Chinese television a site of dissonance. Tensions were relieved when producers were able to make programs that kept all parties happy – namely, audiences, advertisers and the Party leadership. Indeed, a prominent feature of commercial television culture in China has been the merging of the official and the popular. To some extent commercialization for producers, writers, journalists and bureaucrats at television stations meant playing smart. A great deal of improvisation and ingenuity goes towards balancing commercial interests and pushing limits without alarming censors (Bai 2012). Many programs were highly profitable, thus making it possible for broadcasters to maximize economic returns through advertising, sponsorship and product placement. As long as broadcasters supported the political agendas of the day, they were able to justify these profits. Contradictions rooted in the dual identity were largely contained and absorbed at the programming level; at the structural level, however, they pose problems far removed from media industries elsewhere.

The history of media industries in advanced capitalist countries is one of concentration through horizontal and vertical integration. Transnational media firms grow bigger not only to secure a dominant position in each media sector but also to seek synergistic effects across all media platforms. Chinese television, however, existed in a four-tier system, which around the mid-1990s consisted of thousands of cable and terrestrial television stations. Cross-region or cross-media movement of capital was virtually impossible. Furthermore, for a long time, capital outside the system, whether private, state, or foreign, was denied formal access to television production except through advertising and program sponsorship. By the close of the century larger broadcasters that had profited during the previous decade of commercialization as well as businesses operating quasi legally by making television dramas, had become impatient for a new round of deregulation and expansion. There was another important factor in play. Party leaders and media officials were seeking to modernize and expand the media industry in order to contain the threat of Hollywood as China geared up for entry into the World Trade Organization. These twin forces of industry impatience and the threat of cultural globalization led to waves of state-led restructuring of Chinese media.

From the mid-1990s to the time when the 'cultural system reform' was launched in 2003, the dominant way of thinking concerning media restructuring was consolidation aimed at reducing the number of television stations and creating media conglomerates (see Zhao 2008; Zhang 2011). In the spirit of Document No. 82 ('Circular on Strengthening the Construction and Management of Cable Networks'), county-level stations were repurposed primarily as transmission stations with restricted programming power. The number of terrestrial stations decreased from 923 in 1997 to 347 in 1998 (Xu 2013: 377), and further down to 247 in 2010 (National Bureau of Statistics 2011). Cable stations, totaling more than 1,200 in 1997, were divested of cable network assets, which were to be taken over by newly formed broadcast network companies. After divestiture they were then either eliminated or merged with terrestrial stations. Then Document No. 17 ('Some Opinions about Deepening the Reform of the Press, Publishing, Broadcast and Film Industries') was issued in 2001, which laid the groundwork for media conglomeration. A number of television stations, radio stations, and film companies merged into media conglomerates between 1999 and 2004. The result was rapid concentration of media assets and resources, previously widely distributed across an administratively segmented system. In this process provincial and national media were privileged and legitimatized as preferred players while city and county broadcasters, having neither access to the national market nor strong programming power, became weaker and were marginalized. One primary goal and result of the restructuring in this period was divesting power of local governments at the municipal and county levels so that regional horizontal integration and market expansion became possible.

Conglomeration came to a halt in 2004 when the SARFT suspended the formation of any more broadcast conglomerates. The SARFT recognized that conglomeration was failing to produce synergy and market efficiency. Broadcast conglomerates were far from full-fledged businesses. Internally the conglomerates were beset by complicated relations with local governments and conflicts of interests and business cultures between different media entities that were forced together by administrative orders; externally, trans-provincial operations, cross-media movements or activities in the capital market were few and far between. As Keane (2015: 93) notes, [conglomeration] both 'strengthens regional media monopolies and constrains companies from expanding.' The *shiye* status of the conglomerates was identified as the core problem, which became a central theme in the next round of restructuring (Zhao 2008).

The reform of the cultural system was foreshadowed in the 'Report of the Party's 16th National Progress' in October 2002, piloted in 2003, and officially launched in January 2006 with the issuance of the 'Several Opinions on Deepening Cultural System Reform.' Bifurcation was at its core. Bifurcation refers to the separation of the media and cultural sector into public interest institutions and market-oriented businesses. In this design broadcast rights, the CCP's propaganda, and news programming should retain the *shiye* attribute. Other functions such as entertainment production, information services, advertising, program trade, online businesses and so on should be taken over by 'relatively autonomous market entities that are free to absorb outside capital and pursue market-oriented expansion' (Zhao 2008: 112). In 2009, the SARFT issued 'About Promoting the Reform of Separating Production from Broadcasting', according to which television stations should purchase at least 30 per cent of non-drama programs from the market. The document also specified that television stations should form market-oriented program production firms around their existing assets and capacities and that these firms may recruit private capital as long as they are majority-owned by the stations. CCTV and several leading provincial broadcasters in Beijing, Hunan and Shanghai were among the first pilot trials.

The Shanghai Media & Entertainment Group (SMEG) provides an illustrative example of the process. Formed in 2001, the ambitious SMEG consisted of a wide array of media operations ranging from television and radio broadcast to Internet and mobile TV services. Not only did it produce and distribute television programs, films and animation, but it also expanded into tourism, performing arts and exhibitions. Created before the CCP's 16th National Congress, SMEG wore the hat of a 'party-state institution.' In 2009, SMEG became the first broadcaster to launch wholesale 'separation of production and broadcasting' under the auspices of the SARFT. SMEG's broadcast core (Shanghai News and Media Group) was renamed Shanghai Radio & TV, which in turn created its own subsidiary firm, Shanghai Media Group (SMG or *dongfang chuanmei jituan*). Shanghai Radio & TV took over all broadcast and news production assets, including the Programming and Editorial Board, the General Programming Office, radio spectrums and television channels, and television and radio news centers. SMG was assigned all the production capacity of SMEG except for news so it now was free to corporatize its production departments in drama, animation, children's programming, general entertainment programming, sports, lifestyle, science, and business information and data services. Shanghai Radio & TV was the controlling shareholder of SMG.

In the wake of the passing of 'Plans for Furthering the Cultural System Reform' in 2014, SMEG, Shanghai Radio & TV, and SMG underwent another major restructuring. SMEG was reduced in size by letting go its film and Internet businesses so that the latter might more freely tap into the capital market through IPO, transferring not-for-profit television operations to Shanghai Radio & TV, and handing over its administrative functions such as hosting Shanghai International Film Festival and administering film archives to Shanghai Culture, Film and Broadcast Bureau. What was left of SMEG merged with SMG to form a new SMG. In this incarnation Shanghai Radio & TV and the new SMG share the same administrative board, although how the two bodies are to 'act in concert' (*yitihua yunzuo*), as claimed by the management, was not entirely clear. In principle, the former is a *shiye* institution whereas the latter is created for the market. According to the then head of SMG, Li Ruigang, the new SMG is going through asset liquidation and consolidation to ready itself for public listing (He 2014). The movement had started: across the country, *shiye*-status broadcast conglomerates were being replaced by two-body structures consisting of not-for-profit broadcasters and for-profit media groups. The latter are increasingly deregulated and commercializing. They engage in cross-media operations such as Internet TV and online audio-visual businesses, and tap into the stock market through publicly listed entertainment and new media subsidiaries.

Bifurcation as a principle for Chinese media restructuring not only allows deregulation of broadcasters but also extends to the industry in general. In 2003, the SARFT licensed eight private television drama production firms, sending out the first signal that the production of television dramas was now formally opened up to private capital (Bai 2014a; Zhao 2008; Liu 2010; Keane 2015). Although television stations had depended upon private firms for television drama supply in the previous decade, a private firm could only be in the game as partner of a drama production licensee, which was most likely a television station, a film studio, an audio-visual publishing house or the army. While undertaking the lion's share of work in the production of thousands of hours of drama, private firms did not have the legal right to produce television dramas and did not enjoy copyright protection. The SARFT's legitimatization of private capital was in line with the policy orientation in favour of differential treatment of production on the one hand and broadcasting on the other. The orientation was further reinforced in the following years by a series of policy statements advocating the entry of private capital into the cultural industry and encouraging private firms to be publicly listed. In 2009, Huayi Brothers, which was among the first private drama production licensees in 2003, became the first private production firm to be listed (Bai 2014a). It was followed by a few others, including Huace Film & TV and Guangxian Entertainment Media.

State-owned media firms have also sought access to the stock market. In the late 1990s, CCTV's subsidiary firm, China Television Media or *zhongshi chuanmei*), and provincial television operations such as Hunan TV

& Broadcast Intermediary Co. and Shanghai Television's Oriental Pearl were the earliest examples that television stations tried to access the capital market through subsidiary firms (Zhong 2010). Having separated from television stations under the auspices of the cultural system reform, some powerful media groups are more eager than ever to seek listing opportunities. Though barred from the stock market, their subsidiaries stand a better chance of becoming individually listed. SMG's IPTV arm, BesTV, was listed in 2011. To expand its presence in e-commerce, SMG announced its plan to merge its TV shopping firm, Oriental CJ (a subsidiary of Oriental Pearl), with BesTV in 2014.[1] Hunan Broadcasting Service's TV-online shopping arm, Happigo or Happy Shopping, was listed in January 2015. Considering that Internet businesses are less regulated than television, it is not surprising that media groups are breaking new grounds of capitalization through the venue of new media. More frequently, television-based media groups settle for other venues of expansion such as establishing alliances or joint ventures with other entertainment businesses.

THE DIGITAL AS AGENT OF COMMERCIALIZATION

The digital revolution has had a profound impact on television. Giving rise to new storing, recording and distribution modes, digital technologies have revolutionized the consumption of television content by 'divorc[ing] the transmission of television from broadcast signals, cable wires, and satellite feeds' (Lotz 2009: 53). At first, cheap compression and reproduction technologies made it possible for people to access pirated dramas on DVD or via unauthorized free downloading or streaming services. Unauthorized downloading services were closed down during a large-scale government crackdown on peer-to-peer video-sharing sites in China in 2008 (Zhao and Keane 2013), in the wake of which a few online video service providers emerged such as Youku Tudou, Baidu, and LeTV. Chinese viewers, especially youth, have increasingly abandoned television for these online video sites. Concerning the impact of digital technologies on US television, Amanda Lotz notes that 'the extent of changes introduced by new technologies and viewers' response to them has made it increasingly difficult for long-established industrial practices to maintain their grip on the processes of production and the norms of textual output' (Lotz 2009: 54).

New ways of producing, delivering, storing, and consuming television content and new entrants into the audio-visual entertainment market also constitute the new reality for Chinese television. It may be argued that digital technologies such as the Internet, cloud computing, mobile apps, and social media have empowered ordinary consumers to participate in the production and distribution of television and other video-based entertainment. It is also undeniable that the same technologies also serve as key agents for the 'commercial revolution' of television. Next I will examine (1) the pivotal importance that the CCP gave to Internet technologies in the transformation of Chinese mainstream media and culture; (2) how broadcasters are integrating into the digital – in its technological, institutional, and cultural forms – to maximize the value of programs and involve audiences/users in many aspects of capital accumulation.

In light of how the Internet has taken over television and newspaper as the most prominent means of media consumption for many Chinese, the CCP recognized the need for traditional media to adapt to the new media environment by embracing the Internet. In August 2014, the CCP's Leading Group for Overall Reform issued a document known as 'Guiding Opinions about Integrated Development of Traditional and New Media.' The document called for new-type media groups to emerge in the near future; these new mainstream media would be characterized by highly advanced technologies and a greatly enhanced communicative capacity. This document is part of the Xi Jinping administration's reform package and a core component of the new round of media reform. The CCP's zeal for media convergence is part of the state strategy called 'Internet+.' Internet+ was officially inaugurated when Premier Li Keqiang made his 'Government Work Report' in March 2015. It is defined as

> a new type of economy, in which the Internet will play an optimizing and integrative role in allocating factors of production, Internet-related innovations will integrate into all economic and social spheres so as to enhance the innovative and productive power of the economy, and a new kind of economic development will be achieved using the Internet both as infrastructure and as tool (National Development and Reform Commission 2015)

More specifically, the Internet+ initiative focuses on 'convergence and innovation surrounding the new generation of information technologies of cloud computing, the Internet of things, and big data on the one hand and modern manufacturing industries and service industries on the other' (ibid.). So for the 'cultural system reform,' the new question has become how to integrate the Internet and the traditional mainstream media; in other words, how to digitize the mainstream and mainstream the digital so that a new mainstream would be achieved. What the new mainstream would look like and how it would be formed are not specifically envisioned; across various media sectors, people are debating what 'integrated development of traditional and new media' can actually mean. However, developments in the past five years or so indicate that traditional media dominants are evolving into multi-sector new media groups, and that they are actively seeking partnership with Internet giants (or the so-called BAT firms, Baidu, Alibaba and Tencent). Big media, the Western-type (vis-à-vis the type created by administrative orders), seem to be in the making. Sectoral and administrative barriers that used to fragment the Chinese media system are still in place, but cross-sector mergers and cross-regional alliances and operations are on the increase, especially where Internet businesses and services are concerned.

The initiatives that broadcasters are trying out in media convergence are mostly at the experimental stage. Most operate their own websites as an additional platform for their programs; in recent years, they have turned to mobile devices and offer mobile TV services through various apps. More powerful broadcasters such as CCTV, Hunan TV and SMG also seek deeper-level integration with new media. They hope to remold themselves by exploring synergistic opportunities with digital media and communication technologies, and/or entering into strategic alliances with digital media giants. One way of establishing a presence in the online audio-visual market is for broadcasters to launch online video services backed by their own powerful content creation engines. For example, Hunan SATV (subsidiary of Hunan TV) created its new media arm, Happy Sunshine Entertainment, to develop Internet businesses in 2006. In 2014, Happy Sunshine launched an online video-streaming business, Hunan TV.com (also known as 'Mango TV' in China). Not simply an online presence for a traditional broadcaster, Mango TV is more of a new media firm than a television business, and for executives at Hunan TV it is where commercialization will forge ahead for the Hunan Broadcasting System.

Soon after Mango TV was created, Hunan SATV announced its plan of streaming a few of its popular dramas exclusively on the platform. This is deemed an expensive and risky business model by many industry insiders: by stopping licensing copyrights to other online video providers, Hunan SATV loses a lucrative source of revenue and risks relying too much on a fledgling Internet business vis-à-vis the much more powerful and established popular websites such as Youku Tudou, Tencent and iQiyi. However this business model seems to be a response to the perception that the traditional delivery platforms owned by broadcasters are quickly losing value to new media so broadcasters have no other choice but to integrate with new media. In interviews between Hunan TV's officials and the press, a consensus within the senior management surfaces that 'although television will not die right away, it has a shrinking market and will come to a dead end sooner or later if it does not engage with the new media' (Fan 2014). Accordingly, the media group redefines its core activity as in the area of production – in the words of Happy Sunshine's CEO, Zhang Ruobo, 'in the future Hunan TV as a production unit will be supplying programs both to the broadcaster and Mango TV' (Xu et al. 2014). This repositioning reflects the recognition that conventional television is just one type of content while the intellectual property associated with it may be developed via a number of outlets such as online, mobile, and interactive games (Zhang Ying 2014: 37). It also underlies a desire for a new business model that will reduce the media group's reliance on broadcasting and also allow the group to fully exploit its copyrighted materials in the digital environment.

Another path of media convergence that Chinese broadcasters pursue is to cooperate with Internet incumbents. The rationale for such cooperation is that broadcasters will draw on new media firms' strengths in technological support, data analysis, interactive content and Internet-based merchandising, and new media firms will have access to premium content and use such content to draw online traffic. Cooperation might take the form of exclusive digital rights sale of television dramas and reality shows to one or more online video streaming businesses. Prices charged for exclusive online streaming rights to the most popular shows have regularly become fodder for news in the 2010s, ranging from tens to hundreds of million yuan (RMB). Cooperation may also proceed with online video businesses becoming involved or integrated in the production, marketing, and financing of TV shows. These digital mega-firms are able to mobilize news portals, online forums and social media under their umbrellas to generate audiences for broadcasters and for themselves. A typical example is *The Voice of China* (*Zhongguo hao shengyin*), which will be briefly examined in the next section. A more novel form of cooperation is that between Dragon SATV of SMG with the e-commerce giant Alibaba in 2014. The alliance allows Alibaba's customers to use its Digital Entertainment Service to invest modest amounts of money in Dragon TV's hit reality shows, *China's Got Talent* (*Zhongguo daren xiu*) and *Chinese Idol* (*Zhongguo meng zhi sheng*). It not only allows Alibaba to become involved in content production by working with Dragon TV to design interactive content for online, mobile and gaming services (Zhang Yi: 2014), but also turns fans into voluntary marketers for the producers through being given an illusory sense of control and ownership. For both Alibaba and Dragon TV, the large amount of personal data about the fans constitutes valuable commodities deposited in data banks for future exploitation.

Increasingly, broadcasters find it lucrative to work with social media and high-tech data firms to enhance the interactivity of television so as to lure younger audiences back to television. On the night of CCTV's

Annual Spring Festival Gala in 2015, CCTV made the live broadcast of the Gala interactive by cooperating with Tencent, developer and owner of the most prominent instant messaging mobile app, WeChat. The 'shake' function of WeChat connects the television set and the mobile phone in the same living room. Very simply, shaking a mobile phone near a TV set while a TV program is on allows WeChat to recognize what is on television and hence take the audience/user to a mobile site where s/he can interact with and/or participate in the program. This is above all a commercial success. By offering cash prizes through electronic 'red packets,' advertisers on the Gala directly connected with audiences/users. For CCTV, to say the least, the new component of 'red packets' added some fun and participatory feel to the annual gala that is enjoying decreasing popularity among the Chinese. It was reported that a total of eleven billion 'shakes' were recorded during the Gala, that the frequency of interaction reached its peak at 810 million shakes per minute, and that because of this new feature, more youths and more high-income Chinese came to watch the Gala in 2015 than in 2014 (Anonymous 2015).

A few provincial satellite channels also employed this interactive feature for their own Spring Festival galas in 2015. Because users must use Tencent's own electronic payment system called 'WeChat Pay' to receive the 'red packets,' Tencent rapidly popularized 'WeChat Pay,' gaining 100 million users overnight (ibid.). In doing so, Tencent accomplished a crucial step towards commercializing the instant messaging app with 600 million users. Following the successful cooperation between broadcasters and Tencent, Tencent made 'Shake TV' a regular function for WeChat users, and soon dozens of local broadcasters signed agreements with Tencent to embed this interactive feature into hundreds of programs. Broadcasters, Tencent, and advertisers all stand to gain from the new feature as it provides highly accurate data about consumers by connecting what consumers do with their TV and mobile devices with all the data that the social media giant has collected and stored in its clouds. The impact of partnership with Baidu, Alibaba, and Tencent on Chinese television is just beginning to be unveiled.[2]

COMMERCIAL EXPLOITATIONS OF TV PROGRAMS

Intensified commercialization is manifested in the increasingly heavier exploitation of television programs through spot advertising, business sponsorship, product placement, merchandising, and franchising. As of 2013, China had become the world's third-largest advertising market and is soon to become the second largest behind the US, followed by Japan,

Germany and the UK (Yeh and Zhang 2013). Like in other countries, television remains the largest single category of all media (about 40 per cent) in advertising spending. CCTV accounts for about 20 per cent of the total advertising spending on television in the country. In recent years a small number of provincial television networks have enriched themselves with their highly lucrative satellite channels, including those in Hunan, Zhejiang, Jiangsu, Shanghai, Anhui and Beijing. Hunan TV, for example, earned RMB 5.3 billion (almost US$1 billion) in advertising revenue in 2012, more than ten times that in 2004, though still a distant second to CCTV with an earning of RMB 27 billion (US$4.5 billion) (Wang 2013). Elsewhere I have examined the centrality of drama programming to commercial television in China (Bai 2005). I explained how television drama has long been the top genre, generating the most advertising revenue, with more than 15,000 episodes of drama made annually (as of this writing).

During the past decade broadcasters and advertisers have increasingly turned to reality shows, especially as the SARFT stepped up its efforts to curtail excessive commercialism in drama programming (see Bai 2014b). In 2009, the SARFT's No. 61 Document stipulated how many commercial breaks, as well as the maximum lengths of the breaks that may be inserted in each drama episode respectively in and outside of primetime slots.[3] In October 2011, the regulator added that commercial breaks shall not appear right after opening credits or right before end credits, and that commercials shall not be shown as end credits are played.[4] Then about a month later it issued a revision to No. 61 Document, known as the 'Restraining Order on Commercials' (*xian guang ling*), by which television stations are forbidden to program any commercial break within a drama episode.[5] These measures targeting commercialism in drama programming give television stations incentives to pursue other means of monetizing programs, such as replacing some drama programming with reality shows and increasing product placement, which as of now remains an unregulated area.

Businesses may choose to advertise through sponsorship of TV shows. Business sponsorship of television programs in China started in the 1980s, when enterprises funded the production of television dramas either for public relations purposes, in the case of television manufacturers, to boost the sale of TV sets (Wen 2014). Exclusive naming rights in Chinese television can be traced to CCTV's famous weekly variety show, *Zhengda Variety* (*zhengda zongyi*). The Zhengda Group (*Chia Tai*) is a Thailand-based agricultural transnational corporation, which started trade in seeds with China in 1979 and has been sponsoring this show from 1990 till the present. CCTV started auctioning its primetime commercial slots in 1994, and added in 2002 a 'Brought to you by . . .' item so that the winning company would have its name appear as special sponsor of CCTV-1's primetime drama programs for a half-year period. Such sponsorship is in addition to conventional spot commercials surrounding the dramas. Exclusive naming rights have become an important source of revenue for television stations as 'theatres on air' (regularized slots for drama and film programming), reality shows, talk shows, sports programs, and Spring Festival Galas readily lend themselves to special sponsorship. CCTV's drama sponsorship program alone generates a profit that rose from RMB 50 million (US$8.3 million) in 2002 to more than RMB 300 hundred million (US$50 million) ten years later.[6]

Provincial television stations, however, are closing in. In 2005, Hunan TV garnered a staggering RMB 25 million (US$4.2 million) by selling the exclusive naming right of *Super Girl* (*chaoji nüsheng*) to Mengniu Yogurt, but the growth rate of exclusive sponsorship fee is no less staggering. A popular reality show may generate RMB hundreds of millions through the exclusive naming right alone. For instance, Hunan TV sold the rights for *Where Are We Going, Dad?* (*baba qu nar?*), a reality program based on an imported South Korean format featuring celebrity fathers and their children, to a dairy firm, Yili, for RMB 312 million (US$52 million) for its second season in 2014, and for RMB 500 million (US$83.3 million) for the third season in 2015.

Product placement, by which products are integrated into television programs or movies to achieve a more subtle and effective advertiser-audience relationship, was first introduced into Chinese television in 1991, when a mineral water dispenser appeared as part of the set for *Stories from the Editors' Office* (*bianjibu de gushi*), sometimes called China's first sit-com. Compared with spot advertising and exclusive sponsorship, product placement represents a small portion of the television advertising market. But like many other recently deregulated media markets, China is witnessing a rapid growth rate in product placement, with a total spend of US$103 million in 2012 as reported by a global marketing firm (Anonymous 2013). Dramas, sport events and reality programs provide ideal vehicles for product placement. During the 18-day period of the World Cup in 2014, for example, the amount of product placement on the sports channel, CCTV-5, totalled 91 hours, an average of 5.1 hours per day, more than doubling the amount of conventional commercials of 2.6 hours per day.

Provincial television channels are no less aggressive. According to a CTR report[7] based on the monitoring of product placement for May 2014, of the twelve CCTV and top ten provincial satellite channels, the three channels with the largest amount of product placement in terms of exposure time for products were Hunan SATV, Jiangsu SATV, and Shandong

SATV. Zhejiang SATV, Jiangsu SATV, and Beijing SATV used product placement with the highest frequencies, no doubt a feature of their highly successful formatted talent and reality shows (Keane 2015). In one month, 96,145 instances of product placement occupied these CCTV and provincial channels for 413 hours, with a daily average of 36 minutes of product placement per channel on 141 occasions (Zhong 2014). As products find their ways into dialogues among characters, costumes, plots, props, prizes, awards and other venues, television programs are impacted in the way they look and the way they are produced, raising the integration of television and commodities to a whole new level.

Because of the segmented nature of China's media system, cross-media operations have been spontaneous and rudimentary until recently. Earlier forms of cross-media operations existed in businesses marketing products – music, novels, tabloid stories, consumer products, etc. – associated with a popular television drama. Perhaps the earliest example of merchandising in post-Mao China can be traced to 1980, when CCTV broadcast an NBC television series, *The Man from Atlantis*. The show became so popular that sunglasses copied from those of the protagonist Mark Harris were marketed and became a fad. Prior to the 1990s, cross-media operations usually occurred independently of and frequently without permission from television stations/producers. The 1990s witnessed increasingly market-oriented television stations diversifying business lines in program trade, advertising, marketing, tourism, and real estate. Subsidiaries were created to commercialize existing assets and resources – programs were traded overseas as well as in the domestic audio-visual market; advertising and marketing services were provided for clients or potential clients of television stations; and locations services as well as paid tours were available at station-owned film and TV production bases. These initiatives took place largely within the television industry, but did not specifically facilitate cross-media synergistic planning and practice.

Against the backdrop of China's entry into the WTO, the reform of the cultural system, and the state's push for media digitalization and convergence, the term 'value chain' (*jiazhi lian*) is now a sacred word in the television industry. Maximizing the value of a program through spin-off merchandising and cross-media promotion has become a goal embedded in many television productions. *The Voice of China* illustrates the extent of synergy in Chinese television. First aired in 2012, the show is a joint production by Canxing, an independent production firm and Zhejiang SATV. It is also a format that is licensed from the parent company Talpa in the Netherlands (see Keane 2015). Its carefully coordinated promotional campaign mobilized all kinds of media – establishing an official website and opening up an official Weibo account, signing distribution agreements with multiple online audio-visual content providers, using social media as free publicity and distribution venues, and inviting representatives from major media organizations to participate in the show as 'media assessors,' so free publicity of the show is easily secured in the traditional media. TVOC generates revenues not only through advertising, sponsorship and product placement but also 'downstream' along the value chain. Spin-off products of *The Voice of China* include new spin-off competition shows, ringtone music downloads, and stars whom Canxing signs and manages for commercial performances and endorsements (Zhang and Chen 2013).

CONCLUSION

As Michael Keane (2015) argues, Chinese television is becoming 'more like its international counterparts despite the tight rein of state regulators: it is professionalizing and consolidating, while at the same time building alliances with digital media companies' (p. 12). In this chapter I have shown that similarities between Chinese and other television systems are more evident than before. The intensity of commodification and the transformative effects of digitalization are forces that are further entrenching the logic of capital in Chinese television and the broader field of cultural production. China is not exceptional. Yet at the same time the Chinese path of commercialization has been distinctive, fraught by cautious reforms and uneven performances among stations. Commercialization began when the market mechanism was injected into state television; this led to an astounding growth spurt throughout the 1990s and beyond. Yet despite growth, the actual capitalization of China's television industry was miniscule in comparison with Western-based transnational media companies; a comparison that caused CCP leaders to worry about the implications of global competition in the wake of China's entry to the World Trade Organization. Expanding the television industry and cultural industry in general thus became a priority on the Party's agenda, and this ambition was certainly shared by national and provincial broadcasters. Yet further market expansion met with institutional and ideological obstacles rooted in the dual identity of Chinese television. To break this impasse 'the reform of cultural system' was launched, the centerpiece of which was breaking down the dual identity so the highly valued assets and capacities in the broadcasting system could now be fully commercialized.

This chapter has shown how Chinese television has been re-formed and restructured so as to allow freer movement of capital trans-industrially and trans-sectorally in the years to come. Significantly, the recognition of the identity of Chinese television as business, that is, a cultural industry, takes place at the same time that the future of television is clouded by rapid technological advances that threaten to challenge television's preeminence. At the time of writing, terms like 'media convergence,' 'all-media,' 'multi-platform' and many others have entered into official and public discourses, lending urgency, justification, and legitimacy to further marketization of television. Perhaps we can say, in the light of the government's new Internet+ initiatives that the Internet is now a 'special economic zone' for broadcasters, the more aggressive of which are tagging to it to sail into the 'wonderland' of capital.

The identity of Chinese television is in great flux due to changing institutional and technological conditions. When the dust settles, its commercial nature will be solidified more than ever. A lingering set of questions concerns the public or *shiye* counterpart of commercial television. What would be the nature of the relationship between non-marketizable television operations such as management of spectrums and channels and profit-driven media groups? Is the traditional broadcaster emptied out as a result of bifurcation? In the case of SMG, reorganization along the line of bifurcation has resulted in the *shiye* broadcaster being the parent company of the media group. There may be variations in practice across different broadcasters but some kind of relationship between the two bodies is invariably retained. If so, is it possible for the broadcaster, in control of highly profitable channels, to become insulated from the market force? Is it unreasonable to expect a porous boundary between broadcasters and their commercial children? Is the dual identity issue going to return in a different form?

The future of the television industry is a question that necessitates a broader, or in Keane's words, 'cross-platform, transcultural' (2015: 11) approach, one that is willing to let go of conventional television per se as an object of study and refocus on the disappearing boundaries between television and other media industries. For example, we cannot afford to lose sight of how Internet giants such as Alibaba (e-commerce), Baidu (search engine), and Tencent (social media) are becoming major forces in cultural production, in the process transforming China's audio-visual market. Indeed, new commercial media conglomerates not unlike those in the West are now forming to take advantage of synergistic opportunities. Considering the continued existence of administrative barriers prohibiting mergers and takeovers of regionally based media, it is interesting to observe how the tensions between capital, and administrative obstacles to capital, play out.

NOTES

1. 'BesTV Plans to Merge with Oriental Pearl and Take over Four Other Companies', accessed 20 September 2015 at http://cn.reuters.com/article/chinaNews/idCNKCS0J 803720141124.
2. For this section, I benefited a lot from extended discussions with my friend, Wu Jing, an editor at Henan TV station, about Tencent and 'Shake TV.'
3. Accessed 20 September 2015 at http://www.sarft.gov.cn/articles/2009/09/10/2009091 0112458240601.html.
4. Accessed 20 September 2015 at http://www.sarft.gov.cn/articles/2011/10/12/20111012 092247790975.html.
5. Accessed 20 September 2015 at http://www.sarft.gov.cn/articles/2011/11/28/20111128 125509340939.html.
6. See 'CCTV's Bidding Prices Keep Growing,' a report of the Cultural Industry Center of 'Chinese Economy Net,' accessed 20 September 2015 at http://www.ce.cn/culture/whwx/ wz/201311/21/t20131121_1785416.shtml.
7. CTR (CVSC-TNS Research) is a major market research and media analysis company, a joint-venture between CCTV and Kantar, a UK-based media consultancy firm under the transnational advertising group, WPP.

REFERENCES

Anonymous (2013), 'Global product placement spend rises', April, accessed 10 September 2015 at http://www.warc.com/LatestNews/News/BRICs_drive_product_placement_growth_. news?ID=31278.
Anonymous (2014), 'The SARFT publicized the 2014 list of television drama production license holders', 29 April, accessed 6 May 2015 at http://zgbx.people.com.cn/n/2014/0429/ c347565-24956937.html.
Anonymous (2015), 'WeChat "Shake TV" was officially launched; more than fifty television stations have been connected', 12 March, accessed 20 June 2015 at http://news.sina.com. cn/m/2015-03-12/110231598585.shtml.
Bai, Ruoyun (2005), 'Media commercialization, entertainment, and the Party-State', *Global Media Journal* **4** (6), accessed 6 September 2015 at http://lass.purduecal.edu/cca/gmj/sp05/ graduatesp05/gmj-sp05gradinv-bai.htm.
Bai, Ruoyun (2012), 'Cultural mediation and the making of the mainstream in postsocialist China', *Media, Culture & Society* **34** (4): 391–406.
Bai, Ruoyun (2014a), *Staging Corruption: Chinese Television and Politics*. Vancouver, BC, Canada: University of British Columbia Press.
Bai, Ruoyun (2014b), '"Clean up the screen": Regulating television entertainment in the 2000s', in Ruoyun Bai and Geng Song (eds.), *Chinese Television in the Twenty-First Century: Entertaining the Nation*. London and New York: Routledge, pp. 69–86.
Fan, Xiaodong (2014), 'Hunan SATV seeks gold from the Internet: Mango TV estimated worth more than six billion yuan', *Tencent Science and Technology* 23 October, accessed 15 May 2015 at http://tech.qq.com/a/20141023/009858.htm.
He, Tianjiao (2014), 'President of Shanghai Media Group, Li Ruigang: pushing for the whole company to be publicly listed', *First Business Daily (diyi caijing ribao)* 7 November, accessed 6 May 2015 at http://finance.sina.com.cn/chanjing/gsnews/20141107/020620754524.shtml.
Huang, Yu (1994), 'Peaceful revolution: the case of television reform in post-Mao China', *Media, Culture & Society* **16**: 217–41.
Keane, Michael (2001), 'Broadcasting policy, creative compliance, and the myth of civil society in China', *Media, Culture and Society* 23: 783–98.
Keane, Michael (2015), *The Chinese Television Industry*. London: BFI, Palgrave.

Lee, Chin-Chuan (2000), 'China's journalism: The emancipatory potential of social theory', *Journalism Studies* **1** (4): 559–76.

Liu, Bonnie Rui (2010), 'Chinese TV changes face: The rise of independents', *Westminster Papers in Communication and Culture* **7** (1): 73–91.

Lotz, Amanda (2009), 'What is U.S. television now?', *The ANNALS of the American Academy of Political and Social Science* 625: 49–59.

Ma, Eric Kit-wai (2000), 'Rethinking media studies: The case of China', in James Curran and Min-Jung Park (eds.), *De-Westernizing Media Studies*. London and New York: Routledge, pp. 21–34.

National Bureau of Statistics (2011), 'Report of Statistics about National Economic and Social Development', accessed 29 January 2014 at http://www.stats.gov.cn/tjsj/tjgb/ndtjgb/qgndtjgb/201102/t20110228_30025.html.

National Development and Reform Commission (2015), 'Report of the Implementation of the 2014 Plan for National Economic and Social Development and the 2015 Provisional Plan for National Economic and Social Development', quoted by Chinese National Radio, 'Key Figures of the Internet discuss 'Internet +': increasing the innovative capacity and productive power for the Chinese Economy,' published on 16 March 2015, accessed 6 September 2015 at http://tech.cnr.cn/techds/20150316/t20150316_518011009.shtml.

Spigel, Lynn (2004), 'Introduction', in *Television after TV: Essays on a Medium in Transition*. Durham, NC: Duke University Press, pp. 1–40.

Wang, Xiaofeng (2013), 'Wars among provincial satellite television channels: Hunan SATV leads the others by 10 years', *Sanlian Life Weekly* (*sanlian shenghuo zhoukan*), accessed 6 May 2015 at http://news.ifeng.com/shendu/slshzk/detail_2013_04/07/23935939_0.shtml.

Wen, Huike (2014), *Television and the Modernization Ideal in 1980s China*. Lanham, MD: Lexington Books.

Xu, Minghua (2013), 'Television reform in the era of globalization: new trends and patterns in post-WTO China', *Telematics and Informatics* 30: 370–80.

Xu, Qinghong, Menglin Gu, Feng Liao and Yufei Gao (2014), 'Hunan SATV no longer sells rights to audio-visual service providers', *Jinghua Times* (*jinghua shibao*), 10 May, accessed 6 September 2015 at http://media.people.com.cn/n/2014/0510/c40606-24999452.html.

Yeh, Johnson, and Ming Zhang (2013), 'Taking the pulse of China's ad spending', *McKinsey Quarterly*, June, accessed 6 May 2015 at http://www.mckinsey.com/insights/media_entertainment/taking_the_pulse_of_chinas_ad_spending.

Zhang, Xiaoling (2011), *The Transformation of Political Communication in China: From Propaganda to Hegemony*. Singapore: World Scientific Publishing Company.

Zhang, Yi (2014), 'Alibaba makes inroads into the entertainment industry, signing agreement of alliance with Dragon TV', *Yangzi Evening News* (*yangzi wanbao*) 11 June.

Zhang, Ying (2014), 'Broadcasting consortia: Seeking a breakthrough by borrowing strength from the Internet', *Chinese Radio, Film and Television* (*Zhongguo guangbo yingshi*) 565: 36–41.

Zhang, Lei, and Bo Chen (2013), 'An analysis of the business strategies of *The Voice of China*', *Journal of Zhejiang University of Media and Communications* **20** (4): 79–82.

Zhao, Yuezhi (2008), *Communication in China: Political Economy, Power and Conflict*. Lanham, MD: Rowman & Littlefield.

Zhao, Elaine Jing, and Michael Keane (2013), 'Between formal and informal: the shakeout in China's online video industry', *Media, Culture & Society* **35** (6): 724–41.

Zhong, Yong (2010), 'Relations between Chinese television and the capital market: three case studies', *Media, Culture & Society* **32** (4): 649–68.

Zhong, Jiaqi (2014), 'CTR: Limited TV cake, unlimited possibilities for product placement', a report by CTR, accessed 20 September 2015 at http://www.prnasia.com/story/100690-1.shtml.

26. Between sustaining and disruptive innovation: China's digital publishing industry in the age of mobile Internet
Xiang Ren

Among China's cultural and creative industries digital publishing has the potential to change the boundaries that have previously constrained reading publics in China. Most of these boundaries are administrative, intended to channel the Chinese reading public into state approved formats and genres. Digital publishing, and more recently mobile Internet reading practices, are challenging institutional arrangements and generating disruptive technological innovations, not only in respect to publishing business models, but also administration, censorship, and reading cultures. In changing the game rules of connecting readers, content, and publishers, they broaden the scope of genres, and in doing so provide seeds of digital activism.

Yet, while there is cause for optimism, there is uncertainty about the extent to which disruptive technologies can transform established publishing models and how the relations between digital publishing, reading publics and digital activism will play out. Uncertainty exists especially when the core consumer market of mobile publishing is the *diaosi*, a demographic sometimes referred to a 'lost generation'.

In this chapter I review the development of China's digital publishing industry. I explore economic and cultural changes brought about by mobile reading as well as its role in the development of new reading cultures in China. In the first section I look at problems facing publishing more broadly before turning to the rise of digital publishing, the mobile Internet and the various industry players. Following this I examine the digital disruption in China's mobile Internet publishing industry and the digital activism of emerging reading publics.

PUBLISHING INDUSTRY IN CHINA: FROM MARKETIZATION TO DIGITIZATION

The Chinese government is proposing market-oriented reforms to upgrade the publishing sector with a focus on the transition to digital publishing

(Liu 2008). Digital publishing has achieved vast scale. According to official statistics, total revenues generated from digital content business such as e-books, e-magazines, and e-newspapers in 2014 was RMB 6.98 billion (roughly $US1.12 billion).[1] However, the digital transition presents many challenges. Compared with international publishing corporations such as Pearson, Penguin-Random House and Harper Collins, Chinese publishers, even the big publishing groups, have less technical and commercial capacity and human resources in digital publishing. In addition, government intervention and the bureaucratic administration of state-owned publishers reduce their independence and capacity to exploit digital opportunities.

The marketization of the publishing sector has gathered momentum over the past three decades and private publishing is on the rise. Regulatory barriers that previously hindered private publishers are gradually being removed, though some restrictions still exist, such as the control of publishing numbers.[2] Private publishers are dominant in genre fiction, self-help and popular culture. Despite their superior commercial competence, however, few private publishers have sufficient financial and technological capacity or relevant human capital to move proactively and confidently in digital publishing. Instead, they have to depend on digital intermediaries and aggregators and make money mostly from licencing copyrights.

Overall the publishing system in China is immature, even in the print sector. Weaknesses exist in public reading culture, copyright enforcement and publishing services. On average Chinese adults read only 4.56 print books in 2014.[3] This figure is lower than the US (7 print books), South Korea (11 print books), and Japan (8.4 print books).[4] Chinese readers spent an average of $4.30 purchasing e-books in 2014, while the figure was $46 in the US, $84.4 in the UK and $86.5 in Japan.[5] Moreover, the content of public reading is practical rather than intellectual. Chinese bestsellers are mostly about cooking, health, self-help, exam preparation and fan-generated literature. While digital publishing is the future, rampant piracy and copyright infringement threaten its commercial viability. In China the estimated number of pirated e-book websites in 2014 was 14,000; revenue generated through digital piracy was about 8–10 times the copyrighted e-book business.[6] Moreover, important publishing services and intermediaries like book clubs, book reviews, and literary agents that connect authors, readers, and content socially are absent in China (Ren 2011).

Within this environment of uncertainty the digital publishing industry is struggling to establish commercially viable and financially sustainable business models (Liu and Sun 2009). The uncertainty of the digital publishing market and difficulties in monetizing digital content place many Chinese publishers in a dilemma: they either 'have one foot in the grave' – because going digital is an irresistible trend; or, they risk self-decimation by entering the digital publishing business without reliable business models (in Chinese: *zhaosi huo dengsi*).

New technologies (either physical or social technologies) are disrupting business models, as well as administration, cultures and mindsets in China's publishing industry. The mobile Internet – and with it the mobile publishing business, delivers a new generation of disruptive technologies. Mobile publishing is a fast growing market: it provides one of the most reliable revenue sources for the emerging digital publishing industry. Mobile reading refers to 'the act of reading and consuming digital content on mobile devices', such as smart phones, tablets, and e-readers. The content of mobile reading includes e-books (digitized print book titles and born-digital online literature), e-newspapers, e-magazines, and cartoons. A wide variety of business models and innovations have been developed, harnessing the technical, social, and commercial dynamics of mobile Internet and adapting to the regulatory environment and cultural market in China. The innovations are changing the ways content is created, distributed, consumed and monetized and are making reading interactive, social and personalized.

By enabling readers to read anywhere and anytime, mobile reading has widened access to digital content and enlarged the scale of public reading in China. It provides a platform for readers to access and consume content in portable and flexible ways, during both focused and fragmented time. Mobile reading also widens knowledge access in the digital age for people from low socioeconomic backgrounds, resulting in a new generation of reading publics. While mobile reading has created new markets for digital publishing it is also profoundly changing public reading. The rise of young readerships with low-income levels and/or low-level education is shaping the business and culture of digital mobile publishing in China. In fact, some interesting tensions have become evident. With reading publics expanding, the decreasing average levels of education, income, and literacy of readers (and authors) is crucial to the future of the market. *Diaosi*, sometimes interpreted as 'China's lost generation' (Kan 2013), is one of the most noticeable cultural characteristics among emerging reading publics. The rise of *diaosi* in digital public reading requires us to revisit the historical view of publishing as enlightenment (Darnton 2009) and the belief of the power of Internet in digital activism (Yang 2013).

MOBILE INTERNET AND THE DIGITAL PUBLISHING INDUSTRY

According to the China Internet Network Information Center (CNNIC), by June 2014 China had over 527 million active mobile Internet users and for the first time the percentage of users who access Internet via mobile devices surpassed those via PCs (CNNIC 2014). 53.67 per cent of Chinese mobile Internet users read on mobile devices (Enfodesk 2013). The portability of mobile reading expands the scale and scope of reading. Chinese people exhibit highly flexible and diverse mobile reading behaviour in terms of where and when to read: public transport, office, and even toilets are places where people prefer to read via mobile devices; night time, lunch break, and bed times are the peak periods of mobile reading (CNNIC 2014; Enfodesk 2013).

The touch screen-based mobile Internet is easy and convenient to use; moreover, the price of mobile hardware is increasingly low, which greatly widens Internet access for people with low educational levels, low digital literacy and low incomes. Mobile Internet enables hundreds of millions of rural migrants working in big cities and people in rural areas to connect with the online world. Studies show that 74.3 per cent of the new generation of migrant rural workers (*nong min gong*) in cities use mobile phone to access Internet (Zhou and Lü 2011); an average of 75.3 per cent of rural people use mobile Internet, slightly higher than their urban counterparts.[7] The increase in the mobile Internet population has created a booming and potentially huge market for mobile reading. The mobile reading market in China topped total revenues of RMB 8.23 billion ($1.32 billion) in 2014 and will reach RMB 10 billion ($1.61 billion) in 2015 (Enfodesk, 2013).

The rise of mobile Internet together with the emergence of mobile reading provides publishers with a promising opportunity. According to a 2014 national survey on reading habits, a total of 41.9 per cent of people in China have read published content on mobile phones.[8] Among those who read digital content, the percentage of mobile reading is as high as 87.4 per cent (iResearch 2014). Mobile reading has stronger portability and a more easy-to-use interface than desktop-based digital publishing, which makes screen-based reading an enjoyable and convenient experience. Because it is more social and interactive mobile reading adds to readers' compulsion to read. More importantly, the mobile reading business benefits from viable electronic payment systems, either combined with mobile phone fees or through various mobile payment methods. The ease-to-pay of mobile reading removes a bottleneck in monetizing popular digital content.

Among all in-app purchases in China, online literature is the third largest category, accounting for 30.8 per cent, only less than games and social media (CNNIC 2014). The revenues generated from mobile reading accounted for on average 60–70 per cent of Chinese publishers' e-book businesses in 2014 (Yuan 2014). On all accounts mobile reading has become an essential and even leading sector of China's digital publishing industry.

MAJOR PLAYERS IN CHINA'S MOBILE READING INDUSTRY

The industry has a variety of established players and new entrants. A relatively low degree of concentration, together with a high level of firm specialization, characterizes the structure of the mobile reading industry. Despite intensive competition mobile reading in China is not an open market. Government intervention and government-backed monopoly in a number of relevant fields increase entry barriers and render the power structure of China's mobile reading industry quite complex. The players involved in the Chinese mobile reading business can be categorized into eight major forces.

Content Providers

Three types of content providers dominate in the mobile reading industry in China: state-owned publishing houses, private publishing companies and online literature sites. As a result of government control over publishing, state-owned publishing houses, magazine publishers and newspapers are the biggest copyright owners of published content. State-owned publishing houses have a monopoly in the professional and educational publishing sectors and generate reasonable digital publishing revenues through institutional markets. Government subsidies and funds raised in the stock market enable some state-owned publishers to invest heavily in expanding their digital publishing businesses without much consideration of short-term profits. In taking advantage of the monopoly and policy benefits, many state-owned publishers have generated reasonably large amounts of revenue from digital publishing. For example, Phoenix Publishing Group made over RMB 400 million ($64.41 million) through digital publishing and software services in 2014; the annual e-book sale of CITIC accounted for sales of over RMB 40 million ($6.44 million) (Yuan 2014).

As leaders in the mass market, private publishers have been proactive in harnessing the digital and mobile dynamics to expand their readership in the digital environment, particularly in their advantaged areas such as self-help, health, popular culture, business and history. The private publishers face more restriction from bureaucratic administration than state-owned publishers and thus have developed more flexible and effective collaboration with digital intermediaries and Internet companies. The sale of e-books in leading private publishing companies was around RMB 20 million ($3.22 million) in 2014 (Yuan 2014).

It is worth mentioning that the percentage of digital publishing revenue only accounts for about 5–10 per cent of total sales for publishing companies in China. Publishers still depend on print publishing sales. Generally, they are reluctant to license bestselling and new titles to digital channels due to a fear of threatening print publishing sales. Moreover, due to their lack of technological and commercial capacities, traditional publishers are disadvantaged in negotiating with digital distributors and aggregators on licencing and revenue share. This further reduces the willingness of publishers to license best content to digital channels.

Online literature is the dominant content source for the digital publishing industry and the most attractive content for readers. Its success results from a systemic coincidence: the inability of the heavily regulated and censored print publishing to service public reading demand and the dynamics of self-publishing based on millions of creative users (Ren and Montgomery 2012). It has also achieved success because Internet censorship has lagged behind the fast evolution of 'born-digital' content. According to conservative estimates, the total number of authors in online literature numbers over two million, publishing a million words each day. After Tencent acquired Shenda in 2014, the online literature industry became increasingly concentrated and formalized, compared with the early grassroots period. This formalization increased the status of content providers in the mobile reading value chain. More than that, the new monopoly company with 70 per cent market share in online literature industry, known as Yue Wen Group, will adopt more ambitious and aggressive business models based on its vast amount of copyright in bestselling fiction.

Telecommunication Companies

Three telecommunication companies between them have acquired 70 per cent of the market share in the mobile reading industry; China Mobile's He Reading has 49.1 per cent, followed by the China Unicom's Wo Reading with 12.5 per cent, and China Telecom's Tianyi Reading with 6.3 per cent.[9] The monopoly of the state-owned telecommunication companies provides a unique advantage for building their distribution dominance in the mobile reading industry. By pre-installing reading apps in smart phones, the telecommunication companies can expand the mobile reading market in extremely efficient and cost-saving ways. Further, combining mobile reading charges with other mobile phone fees makes it extremely easy for readers to pay for digital content. Telecommunication companies have also launched several popular bundles combining e-books with other value-added information services, for example, China Mobile's *Donggan Didai*.[10]

The competition between the big three is increasingly intense. China Mobile entered the mobile reading market earliest in 2008, followed by China Telecom in 2010 and China Unicom in 2011. Their business models are similar in that they take advantage of their existing infrastructure and capacity to reduce costs and build super value bundles for consumers. On the other hand, cash revenue and direct profit is not the top priority of the telecommunication corporations in mobile reading. Rather, they expect mobile reading to attract users, improve user addiction, and increase Internet traffic, which will benefit their commercial ecosystem as a whole and generate new revenue sources.

App-based Digital Distributors

Thousands of 'book apps' are transforming e-books into interactive apps, either based on individual titles or collections. Publishers, individual developers or small start-ups are major creators of these 'book apps'. It is unavoidable that a large number of book apps contain unauthorized content in China. However, these book apps have played an important role in popularizing mobile reading and connecting mobile phone users with book content, particularly in the early years. Compared with complicated digital reading based on desktop computers, the user-friendly interfaces of book apps make it extremely easy for average users, even those with low digital literacy, to access and consume digital content with simple gestures on a touch screen.

As the mobile reading market has matured, integrated mobile reading apps have gradually replaced individual book apps and become a leader in the reading apps market. The top mobile reading apps include Shuqi Novel, iReader, QQ Reader, 91 Panda Reader, Sogou Reading, Duokan and Tang Cha. They adopt one-stop-shop models, combining an e-book store (e-commerce through in-app purchases), an e-book reading app, and digital reading services like syncing highlighting and taking notes. Behind a small mobile reading app in appearance is often a large company and even an ecosystem. For instance, QQ Reader is by nature the end-user-interface of Tencent's digital publishing ecosystem, which includes the most popular social media QQ and Wechat and the monopoly online literature company Yue Wen. Likewise, iReader is a strategic partner with China Mobile: the app is pre-installed in millions of smart phones sold by the monopoly telecommunication corporation.

Internet Retailers

Internet retailers like Amazon, Dang Dang, and Jing Dong are becoming an important distribution channel for digital content in China's mobile reading industry; so are platforms that sell digital goods such as Apple App Store and Google Play Store.[11] Compared with their dominant role in the West, however, Amazon Kindle, Apple iBook, and Google Book have limited market share in China's digital content industry. In China directly purchasing an English language e-book from international e-retailers often requires Internet censorship circumvention (*fan qiang*), which presents difficulties for readers. Moreover, most mobile reading consumers are not capable of reading English language titles. Nevertheless, the readership still has a scale of millions, making China a potentially large e-book market international publishers should not neglect.

Kindle has successfully launched a local e-book store in China, partnering with Chinese All (*zhong wen zai xian*). However, the development of Kindle China, particularly the growth of market share, is not as rapid as in other international markets like Japan and Brazil. The restrictions on content and threats of digital piracy are important reasons for the lack of penetration. Kindle faces intensive competition from domestic e-commerce sites like Dang Dang and Jing Dong, which between them have accumulated large-scale readerships though selling physical books online. However, it is still difficult for these companies to transform the purchasers of print books to digital content consumers. For this reason e-commerce distributors are attempting to use e-books to attract Internet traffic of consumers and generate profit through follow-up online shopping. In 2013, Dang Dang launched a three-day storewide free e-book promotion as part of the price war among the Chinese Internet retailers. Many publishers publicly criticized this strategy for reaping commercial benefits at the expense of publishers' sustainability. This exposed the divergence between Internet retailers and publishers in the e-book business.

Digital Aggregators

Digital aggregators in China normally focus on institutional or B2B markets and for this reason they are not as visible as other forces in the mobile reading industry. However, due to the large amount of copyright they obtain from publishers and authors, they are influential powerhouses in the infrastructure of digital publishing and mobile reading industries. CNKI, Wanfang, and Weipu have been leading aggregators in academic and professional publishing industries. Chinese All (*zhong wen zai xian*) is one of the leading aggregators in trade publishing; it collaborates with nearly 300 publishing houses and 2,000 well-known authors; it was the first digital publisher to successfully file for IPO in China's stock market.

Technology Providers

China's state-owned publishers normally outsource the business of publishing technologies. Founder, a state-owned high-tech company associated with Beijing University, has been a monopoly company in the market of software solutions for Chinese language editing, publishing, design and printing. As a result the electronic files of almost all print content published in China are stored in Founder's software system. However, Founder software has a unique technical standard that is not compatible with mainstream e-book standards and software. Founder thus has a unique role in shaping the infrastructure of digital publishing in China. In recent years, new technology providers have entered the market and are challenging Founder's monopoly although it remains difficult and costly for other technology companies to transform electronic book files in the Founder formats to e-book products due to software incompatibility.

Hardware Manufacturers

Hardware manufacturers used to lead mobile reading in the very early years. Hanvon launched its e-readers with an e-ink screen in 2008 soon after Amazon's first generation Kindle in 2007. Unlike the Amazon model, Hanvon defined its e-readers as an expensive commercial gift. Yi Ren Yi Ben adopted similar strategies. This model achieved commercial success but soon encountered challenges from Apple iPads in the high-end business gift market. On the other hand the incapability of establishing an ecosystem combining digital content and hardware like Kindle further eliminated the comparative advantages of hardware manufacturers. Interestingly, the commercial success of the Kindle model stimulated a number of leading publishing groups in China to copycat through launching their own brand e-readers around 2009; for example, Reader Group and Shanghai Publishing Group. All failed very soon. After 2010, smart phone manufacturers began to show great interest in entering the mobile reading industry; for example, Xiaomi acquired mobile reading start-up Duokan and integrated mobile reading into its long-term ambition of building an ecosystem as comprehensive as Apple. When we consider

China's advantage in manufacturing, there will no doubt be opportunities and room for innovation for hardware companies in mobile reading in the future.

Networking Sites

Social media websites like Douban, Wechat and Weibo play a significant role in connecting readers with content, publishers and other readers in the mobile reading system. Douban is a SNS website allowing users to comment and rate film, books and music and share reading experience. Readers' collective opinions become important quality indicators for others to choose digital content. The popular social media Wechat and Weibo have become popular and important for e-book marketing and have the potential to transform into powerful distribution channels. The rise of social networking also enables readers to share digital content widely; as a result social media have become an essential distribution channel of unauthorized digital content in China. There are a number of popular accounts in Weibo and Wechat that function as a social hub for readers' online unauthorized sharing. One account even calls itself 'there is no e-book I can't find'.

BUSINESS INNOVATIONS IN MOBILE PUBLISHING

As a theory of change 'disruption' aptly describes transformation driven by digital technologies. Christensen uses the term 'disruptive innovation' (in contrast to sustaining innovation) to explain why already successful companies failed to adopt new technologies and business models. He believes that the operation, management and decision-making systems, and even the culture of successful companies, are barriers against adoption of disruptive technologies/innovations: these companies have lost ground to disruptive innovators (Christensen 1997). However, the theory of disruptive innovation tends to simplify the role of enterprises in a digital transformation as either disrupting or being disrupted and encounters difficulty when explaining disruptive changes in complex social and economic systems (Lepore 2014).

China's digital mobile publishing industry is characterized by the complex interplay between new entrants, established players and government regulation. The separation between content providers and digital intermediaries facilitates disruptive innovations led by Internet companies, telecommunication corporations, and various digital start-ups coming from outside the traditional publishing domain, and which are less restricted by the established publishing business, culture, and regulation. On the other hand, traditional publishers with exclusive content/copyright resources remain powerful in shaping digital transformations. As such, both sustaining and disruptive innovations (Christensen, Horn, and Johnson 2008) exist. The sustaining innovations aim to improve the models based on digitizing print content and selling individual titles similarly to physical publications. By contrast, disruptive innovations are transforming the ways content is created, distributed, and consumed in the mobile Internet environment and are creating new reading markets.

Digital publishing in China was defined and developed as a digitized print publishing system. The 'traditional' models that sell e-books in the same ways as print ones represent publishers' favoured business models in the mobile publishing age. However, many have encountered difficulties and have failed to generate reasonable revenue (Liu and Sun 2009). Fanshu, the online e-book store built by Founder, a dominant publishing technology provider, is a representative example.[12] According to iResearch (2014), over 80 per cent of Chinese readers are willing to pay for high quality digital content, but they are not satisfied with what the digital publishing industry has provided so far. The Fanshu model shows strong producer-oriented thinking, one that builds an e-book system based on what publishers and intermediaries want, and which technologically easy to provide, instead of what readers want and like.

Elsewhere, digital start-ups like Duokan and Tangcha are trying to innovate in the traditional e-book selling models by improving content quality, information services and reading experiences. Digital technologies have been used to optimize visual designs for small screen reading, personalize reading experience, enhance cloud-based syncing and sharing and upgrade social media functions. These start-ups believe that reader habits of consuming copyrighted content and paying for it can be gradually cultivated through good reading experiences in spite of the existing free pirated alternatives. However, the growth of e-book sales is too slow to satisfy copyright owners and investors. Tangcha was closed in 2014. Duokan, though acquired by mobile phone giant Xiaomi, has continued to suffer from poor revenues generated from e-book business (Li 2014).

Disruptive models showed stronger commercial viability in the Chinese mobile reading market. China Mobile Reading Base is a typical example. Those who attribute its commercial success simply to the monopoly of China Mobile tend to neglect the significance of business innovations. China Mobile Reading Base adopted an e-book subscription model as early as 2010, which is similar to the widely debated Kindle Unlimited in the West. China Mobile Reading Base prices the e-book subscription services extremely low (the lowest is only RMB3, roughly $0.5 per month).

However, based on the huge amount of users, monthly revenue reached RMB 100 million ($17 million) by 2012. Compared with the models that sell individual e-book titles, subscription spreads the risk of uncertain market demands through the economics of scale and scope. It is also easy and convenient for readers as they pay once and enjoy full access. Sometimes, readers even do not realize their purchases because e-book subscription is often combined with everyday phone charges or value-added information services. Through cheap price and super value bundles, China Mobile has successfully created a new reading market, in particular among the less educated and low-income populations in China.

Free content models are even more disruptive than e-book subscription. In China's weak copyright environment (Montgomery 2010), digital publishers need to give serious thoughts to the possibility of free content. In fact, thousands of digital piracy websites have already proved the commercial viability of free content. The question remains as to how can be formalized. Limited time free model is popular in the Kindle platform and Apple App Stores in attracting users and improving their addiction. The three day store-wide free e-book promotion launched by Dang Dang in 2013, though widely criticized, attracted thousands of millions of downloads and showed the enormous market potential of 'free' in digital publishing industry.

In late 2014, Baidu launched its free digital reading platform. For some time copyright owners had been criticizing Baidu for supporting digital piracy and reaping vast commercial benefits from online advertising boosted by free unauthorized content. The free e-book initiative is an important step taken by Baidu to formalize the piracy-related digital publishing value chain. Baidu provides readers with free copyrighted content with assured quality and promises to subsidize copyright owners based on the total clicks and download times of their content. Online advertising is the fundamental revenue-generating source. By 2013 the scale of online shopping in China reached RMB 1,850 billion (roughly $308 billion). During the 2014 Chinese online shopping festival 'the double eleven', over 60 per cent of purchases were transacted through mobile devices. In 2013, mobile marketing revenue surged to RMB 15.52 billion ($2.5 billion) in China. All these statistics[13] show tremendous potential opportunities for cross-subsidies through online advertising in the mobile publishing business.

'Big IP (Intellectual Properties)' is a popular term to describe the emergent digital content models that explore and monetize the IP resources of popular content through multiple channels. Copyright owners have realized that the revenues generated from licensing copyright to film, TV, and game industries are much more profitable than selling e-books to readers.

This is especially evident as venture capital companies and vendors have spend large amounts of money acquiring valuable IP in recent years, pushing the average price for popular online fictions to seven digits (roughly $160,000) each. The 'Big IP' strategy is now widely adopted in the Chinese online literature industry: directly charging readers for accessing content is not prioritized whereas accumulating popularity and fans has assumed far greater importance.

There is at present a standoff between 'sustaining' and 'disruptive' innovations in China's mobile publishing industry. Disruptive models expand channels for distribution and monetization of digital content in markets where piracy is rampant and readers are not willing to pay much for purchasing digital content. However, the established players (publishers particularly) in China have not been significantly disrupted: sustaining innovations are still the mainstream. The classic story of digital start-ups disrupting big corporations has rarely occurred in China's mobile publishing industry; rather, successful disruptive innovations are usually supported by monopolies (e.g. China Mobile taking advantages of its monopoly or where Baidu exploits its online advertising resources). Increasingly it is competition between traditional publishers that have the monopoly in content creation and Internet or telecommunication corporations that dominate the digital distribution channels. There is not much space for new entrants, especially digital start-ups to drive industry-wide digital disruption in China's mobile publishing industry. The heavy hand of Chinese government is another reason. All these factors discourage disruption. In the long term without open competition and disruptive start-ups digital transformation is at considerable risk of undermining economic efficiency, market dynamics, and the healthy development of China's mobile publishing industry.

DIAOSI AND THE NEW READING PUBLICS

Aside from the cultivation and marketization of mobile reading publics there is an argument that mobile reading provides seeds of digital activism in China, essentially a modality of 'digital enlightenment'. It is widely believed that the growth of public reading has contributed to the democratization of knowledge and mass enlightenment (Leavis 1939). The rise of mobile publishing and reading aligns with China's dynamic socio-economic transition, notably urbanization, the creative economy and the knowledge-based society. This transformation has generated new demands for knowledge, represented by the fast growing markets for new forms of public reading. Mobile reading has also made an unparalleled contribution to connecting traditionally disadvantaged reading populations to digital content, bridging knowledge gaps and digital divides, while nurturing digitally literate consumers for China's booming cultural industries and creative economy. Moreover, digital mobile technologies have circumvented government censorship of print publishing content and 'enlightened' digital reading publics with previously unapproved formats, genres and ideas.

In the post-Web 2.0 age mobile Internet further democratizes knowledge creation and facilitates population-wide creativity whereby creative users play an essential role in co-developing knowledge (Potts et al. 2008). Mobile publishing lowers the entry barrier of online self-expression and enables everyone from public intellectuals to common netizens to publish their creativity and opinions. It has changed the lives of millions of creative 'grassroots' people. Wang Puning (Pen name: Qiu Wuyu) was a worker who raised a family of eight by delivering bottled water. When he wrote his first online fiction, he typed 3,000 words everyday through a cheap smart phone that was perhaps the only digital device he could afford then. Now he is celebrated and wealthy through his bestselling thrill fiction. Though Wang is in the lucky top 5 per cent of grassroots authors who earn fame and decent income from writing, his story is a snapshot of China's dynamic population-wide literary creativity in the age of mobile publishing. Grassroots creativity becomes a major source of digital content for mobile reading, not only online literature (genre fictions), but also journalism and political content. The impact of the democratization and decentralization of authorship is beyond the publishing domain, creating an informed population for digital activism in China.

On the other hand, while over one third of the Chinese population has access to the mobile Internet, the Internet is no longer an elite medium. Demographic changes are shaping the culture of digital mobile reading as well as digital enlightenment and activism. Over 60 per cent of Chinese smart phone users have only high school education and below; nearly 90 per cent have a monthly income less than RMB 5,000 (roughly $800); moreover, over half of the mobile Internet population comes from non-capital cities (*er san xian chengshi*) (Gao 2013). Further, 31 per cent of Chinese Internet users are below 24 years old (Gao 2013). For these reasons the Chinese digital publishing industry categorizes the demographic features of the new reading population by the 'three lows', namely, low income, low education, and young (low age, *diling* in Chinese).

The CEO of mobile phone giant Xiaomi once remarked that the Chinese mobile Internet industry belongs to the *diaosi*. The *diaosi* demographic, with its large overlap with the 'three lows', feels desperate in moving upwards in the Chinese social hierarchy. Career advancements and life success depends more and more on social connections and the socio-economic capacities of their families. They often express their dissatisfaction in various ways in the digital public sphere. While fun-poking as explicit political participation is discouraged in China (Cheng, Liang, and Leung 2014), *diaosi* cultural elements such as anti-elitism, digital activism and populism are influencing digital culture. Yet at the same time, *diaosi* are treated as potential consumers in the Chinese Internet environment. Internet giants and digital start-ups are increasingly keen and skilful in understanding *diaosi* culture and mobilizing this demographic as consumers. *Diaosi* activism and *diaosi* consumerism are therefore key cultural elements of mobile publishing and reading.

This phenomenon demands a reconsideration of the arguments referring to China's mobile Internet in terms of enlightenment, civic participation and digital activism originating from 'elites'. It would be misleading and naively optimistic to exaggerate the potential of mobile Internet in transforming the Chinese people and society simply because of a combination of disruptive technologies and millions of active netizens. In the context of mobile reading, the complexity of digital activism engaged in by the *diaosi* reflecs the classic distinction between serious and entertaining reading and between high-brow and low-brow content.

Chong et al. (2012) assert that entertainment is one of the most significant perceived values for Chinese mobile Internet users. This trend has inevitably led to criticism that screen-based digital reading leads to shallow and fragmented content consumption. Indeed, the proportion of serious and high quality content is seriously declining. The for-profit Internet companies whose Key Performance Indicators are traffic and 'click rate' further enhance the trend of entertainment-oriented shallow reading. Adding to this argument is the fact that fan-created online literature has dominated mobile reading content: 42 per cent of smart phone users read online fiction and 30.8 per cent have paid for online literature (only less than mobile game and social media) (CNNIC 2014). Globally the prevalence of porn, pulp, and vulgar content is a defining feature of online literature and to some extent this makes online literature a synonym of trash in China.[14] Many are worried that the consumption of such content will reduce reading publics' capabilities in critical thinking and in-depth learning.

Undeniably mobile reading makes digital content (and online interactivity) that was previously mostly accessed by 'elites' (the rich, educated, digitally literate) accessible for the mass online population (the 'everyperson'). However, the dominance of entertainment distracts mobile Internet users from seeking out uncensored digital content and this reduces political dynamics like 'connecting citizens to civil society' (Cheng et al. 2014).

Estimated suggest that only 18 million Internet users in China use censorship circumvention tools, compared with a total of more than 600 million Internet users. Furthermore, Mou and Atkin (2014: 16) believe that accessing politically sensitive content is not the major reason for using circumvention tools (keeping social connections and fluent information flows are), which 'may counter the expectations of social activists and even policy makers'.

Public reading studies have identified a gap in cultural consumption and tastes among different classes in society (Hart 1950). The divergence between elitist and massive public reading is enlarged in the mobile age in China. Meanwhile Chinese consumers who buy English e-books from Amazon Kindle, Apple and Google and users of high quality serious content are growing in the mobile age. However, the majority of mobile readership is the so-called 'three low' or *diaosi* population and their preferences for entertaining, easy-to-follow, and so-called 'low browse' content are shaping the Chinese digital content ecosystems. The dominance of the less-educated, low-income readership combined with low quality content in digital public reading raises questions about the 'quality' of China's creative economy and knowledge society. In addition to severe Internet control by the Chinese government, the depoliticization of public reading caused by entertainment represents a direct threat to digital enlightenment and activism.

CONCLUSION

The Chinese government is investing heavily and promoting public reading. However, the motivations behind official public reading agendas are more about ideological concerns and economic benefits, ensuring the dominance of official values in digital content systems, creating markets for emerging cultural industries and training new labour forces for economic transitions. Digital censorship in mobile publishing and reading has coevolved with technological developments. The Chinese government issues licenses for e-book business and increasingly restricts market entry in the online content industry. Officials have realized the difficulties of pre-publication control in the digital age and have gradually shifted the responsibility of censorship to post-publication controls and self-censorship. Campaigns like 'Cleaning Up the Web' are frequently used to delete 'unhealthy' content and deter digital publishing companies. In 2015, Chinese regulators required online literature authors to register with their real names, aiming to enhance self-censorship of fan-generated-fiction.[15]

Despite the trend towards entertainment and the response of the government, mobile reading is providing a significant boost for the digital publishing industry in China. In addition to established publishers, a wide range of telecommunication corporations, Internet firms, and digital start-ups are involved in mobile publishing. Both sustaining and disruptive models are emerging; these are transforming the creation, distribution, consumption and monetization of digital content. As I have shown, mobile reading greatly enlarges digital reading publics, engaging previously excluded populations with low education, low incomes and low digital literacy. This process helps to democratize arts and knowledge in a highly controlled media system and contributes to the Chinese creative economy. However, the potential of digital enlightenment is being constrained by a variety of commercial, cultural and political forces. The complexity has resulted in uncertainty about the future of mobile reading in China. It remains a question whether mobile reading will lead to an economically efficient digital publishing system and informed, enlightened, and active digital reading publics. Both are crucial in building the Chinese creative economy, especially considering the latest national strategy of 'Internet+' that calls for population-wide creativity and grassroots start-ups.

NOTES

1. According to the 2014–15 annual report of Chinese digital publishing by the Chinese Academy of Publishing and Press, see the brief of the report at http://cips.chinapublish. com.cn/yjsdt/201507/t20150715_168554.html.
2. The ISBN (international standard book number) and ISSN (international standard serial number) are issued through the Chinese governmental institution only in China, and function as a license to publish an individual title legally. At the moment, state-owned publishers and a very small number of approved private publishers are issued publishing numbers while other private publishers have to buy numbers from them and have their content edited and censored by the issuers as well.
3. See the brief report of the 12th National Reading Survey in China at http://www. chuban.cc/yw/201504/t20150420_165698.html.
4. See 'China is facing a crisis of public reading' at http://edu.people.com.cn/n/2014/0425/ c1053-24940454.html.
5. See 'Japanese readers spend the most on electronic books' at http://www.donotlink. com/framed?756730.
6. See 'Making money through digital piracy will not be allowed' by Yang Yang, accessed 25 September 2015 at http://www.eeo.com.cn/2014/0525/261030.shtml.
7. See an investigation of Internet use by rural people, accessed 20 September 2015, http:// it.21cn.com/tel/a/2014/0211/16/26364581.shtml.
8. See a press release of the report, accessed 25 September 2015 at http://mil.chinanews. com/cul/2014/04-21/6088016.shtml.
9. See detailed statistics, accessed 20 June 2015 at http://news.xinhuanet.com/zgjx/2014-10/16/c_133720868.htm.
10. It is a bundle of mobile telecommunication services provided by China Mobile. With a monthly minimum fee of RMB 10, users have complimentary 120 text messages, access to digital content like e-books, mobile music, and so forth.

11.   The difference between e-retailers and app-based distributors is that the former also sell other digital content commodities while the latter mostly focus on digital publishing products and particularly e-books only.
12.   Though Fanshu has over 600,000 e-book titles, it had an annual revenue of only 1.14 million RMB yuan with over 21 million RMB yuan loss in 2010. Baidu acquired it in 2011, but has not changed its difficult situation. The difficulties could be attributed to rampant piracy and copyright infringement in China. However, the low quality of content, over-priced e-book titles, poor compatibility with mobile devices, and DRM-caused inconvenience for readers are also reasons for the failure.
13.   See relevant statistical information, accessed 20 July 2015 at www.diankeji.com/news/7998.html http://a.iresearch.cn/onm/20140920/238309.shtml.
14.   See some criticism by leading newspapers in China, accessed 25 September 2015 at http://www.infzm.com/content/101017 epaper.gmw.cn/gmrb/images/. . ./2011120209_pdf.pdf.
15.   See the governmental guideline for improving healthy development of online literature, accessed 15 August 2015 at http://www.gapp.gov.cn/news/1663/236795.shtml.

REFERENCES

Cheng, Yang, Jingwen Liang, and Louis Leung (2014), 'Social network service use on mobile devices: An examination of gratifications, civic attitudes and civic engagement in China', *New Media and Society* **17** (7): 1096–1116.
Chong, Xiaoli, Jinlong Zhang, Kin-Kueung Lai and Lie Nie (2012), 'An empirical analysis of mobile internet acceptance from a value–based view', *International Journal of Mobile Communications* **10** (5): 536–57.
Christensen, Clayton M. (1997), *The Innovator's Dilemma: When New Technologies Cause Great Firms to Fail.* Boston, MA: Harvard Business Review Press.
Christensen, Clayton M., Michael B. Horn, and Curtis W. Johnson (2008), *Disrupting Class: How Disruptive Innovation Will Change the Way the World Learns.* New York: McGraw-Hill.
CNNIC (2014), *2014 Chinese Mobile Internet Research Report.* Beijing.
Darnton, Robert (2009), *The Business of Enlightenment: a Publishing History of the Encyclopédie, 1775–1800.* Cambridge, MA: Harvard University Press.
Enfodesk (2013), *2013 Research Report on China's Mobile Reading Industry.* Beijing.
Gao, Chunmei (2013), *2012 nian zhongguo yidong hulianwang yonghu baogao* ('2012 report on China's mobile Internet users'), in Jianwen Guan and Shenhong Tang (eds.), *Zhongguo yidong hulanwang fazhan baogao 2013* (*Annual Report on China's Mobile Internet Development 2013*). Beijing: Social Science Academic Press, pp. 61–81.
Hart, James David (1950), *The Popular Book: A History of America's Literary Taste.* London: University of California Press.
iResearch (2014), *China Mobile Digital Reading Report.* Beijing.
Kan, Karita (2013), 'The new "lost generation": inequality and discontent among Chinese youth', *China Perspectives*, 2: 67–73.
Kissinger, Jeff S. (2013), 'The social and mobile learning experiences of students using mobile e-books', *JALN – Journal of Asynchronous Learning Networks*, **17** (1): 155–70.
Leavis, Queenie Dorothy (1939), *Fiction and the Reading Public.* London: Chatto and Windus.
Lepore, Jill (2014), 'The disruption machine: What the gospel of innovation gets wrong', *New Yorker* 23 June, accessed 25 September 2015 at http://www.newyorker.com/magazine/2014/06/23/the-disruption-machine.
Li, Nan (2014), *duokan zoudao shizi lukou* ('Duokan is at an intersection'), *Publishers* 7, S: 26–8, accessed 25 September 2015 at http://www.chinadaily.com.cn/hqcj/xfly/2014-07-10/content_11987127.html.

Liu, Binjie (2008), 'Use of digitization to modernize China's publishing industry', *Publishing Research Quarterly* **24** (1): 40–47.

Liu, Zheng and Tan Sun (2009), 'E-books in China: develop and use', Paper presented at the World Library and Information Congress: 75th IFLA General Conference and Council, Milan, Italy.

Montgomery, Lucy (2010), *China's Creative Industries: Copyright, Social Network Markets and the Business of Culture in a Digital Age*. Cheltenham, UK and Northampton, MA, USA: Edward Elgar.

Mou, Yi, Kevin Wu, and David Atkin (2014), 'Understanding the use of circumvention tools to bypass online censorship', *New Media and Society* (online first version), accessed 25 September 2015 at http://nms.sagepub.com/content/early/2014/08/27/1461444814548994. abstract.

Potts, Jason, John Hartley, John Banks, Jean Burgess, Rachel Cobcroft, Stuart Cunningham and Lucy Montgomery (2008), 'Consumer co-creation and situated creativity', *Industry and Innovation* **15** (5): 459–74.

Ren, Xiang (2011), *shuzi chuban yao ti chuantong chuban huan san bi zhai* ('Digital publishing needs to pay debts for traditional publishing'), *chuban cankao* (*Information on Publication*) 7: 18.

Ren, Xiang and Lucy Montgomery (2012), 'Chinese online literature: creative consumers and evolving business models', *Arts Marketing: An International Journal* **2** (2): 118–30.

Yang, Guobin (2013), *The Power of the Internet in China: Citizen Activism Online*. New York City: Columbia University Press.

Yuan, Yewei (2014), *chuantong chuban jigou shuzi chuban shouru da pandian* ('How much money traditional publishers made in digital publishing'), *chuban shangwu zhoubao* (*China Publishing Today*) 13 November.

Zhou, Baohua and Shuning Lü (2011), *Shanghai Shi xinshengdai nongmingong xinmeiti shiyong yu pingjia de shizheng yanjiu* ('An empirical study on the uses of new media by new generation of migrant rural workers in Shanghai'), *xinwen daxue* (*Journalism Quarterly*) 2: 145–50.

27. Getting connected in China: taming the mobile screen
Elaine Jing Zhao

The cultural and creative industries in China are more than ever before reliant on content, and less on propaganda. The old image of state-owned cultural institutions (*shiye*) dispensing pedagogic content to a loyal mass audience has ceded to a more dynamic model that closely follows international developments in digital media and the protection of copyrights – although the sustainability of this model and its international competitiveness inevitably relies on state policy. The new players in the market are testing boundaries. The audiovisual entertainment market-place is where we see these tensions playing out. How this impacts on the state's conceptualization of 'national cultural industries' that might con-tribute to China becoming a 'strong cultural power' is unclear. The mass audience is fragmented, nomadic and inclined to be disloyal. Whereas in the past people's lives were physically shaped by face-to-face social rituals, now these same rituals have become part of the digital landscape of 'connected viewing'.

The online audio-visual market in China is witnessing the co-evolution of technology, culture and economy. In this chapter I focus on emerging mobile and social viewing practices, as well as a number of industry innovations. I start with an overview of the rise of mobile and social viewing in China. I provide an illustrative example of the changing viewing cultures around the annual Spring Festival Eve Gala, a well-established ritual in the country. Following this I look at several initiatives in the industry, including text messaging for interactive experiences, the development of innovative mobile apps, the marriage of soft- and hardware, and the integration of social apps in content distribution. I offer an analysis of the impact of socially networked viewing on content production strategies as well as changes in distribution and promotion strategies. In doing so, I draw attention to the structural forces shaping these developments, as well as collaborations and tensions between different forces. Based on these analyses I conceptualise the various modalities of convergence and connectedness in China.

The audiovisual entertainment marketplace has witnessed rapid changes in viewing practices – from traditional TV sets in the 1950s to VCD and DVD players in the 1990s to laptop computers and today's smart mobile devices. This evolution of digital technologies has created alternative temporal and spatial engagement opportunities. Online viewing and time-shifting alternatives has meant that an increasing number of people are now 'connected viewers' (Holt and Sanson 2014). Viewing practices have changed with the adoption of media technologies, extending from the living room to the bedroom and from the bus to the metro. What used to be a family or communal entertainment activity becomes more individual-ized, yet social in new ways.

Both academic and industry understandings of convergence have gone beyond the technological level. As Henry Jenkins argues, convergence is not an end result but rather a *process* that changes how media is con-sumed and produced (Jenkins 2006). The broadcasting era, previously dominated by one-to-many distribution strategies, has transitioned to a moment characterised by 'interactive exchanges, multiple sites of produc-tivity, and diverse modes of interpretation and use' (Curtin 2009). In this brave new world of 'connected viewing', media companies are deploying multi-platform programming strategies, revaluing digital audiences, and experimenting with interactivity and user engagement (Holt and Sanson 2014: 4). The leaders in the emerging landscape, Google, Netflix, iTunes, Amazon, Hulu, Yahoo and Facebook, what Cunningham and Silver call the 'King Kongs' of the online distribution world, have created new markets and new forms of content: they are challenging the dominance of traditional media (Cunningham and Silver 2013).

As the television industry transforms globally as a result of the techno-logical imperatives of content production, consumption and distribution (Hartley 2009; Turner and Tay 2009), it is struggling to adapt in China. Describing the evolution of the Chinese television industry, Keane (2015) shows how the medium is facing an unprecedented challenge from the numerous online video platforms that have been nurtured by the Internet economy. With their origins in informal media economies, best repre-sented by peer-to-peer sharing and user-generated content, these online players have now become formal legal entities (Zhao and Keane 2013). Indeed, copyright content acquisition and original content production (Zhao 2014) are the main competitive advantages for addressing the market demand for creative content. The proliferation of viewing devices, together with an improved network infrastructure, has nurtured frag-mented viewing cultures, not only facilitating cross-platform, time-and-place shifting viewing experiences, but also increasing viewer engagement with content. The evolution of viewing cultures offers an opportu-nity to re-theorise convergence and the 'connected viewing' experience. Furthermore, they represent a new way of understanding media content production in China, which in the past has largely followed the dictates of the regulators in Beijing, namely SAPPRFT (the State Administration of Press, Publication, Radio, Film and Television).[1]

RISE OF MOBILE AND SOCIAL VIEWING IN CHINA

According to the China Internet Network Information Center (CNNIC) (2014), the user base of online video services in China has maintained an average annual growth rate over 60 per cent between 2007 and 2013, reaching 428 million by the end of 2013. This accounts for 69.3 per cent of total Internet users. While online viewing was predominantly PC-based, the report showed a 12.8 per cent increase in mobile viewing and a decrease of 17.5 per cent in online video viewing on PC during this period (CNNIC, 2014). Bigger-screen smartphones and tablets, and Wi-Fi-equipped homes are cited as the top two reasons for viewing online via mobile devices.

In addition, the stronger capacity of large volume data transmission has facilitated the growth of mobile video viewing in China. In December 2013, the issuance of TD-LTE licences to three major telecom operators in China signalled the trial of 4G services. In June 2014, the Ministry of Industry and Information Technology (MIIT) further issued two FDD-LTE licences to China Telecom and China Unicom to promote the adoption of the 4G network. For users this means better picture and sound quality, but perhaps more important, faster data transmission. In fact, smooth streaming with no hiccups was cited as the top consideration in selecting mobile video platforms (CNNIC 2014). Meanwhile, lowering tariff rates is likely to facilitate the growth of mobile viewing habits. For example, China Mobile introduced several measures to slash the 4G service tariff in June 2014, including lowering the entry barrier for 4G service from RMB 40 to RMB 30, doubling the data traffic of the original price, and introducing quarterly and half-year packages in addition to the monthly packages. In early 2015, Premier Li Keqiang repeatedly called for lower Internet fees and better speed (*China Daily* 2015). Overall, the increasing adoption of bigger-screen mobile devices, the advance of network infrastructure, as well as lower tariffs, have been driving viewership towards mobile platforms.

As multi-platform viewing habits are growing, users are increasingly connected to each other via social media. Such connectedness informs their viewing choice and facilitates exchanges of views. By the end of 2013, Weibo and Wechat had become the two major sites where people share videos (CNNIC 2014). Moreover, users perceive social ratings as more reliable than various 'top charts' provided by online video platforms themselves. This social rating mechanism helps users to discover content that appeals to them. More importantly, the users in turn become a key link in the circuit of distribution, increasing the scope of distribution and expanding the range of content available in what is still a highly regulated market. As such, social platforms function as a site of discovery and discussion of content, both legal and illegal (Kokas 2014).

People increasingly have two screens on at the same time, shifting from one to the other freely. An illustrative example of this multi-tasking practice is the Spring Festival Eve Gala (*chunjie lianhuan wanhui*), broadcast by China Central Television (CCTV) and watched by hundreds of millions on the eve of the lunar New Year. First conceived in 1983, the annual television event adds a distinctively national character to the occasion, transcending immediate families and narrow localities (Zhao 1998). While charged with the mission of wiring families to the state, the Gala has over the years lost touch with the national audience as a result of stringent censorship, packaged official propaganda and a proliferating array of alternative entertainment. This disinterest is especially evident among younger generations, who have grown up in the era of consumer markets and who are materialistic, individualistic and more sceptical than previous generations (Zhao 1998). Overseas drama and variety shows, either acquired by online video distribution platforms or downloaded from illegal sources, appeal more than officially sanctioned entertainment shows.

The wide adoption of Weibo and Wechat, however, has to some extent revived the interest in watching the Gala live. On this important occasion of family reunion and new-year celebration, the Gala is now reconnecting people across the nation thanks to digital media affordances. Mobile screens and social media bring geographically distributed people together, forming a community of connected viewing. In the words of the well-known CCTV host Zhao Zhongxiang, 'I am watching the Spring Festival Gala. I am also browsing Weibo and sending text messages. These are what make Chinese New Year's Eve'.

The Spring Festival Eve Gala is one of the most difficult television shows to produce in China. Targeting a national audience makes it difficult to please everybody. In this institutionalised media event deeply embedded in the culture of Chinese New Year's celebration, today's audience seem to be deriving entertainment more from collectively commenting on the show than simply watching it. From revealing the tricks behind the magic performance to complaining about insipid skits (*xiaopin*) to identifying online sources of witty remarks in cross-talk (*xiangsheng*), viewers are active online, mostly with their mobile phones as a secondary screen. Meanwhile, a large following exists on Weibo who express their feelings with a brief 'Haha' or emoticons. Although the Gala is typically bland and propagandist, commentary is interesting. For many viewers the messages on Weibo are now an important part of the Gala and not to be missed. Moreover, without watching the Gala, they will find it hard to figure out the meaning of message streams on Weibo or Wechat. Similar live shows, such as variety shows based on format adaptations, have also witnessed such trends. *I am a Singer* (*wo shi geshou*), a singing competition adapted by Hunan satellite TV from the original Korean show, has aggregated a fan base of over 2.5 million. Many viewers follow the Weibo accounts of the singer-competitors in the show, resulting in a growing fan base of the program account. The synergistic effect between the social media and the celebrity accounts on Weibo facilitates dialogues about the show. Such interactions grow the viewer base and enhance viewer loyalty.

While social apps have revived people's interest in viewing live shows such as the Spring Festival Eve Gala, such second-screen viewing experiences proliferate beyond 'live shows'. As mentioned previously, Weibo and Wechat are important social platforms for video sharing. Titles of popular dramas often appear in the trending topics of Weibo and comments are shared among circles of friends on Wechat. Considering the evolution of viewing habits, it is critical that industry incumbents respond to these changes by integrating the mobile and social within the viewing experience.

TAMING THE MOBILE SCREEN

Early attempts at integrating mobile and social elements into the viewing experience can be traced back prior to the app age when television stations used text messaging for user interactions, namely through puzzles, quizzes and trivia. Revenue-sharing deals between television stations and telecom service providers were big incentives for both parties. What really resulted in a national sensation, though, was an experiment by Hunan Satellite TV in southern China.

In 2004, Hunan Satellite TV (HSTV) threw out a challenge to the traditional Chinese TV culture. Its singing competition *Super Girl* (*chaoji nüsheng*), modelled after the *Idol* format, allowed the audience to vote for contestants by sending text messages from their mobile phones. This was in sharp contrast to popular entertainment in China, which was subject to direct state intervention, meaning that content was vetted before being broadcast. Now the audience could have their voice heard: they selected and supported their own idols instead of merely appreciating those handpicked by the authorities. The possibility of audience voting via text messages generated tremendous interest among the national audience. To circumvent the top limit of the votes allowed for one mobile number, many fans pooled money together to buy new mobile phone numbers to vote for their favourite singers (Xiao 2005). The program received unprecedented ratings for regional satellite TV. According to data from 2005, when *Super Girl* was at its peak, viewers' votes via text messages generated over RMB 100 million (approximately US$15.66 million) for Hunan TV (Zhu 2011).

This annual wannabe pop star competition gained momentum for several years until the then media watchdog SARFT banned the broadcast of talent shows during prime time and limited votes for talent show candidates to those cast inside the studios (Xinhua 2007). In other words, votes cast outside the studio, including those sent via mobile phones, were banned. *Super Girl* was eventually banned by the government in 2011. While the official announcement cited an overlong program running time as the reason for its cancellation, many believed the real reason was the national voting mechanism via mobile used to determine the winners (Zhu 2011). Such mobile-mediated resemblance to democracy was perceived as subversive by the authorities. In 2009 Hunan Satellite TV launched another similar program, *Happy Girl* (*kuaile nvsheng*), but scaled down text messaging by restricting voting to a studio audience.

While the early innovation in bringing TV and mobile screens together was nipped in the bud, viewing cultures have not stopped evolving, nor have industry strategies. As mentioned previously, mobile devices are both a viewing platform and an interaction tool; they not only connect viewers and content in new ways, but also connect geographically distributed viewers with shared interests. Moreover, while television stations have run up against the policy barrier, major online video platforms have adopted various strategies to facilitate connectedness.

First, industry incumbents have placed increasing emphasis on copyright as a key competitive advantage (Zhao and Keane 2013). In this way mobile distribution is included in the copyright negotiation. According to Gong Yu, CEO of iQiyi, the service provider has witnessed a sharp growth of mobile traffic, accounting for 28 per cent of the total traffic by the end of 2012, compared to less than 4 per cent a year earlier (Shi and Hu 2013). The growth rate is much faster than distribution over PC. Because of such growth on mobile, in 2013 iQiyi began to include mobile distribution in all negotiations over copyright content acquisitions, significantly increasing the amount of content licensed for mobile platforms (Shi and Hu 2013).

Meanwhile, major online distribution platforms have developed mobile applications in order to expand viewership via smartphones and tablets. According to Gu Yongqiang, CEO of Youku Tudou, while the traffic of online video platforms mainly relies on a search engine in PC-dominated viewing, mobile applications have become more important as viewership shifts towards the mobile screen (Wang 2013). The importance of gaining users via mobile has pushed the industry towards further consolidation. In 2013, Baidu acquired PPStream Inc.'s online video business for US$370million, which is now operating as a sub-brand of Baidu's online video arm iQiyi. The move was a strategy to bolster iQiyi's position in the mobile video market, as most of the traffic for PPS was generated by mobile application users (Gao and Chen 2013). It is evident that technological convergence is accompanied by economic convergence.

In addition to developing mobile applications, some online video platforms have joined hands with hardware manufacturers to stake out a position in the mobile video market. For example, in April 2013, Sohu Video sealed an exclusive deal with Samsung to pre-install its mobile app in all Samsung mobile phones and tablets sold in China over the next three years, starting with the flagship product Galaxy S4. The exclusive collaboration with one of the leading mobile brands in China may help Sohu to attract mobile video users.

The strategy of integration between software and hardware targets a defined market. In 2013, Xunlei cooperated with Vivo, a smartphone brand of consumer electronics manufacturer BBK to launch the Xplay3S model. Vivo is well known for its aspiration of delivering premium audio-visual entertainment experience. Under the slogan of 'Hi-Fi and Smart', the Xplay3S model was a flagship of the brand, targeting music and movie fans. On the hardware front, it has launched a 6.0 inch 2560*1440 pixel super high-definition screen with capability to support 4k video (ultra HD) owing to the strong core processor, graphic processing unit and memory. Further, it is the industry's first smartphone featuring DTS Headphone:X technology, which renders up to 7.1 channels of surround sound over any pair of headphones (Vivo 2014).

To put technologies to work, mobile devices need premium quality audio-visual resources. Vivo's collaboration with Xunlei allows users to access a vast library of movies, including over 200 DTS-HD movies, over 400 1080P standard movies and over 1000 720P standard movies (Vivo 2014). Further, Vivo users are entitled to one-year free Xunlei VIP membership, which delivers the advantage of accessing the latest movies and getting rid of interruptive advertising. By offering a cinema on the go, Xunlei's collaboration with Vivo may extend its reach to smartphone users.

Similarly, iQiyi has collaborated with mobile device manufacturer to capture the market opportunity in the shift in viewership towards the mobile screen. Its 'iQiyi inside' strategy, launched in 2013, pre-installs its content resources in hardware devices: in so doing iQiyi hopes to expand its market. Advertising revenue is shared between iQiyi and its hardware partner. Initially, iQiyi cooperated with TCL, a leading consumer electronics manufacturer in China to launch a smart TV named TV+. Then it moved on to attract eyeballs to its service on the mobile screen by partnering with mobile manufacturers including 100+ and Huawei. According to statistics released by iResearch in February 2014, mobile traffic accounts for more than 50 per cent of the total traffic of those accessing its video service, with a monthly mobile viewership reaching more than 99 million (iResearch 2014). The extension of the 'iQiyi inside' strategy to the mobile terminal illustrates the importance of mobile viewership to business growth.

As online video platforms move ahead to cultivate the new market, television stations have started to collaborate with online video platforms to deliver a multi-screen experience for the audience. Audiences can view outtakes, uncut versions and mini versions on their online and mobile devices, which extend and enhance their interaction with the content across platforms (Keane and Zhao 2015). *Hero of Chinese Characters* (*hanzi yingxiong*), a game show focusing on Chinese characters broadcast by Henan Satellite TV, allows viewers to access content via PC or mobile 1.5 hours after the TV broadcast.

While advertising remains the major revenue source for both television stations and online video service providers, some are trying to cultivate paying users. In April 2013, Sohu agreed upon a deal with China Unicom that allowed China Unicom users a RMB 15 monthly data package for unlimited audio-visual content via mobile browser and mobile app. As a first data package for mobile video, it may dispel users' concern over the cost of watching mobile video, and thus cultivate their mobile viewing habits and expand the user base. For the telecom operator, the collaboration with the online video distributor enhances its competitiveness in content and increases its revenue streams. Both the collaborations with mobile device manufacturers and with telecom service providers have signalled Sohu's determination to tame the mobile screen. The latter offers more possibility of additional revenue streams. The question still remains as to whether or not users are willing to pay for mobile video service as a stand-alone service.

Having applications on mobile is one thing: the extent that people use them and are willing to pay for services is another; this is a challenge faced by industry incumbents that make considerable revenues from user payments. Founded in 2003, Xunlei established itself as the leading online video download manager in China owing to its acceleration feature, which significantly improves user experience. Its subscription services allow users to enjoy premium download speeds and advertising-free streaming services. According to the financial results of the third quarter of 2014, revenue from user subscriptions accounted for over 50 per cent of the total revenue (Xunlei Ltd. 2014).

With the increasing adoption of Wi-Fi and faster network infrastructure, Xunlei has to reconsider its position in a market where viewers increasingly embrace the mobile platform and where streaming is now more popular than downloading. To adapt to the shifting viewing habits Xunlei launched a streaming app 'Xunlei Kankan', which can run on PCs, mobile phones and tablets. Such a strategy may help Xunlei to grow its user base as people increasingly watch streaming videos on multiple devices. Moreover, premium service subscribers can access synchronised content across multiple devices. This feature accommodates users' habit of place-shifted viewing where, for example, they watch on mobile what they have not finished on PC when going out or lying on the bed. Premium services also include advertising-free content, narrowed release window, and high-definition image quality.

While mobile devices and applications are important for online video platforms to drive mobile video usage, multiplatform distribution is only part of the story. Content and service play a significant role in attracting and maintaining users, especially paying users. For online video service providers, connected viewing thus raises the question of how best to capture the mobile opportunity by updating their screen media practice in content production, distribution and promotion. The emerging trend of connected viewing requires online video service providers to consider a larger ecosystem including hardware manufacturers and telecom service providers as well as their own strategic positions and possible collaborations in the ecosystem.

THE GENERATIVE NATURE OF CONNECTED VIEWING

Whether mobile or stationary, viewers are more than ever socially networked. As new forms of user engagement take shape, the social ecosystem plays a significant role in mobile video discovery and consumption. As mentioned previously, Weibo and Wechat, usually accessed via mobile, have become important sites of conversations about audio-visual entertainment. Some user interactions are synchronous with the viewing of screen content, making viewing a 'shared event' (Lee and Andrejevic 2014: 42). Such multi-screen, socially networked viewing experience has reinvigorated the meaning of 'liveness'. While on-demand viewing through time-shifting technologies allows viewers to circumvent the constraints of broadcast schedule, real-time viewing has to some extent staged a comeback as a networked and social event. Other interactions are asynchronous with the viewing activities, ranging from content search and discovery to after-viewing discussions of plot development and even to inquiries about the clothes worn by the characters.

The socialisation of screen content consumption provides an opportunity for industry incumbents who might carve out a share of the market by responding to these emerging viewing habits. Compared with other leading online video platforms such as Youku Tudou, Sohu and iQiyi, Tencent is a latecomer to the online video market. While some players have to resort to strategic restructuring through mergers and acquisitions to catch the mobile opportunity, Tencent is relying on its social media empire including the mobile app Wechat to boost its position in the online video market. Launched in 2011, Tencent Video is integrated with other social platforms under Tencent, including the messaging service Tencent IM, social network Qzone, and the micro-messaging service Tencent Weibo. For example, the integration with Wechat allows users to click and share videos with their friends on Wechat. While Wechat helps to draw users to Tencent's online video platform through discussions and social recommendation, Tencent has another weapon, a Vine-like app called Weishi. Integrated into Tencent's account system, it allows users to log in with their QQ, Tencent Weibo or QQ Mailbox accounts and create video clips up to eight seconds from their smartphones and share them in Wechat and Tencent Weibo.

Launched with mobile audiences in mind, the micro-video sharing app might increase Tencent Weibo's value proposition to Internet users. The short video app offers content complementary to Tencent's current strategy, which is dominated by big spending in copyright licensing and big productions. Interaction features such as 'comment', 'forward' and 'like' are embedded into the app to exploit user interaction with videos and among viewers with similar interests and taste. The social engine builds on the participatory culture to drive the growth of the mobile audience. Attracting celebrity users is a similar strategy, previously adopted by Sina Weibo in its early days to drive user growth. As the market matures, apart from developing a strong content library of professionally produced content, socialisation of online video consumption gives Tencent a significant competitive advantage in aggregating users and enhancing the advertising value of the platform (Zheng and Zhang 2012).

Further, the generative nature of connected viewing now has a role in content production; for example the micro-video sharing app Weishi has become a platform of talent discovery for reality shows. *Voice of Weishi* (*weishi hao shengyin*), an original music talk show launched by Tencent in 2014, served as a platform for blind audition in the third season of *The*

Voice of China (*Zhongguo hao shengyin*), a smash-hit singing competition adapted from *The Voice of Holland*, produced by Zhejiang Satellite TV, garnering the No.1 viewership rating among shows in its category. The mobile app provides a platform for social dynamics integrated with the talent show and builds upon the previous success of the first two seasons. Tencent used similar strategies for the popular dating show *If You are the One* (*feicheng wurao*), broadcast by Jiangsu Satellite TV and distributed on Tencent in 2014. Before Single's Day (*guanggun jie*), Weishi launched the online activity whereby 'single' users were encouraged to create and upload a micro-video with the tag of 'If you are the One Weishi activity'. Participants may encounter a romance online or walk onto the stage as a participant of the reality TV show. The online activity resulted in numerous submissions and the micro-videos received over a million views within a week (Zhu 2014).

Such user engagement via mobile apps has gone beyond in-program or post-program comment and discussions: it intervenes in the flow of content production. Moreover, online activities prior to the program serve as a 'pre-heat'; they attract attention and engagement from users, and in this way facilitate the expansion of the potential audience base, who may sit before TV sets, laptops or hold mobile phones in hand. Therefore the convergence between the mobile screen and the TV screen constructs a 'matrix' (Curtin 2009), where content is produced and distributed on and for mobile and television screens, facilitating various kinds of user interactions with the content and among themselves before, during and after the program. Compared with other digital distribution platforms which replicate screen content on TV, convergence between micro-video apps and TV screens may be welcomed by TV stations as it complements screen content on TV and helps to elevate rather than threaten ratings. By contrast, online video platforms are more threatening to TV stations, as they may divert from, more than draw audiences to the TV screen.

As well as intervening in content production, social media can yield derivative programs that extend and enrich the lives of TV programs. *The Voice of China* is a notable example here. The program has witnessed lively discussions among viewers, ranging from contestants' personal stories or creative ideas to responses to revelations about the other side of contestants' lives discovered through 'human-flesh search engines'.[2] Such conversations have become fodder for another short-length program, *Cool Me, Real Voice* (*ku wo zhen shengyin*), which focuses on the interviews with individual contestants. For each episode, a ten-minute mini interview is broadcast on Zhejiang Satellite TV, and a complete version of around 20 to 30 minutes is broadcast exclusively on iQiYi, which can be accessed via mobile. Online platforms, without the limit of time slots on TV, provide a wider space for content that cannot be accommodated on TV. Further, the longer version of the program available on online platforms brings the TV audience to online space. Meanwhile, those who have not watched the TV program may be driven to the television after watching the derivative content online. Multiple screens thus cross promote different content to expand the whole audience base of the programs.

It is evident that the socialisation of screen content among consumers is facilitating content production, distribution and promotion. Concomitant with this facilitation is the dissolving of boundaries between formal and informal (Zhao and Keane 2013); that is, formal institutions feed on informal conversations in social networks while social conversations across platforms facilitate distribution and cross-promote content. As content production moves across multiple sites, as in preheat or derivative content, it is important to design distribution modes to accommodate varying viewing habits on different platforms while benefiting from the cross-promotion effect.

TENSIONS BETWEEN THE TWO CAMPS

As both TV stations and online video platforms experiment with new screen practices to respond to connected viewing, some tensions have arisen between the two camps. As discussed earlier, TV stations may perceive simple replication of content for multi-platform distribution through licensing as a threat because it diverts away, more than draws audiences to the TV screen. This is evident in the decision made by Hunan Satellite TV (HSTV) to stop licensing copyrights of its hit shows to online video platforms in May 2014. Although it received no small amount of licensing fee, the management is ambitious to make the revenue alone instead of sharing it with online collaborators (Keane and Zhao 2015).

HSTV's ambition in the digital space is demonstrated in its effort to build its own digital distribution platforms and distribute its hit shows exclusively on its own platforms. In effect, this is a business response to the diversification of mobile and social viewing. Responding directly to connected viewing, Hunan Satellite TV launched its official mobile application *Who? Now!* (*hula*) in July 2013. Its mission, as stated on the official website, is to connect TV with mobile and provide a new opportunity for families and friends to gather before the television set. With the content coming completely from HSTV, the management hopes to complement its TV programs with the interactive engagement via the app and thus expand its audience base and enhance audience loyalty.

As an incentive for viewers to watch television in front of the box, the app allows users to scan the 2D barcode on the TV screen to initiate the interactive viewing experience. The content or activities in the app follow the content and encourage users to sit before the TV set. Within three days the app attracted over a million users (Tencent News 2013). As 2D barcode scanning often requires users to get up and move closer to the screen to have the barcode in the scanning frame, user experience proved unfriendly and discouraged usage. In the 3.0 version launched at the end of 2013, users can scan the screen instead of the barcode to activate the interactive experience.

Moreover, the app has a new feature of chat room during live shows to connect viewers who watch the program at the same time. HSTV also invites relevant TV hosts, guests and behind-the-scene production teams to come to the chat room during the live show to communicate with viewers. This has a strong drawing power. Viewers become active in live events such as the New Year Count-down Concert, the Spring Eve Gala, and format variety shows such as the Chinese version of the popular reality talent show *The X Factor* (*Zhongguo zuiqiangyin*).

Holding its trump card of premium content resources close in hand, the bullish media empire has opted for a selective approach to the opportunities presented by connected viewing, which is evidence of a different approach to the challenges of convergence. Whether or not HSTV has played its cards well is perhaps still too early to tell. Many challenges remain in bringing premium content and technology together to deliver quality user experience to meet or even surpass viewers' expectations.

CONCLUSION

In an age of technological, economic, and cultural convergence, TV is consumed, produced, and distributed differently than it was in the last century. A multiplicity of devices, friendlier network infrastructure and increasingly competitive rates mean that people are watching content on multiple devices and in various scenarios. Mobile screens are integrated into the viewing experience, which might be time- and place-shifted, and increasingly socially networked. Socialisation of screen content consumption permeates content discovery, acquisition and discussions, especially in content with high 'here and now' appeal. For these reasons television in the post-broadcasting era needs to be considered not only as technical devices but also as mobile and social technologies.

Both television stations and online video platforms in China are reconsidering their screen practices to respond to changes in viewing habits.

While some experiments have ended as a result of state interference, the complementarity of convergence and connected viewing continues to manifest new innovations. By developing mobile applications and marrying mobile software with hardware, online video platforms are endeavouring to draw even more audience to the smaller screen. Expanding distribution, however, does not mean just deploying additional platforms; this is demonstrated in the content acquisition strategy that sees the integration of mobile platforms and copyright licensing negotiations. Apart from the value of content resources, user experience is an important factor in attracting users, especially paying users.

Socialisation of screen content consumption cuts across the lifecycle of a program. It not only facilitates dialogue and expands the potential audience base across multiple platforms, but may also intervene in content production, ranging from pre-heat components to derivative content from TV. Such content, produced on multiple sites, demonstrates the dissolving boundaries between formal and informal. Distribution of content also needs to be designed in diverse modes to suit users' viewing habits while facilitating their interactions with the content, and among themselves. Further, the socialisation of screen content consumption generates cross-promotion benefits to different viewing platforms. A bigger ecosystem is evident in the landscape of connected viewing: telecom service providers, mobile device manufacturers, mobile app developers, and the state watchdog all take part, in addition to television stations and online video service providers and the socially networked viewership. Some players in the 'traditional' camp may perceive content licensing to digital platforms as a threat to their own digital lifeline. This further illustrates the significance of considering convergence beyond mere replication of content for multi-screen distribution. Through convergence the whole should be more than the sum of its parts, meaning new possibilities opening up for content production, distribution and promotion to draw a wider audience to diverse screens. While visions of convergence might differ among various players and lead to divergence in some cases, approaching today's connected viewers requires bringing content and technology together to accommodate evolving cultural practices.

NOTES

1. A result of the merger between The State Administration of Radio, Film and Television (SARFT) and the General Administration of Press and Publications (GAPP) in 2013.
2. Human flesh search engine: 'people-powered' search where a large number of online users collaborate in finding more information about a person, as opposed to the likes of Google and Baidu which employ software programs to crawl data.

REFERENCES

China Daily (2015), 'Premier Li wants lower Internet fees, better speed', accessed 15 April 2015 at http://www.chinadaily.com.cn/china/2015-04/15/content_20440545.htm.

China Internet Network Information Center (CNNIC) (2014), '2013 research report on online video applications in China', accessed 1 October 2014 at http://www.cnnic.cn/hlwfzyj/hlwxzbg/spbg/201406/P020140609392906022556.pdf.

Cunningham, Stuart and Jon Silver (2013), *Screen Distribution and the New King Kongs of the Online World*. New York: Palgrave Macmillan.

Curtin, Michael (2009), 'Matrix media', in Graeme Turner and Jinna Tay (eds.), *Television Studies After TV: Understanding Television in the Post-Broadcast Era*. London and New York: Routledge, pp. 9–19.

Gao, Yuan and Limin Chen (2013), 'Baidu to buy PPS' video unit', accessed 12 December 2014 at http://www.chinadaily.com.cn/business/2013-05/08/content_16484057.htm.

Hartley, John (2009), 'Less popular but more democratic? Corrie, Clarkson and the dancing Cru', in Graeme Turner and Jinna Tay (eds.), *Television Studies After TV: Understanding Television in the Post-Broadcast Era*. London and New York: Routledge, pp. 20–30.

Holt, Jennifer and Kevin Sanson (2014), 'Introduction: Mapping connections', in Jennifer Holt and Kevin Sanson (eds.), *Connected Viewing: Selling, Streaming, and Sharing Media in the Digital Age*. New York, NY and Abingdon, Oxon: Routledge, pp. 1–15.

iResearch (2014), 'iResearch: iQiyi, Youku Tudou and Sohu lead mobile video market', accessed 12 December 2014 at http://www.newhua.com/2014/0401/255898.shtml.

Jenkins, Henry (2006), *Convergence Culture: Where Old and New Media Collide*. New York: New York University Press.

Keane, Michael (2013), *Creative Industries in China: Art, Design and Media*. Cambridge: Polity.

Keane, Michael (2015), *The Chinese Television Industry*. London: British Film Institute and Palgrave Macmillan.

Keane, Michael and Elaine Jing Zhao (2015), 'TV or not TV? Reimagining screen content in China', in Larissa Hjorth and Olivia Khoo (eds.), *Routledge Handbook of New Media in Asia*. London and New York: Routledge.

Kokas, Aynne (2014), 'American media behind the Great Fire Wall: social media and film viewing in China', in Jennifer Holt and Kevin Sanson (eds.), *Connected Viewing: Selling, Streaming, and Sharing Media in the Digital Age*. New York and London: Routledge, pp. 144–57.

Lee, Hye Jin and Mark Andrejevic (2014), 'Second-screen theory: From the democratic surround to the digital enclosure', in Jennifer Holt and Kevin Sanson (eds.), *Connected Viewing: Selling, Streaming, and Sharing Media in the Digital Age*. New York and London: Routledge, pp. 40–61.

Shi, Jun and Pan Hu (2013), *shichang yugu 10yi yuan, aiqiyi qiangzhan yidongduan* ('iQiyi seizing the mobile video market with estimated value at 10 hundred million yuan'), accessed 12 December 2014 at http://www.eeo.com.cn/2013/0125/239339.shtml.

Tencent News (2013), *Hunan weishi hula duchuang 'quanping shibie' gaibian erweima shijie* ('Hunan Satellite TV's innovation of "full screen recognition" with Who? Now! changes 2D barcode market'), accessed 12 December 2014 at http://news.qq.com/a/20131226/012081.htm.

Turner, Graeme and Jinna Tay (eds.) (2009), *Television Studies after TV: Understanding Television in the Post-broadcast Era*, London: Routledge.

Vivo Global (2014), 'Industry's first smartphone to offer an immersive DTS Headphone:X™ experience unveiled by premium Chinese smartphone brand, vivo', accessed 27 September 2014 at http://www.vivoglobal.com/news/13.

Wang, Ping (2013), *Youku Gu Yongqiang: wo yanzhong de yidong shipin kehuduan* ('Youku's Gu Yongqiang: mobile video client in my eyes'), accessed 11 December 2014 at http://mi.techweb.com.cn/2013-12-20/1372262.shtml.

Xiao, Shanshan (2005), 'The money game of Super Girl', accessed 11 December 2014 at http://news.xinhuanet.com/ent/2005-08/09/content_3329724.htm.

Xinhua (2007), 'China bans talents show to be broadcasted in prime time', accessed 11 December 2014 at http://news.xinhuanet.com/english/2007-09/22/content_6772701.htm.

Xunlei Ltd. (2014), 'Xunlei announces unaudited financial results for the third quarter 2014', accessed 12 December 2014 at http://ir.xunlei.com/phoenix.zhtml?c=246964&p=irol-newsArticle&ID=1993090.

Zhao, Bin (1998), 'Popular family television and party ideology: the Spring Festival Eve happy gathering', *Media, Culture and Society* **20** (1): 43–58.

Zhao, Elaine Jing (2014), 'The micro-movie wave in a globalising China: adaptation, formalisation and commercialisation', *International Journal of Cultural Studies* **17** (5): 453–67.

Zhao, Elaine Jing and Michael Keane (2013), 'Between formal and informal: the shakeout in China's online video industry', *Media, Culture and Society* **35** (6): 724–41.

Zheng, Weidong and Tianli Zhang (2012), 'The impact of growing online video market on television media', *Rating China* **13** (11), accessed 11 December 2014 at http://www.csm.com.cn/index.php/knowledge/showArticle/ktid/1/kaid/865.html.

Zhu, Chong (2011), 'Why was Super Girl banned? ', accessed 11 December 2014 at http://www.eeo.com.cn/ens/2011/0923/212237.shtml.

Zhu, Yi (2014), *Weishi lianshou 'feichengwurao' wanzhuan duanshipin tuodan xinfengshang* ('Weishi's collaboration with "If you are the one" in leading the trend of using short videos to find a partner'), accessed 11 December 2014 at http://news.163.com/14/1111/02/AAO375O500014Q4P.html.

28. The e-commerce revolution: ensuring trust and consumer rights in China
Ming Cheung

On 5 March 2015, the Chinese Premier Li Keqiang unveiled China's ambitious Internet+ Plan, a strategy ostensibly designed to lift the Chinese economy to a new level in the wake of deteriorating returns in traditional industries and a slowing of GDP growth. As previous chapters in this volume have shown, China's digital transformation comes with a number of caveats. In the cultural and creative industries there are obviously great gains to be made by utilizing big data to gain a better appreciation of audience consumer demands. Cloud computing likewise has the potential to contribute to facilitating work processes and collaborative forms of production, for instance in film, animation and video gaming.

The changes in the cultural and creative industries are therefore part of a broader economic development agenda that encompasses modern logistics, financial services and e-commerce. Building the new engine for economic growth through the application of Internet+ does, however, require government intervention to ensure a fairer playing field for China's new entrepreneurs, the 'e-tailers'. At the same time there is a need to allow the virtual marketplace to take its own course, a point often made by business interests.

This chapter addresses the disparity between the growing e-commerce culture in China and the lack of consumer trust in online purchases. It considers whether or not China's regulatory measures are sufficient to protect the rights of online consumers. If the answer is negative, then what does the gap between expectations and reality imply? The chapter discusses how Alibaba's Taobao.com (Taobao hereafter), one of the leading e-marketplaces in China, has attempted to narrow this gap by designing and implementing a self-regulated consumer rights protection system in its website. The chapter concludes with a discussion of the significance of consumer rights protection and its possible future impact on China's sustainable development in e-commerce and integration into the global online economy.

THE RISE (AND RISE) OF CHINA'S E-COMMERCE MARKETPLACE

Over the past two decades the world has witnessed the economic resurgence of China through manufacturing, and more recently in the e-commerce sector. The latter, which includes the cultural and creative industries, encapsulates China's rapidly expanding commodity and service markets. Riding on the back of a skyrocketing Internet adoption rate and a rapidly developing nationwide courier service, China's online retail sector recorded sales of US$426 billion in 2014; and according to market research transaction volumes are forecast to reach US$1,011 billion by 2018 (eMarketer 2014).

China's e-commerce history begins in 1993, when a number of the country's foreign businesses first deployed electronic data interchange for trade. The following year, China established its first network, the National Computing and Networking Facility of China, thereby connecting the nation to the Internet. Internet-based e-commerce was formally launched in 1997, followed by a leap in the number of dot-com companies operating in the marketplace. As elsewhere, however, the dot-com bubble did not last very long, bursting in 2000. The next few years witnessed the survival of strong dot-com firms and the departure of their weaker counterparts. By 2004, the Internet had permeated the most developed provinces and dot-com businesses reappeared with a new intensity and glamour. The number of online shoppers in China climbed year-on-year from 33.6 million in 2006 to 160.5 million in 2010, reaching 361.4 million in 2014 (Statista 2015a).

China's e-commerce boom has nurtured a consumer-oriented culture, one characterized by frequent visits to e-marketplaces such as Tmall.com and JD.com. These two biggest players together accounted for over 78 per cent of the business-to-consumer (B2C) market share in China by December 2014 (BysoftChina 2015). According to Blackwell et al. (2001: 514), culture refers to 'a set of values, ideas, artefacts, and other meaningful symbols that help individuals communicate, interpret, and evaluate as members of society'. In regard to the evolution of this new cultural phenomenon, commodity and services consumption delineates and defines social and cultural phenomena such as class, community and lifestyle. When a particular consumption channel, method or pattern connects our lives to those of others through shared lifestyle expressions, subcultures of consumption emerge. An example is Taobao, part of the Alibaba Group, which became the biggest US 'initial public offering' (IPO) in history in September 2014 (*The Wall Street Journal* 2014a). Taobao, a widely recognized consumer-to-consumer (C2C) e-marketplace, has become so popular in Chinese people's everyday life that it is not uncommon to hear them saying, 'I am now taobao-ing', which literally means 'digging for treasure'.

In the existing literature, consumer trust is recognized as a critical success factor for e-commerce (Lu et al. 2010). Mayer et al. (1995: 712) define trust as 'the willingness of a party to be vulnerable to the actions of another party based on the expectation that the other will perform a particular action important to the trustor, irrespective of the ability to monitor or control that other party'. One of the major ways to enhance trust among consumers is to provide them with the necessary consumer rights protection that they deserve. While China's online consumption culture is thriving, there is however concern that consumer protection legislation has not kept pace. Scholars have raised concerns over the inadequacies of e-commerce-related laws and regulations, nationwide credit systems and logistics systems (Liao et al. 2009).

ONLINE VERSUS OFFLINE PURCHASES

Distrust of both online and offline purchases is widespread in China. Fake eggs containing ingredients detrimental to human health, contaminated milk powder that has harmed thousands of babies, and harmful food additives designed to give pork the appearance and taste of beef constitute just the tip of the iceberg. It is not uncommon to hear Chinese citizens saying that they need to be very watchful in selecting where and what to eat to avoid ingesting poor-quality or harmful food. Many parents are so concerned about whether their children are consuming unsafe goods that they travel frequently to Hong Kong, line up outside grocery stores, and purchase their daily necessities in bulk. Purchases from physical shopping outlets in China are already characterized by a considerable degree of consumer distrust, not to mention online shopping, which lacks face-to-face interaction between buyer and seller and thus provokes even greater uncertainty about product quality.

Online and offline purchases differ in several ways. For example, when making an online purchase, a consumer cannot physically inspect the genuineness and quality of the product prior to delivery. This constitutes an issue of particular concern in e-marketplaces in China, which are flooded with poor quality and counterfeit goods. In *Puma v. Taobao.com* (2006), the plaintiff, Puma, found a total of 43,932 individually operated vendors on the defendant's website advertising counterfeit apparel and sports equipment. Puma subsequently sent a letter demanding that Taobao remove all Puma shoe listings. However, the Guangzhou Intermediate

People's Court held that Taobao, as an e-marketplace, had no obligation to monitor the goods listed on its website, and further, had no means to determine the genuineness of such shoes.

While Chinese counterfeit products and services can be creative in their appearance and innovative in their functionality (Cheung 2012), many are clones of the original designs – from trademark and content to appearance and packaging. When these counterfeit products or services are put on the market for sale, the consumer is more or less at the mercy of the seller, who may or may not be ethical in providing the true information. Indeed, many counterfeiters in China prefer to risk getting caught in order to make a profit, rather than miss out on an opportunity to capitalize on a lucrative market for their products (Taylor 2009). The potential profits generated from sales can easily exceed the fines and damages imposed when producers are caught and held liable.

Scholars have identified two typical categories of online transaction fraud in China: those arising from uncertainty over trader identity and those arising from uncertainty over merchandise quality (Ba et al. 2003). In the former, the seller remains anonymous or frequently changes identities. The buyer never receives the goods despite having paid for them, but is unable to identify the seller to gain recompense. In the latter, the buyer takes delivery of the goods, but finds them to be counterfeit, of poor quality, or even completely wrong (Gao 2004). An informal survey conducted by Sina back in 2009 revealed that 74.9 per cent of 21,493 respondents had made online purchases that subsequently turned out to be fakes while 83.6 per cent of the respondents reported dissatisfaction with China's consumer protection against fraudulent activities (Sina 2009).

Two questions arise. Can an e-commerce website, which provides a marketplace in which contracting parties can buy and sell goods online, be considered the seller in the event that counterfeit goods are sold? Should such websites be liable for false or fraudulent information transmitted through the platform they provide? In *Yang v. Eachnet.com* (2000), the plaintiff, Mr. Yang, sued Eachnet for his purchase of a cosmetic product from an e-store owned by S Company based on a description he found on a web page link on the Eachnet platform, claiming damages and double compensatory liability under Article 49 of the Law of the People's Republic of China on the Protection of Consumer Rights and Interests (generally known as China's Consumer Protection Law). Upon delivery, Mr. Yang realized that the product, described as made in Japan, was counterfeit. In this case, the Court held that Eachnet was not liable for damages, as the evidence showed the seller to be S Company, the store owner, not Eachnet, the transaction service provider. However, because China's legal system is rooted in the civil law tradition, that is, its jurisprudence is results-oriented with precedence playing a rather insignificant role, the case failed to establish the legal position of companies such as Eachnet, which act as go-betweens transferring information between two parties. Should Eachnet censor all of the daily incoming and outgoing information on its platform even though it is not a party to the sales contracts it facilitates? Is it possible for it to do so? Should Eachnet be held liable for information published by a third party on its platform? Is it easy for a user to judge who the publisher of such information is? And should Eachnet bear joint liability with the seller, as it provides the sales platform and thus, to a certain extent, co-sells the product with the seller? Would that be fair to Eachnet? The Chinese courts allow broad discretion in these issues.

REGULATORY MEASURES ON CONSUMER RIGHTS PROTECTION

At present, consumer rights protection in China is regulated by the Consumer Protection Law, which was adopted on 31 October 1993 and came into force on 1 January 1994. Whether or not a law enacted two decades ago is sufficient to protect consumer rights and interests in today's kaleidoscopic e-commerce era is an issue worthy of investigation. It took some 20 years from the Law's adoption for China's National People's Congress to enforce a major amendment on 15 March 2014. The amendment addresses improvements across seven major areas: (1) regulating the e-commerce industry; (2) strengthening the joint liabilities of false advertisement publishers and e-trade platforms; (3) placing the burden of proof on service providers in the event of a dispute; (4) imposing higher compensation; (5) banning unauthorized disclosures of consumers' personal information; (6) clarifying the role of consumer associations; and (7) establishing a credit file to record illegal acts.

Before the amendment was enacted, China had yet to formulate uniform, substantive national laws or remedies in favour of consumers engaging in e-commerce transactions. The Consumer Protection Law provided no rules regulating e-commerce. Solicitors subsequently found it difficult to advise their clients on the basis of previous judgments, and members of the general public were often confused as to whether certain acts are legal or illegal, what online consumer rights, if any, they enjoy, and what party a misled consumer may sue. Indeed, it was on 1 April 2005 that the Electronic Signature Law, the nation's first law governing e-commerce, was introduced, which aimed to legitimize electronic signatures and protect online transaction security. Although this law recognizes digital signatures as legally binding, it does not close loopholes in the Consumer Protection Law.

The 2014 amendment to the Consumer Protection Law was a positive move, providing online consumers with the right to return purchased goods, except certain categories of items, within seven days from the date of receipt of the goods and with a seven-day money back guarantee to receive the paid amount back from the seller upon the arrival of the returned goods.

A number of other improvements were made; the second one being that advertising agents, e-commerce platforms and product/service endorsers are now required to bear joint liability if the products or services they promoted through false advertising cause harm to consumers. A third improvement to consumer rights requires the business operator to bear the burden of proof if a legal dispute arises from durable goods found to be defective within six months from the date of purchase. This provision has reduced pressure on consumers. A fourth improvement was the imposition of penalties of up to three times the price of a product or service if a business operator is found to have defrauded consumers. In the case of a defective product or service causing injury or death to the consumers, the business operator is liable for damages up to twice the amount of the induced losses in addition to compensating the consumers for their economic and psychological sufferings. Serious cases will lead to criminal investigation.

Over the last ten years studies have brought attention to the immaturity of reliable credit payment and product delivery services in China (cf. Martinsons 2008). As of 2009, only 11 per cent of China's 1.3 billion residents possessed a credit card. Only 15 per cent of online purchases were conducted using a credit card (PCWorld 2009). The low penetration rate of credit cards during this time was the result of an absence of a national credit rating system and the unwillingness among banks to extend credit to the general public. Annual losses amounting to 10–20 per cent of national GDP were estimated to have resulted from China's immature credit system and the immature regulation thereof (Zhao et al. 2008). E-commerce development has been further hampered by logistics shortfalls. In January 2011, it was reported that the warehouses of a number of express delivery services in China had reached their full capacity. Severe staff shortages in the run-up to the Spring Festival shopping season resulted in further delays to the delivery of goods from many of the country's e-marketplaces (*Xinhua News* 2011). This situation underscores the fact that China's infrastructure lagged behind its booming e-commerce market and ever-expanding number of online shoppers.

SELF-REGULATED CONSUMER PROTECTION SYSTEM

Comparing B2C with C2C markets in the e-commerce arena, Xu et al. (2010) note that the risk of experiencing unethical conduct is greater in the latter due to the difficulty in identifying the nature of small, individual or anonymous traders. To enhance consumer trust in their online services, some of the major C2C e-marketplaces in China have designed and activated their own self-regulated consumer protection systems. Three aspects of these systems are particularly significant: electronic payment security, product quality assurance, and online dispute resolution. Because Taobao dominates the C2C e-marketplace with a market share of 96.5 per cent in 2013 (Table 28.1), the following discussion relates primarily to its technology-enabled provisions.

Launched by Alibaba in May 2003, Taobao has defeated international giants such as eBay (iResearch 2011), becoming China's largest C2C e-marketplace; it boasts the greatest number of product listings, registered users and has the largest transaction volume. It reported more than RMB 200 billion (US$31.4 m) in turnover in 2011, creating one million sales-related jobs (*Xinhua News* 2011). The site displayed 800 million products for sale, with 48,000 items sold every minute (*China Daily* 2012). In 2013, it reported 500 million registered users and 60 million daily visitors (TechNode 2013). As China's inflation rate continues to rise, it is expected that the country's e-marketplace will become even more attractive to its millions of netizens, especially the price-conscious among them (iResearch 2010). In recent years Alibaba has been very active in launching themed shopping carnivals, one of the most popular being Singles Day, held on 11.11 (11 November) of each year. In 2015, Alibaba's total sales reached US$14.3 billion on that one day, with around 120,000 orders per minute and 73 per cent of purchases in the first hour made via mobile phones. It took Alibaba only 12 hours to beat its 2014 whole-day record of US$9.3 billion (BBC 2015).

Table 28.1   Major C2C e-marketplaces in China

Ranking	C2C e-marketplace	Market share (%)	Year of launch	Owner
1	Taobao.com	96.5	May 2003	Alibaba
2	Paipai.com	3.4	March 2006	Tencent
3	Eachnet.com	0.1	December 2006	eBay & TOM

Source: Statista 2015b.

Electronic Payment Security

Jones and Leonard (2008) state that third-party recognition is critical to gaining online consumers' trust and to boosting the transaction volume of C2C websites. In order to mitigate the negative consequences of distrust, Taobao has embedded a number of value-added features into its portals. It provides a number of third-party payment instruments to its customers, with its escrow service, Alipay (*zhi fu bao*), particularly well received. This service involves a clear set of payment procedures, which I illustrate in Figure 28.1.

Third-party payment involves an independent institution with a guaranteed good credit standing providing trusteeship services on behalf of a trading platform. Sellers and buyers conduct their payment transactions via this third party. Once a buyer has confirmed an order with the seller, he or she remits payment for the goods to the third party, which then notifies the seller that payment has been received. After the buyer has accepted the goods and confirmed that they are satisfactory, the third party then remits the payment to the seller. Hence, both sellers and buyers engage in trade under the supervision of the neutral platform provided by the third party.

As Taobao is a C2C platform, it has to protect the interests of buyers and sellers, as both constitute its customers. The use of Alipay as an independent and trusted third-party places the two parties to a sales transaction on an equal footing, securing both the payment for and provision of goods on the basis of the parties' adherence to agreed-upon contractual provisions. In addition, if the buyer finds the goods received to be unsatisfactory, then he or she can return them and receive a refund through Alipay.

Product Quality Assurance

San Martín et al. (2011) highlight the importance of warranty in trust building among online consumers. Taobao's consumer protection scheme covers three major scenarios: (1) the items received are of poor quality; (2) the items received are not as described; and (3) the items were not delivered after payment had been made. Taobao provides its customers with a number of warranties; some of the generic ones include seven-day money back guarantee and 30-day repair service for digital and home appliances. Yet there are also warranties that are peculiar to China. To lower customers' perceived risk of deception, the company makes provision for a triple rebate in the case of counterfeit goods (*jia yi pei san*). Sellers who join its consumer protection scheme agree to be bound by its rules, and promise to compensate buyers by paying them three times the product price in

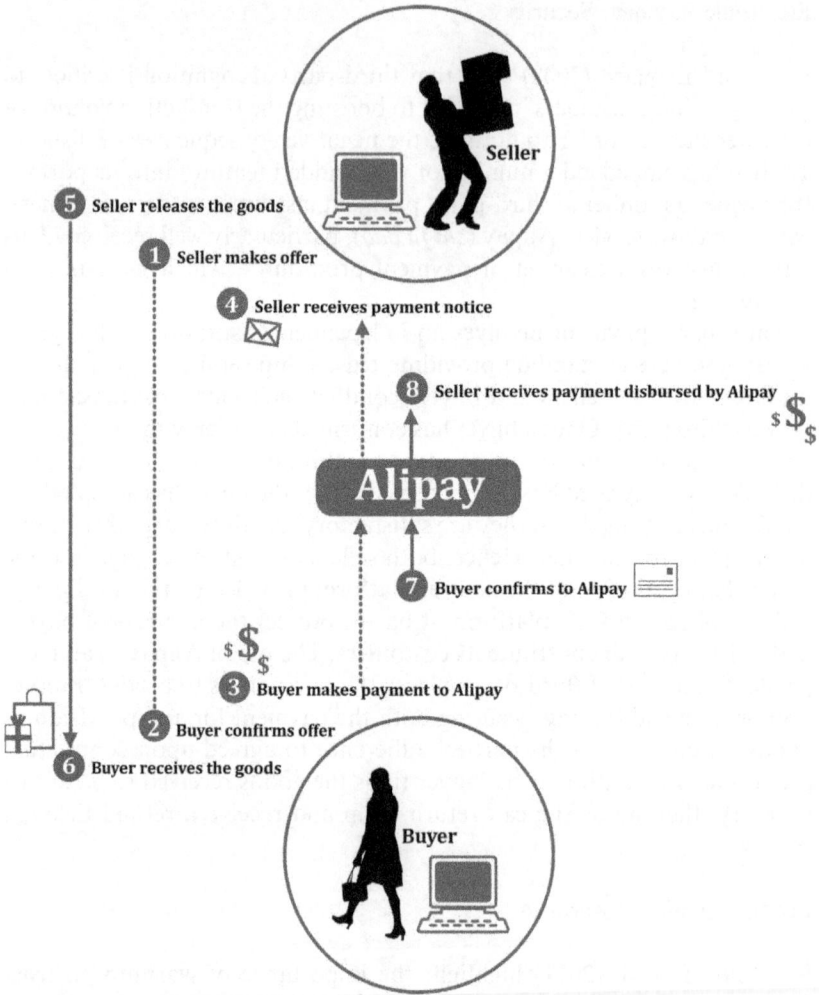

Source: Author.

Figure 28.1 Taobao's Alipay payment procedure

the event that the sale of a counterfeit product is reported and proved. If a buyer complains that he or she has been sold such a product, then the seller bears the burden of proving the contrary. If the seller's proof is not accepted, then he or she must pay the buyer in accordance with this provision. The procedure of this provision is shown in Figure 28.2. It should be noted that this provision offered by Taobao had already been in operation

```
                    Product is suspected
                    to be non-genuine

        Product delivery                  Transaction
        is not confirmed                  completed

        Request a refund due to          Complaint lodged
        receipt of fake product          within 15 days

                Seller requested to provide
                evidence within 3 days

        Proof found                        Proof accepted
        to be inadequate

        Seller issues a rebate worth      Taobao customer service helps
        3 times the product price         the parties to arrive at a compromise
```

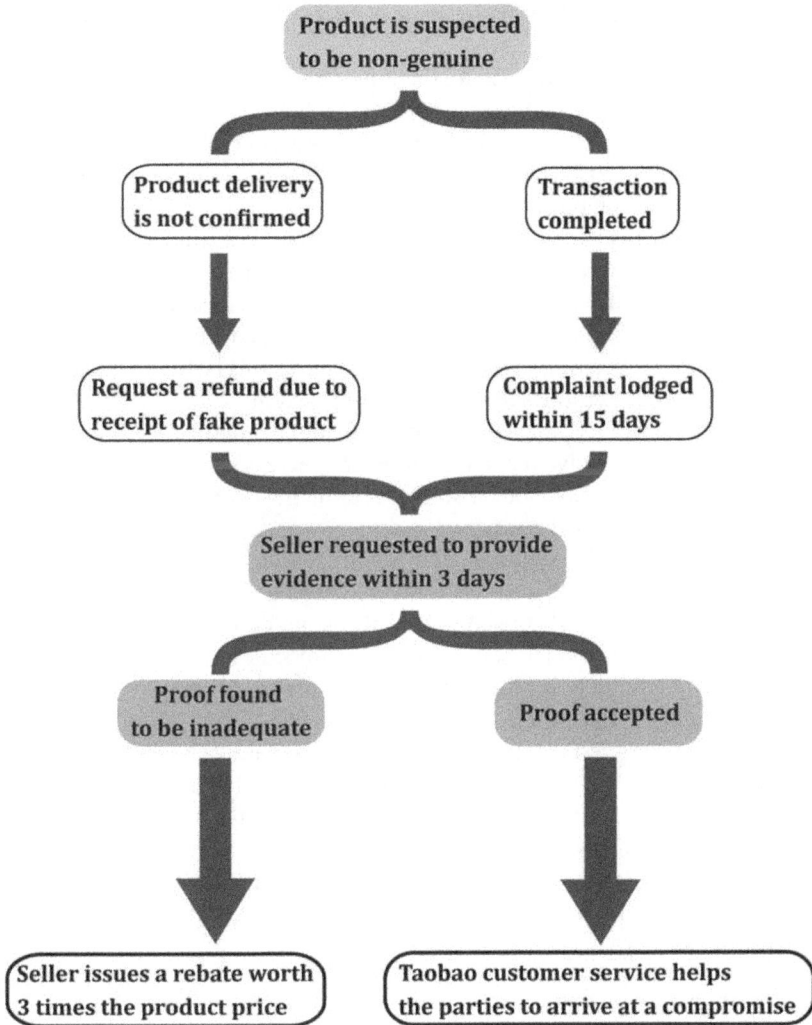

Source: Author.

Figure 28.2   Taobao's triple rebate in the case of counterfeit goods

for many years before the amendment to the Consumer Protection Law came into effect. A report filed by Alibaba with the World Intellectual Property Organization (WIPO) states that the company spent more than US$16 million annually kicking out counterfeit goods, particularly from Taobao. And in 2013, it removed more than 100 million hyperlinks to products suspected of IP infringement from Taobao's platform (*The Wall Street Journal* 2014b).

Once a transaction is complete, the buyer has the opportunity to review the performance of its chosen supplier(s). Such a performance review may lead the buyer to decide to maintain or suspend a business relationship. Taobao, for example, makes a distinction between the reputations of the seller and the buyer, and displays profiles for each separately. The e-commerce platform collects information on all transaction records, including post-transaction feedback, evaluations of the transaction from both the buyer's and seller's perspective and then makes this information available online. Such readily accessible reputation evaluation serves as a valuable reference to online consumers. Of course this is not an innovation as such. eBay has run the same reputational system.

However, a remarkable feature of Taobao's evaluation system is that when examining positive feedback on sellers, buyers see not only that provided by buyers directly, but also the default positive feedback assigned by the system. This is the result of Taobao's special rule: after a successful transaction via Alipay, a seller who solicits feedback but receives no response after 45 days is automatically assigned default positive feedback by the system. Although the charge could be made that the default feedback stipulation provides sellers with a shortcut to higher reputation ratings, this is unlikely in practice, as buyers are given ample time to give neutral or negative feedback on dishonest sellers before the system kicks in. Indeed, sellers, especially newcomers to Taobao, who have a strong desire to build a good reputation, often actively solicit feedback from buyers immediately after transactions. In addition, the system also incentivizes the parties involved (at least the sellers) to provide feedback on transactions. In fact, despite incentives to free ride, feedback is provided on more than half of all transactions on Taobao, a level unheard of on such sites as eBay.

Online Dispute Resolution

Numerous transactions are conducted on Taobao every day, but not all of them proceed smoothly. As a further incentive to buyers, Taobao has established a compensation-in-advance provision (*xianxing peifu*). The e-marketplace requires a deposit from all sellers, which it is authorized to draw on to compensate buyers should it be necessary. In the case of a dispute between buyer and seller, the two parties are expected to reach a compromise solution, and they can use Taobao's integrated instant messaging system, Ali WangWang, to communicate with each other during this process. Indeed, this tool may well enhance the likelihood that a buyer will engage in immediate negotiation or discussion about a product with the seller, although there are cases in which the latter does not respond in a timely fashion. In such cases, Taobao exercises its right to draw funds from the compensation-in-advance scheme to compensate the buyer on the seller's behalf. This scheme came into force in March 2007 as one of the self-regulated protective measures that Taobao has put in place to enhance consumer trust in making online purchases from its sellers.

Turel et al. (2008: 138) write that 'in complaint cases in which two parties are involved, users build trust in the other party, in part, through his or her association with a trusted service provider.' Bewsell et al. (2005) also find that the higher the degree of power a platform or service provider has in resolving disputes between buyers and sellers, the greater the trust consumers will have in online transactions on/with that platform or service provider. When disputes are frequent in the e-commerce world, the establishment of a fair resolution procedure becomes particularly important to ensure consumer trust recovery. Taobao operates its own 24-hour online consumer rights protection platform, which a consumer can visit to review the progress of and any information on his or her claim. The platform plays a third-party role in disputes, intervening only when the buyer and seller parties cannot arrive at a solution. In 2010, Taobao received and processed 2.16 million consumer protection requests, concerning a total of US\$298 million in disputed transactions. The amount related to successful claims that year totalled US\$265 million (Sina 2011).

Yet a number of complaints about Taobao's consumer protection policy can be found on the Internet. According to Taobao's guidelines, the e-commerce platform will intervene in disputes after receiving a request for intervention from a buyer and will inform the buyer of the result within seven days. An Internet forum on Taobao makes clear, however, that numerous buyers had complained about the company's failure to deal with conflicts between buyers and sellers in a proactive fashion, as well as its inability to fulfil its promise to produce results within seven days. Even worse, some complainants reported receiving no reply at all from Taobao (Taobao Forum 2011).

In an attempt to enhance the transparency and accountability of Taobao's consumer protection system, Alibaba launched an online 'User Dispute Resolution Centre' in December 2012. It crowdsources Taobao's millions of users to act as voluntary assessors, effectively playing judge and jury in e-commerce disputes that arise on the e-commerce platform. Each dispute is processed by a panel of 31 assessors; each of them will study the evidence and then cast a vote that would align the case in favour of either the buyer or the seller. The side that receives the majority votes will win. To further strengthen this self-regulated mechanism, each assessor is ranked by Taobao for his or her ability in making reasonable judgments based on how many cases he or she has resolved and how complex those cases are. The assessors are then categorized into different ability groups, aiming to let the most experienced assessors take care of the most challenging disputes. It was reported that the processing time from submitting a dispute to receiving a judgment went down from three to five days when the case was processed by Taobao's customer service personnel to two days when the case was resolved through community arbitration (Alizila 2014a). Since the Centre started its operation in 2012, there have been more than 575,000 amateur adjudicators, each of whom can participate in up to 20 cases on a day, helping to settle 2,000 consumer grievances each day (Alizila 2014b).

DEVELOPMENT OF A CONSUMER-ORIENTED E-COMMERCE CULTURE

Over the past few years, China's reputation as 'the world's factory' has faced strong challenges, as China's land becomes more expensive, labour costs inflate and environmental protection regulations become more stringent. The cost of running a factory is constantly on the rise and has been pushing local and foreign merchants to relocate their production lines to lower-cost countries such as Myanmar, Laos, Cambodia, Vietnam, Indonesia and the Philippines. On one hand, this can be seen as a naturally occurring process as China is experiencing a transformation from a developing country into a more developed economy. On the other hand, this pushes China further along the path to restructuring its economy, making it more sustainable by focusing on generating domestic and global demand for products and services. Indeed the Chinese Government's latest action plan on the Internet+ ecosystem, which integrates mobile Internet, cloud computing and big data together with the online-to-offline (O2O) strategic alliance of virtual and physical stores, reveals its aspiration toward the development of a consumer orientation in e-commerce activities.

As mentioned above, trust is the key to the initiation of an online transaction, and consumer rights protection is at the core of sustainable business relationships. The ultimate goal of China's ongoing economic transition is to establish a consumer-oriented market economy, the fundamental logic of which is to emphasize the creation of superior customer value and business performance. An orientation such as this not only requires an e-marketplace with sufficient knowledge of its target customers but also requires that customers' interests are first priority in the course of identifying market opportunities, accessing data-mining user history, designing user experiences and building long-term relationships for sustainable business growth.

Meanwhile, as Internet technologies accelerate the globalization of business and drive the pervasive diffusion of e-commerce, both nationwide and across regions, competition within China is increasingly dynamic; businesses must compete with both domestic and foreign firms to survive. Among the many factors influencing online consumers' shopping decisions, merchant reputation is arguably the greatest concern. Accordingly, online stores are required to exert considerable effort to establish and maintain a reputation for trustworthiness among consumers. This is not an easy task because China is a nation characterized by a low degree of social trust (*China Daily* 2013); it remains difficult for many Chinese to overcome suspicions that might exist between two potential partners, especially in the initial stages of a business relationship.

While China's e-commerce market is burgeoning, fraudulent transactions are rampant. The State Administration for Industry and Commerce (SAIC), China's competition regulator, reported that authorities processed 61,000 complaints about online purchases just in the first half of 2015, which was a 1.4 times increase against the same period of 2014 (SAIC 2015). This big jump in consumer complaints probably stems from the intense escalation in the number of online shoppers, creating pressure on online stores service capacity. It might also be attributed to rising awareness about the rights consumers now enjoy when making online purchases. Another explanation might be that the e-marketplaces are flooded with poor quality or counterfeit products: some sellers just want to make 'quick' money. Yet it clearly goes against the amendment to the Consumer Protection Law, which requires online sellers to provide complete and true information on the products or services they offer to online consumers.

Nevertheless, it is only since 2014 that China's legal system has started to show more promise in terms of its ability to safeguard online consumer rights or provide recourse for faulty products or negligent payments. And it could take some time to reveal the effectiveness of the amended Consumer Protection Law. Attempts to change the status quo, that is, to alter consumers' propensity for distrust, have fallen into the hands of e-marketplace operators. Taobao, a good representative of the increasingly market-oriented economy of China, has tried to boost consumer confidence in online transactions by designing and implementing a number of self-regulated trust-building measures. The results of the case study reveal how technology-enabled provisions in electronic payment security, product quality assurance and online dispute resolution can, to a certain extent, overcome institutional deficiencies.

Although e-commerce has provided a strong impetus to economic development, it has also given rise to new and often multi-faceted problems. For example, e-commerce has created problems such as the legitimacy and authentication of e-currency, e-contracts and e-billing. What China needs at the moment is a better developed nationwide non-cash payment system, which can help companies to increase inter-provincial trade and cross-regional competition by overcoming geographic obstacles while at the same time providing Chinese consumers access to goods unavailable in their domicile. Consumers also require effective online security systems to verify identities, authenticate transactions, protect their privacy and prevent contract repudiation. In some top-tier cities, the rise in credit card usage has been exponential: according to a 2014 study conducted by Nielsen, 71 per cent of Chinese consumer respondents chose cards over cash as their preferred payment method for everyday spending (Nielson 2014). Yet there is still much room to boost the usage rate nationwide.

Identifying effective methods to protect products and services intellectual property (IP) and to manage and control the export and import of intangible products are among other issues that require immediate attention. Taobao, according to its terms and conditions, is concerned with copyright, trademark and patent infringements and it promises integrity concerning the products and services sold on its platform. If a seller has breached IP regulations or violated other Chinese laws, then Taobao will penalize it by assigning penalty points. The degree of the penalty depends on the severity of the violation. Once a seller accumulates a specified number of penalty points, say 36, Taobao will mask the seller's online store, meaning that users will not be able to find it during a search, with the result that the seller cannot update product information or engage in sales. The seller is also prevented from sending out messages to its members and is prohibited from using certain functions for between seven and twenty-one days. Should the seller accumulate 48 penalty points, Taobao will prohibit it from operating via its online platform until all violations have been rectified, a punishment period has been completed, and the seller proves its intent to comply with the platform's rules and regulations.

However, Taobao's efforts to establish rules and a penalty system to protect IP have not been very successful. In 2011, Taobao was named a 'notorious market' by the US Trade Representative for helping to sustain piracy and counterfeiting (Bloomberg 2011). From foreign investors' point of view, the charge of selling illegal goods is a serious one, with questions of trust and integrity particularly relevant to brand name products. According to Aaron Kessler, an analyst at ThinkEquity LLC in San Francisco, Taobao still needs to devote 'significant effort' to resolving IP infringement problems (Hexun Tech 2011).

Taobao has a number of rules and regulations in place to protect consumer rights, and it also processes and investigates cases of customer complaints made directly to it. However, Taobao's approach to the implementation of its rules and regulations has not been sufficiently proactive. CNN News reported in January 2011 that 50,000 hacked iTunes accounts had been sold on Taobao (CNN 2011). The prices paid ranged from US$15 to US$30 per account, which allowed buyers to purchase products worth up to US$200 from iTunes in a 24-hour period. One of the sellers admitted to a *Global Times* reporter that the accounts were hacked and had been obtained illegally. However, Taobao failed to take any action regarding these suspicious accounts because it claimed not to have received any direct complaints or requests concerning their sale. Further, the company cited its obligation to protect sellers' rights in its explanation for why it could not remove the listings for the hacked accounts. Global public opinion was resoundingly and vocally against Taobao, as the sale of these accounts involved the leakage of personal and credit card information, as well as illegal products being sold in a legal way. Several days after the sale of the iTunes accounts came to light, Taobao declared that it had removed them from its site and was considering an embargo on such products. Consumers were subsequently unable to find 'iTunes' or 'iTunes accounts' on the Taobao search engine.

The iTunes case is a clear example of Taobao's failure to take a proactive approach to the implementation of its rules. As the sale of the hacked iTunes accounts was an obvious violation of both its own regulations and Chinese law, Taobao should have stopped sellers from selling these accounts as soon as possible and/or launched an investigation to find the source of the accounts. However, when reporters asked the company for comments on the case and queried it about what actions it would take, Taobao merely replied that it could take action only if it received a complaint, clear indication of its lack of any intention to tackle the problem proactively. Although Taobao did take action later, the measures it took and the penalty imposed were insufficiently severe to serve as a deterrent. Even worse, it was reported that the hacked iTunes accounts continued to be available on Taobao (*Sina Shanghai Morning Post* 2011), although their sellers were less brazen than before, with customers required to contact them directly and secretly. It was evident that Taobao would need to devote considerably greater effort and to establish a strong deterrent policy if it were to ensure that the products sold via its website are legitimate and their sale is legal and ethical.

CONCLUDING REMARKS

In the time since these issues came to light it appears that lack of progress in combating sales of such goods on its website renders Taobao's policies ineffective, despite the focus on tackling the issue of poor quality or counterfeit goods and protecting consumer rights. Taobao was accused by SAIC, in the 'Alibaba White Paper' released on a state-owned news site in 2015, of allowing its merchants 'to operate without required business licences, to run unauthorized stores that co-opted famous brands, and to sell counterfeit products', of letting its employees turn a blind eye to 'the flaws raised in customer feedback and internal credit-rating systems', and of disclosing to its merchants SAIC's confidential report on counterfeit products in order to let the merchants 'remove the products from shelves before the authority could make its next move' (*South China Morning Post* 2015).

The accusations against Taobao reveal that while Internet technologies empower e-marketplaces to identify and reach potential customers, solid e-commerce standards are still lacking in China. Standardization and the promulgation of specific legislation are difficult but important tasks in the development of e-commerce. For instance, before the e-signature standard was implemented in China, there was no standard specifically aimed at normalizing Internet behaviour. China continues to struggle to establish a business environment that is compatible with international standards, and this is having a huge impact on China's integration into the global economy as well as bilateral trade, including free trade agreements. This chapter provides an understanding of the recent development of e-commerce in China from the regulatory system perspective, an understanding that is also applicable to other emerging markets. The discussion herein is relevant not only to overseas firms wishing to engage actively in the Chinese market, but also to policy makers and the operators of C2C portals in other cultural domains.

REFERENCES

Alizila (2014a), 'Alibaba allows users to play judge in e-commerce disputes', accessed 21 November 2015 at http://www.alizila.com/alibaba-allows-users-play-judge-e-commerce-disputes.

Alizila (2014b), 'How Taobao is crowdsourcing justice in online shopping disputes', accessed 21 November 2015 at http://www.alizila.com/how-taobao-crowdsourcing-justice-online-shopping-disputes.

Ba, Sulin, Andrew B. Whinston and Han Zhang (2003), 'Building trust in online auction markets through an economic incentive mechanism', *Decision Support Systems* **35** (3): 273–86.

BBC (2015), 'China's Alibaba breaks Singles Day record as sales surge', accessed 21 November 2015 at http://www.bbc.com/news/business-34773940.

Bewsell, Glenn, Rodger Jamieson, Adrian Gardiner and Deborah Bunker (2005), 'An investigation of dispute resolution mechanisms on power and trust: a domain study of online trust in e-auctions', in Sokratis Katsikas, Javier López, & Günther Pernul (eds.), *Trust, Privacy, and Security in Digital Business*. Berlin, Germany: Springer, pp. 288–98.

Blackwell, Roger D., Paul W. Miniard and James F. Engel (2001), *Consumer Behavior*, 9th edition. Fort Worth: Harcourt College.

Bloomberg (2011), 'Baidu, Taobao identified as "notorious markets" by U.S. for helping piracy', accessed 21 November 2015 at http://www.bloomberg.com/news/2011-02-28/u-s-says-baidu-a-notorious-market-for-pirated-materials-1-.html.

BysoftChina (2015), 'In China, the top e-commerce sites control a market share of over 92%', accessed 21 November 2015 at http://www.bysoftchina.com/marketplaces.

Cheung, Ming (2012), 'Shanzhai phenomenon in China: the disparity between IPR legislation and enforcement', *International Review of Intellectual Property and Competition Law* **43** (1): 3–20.

China Daily (2012), 'Turnover at Tmall.com and Taobao.com tops 1 trillion yuan', accessed 21 November 2015 at http://news.alibaba.com/article/detail/news/100956282-1-turnover-tmall.com-taobao.com-tops-1.html.

China Daily (2013), 'Trust among Chinese "drops to record low"', accessed 21 November 2015 at http://www.chinadaily.com.cn/china/2013-02/18/content_16230755.htm.

CNN (2011), 'Taobao sells hacked iTunes accounts', accessed 21 November 2015 at http://www.cnngo.com/shanghai/shop/buy-anything-tabao-hack-itunes-account-605066.

eMarketer (2014), 'Retail sales worldwide will top $22 trillion this year ecommerce eclipses $1.3 trillion, led by China and US', accessed 21 November 2015 at http://www.emarketer.com/Article/Retail-Sales-Worldwide-Will-Top-22-Trillion-This-Year/1011765.

Gao, Fuping (2004), 'The e-commerce legal environment in China: status quo and issues', *Temple International and Comparative Law Journal* **18**: 51–75.

Hexun Tech (2011), *mei maoyi daibiaoshu jiang baidu taobao lie ru e ming shichang mingdan* ('U.S. Trade Representative blacklisted Baidu and Taobao as notorious markets'), accessed 21 November 2015 at http://tech.hexun.com.tw/2011-03-01/127634376.html.

iResearch Consulting Group (2010), 'iResearch: 2009 China online shopping market scale nearly 250 billion yuan', accessed 21 November 2015 at http://www.iresearchchina.com/view.aspx?id=9083.

iResearch Consulting Group (2011), *2010 nian zhongguo wangluo guowu niandu shuju fabu* ('2010 China online shopping annual figures'), accessed 21 November 2015 at http://www.iresearch.com.cn/View/131768.html.

Jones, Kiku and Lori N.K. Leonard (2008), 'Trust in consumer-to-consumer electronic commerce', *Information & Management* **45** (2): 88–95.

Liao, Huafei, Robert W. Proctor and Gavriel Salvendy (2009), 'Content preparation for e-commerce involving Chinese and US online consumers', *International Journal of Human-Computer Interaction* **25** (8): 729–61.

Lu, Yaobin, Ling Zhao and Bin Wang (2010), 'From virtual community members to C2C e-commerce buyers: trust in virtual communities and its effect on consumers' purchase intention', *Electronic Commerce Research and Applications* **9** (4): 346–60.

Martinsons, Maris G. (2008), 'Relationship-based e-commerce: theory and evidence from China', *Information Systems Journal* **18** (4): 331–56.

Mayer, Roger C., James H. Davis and F. David Schoorman (1995), 'An integrative model of organizational trust', *Academy of Management Review* **20** (3): 709–34.

Nielsen (2014), '71 percent of top-tier Chinese consumers choose cards over cash as preferred payment method for everyday spending', accessed 21 November 2015 at http://www.nielsen.com/cn/en/press-room/2014/nielsen-71-percent-of-top-tier-chinese-consumers-choose-cards-over-cash-as-preferred-payment-method-for-everyday-spending.html.

PCWorld (2009), 'China's online payment services ride e-commerce boom', accessed

21 November 2015 at http://www.pcworld.com/businesscenter/article/162560/chinas_online_payment_services_ride_ecommerce_boom.html.

Puma v. Taobao.com (2006), Guangzhou Intermediate People's Court, China.

San Martín, Sonia, Carmen Camarero and Rebecca San José (2011), 'Does involvement matter in online shopping satisfaction and trust?', *Psychology and Marketing* **28** (2): 145–67.

Sina (2009), *xinliang diaocha cheng yu qi cheng wangyou ceng zai wangshang maidao jiahuo* ('Sina survey reveals that over 70 per cent of web users found their online purchases had turned out to be fake'), accessed 21 November 2015 at http://www.kuqin.com/shuoit/20090313/39603.html.

Sina (2011), *taobaowang cheng xiaofeizhe nian weiquan chenggong jin e da 1.69 yi* ('Taobao stated that its consumer protection amount reached RMB 1.69 billion this year'), accessed 21 November 2015 at http://finance.sina.com/bg/tech/sinacn/20110106/0441207140.html.

Sina Shanghai Morning Post (2011), *taobao dianjia huan ge ming jixu shou iTunes zhanghao jiage zhang le yi bei*, ('Taobao sold illegal iTunes accounts. Sellers continued to sell the accounts by renaming them and pushing up the price'), accessed 21 November 2015 at http://sh.sina.com.cn/news/f/2011-01-13/0837169388.html.

South China Morning Post (2015), 'Regulator releases damning report on Alibaba over fake, substandard goods on Taobao', accessed 21 November 2015 at http://www.scmp.com/news/china/article/1694077/state-commerce-regulator-releases-damming-account-tabaocom-day-alibaba.

State Administration for Industry & Commerce of the People's Republic of China (SAIC) (2015), *2015 nian shangbannian quanguo shichang zhuti fazhan, shichang jianguan, xiaofei weiquan youguan qingkuang* ('Chinese market development, market monitoring and consumer rights protection in the first half of 2015'), accessed 21 November 2015 at http://www.saic.gov.cn/zwgk/tjzl/zhtj/xxzx/201507/t20150715_158914.html.

Statista (2015a), 'Number of online shoppers in China from 2006 to 2014 (in millions)', accessed 21 November 2015 at http://www.statista.com/statistics/277391/number-of-online-buyers-in-china/.

Statista (2015b), 'Market share of leading C2C e-commerce platforms in China in 2013', accessed 21 November 2015 at http://www.statista.com/statistics/225875/market-share-in-c2c-online-shopping-in-china/.

Taobao Forum (2011), accessed 21 November 2015 at http://bbs.taobao.com/catalog/thread/513886-250582652-1.htm.

Taylor, Phil (2009), 'Copy culture', accessed 21 November 2015 at http://www.chinalawandpractice.com/Article/2194870/Channel/9937/Copy-culture.html.

TechNode (2013), 'How does Taobao use user data?', accessed 21 November 2015 at http://technode.com/2013/06/14/how-does-taobao-uses-user-data/.

The Wall Street Journal (2014a), 'Alibaba's IPO priced at $68 a share', accessed 21 November 2015 at http://www.wsj.com/articles/alibabas-ipo-priced-at-68-a-share-1411075675?mod=WSJ_hp_LEFTTopStories.

The Wall Street Journal (2014b), 'Knockoffs thrive on Alibaba's Taobao: critics say Chinese e-commerce giant needs to do more about counterfeit goods', accessed 21 November 2015 at http://www.wsj.com/articles/SB10001424052702304049904579517642158573008.

Turel, Ofir, Yufei Yuan and Catherine E. Connelly (2008), 'In justice we trust: predicting user acceptance of e-customer services', *Journal of Management Information Systems* **24** (4): 123–51.

Xinhua News (2011), 'China's e-commerce boom hits a bump', accessed 21 November 2015 at http://www.china.org.cn/business/2011-01/25/content_21815506.htm.

Xu, Bo, Zhangxi Lin and Bingjia Shao (2010), 'Factors affecting consumer behaviors in online buy-it-now auctions', *Internet Research* **20** (5): 509–26.

Yang v. Eachnet.com (2000), Hong Kou Intermediate People's Court, Shanghai, China.

Zhao, Jing, Shan Wang and Wilfred V. Huang (2008), 'A study of B2B e-market in China: e-commerce process perspective', *Journal of Information and Management* **45** (4), 242–48.

29. Elderly people and the Internet: a demographic reconsideration
Huan Wu

INTRODUCTION

When the business leaders of China's Internet companies talk about the synergies between the Internet and cultural industries, very few references are made to older adults. Most attention is focused on youth demographics, the heaviest consumers of online sites and social media. As other chapters in this volume have shown, the fast adoption of digital technologies by China's one child generation (those born after 1980) provides a partial picture of China's digital cultural and creative industries.

However, if we are to gain a comprehensive understanding of these industries in China, it is important to represent all citizens of China. Elderly people are avid consumers of TV drama; they participate enthusiastically in cultural activities such as communal dancing in parks; and many uphold traditional cultural values. But when it comes to digital culture, the question remains: how do they participate? Moreover, what is the potential of this growing demographic? How is their social capital developed and maintained through digital culture?

These are missing parts of the puzzle.

One of the purposes of this chapter is to analyse how older citizens' participation in virtual communities contributes to our understanding of the digital cultural and creative industries. Through investigating the types of social capital accumulated by elderly net users, I demonstrate how older people make use of the Internet and virtual communities in a creative way. To illustrate the nature of participation I examine a senior-oriented website named OldKids and a selection of people who belong to the OldKids community.

My purpose in this chapter is to show how OldKids members obtain and maintain social capital. The concept of social capital varies from scholar to scholar. I discuss some of these definitions below. In summary, however, social capital is 'the sum of the resources, actual or virtual, that accrue to an individual or a group by virtue of possessing a durable network of more or less institutionalized relationships of mutual acquaintance and recognition' (Bourdieu and Wacquant 1992: 14). Social capital can be understood as productive resources that inhere in social relations (Resnick 2001). Moreover, it can be 'a source of network-mediated benefits beyond the immediate family' (Portes 1998: 12). In this chapter I use Lin's conception of social capital, regarded as 'the resources embedded in social networks accessed and used by actors for action' (Lin 2001: 25). This definition highlights the possibility that people mobilize social capital through active action. This can be observed through their use of the Internet.

ELDERLY CHINESE, THE INTERNET AND SOCIAL CAPITAL

According to the report released by National Bureau of Statistics of the People's Republic of China in January 2015, by the end of 2014, the number of people over 60 was 212.42 million, or 15.5 per cent of the population; at the same time the number of people over 65 totaled 137.55 million (constituting 10.1 per cent of the population).[1] The current 'older generation' in China was born between the 1930s and the 1950s; they were witnesses to momentous historical change in China. Their life paths are drawn directly from the history books of China. Most experienced the People's Commune Movement of the 1950s, as well as the 'Down to the Countryside Movement' (late 1960s to early 1970s),[2] which was part of the so-called Cultural Revolution (1966–76). Following the chaos of these turbulent times, the Economic Reforms beginning in 1978 saw a focus on productivity. Another social transformation occurred: the family structure underwent change, effectively loosening the strong ties between older adults and their families.

As a consequence of more nuclear families (e.g. one child), many elderly people have sought to develop social ties and find emotional support from outside the family, just as young people do on a day-to-day basis with social media, (be-)'friending' others. However, getting elderly people to become comfortable with digital technology presents a real challenge. Research shows that China's population is aging: there will be a higher proportion of elderly people in the future than at any time in the past. Because of the impending distortion in the makeup of China's population base, largely due to the demographic effects of One Child Policy, it is vital that technology facilitates a greater sense of wellbeing for all. But putting young technology in the hands of older people is something that many businesses just don't consider: gadgets, gizmos and apps are targeted at the young and used to enhance social network consumption.

The World Health Organization (WHO) refers to those over 65 years old as 'older people', but according to social conventions in most countries, 'old' is defined by the retirement age. The Chinese retirement age was determined in the 1950s: 60 for men, 55 for female white-collar workers and 50 for female manual labourers (Dong 2007). Older adults are often represented in peripheral roles in society and portrayed in a negative stereotypical fashion (Harwood 2007; Tsai and Tsang 2012). However, it is time to discard such stereotypes, including seeing older people as digital laggards. In the past, older adults who engaged in online activities had high education levels and good incomes (Harwood 2007). With the pervasive influence of computer technology, lower prices and convenient applications (apps), the relationship of digital technology to older adults' daily lives has changed. This change is reflected in international usage of the Internet. By April 2012, 53 per cent of American adults over 65 were Internet or email users (Zickuhr and Madden 2012).

The *36th Statistical Report on Internet Development in China* issued by China Internet Network Information Center (CNNIC) showed that, by June 2015, the number of net users had risen to 668 million in China. As one would expect the majority are still young people; 23.8 per cent are in the age group of 10 to 19, and 31.4 per cent are aged between 20 and 29. Net users belonging to the age groups 50 to 59, and over 60, account for 4.3 per cent and 2.4 per cent of the total amount respectively (CNNIC, 2015). Over 50s therefore constitute 6.7 per cent or almost 45 million, a sizeable figure.

When researching Internet use of older citizens, Blit-Cohen and Litwin (2004) found that the virtual world functions as a site for older adults to build up social capital. Compared with non-users, older net users have more channels for obtaining or exchanging social capital. Similar findings turn up in a comparative study, based on comparing two senior-oriented online communities (OldKids in China and SeniorNet in the US); for instance, Xie (2006) found that Internet usage can promote older adults' civic engagement and social interaction in online communities. Moreover, offline computer clubs facilitate the formation of mutually supportive social relationships among elderly net users. Other research has revealed that how elderly people use the Internet impacts on their wellbeing: while using the Internet for information seeking and social interaction may positively influence older adults' wellbeing and social capital, using it for entertainment or for meeting with strangers can decrease the level of wellbeing (Sum et al. 2008).

Many older adults are losing social capital in the real world and there are various reasons attributed to this, including retirement, declining health, and poor living conditions (many live alone or in a community lacking a sense of community). Although older people in China hold various attitudes toward the Internet, many studies have demonstrated that the Internet can assist them to access extra-familial networks. Moreover, the nature of older people's usage of the Internet attributes new understandings and dynamics to the digital cultural and creative industries.

Although many researchers have different focuses on the 'resources' of social capital, there are some stable and agreed upon components, namely: a shared sense of collective identity, obligation, networks of social relationships, norms and trust (Blanchard 2004; Resnick 2001). Social capital may be classified into strong ties and weak ties (Granovetter 1973). The former refers to close ties between people who are emotionally connected with each other, where ties are maintained regularly. The latter refers to loose ties between people who are emotionally distant from each other: these ties are maintained infrequently (Ferlander 2007).

Scholars also categorize social capital into 'bonding' and 'bridging' social capital (Gittell and Vidal 1998; Putnam 2000). While bonding social capital indicates ties between similar people in terms of demographic factors (i.e. age and ethnicity), bridging social capital incorporates more distant ties of people from different social groups (Putnam 2000; Ferlander 2007). Williams (2006) states that strong-tie networks lead to bonding social capital while weak-tie networks produce bridging social capital. Woolcock (2001) proposes another dimension of social capital – 'linking social capital', which refers to establishing linkages with people outside the community. As I will show, 'linking social capital' provides the means for many communities to accumulate resources.

OLDKIDS' STORY

OldKids website (www.oldkids.cn) was established in Shanghai in late 2000; its founders are three inspiring men – Wang Yong, Wu Hanzhang and Zhang Zhi'an. At the time they were in their mid-twenties. Before starting a company named Qi Feng Technology Co. Ltd., they were white-collar workers. The company was established primarily to help older people to connect with each other and to provide better services for older adults. At that time there was little interest in the interactions between older adults and the Internet. Since its establishment the founders have taken up the challenge of helping older people to use computer technology and the Internet. When the project began elderly people constituted a sizeable demographic in China but many were digitally illiterate; many others had basic literacy. In 2000, there were only 22.5 million net users in Mainland China. Among these, 41 per cent were in the 18–24 age group; only 3.3 per cent were aged over 50 (CNNIC 2001).

Since its inception more than a decade ago, OldKids website has experienced several redesigns. While its interface has changed significantly, its founders still insist on using the portal to teach older people to make good use of information and communication technologies and to create a virtual community presence. During my interviews, I realized that most OldKids members shared a sense of belonging to the website. The 'spirit of OldKids', which is always mentioned by OldKids founders and members, can be regarded as the sense of community. The core meaning of this spirit includes making older adults younger and helping them realize their dreams. In addition to virtual communities, OldKids helps older adults through its offline applications and activities.

The settings of OldKids website change from time to time. Before 5 July 2013, there were five types of online platforms in OldKids website: chat rooms, bulletin board systems (BBS), blogs, micro-blogs and discussion groups. BBS and blogs are the most popular uses. Set up in 2001, the OldKids BBS was the earliest and the most popular online application. In 2010, 18,000 OldKids members registered in the BBS while more than 4,000 users set up their blogs in the OldKids Blog Channel. Although the BBS's place in popularity was replaced by the blog channel in 2006, many older people like expressing their opinions and communicating with others in BBS. On 5 July 2013, the website designers canceled BBS and moved the original discussion groups in BBS to 'Group' channel. Members can set up groups freely based on their common interests and organize offline activities in the name of a certain group. According to OldKids manager, Wang Yong, by 11 December 2014, OldKids had 100,000 registered users and its daily visits rate was close to 10,000.[3]

Of course OldKids is not the only website catering to elderly communities. However, what make it distinctive among other senior-oriented websites are its offline organizations. In addition to the OldKids computer training centre, the founders set up OldKids club in 2001; its main task is to organize different kinds of activities such as annual meetings of OldKids members. From 2001 to 2008, OldKids members had set up 19 salons throughout China. Each salon has a unique name. Compared with OldKids club, salons are place-based: their advantages lie in organizing small-scale activities, such as computer training, dinner parties, karaoke and travel. The connection between the OldKids online community and its offline communities has provided more chances for older users to obtain new networks of social relationships.

OLDKIDS MEMBERS' STORIES

The following findings are based on my observation of OldKids over six years. I had known about the OldKids website since 2001. I conducted offline fieldwork on its members from 2008 to 2009, and from 2012 to 2013. My fieldwork was primarily in Shanghai but I had the opportunity to travel with my research subjects to six other cities. I used in-depth interviews (on average each interview last 60 minutes) on 40 elderly net users (OldKids members) and the three founders of OldKids. I conducted analysis of approximately 1,800 online posts (incl. BBS posts, microblog/ blog articles).

The first member I will introduce is Wanting.[4] Aged 68 at the time of my interview, Wanting had lived in Shanghai alone for over ten years. Her two children live in Guangdong province and Hunan province. By December 2014, Wanting had written and posted a series of articles in OldKids BBS and blogs (1,235 blog articles in total). From 2006 to 2007, she published 227 diary entries in BBS, recording her life in Manchester with her daughter's family. At that time her daughter and her son-in-law, an Englishman, were living in Manchester. Her vivid description about the growth of her granddaughter in the diaries attracted a large amount of interest, creating the highest reading rate and response rate in OldKids website.

In Mainland China nearly 50 per cent of urban older adults live in empty-nest households (Guo 2012). News reports about the lonely and bleak lives of elderly people whose children have 'left the nest' keep increasing. Although living in an empty-nest household, Wanting said that she enjoyed her life every day and rarely felt loneliness because her OldKids net friends were always with her. Logging into OldKids is a routine for Wanting and other OldKids members after getting up in the morning. Wanting checks if there are messages left for her then she checks the latest posts or articles published by other net friends. Most of the time Wanting and her friends keep their online status 'live' even when they are busy with their housework. They treat each other's online status (which is shown in their web pages) as a kind of company. When Wanting was ill, she mentioned this in her blog; it was always her net friends rather than her children who sent their concerns to her first. During an interview, she said:

> Two days ago I got cold and mentioned that in one of my blog articles in the morning. I received a lot of online messages and calls from my OldKids friends from morning to evening on that day. Xiaohong (Wanting's net friend in OldKids who also lives in Shanghai) directly came to visit me in the afternoon with medicine. . .Moreover, when I went to my son's city for an operation on my leg in 2013, I received online messages and mobile messages from my net friends in OldKids from time to time. They cared about me very much.[5]

After learning about the meaning of strong ties during the interview, Wanting said that she had built up strong ties with at least ten OldKids members. It is through reading each other's posts online and meeting offline that they became close friends. Wanting said that she and her net friends trust each other and could provide emotional and practical support to each other. Wanting regularly meets her net friends offline through the activities organized by OldKids salons or clubs. As for the net friends who live in different cities, they mostly communicate with each other online. Nevertheless, the friendships formed online can also be transferred offline under certain circumstances. Wanting told me a nice story about her net friend Jingkui, who was living in Sichuan province:

> Jingkui always left comments in my blog but we were not familiar with each other for a long time as we lived in two different cities. When I planned to travel in Sichuan last October, I asked Jingkui for travelling information online. She not only gave me advice very patiently but also arranged the whole journey for me and invited me to live in her apartment. I accepted her invitation. When I first met with her husband and son, she told them that: 'this is my nominal mother.' In fact, I am only 13 years older than her; but I am happy to have a daughter like her. Since then, we become good friends both in the website and in real life.[6]

The above stories of Wanting and her net friends prove that interpersonal relationships formed online can be transferred offline. Similar stories among OldKids friends are numerous. The firm connection between OldKids online community and offline communities (salons and clubs) has provided opportunities for older netizens to build up strong ties face to face with net friends. No doubt, most older adults still believe that 'seeing is believing.'

Nowadays in Chinese cities the sense of community in most place-based communities has not been fostered. In addition, social services for the elderly fall short of requirements. By comparison, the strong ties formed in virtual communities among net friends can provide emotional solace and instrumental support for older adults. More importantly, the cost of obtaining/maintaining social ties online is much less than the cost of obtaining/maintaining the social ties offline.

MAINTAINING WEAK TIES WITH NET FRIENDS

Shouzhong, aged 71 at the time of my interview, is a productive blog writer in the OldKids Blog Channel. He was a teacher in middle school before retirement. From 17 December 2006 to 8 December 2014, he published 1,113 blog articles in OldKids. He wrote one blog article every two days on average since he opened his blog in OldKids. As Shouzhong can write in an easy and fluent way, and his articles often contain unique insights, he is a celebrated blogger among the OldKids members. He won the title of 'Top 10 Most Popular Elderly Bloggers' in 'The First National Blog Contest among Older Adults' organized by OldKids website in 2008. Shouzhong has obtained a new network of social relationships through participation in virtual communities since he joined OldKids in 2006. By 2014, he had made at least 280 net friends (whose faces are displayed on his webpage) in OldKids; and most of his net friends are loyal readers of his blog. Shouzhong told me that one of his net friends in OldKids, Xixu, insisted on writing a comment on each of his blog article for eight years.[7]

Shouzhong maintained weak ties with other OldKids members; he believes that face-to-face communication can degrade online relation-ships. While quite a lot of OldKids members are fond of participating in offline get-togethers, Shouzhong rarely joins offline activities. When he joins offline get-togethers organized by OldKids salons, he likes to talk about blog articles in the OldKids website with other net friends, at the same time avoiding discussion of friends' private affairs. During the inter-view, he said that:

> It requires capital for making friends: energy, time and money. . .this time he invited me for dinner, I have to invite him the next time. Although joining offline get-togethers was happy, when I got home after the parties, nothing left.[8]

In one of Shouzhong's blog articles 'When cyberspace is no longer inno-cent',[9] he wrote:

> What attracts older adults most in cyberspace is its innocence. . .In the real world, there are clear boundaries between people, even the interactions between relatives are always involved with interest. But in cyberspace, people treat each other equally, politely and honestly. I can speak out freely online and I find that it is an 'enclave' far from the real world.
> However, I gradually realized that cyberspace is also a vulgarized place. . .You can feel the grouping although you can't touch it. Even if you might not treat your net friends' friends as your own friends, you have to share a bitter hatred of the 'enemy' of your net friends.

When Shouzhong refers to 'grouping', he is pointing out the negative effects of social capital. Portes (1998) claims that social capital (strong ties) within a group may restrict an individual's freedom and exclude outsiders. Cyberspace is not an enclave; instead it contains countless ties with the real world. Nevertheless, cyberspace has provided more possi-bilities for the elderly to obtain benefits through extra-familial networks. Furthermore, it is easier for older adults to achieve and maintain weak ties in a virtual community than in real life, and one of the positive effects of weak ties lies in the provision of wide informational support.

Through my interviews I found that many OldKids members realized the limitations of strong ties among net friends like Shouzhong. They worried that close connections between net friends or within a group (i.e. an OldKids salon) might restrict their freedom, which is important especially after their retirement. Most of today's Chinese older adults were bound to their work units (*danwei*) for several decades. To avoid the negative impacts of strong ties, some OldKids members focus on dealing with online interpersonal relationships while restricting the time spent on participating in offline activities. Moreover, some seldom make comments on net friends' words or behaviour. However, it doesn't mean that OldKids members refuse sincere friendships and cannot build up strong ties with other older netizens. The fact is that they choose net friends carefully, always based on similar interests; and once mutual trust is established between them and their net friends, the weak ties can be gradually transferred to strong ties.

ACCUMULATING BRIDGING AND LINKING SOCIAL CAPITAL ONLINE

Yangliu, 67 at the time of interview, was an archivist working in a hospital in Shanghai before retirement. In her 'real world', she is an ordinary retired woman who looks after her young grandson with her husband at home. In the world of OldKids, however, she is a charming and modern woman who happens to be a forum moderator in the site's BBS from 2003 to 2013. When Yangliu was in high school in the 1960s in Shanghai, she dreamed of entering into the Shanghai Theatre Academy. However, her dream fell apart when the Cultural Revolution commenced in 1966. She was one of the eighteen million 'sent down youth',[10] spending 13 years in Heilongjiang province, which is in the farthest northeast of China.

In August 2007, Yangliu set up 'OldKids Hip-hop Group', possibly the first hip-hop group consisting of elderly women in Shanghai (the members' average age was over 56 in 2013). In 2009, Shanghai Dragon TV screened a program called 'Making you younger.' Featuring in a segment on 5 August 2009 were Grandma Yangliu and the hip-hop salon she led. During the interview, Yangliu described how she obtained the necessary resources for the OldKids hip-hop group. The group members did not have their own costumes for a long time due to a shortage of funds. In 2008, a reporter working for *City Weekend*[11] found out about Yangliu through her blog in OldKids website and wanted to interview her. Yangliu refused the invitation at first, worried that other people might wrongly assume that she wanted to become well known. Finally, she accepted the invitation with a precondition that the reporter help the hip-hop group seek financial support. Through the recommendation of the reporter, OldKids hip-hop group had won their first pot of gold. Yang recalled the experience:

> One day a middle-aged man called me and told me in Chinese that he was a person from overseas. I asked him 'Why you call me? I didn't know anybody overseas.' Suddenly, I thought of the reporter of *City Weekend*. I said to him 'I am Yangliu who dances hip hop; you want to ask us to perform?' The man laughed and said yes. He provided a chance for us to perform in the opening ceremony of a company. After our performance he asked me what I wanted as a reward. As he was a manager of Converse Company at that time, I asked him to give one pair of shoes to each of our group members. The manager agreed and he also gave one T-shirt to each of us. Our group members have uniform costume since then. I began to make use of both the online and offline platforms of OldKids to show the latest development of the hip-hop group. And we indeed earned more performing opportunities and support from enterprises or neighborhood committees of different districts of Shanghai.[12]

The OldKids hip-hop group members weren't professionally trained at the beginning and Yangliu said that the audiences who watched their first performance responded that it was like watching exercises to radio music. In September 2007, under the advice of OldKids founders, Yangliu put forward her plan to invite a professional hip-hop instructor to the OldKids hip-hop group in a website named Xiaoxishu (news tree), which collaborated with OldKids website at that time. Yangliu's plan attracted RMB 5,000 (around US$1,000) in a crowdfunding competition in the Xiaoxishu website with the support of OldKids members. Yangliu was impressed by the fact that many OldKids members mobilized their family members to vote for OldKids hip-hop group. With the funds, elderly hip-hop dancers were able to receive professional training and improve their performance.

Based on my interviews with OldKids members, most of those who voted for the hip-hop group didn't have strong ties with Yangliu or other group members; some of the voters did not even know about Yangliu personally. However, as they all shared the sense of belonging to OldKids, including the virtual community and offline communities, and were contemporaries with similar life experiences, they wanted to help OldKids members who were in need. This demonstrates that although the social ties between most OldKids members are weak, they can still produce bridging social capital. It is the bridging social capital that helped Yangliu receive support from numerous unfamiliar OldKids members. Field (2003) has pointed out that bridging social capital enables people to access resources and information outside their close social network.

Like Yangliu, another OldKids member, Yixiuge,[13] 71 at the time of my interview, managed to obtain resources for *jinshi* salon, one of the 19 OldKids salons. It was set up in 2004 drawing on 'bridging social capital' among salon members and through 'linking social capital' from the local government. Yixiuge learned how to use computers by himself after retirement; he said that it was the net friends he met in OldKids who taught him various Internet applications online. He is also fond of teaching other older adults, especially the members of *jinshi* salon to master different computer and Internet-related applications. On several occasions Yixiuge led salon members to participate in senior-related digital competitions as representatives of the Jinshan[14] District Committee on Aging. In response the district officials provided a room for the *jinshi* salon to hold its activities. In fact, a lack of places for holding offline activities is one of the biggest problems faced by most OldKids salons. Through building up linking social capital with the district government, Yixiuge solved this problem.

Many senior-oriented websites in China, like OldKids, have managed to obtain linking social capital from the outside world. It is found that through joining the activities co-organized by OldKids website and governments either online or offline, more senior netizens have learned how to elicit support from local government or companies (especially the dot-com companies and companies producing older persons' products). For example, nearly 500 OldKids members worked as volunteers in the 'Help older people use the Internet' project, a public welfare project conducted by the Shanghai Working Commission on Aging and OldKids website, from 2003 to 2006; at the same time, these elderly volunteers received more chances of social engagement provided by the government.

DISCUSSION AND CONCLUSION

Social capital is not only one of the most significant benefits senior netizens have obtained through assimilating themselves into digital culture but also an important driving force to go online. Hjorth and Arnold (2013) translate the traditional concept *guanxi* in Chinese into 'social capital' when analyzing the development of social media in China. In Mandarin *guanxi* also points to 'social ties' which has an instrumental sense of maintaining one's existing connections (Keane 2013). Chinese people treasure social ties very much. For older people, abundant social ties can bring both information and emotional support. However, in a digital and fast-changing world, maintaining and creating social ties in the real world has become harder for Chinese older adults than ever before. By comparison, virtual communities provide older adults convenient platforms to maintain existing social ties and chances of creating social ties.

While many senior-oriented websites have closed down, OldKids has developed smoothly. During my research on OldKids, I realized that it is a special case because of the social environment that 'nourishes' it. OldKids is headquartered in Shanghai, a city that has the largest proportion of people over 60 years old in China (Shen 2012). As of 31 December 2014, the total population in Shanghai was 14.38 million; people at the age of 60 or above constitute 28.8 per cent of the city's total population (Shanghai Research Centre on Aging 2015). Moreover, OldKids founders have found out an effective way to achieve financial and policy support from the Shanghai municipal government. Both parties aim to help older adults enjoy the benefits brought about by the Internet. In 2011, OldKids' parent company transferred from being a private company to social entrepreneurs[15] which means it could gain more stable support from municipal government.

OldKids members are not representative of all elderly Chinese. Most are in good economic conditions and their health allows them to join online and offline activities. Nevertheless, the stories of OldKids and its members are typical in today's China: they show the diffusion of digital culture among older people and how the lives of Chinese seniors are changing. With the Internet penetrating into every corner of society and changing people's lifestyles, the OldKids members' stories demonstrate how older adults are adapting. They learn to use computers and the Internet, and obtain social capital by virtue of virtual community; and what is more, they choose different forms of social capital according to their understanding of digital cultural industries.

'My dream makes me young,' Yangliu says, 'but without the Internet, without OldKids, I cannot realize my dream.'

NOTES

1. Anon (2015), Guojia Tongji Ju: zhongguo 65sui yishang renkou zhanbi shouchao 10% ('National Bureau of Statistics of People's Republic of China: the proportion of people over 65 among the total population exceed 10 per cent'), data accessed 20 May 2015 at http://www.ce.cn/xwzx/gnsz/gdxw/201502/26/t20150226_4653796.shtml.
2. Literally 'Up to the Mountains and down to the countryside'.
3. Interviewed 16 December 2014.
4. In this chapter, all the interviewees' names are their nicknames in OldKids website.
5. Interviewed 21 April 2014.
6. Interviewed 25 September 2008.

7. Interviewed 25 August 2013.
8. Interviewed 7 October 2009.
9. Shou Z. (2008), *Dang wangluo buzai chunqing* ('When cyberspace is no longer innocent'), OldKids blog, 15 October, accessed 15 October 2008 at http://www.oldkids. cn/blog/blog_con.php?blogid=61924.
10. The data is an estimate, accessed 30 November 2014 at http://en.wikipedia.org/wiki/ Sent-down_youth.
11. City Weekend is an English-language lifestyle and entertainment magazine and website, which belongs to the Ringier Publishing Group.
12. Interviewed 19 June, 2009.
13. Interviewed 18 March 2012.
14. Jinshan is a suburban district of southwestern Shanghai.
15. According to Zhao (2012), the term social enterprise used here points to the enterprise applying business strategies to achieving philanthropic goals.

REFERENCES

Blanchard, Anita (2004), 'The effects of dispersed virtual communities on face-to-face social capital', in Marleen Huysman and Volker Wulf (eds.), *Social Capital and Information Technology*. Cambridge, MA: MIT Press, pp. 53–73.
Blit-Cohen, Edith and Howard Litwin (2004), 'Elder participation in cyberspace: A qualitative analysis of Israeli retirees', *Journal of Aging Studies*, **18** (4): 385–98.
Bourdieu, Pierre and Wacquant, Loïc (1992), *An Invitation to Reflexive Sociology*. Chicago: University of Chicago Press.
CNNIC (2001), *di 7ci zhongguo hulian wangluo fazhan zhuangkuang tongji baogao* ('The 7th Statistical Report on Internet Development in China'), 31 January, accessed 10 May 2014 at http://www.cnnic.net.cn/hlwfzyj/hlwxzbg/hlwtjbg/201206/P020120612485130956920.pdf.
CNNIC (2015), *di 36ci zhongguo hulian wangluo fazhan zhuangkuang tongji baogao* ('The 36th Statistical Report on Internet Development in China'), data accessed 23 July 2015 at http://cnnic.cn/hlwfzyj/hlwxzbg/hlwtjbg/201507/P020150723549500667087.pdf.
Dong, Yanjie (2007), *60/50 tuixiu nianling xian* ('60/50 retirement line'), *Society Observation* 4: 16–19.
Ferlander, Sara (2007), 'The importance of different forms of social capital for health', *Acta Sociologica* **50** (2): 115–28.
Field, John (2003), *Social Capital* (2nd edn.). Milton Park, Abingdon, Oxon; New York: Routledge.
Gittell, J. Ross and Avis C. Vidal (1998), *Community Organizing: Building Social Capital as a Development Strategy*. Thousand Oaks, CA: Sage.
Granovetter, S. Mark (1973), 'The strength of weak ties', *American Journal of Sociology* **78** (6): 1360–80.
Guo, M. (2012), *quanguo laoling ban: woguo chengshi laonianren kongchao jiating bili da 49.7%* ('China National Working Commission on Aging: the proportion of 'empty nest' families reach 49.7 per cent'), 23 September, accessed 20 January 2014 at http://politics. people.com.cn/n/2012/0923/c70731-19082699.html.
Harwood, Jake (2007), *Understanding Communication and Aging*. Thousand Oaks, CA: Sage.
Hjorth, Larissa and Michael Arnold (2013), *Online @ Asia Pacific: Mobile, Social and Locative Media in the Asia–Pacific*. New York: Routledge.
Keane, M. (2013), 'A review of Online Asia-Pacific by Larissa Hjorth and Michael Arnold', accessed 8 May 2015 at www.creativetransformations.asia/2013/09/ technology-media-and-asia/.
Lin, Nan (2001), *Social Capital: A Theory of Social Structure and Action*. New York: Cambridge University Press.

Portes, Alejandro (1998), 'Social capital: Its origins and application in modern sociology', *Annual Review of Sociology* 24: 1–24.
Putnam, Robert D. (2000), *Bowling Alone: the Collapse and Revival of American Community*. New York: Simon & Schuster.
Resnick, Paul (2001), 'Beyond bowling together: sociotechnical capital', in J.M. Carroll (ed.), *Human-Computer Interaction in the New Millennium*. New York: ACM Press; Boston, MA: Addison-Wesley, pp. 647–72.
Shanghai Research Centre on Aging (2015), *2014 Shanghai shi laonian renkou he laoling shiye jiance tongji xinxi* ('2014 statistical information about Shanghai's aging population and elderly services'), accessed 15 June 2015 at http://www.shrca.org.cn/5742.html.
Shen, H. (2012), *2015 niandi Shanghai laonian renkou bili yuji jin 30 %* ('The proportion of older people in total population of Shanghai will reach 30 per cent by the end of 2015'), 20 July, accessed 30 January 2013 at http://china.caixin.com/2012-07-20/100413329.html.
Sum, Shima, Mark R. Mathews, Mohsen Pourghasem and Ian Hughes (2008), 'Internet technology and social capital: How the Internet affects seniors' social capital and wellbeing', *Journal of Computer-mediated Communication* 14: 202–20.
Tsai, Yean, and Kuo-Jen Tsang (2012), *Aging and Communication: Theory, Research, and Teaching Applications*. Taipei: Wunan Book Inc. Press.
Williams, Dmitri (2006), 'On and off the Net: Scales for social capital in an online era', *Journal of Computer Mediated Communication* 11: 593–628.
Woolcock, Michael (2001), 'The place of social capital in understanding social and economic outcomes', *Canadian Journal of Policy Research* **2** (1): 11–17.
Wu, Yushao (2013), *Zhongguo laoling shiye fazhan baogao* (*China Report of the Development on Aging*). Beijing: Social Sciences Academic Press.
Xie, Bo (2006), 'Growing older in the information age: civic engagement, social relationships, and well-being among older Internet users in China and the United States', unpublished doctoral dissertation, Rensselaer Polytechnic Institute, New York.
Zhao, Meng (2012), 'The social enterprise emerges in China', *Stanford Social Innovation Review* Spring: 29–35.
Zickuhr, Kathryn and Mary Madden (2012), 'Older adults and internet use', 6 June, accessed 12 November 2014 at www.sainetz.at/dokumente/Older_adults_and_internet_use_2012.pdf.

PART V

RECALIBRATING SPACE, TRADITION AND REGIONAL IDENTITY

30. Editor's introduction
Michael Keane

The final part of this volume concerns itself with notions of place and identity, illustrated in design, film festivals and urban development strategies. As mentioned in the introduction to the book, and in more detail in Part II, the cultural and creative industries have become an abiding preoccupation of central, provincial and local governments, both from an economic development perspective and a nationalistic 'strong cultural power' strategy. The tangible elements of these 'soft power' industries have assumed priority: things that can be seen, measured, and ultimately exported signify that Chinese cultural power is on the ascendancy. While the 'national project' benefits from the labours of China's cultural workers and artisans, the question of regional identity has assumed growing importance in a nation that is transforming while diversifying (see Sun 2012).

By way of conclusion, the issues that we return to in this section are first, can China use culture and creativity to redesign and rebrand its global image; and second, how is creativity transferred within and across locales? The chapters that follow show that indigenous and grassroots identities are consolidating despite the tendencies to homogenize that have dogged development since the 1980s. In setting out the context for the discussion of cultural identity it is therefore worth briefly considering the notion of design. Attention to design can inject new life into mature markets and bring about diversification that leads to more profitable markets (Bruce 2009). From a broad perspective design embraces pursuits that involve differing degrees of technique, and, as Bjarke Liboriussen has shown in chapter 5, different uses of 'tools' by different generational cohorts. The applied arts cover fields including industrial design, graphic design, fashion, interior design, decorative arts and functional art. As we have also seen in the discussion of ethnic cultural and creative industries (Li and Huang this volume), China has a long tradition in the design and replication of crafted decorative arts.

Design, as well as design education is a growth industry. A potent symbol of China's modernization on the one hand and Chinese modernity on the other, design is the prototypical creative industry, adding value to commodities and services. As China attempts to move up the value chain, replacing quantity with quality, design has an important role to play. In China the top eight universities all have design courses, usually under the umbrella description of 'fine arts'. The best-known design education institutions are Tsinghua University Art College and the China Central Academy of Fine Arts (both in Beijing), the Guangzhou Academy of Fine Arts, Hunan University School of Design, the Sichuan Academy of Fine Arts, the Hangzhou Academy of Fine Arts (Zhejiang Province), the Xi'an Academy of Fine Arts, the Lu Xun Academy of Fine Arts (in the city of Shenyang) and the China Academy of Fine Arts in Hangzhou.

Another side of the regional development equation, and not dissimilar from design, is the cluster, spaces designed to accommodate people working together, sometimes on design-related products, other times on fine art. Many scholars have explored how this remarkable manifestation of Chinese urban development has become the *de facto* logic of the cultural and creative industries in China (O'Connor and Gu 2006; Wang 2007; Zheng and Chan 2013; Zhong 2012; Gu 2015). As I have discussed in detail (Keane 2011), China is a kingdom of clusters, theme parks, cultural quarters, media bases and incubators. The cultural (and creative cluster) according to Xin Gu (2015: 251) represents a kind of 'boiled down' science park model in which 'the notion of culture was replaced with the notion of innovation in its attempt to access capital'.

Of course innovation is much sought after: moreover, in the quest to show allegiance to the principles enshrined in the 11th Five Year Plan, the creative cluster has morphed into an up-scaled version of the factory system, churning out cheap rather than novel products (see Keane 2011; Zheng and Chan 2013; Wang 2007). The cluster model first came on the radar of China's leaders in the early 1980s, a time when the enforced 'peoples' communes' of Mao Zedong's revolutionary socialism gave way to a different form of collective organization under the more pragmatic stewardship of Deng Xiaoping. Town and Village Enterprises (TVEs) were concentrations of light industrial activity, generating cheap household goods. Often outside city and town areas, many TVEs were owned and run by government; others were joint ventures with investment from local, national and even international sources (Gu and Lundvall 2006). From 1988 Economic and Technology Zones appeared, beginning in the more open southern provinces and free trade zones, later extending to so-called 'open cities' (McGee et al. 2007). Most of these parks were aimed at low-end manufacturing, a problem that has plagued China's clustering landscape. Even in the creative sectors like design and animation much of the work conducted is OEM (Original Equipment Manufacture); in other words service work where there are no real 'gains of trade' in IP acquisition. Working for foreign companies has two sides, however. Workers can just work and not worry about being creative or, if they want to learn, they can acquire 'know-how', leave and start up their own venture.

THE CHAPTERS

In the first chapter Christiane Herr discusses contemporary architectural developments in China in the context of China's simultaneous desire to modernize and maintain tradition. Herr says that since the early 20th century the relationship between modernization and tradition has aroused robust debate among Chinese architects. Some of the debates have explored a mission to find, or rediscover a Chinese architectural identity. The concern for a 'new tradition' is not new, however; it has resurfaced many times over the past century. In the chapter Herr argues that modernization and tradition in Chinese architecture are not at odds with each other; rather that architectural modernization in China is linked on many levels to a reinvention of tradition in architectural terms. In making this point she frames recent Chinese architectural developments within their own context rather than comparing them to Western precedents. Citing the examples of the contemporary Chinese architect Wang Shu, who has explored 'vernacular styles' in his work, the chapter shows how the search for a new tradition is drawing on different perspectives on the relations between architecture and art.

Fashion is fundamentally a consumer activity that gravitates towards places of financial activity and creative capital, hence the history of traditional fashion centres such as Paris, Milan, London and New York. Yet this was how the system was in the past. Tim Lindgren, a practicing fashion designer who has produced garments in Shanghai, argues that the concept of Eurocentric hegemony, originally founded on industrial might, is now a myth perpetuated by large corporations headquartered in Europe. Now the hollowing out of European markets and the need for consistent revenue streams has led to a strategic focus on the emergent Chinese consumer and encroachment upon the territory of the domestic Chinese designer.

Traditionally profits were repatriated to Europe, yet increasingly financial capital now flows in reverse to Asia for the benefit of Asian investors. In this way, China's reputation as manufacturer to the world is being reshaped by a political mandate that underpins a new creative and financial impetus. Lindgren contends that by emphasizing the economic flows of fashion instead of the aesthetic field, an alternate view of a fashion system is emerging that focuses on the increasing importance of Chinese fashion design to the domestic economy and an intensifying presence on the global stage. In this new dawn digital media is allowing Chinese designers to move from mass production while consumers enjoy the customization of production. New technologies provide a more efficient way of working and purchasing product. With the advent of the online market place for distribution there is a sense of optimism that China can move away from the 'world factory' image.

In the next chapter, Ran Ma and Cindy Wong examine how theories of cultural industries might be applied to film festivals. Cities have become identified with festivals and vice versa. Moreover, film festivals have always been alternatives to mass cinema, aimed at selective local and global audiences. Since the 1980s increased efforts by government, sponsors (oftentimes multinational corporation) and local creative personnel have conspired to turn film festivals into viable cultural institutions, in this way creating global networks of production, distribution and curating that extend over non-mainstream cinema globally. One of the aims of the chapter therefore is to investigate the alternatives to state-defined creativity, illustrated by large urban festivals such as the Shanghai International Film Festival. Since the early 2000s, a number of grassroots-level independent film festivals have emerged in culturally vibrant cities such as Kunming (the Yunnan Multi Culture Visual Festival, documentary biennale, known as YunFest), Nanjing (the China Independent Film Festival) and Beijing (the China Documentary Film Festival; and the Beijing Independent Film Festival).

As mentioned above, creative clusters have become the default setting for urban development and cultural policy in China. Some like Beijing's 798 Art Zone and Shanghai's Tianzifang, have acquired brand identity, primarily as tourist markets. Noting the success of these clusters, governments have 'jumped on the bandwagon'. The logic of industrial clustering offers an irresistible development lure, which more often translates into real estate speculation than intellectual property. In this chapter Juncheng Dai and Michael Keane examine the momentum to turn China into a kingdom of cultural quarters and clusters. One of the attractions of clustering is the belief that they lead to knowledge spill-overs, in other words communication between the participants and co-workers leads to sharing of knowledge. The question is: who is the knowledge gatekeeper in a creative cluster? The chapter begins by critiquing the proposition that knowledge is widely shared in China, drawing on previous studies on animation parks in Suzhou and Beijing, and creative clusters in Shanghai. Then utilizing relational economic geography and Mark Granovetter's seminal work on 'strong ties-weak ties' (Granovetter 1973), the chapter offers empirical data to show how innovation occurs, or doesn't occur, in an industrial design cluster, the case being the Guangdong Industrial Design City.

The final chapter, by Jane Zheng, extends the discussion to Shanghai. Zheng looks at the role of intellectuals and creative workers in Shanghai, tracing the development of applied and commercial art in modern China to a group of artists and art scholars during the Republican period (1912–49). She shows how the publication of art related studies during the 1920s and 1930s pioneered awareness of the relationship between art and industry in China. The contrast is drawn with the late 1990s, when the concept of industrializing art and culture re-emerged within a globalizing policy framework of 'culture as industry'. Shanghai embraced the creative zeitgeist, channelling workers into so-called 'creative industry clusters' (*chuangyi jijuqu*). While the ethos of creative industries in most international cases is small-scale business, many of the clusters in Shanghai have targeted large-scale commercial organizations with a view to profiting from culture. Rather than build creative communities, Zheng argues that these clusters have done little to help foster awareness of art and culture and have not served local communities of intellectuals and creative workers. In effect, the contrast between the Republican period and the contemporary era is starkly drawn, problematizing contemporary Chinese cultural policy for cultural and creative industries.

REFERENCES

Bruce, Margaret (2009), 'Unleashing the creative potential of design in business', in Tudor Rickards, Mark A. Runco and Susan Moger (eds.), *The Routledge Companion to Creativity*. London: Routledge, pp. 37–45.

Granovetter, Mark S. (1973), 'The strength of weak ties', *American Journal of Sociology* **78**: 1360–80.

Gu, Xin (2015), 'Cultural economy and urban development in Shanghai', in Kate Oakley and Justin O'Connor (eds.), *The Routledge Companion to the Creative Industries*. London: Routledge, pp. 246–56.

Gu, Shulin and Lundvall, Bengt-Åke (2006), 'China's innovation system and the move towards harmonious growth and endogenous innovation', *Innovation, Management, Policy and Practice* **8**: 1–26.

Keane, Michael (2011), *China's New Creative Clusters: Governance, Human Capital and Investment*. London: Routledge.

McGee, T.G., Lin, C.S., Marton, A.M., Wang Y.L, and Wu Jiaping (2007), *China's Urban Space: Development Under Market Socialism*. London: Routledge.

O'Connor, Justin and Xin Gu (2006), 'A new modernity? The arrival of "creative industries" in China', *International Journal of Cultural Studies* **9** (3): 271–83.

Sun, Wanning (2012), 'Localizing Chinese media: a geographic turn in media and communication research', in Wanning Sun and Jenny Chio (eds.) *Mapping Media in China: Region, Province, Locality*. London: Routledge, 13–28.

Wang, Jici (2007), 'Industrial clusters in China: the low road versus the high road in cluster development', in A. Scott and G. Garofoli (eds.) *Development on the Ground: Clusters, Networks and Regions in Emerging Economies*. London: Routledge, pp. 145–64.

Zheng, Jane, and Roger Chan (2013), 'A property-led approach to cluster development: "creative industry clusters" and creative industry networks in Shanghai', *Town Planning Review* **84** (5): 605–32.

Zhong, Sheng (2012), 'New economy space, new social relations. M50 and Shanghai's new art world in the making', in Peter W. Daniels, K.C. Ho, and Thomas A. Hutton (eds.), *New Economic Spaces in Asian Cities: From Industrial Restructuring to the Cultural Turn*. London: Routledge, pp. 166–83.

31. Between contemporary and traditional: the ongoing search for a Chinese architectural identity
Christiane M. Herr

MODERNIZATION AND TRADITION IN CHINESE ARCHITECTURE

Ever since wide-ranging political and economic reforms began in the 1980s, China has invested great effort in its continuing modernization. Rapid development and urbanization have affected society on almost every level and have shaped recent architectural history. In contemporary China, architecture and urbanization embody and display collective achievements on China's road to becoming a modernized nation. The allure of modernization is empowering for those who are part of it; newer districts in Chinese cities proudly display the names of major urban thoroughfares such as 'Modern Avenue' and major commercial landmarks like 'Contemporary Plaza'.

Modernization has however also brought with it the destruction of centuries-old material and immaterial traditions, as contemporary urban landscapes throughout China make glaringly obvious (Figure 31.1). Although much of China's architectural development over the past three decades has centred on modernizing through opening up to and importing Western ideas, a parallel discourse addresses the continuation or reinvention of tradition.

Figure 31.1   Self-contained large-scale suburban quarters in Suzhou replace villages and farms

In this chapter I discuss contemporary architectural developments in China in the context of simultaneous desires to modernize and maintain tradition. Since the early 20th century the relationship between modernization and tradition has aroused great interest, as well as generating robust debate among Chinese architects. It continues to drive the quest for a Chinese architectural identity today. The concern for a 'new tradition' has resurfaced at every stage of China's architectural development over the past century in spite of reoccurring abrupt and politically charged breaks with tradition.[1] In this chapter I will argue that modernization and tradition in Chinese architecture are not at odds with each other; rather that architectural modernization in China is linked on many levels to a reinvention of tradition in architectural terms. In making this point I frame recent Chinese architectural developments within their own context rather than by comparison with Western precedents, echoing Rowe and Kuan (2002: 201), who argue that modernization in China is self-determining and different in significant respects from processes of modernization experienced in the West.

CHINESE ESSENCE, WESTERN FORM

The search for authenticity and identity in architecture began more than a century ago, a consequence of China's encounter with the West. Faced with the challenges of increasing contact with technically advanced imperialist powers during the late 19th and early 20th centuries, concerned scholars began to advocate ways by which China might adapt to this cultural challenge (Li 2012). In an influential essay ('Exhortation to Study') published in 1898, Zhang Zhidong argued that the survival of Chinese culture depended on using Western knowledge in a way that could maintain and enact a core of Chinese learning (*zhongxue weiti xixue weiyong*) (Zhang, 1901). Following this trajectory of thinking, a self-conscious attachment to, and concern for tradition among Chinese architects during the early decades of the 20th century resulted in a perspective that framed 'essence' (*ti*) – or Chinese architectural identity – in the Chinese tradition, whereas 'form' (*yong*) could be derived from emulating imported technologies and precedents (Rowe and Kuan 2002: 207).

Perspectives similar to Zhang Zhidong's underlie architectural discourse in China today: they exert a major influence on the development of contemporary architectural expression. Despite China opening to international ideas, Chinese culture remains introspective and self-centred; this may be due to historic reasons as well as restricted opportunities for international travel and exchange. With the question of 'Chineseness' – or

'Chinese essence' – in architecture so inextricably connected with interpretations of tradition, architectural modernization in China may paradoxically generate (and be generated by) a rediscovery, reinterpretation and reintegration of the past.

In this chapter I discuss contemporary Chinese architecture, its associated discourses and building practice in light of the long and enduring search for a 'new tradition'. After briefly charting the development of Chinese architecture in the 20th century, I outline several central concerns within contemporary discourses surrounding Chinese architectural identity, including: architecture as an imported profession, commercialization, cultural values, the distinction of art from architecture, the role of leaders and lineages in the Confucian tradition as well as questions of national identity. As the scope of this chapter is limited, I present these aspects in breadth rather than in depth, hoping to provide those not familiar with contemporary architectural discourse in China a glimpse of architectural developments as seen from within.

ARCHITECTURE AS IMPORTED PROFESSION WITH AN IMPORTED SENSE OF HISTORY

In traditional Chinese society professional architects did not exist. Buildings were designed and built primarily by craftspeople, based on knowledge handed down orally from master to apprentice, or in the case of official buildings, strictly following government codes (Liang 1934). Architecture was not a part of the classical canon of accomplishments expected of gentleman scholars (*junzi*): such skill-sets included playing a string instrument (*qin*), Chinese chess (*qi*), calligraphy (*shu*) and painting (*hua*) (Clunas 1997). Similarly, traditional Chinese architecture primarily relied on stylistic as well as technological forms that changed only slightly over the centuries: moreover architecture was not seen as a means of personal expression. With increasing contact and exchange with the West, the profession of architecture was introduced into China, first by foreign professionals working in the Western settlements of the trade ports in the late 19th century, and later by those studying architecture overseas and returning to China (Kvan et al. 2008).

After the fall of the Qing government in 1911, Chinese architecture was included in the search for a new national image, one that would suit the newly established Republic of China. Buildings combining new materials with traditional Chinese stylistic elements were identified with the image of the Chinese Nationalist government (*guomindang*) during the 1920s, with steel and reinforced concrete increasingly replacing traditional timber constructions. This new style developed to a great extent through the works of Henry K. Murphy, an American architect working as architectural advisor to the Chinese government at the time (Cody 2001). The introduction of Western building forms and techniques and later, architectural education modelled on Western precedents, gradually led to the establishment of professional architectural practices in China in the early part of the 20th century (Kvan et al. 2008).

In effect, the importation of the architectural profession constituted a sharp break with existing modes of building. Traditional architecture was associated with craftspeople, whereas Western-style professional architects pursued different ways of working and enjoyed a higher social status. Somewhat ironically, the concern for architectural history was only established through the efforts of returning overseas-educated Chinese such as Liang Sicheng and his wife Lin Huiyin, who proposed the study of the history of traditional Chinese architecture as a parallel to Western architectural history (Steinhardt 2002: 537). There seems to have been little concern for a linearized, documentation- and preservation-oriented account of architectural history in China until well into the 20th century (Li 2002: 35). Liang Sicheng's work in establishing a historical account of Chinese architecture based on a Western-style historic framework eventually led to him being considered the 'father of Chinese architecture' (Steinhardt 2002: 540).

THE BIG ROOF DEBATE

The self-consciousness emerging from the importation of Western approaches to design and construction led to new architectural concerns in the Republican and early Communist eras, surfacing as the 'big roof debate.' This debate first accompanied the development of architecture representative of the Nationalist Chinese government in the 1920s, and resumed after the establishment of the People's Republic of China (PRC) in 1949. Already Henry K. Murphy had drawn on traditional palace typologies that emphasized large tiled roofs for his design of universities and municipal buildings. In a similar manner, Liang Sicheng – by now an influential figure in Chinese architectural circles – saw the large tiled roof with curved eaves as the salient feature of traditional Chinese architecture (Liang 2007). The big roof formed an essential element in Liang Sicheng's proposal for a 'national architecture' that was invited by the Communist Party of China in 1953 (Fairbank 2009: 172). In the works of Liang and his generation of architects such as Yang Tingbao, as well as his students such as Zhang Bo, Wu Liangyong, Dai Nianci and Zhang Jinqiu, this 'national' turn led to designs that aimed to create contemporary yet recognizably Chinese architecture by blending new materials and functions with large tiled roofs adapted from classical formal temple and palace architecture.

In the late 1980s and early 1990s, the municipal government of Beijing encouraged the big roof style as a way to 'recover the style of the old capital' (Xue 2005: 21). The approach was influential and generated a number of characteristic buildings such as the National Library and the West Beijing Railway station. The latter, constructed in 1996, for example, remarkably resembles the large construction projects of the 1950s. Coastal cities such as Shanghai or Guangzhou were more exposed to foreign influence and adopted more Westernized building types and styles than Beijing and inland cities. This difference remains visible today, although Beijing has added Westernized landmark architecture to its portfolio in recent years. Still, tradition-based approaches to design based on Liang Sicheng's analysis of traditional architecture can even be traced in new building types such as high-rise office towers in coastal cities. Within China's architectural community, high-rise towers were (and often still are) assumed to consist of a base, a middle and a 'hat', an analogy to traditional temple and pagoda typology. This parallels similar approaches in the West in which high-rise buildings were composed in analogy to classic column orders in the early 20th century. The effects of this approach are clearly visible in the skyline of Shanghai today, particularly in buildings built between the 1980s and the 2000s.

COMMERCIALIZING ARCHITECTURE IN THE SPIRIT OF INDUSTRIAL PRODUCTION

Whereas the Cultural Revolution (1966–76) had brought architectural development and discourse to a complete halt, the opening up of China in the early 1980s brought widespread enthusiasm for commercial, as well as new foreign ideas (Zhu 2011). The rupture with tradition enforced during the Cultural Revolution also led to a widely shared interest in, or even a yearning for a nostalgically embellished past among the general population. Architectural references to tradition soon made a comeback. The question of 'Chineseness' in architectural design resurfaced in two different forms: architects pursued tradition in discourse and in built work; moreover it was frequently employed for commercial purposes. Traditional references in architecture gained considerable commercial value. With national and international tourism increasing steadily, newly constructed or reconstructed picturesque 'old streets' (*lao jie*) became lucrative investments in many cities (Figure 31.2, right). In residential

Figure 31.2   False timber structures in a newly constructed commercial 'old street' in Suzhou, China

estates and interior design, 'Chinese style' is similarly popular but typically follows shallow and simplified understandings of tradition. Many of the new references to traditional architecture remain superficial in nature, consisting mostly of the application of traditional building materials such as timber and roof tiles to contemporary reinforced concrete constructions. A typical expression of this treatment of traditional materials is the attaching of false timber columns to concrete walls and false timber brackets to concrete roof constructions (Figure 31.2). As a consequence, the traditional relationship between building form, materials and human scale is increasingly lost.

The structuring of the profession into large Design Institutes has significantly influenced architectural discourse and practice (Kvan et al. 2008); most institutes are commercially oriented and since their establishment in the early years of the Communist era, closely connected with the government. From the 1950s until the 1980s, all private architectural practices in China were subsumed into state-controlled Design Institutes, which still produce most of the planning and design work in China today. Architects working in the Design Institutes tend to adopt a conformist stance in order to meet expectations; as a result little design experimentation and exploration are pursued. Much design work produced by the Design Institutes continues a pragmatic, simplified classical style mixed with modern elements – a style that was acceptable even throughout the more ideologically charged phases of Chinese recent history (Li 1999). Small private practices are starting to change this state of affairs but their work, although highly publicized and often well-known overseas, is typically of small scale and little influence within China itself.

Furthermore, design work conducted by private practices needs to be submitted for planning approval through a Design Institute; this ensures continuing government control over independent – and possibly critical – design approaches. Division of labour throughout design processes and a focus on the functional and economical elements of practice are deeply entrenched in the working modes of the Design Institutes. Architects typically design large-scale plans up to the scale of 1:100 within short time spans and leave responsibility and control over more detailed planning, as well as the routine construction process, almost entirely to contractors. This disjunction between architectural design and construction is to a great extent responsible for the lack of holistic design quality frequently found in Chinese contemporary architecture. Even within the Design Institutes the compartmentalization of design processes into factory-style distinct linearized workflow stages, usually overseen by different person-nel, creates a similar disjunction between designers and outcomes. There are few feedback loops ensuring that problems occurring during detailing or construction are addressed in the spirit of the overall design intention, and designers typically do not take responsibility for the specific outcomes of their design activity. Architectural design is understood primarily as a form of drawing up plans in a short time, addressing first and foremost economic and functional concerns of clients.

CULTURAL VALUES AND CONFUCIAN VENERATION OF LEADERS AND LINEAGES

In spite of functional imperatives architecture is appreciated and assessed within an emotional framework. Composition, comfort, appropriateness, a sense of poetry, and art all play a part, and are expressed in personal, emotional language in addition to abstract rational reasoning (Herr 2013). In the case of building design, for example, the focus on functional layout described above at the level of individual buildings is often complemented with a loose and irregular site layout reminiscent of pavilions in a classi-cal Chinese garden. Even the temporary nature of most buildings built in China today, many of which will not be operational for longer than 30 years, is evocative of China's long timber building tradition, which saw buildings and even entire cities routinely destroyed and rebuilt.

Chinese contemporary discourse on architecture features character-istic ways of speaking and writing that derive from traditional Chinese philosophical, artistic and epistemological frameworks of thought (Li and

Yeo 2007; Herr 2011). Discourse is conventionally framed less in terms of Western-style dialectics and more as an exchange of expressive comments that primarily appeal to emotion and elicit agreement through empathy, for example by appealing to the reader's sense of appropriateness, values or personal concrete experience. In a 2011 lecture to a Harvard University audience, architect and 2012 Pritzker Prize winner Wang Shu presented a series of images showing one of his buildings with the comment that the shown images may not appear special, advising the audience to visit the building in person to experience that it was indeed a very special place (Shu 2011). This appeal to the emotional response of the audience is quite different from the typical Western reliance on abstract argument. Even critical essays employ this way of appealing to emotion, such as Zhu Tao's 'Traditional and modern, tradition and us' (Zhu 2002).

Thinking, as well as the expression of viewpoints within contemporary Chinese architectural discourse, takes place based on cultural values that condition specific ways of appreciating and evaluating architecture. Confucian values of respecting leaders, teachers and elders generate a culture of valuing continuity and a respect for tradition unaltered even by breaks as radical as the Cultural Revolution (Steinhardt 2002). As in the traditional arts, students of architecture are expected to learn first by following and studying the masters – often by copying their work – and to make their own contributions to a field once they progress to artistic maturity. Teachers tend to discourage the challenging of established modes of practice by students; likewise students express deep respect for their teachers and expect them to authoritatively direct their work. Judgements of appropriateness are thus typically dependent on lineages that implicitly determine loyalty to a particular body of work or thought. Individuals tend to see their contributions within the framework of such lineages and relationships rather than as outcomes of their personal self-realization.

The focus on architectural 'isms' expressed in terms of abstract ideas that can be observed in Western discourse is not nearly as strong within Chinese architectural discourse. Instead, Chinese design culture seems to value personal experience over theoretical concerns (Herr 2011). Chinese students returning from overseas education, however, often experience a break in this lineage thinking and reposition themselves in a more individualist framework. Among architectural practitioners, Ma Yansong of MAD and Hua Li of Trace Architecture Office have followed this pattern. Some of those returning from overseas maintain Confucianist loyalty to a particular tradition of thought while adopting a Western teacher and Western body of thought. Gu Daqing, Wang Junyang and Zhu Tao are influential scholars whose work introduces Western-style thought, in particular, notions of tectonics and critical regionalism, into the Chinese context in this manner.

Judgements of architectural appropriateness within China are influenced by, and derived from recommendations made by political leaders. When the newly established People's Republic of China faced dire times and lack of resources, Premier Zhou Enlai encouraged architectural development according to the dictum of 'suitable, economical and beautiful if circumstances allow' (*shiyong, jingji, zai keneng tiaojian xia zhuyi meiguan*) (Liang 1959). These priorities have become entrenched in architectural thinking in China and are invoked even today by figures as influential as Wu Liangyong as a moral framework for architectural practice. Such priorities also underlie the Design Institute's constant focus on pragmatic and economic aspects of architecture in an ideologically sanctioned framework of 'appropriateness'. Severe scarcity of resources combined with intense political pressure faced by Chinese architects from the 1950s until the early 1980s resulted in an industrialized, reduced and simplified architectural language that, while stemming from quite different motivations, may be interpreted as Modernist from an outside perspective. This enduring focus on functionality and economy has had far-reaching impact on Chinese architectural design culture. Architectural design teaching and practice typically focuses on plan-based functional layout, which creates a characteristic design language of buildings consisting of compact clusters of compartmentalized spaces dedicated to particular functions. The design of building elevations is typically an additive embellishment and consequence of plan layouts, and is often done only when plan design has been consolidated.

DISTINGUISHING ARCHITECTURE FROM ART THROUGH LINEAGE AND ASSOCIATION

Although architecture was not part of the canon of arts pursued by traditional Chinese scholars (Clunas 1997), architects such as Liang Sicheng (2007) tended to present it in a framework that referred to classical rules and types, or to Chinese garden design. This initially positioned the architect as a traditional scholar and contrasts with the more pragmatic understanding of architects as providers of functional and economical buildings that is common among architecture professionals in China today, in particular those working in the Design Institutes. The differentiation between architecture understood as a profession and architecture understood as a form of scholarly art seems quite strong within China: it recently became explicit with the awarding of the prestigious international

Pritzker Prize to Wang Shu in early 2012. In its citation, the international jury commented:

> The question of the proper relation of present to past is particularly timely, for the recent process of urbanization in China invites debate as to whether architecture should be anchored in tradition or should look only toward the future. As with any great architecture, Wang Shu's work is able to transcend that debate, producing an architecture that is timeless, deeply rooted in its context and yet universal. (Pritzker Prize announcement 2012)

After initial disbelief, the news of a Chinese architect being awarded the Pritzker Prize provoked great pride and enthusiasm among Chinese architecture students. Among the professional architecture community, however, response to the award was mixed. Wang Shu tends to be perceived as too young to receive such a prestigious prize, and as such not representative of contemporary Chinese architecture; instead, he is often described as an artist, implying that his work is removed from professional architectural practice. In February 2012, in the same month as Wang Shu's Pritzker Prize award, the Chinese President Hu Jintao personally presented the country's top architectural honour, the 2011 State Supreme Science and Technology Award of Chinese Academy of Sciences, to 89-year-old Wu Liangyong, a former student and collaborator of Liang Sicheng. Among Chinese architecture professionals, this award was greeted with wide approval. The difference between the two awards illustrates differences in appreciating and valuing architectural work from within and from outside China, and shows the ongoing lineage based tradition within the profession.

Both Wang Shu and Wu Liangyong are engaged in the collective search for a 'new tradition' in Chinese architecture. However, the two architects have different perspectives on what constitutes traditional architecture. Wu Liangyong is primarily concerned with traditional architecture and urban planning that orients itself towards large scale government projects. Wang Shu in contrast consistently invokes vernacular architecture when calling for a rethinking of traditional architecture and presents himself as an 'amateur', suggesting an identification with the unknown craftsman-builder of ancient times rather than with contemporary architecture professionals. Whereas the formal architecture of previous generations stressed rules and grammar, and thus lent itself to the Beaux Arts-educated generation of architects thinking in terms of styles and types, the younger generation of contemporary Chinese architects, exemplified by Wang Shu, seems to find tradition primarily in vernacular architecture and locally sourced materials (Figure 31.3). Wang Shu, for example, characteristically employs timber, rammed earth and recycled local brick in his designs.

*Figure 31.3   Vernacular references integrated with contemporary
                construction materials in the Xiangshan campus of the
                Chinese Academy of Art, designed by Wang Shu*

The two approaches are different in so far as the former emphasizes the rule-governed style of official buildings and thus uniformity in form and material, whereas the latter allows for variety generated through local conditions and context. In addition, vernacular references often address social and cultural issues characteristic of specific locations.

   Until today, the formal style is common in 'official' buildings such as the Chinese Shanghai Expo Pavilion 2010, whereas younger and more experimental practices such as URBANUS explore vernacular references, such as the urban Tulou building for lower income residents in Guangdong. As employed in young practices, vernacular references and inspiration also serve as a way to avoid the stiffness and grandeur that often goes along with work produced by the Design Institutes. Beyond architecture as art or architecture as profession, the reference to vernacular architecture results in a new category: architecture as local craft. Based on contemporary discourse found in Chinese journals such as *Architecture and Culture* (*jiazhu yu wenhua*), this direction seems to hold more promise for future architectural developments (Chakroff 2012). In this context Kenneth Frampton's call for a critical regionalism, introduced to China through overseas-educated students, is highly relevant to contemporary Chinese architecture and his works are widely read in their Chinese translations. The notion of 'tectonics' – although interpreted in a different way to original intentions – is perceived as an appropriate way of addressing the issue of critical regionalism in terms of structural and spatial expression of local contexts (Zhu 2002; Gu and Bertin 2010).

TRADITIONAL ARCHITECTURE SUPPORTING THE NATIONAL SELF-IMAGE

Underlying the widely echoed sentiment that Chinese architecture should recover its traditional 'Chineseness' in the face of a strong overseas design impact on the built environment is a tendency to think of architecture as an expression of national identity. From the distinction of Chinese 'essence' and Western 'form' at the beginning of the 20th century, to Mao Zedong's call to 'make the past serve the present and the foreign serve China' (*gu wei jin yong, yang wei zhong yong*), priority is consistently given to a national focus. Thinking in these terms is motivated in some contexts by political ideology, but to an even greater extent by ethnocentrism and a shared desire for national pride.

The historical background of this desire is a long struggle to develop China from a feudal society into a modern nation at eye level with other developed countries. In this struggle, calls for more development and progress typically appeal to an ethnically framed 'we' (*women*) as a pre-condition for national identity. In Chinese language architectural essays and journal articles, authors frequently invoke such a 'we' that refers to those of Chinese ethnicity, in particular to those born in Mainland China. The notion of 'my/our country' (*woguo*) is often substituted for the term 'China' (*zhongguo*). In Chinese articles, emotional appeals are often made, while in similar Western articles, abstract argument or critical discourse is the preferred form of connecting to the audience. Zheng Chaocan charac-teristically writes in a typical scholarly paper:

> Unless we understand the core content of our architectural culture in sufficient breadth and depth, the artistic style and form of cultural meaning cannot be expressed thoroughly. Today Western culture strongly influences and stunts our country's culture, which is evident from Western architects being in charge of a great number of domestic Chinese architectural projects. (Zheng 2012, translation by the author)

It is only recently that Chinese President Xi Jinping has publicly criti-cized extravagant Western-style buildings such as the CCTV tower by OMA. Xi emphasized that art should serve the people and be morally inspiring (Stott 2014), thus anchoring judgements of architectural quality once again within a socio-political context. This move is consistent with Confucian traditions that see the role of the individual as subordinate and loyal to leading figures: it is also continued in the Communist emphasis on self-efficacy in serving a larger community. A recursion to tradition in establishing a national image is thus perceived as more safe and stable compared to encouraging individual expression. The emphasis on national

Figure 31.4   New buildings modelled on traditional precedents in the 'fang gu' style in Xi'an, China

identity and national pride has transcended political changes over the past decades and forms the basis of a recent tendency to foster recovery of national treasures and icons. In many cities, for example, traditional temples are currently reconstructed or even newly constructed in adherence to old examples despite China's cautious attitude towards religion. In some cities, ancient city walls are reconstructed to recover lost historic grandeur and pride. Similar to the early years of the People's Republic of China, explicit references to traditional architecture are put to work to appeal to politicians, tourists and the general public alike.

Moreover, as tradition appeals to the general public, references to architectural tradition in contemporary buildings have commercial value. Besides establishing commercial 'old streets', cities such as Xi'an seem determined to pursue a *fang gu* style on a larger scale. 'Fang gu' refers to the modelling of the new on tradition, which has a range of possible interpretations. On the one hand it can imply construction as in traditional times but it can also mean a much more superficial disguising of reinforced concrete structures – like shopping malls disguised as traditional timber structures with tiled roofs (Figure 31.4). These developments, however, often are quite crude and do not contribute much to further development of contemporary 'Chineseness' in architecture. Overall, the concern and quest for a new yet traditional architecture remains bound to a national level: even though Wang Shu has received a great deal of international exposure since his Pritzker Prize award, the internal Chinese discourse on contemporary architectural 'Chineseness' has received little attention from outside. Many architects well known in China, such as Li Xiaodong, Liu Jiakun, Zhang Lei and Tao Lei remain mostly unknown in the international architectural community and very few have built outside China.

TOWARDS A NEW VERNACULAR?

With the experience of globalization following China's joining the World Trade Organization in 2001 and a persistent concern regarding the maintaining of identity in times of rapid change, the call to recover traditional values has intensified in recent years. In this context, a return to cultural foundations is seen by many to provide a source of 'Chineseness'. Among different generations of Chinese architects, however, views on what constitutes tradition vary. The generation of architects who returned from overseas education before the establishment of the People's Republic of China was primarily concerned about the preservation and documentation of traditions that were still in existence but changing rapidly with the ongoing modernization of China. Their focus was primarily how to import new ideas in a way that would continue old traditions by new means. This generation also brought with them a sense of architectural appropriateness that was based on the Beaux Arts education they had received overseas. For some time, traditional references were employed as part of a building style that, as Chairman Mao Zedong suggested, could help to appeal to the population at large and show the continuity and stability of the newly founded People's Republic of China (Rowe and Kuan 2002).

Following a complete break with tradition during the years of the Cultural Revolution, and a rapid development of Chinese architecture following the political and economic reforms of the 1980s, China experienced modernism and postmodernism more or less simultaneously. After this period of eclecticism, the quest for 'Chineseness' in architecture is once again at the centre of architectural discourse within China. Among contemporary Chinese architects, the search for a new Chinese architecture increasingly involves inspirations from and reinterpretations of Chinese vernacular architecture rather than reliance on classical temple and palace architecture. In vernacular architecture a new generation now finds a wealth of inspiration to address the relationships between human inhabitation and local context. Vernacular architecture also offers new considerations of architectural scale in relation to human scale, which is increasingly lost in conventional building practice. New directions are derived from observing and adapting local ways of building, and often from addressing social dimensions of architecture. The work of the Design Institutes is unlikely to foster such exploration due to their organizational size and structure. With an increasing number of independently thinking and working small- to medium-size practices actively pursuing the question of the relationship between the modern and the traditional in innovative ways, however, the development of a new, yet 'Chinese' architecture is well under way.

ACKNOWLEDGEMENTS

I gratefully acknowledge the support I have received from my colleagues at the Department of Architecture at Xi'an Jiaotong-Liverpool University, in particular Jessica Sewell and Yiping Dong. This research is supported by the Xi'an Jiaotong-Liverpool University Research Development Fund (RDF 11-01-12).

NOTE

1. For instance the Cultural Revolution (1966–76) saw a break in the continuity of architectural discourse.

REFERENCES

Chakroff, Evan (2012), 'Amateur architecture: a new vernacular?', accessed 12 August 2012 at http://archinect.com/features/article/41080183/amateur-architecture-a-new-vernacular.

Clunas, Craig (1997), *Art In China*. New York: Oxford University Press.

Cody, Jeffrey W. (2001), *Building in China: Henry K. Murphy's 'Adaptive Architecture,' 1914–1935*. Hong Kong: Chinese University Press.

Fairbank, Wilma (2009), *Liang and Lin: Partners in Exploring China's Architectural Past*. Philadelphia, PA: University of Pennsylvania Press.

Gu, Daqing and Vito Bertin (2010), *Space, Tectonics and Design*. Beijing: China Architecture and Building Press.

Herr, Christiane M. (2011), 'Mutually arising abstract and actual', *Kybernetes* **40** (7/8): 1030–37.

Herr, Christiane M. (2013), 'Architectural design education between poetry and prose', *Kybernetes* **42** (9/10): 1404–12.

Kvan, Thomas, Binqing Liu and Yunyan Jia (2008), 'The emergence of a profession: development of the profession of architecture in China', *Journal of Architectural and Planning Research* **25** (3): 203–20.

Li, Bao (1999), 'Searching for a new Chinese architecture: an investigation of architecture in China since 1949', Master's thesis, The University of Hong Kong.

Li, Lin (2012), 'Disciplinization of history education in modern China: a study of history education in the Imperial University of Peking (1898–1911), *Creative Education* **3** (4): 565–80.

Li, Shiqiao (2002), 'Writing a modern Chinese architectural history: Liang Sicheng and Liang Qichao', *Journal of Architectural Education* **56** (1): 35–45.

Li, Xiaodong and Kangshua Yeo (2007), *Zhongguo kongjian* (*Chinese Conception of Space*). Beijing: China Architecture & Building Press.

Liang, Sicheng (1934), *qingshi yingzao zeli* (*Qing Structural Regulations*). Beijing, China: Qinghua University Press.

Liang, Sicheng (1959), *cong 'shiyong jingji zai keneng tiaojian xia zhuyi meiguan' tandao chuantong yu gexin* ('Discussing tradition and innovation from the viewpoint of suitability, economy and beauty if circumstances permit'), *Architectural Journal* **6**.

Liang, Sicheng (2007), *dazhuo zhimei* ('Art and architecture'), in Z. Lin (ed.), *Liang Sicheng's Most Beautiful World Architecture*. Beijing, China: China Qingnian Press.

Pritzker Prize announcement (2012), accessed 27 February 2015 at http://www.pritzkerprize.com/2012/announcement.

Rowe, Peter G. and Kuan, Seng (2002), *Architectural Encounters with Essence and Form in Modern China*. Cambridge, MA: The MIT Press.

Shu, Wang (2011), 'Geometry and narrative of natural form', Kenzo Tange Lecture at Harvard GSD, accessed 27 February 2015 at http://www.gsd.harvard.edu/media/kenzo-tange-lecture-wang-shu-geometry-and-narrative-of-natural-2.html.

Steinhardt, Nancy Shatzman (2002), 'China: Designing the future, venerating the past', *The Journal of the Society of Architectural Historians* **61** (4): 537–48.

Stott, Rory (2014), 'Why China's President says "No More Weird Buildings"', accessed 27 February 2015 at http://www.archdaily.com/559456/why-china-s-president-says-no-more-weird-buildings/.

Wang, Xiao and Li, Baihao (2008), *lun xiandai jianzhu 'yijing' zhi zhongguo tese* ('Chinese characteristics of artistic conception in modern architecture'), *Huazhong Architecture*, **26** (6): 5–7.

Xue, Charlie Q.L. (2005), *Building a Revolution: Chinese Architecture Since 1980*. Hong Kong: Hong Kong University Press.

Zhang, Zhidong (1901), *China's Only Hope: An Appeal by Her Greatest Viceroy, Chang Chih-tung, with the Sanction of the Present Emperor, Kwang Sü*, translated by Samuel I. Woodbridge. Edinburgh: Oliphant, accessed 27 February 2015 at http://openlibrary.org/books/OL13999713M/China%27s_only_hope.

Zheng, Chaocan (2012), *yongbao chuantong-dangxia dui jianzhu chuantong de sikao* ('Embrace the tradition – rethinking of the architecture tradition currently'), *Architecture and Culture*, 97: 64–5.

Zhu, Tao (2002), *'jiangou' de xunuo yu xushe: lun dangdai zhongguo jianzhu xue fazhan zhong de 'goujian' guannian* ('The promises and assumptions of "Tectonics": on the emerging notions of "Tectonics" in contemporary Chinese architecture'), *Time + Architecture* (5): 30–33.

Zhu, Tao (2006), 'Interview with Zhu Tao, and collected architectural work', in Bing Yu (ed.), *Domus + China: 78 Chinese Architects and Designers*. Beijing: China Architecture and Building Press, pp. 434–37.

Zhu, Tao (2011), *chuantong yu xiandai, chuantong yu women* ('Traditional and modern, tradition and us'), *World Architecture Review*, **26** (6).

32. Chinese fashion designers: rebuilding from the centre of the world
Tim Lindgren

The fashion industry is a potentially dynamic sector of the cultural and creative industries, an area in which China already has a dominant global presence through its mass manufacturing of garments. However, the 'made in China' label that appears on garments through the developed world does not signify a Chinese cultural presence. Fashion is identified with creativity. Chinese designers want to create brands.

In the Chinese coastal city of Qingdao, a local garment manufacturer has invested RMB 1 billion (US$163.6 million) over the past several years in cloud computing. Red Collar's online platform allows it to respond to the increasingly specialized and sophisticated needs of its global clients. The platform enables Red Collar to flexibly organize manufacturing capacities; for instance, it produces some three thousand tailored garments each day for clients in New York and has plans to double the availability of this kind of customizable production in the future. Red Collar illustrates the possibilities of cloud computing in transforming China's garment manufacturing industry (Xinhua News Agency 2015). While the company is changing long established industrial manufacturing processes, at the creative end of the value chain Chinese fashion designers are seeking out a presence on the world stage.

Every year designers around the world come to France to show their clothing collections at Paris Fashion Week. This prestigious event is held in March. Ma Masha, known better as Masha Ma outside China, is among a new wave of fashion designers from Mainland China with eyes firmly fixed upon this prize. This sophisticated cohort contributes to a growing momentum that challenges the perception that China is better at making consumer products than creating them. Ma works between a studio on the Bund in Shanghai and an office in Paris, commuting regularly between Asia and Europe. According to Angelica Cheung, the editor-in-chief of *Vogue China*, 'For many generations we Chinese were not encouraged to think creatively, so there's a certain element of truth to say that the Chinese were not great designers' (Chen 2014).

Ma Masha is often mentioned alongside her contemporaries Qiu Hao

(Hao Qiu), Xander Zhou (Zhou Xander) and Huishan Zhang (Zhang Huishan).[1]

They collectively share a foreign education, a contemporary design aesthetic and are prolific on the global stage. Ma was born in Beijing and later studied at the prestigious Central Saint Martin's College in London. She was inspired to follow in the footsteps of the late English designer Alexander McQueen for whom she briefly interned. Ma's growing successes stem from her business-oriented outlook. Despite the growing popularity of designer ateliers offering couture and made-to-measure fashion in Mainland China, Ma has sought to create a business model that would eventually sustain itself. In 2013, she established a diffusion line called 'MA by MA Studio', with plans for expansion into five commercial lines, and an increased presence in more global fashion cities.

Some key elements are important in developing a style for success beyond China's cultural borders. Ma speaks of colour and the simple silhouette of the design; another requirement is more difficult to define as it denotes an almost religious experience or a sense of spirituality. 'For me, Chinese elements are something philosophical', she explains: it's not the appearance but the meaning behind that matters. Indeed the age of Chinese 'red and gold' is well and truly over. 'The figurative dragon and phoenix motifs are simply exotic points of view from the Western world' (Chen 2014). Edward Said's (2003) ground-breaking book *Orientalism* pointed particularly to the problem of creative works deemed 'orientalist', noting the reliance on patronising racial stereotypes of exotic or mystical Eastern cultures and the tendency to portray them as static or regressive. According to Said, orientalism was out of touch with on-the-ground realities in Asian and Middle Eastern countries. Moving forward, one might argue that the rubric of orientalism has now been reshaped. Where this once represented an exchange of ideas and China's role as a source of influence, or perhaps as evidence of a reciprocal relationship between the East and West, the balance has now tipped in favour of the Chinese market and the potential it offers in the field of design.

Stereotypes and misconceptions persist in accompanying Chinese fashion design. In recent years however a surge of designers of Chinese descent has taken the helm at major fashion houses. Increased numbers of Chinese celebrities are seated in the front rows at presentations, not to mention Chinese models opening runway shows, and why should this not be so? Ma Masha sees no point in contributing to the argument. 'Being labelled a Chinese designer is not something you get to choose. It comes along with the package, it's automatically attached to you' (Chen 2014). Nevertheless, the reality is that without the solid infrastructure of a fashion industry in China, Chinese fashion designers must gravitate to traditional fashion centres for education and experience before returning home. The businesses they build are in turn enriching the 'fashion system' in China.

In this chapter I argue that the gathering momentum of Chinese fashion design, as well as the coming together of the Chinese fashion system has reached an irreversible tipping point. Moreover, this is occurring at a time when the Chinese fashion industry is seeking to reinvent itself. Typically new impetuses are constrained by a combination of several key forces. Culture and politics have an almost insurmountable presence in many aspects of daily life, including limits imposed on creative expression; however this legacy is changing rapidly in part due to China's global ascendency as an economically powerful nation. Access to the Internet since the 1990s has paralleled the nation's rise on the world stage. Connectivity to digital and social media platforms has great implications for Chinese fashion design and for the perpetuation of creative activity.

Yet questions remain about the nature of creative identity and the ongoing relevance of political culture to the field of design. Concern with China establishing a creative identity is particularly acute in a nation where new and unsaturated consumer markets are attracting the attention of foreign fashion brands. The calls for a creative identity are occurring at a time when the country's domestic economy moves inexorably from 'made in China' to 'created in China'. While the rhetoric of this turn of phrase may be well trodden, I argue that it has only recently gained momentum. In May 2015, the State Council unveiled a 10-year plan for improving the nation's manufacturing capacity. The Ministry of Industry and Information Technology (MIIT), which instigated the 'Made in China 2025' plan, intends to give China an edge in innovation, green development and quality consumer products. Sha Nansheng, the vice-director of MIIT's Department of Science and Technology, has said Chinese manufacturing industries face pressure on dual fronts: competition from other developing countries with lower labour costs, and a renewed push by developed nations of the West seeking an advantage in industrial manufacturing (Wang and Li 2015).

While most of the sectors listed in the plan are categorized as 'emerging' high-tech industries, the focus on information technology, along with the rhetoric of Internet+, signals a sea change from productivity for its own sake. Upgrading the manufacturing industry in the manner of Red Collar is an urgent priority in China at a time when its status as the mass production centre of the world is undermined by less developed countries. Chinese leaders in particular often champion the cultural (and creative) industries as a new engine of growth amid a slowing economy. In the context of the production of fashion, this recognition is important only if it aligns with the development of innovative technologies that incorporate sustainability and environmental initiatives and that can forge a new kind of contemplative fashion design.

In order to frame this discussion, I distinguish the commercial, financial and logistic implications of the 'fashion industry' from the 'fashion system'. The fashion industry refers to the production of garments by diverse manufacturing processes. The fashion industry is no longer located as it once was in Europe; like a constantly moving nomad, it relocates frequently to geographic sites with low labour costs, mainly in Asia. The 'fashion system' on the other hand refers to how fashion is legitimized, provided with value and disseminated to consumers through various sales channels (Craik 2009; Kawamura 2005). At this point in time the Eurocentric fashion system that originated in France during the period of industrialization remains dominant; maintaining its hegemony provides an important source of income to the European economy. This contrast between 'industry' and 'system' provides a more nuanced focus on the underlying business of fashion, as well as providing a means to discuss how technology and communication media serve as inputs into production and as facilitators of consumption. In this understanding, while a global system of legitimization exists, there is no identifiable global centre of fashion production.

In many ways the global fashion business, when represented by the movement of money, behaves like the ebb and flow of an ocean tide and is motivated by forces of consumption. As it moves into new national markets processes of cultural adaptation occur; in retreat the tide takes with it fresh actors who in turn influence its own constitution. As a result of this recurring process knowledge is shared. In the overlapping areas of Figure 32.1 the state of flux becomes most apparent. In the meeting of the tides Chinese companies move outwards into the global economy to revitalize ailing foreign brands. Here the boundary is blurred because new ideas are assimilated often before the infrastructure of the legal system can keep up.

It is against this backdrop that some new perspectives have emerged in Chinese fashion design: they include the shifting commercial momentum from 'made in China' to the value-adding properties of 'created in China'; the rise of the globetrotting Chinese consumer; and the almost ubiquitous access to knowledge via digital media that has transformed the global landscape for fashion consumption.

Soon after China opened its doors for trade in 1978, 'foreign' fashion companies were attracted to the economies of scale and competitive costs of garment production, leading to China becoming garment manufacturer to the world (Zhang 2006). A government controlled industry body, the China National Garment Association (2013) provides revealing data.

Global Fashion System

National Fashion System

Global Fashion Industry

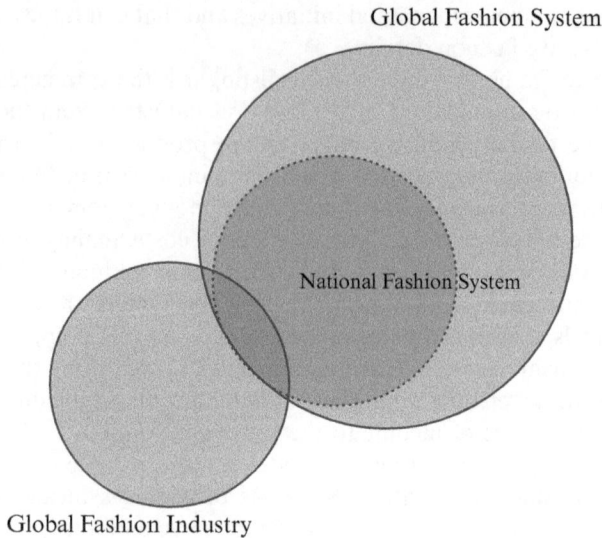

Source: Author.

Figure 32.1   Global fashion industry

In 2012, these industries contributed RMB 1.7 trillion (approximately US$283 billion) to the Chinese domestic economy, in addition to an export value of US$153 billion.[2] The Chinese textile and clothing industries employ approximately 10 million people and are rapidly improving their infrastructure so as to take part in a new phase of development, which correlates to improved brand development and profitability.

In contrast, the global fashion system contributed US$1.3 trillion to the global creative economy (Elliot 2014). It follows that a strong domestic fashion system means China's internal economy will retain a greater share of the profit margins that occur from the increased values of Chinese clothing, as these products move through the fashion system and become 'legitimized' as Chinese fashion design; this is especially the case as Chinese fashion designers move to form international brands.

THE ROLE OF GOVERNMENT

The Chinese government is increasingly aware of the importance of moving beyond the industrial processes of garment production, particularly as it refocuses the economy towards consumption. The 12th Five-Year Plan, implemented in 2011, clearly articulates a renewed focus on the domestic economy. This planning moves China's economic momentum from an export-led income to domestic-led consumption. Furthermore, the Plan stresses less reliance on foreign technology, and the importance of domestic innovation, known as 'endogenous innovation' (*zizhu chuangxin*).[3] Point eight of the ten-point plan specifically encourages cultural production in order to increase China's 'soft power' (Harris 2011). In the field of fashion, soft power is epitomized by the renowned Chinese fashion designer Ma Ke who provided clothing for Peng Liyuan, the Chinese First Lady for her initial state visits, or by the dress that Chinese couturier Guo Pei provided for Barbadian singer Rihanna to wear at the annual Met Ball in 2015 (London 2015). On the other hand, 'Made in China 2025' focuses specifically on innovation. Yet, for China to truly transition from 'Made in China' to 'Created in China', success is needed in its design industries.

In robust Asian design economies such as Japan, design has flourished; for example the global lifestyle brand Muji, the carmaker Toyota, and the fashion designer Issey Miyake. In general, 'Made in Japan' has come to represent an attention to detail and a quality that was previously understood as industrial manufacturing capacity. Creative sectors such as architecture and product design have high barriers to entry, for instance the amount of time and money needed for investment in research and development. These restrictions mean the architectural and industrial design sectors tend to form around the collaborative work and investments of a firm. Fashion, on the other hand, requires less investment and in China a robust clothing industry infrastructure already exists. Yet the business of fashion is fundamentally concerned with anticipating the needs of the consumer in a free market, a relatively new idea in China.

Because of the potential consumer market in China, great financial value is yet to be realized from the existing infrastructure. At the same time the need to provide employment for a domestic populace is increasingly urgent. The accompanying demands of consumption means rethinking how these processes will take place and what the implications are for the established Eurocentric fashion system. Michael Keane (2007) has previously explored this transition phase in terms of the Chinese government's early grasp of the economic importance of the creative industries, a concept that originates from the British government's mapping of its own creative sector. In the United Kingdom, the exploration was undertaken as a means of identifying key aspects of the creative economy, so as to understand and better manage its flows of financial and aesthetic capital (DCMS 1998).

The Chinese government is pursuing a similar purpose. Not only does China desire to transform into a largely urbanized society that enjoys consistent growth, it desires such growth to be measured in qualitative as well as quantitative terms. Rising incomes, demonstrated particularly by the burgeoning middle class are to be accompanied by increased leisure, a better physical environment, expanding arts and cultural activities, and a greater sense of economic and social security. A recent report suggests that by 2022 more than 75 per cent of China's urban consumers will earn RMB 60,000 to 229,000 (US$9,000 to 34,000) per annum (Barton et al. 2013). It is apparent that moving forward, the domestic Chinese economy will need to create social conditions supportive of growth and development. According to another report from the World Bank (2013), the core tenet of this mandate also demands a basic level of security for the domestic populace.

As a result of these significant shifts in policy, and the symbolic importance of design to the spread of Chinese soft power, fashion designers are well placed to move into roles where they will have a greater say about the lifestyle representations of their emergent brands, and where they will become soft power ambassadors in the same way that Giorgio Armani is inextricably linked with the Italian fashion design sector, or that Chanel is to Paris. Designers increasingly have the opportunity to include new global values in their practice that reflect not only a growing pride in their accomplishments, but provide commentary on some of the environmental and cultural problems the country faces on a daily basis. As Ma Masha has indicated, Chinese fashion designers have new opportunities to consider the human condition by thinking about the philosophical underpinnings of design.

CHINESE TOURISTS AND TRAVELLING DESIGNERS

Some of these problems are made more apparent by comparisons with the quality of life in other countries. The Chinese traveller is a relatively recent phenomenon, accelerated by a relaxation in visa application procedures by the European Union and Asian countries. Rapid urbanization and rising incomes mean that more Chinese residents can afford to travel. Increasingly this is an individual effort, where the focus is on an experiential appreciation of European cultures. Fundamentally though, this becomes an economic equation, measured in terms of the spending power of this relatively new and mobile demographic. Until now the transfer of knowledge that occurs as people explore new cultures and undergo new experiences has been undervalued, yet this is arguably the most important aspect of these experiences; upon their return these intrepid travellers bring new expectations of the permutations of fashion, of the hierarchy of fashion brands and their importance for the creation of identity along with improved ideas about product quality, as well as raised expectations of consumer service. These experiences also indirectly serve to draw comparisons with their domestic living conditions. Yet there are further implications.

More than two thirds of Chinese luxury purchases are now conducted outside Mainland China: moreover, every major market is eager to attract Chinese tourists and their disposable income (Solca 2015). Several factors have contributed to the change. Enormous price barriers in China are caused by high tax and import duties and have combined with a weak Euro. As well, booming outbound Chinese tourism and the explosion of Chinese luxury e-commerce has been facilitated by *daigou*[4] websites. All indicators point to more Chinese luxury spending moving from Mainland China, further draining Mainland Chinese stores of traffic and negatively impacting sales densities. As a consequence, European luxury brands may take advantage of relatively short-duration leases to trim their local retail infrastructure. In regions such as Hong Kong, this has already occurred, as some luxury retailers close their shops (Lee and Kwok 2015).

Like Ma Masha, many Chinese fashion designers travel frequently. In the early stages of their careers some relocate for education at prestigious institutions such as Central St Martins in London and Parsons in New York. Parsons, like some other schools has taken advantage of the tidal flows and established an academic centre in Shanghai. In turn an increasingly large cohort of Chinese students have returned to Mainland China to establish new businesses and fashion brands replete with a fast tracked fashion education and an entrepreneurial bent – and importantly, with a greater sense of their place in the global fashion system. In this fleeting phase they are 'of the moment', equipped with the kind of tacit knowledge only found in the most recent iterations of the fashion construct. Upon their homecoming, they become responsible for shaping the structure of the Chinese fashion system with new cultural and aesthetic messages.

However, there are some difficulties in the implementation of this process: these are brought about by rapid urban growth, social unrest and the difficult and often utopian nature of the Government's vision to build a modern, harmonious and creative society with coherent social values. As Janet Wolff (1993) has explained, the aesthetic vision of a fashion designer is like that of many other creative practitioners and is shaped in a mutually dependent relationship between the structures of culture and the manifestations of creativity produced in a social system. As mentioned above, the Chinese social system is undergoing dramatic change. Furthermore, the aesthetic sensibilities of fashion designers in tune with their cultural surroundings are important for recognition within a fashion system: these intangible representations or creative signatures form the core of a creative business; they allow ideas to materialize as tangible products for the consumer market. Importantly, the strength and unique characteristics of their creative signature in a crowded marketplace foretell their viability.

Howard Becker (2008, 96–7) describes self-support or independence as an important stage in the development of an art career. Possessing this capability allows designers to develop their own aesthetic, independently of the aesthetic gatekeeping that occurs in established fashion systems. Developing an aesthetic, or in other words, a refined capacity to use one's senses to make a critical observation about one's culture in the pursuit of beauty, is an individual attribute; yet this is a difficult task in the kind of global culture of dislocation that Zygmunt Bauman (2005) describes. For instance Ma Masha described this process as implementing her key elements of colour, silhouette and philosophy. As Becker (2008: 132) explains, 'artists create an unformalized aesthetic through workday choices of materials and forms'. Forming an aesthetic is therefore a way of making sense of the lived environment. A personal aesthetic defines the terms of engagement with our culture; this aesthetic is used to determine our choice of consumer product, as well as the production of cultural artefacts such as fashion.

THE AUTHENTICITY OF CHINESE FASHION

The onset of the digital era challenges accepted ideas of the linear progression of time; in doing so it alters perceptions of historical or cultural heritage. China's historical legacy has also been disrupted numerous times since the end of the last ruling Chinese dynasty, the Qing at the turn of the twentieth century, causing many people to ask what Chinese identity is. In rethinking what it is to be a Chinese fashion designer, the question of what comprises China's boundaries must be considered briefly. From its northern borders with Russia, and Mongolia, India and Kazakhstan to the west, and to its Westernized port of Hong Kong in the far south, China is an ethnically diverse and geographically large country that contends with the close proximity of other Asian countries such as Korea, Japan, Taiwan and Vietnam.[5] Indeed, these regional Asian neighbours exert a great deal of influence on Chinese popular culture including fashion, music and television and film. Nevertheless, it would appear that for some China has become an amalgam of ideas and ideology and is perhaps a state of mind, rather than a nation fixed in a singular geographic location.

Consequently, as Chinese designers establish and enlarge the financial underpinnings of their fashion brands, they must focus on the development of a unique aesthetic signature, one that resonates with a sophisticated global consumer. In the Western model the design and production of fashion is often reliant upon renewing the contextual position of previously established creative ideas, which are recast as a new version of one's creative identity or an aesthetic signature in line with changes in the immediacy of popular culture. This model is fundamentally based upon anticipating the desires of one's consumer. Yet the Chinese philosophical model often looks to the craft of making and the relationship of people to the natural environment, as a similar representation of one's self in culture (Lindgren 2014). Recent shifts by some Chinese consumers toward more discreet fashion products, for instance items without an obvious logo, is an indication of change. The consumers' redirection from an outward manifestation of identity to the inward concept of self demonstrates this idea, providing that ultimately fashion is associated with lifestyle, and in turn one's lifestyle is determined by the culture in which one lives.

Thus a new attraction to the rigours of craftsmanship, a desire for quality in Chinese fashion products, a well expressed design aesthetic, and a respect of time for brand-building means some designers are stepping away from the irrational 'gold-rush with Chinese characteristics' (Liu 2000: 142) that mobilized earlier groups to concentrate on a lucrative yet perhaps not-so-authentic manifestation of their creative vision. In this way these designers ask their consumer to reconsider the values of living and consumption. However while the fashion system provides structures, institutions and behaviours for fashion designers to cling to, as Wu Juanjuan (2009: 181) has posited, ultimately it is an aesthetic content that fills these structures and which will differentiate Chinese fashion designers. As domestic consumption increases and more products are designed rather than simply manufactured in China, new actors, new systems, methods and new processes of legitimization will arise to challenge the hegemony of the dominant Eurocentric fashion system in which the flows of economic capital currently leave China to become profits for foreign companies. This is exactly the response that the Chinese government is planning for.

However, Chinese fashion designers face a difficult challenge as they move toward legitimization in the fashion system. While the Chinese government is focusing on the 'money' and retaining more of the value-added capital from economy of fashion, fashion designers are more interested in turning their creative visions into brands. This brings to mind Michael Polanyi's (1966) insight that the universe is always seen from a centre within ourselves and that truth is always personal. However, is truth the same as authenticity? As Hobsbawm and Ranger (1983) explain, authenticity is malleable and open to coercion and, as Richard Peterson (2005) contends, it is a very different concept when compared to the freedom of pure creativity. In the conceptual space between Hobsbawm and Peterson reside the magic, malleability and mythology that perpetuate the legitimization of fashion: here also is the opportunity for Chinese fashion design. Authenticity might be described as a cultural manifestation, while creativity through the process of design is an intrinsic process that is driven by the search for a personal truth, a desire to achieve harmony, or balance, most often reframed in the context of the 'commercial market'. In this situation Chinese fashion design would appear to be less about the nationality of the designer and more about the designer's ability to attract a global audience while imparting a strong sense of cultural value.

In this regard, the oft-observed Chinese designer Ma Masha who attended Central St Martins and interned in Europe seems focused more on the development of a sustainable global business model in conjunction with her adept usage of digital and social media. In Ma's view, being labelled a Chinese designer is not a matter of choice without the solid infrastructure of a fashion industry in China: one must go elsewhere to sell one's wares (Chen 2014). Likewise, the designer Qiu Hao suggests that this question of a national label may no longer be relevant. His global mobility means that although he is a Chinese national, he regards this as an external label that in actual fact bears little relation to his design philosophy. Accordingly, 'China', may be conceived of both as a geographic location, and yet another place where the concept of 'China' differs, depending on one's life experiences (Lindgren 2014).

FAKES, COUNTERFEITS AND THE RISE OF ONLINE PLATFORMS

However, there is another much talked about social issue infiltrating the fashion system: that of trust, and this is often the reason for the preference of buying consumer goods abroad. Genuine safety concerns exist with the quality of domestic products ranging from food to cars, clothing and electrical goods. These trust issues include the ubiquity of *shanzhai* (knockoff) designs, localization, and the grey market for clothing: all are effects of innovation and fast-tracked production that depend on the value-generating properties of the fashion system. They raise further questions about the role of intellectual property enforcement in the Chinese creative industries (Montgomery 2010).[6] Another interesting market activity involves representing a Chinese domestic product as foreign in origin. Described as lobalization (Chew 2009), the intent is to simulate a foreign brand identity. All these activities are contentious because they taint nearly every activity in daily life in China, and while they are not consigned solely to the clothing industry, their impact contributes to an undermining of national reputation as well as an ongoing societal disquiet.

Counterfeit versions of almost anything can be found in markets in China, including fake luxury goods, electronics, household goods, food and beverages, certificates, official documents, receipts, and even counterfeit Apple stores. The tainted milk scandal that was widely viewed in global media in 2008 still resonates, epitomizing the deep mistrust the Chinese public have for their government's ability to provide food security (Roubini 2014).[7] In a recent research project concerning Chinese fashion (Lindgren 2014), many interviewees indicated how these activities cause ongoing concern about the basic tools, materials and components required by a fashion designer and contribute to many problems that undermine the structure of the Chinese fashion system. When considered in conjunction with the oppressive and relentless daily vista of visible levels of pollution, the routines of tainted food, and the relentless official pursuit of corruption, the reaction of many designers is to import fabrics and other components of their garments.[8]

The international fashion business now operates without the constraint of seasons, and this fact is illustrated by the rise of fast fashion and the 24-hour cycling of the Internet. The sustained growth of online shopping, or e-tail, encourages fashion designers toward seeking global connections as well as forming symbiotic engagements with consumers. The Chinese e-commerce giant Alibaba facilitates this mechanism as a great tidal arbiter with T-Mall, an online shopping mall. As the chapter by Cheung in this volume shows, this powerful corporation is attempting to mitigate cultural barriers and safeguard consumer trust, a particularly problematic quest, as well as ensure certainty of payment for foreign and domestic brands alike.[9] Alibaba has competition in the form of Shangpin, a dedicated fashion e-tailer, as well as Baidu and Tencent; these online players are all vying for market share in the rapidly expanding space of product mediation. These online platforms provide domestic shoppers access to global fashion brands at cheaper prices than in China, where imported brands are comparatively expensive due to a variety of government taxes on consumer goods.

In addition, changing consumer tastes are reshaping the expectations of well-established brands – and as consumers become more sophisticated so do their expectations. To put the digital environment in context, in 2013 online spending in China totalled approximately US$307 billion. Yet growth is expected to compound at 20 per cent per annum until 2019, at which point an excess of US$1 trillion will be spent across a variety of platforms including mobile commerce, where growth is forecast to be a compounding 44 per cent (Zeng et al. 2015). Cultural change has never been more evident in the field of consumption. For example, 'Singles Day', sometimes called 'Anti-Valentines' day, began on the campus of Nanjing University in 1993, initiated by mainly male students who visited bars to meet other single people. November 11th became the official day for this activity, as the date of 11/11 is a simplified visual representation of single people. The celebration evolved to include women and special singles-only parties arose that involve eating a Chinese snack called *youtiao*, a fried dough stick that also resembles the number 1. Now the combination of growing consumerism in China, a growing bachelor population thanks to the One-Child Policy and access to the Internet means Singles Day has become a nationwide shopping phenomenon. Alibaba alone recorded more than US$9 billion in revenue on this one day in 2013 (Jourdan 2014).

In the field of fashion production and consumption, domestic Chinese fashion designers like Ma Masha and her contemporaries have numerous opportunities to move quickly in their attempts to navigate the digital realm; some have proven particularly adept, despite vigilant and authoritarian intrusions into the use of the Internet in China. In this way they are renewing China's design presence at the centre of a new world of Asian design, and with the gathering momentum of Asian consumption and population growth China is on track to assume the mantle of the Middle Kingdom once again. In many ways, contemporary Chinese fashion designers have been fast-tracked because of their familiarity with the Internet, and because fashion is such a fast moving consumer good the knowledge base moves rapidly. Culturally China's digital revolution is greatly enabling; however, the most important ramification is that because they now compete globally for exposure Chinese fashion designers must first become proficient at their craft before they can draw upon their heritage to create a point of distinction.

To conclude, instead of considering the Chinese domestic fashion system in its current nascent form to be an independent entity, it is clear that it is integrated with a global fashion system, one in which the components (of the system) are geographically separated yet come together to form a whole supported by disparate fashion industries that have coalesced in regions with the lowest manufacturing costs. National identity is less concerned with national borders. Cultural differences merge. Good design is good design – regardless of nationality. Yet good design must also serve to improve the human condition.

In addition, it is evident that the digital creative economy has facilitated the spread of a new kind of virulent tacit knowledge, one that enables the learning processes of fashion producer and consumer alike. Accordingly, emergent Chinese fashion designers are in many ways now born global, laden with easily accessible knowledge gleaned from social media and the Internet, but lacking experience and industry structure while burdened by the need to reframe the rhetoric of 'Made in China' as an asset for the national good.

Chinese designers are able to draw upon deeply ingrained cultural philosophy for its incorporation in a fresh Chinese design aesthetic. Nevertheless in pursuing success, agile and responsive business models that bypass cultural and national boundaries are necessary, even vital for engagement with a global fashion system. Here a multi-channel portfolio strategy is required to gain traction in a diverse global marketplace in order to connect with similarly sophisticated and borderless consumers.

Although Chinese fashion will likely remain within a relatively constrained commercial infrastructure, there is now considerable optimism for new ways of living that include the adoption of more inclusive, sustainable and responsible behaviours. Because of this 'evolution', fashion designers can have great input into the production of a new kind of Chinese culture. Instead of the kind of cultural dislocation espoused by Bauman (2005), a new space for this kind of creativity is appearing in the digital realm where nationality is less important than authenticity and transparency. China's reputation as manufacturer to the world has moved on and a new political mandate now underpins a powerful creative and financial impetus that challenges established models, offering China hope as a future powerhouse of global fashion.

NOTES

1. These Chinese designers trade under their Anglicized names illustrated in brackets.
2. At the time of writing, US$1=approximately 6 RMB (Renminbi).
3. Sometimes referred to as indigenous innovation.
4. A *daigou* website is a channel of commerce that facilitates the overseas purchases of luxury goods on behalf of a Mainland Chinese customer to avoid onerous taxes.
5. The Han is the largest group (91 per cent), and 55 other ethnic groups are recognized in China.
6. Shanzhai is the adaptation of a foreign product by domestic entrepreneurs to meet a localized need. Localization is the cultural adaptation by a foreign brand of a global product to a local market. The grey market demonstrates a logistical problem where clothing is sold through unofficial channels, without the permission of the brand owner. Lobalization is the unofficial adaption of a global brand's intellectual property to a local market, where it purports to be official, imported or foreign.
7. In 2008, a significant public scandal erupted over powdered milk that had been contaminated with melamine. Officially 300,000 children were harmed, with numerous deaths, however unofficial accounts allude to multiples of this figure (Roubini 2014).
8. In a trend called 'face mask fashion', young Internet users post photos of themselves wearing air filtration facemasks. One popular mask is hot pink and another looks like a panda bear (Kaiman 2013).

9. It is interesting to note that Alibaba's initial public listing was on the New York Stock Exchange, away from the volatility of the Mainland Chinese stock market.

REFERENCES

Barton, Dominic, Yougang Chen and Amy Jin (2013), 'Mapping China's middle class', accessed 3 February 2015 at http://www.mckinsey.com/insights/consumer_and_retail/mapping_chinas_middle_class.

Bauman, Zygmunt (2005), *On Living in A Liquid Modern World*. Cambridge: Polity Press.

Becker, Howard Saul (2008), *Art Worlds*. London and California: University of California Press.

Chen, Vivian (2014), 'Masha Ma talks about the future of fashion in China', *South China Morning Post*, accessed 6 July 2014 at http://www.scmp.com/magazines/style/article/1500726/designed-succeed.

Chew, Mathew (2009), 'Delineating the emergent global cultural dynamic of "lobalisation"; the case of pass-off menswear in China', *Continuum* **24** (4): 559–71.

Craik, Jennifer (2009), *Fashion: The Key Concepts*. Oxford; New York: Berg.

DCMS (1998), *Creative Industries Mapping Document 1998*. London: Department of Culture, Media and Sport, accessed 8 February 2012 at http://www.webarchive.nationalarchives.gov.uk/+/http://www.culture.gov.uk/reference_library/publications/4740.aspx/.

Elliot, Larry (2014), 'Financial storm clouds cast a deep shadow over IMF summit', *The Guardian*, London, accessed 10 October 2014 at http://www.theguardian.com/business/2014/oct/12/imf-world-bank-washington-financial-storm-clouds.

Harris, Dan (2011), 'China's 12th Five year plan', *China Law Blog*, accessed 7 April 2011 at http://www.chinalawblog.com/2011/03/http://www.chinalawblog.com/2011/03/chinas_12th_five_year_plan_infrastructure_infrastructure_infrastructure_did_we_say_infrastructure.html.

Hobsbawm, Eric and Terrance Ranger (1983), *The Invention of Tradition*. Cambridge: Cambridge University Press.

Jourdan, Adam (2014), 'Alibaba reports record $9 billion Single's Day sales', Reuters, accessed 8 June 2014 at http://www.reuters.com/article/2014/11/11/us-china-singles-day-idUSKCN0IV0BD20141111.

Kaiman, Jonathan (2013), 'Chinese struggle through "airpocalypse" smog', *The Guardian*, London, accessed 12 March 2013 at http://www.guardian.co.uk/world/2013/feb/16/chinese-struggle-through-airpocalypse-smog.

Kawamura, Yuniya (2005), *Fashion-ology*, 1 ed. New York: Berg.

Keane, Michael (2007), *Created in China: The Great New Leap Forward, Media, Culture and Social Change in Asia*. London and New York: Routledge.

Lee, Yimou and Donny Kwok (2015), 'Hong Kong retailers shut shops as Chinese tourists stay away', Reuters, accessed 9 June 2015 at http://www.mobile.reuters.com/article/financialsSector/idUSL3N0YA1CV20150603.

Lindgren, Tim (2014), 'Fashion in Shanghai: The designers of a new economy of style', Ph.D, A.R.C Centre for Innovation, Queensland University of Technology.

Liu, Kang (2000), *Popular Culture and the Culture of the Masses in Contemporary China, Postmodernism and China*. London: Duke University Press.

London, Bianca (2015), 'Is Guo Pei the next big thing?', *Daily Mail*, London, accessed 16 August 2015 at http://www.dailymail.co.uk/femail/article-3070057/Is-Guo-Pei-big-thing-Meet-designer-spent-TWO-YEARS-hand-making-Rihanna-s-Chinese-couture-Met-Gala-gown-commands-500-000-outfit.html.

Montgomery, Lucy (2010), *China's Creative Industries: Copyright, Social Network Markets and the Business of Culture in a Digital Age*. Cheltenham, UK and Northampton, MA, USA: Edward Elgar.

National Garments Association (2013), 'An overview of China's garment industry', accessed 10 April 2013 at http://www.cnga.org.cn/engl/about/Overview.asp.

Peterson, Richard A. (2005), 'In search of authenticity', *Management Studies* **42** (5): 1083–98.

Polanyi, Michael (1966), *The Tacit Dimension*. London: University of Chicago Press.

Roubini, Nouriel (2014), 'The world economy is flying with only one engine', *The Guardian*, London, accessed 7 July 2014 at http://www.theguardian.com/business/2014/nov/02/world-economy-flying-one-engine-us-growth.

Said, Edward (2003), *Orientalism*. London: Penguin.

Solca, Luca (2015), 'The Great Mall of China', *The Business of Fashion*, accessed 8 June 2015 at 08/06/2015.http://www.businessoffashion.com/articles/intelligence/the-great-mall-of-china.

The World Bank (2013), *China 2030: Building a Modern, Harmonious, and Creative Society*, accessed 18 July 2012 at http://documents.worldbank.org/curated/en/2013/03/17494829/china-2030-building-modern-harmonious-creative-society.

Wang, Liwei and Rongde Li (2015), 'Chinese cabinet unveils "Made in China 2025" master plan', Beijing: Caixin Online, accessed 4 June 2015 at http://www.marketwatch.com/story/chinese-cabinet-unveils-made-in-china-2025-master-plan-2015-05-20.

Wolff, Janet (1993), *The Social Production of Art*. New York: New York University Press.

Wu, Juanjuan (2009), *Chinese Fashion: From Mao to Now*. London: Oxford International Publishing.

Xinhua News Agency (2015), 'Made in China, reincarnated', Beijing: *China Daily Online*, accessed 8 June 2015 at http://www.chinadaily.com.cn/business/2015-05/21/content_20785253_2.htm.

Zeng, Vanessa, Brian Wang, Michael Barnes and Di Jin (2015), *China Online Retail Forecast, 2014 to 2019*. Forrester, accessed 27 August 2014 at https://www.forrester.com/China+Online+Retail+Forecast+2014+To+2019/fulltext/-/E-RES118544.

Zhang, Kevin Hongling (2006), 'Is China the world factory?', in *China as the World Factory*, edited by Kevin Hongling Zhang. London: Routledge, pp. 257–74.

33. Spectacles, showcases, marketplaces (and even public spheres): Chinese film festivals as cultural industries

Ran Ma and Cindy Hing-Yuk Wong

INTRODUCTION: THE FILM FESTIVAL AS A CULTURAL INDUSTRY

Different levels of government in China are actively involved in supporting cultural industries; however, governmental interventions often compete. In focusing on film festivals, both state-sanctioned and independent, this chapter reveals the intricate processes through which Chinese film festivals and their different stakeholders negotiate amongst themselves *and* with the state about an entity, the festival, that itself embodies contesting demands: namely, commerce, projections of soft power, control and freedom of expression.

Film festivals have never been 'mass' events but rather alternatives to mainstream cinema aimed at selective local and global audiences, favouring both artistic merit and oppositional inclinations. Globally, since the 1970s, concerted efforts from governments at different levels, the investment of corporate sponsors, and the participation of creative personnel have made such festivals important cultural institutions, generating international networks that wield power over non-mainstream cinema worldwide. Moreover, cities have become identified with festivals and vice versa, a symbiotic characteristic of contemporary urban policy.

Film festivals in China are a fairly recent phenomenon despite forerunners to be found in Greater China. In Taipei, while the Golden Horse Film Awards began in 1962, it only became international in the 1980s. The Hong Kong International Film Festival was established in 1977 when Hong Kong was still a British Crown Colony; it grew in reputation in later decades (Wong 2011). Film festivals (*dianyingjie*) in the People's Republic of China (PRC), on which this chapter focuses, came even later.

Events known as 'film festivals' (*dianyingjie*) did not occur in the PRC until the late 1980s; when they did emerge they were, unsurprisingly, state-sanctioned. The first continuously run official film festival was the Changchun Film Festival, established in this northeastern city in 1992.[1]

The Shanghai International Film Festival (SIFF), established a year later, became the nation's flagship festival; it remains heavily supported by the local authorities. Of the early state-run film festivals, no others had the momentum of Shanghai. Only in 2011 did a new rival emerge – the Beijing International Film Festival (BJIFF). The inauguration of the BJIFF was in effect a response to former president Hu Jintao's keynote speech to the 17th National Congress of the Communist Party of China (CCP) in 2007 in which he emphasized the importance of Chinese culture and the cultural industries 'as part of the soft power of our country to better guarantee the people's basic cultural rights and interests'.[2]

Since the early 2000s, further away from the spotlight of state-defined creativity, a number of grassroots-level independent film festivals have prospered in culturally vibrant cities including Kunming, Nanjing and Beijing, powered by local cinéphile culture. These independent festivals have used Chinese terms equivalent to those of 'forum' or 'exchange week' to dodge the censorship procedures for a *dianyingjie*. They attract cinéphiles, film scholars, critics, journalists and even buyers worldwide since their programming promises a much more updated and exciting vision of contemporary Chinese films, with a much larger proportion of independent works screened.[3]

Local governments are not always opposed to such festivals; some promote them at different times within designated artistic clusters. Smaller independent Chinese festivals have been co-opted or even used in tandem with tourist attractions, like Sichuan's Ya'an Panda, Animal and Nature Film Festival.[4] The diversity of film festivals therefore provides a challenge when it comes to generalizing such practices. Only some, like the Shanghai festival, come closer to the 'official' cultural and creative industry (*wenhua chuangyi chanye*) model that the municipal government uses to promote the image of Shanghai. In contrast, the Hong Kong International Film Festival (HKIFF) has acted as a major promoter of Chinese cinema to the world, echoing the manager/middle man role that the city itself has developed within China. It has promoted the careers of many film directors and producers as well as enhancing the global stature of Chinese cinema. Yet, through the years, even after the polity's return to the PRC, the HKIFF has continued to irk Chinese censoring authorities – reminding us of that city's 'special status' within the PRC.

We have chosen to categorize festivals in order to show how they embody contradictions inherent in the term 'cultural industries' (*wenhua chanye*). We first focus on the Shanghai and Beijing festivals, exemplars of state-sanctioned events; we examine how national and local cultural and commercial policies work together to promote these events. In doing so we consider the relationship between festivals and the film industry itself. We then explore grassroots film festivals in China, drawing on examples from Beijing municipality (Songzhuang) and Yunnan Province (Kunming).

One question we need to ask is: what tensions play out amongst industry, creativity and resistance within this emerging landscape of film festivals in China? If the mainstream festivals are about soft power and the powerful profiles of their host cities, what other relationships exist with film industries, both domestically and internationally? In fact, while official and grassroots film festivals seem to occupy very different cultural and commercial locations, they are nevertheless made up of intermediaries who inhabit both worlds, and who ultimately rely on the same pool of human resources.

A GENEALOGY OF OFFICIAL FILM FESTIVALS IN POST-TIANANMEN CHINA

It is tempting to trace the genealogy of the film festival to September 1989, when the first China Film Festival (*Zhongguo dianyingjie*) opened. In the wake of the June Fourth Incident in Beijing, this gala event showcased newly produced films – ostensibly a line-up of leitmotif works eulogizing the CCP's revolutionary history.[5] If we were to consider film festivals as promoters of Chinese cinema, however, the 1985 screening of *Yellow Earth* (*huang tudi*) at the Hong Kong International Film Festival stands out as a more significant milestone for Chinese cinema and its ascendance to the global film festival circuit, as well as global markets (see Wong 2011). Another decisive turning point was 2001, when the first independent film festival, Unlimited Image Festival (*Zhongguo duli yingxiangjie*) was held in Beijing: this was 'independent' not just because the line-up was composed of contemporary Chinese independent films, but because it was a grassroots-level film festival that was not submitted to the State Administration of Radio, Film and Television (SARFT) for authorization; in other words, it did not seek relevant permits, a topic we shall return to later.[6]

Although a second China Film Festival never followed, two highly prestigious, national film awards, the 'Hundred Flowers Awards' (*baihua jiang*, est. 1962) and the 'Golden Rooster Awards' (*jinji jiang*, est. 1981) were integrated into one national film event in 1992. Awkwardly titled the 'China Golden Rooster and Hundred Flowers Film Festival', this event had variable locations. In the same year, with the approval of SARFT and co-hosted by the provincial government of Jilin and the Changchun municipal government, the Changchun International Film Festival was instigated, utilizing its close association with the Changchun Film Studio,[7] one of the largest state-owned film studios, also known as 'the cradle of PRC cinema.' This annual festival nowadays presents an unmistakably political selection of Chinese-language films.[8] In many respects these official festivals selectively followed the format of their European counterparts, without their independence or global reach.

Other festivals were short-lived. A film festival was established in the Zhuhai Special Economic Zone[9] in 1994, branded as 'Across the Taiwan Strait and Hong Kong Film Festival (*Zhongguo zhuhai haixialiang'an ji xiang'gang dianyingjie*)'. At the time, it was highly regarded not only because of the sheer value of its cash prize and the media hype of the Hong Kong stars who attended, but also for its vision in bringing together Chinese-language films from three Chinas even before the return of Hong Kong to PRC in 1997, a maneuver considered 'adventurous' but significant.[10] Unfortunately it disappeared after two successful events. As the Zhuhai festival indicates, a successful launch does not ensure success: revisions of policies can interrupt or even terminate a festival.

The process of initiating an official film festival in PRC is invariably top-down. Even in the 1990s, when economic reform (*jingji gaige*) was the mantra of development, the film festival assumed political significance; every aspect had to be handled with great precaution. Locally run film festivals in the 1990s were not without tension, indexing the host cities' difficulties negotiating the drastic socioeconomic transformations in the post-Tiananmen era.

Festivals were, in turn, related to changes in the status of culture. Even before 'cultural industry' (*wenhua chanye*) became the buzzword widely endorsed and circulated in official discourse, the marketized/commercialized cultural terrain of post-socialist China provided new conditions for the film festivals in Changchun, Shanghai and Zhuhai. Early in the spring of 1992, Deng Xiaoping conducted his Southern Tour of the Special Economic Zones; his speeches underscored the China Communist Party's (hereafter CCP) guidelines in respect to economic reform. Deng's message 'signalled a new more friendly political climate for rapid capital accumulation and the development of mass consumption. This new biopolitical regime de-totalized socialist society by reconfiguring socialist power in relation to self-enterprising powers' (Ong and Zhang 2008: 14). In 1993, a number of crucial policies were launched to speed up the marketization of China's film industry. These specifically aimed to dissolve the rigid industrial hierarchy within the China Film Group Corporation that had monopolized film import and export. Official film festivals were envisioned partially as strategies to facilitate urban regeneration and industrial restructuring.

In the initial wave of establishing (international) film festivals in

Mainland China during the 1990s, local governments, like many around the world, tended to equate these to other successful cultural events, such as the Asian Olympic Games or the World Expo. Despite recurrent failures, municipalities believed that these events would enhance local/regional cultural and economic profiles, facilitate urban branding and extend international connections. Yet, while official film festivals in the PRC were complicit with capital, they also were subject to totalizing control from the authorities. Festival organization committees were dominated by government officials and party cadres; presumably not a single film programmer or consultant should stand out. While ideological statements have assumed a much softer presence at more recent festivals, the artistic vision in programming remains compromised by politics. Therefore, it is tempting to argue that the ways in which the official film festivals negotiate with both the rigid 'planned' system and the market economy illustrate their creativities in carving out space *as* and *for* cultural industries.

Official film festivals gradually attained new discursive legitimacy within the policies that came to frame cultural industry reform by the end of the decade. In the 2000s, the National People's Congress, the National CCP Congress and the 'Five-Year Plans' provided crucial guidelines and vocabularies for local and regional governments to stipulate specific instructions and policies to promote cultural industries.[11] Host cities could now conveniently categorize and position their film festivals within municipal and provincial policy-making frameworks for stimulating local cultural industries. Meanwhile, film festivals used cultural industry policies to generate further opportunities and support from the public sector and the market. The significance of, and economic support for film festivals is therefore contingent on short and long-term cultural industry plans.

THE SHANGHAI INTERNATIONAL FILM FESTIVAL

The Shanghai International Film Festival (SIFF), established in 1993 under the supervision of SARFT's Film Bureau and the municipal government of Shanghai, illustrates the significance of official film festivals in relation to China's cultural industries.[12] SIFF is the only state-sanctioned film festival that is recognized by an international body; structurally it appears closest to the international film festival model, complete with marketing opportunities and industry fora. However, deeper analysis shows that the Shanghai festival differs from this international model because of the state's continuing control of cultural production and its manifest relationship to the film industry.

The festival currently is composed of four major sections: the Golden Goblet Award (*jinjue jiang*) is the top competition segment, usually composed of 16 films selected globally, for which several *jinjue* awards will be given, including that of Best Film and Best Director. The Asian New Talent Award, established in 2004, is its second competition category; this consists of 10 films from Asia. Its third competition category, MOBILE SIFF, is dedicated to short films submitted internationally and an International Film Panorama showcases films under various sidebars. In addition to these sections, there also is a film market, SIFF Mart, and SIFFORUM (consisting of lectures, seminars, roundtables and so forth for film professionals).

Much like Changchun's film festival, SIFF was established to rejuvenate the heritage of Shanghai film culture. Leveraging its extraordinary status in the Chinese film history, Shanghai elites had harboured the idea of hosting a film festival since the mid-1980s.[13] Though desiring to highlight the film festival's connection with the Chinese film industry as well as Shanghai's city-branding advantages, the Shanghai city government and the festival committee lacked an effective framework and vocabulary to coordinate and address the festival's multiple roles. Instead, the vaguely defined and unevenly realized slogan 'Going International' (*guojihua*) has embodied the festival's strategic orientation since an early stage. For example, under such a banner, SIFF took the initiative to apply for FIAPF accreditation and was quickly approved, a decision not without controversies, however.[14] This strategy has arguably positioned the Shanghai festival within the world film festival system – with its A-list status constantly emphasized in the festival publicity campaigns. At the same time, this strategy shows how urban elites position the city within the network of rival global cities, which affirms Julian Stringer's argument that it is cities rather than national film industries that 'act as nodal points' on the international film festival circuit (Stringer 2008: 138).

'Going International' has further defined the SIFF's positioning within the official mapping of creative industries at Shanghai into the 2000s. As Michael Keane has noted, in the early 2000s, the idea of 'creative industries' caught the attention of China's city-makers; while Beijing's officials argued about the distinction between cultural and creative industries, Shanghai 'seized the moment' and took the lead in founding Shanghai Creative Industries Center and the Shanghai Creative Industries Association in 2005. Thereafter, 'operating under the combined management of the city's Propaganda Department and Economic Commission, these bodies instigated the development of a range of creative clusters in Shanghai' (Keane 2009: 79). Justin O'Connor and Xin Gu further suggest that, 'the creative industries agenda in Shanghai was particularly embraced as part of its claim to be a global cultural metropolis, one based on its distinctive history as the site where urban modernity made landfall in China' (O'Connor and Gu 2012: 2).

Since 2011, in response to the central government's 'decision' in cultural reform,[15] the Shanghai government has emphatically proposed that the city would be built into an 'international cultural metropolis' (Shanghai Municipal Committee 2011). SIFF claims to be as important as other international cultural fairs in 'strengthening international cultural collaborations and exchanges' (ibid.).[16] According to the 'Shanghai Cultural Industries Report 2013' that reviews the achievements of 2012, the SIFF has been spotlighted as one of the major events for branding local cultural tourism: 'in 2013, there were 1655 films from 112 countries and regions screened at the SIFF, which has received the most attention among all the film festivals in Asia' (Shanghai Cultural Affairs Bureau, 2014). Nevertheless, no further data have been provided to corroborate how successful SIFF is among its regional competitors, such as the major, competing international film festivals at Busan, Tokyo and Hong Kong. To interpret the festival's incremental progress throughout all these years vis-à-vis the burgeoning cultural/creative industries, a more productive approach is to examine some fundamental components of the SIFF in connecting with the film industries home and abroad.

Although SIFF is not renowned for its programming, it is noteworthy that the festival has shown autonomy and creativity in initiating diverse fora and seminars as well as master-classes to facilitate dialogue among film professionals on a wide spectrum of subjects (usually with the geopolitical emphasis on Greater China Region and regional film cultures and industries). SIFF's Film Market, which has grown to be one of China's 'major' film markets, illustrates how this state-sanctioned film festival endeavours to negotiate with market initiatives.

Globally, such 'Film Markets' are one of the defining elements of the success of film festivals (Cheung 2011: 41). SIFF's strategies reflect this worldwide trend. The film market was established as early as 1995, but did not function well as a platform for film business due to the lack of policy support for film import and exhibition, particularly with the state-owned China Film Group Corporation (CFGC) acting as the sole film importer. Since 2012, SIFF Mart has been restructured to include both the SIFF Market and the SIFF Project. In 2012, several high-profile funds (including the state-run National Film Capital) signed contracts worth RMB 3.2 billion (US$ 0.5b.) at the Market (Pudong Media 2013). In 2013, SIFF Market attracted 819 organizations and companies, with 2718 buyers from 106 countries and regions. According to the festival, 750 deals have been achieved by agreement, even though agreements do not always materialize. Judging by the publicity numbers from the film festival, we can assume 'these promising figures present a rather positive picture for the survival and even prosperity of the film market alone' (Cheung 2011: 51). However, these numbers do not explain if the deals are national or international transactions, which leaves questions open about how successful the SIFF market is as an international film festival market.

For overseas exhibitors China is regarded as a potential shooting location and an attractive film market because of its massive population and gradually evolving policies to accommodate transnational capital flows. Nevertheless, even while the CFGC promises to selectively import popular films that are screened at SIFF, coupled with the former point on the film market, it remains questionable how effective the SIFF Market is in facilitating concrete connections between the Chinese film market and overseas film exhibitors, despite the 2014 news that a second state company has obtained the license for importing and distributing overseas films in China.[17]

Meanwhile, media reports have highlighted a highly diversified group of exhibitors now taking part in the Market, which covers 'post-production, new media, shooting location, branding, special-effect makeup, film financing and legal service' (Zhou 2013). If there is any reason to feel the deals are 'promising,' as Cheung claims, this underscores the diversified industrial backgrounds of exhibitors, who cover various sectors of the cultural and creative industries. For instance, at the 15th SIFF in 2012, Xunlei Networking Technologies, a Chinese video and music file-sharing company partly owned by Google Inc., signed deals with Airmedia, One Film Fund and KH Media to invest RMB 500 million (US$78.5m) collaboratively in developing a cross-media movie platform providing service via Internet or Video-on-Demand (Eastday 2012).

The SIFF Project, comprising two pitching programs, Co-production Film Pitch and Catch (Co-FPC) and China Film Pitch and Catch (CFPC), has generated somewhat different dynamics for industrial networks. In 2006, Co-FPC was established with an eye to coproduction opportunities globally, drawing on the former Sino-European Co-production Film Forum. Thirty-two projects are selected annually (see SIFF site). In 2007, SIFF integrated CFPC into its film market to cultivate rising Chinese filmmakers. At CFPC, eight filmmakers have the chance to brainstorm with and to seek advice from a group of veteran film professionals (such as producers, investors, directors), while the filmmakers and their producers also have to pitch their ideas to a jury and industry financiers.[18] CFPC echoes SIFF's strategy in co-opting the independent film community into the film festival, a far-sighted maneuver. In a sense, the SIFF aspires to become one of those 'business festivals' as Mark Peranson keenly observes

(2009). International and domestic film professionals see travelling to cosmopolitan Shanghai as good networking opportunities with the mega Chinese market even if they cannot make deals at the Mart.

THE BEIJING INTERNATIONAL FILM FESTIVAL

As a new addition to state-sanctioned film festivals in 2011, the Beijing International Film Festival (BJIFF) is an official film festival essentially designed to cater to the latest policies in boosting cultural industries.[19] At the press conference announcing the launch of the first BJIFF (April 23–28, 2011), officials pointed out that not only does an international film festival fit the municipal government's plan in building Beijing into a 'world city' (*shijie chengshi*), but it also responds to vital policies such as the 'Plan for the Reinvigoration of the Cultural Industry' and the 'Guidelines on Promoting the Prosperous Development of Movie Industry'.[20] This project highlights the fact that Beijing aims to enhance its cultural soft power and become 'the film and TV Capital of the Orient' (*dongfang yingshi zhidu*), all of which makes the launching of an international film festival a promising strategy. At the same time, official statistics have foregrounded Beijing's unparalleled industrial development in terms of film production and distribution, human capital and cinema infrastructure (such as the number of film theatres, film museums and pedagogical institutes and so forth), which they claimed to prepare the city well for hosting an international film festival (State Council 2010).

Reportedly, the inaugural festival managed to showcase 160 films at 20 cinemas for its main exhibition program, 'Beijing Film Panorama'. Nevertheless, the organizer paid most attention to its red carpet ceremony and the 'Beijing Forum', where 22 festival directors and programmers from major international film festivals were offered a platform to participate in a dialogue on topics such as 'Film Festivals and Host Cities' Influence'. Not unfamiliar with the practices of Chinese official festivals, *Film Business Asia*'s Stephen Cremin, after participating in the 2011 BJIFF, lamented that 'it would be wrong to assume that the Beijing festival is targeted at film lovers', since VIP visitors were not even allowed adequate time to attend screenings. Chaotic organization of the festival screenings was reported on Chinese microblogs such as Weibo, which noted that some public screenings were cancelled without any notice, and the exact situation of attendance for its scheduled 289 screenings was thrown in doubt. Cremin might not be exaggerating in pointing out that the major target for the inaugural festival were the government bureaucrats who would be 'called upon to finance future editions' (Cremin 2011).

The inaugural international film festival at Beijing in 2011 shared the same imbalance between film market and the exhibition that had characterized the SIFF. The BJIFF has included the Beijing Film Market (BFM) since its inception. Indeed, both the festival's film line-up and market have benefited from a unique market event known as Beijing Screenings, which had to move from October to April to coincide with the film festival. Beijing Screenings – organized by CFGC's overseas sales arm since 1996, offer a series of promotional screenings for Chinese films targeting at overseas buyers. They mostly showcase state-run studios' 'model products' that are not considered favorably by 'buyers with commercial bent' or 'international film festival programmers'. Nevertheless in recent years this event has attracted increasing numbers of producers who 'try to get to know China's film industry establishment on its home turf in hopes of cementing relations with the bureaucracy of the world's fastest-growing film market' (Landreth 2011). The BFM has utilized the resources of Beijing Screenings to attract an already existing body of international buyers, programmers and exhibitors, while the festival also maneuvers to diversify cultural industries-related products and services at its freshly launched, highly privileged market interface.

Since the 4th BJIFF in 2014, the BFM has been further divided into two major segments, a Film Factor Market that facilitates business 'covering the whole film industry chain' and a Film Project Market, which aims to 'select and nurture film projects with strong commercial potential' (see BJIFF site). According to reports of the government mouthpiece, *Beijing Daily*, on new achievements in Beijing's creative industries, the 'numbers' generated by the first BJIFF in 2011, particularly its market deals worth RMB 2.794 billion, have indicated that 'a cluster of film industries is in formation' (Zhou and Wan 2011). The festival's official site also highlights that in 2013 major deals for 27 projects worth RMB 8.731 billion (US$1.38 b.) were accomplished at BFM (BJIFF site). Since its third edition in 2013, the festival has added a new competitive category featuring the *Tiantan* (the Temple of Heaven) Award. While many believe this strategy is crucial for the festival's branding, it also recalls Cremin's expectation that the existence of a new, better-financed BJIFF as SIFF's competitor 'could be the best thing ever happened to the Shanghai event,' since it should encourage the SIFF 'to develop its programming, its market, its forums and its publications to the next level' (Cremin 2011).

These two major official film festivals project a China apparently on par with other global powers. Officials in Shanghai and Beijing, whether connected to cultural affairs and cinema or not, view these as branding opportunities. Film festivals, like arts festivals, film markets and other cultural fairs, are essential components of a commanding global city. For this volume we are merely evaluating how these film festivals further the goals laid out by the Chinese central government in its effort to promote cities as well as the nation's cultural/creative industries. Judging from one benchmark, namely, the Western standard on international film festivals, these two festivals cannot compete with the A-list festivals, like Cannes, Venice or Berlin. However, from the Chinese point of view, these cities are asserting their global credentials by assembling all the trappings of the international institutions of cultural exchange. Film festivals as cultural industries are not only about commerce, but also soft power exerted upon the cities' local constituents.

In Shanghai and Beijing, while both municipal governments associate the festivals with state-designated categories such as 'Convention and Exhibition' (*huizhan*) and 'TV and Film Industries' (*yingshi gongye*), the festivals' achievements and contributions to the creative industries usually constitute statistics and numbers generated during the festivals. This interpretative prism partially explains why the festival's function as marketplace is magnified. For instance, according to Cremin, like the SIFF, BJIFF is 'a festival of numbers': the festival reports convey 'how many foreign festival presidents, how many films on how many cinema screens, how many exhibitors attended the market, how much money promised at how many deals at the close of the project market' (Cremin 2011). Although quantitative evaluations are inadequate to understand a film festival's creative presence, nevertheless, numbers and 'lists of statistics' as econometrics 'operate as persuasion devices for government, potential investors and insecure populations' (Rossiter 2008). They affirm the market potential of the film festivals, which may ultimately prove their value within the state's mapping of cultural and creative industries.

INDEPENDENT FILM FESTIVALS: UNMAPPED CREATIVITY AND CULTURAL INDUSTRIES

As mentioned by Qiu (this volume), a great deal of pressure is placed on assembling evidence for official projects; such data are usually collated in official Blue Books (*lanpi shu*). In his contribution titled 'Counter-Mapping Creative Industries in Beijing' featured in a special themed issue of *Urban China* (*chengshi Zhongguo*), Ned Rossiter questions the 'cluster' model that is used to underpin the 'government policy and infrastructural development' and instead promotes the idea of 'counter-cartographies' in shifting attention to constituents that are not usually considered as integral to Beijing's creative industries by the authorities. As Beijing-based artist Elaine Ho echoes, 'what are the exchanges, encounters and hidden productivities left out of this kind of map?' given that 'standard approaches to mapping creativity actively reduce and neatly contain the power of creativity' (Ho 2008: 71).[21] In following this provocative vision, we argue that grassroots-level independent film festivals figure as part of the innovative cartographic experiment in highlighting the unmapped creativity of Chinese cinema.

As mentioned earlier, since the early 2000s, grassroots level independent film festivals have emerged in Kunming, Nanjing and Beijing. Most independent film festivals take shape from the networking and screening activities of local cinéphile groups. In particular, the popularization of digital video (DV) formats since the early 2000s has enabled a wider spectrum of the general public to engage with image making creatively as amateur filmmakers. The ensuing increase in both the quantity and quality of independently produced works has necessitated the creation of more professionalized exhibition and screening platforms in addition to film festivals and overseas niche markets. Cine-groups have found it necessary to expand their screening venues beyond salons, pubs, bars and classrooms.

The earliest attempts to launch independent film festivals occurred in 2001 but both the Unlimited Image Festival in Beijing and the inaugural Beijing Queer Film Festival closed prematurely due to pressure from authorities. Rather than merely framing grassroots film festivals as oppositional to official film festivals, we examine how they are positioned within power relations configured by the party-state (censorship), the international film festival network and the Chinese film industry. A number of key points can be drawn out of this relationship.

First, although mostly driven by players in non-official, nongovernmental and private sectors, these festivals take place in the public realm, using alternative venues such as cafes, bars, cinemas and universities. These grassroots festivals are permitted but are subject to close surveillance. Moreover, there are cases in which local and regional authorities support such alternative cultural events as part of their efforts to boost cultural industries initiatives, a point to which we shall return later.

Second, alternative film festivals are not founded simply for ideological contestations: they serve as a means to link Chinese independent cinema to the hierarchical international film festival system, and to support new visions and new auteurs. In recent years, international festival programmers, film scouts and even producers and buyers have visited grassroots festivals. Still, it is significant that a standardized format for international film festivals does not apply to grassroots events: not only are they under-resourced (despite occasional partial funding by overseas cultural foundations and film commissions), but sustaining such festivals proves particularly challenging since their operations are subject to multiple layers of political interference.

Third, as indicated above, standardized cultural industry reports do not capture the creative contribution of such festivals. Many independent films have not been submitted to the censors and therefore remain in the grey area of official statistics. At the same time the political significance of independent films is well known and capital from a wide spectrum of sources, including private sectors and overseas funds (sometimes via their agencies and arms in the PRC) has been financing these films.

The emergence of grassroots film festivals is evidence of the demand on the part of the independent film sector for regularized exhibition channels and their yearning for a general public as audience. Although independent cinema registers the contingencies, the 'exchanges, encounters and hidden productivities' (see Ho 2008) left out of the official Blue Book reports, grassroots film festivals and their connected entities and organizations delineate film's multiple industrial configurations and linkages. Beyond analyzing these film festivals' artistic visions, structure and organization, it is also important to examine their creative initiatives and cultural resources.

CREATIVE SONGZHUANG AND THE INDEPENDENT FILM COMMUNITY

Located in Beijing's southeastern Tongzhou District, the township of Songzhuang once hosted two major grassroots film festivals – the Beijing Independent Film Festival (*Beijing duli dianying luntan*, BiFF, est. 2006) and the China Documentary Film Festival (*Zhongguo jilupian jiaoliuzhou*, DOChina, est. 2003). Several major organizations closely related to independent cinema are clustered there, making this peripheral town the heartland of China's independent film community. Crucially, Songzhuang lays claim to the largest contemporary art community in China, more than 3000 artists and art professionals. Independent art critic Li Xianting, celebrated as the 'godfather of Chinese contemporary art', was among the first of the community of artists to move to Songzhuang. Many purchased peasants' houses around 1994 after they were evicted from another spontaneous artist community, Yuanmingyuan, in northwestern Beijing. Witnessing the continuous influx of artists and professionals (critics, traders, auctioneers and collectors) into Songzhuang and the cultural and economic benefits such migration was generating locally, in 2004 the township government proposed the idea of 'town-making by culture' (*wenhua zaozhen*) (Songzhuang Art Development, 2010). In

2006, Songzhuang was nominated one of the inaugural Ten Cultural and Creative Industry Clusters (CCIC); for many cultural planners in the nation's capital 'Beijing's coming of age in the creative economy signified a deepening of the creative zeitgeist' (Keane 2009: 85).

Songzhuang's evolving trajectory has been underwritten by constant negotiations among the artists (and their community), local, municipal as well as the central government.[22] The township's policy in luring educational institutions, companies and related entities specializing in visual production and digital filmmaking into Songzhuang has paved the way for its connection with the independent film sector. Li Xianting also figures prominently as a mediator among the independent film community, the artist community and the township government. In the 2000s, Li shifted his attention to Chinese independent cinema, particularly documentaries, since he believed that 'contemporary art lost its significance and meaning after the artists all got rich and famous' (Shaffer 2011).

2006 marked Songzhuang's evolution as an independent film zone. In this year the BiFF was launched and Li Xianting's Film Fund (LFF) was founded. A non-governmental organization dedicated to promoting and financing Chinese independent cinema from production/exhibition to archiving and research, LFF gained its startup funding from the donation of contemporary artist Fang Lijun, one of Li's protégés. The Fund has built a film archive collection and has publicized Chinese independent films. There is a digital library supporting online streaming of their collection, which is open to the public free of charge.

The infrastructural expansion of LFF and its related entities coincided with pivotal events marking Songzhuang's transformation into a designated Cultural and Creative Industry Cluster (CCIC), which has in turn provided an environment for hosting grassroots film festivals. For instance, largely funded and planned by the CCP committee of Songzhuang's Xiaopu Village and partially financed by the donations from the artists, the Songzhuang Art Museum was opened in October 2006. Primarily intended as public exhibition space for local artists, this art museum became a major venue for BiFF and DOChina. The fact that both festivals were strategically (re)located to Songzhuang (DOChina since 2007) indicated that the 'clustering' of independent cinema within the festivals functions as a crucial networking platform for independent filmmakers and film professionals. As indicated, although such film festivals are not equipped with any film market or pitching projects, a number of international film programmers, curators and even producers and buyers regularly travel to Songzhuang expecting new discoveries.

In 2011, in the wake of dissident artist Ai Weiwei's arrest in April, both festivals encountered great challenges. DOChina was cancelled because of official pressure, and BiFF was forced to find venue partners outside of Songzhuang. In the following year DOChina merged with BiFF into a new Beijing Independent Film Festival (or BIFF) to resist official interference. Although Tongzhou and Beijing Municipality authorities threatened again to close this festival, BIFF was able to run its full program by shifting the venues to the artists' studios as closed-door, semi-underground screenings. Li Xianting believes that 2012 marked 'the most critical moment' for Songzhuang's artistic environment.[23]

In his observations on creative clusters in Beijing, Keane indicates that 'cultural creative industries' has become an expedient term to justify real estate speculation and the construction of creative training centres, often based on bureaucratic models but lacking real imagination and a sense of risk-taking' (Keane 2009: 94.) Similarly, Li (2013) concludes that to some extent the development of cultural industries in Songzhuang has ended up as the advertising campaigns for real estate companies. Towards the end of 2013, waves of demolition at Songzhuang targeting artists' studios and houses caused panic and pessimism towards the township's CCIC turn.

We argue that grassroots film festivals' engagement with the local governments' cultural industries initiatives is often contingent and constantly subject to change: at the same time it is flexible and open-ended. While the grassroots festivals at Songzhuang have indexed the independent cinema's advances in community building and cultivating industrial strengths, it is difficult for local governments to defuse their surveillance and ideological bias against such public events. In other words, even if the grassroots festival's creative potential could be recognized and leveraged by the local authorities, the festival itself remains a shadowy presence in the official agenda. Therefore in most cases, the collaboration takes a rather passive and indirect format. For the grassroots film festival, being open to the (semi) official bodies' participation and support does not necessarily mean subordination to the latter. Usually it entails makeshift strategies to fit the festival into the cultural industry-framed discourses and policies.

YUNFEST

The biennial Yunnan Multi Culture Visual Festival (*yunzhinan jilu yingxiangzhan*, Yunfest) in Kunming took shape in a city geographically and culturally distant from Beijing: more than 2000 kilometres from the capital in a region more closely linked to Southeast Asia than the Han north. The inaugural Yunfest in 2003 carried the title of 'Yunnan Anthropology

Documentary Festival.' From its second iteration in 2005, the biennial adopted its current name, with its organizing entity a research-based NGO supervised by the Yunnan Provincial Academy of Social Science (YASS). This support has enabled the festival to find venue partners, sponsors and apply for various sources of funding, including the Ford Foundation, the Nature Conservancy and other global NGOs. The visionary founder of Yunfest, the anthropologist Guo Jing, actually leveraged his official identity as the head of Yunnan Provincial Museum to stage the first Yunfest, which had its open air opening screening in the courtyard of the museum building. This first festival highlighted rare Chinese ethnographic documentary films produced before the Cultural Revolution by the state-owned studios, which while little known within China were highly regarded by anthropologists overseas. For Guo, Yunfest's vision of anthropology linked the audience with documentary traditions and current practices in Southeast Asia, particularly of the nations near Yunnan, including Thailand, Vietnam, and Cambodia. Since its 4th event, Yunfest has attempted to collaborate with documentary entities in the Philippines, Thailand, Indonesia and Vietnam in presenting Southeast Asia-themed sidebars such as 'Media Mélanges'.

Since 2005, the festival has further leveraged its embedded anthropological focus by presenting a sidebar of 'Participatory Visual Education'. For this sidebar, ethnic minority villagers from Yunnan and even participants from Southeast Asian regions are given digital video cameras by NGOs to make films about their own communities and to reflect their own lives. Yunfest's programming idea, linking ethnographic documentaries with the latest works of Chinese independent cinema, has gained discursive legitimacy in registering the official rhetoric highlighting Yunnan's ethnic culture and the governmental project of opening up Yunnan as the gateway to Southeast Asia. These are also the leitmotifs in promoting Yunnan's cultural industries.

Of course, what has decisively placed the Yunfest into the international film world spotlight is its strong line-up of Chinese independent documentaries. The festival has become a preeminent platform within China for aspiring documentary auteurs to launch their career: the biennial gatherings similarly attract many film scouts, programmers and scholars from overseas. For each edition, Yunfest receives from 100 to 130 works submitted to its three major sections (Competition, Showcase, and Youth Forum); this number reached 200 in 2011. It thus maps the continuous, unstoppable creativity of contemporary independent documentary filmmakers, but it also shows how limited the public platforms/channels are for the filmmakers to exhibit and circulate their works.

Free entrance and convenient screening venues in the city centre have made it easier for the Yunfest to find its most dedicated audience, most of whom are ordinary citizens. In 2011, the festival extended screenings to two brand new multiplex cinemas in town (still with free admission).

While Yunfest had its moment as a public sphere where it was relatively free from government as well as commercial interference, the consecutive forced cancellation of two editions in 2011 and 2013 was a huge blow to Chinese independent cinema. This government crackdown epitomized the worst time for grassroots film festivals. More established grassroots festivals in Nanjing and Beijing were shut down and driven underground in the same period. Yet it is intriguing to observe that in 2012, for instance, an increasing number of film festivals across various genres – including official, semi-official and grassroots ones – were still emerging. According to the incomplete statistics, in 2012 a total of 32 film festivals were scheduled at nineteen Chinese cities, although some did not take place. Among these, cities such as Shenyang, Urumqi and Xi'an all held their own festivals for the first time.[24]

Into 2014, the momentum in installing film festivals nationwide for city branding and campaigning for local cultural industry does not seem to have abated. For instance, the Guangxi Museum of Nationalities, its local normal college and TV station have created the semi-official Guangxi Documentary Film Festival (*Guangxi jilu yingxiangzhan*) since 2012 with a programing layout resembling Yunfest. It even boasts a similar 'Participatory Visual Education' program and a geopolitical focus on Southeast Asia. This festival interestingly mirrors how the local government of Guangxi has been inspired by Yunfest to set up an ethnography documentary film festival to match its own status as a province equally proud of its colourful ethnic culture and geographical closeness with Southeast Asian countries. It also reaffirms the grassroots festival's potential in initiating fresh horizons for local governments to brainstorm for strategies in boosting cultural industries.

Alternatively, this potential for urban branding might also explain why even with the occasional strengthened supervision and regulation of film festivals by the central government, new festivals still emerge nationwide. Again, positioning the grassroots film festivals not in opposition to the official festivals but rather within the frictions, grey areas and buffering zones configured by the negotiations between the various stakeholders, we see that the grassroots festivals engage with the cultural industries in ways neither predesigned for them nor imposed on them.

CONCLUSIONS

Our review of Chinese film festivals has shown how cultural and creative industries strategies have been applied differently in the various film festivals of China. Taking into account China's unique situation as a large country practicing a socialist market economy, film festivals have negotiated complicated terrains where creative concerns need to be circumscribed with regard to censorship, both in terms of government imposed censorship and self-censorship. At the same time, the urge to grow cities and to project national soft power means that different authorities use these festivals to further city brands while allowing varying degrees of autonomy.

While the glamorous international festivals in Shanghai and Beijing seem like the typical mouthpieces of their respective cities in bids to become world cities (and world recognized capitals for cinema), smaller grassroots film festivals, those not sanctioned by different governments, also participate in the workings of cultural industries. These festivals incorporate the demands of artists and their works as integral parts of the metropolitan cityscapes and can evoke a Chinese formation of alternative public spheres. They also reveal creative partnerships across smaller cities and different stakeholders that work around government restrictions to give platforms to new voices and maintain the vitality of Chinese cinema on national and international screens.

Indeed, nowadays in the PRC, festivals that mainly screen and promote microfilm (*weidianying*) – namely 30–300 second long digital short films – are mushrooming. These Internet based, highly market oriented exhibition events are self-labeled as 'microfilm festivals' and they are considered innovative practices that further unlock the potential of the cultural industries. The Wanda group is launching the Qingdao International Film Festival in 2016, a festival tied less to the government than to private sources, obviously with a view to branding the mega movie studies bankrolled by China's richest man, Wang Jianlin. Hence, new chapters remain to be written in the people, spaces and products of China's cultural industries.

NOTES

1. During the formative period of the socialist regime in the so-called Seventeen Years ('*shiqinian*', 1949–66), the Chinese state regularly held a type of film festival titled as 'Film Week' (*dianyingzhou*) as part of its extensive programs of cultural diplomacy both with socialist countries and those outside of the communist bloc.
2. In his keynote speech for the 18th National Congress of the CCP, Hu again stresses

that the flourishing of cultural industry would 'enhance the overall strength and overall competitiveness of Chinese culture', see Hu Jintao, 'Full text of Hu Jintao's report at 18th Party Congress', 17 November 2012, accessed 20 October 2014 at http://news.xinhuanet.com/english/special/18cpcnc/2012-11/17/c_131981259_7.htm.

3. According to the state 'Film Regulations', in particular in terms of Item No. 35, film festival held domestically should obtain permission from the SARFT. Because a large number of independent films are not legitimized, independent film festivals' Chinese titles never contain the term of 'film festival/*dianyingjie*' to save trouble dealing with the bureaucratic process. Not only independent film festivals evade the term of '*dianyingjie*' in the Chinese title; for instance, the Chinese title of the officially run Guangzhou International Documentary Film Festival obviously prefers 'festival/*jie*' rather than that of 'film festival/*dianyingjie*'.

4. For details refer to the festival site, http://www.film-yaan.com/yaanen/.

5. In 1987, the International Scientific and Education Film Festival (ISEFF) was held at Beijing, although the leading organizing entity was the International Scientific Film Association and the film exhibition was dovetailed with the association's convention. A second ISEFF took place at Shanghai in 1989. Also see *China Film Yearbook* (*Zhongguo dianying nianjian*), China Film Yearbook Press, 1988, p.457. Since 2000, a semi-international film exhibition titled China Conference of Science and Education Producers (CICSEP) was launched as a biannual event which toured around Chinese cities, and the organizer in 2014's news press admitted that this exhibition was somehow connected with the discontinued International Scientific and Education Film Festival. See CICSEP (2014), 10 December, accessed 11 January 2015 at http://www.cicsep.com/cms (in Chinese).

6. Since March 2013, SARFT has merged with General Administration of Press and Publication to form the General Administration of Press and Publication, Radio, Film, and Television (SAPPRFT). We mostly stick to the name SARFT in this chapter.

7. It was reshuffled into Changchun Film Group Corporation in 2000.

8. Essentially a platform showcasing Mainland Chinese films and Main Melody films in particular, in 1996 (the 3rd edition) the festival introduced the Golden Deer Award for 'best foreign film'. Apparently it was also in this year that the film festival introduced awards for films produced in other regions of Greater China. A growing number of mainland-Hong Kong co-productions as well as foreign-language films have been programmed to enhance the film festival in recent years.

9. Established in May 1980, Zhuhai is one of the five special economic zones in the People's Republic of China. Originally comprising a territory of 6.1 km² in Zhuhai City, it was expanded to 15.16 km² on 29 June 1983, and 121 km² on 5 April 1989.

10. According to the key organizer of the festival, the former vice secretary of the CCP Zhuhai Municipal Committee Li Huanchi, who candidly talked to the media ten years after the festival's termination. It was called off mainly because around 1992 and 1993 film festivals or semi-festivals proliferated within China, and the Publicity Department of CCP Central Committee, which took the place of SARFT in supervising domestic film festivals, decided to downsize the number of festivals to facilitate the management, a decision not without its political concerns. Unfortunately among the three running film festivals, the Publicity Department decided to retain those in Shanghai and Changchun but not the one in Zhuhai, for causes never disclosed. Refer to 'Splendid Zhuhai Film Festival' (*xingguang shanyao Zhuhai dianyingjie*), 31 December 2008, accessed 20 October 2014 at http://zh.cnr.cn/xwzx/zhft/20081231/t20081231_505196311.html.

11. In 2000, the Communist Party of China's Fifth Plenary Session of the 15th Central Committee announced the 'enhancing of cultural industry development'. This was the first time that such statements appeared in CCP's public documents. See 'Creative Industries Timeline', *Urban China (Creative China: Counter-mapping the Creative Industries)*, No. 33, 15 Dec 2008: 22.

12. Between 1993 and 2003, SIFF was biennial; since 2004 (7th SIFF) the festival has been held annually.

13. In 1988, well before Shanghai attempted its 1993 international film festival, the city launched an international animation film festival, which was also a self-styled '*dianyingjie*'. This festival however stopped running after its second edition in 1992. For the details of this animation film festival, refer to the Office of Shanghai Chronicles (*Shanghai difangzhi bangongshi*), accessed 20 November 2014 at http://www.shtong.gov.cn/node2/node2245/node4509/node17931/node18032/node63955/userobject1ai12054.html.
14. The Paris-based organization FIAPF (Fédération Internationale des Associations de Producteurs de Films), founded in 1933, is an international regulating body that supervises and accredits international film festivals based on mutual agreements. Till 2009, it adopted the accreditation system with several international film festivals, including Venice, Berlin and Cannes in its A-list; later on the A-category evolves into a neutrally titled section of 'Competitive Feature Film Festival'. Refer to the official site of FIAPF for more information, http://www.fiapf.org/.
15. The Sixth Plenary Session of the Seventeenth CCP Central Committee passed 'Decision Of The CCP Central Committee On Major Issues Pertaining To Deepening Reform Of The Cultural System and Promoting The Great Development and Flourishing Of Socialist Culture', shortened to 'decision' here.
16. Unless otherwise indicated, all translations from Chinese to English are ours.
17. It was said that China National Culture & Art Corp. (CNCAC) would obtain a second distribution license. See Patrick Frater, 'China Expected to Confirm Second Theatrical Distribution License (EXCLUSIVE)', deadline.com, March 2014, accessed 20 December 2014 at http://deadline.com/2014/04/a-2nd-film-distribution-license-in-china-not-so-fast-as-watchdog-denies-knowledge-708275/.
18. In 2014 the SIFF Project was restructured, with CFPC substituted by and upgraded into a sector of New Talent Project, which expanded to accommodate ten Chinese-language projects and became open only to debutant or sophomore directors, whereas their pitching process remains basically the same.
19. The festival is hosted by the SARFT and Beijing municipality, presented by the Film Bureau and the Beijing Municipal Bureau of Radio, Film and Television and organized by the state-run Beijing Gehua Cultural Development Group.
20. Full name 'Guidelines of the General Office of the State Council on Promoting the Prosperous Development of Movie Industry', which became effective in 2010.
21. While Elaine Wing-ah Ho's article for *Urban China* is translated into Chinese, this chapter quotes the English version as offered by Ho.
22. As of 2012, within the cluster there are 'altogether 14 large art museums, 113 galleries, over 4,500 artist studios, 50 cultural manufacturers, 25 cultural service providers, with a total exhibition and operation area of over 100,000 m². ' According to the corporation site of the real estate developer of Tongzhou district, the state-owned Beijing Tongzhou Modern International New City Investment & Operation Co., Ltd, Songzhuang 'will be developed into the international culture creation industrial park and creation culture and tourism district with its own characteristics' by 2020. The first China Art Industry Expo smoothly opened at Songzhuang in 2012, and the township also has three major construction projects under way: Beijing Songzhuang Creativity Valley, Songzhuang Cultural Originality Industrial Park, and Beijing World Art Trade Center. Refer to Tongzhou New City, 'The Booming of Tongzhou New City Cultural Originality Industrial Cluster', January 2012, accessed 20 November 2014 at http://xctz.bjtzh.gov.cn/n5560366/n7925814/n7925952/c7981044/content.html.
23. Although the BIFF went smoothly in 2013, governmental interference escalated and the festival was forced to cancel in 2014 and 2015.
24. The statistics have referred to film critic Shuiguai's piece posted on his Douban page titled '2012 *Zhongguo dalu yingxiangjie ditu*' ('2012 Map of Image and Film Festivals in Mainland China'), 16 February 2012, accessed on 22 December 2014 at http://www.douban.com/note/262624173/.

REFERENCES

Beijing International Film Festival, accessed 20 November 2014 at http://www.bjiff.com/.
Cheung, Ruby (2011), 'East Asian film festivals: film markets', in Dina Iordanova and Ruby Cheung (eds.), *Film Festival Yearbook 3: Film Festivals and East Asia*. St Andrews: St Andrews Film Studies, pp. 40–61.
Cremin, Stephen (2011), 'A tale of two festivals', *Film Business Asia* 28 April, accessed 20 December 2014 at http://www.filmbiz.asia/news/a-tale-of-two-festivals.
Eastday.com (2012), 'Alternative ways to see movies', 19 June, accessed 20 December 2014 at http://english.eastday.com/e/120619/u1a6636775.html.
Ho, Wing-ah Elaine (2008), 'HomeShop series number one: game 2008 off the map', *Urban China* (*chengshi Zhongguo*) 33: 70–71 (original English text courtesy of Ho).
Keane, Michael (2009), 'The capital complex: Beijing's new creative clusters', in Justin O'Connor and Lily Kong (eds.) *Creative Economies, Creative Cities: Asian-European Perspectives*. London: Springer Media, pp. 77–98.
Landreth, Jonathan (2011), 'Beijing screenings event moves from October to April', *The Hollywood Reporter* 21 March, accessed 20 November 2014 at http://www.holly woodreporter.com/news/beijing-screenings-event-moves-october-169550.
Li, Xianting (2013), *mengyan Songzhuang* ('Songzhuang nightmare'), Li Xianting's blog, 21 July, accessed 20 November 2014 at http://blog.artintern.net/article/370269.
O'Connor, Justin and Xin Gu (2012), 'Creative industry clusters in Shanghai: a success story?', *International Journal of Cultural Policy* **20** (1): 1–20.
Ong, Aihwa and Li Zhang (2008), 'Introduction', in Aihwa Ong and Li Zhang (eds.), *Privatizing China: Socialism from Afar*. Ithaca: Cornell University Press, pp. 1–19.
Peranson, Mark (2009), 'First you get the power, then you get the money: two models of film festivals', originally published in *Cineaste* 33:3 (2008): 37–43. Reprinted in Richard Porton (ed.), *Dekalog 3: On Film Festivals*. London: Wallflower, pp. 23–37.
Pudong Media (2013), *Shanghai guojidian yingjie guancha yu qishi* ('Observations of and inspirations from the SIFF'), 4 June, accessed 22 November 2014 at http://www.pmg. sh.cn/info/178/view.
Rossiter, Ned (2008), 'Introduction: counter-mapping creative industries in Beijing', 25 November, accessed 20 November 2014 at http://orgnets.net/urban_china/introduction_ rossiter.
Shaffer, Benny (2011), 'The philosophies of independence: the Li Xianting Film School', *LEAP: The International Art Magazine of Contemporary China*, 28 April, accessed 20 December 2014 at http://leapleapleap.com/2011/04/philosophies-of-independence/.
Shanghai Cultural Affairs Bureau (2014), *2013 Shanghai wenhua chanye fazhan baogao* (*Shanghai Cultural and Creative Industries Report*) 20 January, accessed 20 November 2014 at http://shcci.eastday.com/c/20140120/u1a7896916.html.
Shanghai International Film Festival, accessed 20 November 2014 at http://www.siff.com/.
Shanghai Municipal Committee (2011), *guanyu guanche zhongyang jueding de shishi yijian* ('Suggestions on how to implement the decision of the CCP Central Committee on major issues pertaining to deepening reform of the cultural system and promoting the great development and flourishing of socialist culture'), 24 November, accessed 23 November 2014 at http://www.gov.cn/gzdt/2011-11/24/content_2002318.htm.
Songzhuang Art Development Foundation (2010), 'Artistic, attractive and active Songzhuang', accessed 10 December 2014 at http://www.sz-fund.com/contents/28/28. html.
State Council (2010), *diyijie Beijing guoji dianyingji xinwen fabuhui* ('The news conference of the First Beijing International Film Festival'), 6 December, State Council Information Office of the People's Republic of China, accessed 20 December 2014 at http://www.scio. gov.cn/xwfbh/gssxwfbh/fbh/Document/819998/819998.htm.
Stringer, Julian (2008), 'Global cities and the international film festival economy', in Mark Shiel and Tony Fitzmaurice (eds.), *Cinema and the City: Film and Urban Societies in a Global Context*. London: Wiley-Blackwell, pp. 134–46.

Wong, Cindy Hing-Yuk (2011), *Film Festivals: Culture, People and Power on the Global Screen*. New Brunswick NJ: Rutgers University Press.

Zhou, Ruyun (2013), *dianyingjie shichang jinjuxing, chanye zhishu baogao jijiang fabu* ('SIFF Market is to kick off today, industrial index to be announced'), 17 June, accessed 20 December 2014 at http://money.163.com/13/0617/11/91IMHO4000254TI5.html.

Zhou, Ning and Yi Wan (2011), *Beijing wenhua chuangyi chanye fazhan diaocha* ('An investigation of Beijing cultural and creative industries'), 19 July, accessed 23 December 2014 at http://www.bjqx.org.cn/qxweb/n29791c747.aspx.

34. Who is the knowledge gatekeeper in the creative cluster? A case study of Guangdong Industrial Design City
Juncheng Dai and Michael Keane

INTRODUCTION

Nowadays, scholars, policy makers and managers pay increasing attention to the role played by knowledge in sustaining the innovation and competitiveness of firms and regions. In the People's Republic of China over the past decade the cluster has become the default setting of the cultural and creative industries. The thinking behind many cluster projects is to 'pick winners'. In this sense the rapid expansion in the number of creative clusters in China over the past decade is not so very different from the late 1980s and early 1990s, a period that witnessed a growth surge in innovation parks, most of which inevitably failed to deliver measurable innovation, ultimately serving as revenue generating sources for district governments via real estate speculation (Wang 2007; Keane 2011).

In this chapter we examine 'knowledge gatekeepers'. Our contribution is directed towards understanding the proclivity of actors in Chinese creative cluster projects to interact and share knowledge, thereby enhancing innovation. The specific aim is to identify those actors that play the role of knowledge gatekeepers. The first section introduces a theoretical approach from relational economic geography and discusses elements of the clustering phenomenon in China in contrast to its international counterparts. We draw on studies that have identified a tendency on the part of Chinese cluster participants to refrain from sharing information and resources. Then by examining the case of the Guangdong Industrial Design City (GIDC), we provide empirical insights into the role played by knowledge gatekeepers. Finally we draw some theoretical and policy implications.

A RELATIONAL ECONOMIC GEOGRAPHY APPROACH

In advocating a 'relational approach' to economic geography, Fløysand and Jakobsen (2011) utilize the concept of 'social field' to explain the different behaviour of actors within networks and the likelihood of innovative success. The term 'relational' implies that 'innovative success needs to be explained by performance in relation to other firms and networks – i.e. their relational position in networks' (Fløysand and Jakobsen 2011: 332). The idea of social field emphasizes that agents are embedded in various fields, including economic, political, the family and community relations. Bathelt and Glücker note that much economic action is therefore embedded. The focus in relational economic geography is on processes such as 'institutional learning, creative interaction, economic innovation, and inter-organizational communication'. (Bathelt and Glücker 2003: 125).

Bathelt and Glücker provide three propositions underpinning a relational approach. The first of these is 'contextuality'; that is, economic agents are situated in social and institutional contexts or relations. Second, such contextuality leads to a degree of 'path-dependence'. Economic decisions made by others, and in the Chinese context this entails policy restrictions, impact on enterprises' decision making. In China a follow-the-leader approach has been evident. Third, economic processes are 'contingent'; there will always be deviation from existing development paths. Again in China the government uses some places and regions to experiment with new approaches and 'models.'

In other literature consideration is directed towards those actors identified as knowledge gatekeepers (cf. Tushman and Katz 1980) for their capability to interact with others in the network, to collect knowledge, foster its diffusion, then act as a focal point for the innovation capability of the whole network. The role of the knowledge gatekeeper and its effect on knowledge diffusion is reported at the level of both individuals and organizations (e.g. Burt 2004; Giuliani and Bell 2005). However, less attention has been paid to the question of which actor should assume the role of gatekeeper in a creative cluster. In understanding the relational effects within creative clusters this chapter draws on Granovetter's (1985) seminal work on the embedded social relations that constitute networks. We show how Granovetter's strong ties/weak ties model can be usefully applied to understand how knowledge is conveyed and shared in creative clusters in China; or alternatively why certain knowledge is not shared.

There is no doubt that the cluster model offers advantages. In many countries and regions firms take advantage of spatial co-location within clusters to exploit external economies. Michael Storper describes these external economies as 'complex outcomes of interaction between scale, specialization, and flexibility in the context of proximity' (Storper 1997: 27). External economies can accrue in several ways. The pooling of human capital is one of the principal ways. Successful clusters provide a variety of employment and opportunities for career development; for instance,

Hollywood attracts technical workers (programmers, animators and film crews), core intellectual property creators (artists, writers, designers) and cultural intermediaries (entrepreneurs, entertainment industry lawyers, and business facilitation services).

In open economies clusters form naturally: the successful ones drive innovation through heightened competition and the ability of firms and actors in the cluster to observe and learn from each other. Organic 'inter-actor networks' are a much sought after 'cluster effect' (Zheng and Chan 2013). In clusters with mature technology this effect may be less important but in industries characterized by the never-ending search for novelty – namely, the creative industries – it is likely to be the rationale of the cluster (Potts 2011). Hollywood is a classic example of strong inter-actor networks. Knowledge is highly embedded and employees are mobile. Silicon Valley is similar. The success of creative regions like Hollywood and Silicon Valley is to a large extent due to the mobility of ideas despite the ubiquity of IP lawyers.

According to a study of China's Town and Village Enterprises (TVE) (Marangos 2009) Chinese people are predisposed to cooperate because there is a greater degree of trust amongst people due to the legacy of traditional Confucian value systems. The author argues that where a low degree of trust exists (i.e. in the individualistic West) there is a higher reliance on well-defined rights and contracts; the contrast is drawn with the international IP system (Montgomery and Potts 2009). Of course arguments promoting 'weaker' intellectual property rights as a well-spring of innovation in the creative industries have been common in recent times. One might then expect China's creative clusters to be places where ideas spill over and where people cooperate in different ways. However, this is not borne out by research.

A study conducted by Zheng and Chan between 2008 and 2010 identified superficial forms of cooperation in Shanghai's creative clusters. In particular they found that inter-company cooperation was limited: where it occurred it largely involved 'buyer-supplier relations, business introduction within friends' circles and working separately on different parts of a product without intellectual interactions. . .' (Zheng and Chan 2013: 619). Whereas successful clusters drive innovation, for instance through heightened competition and the ability of firms and actors to observe and learn from each other (as in the example of Silicon Valley), this does not translate so easily into the Chinese context despite extant scholarly debates about the benefits of 'spillover' effects. Furthermore the research by Zheng and Chan found that the extent of connections was affected by physical conditions, including the image of the cluster as well as management styles and rents. A second finding was that while respondents acknowledged the importance of cooperation, in actual fact a stronger sense of competition prevailed: this was 'embedded in protective measures to prevent business ideas and plans being disclosed' (Zheng and Chan 2013: 627).

It seems that people openly identify with the principles of sharing but in practice they avoid cooperation unless it is in their interests. Another study by Keane (2011, 2014) looked at animation parks in Suzhou and Beijing. The results showed that animation workers had less enthusiasm for knowledge sharing than those in 'mixed enterprise' clusters[1] where a majority (55.36 per cent) recorded positively that they freely shared ideas. This reluctance to share in animation can be explained by the nature of the industry and the high degree of outsourced work and hence competition for contracts.

THE GUANGDONG INDUSTRIAL DESIGN CITY

While the above-mentioned cluster studies demonstrate a willingness to celebrate creativity on the one hand and a reluctance to share ideas on the other, the next part of the chapter concerns industrial design. The cluster investigated is in the town of Beijiao, located in the Shunde District of Foshan City in southern Guangdong Province (Figure 34.1). The key industries are household appliances, metal materials and mechanical equipment manufacturing. Midea, Whirlpool, and Sienhua are the leading firms (hereafter enterprises). The Guangdong Industrial Design City (GIDC) was established in an old factory reconstruction by Midea. The first stage of this project covered an area of 60,000 square metres; further construction reached 22,500 square metres, providing industrial design services sectors in household appliances, furniture, machinery, clothing and moulding. At present there are over 50 industrial design enterprises or related organizations with a total number of over 500 designers in the industrial park.

The study employed a questionnaire followed by semi-structured interviews. The questionnaire comprised four parts: the enterprise's general information, networked connectivity, creative atmosphere and innovation capability. The survey was conducted from 10th April 2011 to 18th April 2011. There were 56 enterprises on the registration list provided by the GIDC management committee. Due to the fact that some enterprises registered with different names, the sample size of actual enterprises was 52. Because some enterprises had not physically established in the GIDC, the actual number of questionnaires was subsequently further reduced to 45. Twenty-five of these were interviewed with the help of the GIDC management committee. The respondents of the questionnaire survey and the interviewees were generally the heads of the enterprise; if this person was

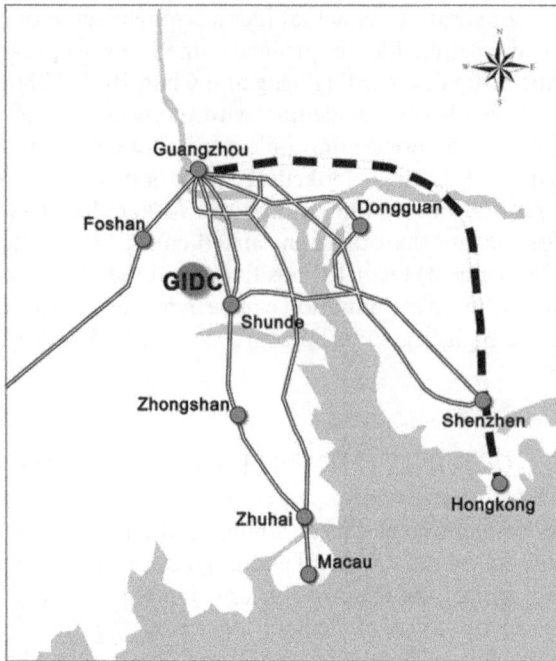

Figure 34.1   Location of Guangdong Industrial Design City (GIDC)

not available, we interviewed the project director or a person familiar with the enterprise's social network.

   The questionnaire identified 33 industrial design enterprises. In addition, there were another twelve related design enterprises including advertising design and architectural design services. Seven 'support organizations' included government management organizations, GIDC operating organizations and patent services. Most (90. 9 per cent) were domestic private enterprises; the other 9.1 per cent were foreign-funded enterprises. Most (90.9 per cent) had less than 50 staff.

THE DIFFERENT ACTOR NETWORKS IN THE CLUSTER

Enterprise Networks

In order to study the social network among industrial design and related enterprises in the GIDC, we disregarded the seven enterprises that belonged to service support organizations and examined the social networks of the remaining 45. Generally according to Granovetter's weak ties theory, we were able to categorize enterprise networks into strong and weak ties based on connection frequency and the content of the connection (Grannovetter 1973). Strong ties networks had frequent connections (i.e. 'often' and 'a lot') and the content included cooperative relationships (i.e. 'project cooperation') or emotional relationships (e.g. a 'private party'). Weak ties were those with low frequency (i.e. 'seldom' and 'little'), where the content was consultation relations (i.e. 'project consultation', 'employ specialist', 'output specialist') and intelligence sharing relationships ('trade union').

Strong Ties Networks

Strong ties networks engender trust: this allows enterprises to obtain deep and complex knowledge, speed up information processing and identify new methods, in this way expanding existing innovation resources (Uzzi 1996). This study used a 'degree centrality' index to measure if the enterprise was in the central position of a strong ties network. It assumed that enterprises located at the central position of a strong ties network had stronger innovation, while enterprises located at the outskirts had weaker innovation. We found that the strong ties network was made up of two aggregations (Figure 34.2). Aggregation 1 was formed by local emotional

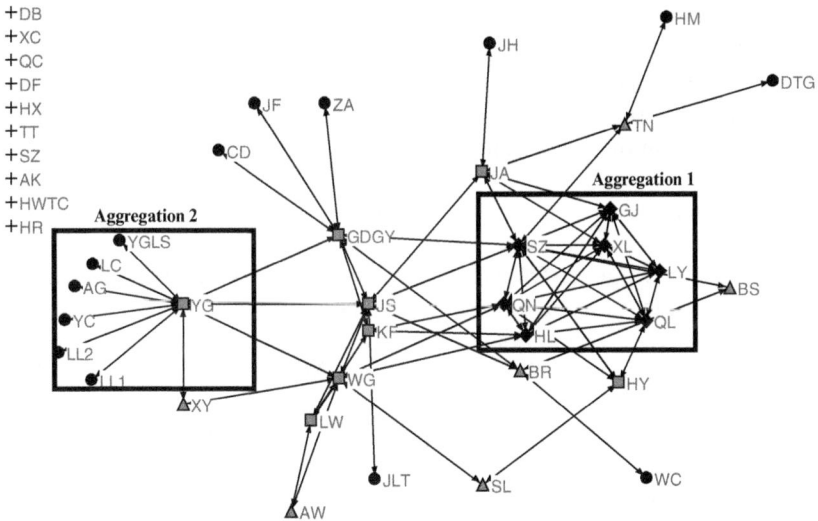

Figure 34.2   Strong tie networks of GIDC enterprise

and cooperative relationships, the so-called 'Shunde Gang' (made up of enterprises: QN, HL, GJ, XL, QL, SZ, LY, and HY).[2] According to one interviewee, the manager of GJ, 'The founders of a few enterprises originally worked in Midea; they started a partnership; although they separated later, they still maintain good relations with each other'. Another interviewee, the manager of HY, remarked that 'local people are more honest, and would also communicate with each other about internal management and projects, besides party gatherings'.

Cooperative relationships among local enterprises and those with foreign, Hong Kong and Macau technology backgrounds (like YG) showed different results in Aggregation 2. Typically local enterprises believed that foreign enterprises were more powerful and they wanted to cooperate on projects that they considered difficult to finish on their own.

Weak Ties Networks

In his 'weak ties theory', Granovetter noted that during the process of delivering messages and knowledge resources, actors with weak ties might deliver newer and more heterogeneous knowledge or information, and this was valuable in the network environment (Grannovetter 1973). In order to judge weak ties, the study used Freeman's (1979) Betweenness Centrality Index (BCI). The study assumed that enterprises located at the centre position in a weak ties network had stronger innovation, while enterprises located at the fringes illustrate weaker innovation. The results (Figure 34.3) showed that JS (BCI=144.20), BR (64.69), YG (37.71), and GDGY (27.50) had the largest Betweenness Centrality Indices. JS undertook the planning and building design for the GIDC and was also a primary industrial design enterprise linked with others. BR, YG and GDGY took on the role of knowledge acquisition channels in the GIDC.

Client Networks

It was observed that GIDC was a client-driven design industry network, mainly dependent on the household appliance industry in Beijiao Town. The 25 enterprises we interviewed all had some form of business cooperation with Midea Group, Welling Electrical Machine, Sienhua and other well-known enterprises. The client-driven network's important role in innovation was supported by empirical studies. For instance, Krätke (2010) analyzed the services and client networks of firms in the Hanover-Brunswick-Götingen region and proposed the concepts of 'supra-regional links' and 'international links', indicating wider client networks with stronger innovation capabilities.

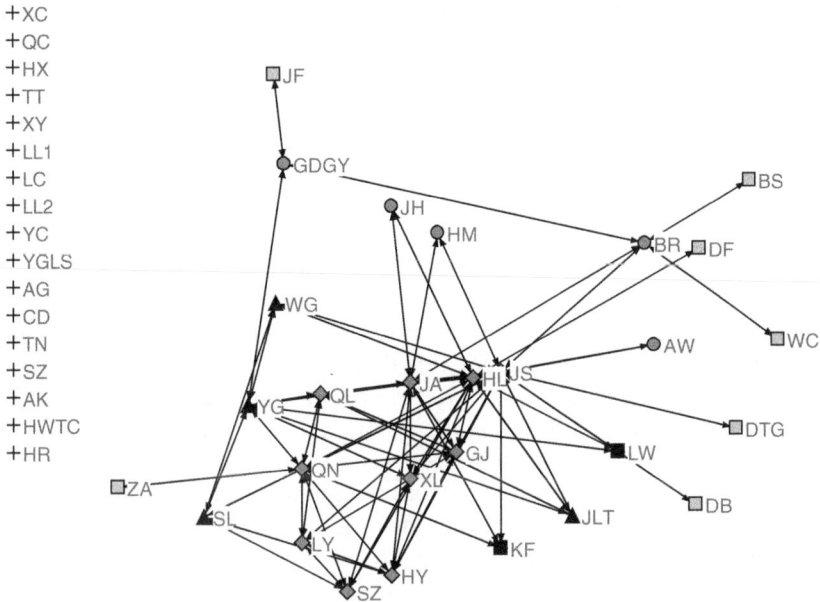

Figure 34.3   Weak tie networks of GIDC enterprise

The expansion of clients of the design enterprises in GIDC began in Shunde in the Pearl River Delta, then later expanded to the Yangtze River Delta and the Beijing–Tianjin–Hebei regions; some now serve international clients. Accordingly this study designed a 'Client Network Index'[3] to evaluate client networks in GIDC.

Networks with Universities and Scientific Research Institutions

Universities and scientific research institutions have maintained connections with local enterprises, governments, and organizations, and for this reason they can function as a bridge connecting local and global innovation (Bathelt et al. 2004). To measure the influence of innovation networks between enterprises and universities and scientific research institutions, this study utilized two indexes: 'Derivation Network Index'[4] and 'Connection Frequency Index'[5].

According to the 'Derivation Network Index', the research found that 27.2 per cent of enterprise founders were employees of scientific research institutions. Scientific research institutions had subsequently established industry-university-research bases in GIDC. From the Connection Frequency Index, it was observed that Shunde Vocational

Technical Institute (index=13), the Academy of Fine Arts in Tsinghua University (9), Guangdong University of Technology (9), Guangzhou Academy of Fine Arts (5), and Wuhan University of Technology (5) were the top five colleges that connected most frequently with industrial design enterprises in GIDC. In addition, 9.61 per cent of enterprises in GIDC had connections with more than five universities and scientific research institutions.

Enterprise Service Support Organization Networks

Government can play an important role in local innovative network construction. In China government functions as a core node of networks, providing key resource allocations for R&D, technological transmission, knowledge diffusion, information dissemination, and the industrialization and marketization of technical products. In this study the operational management function of the government management committee in GIDC to a large extent was replaced by professional operational enterprises (like TT). Accordingly, the government and intermediary organizations are classified together as service support organizations.

The study utilized a 'Service Diversification Index'[6] to evaluate the enterprise's service support organization network and found that administrative approval agents, operational management agents, design awards application and patent service agents are the four most critical professional services in GIDC.

CONCLUSIONS AND DISCUSSION

This study utilized an Industrial Design Enterprise Innovation Index[7] as dependent variable and constructed a regression equation.[8] From the regression equation it was observed that different actor networks had a significant influence on innovation (Table 34.1).

The first finding was that the influence on structural holes (Burt 1992) within the network was not significant in the GIDC creative industry cluster. This presumably was due to the fact that foreign firms were subsidiaries and didn't display sufficient 'independent innovation' to function as the 'structural hole' and attract other industrial design enterprises. However, the 'Shunde Gang' remained connected with outsiders of the GIDC, which in turn influenced knowledge transfer among different enterprises in the cluster.

The Client Network Index, Scientific Research Derivation Network Index, Scientific Research Institutions Connection Frequency and Service

Table 34.1   Regression results of different networks and enterprise innovation

	Beta	P
Constant		0.000
Degree centrality	0.255	0.204
Betweenness centrality	0.029	0.889
Client network index	−0.369*	0.041
Scientific research derivation network index	−0.635**	0.002
Scientific research institutions Connection frequency	−0.458*	0.021
Service support network index	−0.425*	0.034
Numbers of enterprises' designer	0.442*	0.018
R^2	0.714	
Adjust R^2	0.572	
F	5.003**	
P	0.005	
Std. Error	1.196	

Note: ** means $P< 0.01$; * means $P< 0.05$.

Support Network Indices presented negative correlation status. The Client Network Index, which was based on the territorial expansion of clients, displayed significant negative correlation (Beta value was −0.369 under 0.05 confidence level). Because the enterprises with stronger innovation ability focused more on Shunde clients, local enterprises with weaker innovation ability had little chance to embed into the local market and instead chose to expand into markets outside Shunde.

The Scientific Research Derivation Network Index displayed a significant negative correlation (the Beta value was −0.635 under 0.05 confidence level): the reason for this was that founders of enterprises took part-time teaching jobs in universities or scientific research institutions and paid limited attention to the innovation of enterprises. The Scientific Research Institutions Connection Frequency also displayed significant negative correlation (Beta value was −0.458 under 0.05 confidence level): this occurred because enterprise founders preferred to lock into universities or scientific research institutions from where they graduated. However, because Beijiao cannot supply enough human capital nor attract creative workers out of Shunde easily, the local design enterprises have had to focus on local labour pools and limit frequency of connections with university and scientific research institutions.

The Service Diversification Index displayed significant negative correlation (Beta value was −0.425 under 0.05 confidence level): this was due to the fact that the foreign enterprises with stronger innovation capability are able to obtain technical service support from their national headquarters: for instance, ZA could receive support from their Korean headquarters.

Finally, this study adopted a relational approach in order to evaluate how different actors assume roles in the innovation network. In the GIDC case the separation between local design enterprise networks and foreign enterprise networks impacted on knowledge transfer in the cluster. The research identified that universities and scientific research institutions could assume the key role of knowledge gatekeeper to connect local and global innovation networks but in the context of China's economic development, universities and institutions are now competing in the market and naturally they seek to limit their knowledge sharing. During the transformation process from government as manager to a service provision orientation, governments are gradually separating public administration functions from operational service functions. This study concludes moreover that operational service organizations in creative clusters can best function as knowledge gatekeepers.

ACKNOWLEDGEMENTS

We would like to thank GIDC officers, especially Tianjing Feng, for helping to collect data for the paper. Thanks to Professor Shangyi Zhou, Huasheng Zhu and Dr. Kean Fan Lim who provided inspiration and sincere comments.

This research is supported by the National Natural Science Foundation of China (41501149) and China Postdoctoral Science Foundation (2015T80053).

NOTES

1. A mixed enterprise or 'related variety' cluster is made up of a mix of businesses with some degree of potential interaction e.g. advertising, design and media. For a discussion see Keane (2011).
2. Abbreviations for enterprises: TT: Tong Tian; DKT: Di Ke Te; JLT: Jia lan Tu; LW: Liu Wei; XL: Xin Lei; YG: Yue Gang; GDGY: Guang Dong Gong Ye; AW: Ai Wang; BR: Bei Er; SL: Shun Ling; HY: Hong Yi.
3. 'Client Network Index' is the weighting of the number of clients in different hierarchical regions, for instance, 'clients distributed in Shunde district', 'in Guangdong province except for Shunde', 'Domestic area except Guangdong province', and 'in Foreign countries'. Correspondingly, the study gave a weighting to four level regions '1', '2', '3', '4'.

Finally, we multiplied the number of clients of each level/ region by its weighting, then calculated the 'client network index' of the enterprise.

4. The 'Derivation Network Index' hypothesized that 'the closer the connection between enterprises and colleges and scientific research institutions, the higher the enterprises' innovation ability': we designed a binary variable 'whether or not the enterprise founder (was or is) the staff of university or scientific research institutions'.

5. The 'Connection Frequency Index' counted the number of colleges and scientific research institutions that connected with enterprises. The study hypothesized that 'the greater the number of colleges and/ or scientific research institutions connected with an enterprise, the stronger the enterprise's innovative capacity'.

6. The 'Service Diversification Index' evaluates how many kinds of support services were used by enterprises. In GIDC professional support services include agents of administrative approval, operational management of GIDC, design award application and patent service agents, brand marketing, scientific consultation and designer associations.

7. Industrial Design Enterprise Innovation Index = Objective Index score * 50% + Subjective Index score * 50%;
   Objective Index score = (annual average turnover score + annual average projects quantity score) / 2 + awards score (among them, every red star award is 0.2; four major international awards is 0.5);
   Subjective Index score = average of five major indexes score.

The five major indexes included 'concept innovation ability, degree of product satisfaction, ability to identify talented personnel, company innovative atmosphere and technical innovative capacity. The Likert five-point scale method was adopted.

8. Regression equation used to build model:

$$Y = \alpha + \beta 1 X 1 + \beta 2 X 2 + \beta 3 X 3 + \beta 4 X 4 + \beta 5 X 5 + \beta 6 X 6 + \gamma 1 Z 1 + \varepsilon$$

Y is dependent variable, the Industrial Design Enterprise Innovation Index, referring to the innovative capacity of an enterprise in a creative industry cluster;

$X1$ is the Degree Centrality Index, refers to the centre position of a strong connection network of an enterprise within a creative industry cluster;

$X2$ is Betweenness Centrality Index, refers to the centre position of a weak connection network of an enterprise within a creative industry cluster;

$X3$ is Client Network Index, refers to strength or weakness of the client network of enterprises in the cluster;

$X4$ is Scientific Research Derivation Network Index, refers to whether or not enterprises derive from colleges and scientific research institutions networks;

$X5$ is Scientific Research Institutions Connection Frequency Index, refers to the number of connections through which enterprises connect with colleges and scientific research institutions;

$X6$ is Service Diversification Index, refers to the quantity of service support types in creative industry cluster;

$Z1$ is a control variable, Numbers of Enterprises Designer Index, refers to the professional level of enterprises. There was significant correlation between enterprise scale and numbers of designers (under 0.01 confidence level, correlation coefficient is 0.764). Numbers of Enterprise's Designer Index thus reflect innovative capacity.

REFERENCES

Bathelt, Harald, and Johannes Glückler (2003), 'Toward a relational economic geography', *Journal of Economic Geography*, **3** (2): 117–44.
Bathelt, Harald, Anders Malmberg and Peter Maskell (2004), 'Clusters and knowledge:

local buzz, global pipelines and the process of knowledge creation', *Progress in Human Geography* 28: 31–56.

Burt, Ronald S. (1992), *Structural Holes: The Social Structure of Competition*. Cambridge, MA: Harvard University Press.

Burt, Ronald S. (2004), 'Structural holes and good ideas', *American Journal of Sociology* 110: 349–99.

Fløysand, Arnt and Stig-Erik Jakobsen (2011), 'The complexity of innovation: A relational turn', *Progress in Human Geography* 35: 328–44.

Freeman, Linton C. (1979), 'Centrality in social networks: conceptual clarification', *Social Networks* 1: 215–39.

Giuliani, Elisa, and Martin Bell (2005), 'The micro-determinants of meso-level innovation and learning: evidence from a Chilean wine cluster', *Research Policy* 34: 47–68.

Granovetter, Mark S. (1973), 'The strength of weak ties', *American Journal of Sociology* 78: 1360–80.

Granovetter, Mark (1985), 'Economic action and social structure: the problem of embeddedness', *American Journal of Sociology* 91 (November): 481–510.

Keane, Michael (2011), *China's New Creative Clusters: Governance, Human Capital and Investment*. London: Routledge.

Keane, Michael (2014), 'The cluster effect in China: real or imagined', in K. Shao and Xiaoqing Feng (eds.), *Innovation and Intellectual Property in China: Strategies, Contexts and Challenges*. Cheltenham, UK and Northampton, MA, USA: Edward Elgar, pp. 136–59.

Krätke, Stefan (2010), 'Regional knowledge networks: a network analysis approach to the interlinking of knowledge resources', *European Urban and Regional Studies* 17: 83–97.

Marangos, John (2009), 'Why is China a high-lambda society?', *Journal of Economic Issues* **39** (4): 933–50.

Montgomery, Lucy and Jason Potts (2009), 'Does weaker copyright mean stronger creative industries? Some lessons from China', *Creative Industries Journal* **1** (3): 245–61.

Potts, Jason (2011), *Creative Industries and Economic Evolution*. Cheltenham, UK and Northampton, MA, USA: Edward Elgar.

Scott, Allen (2001), 'Capitalism, cities, and the production of symbolic forms', *Transactions of British Geographers* 26: 11–23.

Storper, Michael (1997), *The Regional World: Territorial Development in a Global Economy*. New York: Guilford.

Tushman, Michael L., and Ralph Katz (1980), 'External communication and project performance: an investigation into the role of gatekeepers', *Management Science* 26: 1071–85.

Uzzi, Brian (1996), 'The sources and consequences of embeddedness for the economic performance of organizations: the network effect', *American Sociological Review* 61: 674–98.

Wang, Jici (2007), 'Industrial clusters in China: the low road versus the high road in cluster development', in A. Scott and G. Garofoli (eds.), *Development on the Ground: Clusters, Networks and Regions in Emerging Economies*. London: Routledge, pp. 145–64.

Zheng, Jane, and Roger Chan (2013), 'A property-led approach to cluster development: "creative industry clusters" and creative industry networks in Shanghai', *Town Planning Review* **84** (5): 605–32.

35. A comparative perspective on the industrialization of art in the Republican period in Shanghai and today's creative industry clusters
Jane Zheng

INTRODUCTION: TWO CONTRASTING PERIODS

Much of the current work on cultural and creative industries in China begins in the 1990s and focuses on the shift of state-managed culture towards the market. However, there is an important legacy that is often overlooked.

This chapter looks at the role of intellectuals and creative workers in Shanghai. It traces the development of applied and commercial art in modern China to a group of artists and art scholars during the Republican period (1912–49). An increase in the number of art-related studies during the 1920s and 1930s pioneered awareness of the relationship between art and industry in China. Successive wars and political movements disrupted these endeavours. Then in the late 1990s the concept of 'industrialized' art and culture remerged within a globalizing policy framework of 'culture as industry' and creative industries. Shanghai, perhaps more than any other city, witnessed a concentration of workers in so-called 'creative industry clusters' (*chuangyi jijuqu*). Many of these clusters have targeted large-scale commercial organizations with a view to profiting from culture. In this chapter I argue that they have done little to help foster awareness of art and culture and have not served local communities of intellectuals and creative workers. I show how the contrast between the Republican period and the contemporary era problematizes contemporary policy in relation to cultural and creative industries.

ART AND INDUSTRY IN REPUBLICAN SHANGHAI

The industrialization of art in Shanghai began in the Republican period (1912–49), often considered a golden age of scholarship in the arts. Commercial art, and applied art in particular, gained momentum.

Research on art-related subjects was almost as important as art history and art theory in the literati tradition. In the 1920s many publications covered topics that went beyond the traditional scope of Chinese art history and art theory; such topics included commercial art studies, art education, public art facilities, cultural heritage preservation, cultural policies and international art exchanges.

These research publications responded to issues central to art and its relationship to the livelihoods of ordinary people. Applied art was deemed a major research area. From 1924 to 1932, Jiang Danshu taught art at the Shanghai Art College as head of the Art Education Department. In regard to commercial and industrial art studies, he said:

> Commerce and industry is the lifeline of a country and art is the lifeline of commerce and industry. If commerce and industry stay away from art, these products will no longer be attractive to the consumers. Commercial and industrial products without artistic designs will constantly fail. (Jiang 1991: 30–32)

Wang Yachen was an art educator and critic. He published a series of articles discussing commercial and industrial art during the 1920s and 1930s. The topics covered such fields as modern decorative art, design, industrial design, design education and industrial art: published articles included titles such as 'Industry and design' (*gongye yu tu'an*) (Wang and Rong, 1990: 301–2), 'The relationship between design education and commercial art' (*tu'an jiaoyu yu gongyi de guanxi*) and 'Studies on aesthetics in advertising' (*guanggao xue shang mei ren de yanjiu*) (Wang and Rong 1990: 303–9). Wang stated:

> Various fashionable objects are the signature items of a metropolis, especially the modern metropolises of the world. Shanghai for example, includes intentionally artistic elements as well as artistic yet functional elements such as clothing, food, housing, and the transportation system. Without art there could be no metropolis (Wang [1934] 1990: 295–6).

Wang believed that the term decorative arts should not only be applied to luxury goods, but to common commercial and industrial products as well. 'Industry can never stay away from decoration. Neither can commerce' (ibid.). Another artist and critic, Feng Zikai observed that skyscrapers, advertising designs, graphic design for book jackets and commodity packaging all commanded people's attention in a modern metropolis such as Shanghai. All of these instances, he said, reveal a close connection between commerce, industry and art (Feng 1976: 20–42).

Commercial art education developed in concert with the reforms in the national education system in the 1930s. Jiang Danshu believed that the purpose of handicraft courses was to nurture frugal habits in children as well as fostering their moneymaking ability (Jiang 1991: 22). Furthermore, he believed handicraft courses developed civic virtues and fostered equality among the citizens of the nation (Jiang 1991: 39–40). Handicraft courses also aided the process of popularizing art. Lü Fengzi, an art educator and artist, maintained that the purpose of art education was to empower ordinary people with the ability to appreciate art (Lü 1925: 14). The pedagogies for art education were also examined. Wang Yachen drew attention to existing problems in art education within primary and middle schools (Wang [1933] 1990: 334). He suggested that a better teaching method for art education was to study Western painting practice, design and plaster-cast life drawing before conducting *guohua* (traditional style painting) practice (ibid.).

In 1925, the Jiangsu Province Art Education Association investigated the status of art education within the province. A survey was conducted, which addressed art courses taught inside art schools, music schools, other common schools, art exhibitions, research institutions, public art facilities, cultural heritage education, folk art and handicrafts.[1] In the 1930s, critics sought to identify and resolve the problems of art education over the previous several decades. Other research topics ranged from arts facilities to cultural policies and cultural exchange. As Michael Sullivan has noted, during the 1920s an increasing number of museums and art galleries opened China's artistic legacy to ordinary people (Sullivan 1996: 24). In research articles members of the Shanghai Art College advocated public accessibility to high culture through the construction of cultural institutions (Munro 1941: 10). Wang Yachen appealed to nationalistic concerns pertaining to ancient Chinese art studies and the establishment of art museums. He stated:

> European countries and America have their oriental art museums displaying art treasures from China, Egypt and Japan. It is rather tragic that there is no professional art museum or art exhibition in Shanghai, the greatest oriental metropolis and the cultural centre of China. (*Newspaper Everyday*, July 4, 1923; in Wang and Rong, 1990: 343–4)

In 1924, Liu Haisu and Wang Yachen jointly submitted a proposal, appealing to the government to invest in one art museum with the Sino-British Indemnity Fund (*zhong ying gen zi peikuan*) (*Newspaper Everyday*, July 13th, 1924; Wang and Rong 1990: 345–346). Liu Haisu, then the principal of the Shanghai Art College, organized contemporary Chinese art exhibitions in Europe in the 1930s while Wang Jiyuan presided over a contemporary Chinese art exhibition in the Philippines. With an increasing number of cross-cultural art exhibitions held in Europe and Asia, cultural policy and examination standards became a hot new topic for art research. Wang Yachen's article titled 'Art for overseas exhibition: a calling for serious examinations' (*yu waihua zhan ying yan ge shencha*) was concerned with the standards and qualifications of examiners (Wang 1932: 3). All of the research clearly served the public interest rather than pastime leisure activities.

The new applied art research utilized a global perspective. Artists not only studied cases within China but also those in other countries. In his study of the design of advertisements one artist compared images of beautiful women in English and American advertisements with those in Chinese ones. The artist noted that the specific function of these advertisements was to attract attention and that the best way to do that was to make an alluring advertisement employing creative composition (*Arts* vol.1, no.1, March 1920).

In addition to learning from other cultures, artists at the College studied how to introduce Chinese art to the outside world. In the 1920s and 1930s, when 'world citizenship' was a slogan advocated in the West,[2] artists at the Shanghai Art College actively echoed this mindset. They acquired a new obligation to propagate Chinese art in the West. Wang Yachen stated:

> The essence of indigenous Chinese art has been admired by the Europeans during their long co-history with Chinese art. Chinese culture has infiltrated modern European culture. However, Chinese people are always reluctant to propagate their arts, particularly internationally. As a result these opportunities are always seized by the Japanese. (Wang 1990)

The new research on art and art-related subjects by artists at the College covered a far wider range of research topics compared with Chinese research prior to the era of formal schools. This new research was indicative of a clear intent to serve society while embodying a resolutely cosmopolitan outlook. One concern often raised was the practical functioning of art in ordinary people's daily lives. An anthropological understanding of art reveals that an integral part of people's lives shifted from the previous 'high-cultural' perspective of the social elites. The researchers were the harbingers of a new age of Chinese art research.

CULTURAL INDUSTRY DEVELOPMENT IN CONTEMPORARY CHINA

Although Shanghai was renowned during the Republican period for its distinctive cultural environment, this is not the case in contemporary Shanghai. The process of industrializing the arts was disrupted during the period of civil wars and subsequent political movements under the leadership of the Communist Party of China (CCP). The repositioning of the state's goals towards economic development in the late 1970s, accompanied by a dissolution of power to the lower administrative levels of city and district governments in political reform, led to the enhanced importance of localities and the emergence of an entrepreneurial style of urban governance. The industrialization of culture and arts, expressed in the terms of cultural and creative industries, entered into the policy discourse during early 2000 (O'Connor and Gu 2006). One major phenomenon has been the designation of 'creative industry clusters', which aim to facilitate the development of cultural and creative industries (Keane 2011; Zheng 2010, 2011).

Compared with the Republican period, the environment in contemporary Shanghai emphasizes economic performance but lacks empathy for cultural diversity and creative expression. As is the case elsewhere in China, Shanghai's competitiveness in the cultural and creative industries is not as strong as its economy. Research has shown that Shanghai is weaker than other cosmopolitan cities in many dimensions. In the early 2000s, Qu applied a quantitative evaluation tool to assess Shanghai's cultural competitiveness and eligibility to be described as international in the fields of publications, cultural facilities, cultural consumption, public cultural expenditure, information media, educational standards, science and technology and medicine.[3] His research shows that expenditure on public education in Shanghai was one tenth of that of Tokyo and one fifth of Hong Kong (Qu 2003: 214–27).

The problem of China's cultural development is essentially rooted in cultural institutions. China's cultural environment exhibits weaknesses, especially in respect to facilitating talent, enabling cultural growth and allowing adequate cultural diversity. Censorship echoes Richard Florida's key point about the importance of talent and tolerance, along with technology, the so-called '3Ts' (Florida 2002). Censorship constrains expression: the aim is to condition people's thinking in line with that of the leadership, which leads to a lack of real cultural diversity. Yorke points out that forcing artists to conform to ideological thinking is a short-term solution. If the role of the artist is predetermined by political constraints not under their control, their works are in many aspects only the symptom rather than the precursor of social change (1989: 188–98). Elsewhere Wu points out that Shanghai lags far behind its goal of reasserting its cultural prominence. He says it is not China's artistic centre despite a large number of cultural facilities in progress. Censorship in both the traditional and progressive art fields has seriously dampened Shanghai's cultural climate (Wu 2004: 174).

This situation has not improved with the emergence of creative industry clusters. Both the institutions and the respective cultural policies reveal a socio-political setting different from most international settings. This socio-political setting in turn impacts upon the rationale for clustering. In 2008, I conducted research that drew attention to the performance of such clusters (Zheng and Chan 2013). I adopted both quantitative and qualitative research methods, namely questionnaire surveys and in-depth interviews. The survey was conducted in March 2007 with help from the SCIC (Shanghai Creative Industry Centre). Of 141 questionnaires distributed, 112 responses were deemed useful. I utilized two statistical tools, T-test and Chi-square, in the data analysis. The main findings were that the support of creative industry clusters for local micro/small companies and individuals is inadequate. Second, cultural policies in creative industry clusters have failed to improve cultural diversity and democracy. In the following section I discuss the ramifications.

LOCAL MICRO/SMALL COMPANIES AND INDIVIDUALS

Micro- and small-sized companies (or small- and medium-sized companies[4]) are the engine of local innovation. Writing about cities in America, Jacobs (1964) points out that small companies rely more on resources such as low-cost old buildings in order to compete with other companies. They are financially weaker than big companies and for this reason cannot afford high rents. This economic imperative explains why many cultural activities were spontaneously incubated in old factory buildings in Shanghai. In China the majority of cultural and creative industries enterprises are micro/small scale; they need economic and other service support in their start-up stage. According to Zhang, most cultural industry companies in the service segment in China are small scale; they are not competitive with transnational companies (Zhang 2001: 39). However, creative industry clusters appear to function differently according to my evidence.

I asked two questions, first regarding annual sales, the second concerning the profession of companies. The surveyed results are presented in Table 35.1 and are categorized into seven grades (A–G) according to annual sales. Among the seven cluster parks investigated, only 11.7 per cent of tenants were micro/small companies. Furthermore there was a wide discrepancy in income of companies. In some examples, such as Chuangyi Yuan, the majority of tenants had annual sales lower than RMB 5 million (US$0.9m); in Creative Warehouse, Jing'an Media and Culture Park, and Zhoujiaqiao, companies reported annual sales ranging from RMB 0.5 million (US$0.08m) to RMB 30 million (US$4.7m). Other creative

Table 35.1 *Size scale (annual sale) of creative industry clusters (RMB)*
(% of firms)

	A	B	C	D	E	F	G	Total
Creative Warehouse	8	8	0	23	23	38	0	100
Chuangyi Yuan	10	20	40	30	0	0	0	100
2577 Creative Garden	0	0	14	28	15	15	28	100
Jing'an Media Culture Park	0	0	15	85	0	0	0	100
Jing'an Modern Industry Mansion	7	23	8	31	8	23	0	100
The Only Creative Park	0	0	3	37	20	10	30	100
Zhoujia Qiao	0	6	23	42	19	6	4	100

Notes: Annual sales in RMB. A: <100,000; B: 100,000–500,000; C: 500,000–1,000,000; D: 1,000,000–5,000,000; E: 5,000,000–10,000,000; F: 10,000,000–30,000,000; G: >30,000,000.

industry clusters (i.e. 2577 Creative Garden and The Only Creative Park) had tenant companies with much larger production scales ranging from RMB1 million (US$0.16m) to higher than RMB30 million (US$4.7m). This indicates that there is no agreed objective to recruit micro/small companies as tenants. In other words, factors other than support of small companies influenced the admission policies of developers (administrators).

Moreover, some clusters house a majority of larger scale tenant companies. In a pilot study, I had identified office buildings as one type of cluster. In Shanghai there were a number of rounds of designation; that is, clusters were officially recognized by the SCIC as qualified cluster parks. According to my interviews with managers and tenant companies, in the first round of SCIC's designation The Only Creative Park was an office building – as was 2577 Creative Garden in the second round of designation. Others were 'spontaneously developing' clusters. Thus, 2577 Creative Garden and Only Creative Park are categorized into Group A and others into Group B. By assigning weight 1 to 7 to the seven grades, a T-test was run to verify the disparity between the means of scale of the two groups. The finding is that clusters in Group A have much larger scale tenants.

Qualitative evidence confirms the lack of support for micro and small companies. In particular incentives (i.e. waiving part of a certain department's tax share) promised by the local government and cluster administrators are often not fulfilled. Comments such as this were found in the returned questionnaires:

> I hope the incentives promised by the government can be fulfilled as soon as possible. Moreover, the government needs to materialize other functions of the quarter to make sure that it really works as a creative industry cluster. (Comments in questionnaire survey, 2007)

The original purpose of providing incentives is to relieve the tenant's financial burden. Such practices are common in enterprise zone experiments in Europe and America that provide support for small start-up companies. The failure of some local governments and cluster administrators to fulfill their promised incentives has shown that these incentives were in fact lures to attract tenants rather than strategies to support start-up entrepreneurs. One SCIC official revealed that supporting small and weak creative industry companies was not their main consideration and described such support for weak start-ups as the business of 'charitable institutions' (Interview 2007). These facts show that SCIC did not aim to foster local start-up entrepreneurship; such policies influenced the development of creative industry clusters especially after Round 2.

According to the above data: (1) we can see a small cohort of micro/small scale companies and an uneven distribution of different-sized tenants; (2) some creative industry clusters contain a high percentage of large companies; and (3) (from the interviews) there is no clear intention to support small companies and individuals.

Artists are facing high economic pressure with the effects of gentrification. Kraus (1995) has noted how the reform of cultural institutions since the late 1980s exposed artists to market pressures, including the threat of unemployment and other forms of economic pressure. The provision of affordable accommodation for artists is also inadequate. Jacobs (1964) writes that cities need old buildings, not only those museum treasures or spectacular buildings with important architectural merit, but 'a good lot of plain, ordinary, low-value old buildings, including some rundown old buildings' (Jacobs 1964: 187). The value of old buildings is important for the clustering of small start-up companies, small neighborhood bars, foreign restaurants and individual artists: they foster cultural diversity, stimulate animation and generate ideas. These points have provided the rationale for using old buildings for culture related activities and small enterprises. However, such old buildings are the least valued and are being rapidly demolished for new developments in China. Creative industry clusters are developing as large-scale 'spectacular projects' through the conversion of historical buildings into real estate office properties. This has resulted in gentrification: the dominant sectors are architecture design, media, planning and consultancy and some other tertiary industry sectors. Art sectors, such as painting, music and performing art, only account for a small section of the tenants' business in creative industry clusters (questionnaire survey at the creative industry clusters, 2008).

IMPROVING CULTURAL DIVERSITY AND DEMOCRACY?

The development of creative industry clusters during the early 2000s was not accompanied by changes in cultural policy that would lead to improved cultural diversity and cultural democracy in Shanghai. Obeying the Party leadership was the priority; for instance, the SCIC emphasized that *Deng Xiaoping lilun* (Deng Xiaoping Theory) and Jiang Zemin's *sange daibiao sixiang* ('Three Represents Thinking') served as the ideological guidance in developing creative industry clusters and creative industries in Shanghai (Xia 2006). This guidance principle was written into the Eleventh Five-Year Plan for the Development of Creative Industries in Shanghai as the major tenet: 'We need to insist on the principle that combines government guidance and market forces' (SCIC 2006a).[5]

SCIC officials appeared to avoid artists who did not actively align themselves with the government. One government official cited an example of an overseas artist who rented several industrial sites, converting them to attractive quarters without taking account of the government's interests: 'The government does not like people like him; if he makes any mistake in ideology, we will shut down his quarters immediately' (interview with SCIC official, 2006). A number of spontaneously developed art warehouses along the Suzhou Creek were demolished by the district government, disregarding artists' appeals;[6] this occurred at a time when local governments were making increasing efforts to reuse historic buildings (e.g. the Sculpture Space project). A number of Shanghai artists questioned the obvious contradiction in the government's action; that is, pulling down artists' warehouses but at the same time preserving and reusing others in projects backed by the government (Anon, 2006a). This suggests that it was not the artists' idea of reusing historic and industrial buildings that annoyed the authorities, but the earlier spontaneous, non-official cultural activities that were not under the direct control of authorities. In this sense, the development of creative industry clusters embodies a suppression of nascent bottom-up cultural democracy and continuous restraint of public participation in urban affairs.

The extension of the government control over new cultural activities and businesses through 'creative industry clusters' is more clearly reflected by the 'Management Regulations of Creative Industry Clusters in Shanghai' (SCIC 2006b: 44–5):

(3) Creative industry cluster administrators need to set up archives for recording their tenants and assist executive departments in collecting statistical data.

(4)   Creative industry cluster administrators need to actively guide their tenants to register in the local district and provide services and management in cooperation with executive departments in the local district.
(5)   Creative industry cluster administrators should timely report to government administrative departments all the activities of their tenants. Those performances and exhibitions that touch on ideologies should be reported to the Culture Department of the government.
(6)   Creative industry cluster administrators should accept the supervision, and guidance of the executive department of the government. At the same time, 'creative industry cluster' administrators also need to sign the corresponding contract with their tenants to clarify their management responsibility and urge their tenants to conform to all the regulations of creative industry clusters.

According to my interviews with administrators, regulations issued by the government were implemented; any artwork or artists that challenged authority would be 'admonished' and discontinued, similar to the situation outside creative industry clusters. In this respect there are evidently no special cultural policies allowing extra cultural freedom inside (interviews with creative industry cluster administrators, 2006–07). By joining a creative industry cluster, artists and creative industry companies have lost a certain degree of cultural freedom compared with their early spontaneous activities in disused old factory buildings away from the interest and control of the government. For instance, in earlier art warehouses along the Suzhou Creek, the procedure of renting spaces was simple, involving only negotiation about rent with landlords (Anon 2006b). In creative industry clusters, however, the procedure is far more complicated. In 2577 Creative Garden for example, administrators require tenants to submit their business licenses and photocopies of personal IDs and sign the contract entitled 'The Property Management and Service Contract in the 2577 Creative Garden', which also includes the government's regulations on tenants' activities (2577CGA, 2007). These administrative regulations have frustrated some creative industry workers and they expressed their unhappiness during the interviews. One written comment given by a tenant company in the questionnaire survey is as follows:

> In my view, what is creative industry? Why do we need the Shanghai Creative Industry Center? Does the established Shanghai Creative Industry Center simply aim to renovate the old buildings to lease to tenants or to promote the development of creative industries in their start-up stage? All these questions have not been clarified. Without really answering these questions, creative industries will not be successfully developed in the current institution under ideological controls. (Questionnaire survey, Shanghai, 2007)

Inadequate tolerance of cultural diversity and democracy has been a phenomenon in China for decades, and creative industry clusters unfortunately have failed to change the situation.

CONCLUSION

Michael Keane (2009) has discussed the concept of 'creative industries' in China from four perspectives, pointing out that many current policies are not rooted in Chinese culture and do not have real capacity to advance social changes. Creative industries are generally seen as cultural industries in China, which allows them to be manipulated by Party officials who are reluctant to admit risk; because of this people working in creative pursuits have not benefited from artistic and intellectual freedom.

Most of the findings in this chapter are consistent with these arguments (Keane 2007, 2009). I have contrasted the industrialization of arts in Shanghai during the Republican period with contemporary times. I showed how this industrialization movement began and how it prospered in Shanghai, drawing attention to the writings of intellectuals and artists during the Republican period. During this period there was considerable literature on applied and commercial art, illustrating a break away from the previous literati painting approach. Subjects ranged from commercial and industrial products, commercial art, commercial art education, to art facilities and cultural policies. The accomplishments of intellectuals and artists during the Republican period contributed to cultural patrimony and cultural ambience in Shanghai, but unfortunately this golden age disappeared over the following seven decades.

Looking in hindsight at the accomplishments of Republican period artists and intellectuals problematizes contemporary cultural policies and creative industry cluster initiatives. Censorship is the dominant instrument of China's cultural policies, restraining expression and thus jeopardizing cultural diversity and democracy. Moreover, the support within creative industry clusters for small businesses and individuals is inadequate. We see a small percentage of micro/small scale companies and an uneven distribution of different-sized tenants while some clusters contain a high percentage of large companies. No clear intention is evident to support small companies and individuals. In addition, a lack of recognition and respect for the capacity of local talent, and their potential intellectual contribution to Shanghai's cultural and creative industries is evident. The creative industries clusters initiative has failed to provide extra freedom for cultural expression beyond existing cultural policy; however, this was probably a 'Chinese dream' that was never meant to be fulfilled.

NOTES

1. Liu Haisu's *Activities in the Jiangsu Province Art Education Association in 1924*, collected in the Shanghai Archive House (Q250-1-23).
2. Thomas Munro (1941) wrote that art oversteps the boundaries, not only of space but time such that the meditation of an ancient Hindu or a Chinese or Egyptian sage may be far more comprehensible today. He also advocated 'the development of cultural inter-changes for all artistic improvements' (ibid.). In this historical background, artists at the college actively echoed the worldwide trend.
3. That article evaluates Shanghai cultural competition using a set of indicators proposed by the author, but does not rank cities.
4. The criteria for micro, small, middle, and large companies are different in various countries and professions. However, a specialized classification for the scale of com-panies in creative industries in China has not been worked out. This research uses the criteria in Europe and defines micro creative industry companies as having annual sales below RMB 0.5 million (Choice A and Choice B), small companies: RMB 0.5–5 million (Choice C and Choice D), medium sized companies: RMB 5–30 million (Choice E and Choice F); big companies (Choice G).
5. Ironically, the plans for creative industry and 'creative industry clusters' involve little concern for cultural democracy. No artist or other creative worker has participated in the planning procedure for this plan.
6. M50 is a rare case where the site was preserved due to artists' appeals.

REFERENCES

2577 Creative Garden Administration (2577CGA) (2007), 'The Property Management and Service Contract in the 2577 Creative Garden', accessed 12 November 2009 at http://www.cg2577.com/.

Anon. (2006a), *bainian diaosu kan jinzhao – Shanghai chengshi diaosu yishu zhongxin kaiguan jishi* ('Come to attend today's sculpture exhibition to know about the one-hundred-year history of sculpture: a report of the opening ceremony of the Shanghai Sculpture Space'), *Xinmin Weekly* (11 January), accessed 25 September 2015 at http://www.sss570.com/chinese/news/list.asp?art_id=144.

Anon. (2006b), *M50 yishu cangku de xianzhuang yu fazhan* ('The development and current situation of the M50 art warehouse'), accessed 5 July 2015 at http://www.yangtze.org.cn/tjlist.asp.

Feng, Zikai (1976), *shangye yishu* ('Commercial arts'), in Bing Sun (ed.), *Feng Zikai Yishu Suibi* (*Feng Zikai, Random Essays on Art*). Shanghai: Shanghai yiwen chubanshe, pp. 20–42.

Florida, Richard (2002), *The Rise of the Creative Class and How it's Transforming Work, Leisure, Community and Everyday Life*. New York, NY: Basic Books.

Jacobs, Jane (1964), *The Death and Life of Great American Cities*. Harmondsworth: Penguin.

Jiang, Danshu (1991), *meishu yu gongshangye* ('Arts, commerce, and industry'), in Jiang Danshu, *yishu jiaosyu zazhi* (*Essays on Art Education*). Hangzhou: yishujiaoyu chubanshe, pp. 30–32.

Keane, Michael (2007), *Created in China: The Great New Leap Forward*. London; New York: Routledge.

Keane, Michael (2009), 'Creative industries in China: Four perspectives on social transfor-mation', *International Journal of Cultural Policy* **15** (4): 431–43.

Keane, Michael (2011), *China's New Creative Clusters: Governance Human Capital and Regional Investment*. London; New York: Routledge.

Kraus, Richard (1995), 'China's artists between plan and market', in D. Davis, R. Kraus,

B. Naughton and E. Perry (eds.), *Urban Spaces in Contemporary China*. Washington, DC: Woodrow Wilson Center Press, pp. 173–92.

Lü, Fengzi (1925), *zhong xuexiao de meiyu shishi* ('Aesthetic education practice in middle school'), in Cai Yuanpei et al. (eds.), *meiyu shishi de fangfa* (*The Methods for Implementing Aesthetic Education*). Shanghai: Shangahi Shangwu Yingshuguan, p. 14.

Munro, Thomas (1941), 'Creative ability in art and its educational fostering', in Guy Montrose Whipple (ed.), *Art in American Life and Education*. Chicago: The University of Chicago Press, pp. 289–321.

O'Connor, Justin and Xin Gu (2006), 'A new modernity: the arrival of "creative industries" in China', *International Journal of Cultural Studies* **9** (3): 271–83.

Qu, Shijing (2003), *Shanghai shi wenhua jingzhengli guoji bijiao yanjiu* ('An international approach to comparing Shanghai's cultural competitiveness'), in Jizuo Yin (ed.), *Shanghai wenhua fazhan lanpi shu* (*The Blue Book of Shanghai's Cultural Development: Culture Development and Cosmopolitan Construction in 2003*). Shanghai: shehui kexueyuan chubanshe, pp. 313–37.

Shanghai Creative Industry Center (SCIC) (2006a), *Shanghai chuangyi chanye fazhan shiyiwu guihua* ('The Eleventh Five-Year Plan for creative industry development in Shanghai'), in Shanghai Creative Industry Center (ed.), *Shanghai peiyu fazhan chuangyi chanye de tansuo yu shijian* (*Shanghai Cultivating Creative Industry: Research and Practice*). Shanghai: Shanghai keji wenxian chubanshe, pp. 29–42.

Shanghai Creative Industry Center (SCIC) (2006b), *Shanghai chuangyi chanye jijuqu jianshe guanli guifan* ('Management regulations of creative industry clusters in Shanghai'), in Shanghai Creative Industry Center (ed.), *Shanghai Peiyu Fazhan Chuangyi Chanye de Tansuo yu Shijian*, Shanghai: Shanghai keji wenxian chubanshe, pp. 43–5.

Sullivan, Michael (1996), *Art and Artists of Twentieth Century China*. Berkeley: University of California Press.

Wang, Yachen ([1924]1990), *Lü Ouguo ren meishu zhanlan hui de ganxiang* ('Impressions of European art exhibition') 1924. Reprinted in Zhen Wang and Junli Rong (eds.) (1990), *Wang Yachen yishu wenji* (*An Anthology of Wang Yachen's Art Essays*), Shanghai: Shanghai shuhua chubanshe, p. 526.

Wang, Yachen (1932), *sui gan* ('Random thinking'), *minbao* (*People's News*) 19 July, 2: 3.

Wang, Yachen ([1933]1990), *jindai yishu yundong yu yishu jiaoyu* ('The modern art movement and art education'), *minbao* (*People's News*) 7 July 1933. Reprinted in Wang Zhen and Rong Juli (eds.) (1990), *Wang Yachen yishu wenji* (*An Anthology of Wang Yachen's Art Essays*). Shanghai: Shanghai shuhua chubanshe, p. 334.

Wang, Yachen ([1934]1990), *xiandai zhuangshi yishu qianjie* ('A general introduction to modern decorative art'), in Zhen Wang and Junli Rong (eds.), *Wang Yachen yishu wenji* (*An Anthology of Wang Yachen's Art Essays*). Shanghai: Shanghai shuhua chubanshe, pp. 295–96.

Wang, Zhen and Junli Rong (eds.) (1990), *Wang Yachen yishu wenji* (*An Anthology of Wang Yachen's Art Essays*), Shanghai: Shanghai shuhua chubanshe, pp. 301–2.

Wu, Weiping (2004), 'Cultural strategies in Shanghai: regenerating cosmopolitanism in an era of globalization', *Progress in Planning* 61: 159–80.

Xia, Yu (2006), *peiyu fazhan chuangyi chanye, zengqiang chengshi chuangxin huoli* ('Fostering creative industries: enhancing innovative dynamism of the city') in SCIC (ed.), *Shanghai chuangyi chanye fazhan shijian baogao* (*Shanghai Creative Industries Development Report*). Shanghai: Shanghai kexue jihua wenxian chubanshe, pp. 3–11.

Yorke, Amanda (1989), 'The role of the artist in contemporary China: traditional and modern Western attitudes to art appreciation', *Journal of the Oriental Society of Arts* **20** (21): 188–98.

Zhang, Yiwu (2001), 'The impact of joining WTO on ideologies and the corresponding strategies', conference paper collected in the Shanghai International Festival of Arts, China, pp. 35–42.

Zhang, Xingquan (2005), 'Development of the Chinese housing market', in C.R. Ding and Y. Song (eds.), *Emerging Land and Housing Markets in China*. Cambridge, MA: Lincoln Institute of Land Policy, pp. 183–231.

Zheng, Jane (2010), 'The "entrepreneurial state" in "creative industry cluster" development in Shanghai', *Journal of Urban Affairs* **32** (2): 143–70.
Zheng, Jane (2011), '"Creative industry cluster" and the "entrepreneurial city" of Shanghai', *Urban Studies* **48** (16): 3553–74.
Zheng, Jane and Roger Chan (2013), 'A property-led approach to cluster development: "creative industry clusters" and creative industry networks in Shanghai', *Town Planning Review* **84** (5): 581–608.

Index